THE TENNIS BOOK

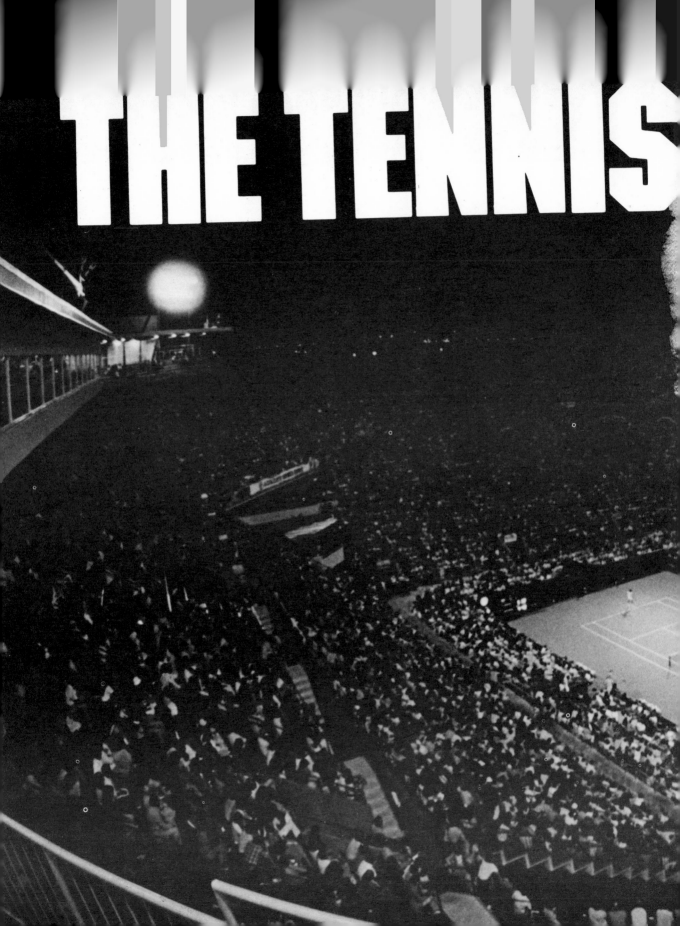

THE TENNIS

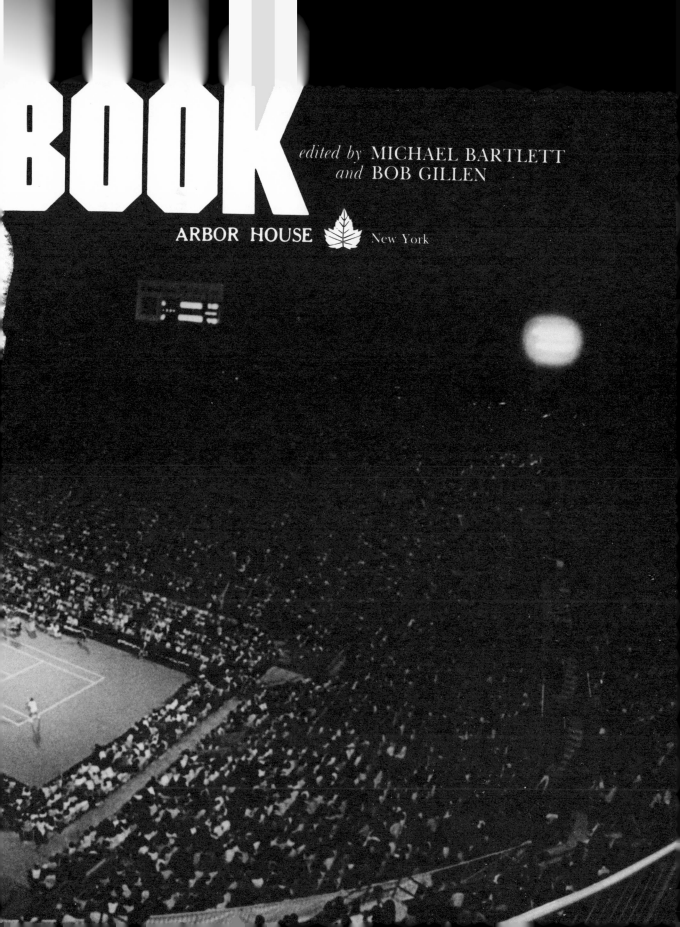

BOOK

edited by MICHAEL BARTLETT
and BOB GILLEN

ARBOR HOUSE New York

AUTHORS' NOTE

Putting this collection together would have been impossible without the assistance of many friends and associates. We would like to express our appreciation to: Shep Campbell and Alex McNab of *Tennis Magazine;* Susan Adams and David Lott of *World Tennis;* Eve Kraft and Ed Fabricius of the U.S. Tennis Association; Szilvia Szmuk, curator of the William M. Fischer Lawn Tennis Collection, St. John's University; Diane Kiffin and Claire Harrison. Our special thanks to Spence Conley for his encouragement and counsel, and to Russ Adams for his photography. And of course Jean King and Betsy Storm.

OTHER BOOKS BY MICHAEL BARTLETT
The New 1969 Golfer's Almanac

Bartlett's World Golf Encyclopedia

The Golf Book

OTHER BOOKS BY BOB GILLEN
Winning Tennis: Strokes and Strategies of the World's Top Pros

Library of Congress Catalog Card Number: 81-67222
ISBN: 0-87795-344-9
MANUFACTURED IN THE UNITED STATES OF AMERICA
10 9 8 7 6 5 4 3 2 1

Designed by Antler & Baldwin, Inc.

TITLE PAGE PHOTO: *Night play at the U.S. Open, Flushing Meadow, New York. (Photo by Russ Adams)*

Contents

Part II THE COMPETITION: CHAMPIONS AND CHALLENGERS

Part III   THE SECRET: STROKES AND STRATEGIES

Part IV   THE IMAGINARY GAME

Part V   THE RECORD OF THE GAME

THE CHAMPIONSHIPS

Acknowledgments

- "Twynam of Wimbledon," from *A Roomful of Hovings* by John McPhee. Copyright © 1968 by John McPhee. This material originally appeared in *The New Yorker*.
- "Rome: Foro Italico," from *Inside Tennis: A Season on the Pro Tour* by Peter Bodo. Copyright © 1979 by Peter Bodo. Reprinted by permission of Delacorte Press. A Delta special.
- "The French Championships," from *The Tennis Set* by Rex Bellamy. Copyright © 1972 by Rex Bellamy. Reprinted by permission of Cassell & Co. Ltd. of London.
- "The Wimbledon Centenary," from *Game, Set and Match* by Herbert Warren Wind. Copyright © 1962, 1964, 1965, 1967, 1968, 1970, 1971, 1972, 1973, 1975, 1976, 1977, 1978, 1979 by Herbert Warren Wind. Originally appeared in *The New Yorker* in slightly different form. Reprinted by permission of the publisher, E.P. Dutton.
- "Forest Hills: The Twelve-Day Week," from *The World of Tennis* by Richard Schickel. Copyright © 1975 by Richard Schickel. Reprinted by permission of the publishers Ridge Press and Random House, Inc.
- "The Australian Open," from *The Education of a Tennis Player* by Rod Laver with Bud Collins. Copyright © 1971, 1973 by Rod Laver and Bud Collins. A Fireside Book reprinted by permission of Simon & Schuster and the International Management Group.
- "Diary Notes: Summer 1955," from *A Handful of Summers* by Gordon Forbes. Copyright © 1979 by Gordon Forbes. Reprinted by permission of the publisher, Mayflower Books.
- "The Road to Nowhere," by Barry McDermott from *Sports Illustrated*. This article is reprinted courtesy of *Sports Illustrated* from the April 21st, 1980 issue. Copyright © 1980, Time Inc.
- "Gladiators and Troubadours," from *Arthur Ashe: A Portrait in Motion* by Arthur Ashe and Frank Deford. Copyright © by Arthur Ashe and Frank Deford. Reprinted by permission of Houghton, Mifflin Company and The Sterling Lord Agency, Inc.
- "The California Comet," from *Covering the Court* by Al Laney. Copyright © 1968 by Al Laney. Reprinted by permission of Simon & Schuster, a division of Gulf & Western Corporation.
- "William Tatem Tilden II," from *The Twenties: The Golden People* by Paul Gallico. Copyright © 1965 by Paul Gallico. Reprinted by permission of the publisher, Doubleday & Company.
- "I'll Play My Own Sweet Game," from *Big Bill Tilden* by Frank Deford. Copyright © 1975, 1976 by Frank Deford. Reprinted by permission of Simon & Schuster, a division of Gulf & Western Corporation.
- "Lenglen vs. Wills," from *A Measure of Independence* by John Tunis. Copyright © 1964 by Lucy R. Tunis. Reprinted by permission of Atheneum Publishers.
- "One for All," from *Love and Faults* by Ted Tinling and Rod Humphries. Copyright © by Ted Tinling and Rod Humphries. Reprinted by permission of Crown Publishers, Inc.
- "The Greatest Match Ever Played at Forest Hills," by Allison Danzig from *Tennis Magazine*. Reprinted by permission from the September, 1974 issue of *Tennis Magazine*. Copyright © Golf Digest/Tennis, Inc.
- "The Greatest Match," from *A Tennis Memoir* by Don Budge and Frank Deford. Copyright © 1969 by Donald Budge. Reprinted by permission of The Sterling Lord Agency, Inc. and Viking Penguin, Inc.
- "The Grand Slam—My Favorite Invention," from *A Tennis Memoir* by Don Budge and Frank Deford. Copyright © 1969 by Donald Budge. Reprinted by permission of The Sterling Lord Agency, Inc. and Viking Penguin, Inc.
- "The Short and Happy Life of Maureen Connolly," from *The Ultimate Tennis Book* by Gianni Clerici. Reprinted by permission of the author.
- "Lone Wolf of Tennis," by Dick Schaap from *Sport*. Copyright © by Dick Schaap. Reprinted by permission of the publisher, Arbor House.
- "Arthur Ashe vs. Clark Graebner," by John McPhee. Reprinted by permission of Farrar, Straus and Giroux, Inc. Selection from *Levels of the Game* by John McPhee. Copyright © 1969 by John McPhee. This material originally appeared in *The New Yorker*.
- "The Intersexual Saga of Tennis," by Bud Collins from *Rod Laver's Tennis Digest*. Copyright © 1975, 1976 by Rod Laver and Bud Collins. Reprinted by permission of the authors and Digest Books, Inc.
- "The Man Who Has to Win," by Al Barkow from *Tennis USA*, January, 1978. Reprinted by permission of the author and the United States Tennis Association, Inc.
- "Dr. Jekyll and Mr. Hyde," from *Nasty: Ilie Nastase vs. Tennis* by Richard Evans. Copyright © 1978, 1979 by Richard Evans. Reprinted by permission of Stein & Day Publishers.
- "Vilas Tries Harder," by Philip Taubman from *Esquire*, May 9, 1978. Copyright © 1978 by Esquire Publishing, Inc. Reprinted by permission of the magazine.
- "The Basic Borg," by Barry Lorge from *World Tennis* magazine. Reprinted from the October, 1977 issue of *World Tennis* magazine. Copyright © 1977 CBS Publications, the Consumer Publishing Division of CBS Inc.
- "True Chris," by Gerri Hirshey from *Tennis USA*, July, 1977. Used by permission of the author and the United States Tennis Association Inc.
- "The Last Tennis Rogue," by Mike Lupica from *World Tennis* magazine. Reprinted from the June, 1979 issue of *World Tennis* magazine. Copyright © 1979, CBS Publications, The Consumer Publishing Division of CBS Inc.

- "Summer 1980: Borg vs. McEnroe," by Neil Amdur from *The New York Times*, July 6, 1980, and September 8, 1980. Copyright © 1980 by *The New York Times*. Reprinted by permission of the author and the publisher.
- "Power Tennis and the Forehand," from *Tennis As I Play It* and *Fifty Years of Lawn Tennis in the United States* by Maurice McLoughlin. Reprinted by permission of the United States Tennis Association Inc.
- "The Spin of the Ball," from *Match Play and the Spin of the Ball* by William T. Tilden II, Kennikat Press, 1969.
- "My Backhand," from *A Tennis Memoir* by Don Budge and Frank Deford. Copyright © 1969 by Donald Budge. Reprinted by permission of The Sterling Lord Agency, Inc. and Viking Penguin, Inc.
- "Pressure Tennis," from *Playing Tennis My Way* by Jack Kramer. Copyright © 1948, 1949 by Jack Kramer. Reprinted by permission of the publisher, Ziff Davis Company.
- "The Serve and How to Vary It," by Pancho Gonzales from *How to Play Tennis the Professional Way*, edited by Alan Trengrove. Copyright © 1964 by Alan Trengrove. Reprinted by permission of Simon & Schuster, a division of Gulf & Western Corporation.
- "The Hoodoo Shot," from *How to Play Championship Tennis* by Rod Laver with Jack Pollard. Copyright © 1964, 1965 by Rod Laver and Jack Pollard. Reprinted by permission of Macmillan and International Management Group.
- "The Inner Game," from *The Inner Game of Tennis* by Tim Gallwey. Copyright © 1974 by Tim Gallwey and Random House, Inc. Reprinted by permission of the author and Random House, Inc.
- "Common Myths and Key Fundamentals," from *Tennis for the Future* by Vic Braden and Bill Bruns. Copyright © 1977 by Vic Braden and William Bruns. A *Sports Illustrated* book.
- "The Tennis Court," from *The Consul's File* by Paul Theroux. Copyright © 1972, 1974, 1975, 1976, 1977 by Paul Theroux. Reprinted by permission of Houghton Mifflin Company.
- "Mixed Doubles," from *Irwin Shaw Short Stories: Five Decades* by Irwin Shaw. Copyright © 1978 by Irwin Shaw. Reprinted by permission of Delacorte Press.
- "Tennis," from *The Stone Arbor* by Roger Angell. Copyright © 1950 by Roger Angell. First appeared in *The New Yorker*. Reprinted by permission of Little, Brown & Company.
- "The 20 Greatest Matches of All Time," from *Tennis Magazine*. Reprinted from the February, 1981 issue of *Tennis Magazine*. Copyright © Golf Digest/Tennis, Inc.
- "The Way It Wasn't," from *The Game: My Forty Years in Tennis* by Jack Kramer and Frank Deford. Copyright © 1979 by Jack Kramer and Frank Deford. Reprinted by permission of G.P. Putnam's Sons.
- "The Greatest Doubles Teams and Players," by George Lott from *Tennis Magazine*. Reprinted from the May, 1973 issue of *Tennis Magazine*. Copyright © by Golf Digest/Tennis, Inc.
- "Some of the Greatest Marathons of History," by Bud Collins from *Rod Laver's Tennis Digest*. Copyright © 1975 by Rod Laver and Bud Collins. Reprinted by permission of the author and Digest Books, Inc.
- "Suppose They Gave a Tournament and Everybody Came," from *Tennis: A Game of Motion* by Gene Scott. Copyright © 1973 by Rutledge Books, Inc. and Crown Publishers Inc. Used with permission of Rutledge Books.
- "The All-Time Tournament," from *The Ultimate Tennis Book* by Gianni Clerici. Reprinted by permission of the author.
- Wimbledon, U.S. Open, French and Australian Championships records and All-Time Champions list from *1981 USTA Yearbook*. Copyright © 1981 by United States Tennis Association, Incorporated. Reprinted by permission of H.O. Zimman, Inc., publisher, and the USTA.

Foreword

by NEIL AMDUR

No sport has undergone a more dramatic change in its character during the last two decades than tennis. Shaken from its clubby consciousness by the introduction of the open era that united amateur and professional in 1968, tennis has moved from the classes to the masses, from an informal lawn party to a lavish spectator show.

At the same time, tennis writing has taken on a new perspective. Before the emergence of highly organized professional tours, the sport catered to the amateur players who traveled the world as ambassadors and discreetly pocketed as much money as they could under the table. Tennis writers knew "shamateurism" existed, just as track and field journalists knowingly hear about huge payoffs being made to so-called amateur runners.

The 1981 Wimbledon championships dramatized just how far tennis and tennis journalism have expanded. John McEnroe's off-the-court behavior was followed almost as intensely as his controversial performances on the court. Irate spectators tossed cushions onto the Centre Court one night to protest a doubles match halted by darkness, a gesture that would have seemed unthinkable at the tradition-minded All-England Club years before. Celebrities and royalty gathered by the dozens in the tented "cha-

lets" on the grounds, while touts outside the club commanded and got $1000 for one Centre Court ticket to the men's singles final. And in the middle of the madness, television was there to record almost everything.

Television's impact on sports has been enormous. Its role in shaping the destiny of tennis and tennis writing has been equally significant. Decades ago, Allison Danzig, Al Laney and other outstanding tennis journalists were the messengers of the sport. Before television, a person who did not go to Forest Hills had to rely on writers to provide pictures of the scene, strategies and stroke production of a match. The writers' stories, the glowingly detailed accounts of Davis Cup classics, Bill Tilden's dominance, Lenglen-Wills or Don Budge's backhand, often were the reader's only link to the reality of the sport at its highest level.

But things have changed. More than 37 million viewers saw Billie Jean King beat Bobby Riggs in the Houston Astrodome at their famous 1973 "Battle of the Sexes." NBC now televises the men's singles final of Wimbledon "live" to the United States, at nine A.M. Eastern time and even earlier to points west. At the U.S. Open, CBS supplements its elaborate weekend coverage with thirty-minute nightly highlights. Hardly a day passes when some cable network is not showing a tennis event—a "live" or taped match, an instructional series or a made-for-TV special. Thus, tennis writers no longer can rely solely on reporting a match. Most people already know the outcome, and many have seen the event. More than ever, the writer must venture behind the scenes to determine what happened, why, and its significance to the sport.

Tennis is not a sport to be covered by amateurs. You understand the game or you don't. In football, basketball and baseball, play-by-play can be definitive, and the box scores or yardsticks usually tell the story. In tennis, the score of the memorable 1980 Wimbledon final between Bjorn Borg and John McEnroe was only a tease to the sustained excitement of that day—from the 18–16 fourth-set tie-breaker to the 8–6 fifth set. Filling a story with quotes, at the expense of detail, gives the reader no insight into the nuances that take place on the court. Frequently, the skilled journalist can observe elements in a match that even a player may be too involved to spot.

But there is more to tennis writing than match description, as this book clearly illustrates. Tennis is played throughout the world, and Rome's Foro Italico is as strikingly different from Paris's Roland Garros, in character and culture, as Wimbledon is from Flushing Meadow. Unlike football or baseball, tennis is international, and the journalist's job is to convey this ambience to the reader.

Fortunately, many of today's top tennis writers—Barry Lorge, Bud Collins, Mike Lupica, Peter Bodo, to name just a few—play the game. Because they understand and enjoy it, their writing is not only informative but enthusiastic and entertaining. They can relate to what Borg or Chris Evert Lloyd is feeling, down a set and a break. Just as Borg, McEnroe, Jimmy Connors and Gene Mayer differ in their playing styles and personalities, tennis writers leave their trademarks, as you will discover in these pages.

Bud Collins is delicately irreverent, the drop volleyer of the profession. Mike Lupica is as brassy as Barry Lorge is thoughtfully detailed. Rex Bellamy's lyricism lingers with the aromatic freshness of his pipe. Frank Deford's royal prose befits his physical presence. Herbert Warren Wind makes us all appreciate how little we know. Gianni Clerici brings the same artistry to words that Rino Tomassi, his Italian countryman, finds in statistics. Tennis's love affair has also enticed such writing geniuses as John McPhee, Richard Schickel, Paul Gallico and Irwin Shaw into the ranks, just as the millions of new players in the late 1960's and early 1970's now have become spectators.

More than any other quality, love permeates the sport's fiber, from writing and scoring to playing and spectating. There will always be petty politics and courtside confrontations, but the record crowds at Wimbledon, Flushing Meadow and Madison Square Garden prove, indeed, that tennis has come a long way, baby.

Introduction

by **BOB GILLEN**

HOW do you decide what constitutes the best tennis writing ever published? The first thing to settle is what is tennis, as a sport. Then you must determine what pieces best illuminate this view of the sport for all time.

Tennis is confrontation, an athletic combat scored across a sharply defined rectangular field of play. Rod Laver compared it to boxing: "Strangely, although they may seem worlds apart, boxing and tennis have a certain kinship. Two individuals head-to-head, probing for weakness and attacking it. Footwork, timing and stamina are essential. Just you and your opponent in there until one of you is beaten."

Obviously, tennis is more subtle—less direct —than boxing, as the placement of ball with a racket scores the point, not a fist in the face. But the physical side is there, certainly at the highest level. Harold Solomon once described returning Bjorn Borg's shoulder-high topspin drives as absorbing body punches—sooner or later the arms, the shoulders, the stomach start to go and the game is lost.

Few sports so effectively pit one player's skill, judgment and will against another's. Virginia Wade has felt that, explaining she could feel Billie Jean King's will bending the outcome of a match as they played. She recognized that she was battling Billie Jean's remarkable force of personality as well as her purely athletic skill.

Tennis isn't a reflective sport like golf; it's reactive. It isn't a terrain sport like skiing, mountain climbing or sailing; the court is a constant (or is supposed to be). Tennis isn't a team sport like baseball or football; it's solitary, even in doubles play.

What does happen out there between the white lines is best understood at the highest level of the game—by observing the world-class players, the superstars. Indeed, the sport can be traced through the years by following the development of the top players, each dominating an era.

I remember a conversation I had in 1972 with a friend shortly after watching the famous Rod Laver and Ken Rosewall World Championship of Tennis match (the one that spilled over into prime time television, gathering ever increasing numbers of first-time tennis viewers). My friend said: "But can either of them beat Pancho Gonzales?" Of course they could—and had—because Pancho was several years past his prime, although even then Pancho was combative enough to dispute the proposition. And indeed, Rosewall was one or two years past his prime at the time of that match, and Laver would never win another major title.

But my friend remembered Gonzales as *the* player and would continue to do so until something—or someone—would come along so consistently brilliant as to jar his judgment. For most fans, Laver's second Grand Slam in 1969 firmly established him as *the* player, to be superseded by Jimmy Connors, who in turn was supplanted by Bjorn Borg. Some purists insist, however, that Connors was merely an interlude between the decline of Laver and the ascendancy of Borg—a false prophet, if you will.

And so it goes in tennis, as it has since the emergence of America's first tennis superstar, "The California Comet," Maurice McLoughlin, in 1913. The confrontation. The cult of the player-personality. The debate.

Thus we have centered this collection on the greats of the game through the last seventy years —stories that tell where they played, what they were like, how the matches went, what the players contributed to technique and how they compare, one to another. So much of tennis writing through the years has been straight-match re-porting: We have included almost none of that here, although much of the material deals with great matches. More than anything, a piece for this collection had to be of quality, giving a view of the game that stood the test of time—as enjoyable and enlightening now as the day it was written.

We begin quietly, behind the scenes at Wimbledon as the groundskeeper prepares Centre Court for the greatest event in tennis. Then we follow the tour through Italy, France, England, the U.S. and Australia, meeting the players and seeing how they live and compete. Then we turn to the superstars and their famous matches and further trace their impact on tennis through the evolution of style and in the record book. Is there a secret to this game? Perhaps the top instructors can explain it, or maybe the essential truth is best captured in the game's fiction.

The discovery is yours.

New York City, 1981

PART I

THE ARENA:
Circuits and Centre Court

"Of all the evocative place names in sport—such as St. Andrews, Green Bay, Madison Square Garden, Holmenkollen Hill, Pauley Pavilion, Fenway Park, the Restigouche, Ascot, Annapurna, Kooyong, Lord's, Old Town, Le Mans, Pebble Beach, Forest Hills, Churchill Downs, Bimini, Wembley, Cooperstown, Aintree, the Solent, Yale Bowl, Saratoga, Stade Roland Garros, Rugby, and Yankee Stadium, to list those that first rush to mind—I do not believe that any holds more significance or rings the bells of memory more loudly and clearly than Wimbledon, the site of the most famous tennis tournament in the world."

—from *Game, Set and Match* by Herbert Warren Wind

Twynam of Wimbledon

by JOHN MCPHEE

If Wimbledon is the cathedral of tennis, then its Centre Court is the game's high, green altar, where each blade of grass was individually nurtured by master groundsman Robert Twynam. In Wimbledon, A Celebration, *writer John McPhee, with his characteristic concern for the value of each word, defines the focus of Twynam's horticultural zeal.*

A weed—in the vernacular of groundsmen in England—is known as a volunteer, and there are no volunteers in the Centre Court at Wimbledon. Robert Twynam, who grows the grass there, is willing to accept a bet from anyone who is foolhardy enough to doubt this. Twynam's lawn—930 square yards, one-fifth of an acre—is the best of its kind, and Twynam has such affection for it that he spends a great deal of time just looking at it. He takes long, compact walks on the Centre Court. At times, he gets down on his hands and knees and crawls on it, to observe the frequently changing relationships among the various plants there. Twynam keeps a diary for the Centre Court ("February 4: Very sunny spells, Centre Court fine," "February 5: Cooler, little sun, Centre Court okay"), and, in the words of one member of Wimbledon's Committee of Management, "Mr. Twynam regards each blade of grass as an individual, with its own needs, its own destiny and its own right to grow on this blessed piece of lawn." Twynam has been at Wimbledon almost fifty years. Nearly all the greatest stars of tennis have played under his scrutiny, and—while he knows a great deal about the game—his appraisals of all of them seem to have been formed from the point of view of the grass. "When Emmo puts his foot down . . ." Twynam will say, in reference to Roy Emerson, of Australia, "When Emmo puts his foot down, he is stepping on forty or fifty plants."

Working alone on his hands and knees somewhere between the base lines, Twynam raises one hand and affectionately slaps the surface of the lawn, which is so firm that an echo, like the sound of a rifle, returns from the roof of the grandstands. It is the third week of June, and the Wimbledon championships will begin in a few days. "This court brings the best out of the players," he comments. "They can make the ball speak, here on this court. The ball sometimes comes through so fast it sizzles. We've had some terrific battles here." The lawns of Wimbledon are his in more than a professional sense, for his own home is within the tennis club's compound, and tennis lawns are around it on three sides. His house has casement windows and a steep slate

16

roof. Red roses grow up its walls. Twynam, his wife and their children are the only people who live within the boundaries of the All-England grounds. At the edge of the grass of the Centre Court is a Lightfoot Automatic Electric Refrigerator, in which—for consistency of bounce and other, more subtle, reasons—tennis balls are chilled up to the moment that they are put into play. The Twynams kept their butter and milk in the refrigerator in the Centre Court until recently, when they bought a fridge of their own.

When Twynam describes tennis players, he is less likely to call them touch players or power players than to call them toe-draggers, sliders, or choppers. A right-handed toe-dragger will inscribe a semicircle in the lawn, with his right toe, as he serves; and by the end of a long match these crescent ruts can be so deep and distinct that they almost seem to have been burned into the ground. "They dig their toes. They drag their toes," Twynam says. "Once they get underneath the surface, away they go. Nothing will hold it." Understandably, Twynam prefers to see non-toe-draggers defeat toe-draggers in Wimbledon championships, but things do not always work out that way. The preeminent toe-draggers of this century have been Jean Borotra, Robert Falkenburg and Jaroslav Drobny, each of whom won the men's singles championship. Borotra won it twice. "Borotra was the worst ever," Twynam says. "He used to cut the court to pieces, he did. He dragged his toe something shocking. He was so awkward on his feet. He used to dig up the turf with his heavy great shoes and make shocking big holes. The Bounding Basque they used to call him. He slid a lot, too, as you can imagine." A slider runs to get into position, then slides a yard or so before executing a shot. "Of course that's what gets on the old court, you know," Twynam goes on. "They all slide to a certain extent, but the *great* players don't slide much. I mean, they know where the ball is coming, don't they? These foreign players do a lot of sliding. Czechs. French. Austrians as a rule are heavy-footed, too. One or two Americans used to slide. Falkenburg was a slider. He was one of our worst enemies all around. But Emmo never slides. Rosewall never slides. Don Budge never

slid. Kramer never slid. Budge Patty—a gentleman player, he was. He played beautiful tennis. He never slid. He never dragged his toe. He was a genteel player, a nice player. He beat Frank Sedgman for the championship in 1950." A chopper, after losing a point, temporarily uses his racket as an ax. There have been so many choppers at Wimbledon that Twynam sees no point in drawing up a list. The effect of the chopping is almost always the same—a depression in the lawn five inches long and an inch deep. When this happens, or when a slider takes a serious divot, play is interrupted while Twynam goes onto the court to repair the damage. He fills holes with a mixture of clay and grass cuttings; and when he replaces divots, he applies fresh clay, then a cupful of water, then the divot itself, which he sutures into place with matchsticks while the crowd and the competitors look on—an operation that usually takes three minutes.

Throughout the Wimbledon championships (known to the Wimbledon staff as The Fortnight), Twynam is close to the Centre Court and is prepared to go into action. He sits on a folding chair in the passage—between the Royal Box and the West Open Stand—that the players use to get from the clubhouse to the court. He places the chair very carefully beside the sloping wall of the grandstand, at the point where he can be as close as possible to the court without allowing his head to protrude into the view of the spectators, or paying customers, as he prefers to call them. Since he is five feet five inches tall, he can get quite close. From time to time, he nips into his house for a cup of tea or something to eat, where he continues to watch the Centre Court, on BBC television. On the salt shaker he uses are the words "Say little and think much." If anything goes wrong on the court, it is only a half-minute walk through his garden and past the Court Buffet, past the Wimpy hamburger kiosk, and into the stadium. The appearance he makes as he moves into the view of the crowds is arresting. He looks like a Member of Parliament. His hair is handsomely groomed, wavy and silver-gray. His mustache is sincere and reassuring, being just halfway between a handlebar and a pencil-line. His face, which has strong and attractively proportioned features, is weathered and tanned. He is trim and in excellent condition—nine stone five. He wears a gray suit, suede shoes, a white shirt, a regimental tie.

Twynam is not a horticulturist or a botanist or a herbarian, and his approach to the growing and care of his grass goes some distance beyond science. He is a praying man, and at least part of the time he is praying for the grass. One June, three days before The Fortnight began, he left all sixteen of Wimbledon's lawn tennis courts uncovered, for he wanted to take advantage of what he believed would be a brief but soaking rain. Imprudently, he did not even get out his tarpaulins against the possibility of a heavier storm. After the rain had been falling steadily for ninety minutes, he began to worry. The courts could absorb only two hours of rain and still be in perfect condition for the opening matches. "If it had gone longer, I would have been in serious trouble," he said afterward. "I got down on me knees and prayed, I did. I got down on me knees and prayed." The rain stopped almost precisely two hours after it had begun, and the lawns were in perfect condition on opening day. Some nights, out of consideration for others, he prays that it will rain, but not until ten-thirty—"when everyone's gone home from the boozer," he explains. "A drop of rain, no more—just to give it a drink, just to cool the grass." The Wimbledon lawns are top-dressed from time to time with miscellaneous loams, and the new soil is eventually pressed into the old with rollers. When asked if the courts are periodically checked to see that they are level, Twynam says, "Oh, no, bloody fear. We haven't got the time. We trust in the good Lord. They're pretty good for level, considering they get such a banging about." Only once every five or six years is the earth of Wimbledon tested for its pH factor. At last count, it was between 5 and 6—slightly acid.

In a drawer of a small chest in Twynam's sitting room are copies of important texts in his field, such as R.B. Dawson's *Lawns* and I.G. Lewis's *Turf.* Twynam has his personal pantheon of great figures in grass. The late William Coleman, one of his predecessors as head groundsman at Wimbledon, trained him and remains to this day something of a hero to Twynam, but not on the level of Sir R. George Stapledon, of whom Twynam speaks with obvious reverence ("He went into this lawn culture in a big way, you know"), and whose name is apparently the greatest one in the annals of English turf. It was Stapledon who developed the superior modern strains of English grasses. There is a passage in *Turf* in which I.G. Lewis writes, "At a seaside town on the west coast of Wales the first steps towards better grasses for this country were taken by a man in whom profound belief mingled with immense vision—a combination which in all ages has been recognized as the precursor of genius. Aberystwyth was the seaside place and R. George Stapledon the man. With the results of a wide survey of grassland in this country uppermost in his mind he set out, as others of his native Devon had set out centuries before, on a journey of discovery. Stapledon, however, sought new grasses, not new lands." These books in Twynam's drawer are used more as talismans than as references. Twynam does not use them in his season-to-season work. Some years ago, he regularly read a journal called *Turf for Sport,* but found it so redundant he gave it up. He does have a look, now and again, at the *Groundsman,* but his way with his lawns is not so much planned or studied as it is felt. He has his experience, his sense of the weather and a crew of twelve, and his lawns are acknowledged by tennis players from everywhere as the best in England and the best in the world.

The men in Twynam's crew, for the most part, are middle-aged and even elderly. Around all of them there is an atmosphere of individuality suggesting that no pressure or persuasion could cause them to wear white monkey-suit uniforms or soft rubber shoes, and they don't. Players are forbidden to go on the courts in anything but flat-soled tennis shoes, but the men of Twynam's crew walk around on the lawns all day in street shoes with sharp-edged leather heels. Typically, they work in their shirtsleeves, with the cuffs turned halfway up their forearms, and now and again they hitch up their braces as they mow or roll the lawns. Most of them have been at Wimbledon for decades, but they appear to

Centre Court, Wimbledon, the perfect stage for tennis drama. (Photo by Russ Adams)

have been pulled in off the street for an afternoon's work. For thirty-seven years, it was Twynam himself who lined out the courts ("If the lines are dead straight and the corners are true, it's a picture; it's not everyone can line a court out—to get it really spot on"), but he has turned over this responsibility to John Yardley, a tall sharp-featured man with a good eye and a steady hand.

Twynam likes to point out that two standard rules of lawn care are "Do not use a heavy roller" and "Do not roll too often." "These rules are always broken at Wimbledon," he says. According to *Turf,* "Occasional rolling with a light roller is permissible, but very heavy rolling packs the surface and prevents healthy root growth." A similar warning appears in *Lawns,* which goes on to say, "For spring use the roller seldom need be heavier than 2 cwt." Twynam and his crew use something ten times heavier than that. They call it the Old Horse Roller. In season, they use it every day, and it weighs 2500 pounds. They drag it around by hand. No power machines of any kind are used on the Centre Court, and only for certain brief autumnal procedures are power machines used elsewhere at Wimbledon. The Old

Horse Roller is equipped with shafts, in which a horse, its hooves padded, was once harnessed, but the horse was phased out long ago and now John Yardley gets between the shafts and four other men drag or shove the roller to help him. They heave like galley slaves. The work is hard. Fights occasionally break out. One day the Old Horse Roller was reversing direction, slightly overlapping its previous path, when one old man got his feet tangled up in the feet of the man next to him. The second man, whose age was about sixty, raised a fist, loudly called the first man a bleeding bastard, then hit him hard, knocking his hat off. The first man, who appeared to be at least seventy-five, hit back. Yardley turned in the shafts and bawled them out. They calmed down, the hat was retrieved, and the Old Horse Roller began to move again. By mid-June, the turf of Wimbledon is packed down so firmly that the daily rolling has little effect. "What the roller does is put a polish on," Twynam said. "The court is firm enough as it is, but the roller makes a nice gloss on the top of the grass."

The lawns are mowed every day in the springtime—with hand mowers, of course. Power mowers frog and rib the courts—"frog" and "rib" being terms for various unkempt results—and, moreover, power mowers cannot be as finely adjusted as hand mowers. The height of the grass at Wimbledon is three-sixteenths of an inch. The mower that keeps it at that level is a sixteen-inch Ransome Certes, which has a high-speed, precision-ground, ten-knife cylinder, makes a hundred cuts every thirty-six inches, costs 41 pounds 12 and 6, and hums with the high sound of a vacuum cleaner while it moves. It throws its cuttings forward into a hooded catching device, the design of which causes the overall machine to look very much like an infant's perambulator and the crewman who pushes it to look like a grandfather in St. James's Park. In the early spring, the courts are cut diagonally. In mid-spring, they are cut from side to side; and as The Fortnight approaches, the cuts are made the long way, end to end. Cutting the long way, the lawnmower is always pushed in the exact swaths that were cut the day before, and it always moves on each alternating swath in the same direction that was followed in earlier cuttings. The effect of this, to an observer at one end of the court, is that the lawn appears to be made of an enormous bolt of green seersucker, the alternating stripes being light and dark. If, in making the cut, the mower was going away from the observer's point of view, the cut appears light. If the mower was moving in the observer's direction, the cut appears dark. The light cuts and dark cuts have no influence on the bounce of the ball, but they follow the line of play and thus remind the players of the direction in which the ball is supposed to be hit.

"Grass grows at night, you know," Twynam says. "With a little warm rain, you can practically hear it growing." He puts his hand on the court. "Feel that. This hasn't been mowed for a day. Feel that little wisp on it." If the weather is warm and humid, the grass will grow as much as an eighth of an inch overnight, but it usually grows much less than that, and the tips that the mower shaves off the grass are often so small that Twynam refers to the aggregate as dust. Sometimes, after the Centre Court has been completely mowed, the removed cuttings can be held in the palms of two hands.

Somewhere in almost any English newspaper story of an opening day at Wimbledon, a poetic reference is made to the appearance of the lawn itself. "The turf was green velvet," said the *Times*. This gratifies Twynam less than one might imagine, for green velvet is the last thing he is trying to grow, and an edge comes into his voice when he describes groundsmen who develop their lawns for cosmetic effect. "These lawns at Wimbledon are not made to look at but to play on," he says—and as long as the lawns are alive and healthy he doesn't care what color they are, including brown. "Other courts are greener than these," Twynam goes on. "This is hard-growing, natural green. There's no nitrogen or phosphates or sulphate of ammonia forcing this green up. Grass that is forced up may look greener, but it is weaker and softer. Overfeed grass and you're not making good base grass. All you're doing is mowing. If you force-feed it, it gets all pappy and there's no guts in it. If you don't give it *any* fertilizer, you're asking for trouble, but don't give it much. One ounce per square yard. Grass doesn't want forcing. Let it grow hard. Leave the grass to struggle for itself. The deepest roots only go down about two-and-a-half inches anyway. If we were to fertilize just before The Fortnight, use a seven-hundredweight roller once a week, and mow to a quarter of an inch, we'd have lovely green beautiful lawns. But we haven't fertilized these courts for three months. These are not ornamental lawns. This is a true hard surface for lawn tennis. This is hard-growing grass. And as soon as it grows, we go down and cut it off. These lawns are not here to be looked at. The world championship is played here." Whatever the reasons, the lawns of other front-line English tennis clubs—Roehampton, Queens, Hurlingham, Beckenham—do not have quite the same texture as the lawns of Wimbledon. Billie Jean King, of California, who has won three ladies' singles championships at Wimbledon, says that the other English courts she has played on "are not half as good" as Wimbledon's. "The bounce varies in the other places," she explains. "One time the ball may skid, another time it may stand and float. But not at Wimbledon."

In Australia, grass courts are very good, and

most players, Mrs. King included, say that the Australian surfaces are almost as good as Wimbledon's. Roy Emerson, who won Wimbledon in 1964 and 1965, goes further than that. He thinks that the center courts at Brisbane, Sydney and Adelaide are the peers of the Wimbledon lawns. "The turf is good in Calcutta, too," Emerson says. "Wimbledon, Adelaide, Brisbane, Sydney, and Calcutta—that's the story on good grass courts throughout the world. Other than that, grass courts are pretty bad. Forest Hills is nowhere near it—very bad." Emerson's reverence for Wimbledon may have been reduced slightly in 1966, when, defending his title, he sprinted after a stop volley and—by Twynam's description—"got his racket tied up in his pigeon toes, bowled over once, and finished up in a ball under the umpire's chair, tangled up in the microphone cables." In the accident, Emerson injured his shoulder, and as a result he lost the match and the chance to win Wimbledon three years in a row. "Wimbledon is fast and hard," Emerson says now, "but Wimbledon is sometimes a little slippery. The first couple of rounds, the courts are a bit green. There is still a lot of juice in the grass. In Australia, there is a bit more heat. The grass is hardier and isn't as slippery."

"I've seen football players hurt worse than that—with their ankles hanging by the cleats—get up and score goals!" Twynam says, remembering Emerson's accident. "It was a shame, that—when Emmo fell. Emmo is as pigeon-toed as a coot, like Frank Sedgman, but he usually has good footwork. He gets the feel of the lawn straightaway. He likes a court really fast. He likes the ball to come through. He's very quick. Emmo is a real machine. And he never makes a mess of a lawn. If Emmo sees a place kicked up, he goes out of his way and treads it back."

Developing a reasonably good tennis lawn in England is not the difficult feat that it is in, say, the United States. The English atmosphere, with its unextreme temperatures and its soft, reliable rains, makes the English land a natural seedbed for grass. At Cambridge, typically, there is a meadow behind St. John's College, on the west bank of the Cam, where cattle graze during much of the year, and where crocuses come shooting

through by the thousand in March. Each year, the crocuses are mowed down, the grass is cut short, the cattle are driven to other meadows, posts and nets are erected, courts are lined out, and all kinds of dons, by-fellows and undergraduates play tennis there. In another part of Cambridge, beside the university gymnasium, is a patch of lawn that basketball players ride their bicycles across all winter long on their way to and from the gym. In the spring, the same lawn is sometimes used for exhibition tennis matches on an important scale. Some years ago, when Vic Seixas was preparing to defend his Wimbledon championship, he played an exhibition match against Tony Trabert on the lawn beside the Cambridge gym. In England, grasses riot on the earth, obviously enough, but what happens after that—the ultimate quality of the playing surface—is a matter of the groundsman's style. Seixas, who was still competing at Wimbledon when he was forty-three, describes the Wimbledon turf as "cement with fuzz on it." Seixas lives in Villanova, Pennsylvania, and plays at the Merion Cricket Club, near his home. He says that the grass courts at Merion—and at Forest Hills and other American tennis clubs—are soft. "We don't have a proper conception of what grass should be," he goes on. "In American clubs, hard-working ground crews produce nice-looking lawns, but that's all they are—nice-looking. The turf has to be hard for the ball to bounce. In our country, the ball just dies. It's like playing it on a cushion. And in the soft ground you get holes and bad bounces. A bad grass court favors a weaker player and makes luck more important than skill. The Wimbledon people obviously feel that it's a very integral part of the game that the ball bounce properly. Surfaces cannot get much faster than at Wimbledon. The smoother the surface, the more the ball will shoot off it. Remember, though, the problems are greater in our country. I can't make grass grow in my own lawn."

For many years, before they were given their present house at Wimbledon, Twynam and his family lived in a small maisonette flat on the Kingston By-Pass, in Surrey. His back garden, which was sixteen feet wide and twenty feet long, was turfed with "a bit of old rough grass," which he mowed with no especial fidelity, since he cared nothing about its botanical origins or its earthly destiny. He has always concentrated on Wimbledon. He was born within a mile of the Centre Court. His father was a construction foreman from Connemara, who had crossed to England at the age of eighteen, and while still a very young man had attempted to emigrate to the United States. For obscure reasons, he was kept at Ellis Island for a number of weeks and then sent back to Britain. "I wouldn't have let him in, either," Twynam says. "He was the biggest bloody rogue that ever set foot in this country." When Twynam was two, his father left home and did not permanently return. Twynam was the youngest of six children. He went to school until he was fourteen and then tried working as a messenger for the General Post Office. He wore a pillbox hat and a black mackintosh, and he went around Chelsea and Battersea in all weathers on a red bicycle. He hated the hat, the coat, Chelsea, Battersea, the bicycle, and the weather, so he applied for a job as a ball boy at Wimbledon. The All-England Lawn Tennis and Croquet Club had full-time, resident ball boys when Twynam joined the staff—a luxury that the club gave up many years ago. Dressed in the club's green and mauve colors, Twynam spent three years retrieving faulted serves and put-aways, and then he was promoted to the ground crew.

"I ball-boyed for Vincent Richards, Jean Borotra, Henri Cochet, Bill Tilden, Sidney Wood, Alice Marble, Helen Wills Moody," he said one June evening, while he was enjoying a walk on the Centre Court. "Wills Moody was playing here when I first came, in the final, here on the Centre Court. Light and dainty, she was. I've never seen a woman take a divot. Alice Marble was tall, blond, strong, and manly—but no damage. Like Althea Gibson—a bit manly and not all that interesting to watch. Suzanne Lenglen was light, like a bloody ballet dancer, and never disturbed the courts at all. Helen Jacobs was a bit heavy-footed, but not bad. Mrs. Susman—Mrs. J.R. Susman—was the only 'worst enemy' we've ever had among the women. She used to drag her toe terrible when she served—

terrible mess—oh, shocking. She used to scuff and slide. Slide on her right heel, drag her left toe. Always sliding she was, Susman. Women play tennis now like men did years ago, but they seldom hurt the grass. Billie Jean is light on her feet for a big girl. Maria Bueno is so light—a very dainty thing, she is."

The evening was quiet, in the extended twilight of the late spring, and the walk was long and helical. As Twynam moved around the court, he stopped from time to time—for no apparent reason—to stare at the turf in the way that some people stare into a log fire. In one of these moments, he said that he himself had once played in the Centre Court—but only briefly, and over forty years ago, with another groundsman. "It was just a knockup," he said, "but it was an odd experience, really. You seem like a lonely soul, stuck out here on your own in the vast arena." He opened a packet of cork-tipped Player's Weights and lighted one. During the Second World War, he said, he was a Leading Aircraftsman in the Royal Air Force, and he spent four years in control towers, "talking in" planes. In Poona, in the State of Bombay, to defeat boredom during a rest period, he organized a group that cleared an area in a grove of mango trees and built a red-clay tennis court. Until 1955 or so, he played tennis forty-five minutes a day, with other groundsmen, at Wimbledon, never sliding —or so he says—and never dragging his toe. The Wimbledon ground staff has its own tournament, and it has always been a professional tournament, for the winner receives, in addition to a fine silver trophy, a merchandise voucher that is convertible into goods in London stores. The competition is therefore without nonsense. Ball boys are used, and, as Twynam describes it, "We have a chap in the chair taking the umpire duty. There are base-line judges. The players wear flannels, slippers—no pure whites. Some wear a bloody collar and tie." Year after year, in the 1930's and 1940's, Twynam got into the final, but he always lacked whatever it is that draws a player together in a championship final and gives him the thrust to win. But 1952, the year of Frank Sedgman, was also the year of Bob Twynam. In the ground-staff final, he defeated William Collis, and won his only Wimbledon championship. "I had quite a decent game in those days," he said. "But now I'm retired a bit. My game is going down." About a dozen times a season, he plays with his son, Robert—almost always on one of Wimbledon's ten hard-surface courts, where the ball bounces higher than on turf and the action is slower. "Yes, these grass courts are too much for me now," he admitted. "I watch the ball go by."

Each year, the opening match of the Wimbledon championships is traditionally played between the men's defending champion and some unfortunate and usually obscure fellow whose name happens to be paired with the champion's in the draw. The match is little more than ceremonial—no test for either the champion or the court. In 1966, for example, Emerson, the defender, was paired with one H.E. Fauquier, of Canada, and Emmo defeated him 6–0, 6–1, 6–2. In 1967, the defending champion was Manuel Santana, of Spain, and the player that came up opposite Santana in the draw was Charles Pasarell, an undergraduate at UCLA. Because Pasarell happened to be an American, his role as the customary opening-day sacrifice was an ironic extension of the humbled status of American men at Wimbledon, for men's tennis in the United States was in such a state of decline then that for the first time in thirty-nine years no American player was seeded in the men's singles championship. All this only moderately interested Twynam. "That should be a good match," he said, "because the court will be in A-1 condition."

The draw was published during Overseas Week, as the Wimbledon staff refers to the seven days immediately preceding the tournament. During Overseas Week, tennis players from about fifty nations come to Wimbledon, unstrap their enormous stacks of rackets, and have at each other from eleven in the morning until deep in the evening, trying to effect ultimate refinements in their styles before the meeting that is regarded by all of them as the world-championship event in the sport. They practice—usually two-on-one—on the courts outside the stadium. No one ever practices on the Centre Court. Twy-

nam walks around among them, watching the lawns and the weather. Given the imminence of The Fortnight, Overseas Week is a surprisingly relaxed and easygoing time, full of chatter and casual gossip. The players all know each other as if they had spent the past ten years in the same small boarding school, and, in a sense, they have. "They love these courts. They would sleep on them if you let them," Twynam says. "They love to come to Wimbledon. If they can't make it, it breaks their hearts. They come back with their children. The atmosphere is so beautiful here." In the air were the scent of roses and fresh-cut grass and the sound of tennis balls like the sound of popping corks. An Australian on court nine hit two drives into the tape at the top of the net. "You hit the ball over the net and into the court," he said to himself. "That's page one, line one." An American girl on court eight shouted at herself, "What's the story with my backhand?" English players kept calling "Sorry" to one another. "Sorry." Twynam saw a girl beside one court with oranges in her hand. "South African," he said. "If she's got oranges in her hand, she's a South African." Santana, practicing with Vic Seixas and Charlie Pasarell, drilled one past Pasarell at the net. "You're out of your mind," said Pasarell. Santana grinned toothily. Other remarks were flying around in Dutch and Danish, German and Polish, Serbo-Croatian. Twynam wandered off to one corner of the grounds and onto the croquet lawn. He said that on Sunday afternoons elderly members play croquet, two at a time. They wear all white, like the tennis players. Twynam tapped the croquet lawn with one foot, and said, "Make a nice nursery for the tennis lawns, wouldn't it, this?" Looking back across the courts, he said, "They're all first-class tennis players here. There are no rabbits here. We don't do this for love, you know. There's no jiggery-pokery. Nothing's too much trouble to cater to the players. They have medical services, masseurs, doctors, free rides to London. They can have anything they want, as long as they're playing tennis. They've got to play good tennis. We must take care of paying customers, not just friends who come in and look around and pay nothing. These players come here to play tennis.

Even the second-rate players play good tennis here. This Wimbledon is not run for love. We English want the money, you know. We're a tight nation, we are. Any penny that's going, we'll have it." He paused a moment and then said he was going to have a look at the Centre Court. In the stadium, he made a close inspection of the turf. He pressed his fingers down on the dense, elastic surface. "Feel the fiber," he said. He withdrew his hand, and the turf sprang back. "The court is as alive as the players are," he went on. "There is an inch of fiber between the surface and the topsoil. Claw it. Claw it. See? There's something there to wear." About two feet down, he said, are the tops of tile land drains, set in a herringbone pattern in the local clay. Ten inches of clinker is above the drains, and over that is an inch of fine ash. Above the ash is ten inches of light and loamy topsoil, and in the topsoil are the roots of the lawn. When the surface of the lawn is looked at from a distance of inches, the differences among the various grasses there become pronounced. Some areas were lighter in shade than the grasses around them and were noticeably tinged with gray, in contrast to the flaring shamrock-green of their neighbors. "The light patches are *Poa pratensis*," Twynam said. "Smooth-stalked meadow grass. The gray color is seed heads. One must mow close to get them. By rights, we don't want smooth-stalked meadow grass any more. The greener patches are Chewings fescue and American browntop—better pedigrees than the *Poa pratensis* now. The smooth-stalked meadow grass is coarse and doesn't make as good a mat as the fescue and the browntop. But it's been here for years. It's self-sowing—and it comes up in these pale-gray patches. We'll phase it out before long. You get a better game of tennis on the browntop and the fescue. The fescue comes up into a tuft, and we mow it right down to the basal level. That forces the grass prostrate and makes it mat. The American browntop is shallow-rooted but hard-wearing. Americans have done a lot for lawns, you know. It's all Americanized. This browntop is actually what they call Oregon browntop. If you were a keen lawnmaker yourself, you'd use these strains. But you don't get a first-class lawn in two

or three years. It takes twenty or thirty years to get a real lawn down. There's also a bit of creeping bent in here, but that's about all. One or two bastard grasses come in, like a bit of rough-stalked meadow grass, a bit of rye grass, a little bit of Yorkshire fog. They blow over, you see. But we pick them out. Yorkshire fog is bloody awful. Prickly. Spiky. Hairy . . . . Volunteers? Parsley piert, plantain, and pearlwort are about all you get in here. We don't let them stay. . . . The only hard thing about this job is, you can't change your court over. The court is static. All the courts are static. We can't move them up or back or sideways. The lines are always in the same places and have been for forty-six years. Same toepieces. Same base lines. Same no man's lands. Same run-ups in the service areas. We get the same problems in the same places every year. In the autumn, on the other courts, we put in new turf—pieces one foot square from our own nursery—along the base lines and the run-ups. The Centre Court base lines and run-ups are almost always resown. The last time we turfed in here was six years ago. We oversow the rest of the court with seed, after pruning the roots with a hand fork and letting in some air and light. This year, we'll be using 80 percent Dutch Highlight Chewings fescue and 20 percent Oregon browntop. Then we give it a light top-dressing with a heavy loam, then a light roll, and it's ready to start germination—we hope. In November, we solid-tine the turf with potato forks, making deep holes two inches apart. Then we top-dress it again, with a ton of medium-to-heavy loam. Luting, it's called. The new soil is spread with a lute, a rake that has no tines. Extra-thick top dressing makes a firmer surface. The soil falls into the legs made by the potato fork. We never hollow-tine here—just a matter of opinion. The top-dressing soil comes from the Guildford area, here in Surrey, and it's a decent bit of stuff. Mow the grass once or twice in late autumn and it stays a half-inch high until spring. You like a good winter, to lift up the roots. A good winter is a cold winter, what they call an open winter. It lifts the roots up and aerates them. The Centre Court is the hardest one to keep in good shape. It is shaded from the sun. Frost stays longer in here. There is less freedom of air. But in the spring we get a good top growth. It's called a good braird.'' He plucked a bit of browntop, or common bent grass, out of the turf and turned it slowly in his hand, describing its flat, hairless, spear-shaped leaves, its short rhizomes and stolons, its notched, blunt-topped ligules. Hunting around a while, brushing past whole colonies of the predominant grasses, he finally came up with a plant he was seeking, its blades like stiff bristles, infolded and bluntly keeled, its ligules blunt, and its auricles rounded like shoulders. ''There you are,'' he said. ''A bit of creeping red fescue.''

On Saturday afternoon, forty-eight hours before the championships began, four women members of the club—Mrs. C.F.O. Lister, Mrs. W.H.I. Gordon, Mrs. P.E. King, and Mrs. N.M. Glover—played on the Centre Court for an hour and twenty minutes so that Twynam, with this light rehearsal, could sense the timbre of the lawn. While the ladies—in pure white, of course —made light but competent movements around the court, driving long ground strokes at one another, Twynam said that a similar ritual occurs every year. ''It gets the court knocked in a bit,'' he explained. ''I watch them to see how the ball really does come up, you see. Then, if necessary, we can get the surface padded down a bit. It's coming through quite well, considering the wet we had yesterday. I've been looking for bad bounds, but there have been none. No trouble at all. It's coming through quite good.''

That night, the court was covered. Twynam and his crew have an enormous tarpaulin—8060 square feet. Winches at either end of the court raise the canvas, between spars, until it is high above the grass, looking like a vast pup tent. Air can circulate inside. Mildew won't form beneath the tent, as it will, sometimes, under a flat tarp. The crew can get the tent up in fourteen minutes. If rain comes during a match, they just drag it over the lawn, flat. Sunday morning, they removed it, then mowed, rolled, and marked the lawn. The white lines, put down with a forty-year-old machine, are made of pulverized chalk, called whiting. Lime is never used. It would burn the grass. The court was covered again at noon. At seven-thirty A.M. on Monday, the opening day,

the court was uncovered. It was mowed again, rolled again, and—although it hardly appeared to need it—marked again.

The gates of the grounds were opened, and the crowds came in. Fourteen thousand five hundred people came into the Centre Court. Twynam looked them over. ''From grocers' boys to kings we get here,'' he said. The sky was a mixture of clouds and blue. ''The court is all right,'' Twynam said. ''The court's okay. We gave it a half-hour's slow roll longways this morning, that's all. It could have had a little more rolling, but the players will pat it down, I hope.'' He set his chair in his accustomed spot, adjusting it so that the top of his head would not quite coincide with the slope of the adjacent wall. Santana and Pasarell walked past him. Pasarell, his hair falling over his forehead, looked sleepy and impassive. Santana's dark eyes were bright and he was smiling. Applause greeted them, and they began to warm up. Both are fairly large but not impressively or even athletically built. In the way they moved, however, and in the way they hit the ball, they showed, even in warm-up, why they were there. ''When they win Wimbledon, they win the world,'' Twynam said. Santana once worked as a ball boy at a club in Madrid. His family had no money. To finance a tennis career, he found a sponsor, and now he has become a national hero in Spain. He is the first Spaniard who has ever won at Wimbledon, and the first tennis player ever to be given an award that the Spanish government annually makes to the nation's outstanding athlete. A touch player, he has been called a genius with a racket, a stylist, a virtuoso, and a master of many shots. He has been said to have thirty-seven shots known to the game and two that no one has ever heard of. He has seven different forehands. When Santana—at the end of the court near Twynam—began to serve in the match with Pasarell, Twynam said, ''Santana is a scientific player, very steady. Watch him now, though. Watch his right foot. He drags his toe something shocking, he does.'' Santana lifted the ball high and swung through for his first serve. His right toe, never coming off the ground, moved in an arc toward the base line and scuffed up the grass. After six or eight serves, Santana had made a light but distinct crescent in the lawn.

Twynam looked at the sky, which was thickening a little but not seriously. "All in all, the Lord has done pretty well for us," he said. Pasarell got ready to serve. Pasarell's father, who is chairman of the board of Philip Morris de Puerto Rico, was once tennis champion of the island. So was Charlie's mother. Charlie grew up in a beautiful house in San Juan and learned his tennis under Welby Van Horn, at the Caribe Hilton. He is very strong, and the dimensions of his game consist of power and more power. He is technically moody, given to flashes of brilliance, and when he is playing well and is fired up he is a beautiful tennis player and almost unbeatable. But his game can fall apart quickly. He relies on speed, the hard ball, the rush to the net. He has four shots: One forehand, one backhand, one serve and one volley—boom, boom, boom, boom. If he could give Santana any game at all, it would be a contest between power and style. As Pasarell was about to serve, Twynam said, "Watch this one now. Watch his foot." Pasarell tossed the ball into the air and swung through. "See how he lifts that foot?" Twynam went on. "See how he puts it down flat? He's all right, he is. First-class. He doesn't drag his foot."

Santana broke through Pasarell's fourth service and soon led 5–3. Lovely, puffy clouds were now moving swiftly overhead. "They're all right, but I'd sooner see a nice blue sky," Twynam said. "Beggars can't be choosers, I suppose." The scuff line under Santana's toe was becoming a small rut. "Shocking," Twynam said. "But the court can take it." Pasarell broke back through Santana's service, and the first set went to 8–8 before Pasarell broke through again. He won the set, 10–8.

Taking his time during the next change of ends, Pasarell walked slowly to the umpire's chair, toweled himself, and looked at the sky. Returning to the court, he spoke to himself. "Come on, Charlie," he said. He said this aloud to himself about once a game, all afternoon. He won the second set, 6–3.

The sky had gone gray, and several minutes later a pouring rain fell. "I'm no God," Twynam said. "I can't stop the bloody weather." His crew had the net down and the court covered in sixty seconds. The rain lasted seven more minutes. The cover came off, the net went up, and, less than ten minutes after play had stopped, the match was under way again. "It al¹ has to do with the paying customers," Twynam said, after directing the operation. "If there was no one watching, we wouldn't give two hoots. Let's have another four or five hours of sunshine, God. Be good to us, please." Three minutes later, the sun broke through and patches of blue appeared in the sky. Santana won the third set, 6–2.

It appeared that Santana had found his touch and had turned the match around. Pasarell, however, seemed stronger in the fourth set than he had been all day. He was leading, 4–3, when more rain began to fall. "This has never happened for donkey's years, this," Twynam said. "It's bad for the public, bad for form." Twynam, as it happened, was referring not to the rain, for his crew has covered and uncovered the Centre Court as many as eight times in one afternoon, but to the match itself. In the ninety years of the Wimbledon tournament, no defending champion had ever lost on opening day, and it appeared that the defending champion was in danger of losing now. Fourteen minutes after the new rain had begun, the sun was out again and there were wide blue patches of sky in the west. Breaking Pasarell's service, Santana tied the set, at 5–5. "Come on, Charlie," Pasarell said as he missed the shot that blew the tenth game. Santana won the eleventh, Pasarell the twelfth. Then, in the thirteenth game, Pasarell broke Santana's service. "He's a bit of a rawboned American, but he's getting there," Twynam said. A few minutes later, in bright sunshine, Pasarell chased a lob, running toward the base line, and Santana moved up to the net. Pasarell stopped, turned, and drove the ball past Santana to win the match, 10–8, 6–3, 2–6, 8–6.

"What did you expect?" Twynam said. "He didn't drag his foot."

Rome: Foro Italico

by PETER BODO

Peter Bodo is an effervescent, freestyle personality who fits well into the highly charged, constantly moving world of professional tennis. During 1978, Peter and photographer June Harrison circled the globe to produce Inside Tennis: A Season on the Pro Tour. *The opening chapter is set in Rome, where the Italian Open is the tennis tour's rite of spring.*

IT is spring again. The soft showers that traveled across the hills of Parioli and the Tiber River have stopped now, leaving the Foro Italico damp, cool and quiet. Torn clouds linger at the crest of nearby Monte Mario, and ribbons of mist rise from the clay courts to mingle with the cries of birds as evening descends.

The courts are empty, the nets slack as the seines of fishermen left out to dry for the night. A groundsman strolls across the *en tout cas* surface, which is composed of pulverized brick over a base of yellow clay and carbon, smoothing irregularities that only his eyes can detect. The courts are dull bronze and grow darker by the moment.

Tomorrow the Italian championships will begin on these courts, opening the spring and summer season of professional tennis. Later, there will be the French championships, the Lawn Tennis Championships of the All-England Lawn Tennis and Croquet Club—also known as Wimbledon—and the U.S. Open. But right now it is spring and it is Rome.

The birds have fallen silent. The roses lashed to the trunks of the parasol pines surrounding the Foro Italico are still visible; each bloom stands out like a bright drop of blood against the gnarled bark.

The players have already arrived in Rome. Tomorrow they will begin competing for a total purse of $175,000. They will be fighting to maintain or improve upon their world rankings on the computers used by the Association of Tennis Professionals and the Women's Tennis Association. They will be hoping that a good performance will either win or sustain contracts with racket companies, clothing designers, or shoe manufacturers. They will be struggling to uphold, reverse, or confirm the opinions of a worldwide public through the medium of the international press. And they will be striving to keep the second serve deep, to take a full, confident swing at break point. They are professionals. One of the reasons they stay at the St. Peter's Holiday Inn is because there are two red-clay tennis courts on the grounds.

Like most tournaments along the tour, the Italian championships has selected an "official" hotel where the players get a reduced rate for promotional reasons. English-speaking players dominate the tour, and most of them are staying at this sprawling bunker of a hotel. Just the name, Holiday Inn, provides a certain measure of reassurance; the players are more than happy to trade ambience for such commodities as good showers, soft, fluffy towels, reliable switchboard operators, and familiar menus. "Chris Evert is the queen of room service," a young player once remarked, and at any official hotel you can tell which floor is occupied by competitors: A trip down the corridor is a hazardous journey through a minefield of teacups, toppled glasses and bottles, and shriveled half-eaten steaks.

Sleep is what counts now; it is the only curative for the wild travel schedule of the tennis pro. In one twelve-month period, Arthur Ashe traveled 165,000 miles by air; he once flew 6,000 miles in four days, trying to fit a good day's practice into a hectic business schedule complicated by a desire to see his girl friend in Toronto. All players appreciate the value of sleep; so it is no wonder that while Rome is just beginning to stir and wake to the balmy night, the Holiday Inn is quiet. Most of the pros are already sleeping behind drawn draperies to the mesmerizing hum of the air conditioner. Some will toss and turn; others will spiral off into thick, dull sleep; and still others will see fabulous creatures come swimming up out of their dreams.

Among those with sufficient cause for anxiety dreams is Vitas Gerulaitis, the defending champion, who has arrived from New York this afternoon. He cannot sleep lightly tonight; there is too much at stake now. Over the last twelve months his game has taken a quantum leap, and suddenly he is in the world top five. There is no comfort in the fact that he has just won the World Championship Tennis title, one of the top ten in the world. Gerulaitis knows that in this day and age, when new rackets are given names like "The Enforcer," "The Intimidator" and "The Smasher," you are only as good as your last win. He has something to lose now, while lesser players only have something to win. And he has drawn Adriano Panatta, the idol of Italian tennis, as his first-round opponent.

Out across Rome, Panatta is at home finishing a leisurely dinner. Disgusted by his bad luck in the draw, he wonders how much worse things can get. Panatta has the talent to reach the world top five. When he won the Italian and French championships back to back in 1976, it looked as if his potential was finally coming to fruition. But his exhilaration led to intoxication, and then came the fall.

Panatta signed on with a clothing manufacturer called General Sports. The failing company could not pay him, so Panatta ultimately bought it. However, the best intentions of a thirty-year-old who had done little but play tennis for most of his life were insufficient to turn the company around. Panatta's assets were drained, and the strain showed in his tournament results. Slowly he sank to the mid-twenties in the rankings. Now he was ready to return to the game with a clearer mind. One more big year would probably be enough to secure the future for himself and his family, and almost any kind of a showing in his home championships would reestablish his stature in the minds and hearts of his countrymen. After all, he was still elegant, soulful, irascible—a perfect hero for Italy.

A few doors away from Gerulaitis back at the Holiday Inn sleeps Bjorn Borg. After a two-year respite from the arduous clay-court circuit, he has come back to play in Italy and France despite the effects his three-week struggle might have on his bid to win a third consecutive Wimbledon. There are rumors that Borg is playing for the Grand Slam—attempting to join Don Budge and Rod Laver as the only men who have won the French, Wimbledon, American, and Australian titles in the same year. Here, as anywhere else, Borg is the man to beat.

And now, as the cups chime in the cafés along the Via Veneto and the idle laugh and gossip the night away, the lights are all out in the players' rooms at the Holiday Inn. The championship vigil is on.

"Come on, why did you do that?" The outraged voice belongs to Greg Halder, a youthful Canadian pro who is struggling through a qualifying match that is not going well for him. He tosses the second ball and strikes a thunderous double fault. His soliloquy can be heard on the terrace of the clubhouse, thirty yards away. Only a few disinterested spectators are on hand for this match, but that doesn't prevent Halder from raging like a Shakespearean hero. When he misses a drop volley from the mid-court, he drops his racket and cries, "No—what a fool, what an unbelievable fool!"

It is a gorgeous, soft and sunny day, but the frenetic quality of this tournament is already evident. The Italian is notorious for its lack of organization and the patriotic fervor of its officials and audience. Nevertheless, the charms of the Foro Italico give the event the most festive ambience of any tournament.

The Foro Italico was built in 1935 as part of Mussolini's plan to revive the athletic glory of ancient Rome. Although it lacks the icy spirit and epic proportions of most fascist sites, the Foro is haunted by marble incarnations of the fascists' human ideal. The main gate is guarded by the towering statue of a young soldier striding off to a war long past.

The Foro is a long oval, like a chariot ring, with deep cavities at either end. One of these craters houses several field courts separated by rows of tall hedges. Massive marble steps overgrown with grass and moss lead down about thirty feet to court level, providing spectator seating. The field courts are rimmed by parasol pines with comical swollen heads. The lightest breeze fills the air with the scent of evergreens.

At the other end of the oval is the stadium, or Campo Centrale, which rears skyward in a maze of black bleachers. The recent expansion of the stadium has left the grotesque statues surrounding it diminished by a superstructure of steel piping. The stadium looks like the skeleton of a pantheon that has been burned out and ravaged, leaving only its marble inhabitants intact. From ground level down to the court, it is terraced with marble steps. A sense of antiquity prevails when the mild spring sun fills this bowl with molten lights and turns the bank of spectators into bands of muted, shifting colors.

Between the Campo Centrale and the field courts are a broad patio with an outdoor café, an arcade of trade booths and the clubhouse, built into the side of a hill. The public restaurant and facilities for the press and players are in the clubhouse.

Color distinguishes the Italian Open; the gold and green field is dotted with the red, white and green of the Italian flag. The marble has an aquamarine tint, and the spectators wear vibrant silks and jewelry that throws sparks in the sun. The Italian is also a tournament of sounds. The birds that find a haven on Monte Mario chirp incessantly. The porcine hawkers, calling their wares in jovial tones, sell colored hats, cushions and miniature flags from wooden footlockers. Vendors urge spectators to buy waxed cartons of mineral water, the rich ice cream known as gelato, espresso and soft drinks whose prices often fluctuate with the weather. There is also the constant rasp of gravel as spectators come and go; they stop to chat or eat mozzarella and tomato salad with oil and vinegar on the sunny patio. And there is the sonorous calling of the score: *Quindici, trenta, quaranta, pari, vantaggio, giuoco.* Another common call from the umpire's chair is *"Silenzio, per cortesia,"* a plea for silence on behalf of the players. Bedlam often erupts in the Campo Centrale, for the Italians are a vocal, partisan crowd. This is their national championships, and they like to see Italians win it.

The players' restaurant overlooks the field courts. During the lunch hour, players in vibrant track suits dine well; a young man accustomed to cheeseburgers and French fries is now eating his way through tortellini, veal in cream sauce, and gorgonzola. His cluttered tray also holds a bottle of San Pellegrino mineral water, the "official" drink of the Italian tournament; the name is painted on the yellow coolers that sit beside the umpire's chair on every court.

Outside the clubhouse I met Bill Scanlon, a young American player who was leaning on a railing watching Harold Solomon and Eddie Dibbs practicing down below. Beside him was a plastic bag containing four tennis rackets. The logo on the bag, an abstract F, stands for Fila, the most prestigious brand of tennis wear. Bjorn Borg, Guillermo Vilas, Evonne Goolagong, Dick Stockton, Harold Solomon, and a host of lesser players wear this sleek, expensive line. They earn a flat fee if they are considered stars; journeymen merely get their clothes free. Lately Fila has also dressed tournament personnel, from ball boys to umpires. At the Italian, the company has given each of 110 linesmen a track suit worth $120, two shirts worth $40 each, and a few pairs of socks. Fifty-nine ball boys each received a shirt, shorts, and socks worth a total of $56. In all, the company distributed $25,000 worth of clothes to peripheral personnel alone.

Scanlon joined Fila's stable under promising circumstances. He emerged at twenty from the faceless mass of college players to win the National Collegiate Athletic Association title, turned pro, and promptly beat Solomon and Panatta in pro tournaments. A smooth, artful player reminiscent of a young Ken Rosewall, Scanlon started 1977 brilliantly. He defeated Nastase twice within a month and reached the finals of Birmingham and the round of sixteen at the U.S. Pro Indoor. He was growing accustomed to the giddy company of the stars. Just as he was gaining attention as the most promising young pro on the tour, along came Fila with a total package: Clothes plus a racket that their new division promised to design to his specifications.

But things began to go wrong for Scanlon in the summer of 1977. There were no big wins. In Italy, his ranking is down to eighty-five and still falling. I noticed that he was wearing blue socks, a green shirt and shorts that did not match. The outfit had a worn look.

"I'm not in Fila's good graces," Scanlon confessed with a laugh. "I haven't won a tournament, and I don't use their racket."

"Is the racket bad?" I asked.

"I tried it for four tournaments." He shrugged. "What can I say? You've got to play with something you like, and this is too stiff in the head for me. They were supposed to make one just for me, but either they didn't bother or it didn't come out right. We're still trying to straighten it out."

"Who do you play in the first round?"

"Tanner," Scanlon said, frowning. He hurried off with the Fila bag containing Wilson rackets to take the practice court he had booked with Billy Martin.

By mid-afternoon, most of the qualifying matches were over. I wandered the grounds chatting with the players—those who had just come from tournaments in Florence or Hamburg, and those who had rested at home to prepare for the European circuit.

Out in the café area, Mima Jausovec squinted up at the ring of flags rippling above the stadium. "Where is my flag?" demanded the short, former Italian titlist. "I make a complaint to the referee. No flag of Yugoslavia!"

The day expired slowly. The pros had taken their first deep breath of spring as they practiced on the forgiving courts of damp clay. The tournament proper would begin the next morning.

The hotel room was silent and cool; it was after three A.M. and Lennart Bergelin—coach, traveling companion and confidant to Bjorn Borg—tossed lightly in his sleep. Beginning at dawn, there would be neither time nor inclination for anything but tennis as his protégé began the quest for a perfect season.

Suddenly there was a muffled ping, similar to the sound of a steel spring jumping its load. Bergelin rolled over, muttering, and switched on the lamp. He knew just what had happened.

Bergelin got up and began to rummage among the twenty-four identical Donnay rackets stacked in the corner. He lifted the cover of each and peered inside until he found the one that had popped a string. This occurs frequently, because Borg likes his rackets strung at eighty pounds, a tonicity that some stringers claim cannot be achieved with the standard lamb's gut and wooden frame. Part of Bergelin's job consists of finding stringers who can get the right amount of tension without shattering the wood or severing the gut. It is no small chore, for Borg often breaks a dozen frames a week and customarily travels with up to forty rackets. On the continent, Borg uses Donnay. In America, he plays with the Bancroft Borg Autograph. It is the same with his shoes—Diadora in Europe, Tretorn in America. Even Bergelin has modest endorsement arrangements because of his relationship to Borg; few people have seen him dressed in anything but his blue Fila track suit.

Bergelin cut the strings out of the frame and set the racket aside. He went to the bathroom for a long drink of water and then returned to bed.

Once again the morning was bright and clear; a sweet breeze fluffed the cypresses beyond the practice courts at the Holiday Inn. A handful of players stood around chatting or waiting to take a court for practice. Ruta Gerulaitis, a pert blond, said that her brother was back to his usual self. Yesterday when she called to wake him up, Vitas had actually spoken a few words, but this morning he answered with a grunt, and when he heard Ruta's voice he replaced the receiver.

Billy Martin staggered out of the hotel, his eyes still puffed with sleep and his wet hair combed neatly. Squinting toward the courts, he shrugged. "I'm going back to bed," he said, taking a few steps. He turned around and added, "I tried, right? I mean I really tried to get a court —you saw me."

Martin is known as one of the indefatigable laborers on the tours; it is not uncommon for him to practice four hours a day, playing every ball with the greatest intensity. But he has yet to wrest the practice title from Gottfried, who once asked Ashe if it would be all right to practice only in the morning on one particular day, because he was getting married in the afternoon. "No problem," Ashe replied magnanimously.

It is staggering to contemplate the sheer number of tennis balls Martin has struck in his young life. By the time he was fourteen, he was a legend in age-group tennis—a prodigy who set the sports pages aflame with his dazzling record. He stopped at college only long enough to collect the national singles title as a UCLA freshman and then turned pro, scoring a number of impressive upsets on his first turn around the tour.

But the subtle advantage of a newcomer, that psychological aura that makes even the most established opponents tentative, soon vanished. A few losses to his equals and then a few more to his inferiors firmly reestablished Martin's mortality. Soon he was just another journeyman

without a single "big" shot to distinguish his game.

But Martin keeps practicing. Each morning he carefully parts his short sun-bleached hair perfectly down the right side and puts on his crisp Fila gear to work at improving his strokes.

Out at the Foro the matches are already underway. On adjacent field courts, Mike Fishback and Brian Teacher are both in danger of losing their first round matches, which are in the decisive third set. The composure of each player has cracked.

Fishback is a bearded youth who likes to wear a heavy, embroidered Mexican sweater suggesting illicit south-of-the-border liaisons. He falls often; nothing gives him greater satisfaction than diving for and returning an impossible ball —even though his opponent usually crowns such an achievement with an insolent put-away volley. Clay cakes Fishback's body; mineral water bottles, rackets, a few spare shirts, and mounds of the sawdust players use to dry their hands are all scattered around his chair. He is that rarity in this decorous game: A sloppy fellow.

Fishback's style is unorthodox: Two-handed off both sides. When he receives serve, he waits with the racket held like a massive broadsword, ready to bludgeon the return. Although he puts his left hand at the base of the grip, he serves with his right arm, so what is he? He himself professes not to know or care. All he wants is to win and enjoy the life of a tennis pro. He growls and snorts and scolds himself to enough wins to remain on the tour.

But now, with break point against Fishback at 3–all in the third, Terry Moor comes in behind a forehand approach shot. Fishback's backhand pass, struck with severe topspin, lands just wide of the line and takes a jackrabbit leap toward the fence. Fishback stares at the spot, then hangs his head for a few moments. After taking a few steps toward his chair for the changeover, he explodes, hurling his racket against the fence. A linesman sitting nearby frowns, turns around to the cluster of spectators, and grumbles about this wild American.

On the next court, Pat McNamee manages

to stay in a crucial game with the help of three let court winners. It seems that each time Teacher is in a position to get the crucial break, McNamee's ball strikes the top of the net and then dribbles over to save him. *Vantaggio,* McNamee. He hits a big serve and comes to net. Teacher's return is just about perfect—low, dipping to force his opponent to half-volley from the dirt. The ball comes off McNamee's strings, hits the top of the net again, and hangs in the air for a moment before plopping over on Teacher's side. Teacher collapses on the clay and lies on his back, looking up at the sun with his wolf-gray eyes.

A few players are sitting on the marble steps near the restaurant, chuckling over this double drama, when a loudspeaker from inside crackles: *"Signore Borg, Signore Ycaza, Campo Centrale, per favore."*

Most of the players have not yet seen Borg, for he spends as little time as possible around the tournament grounds. He comes and goes silently, almost stealthily. Suddenly he is encountered, like an unidentified flying object. He materializes in his corduroy jeans, short-sleeved sport shirt, and navy clogs. In this day of the sculpted blow-dry haircut, Borg's locks are just plain long and unkempt. There is a touch of Howard Hughes about Borg, from his ineffable manner right down to his compulsive privacy. You can visualize him two decades from now, after he has won fifteen Wimbledon titles and made enough money to float a fleet of oil tankers, sitting in his Monte Carlo apartment with sixteen-inch fingernails.

Borg and Ricardo Ycaza, an Ecuadorian, are still in the locker room. They are far enough apart so that they don't have to speak. But in a few moments they will have to leave this haven, and walk through a cool, damp tunnel that leads out to the Campo Centrale, passing beneath the clubhouse, the outdoor café, and the stadium grandstand along the way. The walk is long enough to make a player feel as if he has been born into a different world when he emerges into the rioting colors and din of the stadium. Sometimes the players chat on their way out to the court. This is not the case now; Ycaza can't think of a blessed word to say to the taciturn, confident fellow whose fury he must soon face.

Ycaza is not the only one who cannot pierce Borg's reserve. Hundreds of journalists have also tried with little success. Borg never volunteers any more information on a subject than is absolutely necessary, nor does he show any interest in the movements of his colleagues. When Borg is away from tennis, he likes to lie on a beach or watch television; until recently, he enjoyed the escapades of Kalle Anka (Donald Duck), but he no longer has such literary interests. The wild tales of his taste for the teenage idolaters who used to dog his footsteps were mostly fabrications. He conceals his movements and leaves very little grist for the public gossip mill.

Although Borg is neither articulate nor thoughtful in any discernible way, he is far from stupid. His ways are as simple and impenetrable as those of an animal; the quiescence we associate with the most regal and powerful of wild creatures surrounds him. Borg has a pulse rate of thirty-five beats per minute—less than *half* the human average. Like the bear from which he derives his first name, he is solitary and he loves to sleep. Borg gives nothing away. He is inviolable and passive. Like the bear, he responds only to extreme provocation.

Polite applause greet Borg and Ycaza as they step onto the golden floor of the Campo Centrale. Around them, the low walls are plastered with placards placed to ensure that a camera or still photographer following the action will not miss the advertising. When a tennis fan in Milan, Florence or Palermo picks up a magazine to read about the tournament, the brand names in the background will register on the subconscious.

Ycaza plays with desperate fury when the match gets underway. The Swede looks disinterested; his game is lethargic. On the changeover with Ycaza leading 4–3, Borg peevishly casts a green towel over the lens of a cameraman who has moved in for a close-up. This is Borg's first tournament in weeks; perhaps he is just meeting the spring slowly, like the bear emerging from his dark den after long hibernation.

Ycaza collects the first set, 7–5, on the

strength of an early service break. Borg remains unruffled. He wins the first game of the second set and then takes advantage of a letdown by his opponent to break in the second game. Such letdowns are common, particularly when an underdog like Ycaza has parlayed hope, determination, fear and abandon into a profitable whole. Such feverish emotions cannot be sustained for long; soon the player's whole being aches for a moment's respite. Borg has waited for Ycaza to yield to that moment, and now he strikes. The games begin to flow by . . . two, four, six, nine in a row. The Swede, finding his rhythm, pares down the margin of error on his ground strokes until it is all but undetectable. He wins easily.

Soon they are preparing the court for the match the crowd has been waiting for—Panatta against Gerulaitis.

Ruta Gerulaitis noticed that her brother, the number-two seed behind Borg, was nervous on the morning of his first match. She tried to make small talk on the way over to the Foro, pointing out any number of quaint piazzas and expensive cars, but Vitas was unresponsive. Ruta knew her brother was in trouble.

The match begins at the height of the afternoon; the stadium is filled with over seven thousand Panatta loyalists who greet the appearance of their hero with applause and adulatory shouts. Panatta looks nervous during the warm-up. He has great difficulty finding the grip that has been second nature to him for some twenty years. His hand explores the racket handle continuously as he unlimbers his arms and legs with casual, softly struck strokes.

On the far side of the court, a subdued Gerulaitis mutters and does everything just a bit too quickly. He stares at the clay between shots to avoid looking up at the stadium. He rotates his arm a few times, touches the socket as if he wants to make sure it is still there. Finally they are ready to play.

When Panatta wins the first point that Gerulaitis serves, a massive cheer thunders through the Campo Centrale. But the American wins the first game, and then the second and the third. The cheers turn to jeers as Italy spurns its favorite son. Panatta wins the first two points of

Gerulaitis's serve in the fourth game, but again Gerulaitis keeps him at bay and holds service.

Although his manner is tentative, Gerulaitis plays well. He is an electric shotmaker whose greatest asset is speed. He darts to the net with the grace of a hummingbird to employ one of the best volleys in all of tennis. Although his father admits he has a "baby serve," Gerulaitis manages to win by remaining one step ahead of his opponents. He is always pushing, so that his opponents are forced out of their games and rushed into tentative strokes. Vitas swarms all over the net. He turns tennis into a baffling shell game with the pea always hidden under the least likely shell.

By the time Panatta gets his bearings, Gerulaitis leads five games to love and the stadium is brooding. A love set would imply an insult to the nation itself. But slowly Panatta begins to respond. At his best, he has the ability to dig himself into a big hole and then dig himself back out before the last spadeful of dirt seals his fate. Panatta has a flair for drama; it often seems that he must emotionalize a match before he can produce his best tennis. In the Foro, he has always been a regular Lazarus. In 1976, when he won both Rome and Paris, he saved eleven match points in his first-round match against Kim Warwick in the Foro. Everyone, including Gerulaitis, knows this. So when Panatta wins three games in a row to trail by just 3–5, the American looks up apprehensively at the gathering rain clouds, as if they were an omen.

In the next key game, Gerulaitis serves for the set. His composure is shaken when he punches an easy forehand volley wide at 15–all. At 30–all he moves forward to intercept a floating backhand only to jerk the high volley into the net; this is often the first shot that misfires under pressure.

Up in the players' gallery, Ruta Gerulaitis sees it all coming apart. As the crowd rallies around its hero, her brother's serve grows increasingly tentative. Panatta is playing awfully well now; nothing brings a fine player's game to its peak as quickly as sensing fear in his opponent. "This kid's in trouble," Ruta thinks as she watches Vitas's slow collapse.

It is even now at 5–all. The only sounds during the rallies are the soft popping of the ball and the rasp of feet sliding on the clay. If you shut your eyes, the players sound like two animals moving in the dead of night. The level of the tennis has risen; the match is swollen with pressure. Games reach 6–all, to force the set into the tie breaker.

Gerulaitis serves the first ball and puts away a backhand volley. He returns to the base line to await Panatta's serve. The Italian follows a good first serve to the forecourt, and his opponent's passing shot dies in the net. Panatta serves again —a fault. His next serve is deep and true. Panatta attacks brazenly; although the return is good, a lunging forehand volley keeps the point alive. Panatta faces an awful moment while Gerulaitis chooses his shot off the slow ball. He decides to thread the ball along the line, but Panatta has guessed correctly. He is extended in mid-air, with his racket arm outstretched. The ball strikes the strings and falls across the net. The spectators leap to their feet in a disturbing flash, as if reality has been shifted. They accord Panatta a standing ovation and begin to chant: "Ahhhhhh-dri-aaaano. Ahhhhh-dri-aaaano . . . "

The momentum belongs to Panatta now. Gerulaitis reaches 2–all, but a suspiciously late call of let after a service winner by the American ultimately turns into a point for Panatta. The Italian also wins the next point, and from 4–2 on he retains his advantage. When Gerulaitis hits an errant overhead two points later, he turns and offers the crowd the central digit of his left hand. The crucial let call and the catcalls that helped force him into an overhead error were typical Roman antics, particularly exasperating for the defending champion. "These people are animals," Gerulaitis thinks after Panatta takes the tie breaker 7–4. "Rome is the asshole of the universe."

Gerulaitis tries to shake off the unpleasant feeling that he has been cheated, but it lingers like a kink in his backswing or a wart on the ball each time he draws a bead on it. He extends Panatta in the second set, but to no avail. With his confidence stimulated and his elegant all-court game grooved, Panatta strikes again when the pressure is heaviest on Gerulaitis—at 5–6 in the second set. A volley winner at match point gives the fans the only verdict they would have accepted.

Ruta is waiting for her brother at the club-house after the match. He removes the aviator sunglasses from her forehead and slips them over his own eyes. "I want to go back to the hotel incognito after this," he mutters.

The second day of the Italian Open is over. The spark of life has been breathed into the Campo Centrale.

A succession of days can slip away at the Foro without warning, for there is no end to the attractions during the beginning of a tournament. A memorable match is often produced by two ordinary players whose games happen to blend well. There is a spark of spontaneous combustion—points become luminous moments, the match flowers like a skyrocket.

There is time to sit and sip espresso while the sunshine nuzzles your neck and resplendent Romans drift by, their heads thrown back in laughter. Time to discover *panini,* tiny rolls with soft, pink tongues of prosciutto protruding from the ends. Excited children churn the gravel, chasing anyone who remotely resembles a tennis pro, that nearly mythical creature who occupies the same place in sports that the unicorn does in the bestiary. Young girls in tight pastel slacks huddle and giggle, telling tales of not-quite-chance encounters with players.

But some individuals quickly bring you back to the mundane. "Don't ask me no questions unless you're gonna do an article on me—a cover article," Fast Eddie Dibbs quipped as he rushed by. I started after him but stopped; it's never much use trying to catch up with Dibbs.

Fast Eddie, the son of an auctioneer, grew up playing tennis in the public parks of Miami, Florida. He has rounded shoulders and thick, hairy legs on which he bounces along like a bored kid searching for a game on Sunday afternoon. Dibbs made his television debut at fourteen, when a local station came out to film the final of a junior championship. The crew produced some exceptional footage. "There was me and this kid Hirshey, punchin' the shit outta each

other and rollin' around the dirt. We were arguin' about a line call or somethin'," Dibbs recalled. "Hadda be the best television show about tennis ever."

In 1976, Dibbs was ranked number two in the United States, which surprised everyone but his fellow players, who have great respect for his clever game and his ability to capitalize on any weakness in his opponent. Dibbs can steal a match from under his foe's nose. Ironically, everything about his game suggests baseball. He moves like a gifted shortstop, scooping the ball on his forehead. He prepares to hit his two-handed backhand the way a batter cocks up to swing at an off-speed pitch. Even his antics suggest baseball. During the Masters in Houston one year, the operators of the giant replay screen in the arena were testing their video system during a practice session between Dibbs and Harold Solomon. Suddenly Dibbs dropped his shorts and bent over, and the enormous image of his posterior appeared on the screen overhead.

Dibbs also produced the most perceptive self-analysis that ever passed the lips of a tennis player. When he was asked what he would be doing if he was not a tennis pro, he answered, "I dunno—I'd probably be a bag boy at the Food Fair."

Instead, he earns upward of half a million dollars a year, hitting tennis balls.

John Newcombe is here, making yet another comeback. The thirty-four-year-old player swears this will be his last swing at the game, and here he is preparing for Wimbledon. Clay is an odd preparation for fast grass-court tennis but Newk has his reasons. . . . A few years ago, he lent his name and image to a Far Eastern tennis shoe manufacturer in exchange for part of the company. The Italians like Newcombe, so he plays here to promote the sale of Lotto shoes. But right now, he is not doing a great deal to help his own cause.

The Australian takes the court and immediately imposes his big game on Tom Gullikson, an American whose identical twin, Tim, also plays the tour. But after building a 5–2 lead, Newk falters and lets the youth even the match. It is all he can do to force a tie breaker, and now he has

a good chance to win that with a 5–3 lead. He bounces the ball three times and stops; for a deadly moment, he sights downcourt, planning the route of his thunderous serve. The stadium is hushed. Suddenly, a paper airplane made from a bright orange draw sheet comes wafting down past Newk's head to settle gently on the clay. He smiles and strolls over to pick it up. He sails it toward a nearby ball boy, but the plane makes a leisurely circle, floats by his nose and settles at his feet again. This time, he spreads his arms in annoyance and stands there like a perplexed child while the ball boy retrieves the plane. The big Aussie goes on to win the match; the reputation of his shoes remains intact for another day.

The lot of the natives in this tournament is not enviable, either, because they are under enormous pressure to win. It took Panatta over six years to survive beyond the third round in Rome. His countryman, Corrado Barazzutti, has become a world top-ten player without once performing well in his home championships.

At this tournament, the sullen Barazzutti was vanquished in the first round by Vic Amaya, a gentle giant from Michigan who hits rocketing serves and wears size fifteen shoes. Another gifted Italian, Paolo Bertolucci, lost a 6–4, 2–0 lead when the partisans left the stadium following a Panatta victory and filled the galleries around him. The sudden commotion around the field court shattered his concentration and changed the tone of the match. Bertolucci, a likable cannonball of a man who has been seen "practicing" with a cigarette dangling from between his lips, refused to speak with the Italian press. "The sons of bitch only want me when I lose," he said. By the end of the third round, the only Italian with a place in the quarterfinals is Panatta.

Toward the end of yet another day, Vic Amaya described the special feeling that makes it challenging to play the Italian. "When I got to match point against Barazzutti, I was choking my head off. He hit this routine service return, but for some crazy reason I let it blow by, because I thought it was going out. I just froze. I thought it was going out, but at the same time I knew it was staying in. So the ball falls five feet inside the base line. A couple of people laughed.

"That's how this crowd is—it makes you second-guess yourself. You think about the crowd instead of the game. There were times when I was just playing in a daze. I still can't believe I beat an Italian in that stadium. Maybe the crowd ended up helping me, because it sure scared the hell out of me."

It is an ideal morning for a stroll around the Foro and a visit to the marble sentinels at the Campo Centrale. At the main entrance to the Campo is a blue box similar to the shrines along Alpine roads. The inscription on the box reads *I Famosi Prodotti Colgate-Palmolive*—the famous products of Colgate-Palmolive. The display contains "famous products" like Bancroft tennis rackets, golf clubs, "Ultra Brait" toothpaste, cologne, a menthol shave cream, and a bar of Nordiska soap, which looks suspiciously like the stuff they call Irish Spring in Terre Haute.

Colgate, the largest single sponsor in tennis, has a multimillion-dollar investment in the Grand Prix, a concept that links most of the pro tournaments in the world with a point system. The best performers of the year are rewarded with payoffs from the $2-million bonus pool in proportion to the points they earned on the tour. Also, the eight top-point earners are eligible for the Masters, a mega-tournament that ends the Grand Prix year at about the same time as the Super Bowl closes the football season.

The Grand Prix, spanning the outdoor and indoor seasons, is a $12-million venture incorporating tournament prize money, the bonus pool, and the Masters purse. Although Wimbledon is still the ne plus ultra of tennis, its winner receives "only" $40,000. The top man in the bonus pool gets a $300,000 check at the end of the year, as well as his place in the Masters, where victory brings him another $100,000. A fellow can win the bonus pool and Masters without taking a single major title; his reward for this is more than double the total amount of prize money paid to the winners of the four Grand Slam events.

I leave the famous products behind and go to take a closer look at the grotesque figures caged in the framework of the bleachers. Athletes all, they have shapeless, oversized feet and hair like frozen flames of marble. The blank eyes of each smooth statue gaze off toward an ancient Roman city whose name is engraved on its base. The most appealing of the statues is the tennis player. His pose is tranquil and dignified, free of the icy quality radiated by his peers.

The immediate neighbor of the tennis player is a repulsive skater. Some lout has left a daub of red paint at the tip of his penis. The graffiti on its base is perplexing, for along with the de rigueur swastikas and communist slogans is the message, *"Gino ama la gobba"*: Gino loves a hunchback.

In 1976, Harold Solomon did not complete his semifinal match with Adriano Panatta during this tournament. Whether he was defaulted because he walked off the court during a heated debate over a line call or whether he walked off because he was defaulted for arguing depends on who is telling the story. At the time, Solomon vowed never to play the Italian championships again. But just yesterday he said, "Well, that remark was made back in my immature days."

Solomon is playing Victor Pecci, a six-foot-four Paraguayan whose nation did not field a Davis Cup team until he emerged as a world-class player. The gifts of the twenty-three-year-old Pecci include an earthshaking serve and an artistic conception of the game; his liabilities are emotional—he is a streaky player, given to lapses in intelligence and concentration, especially when somebody begins to bully him. He wears a golden earring that enhances his resemblance to a dangerous gypsy.

Solomon, giving away eight inches in height, won the first set handily, only to have his advantage erased by a long stretch of stunning tennis from Pecci. Drop volleys, blazing serves, acute topspin backhand passing shots streamed off the Paraguayan's racket like sparks off a grindstone.

The third set opened with a fresh offensive by Solomon, who ran down everything Pecci hit and relentlessly moved him around the court. The big man began to tire. His eyes glazed and he began to breathe in long gasps. Sensing the kill, Solly prolonged each point until the time came to wade in and finish Pecci off. By then, it seemed like a mercy killing.

It was evening by the time Solly emerged from the locker room, resurrected by a long shower and massage. He wore tight French jeans and a fitted sport shirt. His eyes gleamed like polished chestnuts, for his match had been a classic example of clay-court prowess.

Solomon observed that the courts played faster this year. Despite his proficiency on slow courts, he was pleased by this because there is a point at which a court is too slow for a good player of any persuasion. The strength of a baseline player like Solomon is his ability to choreograph a rally and ultimately create an opening that allows him to end the point; the masters of clay are primarily counterpunchers who riddle an attack like hidden gunners picking off onrushing infantrymen. When an opponent declines to attack, the game often becomes an exercise in geometry and ball placement. On a very slow court, this often degenerates into a tedious struggle won by the player who keeps the ball in play most consistently, with no premium whatsoever on the quality of the shots.

The Italians use a Pirelli ball. Like the other prominent European ball, the Swedish Tretorn, it is pressureless. Dull and inexcitable, it feels like a stone on the racket and deadens the most powerful strokes. The English and American balls get their resilience from the air pumped into them. In comparison, they are happy as gumdrops and literally bursting with energy.

"They've decided to use Penn balls at the French this year," Solomon said. "I think the tennis is going to be a lot more exciting."

The women players here are unhappy. They are treated as a minor annoyance rather than an attraction, because the top pros—Chris Evert, Martina Navratilova, Billie Jean King, Virginia Wade, and others—are in America playing team tennis. The $35,000 prize money offered by the Italian is a mere pittance compared to the men's purse, but this is still an honored title, especially for European players. One of the least disgruntled of the women at the Foro Italico is Marianna Simionescu, a Rumanian player who has sacrificed her career to advance the fortunes of her fiancé, Bjorn Borg.

Marianna is plump and gregarious; her soft orange hair frames a pleasant face. On any given day, a dozen people will ask what Borg "sees in her," for she is not a beauty. The anxiety this caused Marianna early in their relationship has been displaced by a confidence born of her strong role in Borg's life. She is efficient, supportive and impervious to celebrity. She organizes their life into some semblance of domesticity, cooking Borg's meals and telling him when to shower. They are like a couple that has been happily married for years. Marianna guards their nest ferociously.

At the moment, Marianna is standing on the clubhouse deck, watching her fiancé practice. "I don't like to play when Bjorn's watching," she says without taking her eyes off him. "Sometimes if he comes over when I am losing, I play better. But if he is there from the start it is very different. It is difficult. I think he makes me nervous."

However, this does not apply to practice sessions. Borg often unlimbers his game against Marianna, who pounds the balls back as if she is sticking up for her rights.

Panatta had another narrow escape today, the fifth day of the tournament, against a *Sturm und Drang* player named Hank Pfister. The American did not even *see* a clay court until he was twenty-one years old and ready to venture forth from his hard-court California turf. Still, Pfister led 7–5, 2–0, but from 3–all in the second Panatta took six straight games. During that stretch, Pfister appeared to have been cheated on a let-cord call, and he was hounded by the crowd when he dared to question the decision. *"Scherno,"* they shouted when Panatta ran out for the second set. *"Cotto,"* they shouted when Panatta took the lead in the third. *Scherno* means stupid, and *cotto* is the rough equivalent of "well-cooked."

Pfister, a stout six-foot-four yeoman with a service motion that brings to mind a salmon leaping a falls, withered from the pressure. Panatta won nineteen of twenty-one points in one stretch, prompting an Italian journalist to whisper, *"Pfister nel pallone"*—Pfister's head went out.

However, the American forced Panatta into a final-set tie breaker, in which he held four set points. Panatta staved them off with courageous attacking tennis, further inciting the crowd with his every gesture. A few questionable calls helped swing the match for Panatta.

"I think he used me," Pfister said afterward. "Maybe it wasn't intentional, but it just seemed like he played to the crowd and helped create a situation where any crucial call would go his way. I thought he was playing the hero kind of heavy."

Vitas Gerulaitis has returned to New York to continue with team tennis, but Ruta is still here. She will play the French Open and the women's pre-Wimbledon events. She has lost in the singles, so she is more or less killing time until she leaves for Paris.

"Where are your glasses?" I asked, referring to the pair her brother had borrowed.

"Oh, don't even ask," she answered. "They're gone, and I really liked them, too. . . . That's Vitas. He's always losing things. He picks something up because it catches his eye, and then he loses interest and leaves it somewhere. Every time he comes home, he's left half his clothes behind. My mother looks in his suitcase and says, 'Vitas! Where's your new suit? Your new jacket?' Vitas just says, 'Come on, mom, don't bug me. How do I know where they are?' Vitas doesn't exactly have the longest attention span in the world."

Ruta shook her head and smiled mischievously. She is one of those people who put you at ease immediately; after half an hour, she seems like a lifelong friend. Vitas is different. He is also frank and accessible, but his obvious hunger for stardom creates the impression that he is self-absorbed and vain. He is materialistic as only an immigrant's child can be, and his taste for the finest cars, expensive boots and budding starlets is flushed with the innocence of a hungry child in a sweetshop. The burden—or luxury—of sensible behavior falls upon his kid sister Ruta.

Borg stopped by to say a few words to the pressmen after sweeping Solomon out of the tournament with desultory ease. He was beginning to look like himself again; three matches and three hours of daily practice had tanned his sallow skin and left the customary halo where the headband girds his forehead. He sat at the table used for interviews; within moments he was surrounded by about fifty faces, and the tabletop was littered with microphones and whirring tape recorders. He answered the routine questions, and when he got up to go, I followed him into the corridor.

"Are you enjoying Rome?" I asked.

"For sure." He smiled and took a sip from a bottle of *acqua minerale*. "But I don't go out. Marianna does the shopping for both of us. I just go out when I want to eat, sometimes."

I asked if the house Borg had recently bought in Monte Carlo felt like home yet.

"For sure." He jammed his hands into the front pockets of his tight jeans.

"So you wouldn't go back to live in Sweden?"

"No. Well—maybe in the future . . . " As always, his words were drawn with great deliberation. "Maybe when the tennis is finished, in ten years time, it will be possible."

Back home in Sodertalge, Borg's parents had led a sleepy, suburban life. His father, Rune, had been a clothing salesman until young Bjorn bought him a grocery store with his early professional earnings. When Borg's fortune increased, Sweden's prohibitive tax laws made a move imperative. The tax haven of Monte Carlo became the logical choice; the only hitch was that his parents had to accompany him for legal reasons. Suddenly the couple, who had rarely socialized with anyone but their closest neighbors in Sodertlage, were whisked off to the glamorous playground of European aristocrats. They were established in an apartment house and given the Bjorn Borg Sports Shop to operate.

"It was most difficult for them," Borg said. "When I find out I had to move, I was thinking only of them. I was used to the different places by then—I was already eighteen. It was good they have the tennis shop to stay busy."

Just a few weeks earlier, Borg had purchased a villa on Cap Ferrat, which he characterized as "a nice quiet place." During his most recent rest from the tour, he imported some of his childhood friends from Sweden to help him enjoy his vacation.

I asked him how many rooms his villa contained. "I don't know . . . I don't count them," he replied.

I had been told that Borg was only playing this tournament to fulfill a clause in his clothing contract. I don't know why this seemed important to me, but I felt obliged to ask whether he was playing here only for financial reasons, even though he'd never asked me if I wrote about him only for money.

When I did ask, Borg took a step back and shook his head. "No," he said firmly. "I don't have such a deal with Fila. I am free to play where and when I want."

Gradually the tournament is pared down and a quieter mood prevails. The players who have lost concentrate on doubles, a diversion that provides a little more money to help cover expenses. The idle days in Rome are spent practicing, exploring the city, shopping, and dining out. The obligatory visits to St. Peter's Basilica and the Spanish Steps are usually made and quickly forgotten after a pro's first or second visit to the city, although a shrine like Gucci exerts continual attraction.

"This gets to be a time warp," Billy Scanlon cracked one afternoon, putting his finger on a difficult aspect of his occupation. Tennis is a deceptively easy way of life. Many of its practitioners seek routine and discipline to avoid feeling guilty during idle periods. Some of them linger at the tournament grounds from dawn to dusk even when they are out of all events, feeling the same sense of enforced servitude as the lowliest clerk or laborer. A player who loses in the first or second round faces the bleak prospect of another full week of idleness.

Superficially, the lot of the touring pro is an enviable one, but the great freedom is burdensome and leads many players to seek security in small rituals and superstitions. The Indian player Vijay Amritraj will remember which side of the bed he rose from; if he wins, he will get up on that side each day until he is put out of the tournament. A South African, John Yuill, will never, but never, step on a line when he changes courts, a habit Vitas Gerulaitis also embraced for a while. Scores of players have "lucky" outfits. Jimmy Connors played through his triumphant 1974 Wimbledon with a note from his grandmother stuffed into his sock. Such compulsions

are common; each day is a new test, and a player can never predict how he will perform from one day to the next.

Borg disposed of Dibbs easily to reach the final, in which he will face the winner of the match between Panatta and José Higueras, a Spaniard. The sun floods the Campo Centrale with burnished light as we take our seats for the best-of-five-sets semifinal that will determine Borg's last opponent.

The Italians are aware of the suspicion that surrounds their championships; consequently, the difficult task of keeping a match under control is not always entrusted to native umpires. The Panatta-Higueras confrontation will be chaired by Bertie Bowron, a sixty-nine-year-old Englishman with ruddy cheeks and a head of hair as white as a cloud. Bowron is a chipper, independent fellow who has a mailing address in London and lives in his camper throughout most of the spring and summer. He follows the European tournament trail, welcome at every stop because he is a paladin of the game who accepts only expense money for his services. But his impeccable reputation did not prevent Ion Tiriac from grabbing him by an ear and dragging him around the locker room at the Foro one year because of a misunderstanding during a match.

Great expectations fill the Campo Centrale, for Panatta and Higueras are Davis Cup rivals, and their nations hold that competition in highest esteem. The Spaniard cannot match Panatta's elegance; his service motion is studied and downright unathletic. He prepares for his forehand with a baroque, looping backswing; overall, his style suggests that he is impersonating a world-class player, but his steadiness and accuracy are uncanny. All Higueras lacks is that vital spark of genius that the deity breathes into the most attractive players.

Panatta is nervous again; the grim expression on his face implies that some battle is raging within him. He wins two points in the first game, but then only four more as Higueras, snapping topspin balls at the lines and passing deftly, takes a 5–0 lead in the first set. The crowd broods as its hero wins only nine points and no games in the twenty-five-minute first set. As Panatta prepares to serve the first game of the new set, the familiar chant is taken up with mounting enthusiasm. "Ahhhhh-dri-aaaano . . . Ahhhhh-dri-aaaano . . ."

But Panatta cannot respond. When he hits a forehand too deep to give Higueras the first game, he bounces the racket on its head twice as if to bang some sense into it. Soon it is 3–0, and the prospect of the Spaniard's winning three love sets becomes a possibility. Emboldened by Panatta's struggles, Higueras begins to push his luck. Although he is not a confident attacking player, he begins to press forward at every opportunity. In some players, aggressive play reflects a failure of nerves leading to a premature desire to end a match. With Higueras, a proficient base-line tactician, eagerness undermines his strength.

Panatta finally gets a game, breaking Higueras for 1–3. But the Spaniard breaks back and holds to take a 5–1 lead, four points from a comfortable margin of two sets to none. Panatta holds his service for 2–5, despite three set points for Higueras, and he brushes aside another pair of set points as he breaks Higueras again. When Panatta holds service at love, Higueras finds his margin reduced to a single game. He leads 5–4, and as he prepares to serve the crucial tenth game, the crowd is humming.

Again Panatta attacks. Higueras chips a backhand pass into the net, and the Campo Centrale erupts. The tumult increases through the next point, as Panatta follows a sliced backhand to the net, and it reaches another climax as Higueras misses the passing shot. Now the Spaniard is chagrined. He accepts two balls to serve, but the clamor will not subside; shaking his head in disgust, he rolls the balls to the base line.

"*Silenzio,*" Bowron implores. But the crowd has engaged Higueras, who has been proud enough to stand up to it. Now it provokes and bullies him, accepting no plea and giving no quarter.

"*Silenzio, cretini!*" Bowron commands. The noise abates as the crowd ponders this insult.

Ultimately, Higueras gets to set point again, only to see Panatta's volley return the score to deuce. The Italian is playing brilliant tennis

under extreme pressure. Higueras strikes a good serve, but a let is called. He shakes his head and questions the call, knowing that there is no hope of reversal. Still, he wins the point with a delicious lob that Panatta hits just wide with a backhand overhead.

"*Vantaggio, Higueras.*"

All semblance of restraint vanishes from the Campo Centrale when Higueras squanders yet another set point, his sixth, with a forehand error. Jeers and exhortations cascade onto the court. Again Bowron pleads for silence, but this time "*per carita*"—for pity.

Panatta gains the advantage when Higueras hits a defensive volley and then makes dismal work of Panatta's equally tentative lob. Boos and whistles echo in the stadium as Higueras prepares to serve; he finally hurls his racket to the ground, whirls, and hammers his arm at the galleries. This obscene gesture seals his fate. Within moments, a cola can strikes the clay at Higueras's feet, and a resounding chant of "*Buffone! Buffone! Buffone!*" rises over the still pines.

There is nobody lingering over coffee on the charming patio now, nobody strolling by the field courts to sample doubles matches or the women's semifinals. The awful lust of the crowd rules; the uproar has magnetized the Foro, drawing spectators as if they were steel shavings. Excited youths are perched in the trees and even on the shoulders of the statuary.

In the ensuing mayhem, Panatta's coach takes it upon himself to seize the public address system and plead for silence. He is jeered off the court. Eventually Higueras is allowed to serve. He fends off the break point when Panatta drives a backhand deep after a long rally. But Panatta earns another game point with a fluky forehand that skips off the net cord for a winner.

As Higueras starts his service motion, a 100-lira coin strikes him on the ankle. The Spaniard holds up play to summon the tournament referee, who has been lingering near the side line, to remove the coin. This further angers the crowd.

Higueras's game has gone to pieces; blinded by rage, he denigrates the lineage of the entire audience and nets an easy backhand approach shot to surrender the game for 5–all in the second set. Panatta wins the next game at 15, then holds a set point of his own against Higueras's serve. The first ball Higueras delivers is a fault, but Bowron awards him two serves because of the noise. Higueras wins the next point for deuce. The tumult accompanying his subsequent fault again forces Bowron to award the Spaniard two serves. But this time, the referee steps from the shadows to overrule Bowron.

A moment of discussion between the two officials ends with Bowron announcing, *"Grazie."* He waves at the crowd and climbs down from the chair, refusing to brook this violation of the rules, which clearly state that the tournament referee can only intervene at the request of the umpire. Bowron is replaced by a Roman, but there will be no more controversy. With the only man who stood by him gone, Higueras capitulates; his two feeble backhand errors give Panatta the game and the set, whereupon Higueras stalks to the side line, yanks his jacket from the back of his chair, and quits the court.

There is pandemonium in the passageway beneath the stadium. Tournament officials gesticulate wildly at each other. As Bowron tries to make his way through the tunnel to the clubhouse, Higueras catches up with him. "I want to shake your hand," the Spaniard says. "I want to thank you because you did the right thing."

Kjell Johannsen, the number-two Swedish player, is in the locker room when Higueras barges through the door and cries, "I had to quit or else I would have killed somebody!"

Later Johannsen said, "Higueras is the most honest guy in the world. There's no way he would act the way he did without the best reason. It's unbelievable! Panatta lost every match, but he's in the final!" He shook his head, but he could not deny Panatta his due. "It's incredible how well that guy can play under pressure, isn't it?"

Breathless reporters and amazed officials continued the debate in the pressroom. Marty Mulligan of Fila stopped by, as excited as the rest of the company. "I know Borg only plays here because of his contract with the shoe company, but if this kind of thing happens tomorrow, he

won't come any more. This tournament may be finished forever."

Borg had watched bits of Panatta's matches, and he had been filled in on the wild Higueras affair. Now, on the morning of the final, he felt slightly uneasy as he ate breakfast at the Holiday Inn. "This crowd is tough—very tough," he said. "If they begin to make some problem for me, I stop to play, you know? I quit."

Borg did not want to be struck in the head by a projectile, nor did he fancy losing his concentration because of the crowd. He did not want a reenactment of the Higueras controversy. He did not want sympathy. Justice was no overriding concern. He wanted the title. That was all.

Out at the Foro, a sky as blue as a promise had erased the unsavory memory of the previous day. A breeze tousled the pines, and the sun gilded the grounds. The calm that descends on most tournaments for the final gripped the Foro.

The women's final, scheduled at the same time as the men's, would take place in the "second stadium" field court at the far end of the Foro. "I can't believe it!" cried Virginia Ruzici, a finalist in an important tournament for the first time in her life. "It's an insult." Among the twenty-four spectators would be her parents, who have come all the way from Rumania to watch their daughter, the tennis star.

At the far end of the court, Borg is waiting to warm up. Adjusting his headband and fiddling with the grip of his racket, he does not look up at the crowd. Here on the court is where he feels most at home; soon the obligations of his life as a professional man will be dismissed. He wants to play. He wants to be absorbed in the ball the way a puppy is—with concentration bordering on fixation. His appetite stirs and floods his nervous system. This is what he most loves to do, and what he does best.

Borg is broken in the first game. In the second, Panatta gets the benefit of a close call at love–30. "Now the robbery begins," an Italian friend of mine whispers. However, Borg breaks back. At 15–30 in the next game he suddenly strikes his head with his racket and walks calmly to the side line. He has been bitten just above the right eyebrow by a bee. When they continue after a five-minute delay, Panatta runs out the first set, 6–1, by taking the pace off the ball at every opportunity. He has lured Borg into the forecourt, the place the Swede likes least, with succinct dropshots from the backcourt. Panatta has served well and volleyed precisely, ending many points before Borg could force him to rally. It is a highly conceived strategy.

The afternoon is ablaze with heat and light. The glare bothers the Swede, who has a mild headache centered on the sting above his brow. Each player holds his first service game of the second set. In the third game, Panatta departs from his touch game and begins to rally with Borg. He is promptly broken. In the next game, a crucial one for Borg, he reveals the remarkable fifth gear that none of his opponents possesses. He hits heavily topspun balls that pound the clay and hop out of reach. Each successive stroke has more pace and less margin of error; after three or four such shots, Borg is in the groove, and soon he finishes the sizzling rally with the easy placement offered by the final, desperate retrieve of his opponent. Borg leads, 4–1.

At break point against Borg in the next game, Panatta casts himself into the air and strikes a miraculous forehand drop volley off the frame, just wide of the side line. But there is no call of out. Borg looks at the spot where the ball fell, as does Panatta. The umpire makes a quick gesture indicating that the ball was good. Borg bows and quickly rolls the spare ball in his hand to the umpire's stand. He begins to change court. This act of complete surrender is so disconcerting that Panatta starts to hedge. He asks the linesman to come out and verify his call by examining the mark. The official insists that the ball was good.

Thus far the crowd has been subdued. Borg's reaction to this first loaded moment has been so swift, so cool and effective, that there is no reason to challenge him. A puzzled murmur runs through the galleries. Borg's acquiescence has either disarmed the audience or intimidated it. The lean blond has self-control that would be a credit to the most accomplished of assassins.

Back in the match at 4–2, Panatta returns to his coy, artistic game plan and plays brilliantly to hold for 3–4. The crowd rallies to him now; the chant rises, swamping the cheers of a small cluster of Swedes high up in the cheap seats. But Borg is right on the mark. He wins the next two games to even the match at a set–all. Panatta clings to his strategy through the third set, but a flurry of forehand errors he cannot afford against a player like Borg gives the set to the Swede, 6–1.

Panatta's ambitious strategy continues to pay dividends in the fourth set; when he breaks Borg in the fourth game, the crowd is on its feet again, singing his melodious name. Another stunning game gives Panatta a 4–1 lead. Passive play by Borg increases Panatta's margin to 5–2, but Borg breaks him for 3–5, with the Italian serving for the set.

Borg waits in the deuce court. He spits air onto his hands four or five times and swoops into his crouch. His feet shuffle on the clay as he rocks from side to side. Panatta is about to toss the ball for his first serve when Borg pulls up and raises his palm. He bends over, picks up a coin tossed from the stand, and flips the money to the foot of the umpire's stand. He goes back into his crouch and proceeds to win the game at 15, striking unanswerable winners as he glides across the court.

Now Borg can serve to even the fourth set, but he falls behind 30–40 on the strength of Panatta's volleying. At break point, Panatta hits an imperfect dropshot that Borg reaches easily and sends toward the far base line with a vengeful forehand. Panatta gets to the ball and sends a backhand skimming over the net, past Borg, and deep into the backcourt. In or out? An agonizing moment of hesitation by the linesman is broken when Borg nods toward Panatta and turns his back to the net, signifying that he is yielding the point, game, and set to his opponent.

The final set begins with Panatta holding the first two service points, but then Borg strikes, swiftly as a thunderclap. He wins eight straight points; when his heavy strokes are not pounding the clay, he walks with his head bowed, his hips swinging in cadence to his fastidious steps. He is putting greater effort into his serve now.

Borg plays a few unexpected dropshots and

touch volleys in the next game, but Panatta, impervious to them, holds with relative ease. The players change ends, with Borg leading 2–1. Borg leans forward, bounces the ball, and plans his serve, but then he pulls up. He takes a few steps toward the side line, stops, and inspects the court. He heard the light clink of a coin striking the clay, and he will not be content until he locates it. When he does, he carries it over to the umpire's stand. Then he approaches Bergelin, who is standing in the portal just behind the umpire. "If they throw more things, I will stop to play," he says.

The Swede does not return to court immediately. He stops by his chair, towels off carefully, and takes a long slug of San Pellegrino. He moves at his own pace, oblivious of the crowd. When he goes back out, he loses the first point, but then reels off the next four to lead, 3–1.

Panatta will have to play catch-up for the rest of the match, with Borg clinging to his margin with conservative tennis. He does not exert himself much against Panatta's serve and holds his own so deftly that he keeps the tension from accumulating. Working with the precision of a surgeon, he cuts the heart out of the contest and leaves the crowd with no target. He has not uttered a superfluous word or given the Roman crowd the least sign that it does, in fact, exist. Soon he leads, 5–3.

It is match game, Panatta serving. The score reaches 40–15, but then Borg turns it back. He wins three straight points to reach match point, but the talents that have sustained Panatta are still intact. Four times the Italian has advantage, four times Borg brings the score back to deuce. The crowd is tense and breathless—there will be plenty of time to shout should Panatta hold the game and force Borg to serve for the match at 5–4.

But it will not happen. Eleven points go by with Panatta holding off Borg's onslaught with a series of flying volleys, delicate dropshots, and crackling ground strokes. But then, at yet another deuce, he double faults, presenting Borg with his second match point. Panatta strikes a good first serve, but Borg's pendular backhand snaps it up and spits it back, cross-court.

The Italian's backhand volley strikes the top of the net and dies there.

Borg has won the title.

Only the postmortems remained. Borg appeared first, wearing the familiar yellow-and-brown sport shirt and corduroys. He did not think it was a particularly good match. "Both of us miss very, very easy balls," he said.

Someone asked about the close calls, which all seemed to go Panatta's way. Borg shrugged. "The points were good—very, very close, those ones. I did not want to take them like that. Adriano played well, very well. For me, there was just one important thing—to get a good start in the fifth set, you know? Very important."

Soon Panatta arrived, his face relaxed and thoughtful, drained of the tension that had marked it throughout the week. His chestnut-colored hair, still damp, brushed the top of his blue silk shirt and beige cardigan. He lit up a Muratti and molded the ash against a tin plate while he answered questions. He said he'd thought he could win, but the prospect turned bleak when Borg played two unexpectedly strong games to go up 2–0 in the fifth.

"Do you feel you both played well?" a reporter said.

Panatta was staring into the ashtray. "I played well, yes, but—Borg is Borg even when he isn't playing well. Maybe it wasn't the best Borg."

He began to raise his cigarette for one more drag but changed his mind and snuffed it out. He rose to go.

Outside, the grounds were almost empty. Ruzici, who had lost the women's final to the Czech, Regina Marsikova, sat talking with her parents in the players' restaurant. Chairs were strewn all about; the tables were littered with half-eaten meals. Most of the spectators were gone. Birds began to descend on the Foro Italico, swallowing up the last vestiges of the tournament. The experience of Rome faded with the day; it was time to leave for Paris.

The French Championships

by **REX BELLAMY**

The French Open is recognized by most players as the most difficult tournament in the world to win. Every match, for the men, is the best of five sets contested on red clay, which slows the pace of the ball but quickens the deterioration of the body, mind and soul. Rex Bellamy, one of England's finest sportswriters, chose the French Open as his favorite tournament. In the following excerpt from The Tennis Set, *his summation of a life in the sport, he tells why.*

THE French championships are my favorite tournament. The All-England Lawn Tennis and Croquet Club, ruminating among the ivy of Wimbledon, may suspect a lack of patriotism. But as Albert Camus put it, "a man's love for his native soil can be extended to a wider area without perishing." Moreover, I have French ancestry, though the strain of Gallic blood must now be heavily diluted. In any case, the fact that I like the French and their way of life is of only incidental relevance. On its own merits, their tournament is a pillar of light.

The French championships are the game's finest advertisement. The surface, clay, is grueling to play on. Yet it provides the toughest, most exacting test of all-round ability: And the most satisfying spectacle. The entry is the best outside Wimbledon. In many ways, the tournament brings the season to a peak that can hardly be challenged—much less surpassed—by Wimbledon, Forest Hills or the showpiece summits of the WCT and ILTF Grand Prix circuits.

All is grandeur and pathos. The grandeur is public—the protracted, absorbing exercises in tactics, technique and physical and mental stamina. Except for strained sinews or attacks of cramp, the pathos is usually private—the spent, exhausted bodies, lumps of flesh on the masseur's table or the dressing room benches.

These are cruelly superb championships. Nowhere else is the aesthetic potential of the game so fully explored, nor the physical cost of it so poignantly apparent. The first weekend of the 1969 championships was a striking sample. All the beauty and drama of life, all its passion and suffering, were mirrored in the small world of tennis. The enchantment of the championships settled upon us like a strange and lovely dream.

There was a great match—played on the new "show" court tucked away among the trees by the children's playground. John Newcombe, already champion of the German and Italian clay courts, beat Jan Kodes of Prague by 6–1, 6–4, 0–6, 8–10, 11–9. In the fourth set Newcombe served for the match at 7–6. In the fifth, Kodes led 4–1, had two points for 5–2, and was twice within two points of winning. At the end of it all, after more than four hours, Newcombe somehow managed to summon the strength for two pulverizing blows: Service aces that won him the match from 10–9 and 30–15. He said afterwards that he hit the first ball as hard as he could—and the second even harder. He was so weary that he talked as if in some far-off dream. And as he talked, this young superman sank back onto the massage table as drained as a Samson whose Delilah had been busy with the scissors.

For pathos, there was Manuel Santana of Spain, playing his compatriot, Andres Gimeno, for the first time in nine years. Santana's game shone in its full splendor: All light and loveliness, caressed by the most delicate brushwork. The gifted but nervous Gimeno was made to look like a craftsman enmeshed by baffling artistry. But at the crux of the third set Santana pulled a muscle. At 0–1 in the fifth, he retired.

In the dressing room, Santana, crumpled and broken, sat on a bench with his head in his hands. Newcombe did not so much lie on the massage table as collapse on it, like a crumbling pack of cards. The bounding bundle of whipcord called Kodes sat silently in a corner, looking as fragile as porcelain, hiding his private pain behind a grim, emotionless mask that told us nothing—but everything. There was hardly a murmur save for the birds outside, trilling their evening chorus to the skies.

What a cruel game tennis can be. But all this was for the public's pleasure. On a day that smoldered with heat, the mighty center court was suddenly crowded and colorful and fervent after two rain-swept days. Tom Okker, all tiptoe brilliance, frustrated that tough, brave little Texan, Cliff Richey. Zeljko Franulovic and Fred Stolle respectively thrust aside Roy Emerson (who looked as if he had been on clay too long) and Arthur Ashe (who looked as if he had not been on clay long enough). Ken Rosewall and Rod Laver played like the masters we knew them to be.

The whole weekend, indeed the whole game, was summed up by the contrast between, on the one hand, the crowds and the applause, on the other hand, the crowds and the applause, on the one hand, the crowds and the applause, on the one hand, the crowds and the applause, on the one hand, the crowds and the applause,

the sunshine and the drama, and—on the other—the quiet pain in the men's dressing room as the birds sang their last songs of the day. That contrast was as sharp as the thrust of a dagger.

Abe Segal, a big man with a heart and personality to match, is more down to earth about Paris. "On this stuff," he says, "you got to work your butt off." He has been around long enough to know. The gods were smiling on tennis when they gave it Segal. He is a kind and generous man. His language and character are colorful. He is an eccentric of the best kind, because his eccentricity is completely unaffected. He is tough, forthright and inimitable—whether talking, playing tennis, or simply being Abe Segal.

It is in Paris that, meaning no harm to anyone and seeking nothing but a quiet life, we are unfairly assaulted by a program and an order of play that leave us stuttering in polysyllabic bewilderment. Savor this lot as starters: Szabolcs Baranyi, Massimo Di Domenico, Sever Dron, Harald Elschenbroich, Jurgen Fassbender, Zeljko Franulovic, Wieslaw Gasiorek, Istvan Gulyas, Miroslava Holubova, Jiri Hrebec, Nikola Kalogeropoulos, Jun Kuki, Petre Marmureanu, Alexander Metreveli, Ilie Nastase, Marie Neumannova, Wanaro N'Godrella, Onny Parun, Hans Joachim Plötz, Mieczyslaw Rybarczyk, Junko and Kazuko Sawamatsu, Ion Tiriac, Geza Varga, Vlasta Vopickova, Atet Wijono and Antonio Zugarelli.

In such company, the reporter, copy-taker, sub-editor and printer raise thanks if Mark Cox makes news.

These players are not mugs popped into the draw as first round cannon fodder. True, a few leap from obscurity only during Europe's major clay-court tournaments. But in Paris they can all be hard to beat, clinging like limpets to their chance of a fleeting glory. For Eastern Europe, in particular, the French championships are the pinnacle of the game—the ultimate goal of all hope and ambition and endeavor, all the sweat in training and practice, for the other fifty weeks of the year. Musing on the iron men of Eastern Europe, players with faraway faces and strange-sounding names, thus spake Abe Segal in 1970:

These guys are so fit and strong. They're built like tanks and they run like f——deer. Give 'em a smell of the boodle, and they're off. They should be entered in the Grand National. Some guy, I can't remember his name, was dancing around me like he was Buck Rogers. When you ask your mate who he's playing, he says "Some bloody Rumanian." Ninety minutes later he's back in the dressing room. Some bloody Rumanian's beaten the crap out of him.

You hit the hell out of the ball and they still put it past you. Take Lew Hoad yesterday. He hit four or five balls at a hundred miles an hour and still had to come in and hit a volley. He couldn't do it if he wasn't so strong and hadn't been playing on clay for six weeks. But this tournament is bloody important."

Hoad himself told me once: "You say you don't want to go to the damned place. When you do, your arm nearly falls off. The balls are heavy. They water the courts. You've got to play some guy you've never heard of, and you're out there for three-and-a-half hours. But it's a great tournament."

Rod Laver was eloquent on the subject of Paris in his book, *The Education of a Tennis Player.* Discussing the Grand Slam, he wrote:

I realized that this was the hardest championship for me to win, and because of that it probably meant more than the other three. The Slam is three-quarters grass, and I wasn't worried about myself there. The other quarter, the French, is something else, more challenging than the others, more difficult to win, more satisfying from the standpoint of having survived a terrific test. There isn't as much pressure, perhaps, because it's early in the season and the prestige isn't as great as Wimbledon or Forest Hills. But in Paris you know you've been in a fight. You come off the court exhausted, looking battle-stained, your clothes and body smudged with red clay.

Paris isn't one of my favorite places, but I look forward to it because the French championships is the tournament I enjoy the most from the standpoint of emotional involvement. I love to watch matches in Paris, grim struggles on that slow clay, beauties for the spectators.

When the twelve thousand seats in the stadium are filled and people are hanging from odd ledges, railings and the scoreboard, as they were for the final with Rosewall, it's a very lively, warm, emotional place. Those people give you a transfusion of élan and it's a great joy to play for them—at least if you're playing well. It's not quite the same sensation as a filled Wimbledon court because sometimes the stillness of Wimbledon can drive you crazy. You keep waiting for a noise, an indication that they're alive. In Paris, there's no doubt. The buzz of humanity assures you this is combat as elemental to the people as a duel or a prize fight.

Paris in the spring may mean love to some, chestnuts to others, but to me it signifies the toughest two weeks of the year.

For the reporter, too, the French championships cannot strictly be classified as fun. For one thing, there is the consonantal clatter of all those ludicrous names, which tend to give reporter and copy-taker mental indigestion before they finish the first "take." The tournament also spans fourteen consecutive days, with never a pause to refresh the soul. Then there are the long matches, often spectacles of absorbing beauty—but so protracted that they overlap deadlines and necessitate "adds," "rejigs" and "rewrites."

During the first week, play often spans eleven hours a day. We saunter about for hour after hour through the rising dust. We sit here and there on stone benches in the heat of the day. We get sweaty and uncomfortable, and wish it were not such an obvious abuse of good will to pop into the dressing rooms and use the players' showers.

By the time the long days have finished, the last stories have been written and dictated, and the confounded telephone delays are tomorrow's threat rather than today's frustration, what is to be done about a meal? It is always possible to eat adequately in Paris, even as far out as Auteuil. The Chez Chaumette in the Rue Gros is first class and often richly sensuous (though the resident dogs have been known to regard the floor as a *urinoir*). The Auberge du Mouton Blanc, in the Rue d'Auteuil, is consistently agreeable. But these and similar restaurants are useful only when open—and occasionally, because of the lateness of the hour, we are driven by necessity to formica-topped tables amid the pin tables of suburban bars. It seems such a shame, such a wasted opportunity, when some of the finest food in the world is only a few miles away. Yet that is sometimes the way it has to be during that crowded first week.

It was the French championships that dispelled any illusions my wife had about the glamor of reporting tennis in Paris. In 1960 she labored at my side through all fourteen days. In the evenings we hurried back to our hotel near the Place St. Michel, in a street once well known to the Resistance and the Gestapo. We recharged our batteries with a shower and a change of clothes, and went out for a meal. Late to bed, and early to rise—for another day's work. Except for a few references to the deficiencies of concrete as seating accommodation, my wife has never said much about those championships. Nor has she suggested a return trip, not as a working wife, anyway.

Which reminds me that when Barry Newcombe reported the French championships for the first time, his wife asked him on the telephone one evening: "Is this tournament played on grass, or dirt?"

She knows now. Dirt.

But the truth is that reporters, like players, do not go to the French championships for a holiday. We go to work: And how thoughtfully nature and man have conspired to cushion the severity of our labors. Granted the best company, the best tennis, the best food and the best wine, who could possibly complain, save for a blind misanthropist whose taste buds have withered?

With the help of Abe Segal, Lew Hoad and Rod Laver, I have tried to convey something of

the unique flavor, the transient nuances, of this marvelous tournament. And although the first week tends to be a hard slog for the reporter, the second has its compensations. Unless the weather has unkindly interrupted and congested the program, there are fewer matches. The working day begins much later and ends a little earlier. It becomes possible to sit down to dinner, freshly laundered, in the sort of places where angels would sing songs of praise if they knew what was what in the way of dining out. Moreover, there is no longer any need to hurry.

Reporters, like players, learn to pace themselves through a tournament. Too many late nights in the first week would leave me jaded for the second. But once the first week is over, the reporter can, as it were, go to town. What matter if he clambers into bed at three or four in the morning, if he can sleep till the sun is high?

The glitter of the Right Bank has never dazzled me. It is too worldly, in every sense. The Left Bank has always been my milieu. When I cross the river, it is usually to head for the cobbled slopes of Montmartre rather than the glossy opulence of the Champs Elysées. My temporary home in Paris these days is a small hotel in a little Montparnasse community where, each year, I renew acquaintance with the same news agent, the same greengrocer, the same laundress. I know the Left Bank of Paris better than I know any part of London.

French tennis has some charming people attached to it: Most obviously such couples as Carolyn and Pierre Barthes and Rosa-Maria and Pierre Darmon. In the press box, Judith Elian is always flashing brightly dark smiles and juggling with languages. On distinguished occasions, Dick Roraback—lean and bearded, with pale, questing eyes and a zest for living—turns up to write one of his vivid features for the *Herald Tribune*.

To arrive in Paris is good: But to arrive at the Stade Roland Garros is even better, because it is to arrive among friends. And where better to meet them?

The championships are separated from the Bois de Boulogne by a highway that is all scream-

Every men's match at the French Open is best of five sets on the clay at Roland Garros in Paris—a gritty marathon that many consider the toughest tournament in the world to win. (Photo Courtesy of the USTA)

ing brakes and tall trees. If you travel by *métro,* you emerge into the sunlight at the Porte d'Auteuil amid a whirling mass of traffic. Across the road is the *jardin des fleurs.* Do not pass it: Go in. You will find little plaques scattered about, each offering a few lines of poetry. Each plaque has, as a backcloth, an arrangement of growing things to illustrate the verse. Here, in short, is an imaginative marriage of poetry and horticulture. Your French does not need to be extensive to catch the flavor of the place. In any case, it is a good spot to relax.

On most mornings, you will catch Roland Garros in a warm mood, with little to disturb its drowsy charm except for loud thumping noises from courts tucked away among the trees. It is not the loveliest rendezvous of the tennis set. But it has its own history and character, and there are a lot of trees about, which always tend to lift the eyes and the heart upward. In a rambling sort of way, it offers much solace for the

soul—or the stimulus of excitement, whichever you choose.

My mind is not cluttered with dates and facts and statistics. A cluttered mind is often a closed mind. A reporter needs to leave plenty of room for maneuver between the ears, so that ideas can dart about freely, and impressions can move in, take root, and blossom. All of which is to justify the admission that I cannot remember when I first reported the French championships.

In that first year at Roland Garros, I busied myself collecting facts and doing all the usual chores. I also spent a lot of time sitting and dreaming, looking at the day, and letting the color and beauty of it all flood into the mind—while I made little notes and turned them into the phrases that, with luck, would breathe life into the reports. There was time to spare, because hardly anyone bothered me: For the simple reason that hardly anyone knew me. But the years have left a legacy of kind friends: The mutual aid society of the writing game, or players who know what we are looking for and help us find it. Like anything worth while, such a rapport takes time to grow. The friendship that springs up in five minutes has no anchor to hold it firm in angry tides.

The golden era of open tournaments, between 1968 and 1971, is the basis of reminiscence here. But a glance at earlier horizons may lend perspective to the view. A few fleeting pictures of 1960, for example, still hang fading in the mind. Paris was making world headlines because of a summit conference. And a few miles down the Seine from the throbbing heart of the city—from that rich source of news, the Elysée Palace—the world's leading "amateur" tennis players had their own little summit meeting.

Jaroslav Drobny and Budge Patty were still doing their stuff, though the splendor had gone. Luis Ayala, the muscular Chilean, was dancing around the courts like a rubber ball. The 1959 runner-up, the South African Ian Vermaak, white cap stuck carefully over one ear, was taken to five sets by a highly promising British player, the nineteen-year-old Mike Sangster. A compatriot of Vermaak's, Rodney Mandelstam, who had played through the qualifying competition, lost in five sets to Lew Gerrard amid the gray, echoing vastness of the center court. The sun and the pace became hotter and hotter. There was time to watch the first set, stroll round the outside courts, have a leisurely lunch, stroll round the outside courts again—and then drift back to find Gerrard and Mandelstam still pounding away, still sweating and straining. Roland Garros is like that. Even the first round losers can play enough tennis to make the trip worth while.

The broad canvas of the French championships gives us plenty to talk about as we sit among the rustling trees. Andrzej Licis ("I am zee smallest," he told me once, "but I run quick") gave the fourth seed, Rod Laver, a nasty fright as the first soft shadows of evening were falling across the courts. Laver had a match point against him at 2–5 in the fifth set. But he saved it: And with some new fire of inspiration burning within him, fought back to win. "I had never heard of Licis before, and seldom after," says Laver, "but that afternoon I thought he was one of the greatest players in the world."

In the next round, Manuel Santana beat Laver in five sets. The championships ran into stormy weather, and play was called off shortly before six o'clock. There were pools on the courts, the weeping willows by the painters' tableau of results were even more lachrymose than usual, and the restaurant was bulging at the seams. But by that time Laver had been washed away. In the same round, Roy Emerson was beaten by that strolling giant from Italy, Orlando Sirola.

One more glance at a few fading prints before we leap to the more recent past. The year was 1961. It marked the first appearance at Roland Garros of one of the great players of tennis history—a woman who later achieved an unparalleled record, had a revolutionary effect on the women's game as a whole and the Australian women's game in particular, and, in spite of her reserve, inspired an ever-increasing depth of admiration and respect both on and off court.

Margaret Smith was then only eighteen years old. But she had already been Australian champion twice. In Paris, she was seeded third. But that was the year when none of the top four seeds (Darlene Hard, Maria Bueno, Miss Smith and Christine Truman) reached the semifinals. They were beaten, respectively, by Edda Buding, Suzy Kormoczy, Ann Haydon and Yola Ramirez. It was also the year when the sixth seeds, Manuel Santana and Miss Haydon, won their first major singles championships.

Miss Haydon beat Miss Smith 7–5, 12–10 in a thrilling, agonizing test of mental and physical stamina. They were on court for almost two hours of a sweltering afternoon. When Miss Haydon was leading 7–5, 10–all and 15–love, Miss Smith, suddenly crying quietly, had to stop because of cramp in her feet. Three minutes later she resumed the torrid battle. But she lost the game and, after taking salt tablets, lost the next as well—after saving two more match points (she had already saved three at 9–10).

For Miss Smith, that was a cruel introduction to the ultimate rigors of the chastening clay-court game. It was a fine match, and a harrowing experience for both players. Through the next decade, Miss Haydon and Miss Smith advanced to fame and marriage, to the names Jones and Court. Now we can look back, down the tunnel of the years, and feel that the image of each player is rounded and complete.

Let us take up the story in 1967, when Emerson, that prancing Peter Pan, won the last of his twelve Big Four singles championships—and Françoise Durr, who makes a virtue of heterodoxy, gave France their first women's singles champion since Nelly Landry (French by marriage) in 1948, and their first French-born winner since Simone Mathieu in 1939.

There were some stormy early days. When sunshine eventually succeeded rain, the flowers sparkled with a new brightness. But for a while these were damp, drab and frustrating championships—even in the restaurant, where for some unfathomable reason the staff seldom allowed customers to drink wine sitting down or tea standing up.

A violent wind snapped in two a couple of the giant chestnuts, apparently impregnable, that line the Avenue de la Porte d'Auteuil. One glanced off the radiator of a van. The other smashed through the front of a gleaming new coach. It would be understanding the case to describe the tennis that followed as a travesty of the game.

The courts had been soaked by rain and were strewn with displaced foliage. The players had spent the better part of two drenching days finding out that there is no pleasure in doing nothing when there is nothing to do. Now they were plunged into a tennis nightmare, with crashing noises all around them and tennis balls behaving as tennis balls were never meant to behave. Air shots were commonplace. Anyone who could play a dropshot into the wind was on to a good thing. To toss the ball too high, while serving, was to risk losing it over the back canvas. In circumstances that mocked the conventions, players were forced to desperate improvisation. Some were close to laughter, others to tears.

Peter Curtis, then ranked sixth in Britain, was playing in the championships for the first time. He was blown to obscurity in the first round by Patricio Cornejo of Santiago, one of the early disciples of sideburns. Ask Curtis about wind players and he will talk about Roland Garros rather than the Promenade Concerts. His frustrations were such that he eventually tried an underarm service: And put it in the net. But the match was played in three phases spanning twenty-three hours. So it may be that Curtis had some kind of record to his name after that first match in Paris.

But sunshine and the heat of battle are seldom far away at Roland Garros. In terms of tennis maturity, the adults were soon sorting out the adolescents. The tournament sprang to life on a day when the dignity of Australian tennis was fiercely assailed. Martin Mulligan, John Newcombe and Bob Hewitt lost in straight sets. Owen Davidson saved three match points. Tony Roche had to hang on desperately in his fifth set with a Czechoslovak ten months his junior—and in those days the sight of Roche was making his seniors tremble, never mind his juniors.

At last, Roland Garros was hazy with heat, throbbing with drama, glittering with the thrust and pary of often wondrous strokes.

The match of the day, its quality and its shape equally thrilling, was that between the reigning champion, Roche, and that straining bundle of energy, Jan Kodes. They shared the burning eagerness of youth. They also shared that uncommon attacking stroke, a rolled backhand. They fashioned a match that quickened the often gentle rhythms of the clay-court game, and raised the pulse rate of all those lucky enough to be perched on the soaring tiers of the center court.

There were two main crises. When leading by 6–4, 6–2, and 6–5, Roche came within two points of the match and (as Gail Sherriff, later Mrs. Chanfreau, observed) had Kodes "done like a dinner." But the bulldog from Prague fought his way out of the trap, emerging with blood seeping from his hand and red shale spattered over his clothes. In the fifth set came a shaft of splendor, the sort of stroke that champions play when their titles are rocking. At 5–4 to Roche, with Kodes serving at 30–15, Roche played a cross-court stop volley, a backhand, that died like a whisper in the night.

It was the moment of truth—and Kodes knew it. He made two mistakes, packed his bags, and headed for the dressing room.

Maria Bueno's greatness was then fading, her physical resources afflicted by the wear and tear of the years. But the regal authority of old had not yet exhausted itself. The smoldering fire could still glow with a consuming heat, though its steady flame had gone. On the day she beat Virginia Wade, Miss Bueno's tennis was, for most of the match, irresistibly severe. Her unparalleled flair for the game was in full flow. She was breathtaking to watch. The storm ripped gaping holes in Miss Wade's unwaveringly resolute resistance.

Then came the astonishing day when the top three seeds, the women's singles champions of Wimbledon, France and the United States (Billie Jean King, Ann Jones and Miss Bueno), were all beaten. Miss Melville, only nineteen, had previously survived two match points against Monique Salfati. Now she beat Mrs. Jones 0–6, 6–4, 8–6: After taking only three games as far as deuce in that crushing first set. A rising young player tackling a hardened campaigner, Miss Melville went for her shots with courage and confidence whatever the state of the match. In moments of adversity, she seemed to be smiling ("I wasn't smiling: I was snarling"). At 5–all in the third set, Mrs. Jones would doubtless have responded gladly when the public address system echoed the referee's demand that she should report for a doubles match (the French seldom carry efficiency to excess).

Françoise Durr beat Miss Bueno 5–7, 6–1, 6–4 and Annette van Zyl, later Mrs. du Plooy, beat Mrs. King 6–2, 5–7, 6–4. That was a day when we could have written columns. But for some reason space was tight. We mostly had to make do with inches.

Came a sweltering Sunday afternoon that French tennis as a whole, and the Durrs in particular, will long remember. At four-twenty the crowded center court—its four vast blanks ablaze with color, like giant flower beds—almost burst asunder with noise and movement. A French-

woman, born on Christmas Day, had become French champion. Miss Durr, who knows how to apply pressure without using violence, beat the pretty little Lesley Turner 4–6, 6–3, 6–4. An arduously close match lasted one hour and thirty-five minutes.

Here was a smack in the eye for the purists, a vindication of all those who assert that character is more important than talent. Miss Durr's sunglasses and hair ribbons are distinctive but not elegant. The same applies to her grip and her strokes: Especially that sliced backhand that often takes her down on one knee. What binds all the peculiarities together and makes her such a bonny competitor is her ball control and the unfailingly sharp wits that dictate her strategy and tactics. She knows where the ball needs to go: And she has the ball control to put it there.

The crowd's collective heart went out to her at every crisis. When she squeezed a last decisive error from Miss Turner's backhand, the new champion flung her racket so high that it could have brained her on the way down. She has continued to grace the top table. But the wine has never tasted better than it did that day in Paris.

For the second time Roy Emerson completed the second leg of the Grand Slam, which has always eluded him. The historians may recall Emerson as a superb athlete who never stopped running, a bustling, hustling serve-and-volley specialist who won more Big Four singles titles than anyone else: Six Australian, two French, two Wimbledon and two American. But the Emerson whose memory I cherish is the Emerson of the slow clay courts of Paris and Rome. He was not just a fast-court specialist. He was a tennis player. And if we speak of him in the past tense, it is only because he can no longer climb quite so high as he could in his salad years.

Emerson beat Tony Roche, more than eight years his junior, by 6–1, 6–4, 2–6, 6–2. Emerson needed the interval after the third set. But his was a marvelous performance. He was everywhere. When Emerson was leaping and whirling and booming away at the net, Roche must have thought he was playing against a practice wall that was firing back with interest. It was as if every attempt at a passing shot touched off a charge of dynamite.

The 1968 championships were the world's first major open tournament. Had the organizers been prudent, the whole thing would have been canceled. But the championships were gloriously successful. Riots, strikes and sunshine ensured massive crowds: Because the citizens had nothing else to do. Roland Garros was a port in a storm. We thought of Drake and his bowls, of Nero and his fiddle. In a strife-torn city, the mighty center court blazed with color. Spectators even perched on the scoreboards, which was as high as they could get without a ladder.

The fizz and verve of that fortnight sprang from two sources: A revolution on the courts, and a whiff of revolution in the streets. Roland Garros has seldom been so packed, so animated, so stimulating, so early in the tournament. There was an air of tingling expectancy, because the promoter-controlled professionals, great names of past championships, were returning to active service on these famous courts. The flavor of the occasion was that of a nostalgic reunion. Even Abe Segal (looking slim and fit after training hard to become slim and fit) reemerged from South Africa at the age of thirty-seven, twenty years after working his passage to Europe to enrich the character of the tennis set. There were colorful and convivial scenes as players streamed into Paris from all over Europe.

The city seemed to be cut off from the world. A few players telephoned to say they were not coming. Other withdrawals languished in the strike-bound postal repositories. There was an early announcement that no one would be scratched until Thursday.

Some of the travelers' tales sounded absurd: But they were true. The four women under contract to George MacCall arrived at two A.M. after a nine-hour drive from Amsterdam. That bearded jazz enthusiast from Copenhagen, the blandly serene Torben Ulrich, turned up on a bicycle with a knapsack on his back (a sight that would have been even more remarkable but for the fact that, in any circumstances, it would be no surprise to see Ulrich turn up on a bicycle with a knapsack on his back). Some of the profession-

als landed at a military airfield after flying from New York. One group came by taxi from Luxembourg. Many traveled by bus from Brussels.

Once in Paris, the players were told they had to move close to Roland Garros, because no transport could be provided to and from the Champs Elysées. Abe Segal and Bob Howe decided that Paris had ceased to be fun. So they tested the rumors that tanks were encircling the city. They set off for England in Segal's Mustang, with a massive drum of petrol in the back. But they neglected to pack a tin-opener. There was no means of unwrapping their cargo: And the garages were closed. They eventually found help in some anonymous French village—and Segal, spitting petrol, sucked up the fuel through a rubber pipe.

But the spectators found petrol from somewhere. The roads around Roland Garros were swollen with cars. And when the sun shines on the Bois de Boulogne, riots and strikes and petrol shortages lose much of their damaging effect on the morale. The first of the Big Four tournaments to be open to everyone was played in the sort of environment nightmares are made of—but the tennis was often like a dream.

Came a weekend of roasting enchantment. The huge amphitheater of the center court smoldered with heat. Its steep banks, overflowing with spectators in summer colors, was a dazzling sight. The players must have felt like ants, trapped at the foot of a giant rock garden in full bloom. The promoter-controlled professionals —the old boys coming back to the school of their youth—looked at the brightness and beauty around them and felt, perhaps, that such gloriously open tennis as this was made for the gods.

Ken Rosewall, briefly threatened by Herb FitzGibbon, played some wonderful tennis. The lashing facility of his ground strokes almost stopped the heart. There were puffs of dust as the ball bit into the court like a bullet. The crowd made thunderous noises: And then fell back into those intimidating silences peculiar to vast assemblies.

Even this became a shadow in the memory as Ricardo Gonzales exposed the richest texture of his game in beating Istvan Gulyas 6–4, 6–2,

6–2. The Hungarian had reached the final two years earlier, but he was too modest to fancy his chance against Gonzales. This was a match between a big man and a small man, with Gonzales making tennis look the loveliest of games. He was efficient, but he was romantic. His serving and smashing were explosive. His ground strokes, stop volleys and dropshots had the delicacy of feathers blown by a gentle breeze. At times he seemed to have too much respect for the ball to hit it hard; instead, he whispered to it, like a fond parent lulling a child to sleep. To watch Gonzales was to think in terms of poetry and music. He did not play the game. He composed it.

Then there was the comedy-drama of Ion Tiriac playing Rod Laver. Tiriac is a swarthy, shambling giant with bulging muscles, black curly hair and long sideburns. There is so much hair on him that he seems to have been zipped into a rug. A Heathcliff of a man, he might have stepped straight from the pages of *Wuthering Heights.* This intimidating Rumanian took three falls, two sets, and—eventually—a hiding from Laver.

To look at Tiriac, you would expect him to play a game to match his size and strength. But he is a slow-court specialist, an expert exponent of lobs and looped drives: In short, a good operator on clay. He was new to Laver. "The ball was coming at me twenty feet high," said Laver as he was toweling down afterwards. "I felt like catching the f—— thing, throwing it back, and saying: 'Can't you do any better than that?' "

Laver can be reticent. But that day he had been through the fires of hell and was chattering freely in basic Australian.

The topspin on Tiriac's cross-court forehand set the left-handed Laver awkward problems on the backhand. When the ball did not bounce high and deep (thus depriving Laver of the chance to attack without risk), then like as not it skimmed the net and dipped so sharply that the stooping Laver put his backhand volley in the net. He also found Tiriac's backhand difficult to read. On neither flank was Laver offered the hot pace he likes: Instead, the ball came to him in a mostly gentle variety of mesmeric arcs and angles. Laver became tentative and edgy. He was playing from memory in a strange world that recognized none of the conventions of his own. The assurance drained out of him; the errors seeped in.

Meanwhile Tiriac was lunging and leaping, scrambling and stumbling about the court in a disconcerting way. He flung himself headlong in the rally that won him the first set. The center court seemed to shake with an impact doubtless recorded on the seismographs. Twice in the second set he fell again. When he won that set, his shirt and shorts were strewn with shale, and blood was streaming down his right leg from a cut knee. He was winning, but he looked as if he was losing. Yet for an hour and a quarter his tennis and his expressively menacing character dominated the match.

By the beginning of the third set, Laver was fast losing dignity. He was being drawn to and fro like a puppet on a string. He was running in circles. His legs were getting mixed up. But he kept his head and he kept at work. At the crisis of the third set he played two glittering strokes —a perfect backhand dropshot that spun into the tramlines as it died, and then his pride and joy, a topspin backhand. He was now taking the ball earlier, hitting better approach shots, and visibly gaining confidence. Tiriac, tiring, was beginning to look genially resigned. Laver covered the full width of the court—and more—to win the fourth set with a running forehand, a blazing shaft hit from well wide of the tramlines. In winning the last ten games of the match he played superb tennis against a Tiriac now looking helplessly statuesque. The mesmeric spell had been shattered. In the mind's eye, Heathcliff, still glowering, lumbered back to his brooding moors.

Ricardo Gonzales and Roy Emerson then strode into the dusty arena to delight us. Their match could not equal the melodrama of its predecessor, though the quality of the tennis was higher. With the help of a rain break and a night's rest after the third set, Gonzales won. The busy, fidgety Emerson, covering the court with a predatory, catlike grace, tried to hustle the older man into error or weariness or both. Up to a point, Gonzales was sucked into the slipstream of Emerson's swift aggression. But Gonzales was an artist—the racket his brush, the court his canvas. For most of the match, his game had a caressing charm that Emerson could not resist. Many of the rallies were as finely woven as some gorgeous tapestry. The sun was shining. Gonzales and Emerson were enjoying themselves. The crowd leaned forward. They roared. They hushed. They burbled with bliss.

Laver played thrilling tennis, repeatedly challenging the laws of probability, to beat Gonzales in straight sets. But Rosewall was taken to five by Andres Gimeno. The tall, stiff Spaniard was at his best only when he attacked—and he did not attack often enough. Rosewall was nearly always the more positive player on the important points. But there was many a trembling crisis to tantalize the capacity crowd, whose bright colors soared steeply towards the treetops that peep over the perimeter of the court.

Rosewall won the final 6–3, 6–1, 2–6, 6–2. He gave a masterful demonstration of clay-court tennis. His ball control was as immaculate as his tactical judgment. He struck a perfect length, peppered the lines, and continually made Laver run and stretch. This was cool, clinical professionalism. Yet often Rosewall showed us the one stroke in which he flirts with the flamboyant—a sharply angled backhand stop volley, played with his back to the net when (logically) the ball has passed him. Laver again became a man Tiriac would have recognized. Rosewall was drilling holes in his game, and Laver's errors were seeping through. Only his service, smash, speed, and determination kept him going. He saved seven match points. Then Rosewall nabbed him.

This meant that Rosewall had become the unchallenged monarch of the clay-court game. He had beaten Laver by three sets to one in the finals of the first two open tournaments, in Bournemouth and Paris. Rosewall, of course, had been French champion fifteen years earlier. Someone asked him if he was still the same weight: "Maybe a bit heavier in the pocket."

In 1968, such men as these had all the attention. They were like returning prodigals, or gods popping down from above to remind mere mortals of the difference between margarine and butter. But the women had some fun, too. Françoise Durr and Rosemary Casals were beaten in straight sets by Gail Sherriff, with her discusthrower's forehand, and by that cuddly, golden-haired little Mexican, Elena Subirats. Billie Jean King, who was tactically uncertain, lost to Nancy Richey, who was not. In the final Ann Jones misplaced the tenuous thread of authority—and later tired—after making and wasting two chances of a quick advantage over Miss Richey. In the first set Mrs. Jones led 5–1, but lost eleven of the next thirteen points and had to work hard to take the set. In the second, she led 4–2 but lost fifteen of the next sixteen points. There was to be no third chance. Miss Richey was as steadfast when facing victory as she had been in the darkness of adversity.

A fortnight earlier—freshly arrived in a troubled, threatening and increasingly isolated city—the tough little Texan had asked anxiously: "How do we get outa here?" Now she had won the game's first major open tournament. Like the rest of us, she was glad she had stayed.

The personal memories of that fortnight are etched on the memory for all time. A night drive from Brussels in a hired car. Public scuffles, bred from the irascibility of frayed nerves. Electricity cuts. Garbage rotting in the streets. Long walks to and from Roland Garros, because there was no other way of making the trip. Journalists operating the switchboard, taking their own calls from London. The worried players, who had taken a lot of trouble to get to Paris and wisely decided to get out of it as fast as they could. The sundry extraordinary contacts (including an ex-racing driver with an inexhaustible stock of petrol) who turned me into a sort of last-hope travel agent. Most of all, the repeated doses of tear gas, and a night spent in a candlelit garret with four French youngsters—because my bed, a hundred yards away, was in the middle of a battleground.

I stayed there for the rest of the week. The riots cooled. But then I moved to Auteuil. If you wonder why, try walking from the Place St. Michel to Roland Garros—and back—carrying a weighty briefcase through the rain. It happened too often.

The same combination of circumstances—the same unlikely *mélange* of ugly violence and beautiful tennis, the same omnipresent air of crisis—can never occur again. Those 1968 championships were unique. But another fracas, more private, caused a buzz of chat at the beginning of the 1969 championships. Two days earlier, in a Berlin dressing room, Roger Taylor's left fist had collided with Bob Hewitt's left eye. In Paris, Taylor had to scratch. Bruised knuckles and a swollen hand would not allow him to grip a racket. But Hewitt played, and won a couple of matches. It seemed that Taylor had won the war but lost the peace.

In 1970, for the second time in three seasons, the French championships were played amid a rumble of controversy. In 1968 they were the first major open tournament. In 1970 they were the first to be boycotted by World Championship Tennis, whose players have easier ways of earning a living than playing two weeks of five-set matches on slow clay. Relations between the French and WCT were strained anyway—and the French refused to pay WCT anything except the money their players could earn on court. This was a gamble. But it came off. Crowds and receipts were much the same as in 1969. The absence of WCT had no effect except, inevitably, on the quality of the men's tennis. The prestige of WCT suffered. They ducked the toughest tournament in the game, and it managed very well without them. In the short term, at any rate, the event proved to be bigger than the players. The French shattered WCT's ultimate bargaining weapon: That no big tournament could prosper without such players as Laver, Rosewall, Newcombe and Roche. WCT were wrong. Which was a healthy reminder of the old Irish saying that the only thing worse than being indispensable is being dispensable.

The championships were embellished by fresh thinking and imaginative promotional gimmickry. We had *la journée des fleurs,* when nice young ladies pinned roses on our lapels; *la journée des jeunes,* when the young were given a big welcome; and *la journée de l'élégance sportive feminine,* which produced a slightly embarrassing mannequin parade, on the center court, in weather that must have given the girls goose pimples. But we had to hand it to the French: They were original.

Unfortunately they remained careless about providing such essential personnel as scoreboard operators and ball boys. The tournament was wearing new clothes, but its basic character was unchanged.

The crowds were huge, the sunshine fierce (the mannequins were unlucky). The heat was so merciless that it was a test of fortitude watching tennis, never mind playing it. To sit or stand in the sun was to find out what happens to a steak under the grill. How clement were those evening shadows across the torrid arena! Towards the end, wind blew swirling clouds of dust around the courts. The playing conditions have seldom been as grueling. By comparison, Wimbledon seemed like a garden party.

Inevitably, the straining, dehydrated muscles protested. Lea Pericoli collapsed, shrieking with the agony of severe leg cramp, when 4–5 down in her third set with Lesley Hunt. A cluster of would-be masseurs (men, of course) rushed on court. It was ten minutes before the Italian could be moved to the dressing room. The six-foot-three-inch. Vladimir Zednik, as massively genial as Tommy Cooper, asked too much, too often, of his mighty muscles. He finally sprained an ankle coming down from a smash, was carted off to hospital and did not compete again for eleven weeks. Bob Howe chipped a bone in a foot, an injury that was to end his run of sixteen consecutive years playing in all three events at Wimbledon. Cramp nearly finished Margaret Court in the second round. And the day before the final, she was struck down by the sort of stomach trouble that can afflict any highly trained athlete who enjoys good food and drink.

Georges Goven is a wiry, spry, springy little chap with bandy legs and a jerky, swaggering walk. He bounces around the court so fast you wonder what would happen if his brakes went. He is permanently wound up and gaining time. He gave the French something to shout about (not that they need much encouragement) by reaching the semifinals. On the way he beat Manuel Santana, twice champion but ten years his senior, in a center court match that was a highly emotional Latin occasion. Noisily stiffening Goven's nerves, the crowd eventually seemed to manage the match rather than watch it. Goven was a bright and breezy twenty-two-year-old. Our minds flashed back to a similar scene on the same court nine years earlier—when the young Santana burst into tears after becoming the first Spaniard to win a major championship.

But Jan Kodes was heading Goven's way. The tight-lipped Czechoslovak was taken to five sets by Tiriac in a tempestuously delightful clay-court exercise. It was punctuated by Tiriac's brooding histrionics: And dominated by the fact that Kodes, who has iron concentration, did not let them bother him. Kodes had less trouble with Martin Mulligan, an itinerant, wide-smiling, one-man charm school. At times Mulligan even out-Drysdales Drysdale. He remembers everything about everybody—including the names (and nicknames) of their wives, mistresses, children, dogs, cats, and canaries. He has lived in Italy since 1964, suits the climate, and is now known in the trade as Martino Mulligano. Kodes beat him in straight sets.

Terry Williams (Reuter) put a stop watch on this eighty-eight-minute match and discovered that the ball was in play for only twenty-eight minutes. Does this mean tennis players should take a two-thirds' pay cut?

Kodes was ready for Goven. Or thought he was. Goven led him 6–2, 2–6, 7–5 and was serving for a 3–0 lead in the fourth set. You can imagine what happens when a dashing young Frenchman—the hero of the moment because he has beaten Santana—plays an important match on the center court. There was an explosive din whenever Goven won a point, which was often. With Goven darting about and bearing down on him, and the crowd going wild, Kodes sometimes had a look of glassy-eyed bewilderment. He must have felt like an early Christian hauled out of bed and tossed to the lions. Just in time, he remembered that he was the better player.

At the other end of the draw the tennis Cagney called Cliff Richey beat the top seed, Ilie Nastase. The Rumanian is a resourceful, enviably talented stroke player and a superb athlete, his lank hair flopping as he prances about the court with a slightly pigeon-toed gait. But maybe he was jaded by a long run of success. His length was poor and he did not hit hard enough. The chunky and combative little Richey is less well endowed as a player and an athlete. But this dedicated "loner," an austere introvert with a strong will and a fighting heart, has pushed his abilities to their uttermost limit. He played a fine, well-designed, relentlessly aggressive match that gave Nastase the hangdog look of a man who was second best and knew it.

Zeljko Franulovic, so relaxed that he makes Perry Como seem a fidget (Graham Stilwell's comparison, not mine), beat Arthur Ashe in five sets. These are players of class and character, each with his own mannerisms—Ashe pushing up his glasses with an index finger, Franulovic nonchalantly resting his left hand on his hip between rallies. They often played their best tennis simultaneously, which was bad for the blood pressure. Ours, anyway.

Franulovic, who was earning his money that week, took more than three hours to beat Richey 6–4, 4–6, 1–6, 7–5, 7–5. The match had one of the most astonishing volte-face in the history of the tournament. From a set and 1–2 down, Richey sank his teeth into the match and locked on like a bulldog. The pale-eyed Texan, restlessly eager to punch his way to the net, was all bouncing, surging authority. He hardly missed a shot. It seemed that he could do nothing wrong and that Franulovic could do nothing right. The Yugoslav lost his touch and had no compensating weight of shot.

Richey won sixteen games out of twenty. The seeds of his eventual frustration were probably sown when he was 3–1 up in the fourth set and had a furious argument with a line judge and the umpire over a close decision. That changed the climate of the match and put the crowd behind Franulovic. But Richey reached 5–1. He was two breaks up and twice served for the match. The first time, he served two double faults. The second time he reached 40–15, two match points —wasted by a wayward volley and another double fault. Franulovic accepted his reprieve just as equably as, earlier, he had accepted his sentence.

He regained his touch. Suddenly, his game was sweetly in tune again. Richey lost six successive games—but had a break point for a 5–3 lead in the fifth set. By that time both players had been through so many crises that their nerves must have been numb.

What a match that was, swinging crazily this way and that, with the dust swirling and the crowd roaring—then hushing one another as a fresh point renewed the drama. After those harrowing dog fights with Ashe and Richey, Franulovic was drained of emotional and physical resilience. In Paris a player has to combat both kinds of exhaustion, unless he plays superb tennis or has an easy draw.

Kodes beat him 6–2, 6–4, 6–0 in sixty-six minutes. It was the first time two East Europeans had contested the final. In the absence of WCT, the only Australian in the last eight was the Italianized Mulligan. A year earlier, Franulovic and Kodes had been slapped down by the Australians, who had grabbed five of the last eight places.

Kodes won his first major title and became the first Czechoslovak champion since Jaroslav Drobny in 1952 (this time, Drobny won the veterans' event). The nimble, lusty little Kodes had never played better. He hit fierce passing shots on both flanks, but tossed in a few dropshots to keep Franulovic honest. Yet Franulovic had a chance to get into the match. The crux came in the tenth game of the second set. With Kodes briefly off the boil after an irrepressible start, Franulovic served two double faults in a loose game that put him two sets down. After that, Kodes was too far in front to worry and Franulovic too far behind to hope: He scored only ten points in the third set.

The big noises in the women's event were big women—in ascending order of inches, Margaret Court, Helga Niessen (now Mrs. Masthoff) and Karen Krantzcke. To start at the top, as it were, Miss Krantzcke was confident and bang in form after helping Judy Dalton win the Federation Cup for Australia the previous week at Freiburg (where Miss Krantzcke had not lost a set). She has a brutal forehand and a totally dismissive smash. In Paris she beat Mrs. Dalton, Françoise Durr and Virginia Wade in successive rounds to

reach the semifinals, and then led Miss Niessen 3–1. Miss Krantzcke was to score only seventeen more points. She hit the ball all over the place. She had eight successive wins behind her—mostly good ones achieved under pressure. "The strain of concentrating so hard for so long hit me like a bomb at 3–1. Towards the end I didn't know what was going on."

Miss Niessen is a languidly leggy five feet eleven inches. Her glacially composed court presence ("I never get angry—I can't") nettles many of her opponents, but conceals a sharp sense of fun. For years she had been overshadowed by two equally sophisticated Germans, Edda Buding and Helga Schultze (now Mrs. Hösl). But late in 1969 Miss Niessen began to use metal rackets and beat all sorts of players she was not supposed to beat. Now she became the first German since the war to reach the women's singles final of a Big Four championship.

Sporting her usual chic line in sun caps, she frustrated Billie Jean King by 2–6, 8–6, 6–1 in ninety-three minutes. They played in an oven called the center court, amid blazing heat and a wind that had the players spluttering in clouds of dust. Mrs. King crisply outclassed her in the first set and had sixteen break points in the second. Three times Miss Niessen held her service from love–40 down. Had the Queensberry Rules been in force, the fight would have been stopped. Miss Niessen had only two break points in the set. But her flowing backhand, a lovely shot, won her the second of them. In the third set Mrs. King had a break point for 2–1. But she was promptly afflicted by cramp and hobbled through the rest of the match merely as a formality.

Mrs. Court lost only one set in the tournament. That was in the second round, when she twice had to hold her service to avoid losing to Olga Morozova in straight sets. Attacking with unusual boldness for an East European, Miss Morozova kept hustling Mrs. Court into error and dashing to the net to hit winning volleys or smashes. Mrs. Court was playing only her second match in twelve days. Her legs had lost the habit of running and jumping. Soon she was resisting not only Miss Morozova, but cramp as well. Yet she won.

Mrs. Court beat Miss Niessen 6–2, 6–4 to become the first woman since Helen Wills to win the title four times. The match was played in glowing heat and the players perspired freely under their sun hats. They worked each other cruelly hard and the match was far, far more grueling than the score suggests. In gaining a 6–2, 3–0 lead (she had a point for 4–0) Mrs. Court played some of the most resourceful and accomplished clay-court tennis of her unparalleled career. She had to. But Miss Niessen won four games out of five to draw level at 4–all. Again we admired her length, her dropshots, her cool tennis brain, and her firmness in adversity. But the German lost the tenuous thread of authority with a rash of errors in a loose ninth game —and Mrs. Court eagerly wrapped up an exhausting match that had given us some lustrous rallies.

Mrs. Court, who should know, considers the French championships tougher, physically, than any other Big Four tournament. It certainly was that year. The playing conditions made sure of it. And it was particularly tough for Mrs. Court, who had been keeping two secrets.

She spent a lot of time having treatment from the masseur. Everyone thought the trouble was the injured neck that had kept her out of the Federation Cup competition. But it was her legs she was worrying about. With the masseur's help, she nursed them into condition.

The second secret arose from an evening out, at my suggestion, on the Left Bank. It was carefully planned for the evening of the semifinals, a day and half before her last match (should she succumb, ever so little, to the pleasures of the good life, there would be ample time to recharge the batteries). I piloted Mrs. Court, her husband Barry, and Pat Walkden to a restaurant in a back street behind a back street. With *champignons à la grecque* and *fondue* to be savored, we dined discreetly well. Then, on to the Alcazar, a noisy, bustling, informal night spot with a continuous stage show that is all bounce and verve and gaiety—the sort of place to wind anyone down at the end of a day's work. Finally, a beer at a pavement table on the Boulevard St. Germain.

It was a lucky evening, because wherever we went we seemed to slot into the last vacant seats. Moreover, we were relatively sober. As Miss Walkden would put it, there was no "rough stuff"—if we may except a chatty drunk on the Boulevard St. Germain, who examined Mrs. Court's openwork sandals and told her, at quite unnecessary length, that she had the most beautiful feet he had ever seen. Maybe he was kinky about feet.

That was the whole story until almost two days later. Having dictated a report of the final, I popped into the restaurant to raise a glass with the Courts, who were celebrating with the customary beers. They gently broke the news that for most of the previous day Mrs. Court had been prostrate with a violent stomach disorder. Something she had eaten, perhaps? Had she lost, they added, they were not going to tell me because I might feel bad about it (even an incidental measure of guilt can weigh a man down).

But no wonder Mrs. Court was so desperately eager to win that sweltering final in straight sets. And that, of course, was the year she emulated Maureen Connolly by winning the Grand Slam.

A compromise brought WCT back into the fold in 1971. But Laver, Newcombe, Okker, Roche and Rosewall were missing. Half the WCT stable, including the thoroughbreds, had the strength of will to resist two weeks of physical and emotional torture on slow clay—with not even a tie break to show them a light at the end of the tunnel.

So the men's event looked thin on top for the second year running, though the makeshift WCT team did stiffen the competition in the early rounds. There were no Australians in the last sixteen, which gave the tournament the character of a house without a roof on it. In the women's event, true, there was an all-Australian final, but the women concerned were not from the traditional school. Evonne Goolagong has some aboriginal blood and Helen Gourlay is a Tasmanian of Scottish and Irish stock. Their advance to the final provided Australian newsmen with some sensational copy. Because Miss Goolagong was the first player since Althea Gibson, in 1956, to win the championship at her first attempt, and Miss Gourlay was the first unseeded finalist since Ginette Bucaille in 1954.

In the early days there was the usual scope for peripheral humor. Matches started late. There were not many ball boys about. Blank scoreboards seemed to be hanging beside the courts because there was nowhere else to put them. Everyone was complaining about the balls ("It's like hitting a melon," observed a sardonic Chilean). But there is probably no other big tournament where you can buy a chocolate ice flavored with Grand Marnier. As a distraction beside the center court press box, we also had Titian's reclining maenad—a sunbather who remained glamorously recumbent even when plopping noises and amplified French indicated that players and umpire were on active service. She just wanted a singe, and knew where to get it.

The sensation of the men's event was Frank Froehling, runner-up for the 1963 United States championship, who had returned to the big-time after five years as a businessman. Froehling is a sensation even when he is losing. He is a bony six feet three inches tall and most of him is angles: He plays like a mobile windmill and seems to spread everywhere. When he bends down to receive service, it is like seeing a lamp post melt. Froehling's forehand is the sort of stroke a farm hand might use if he wanted to scythe an entire field with one swing. But he is hugely persistent. Watch what he does to the ball, rather than the way he does it, and you appreciate that he is a rather good player.

Froehling won two matches in straight sets. He beat Jan Leschly in four, though he needed nine match points. That threw Froehling in with his old sparring partner, Marty Riessen—who is almost as tall and bony as he is, but better balanced, because there is a lot of room between Riessen's knees. Neither sees too well in low cloud. For a time these high, spare men looked as if they were flexing their trigger fingers from opposite ends of a broad, dusty street in one of those Western duels. We waited for the bang, the music, and the credits. Froehling gunned his man down by 1–6, 2–6, 6–3, 6–4, 6–2.

Riessen romped through two sets without

any fuss. Then he broke a string on the first point of the third set, and went off the boil. The pace of the match declined, its quality improved, and Froehling played better and better, as if remembering how he used to do it in the old days. "I played so well that I thought I could do anything," said Riessen. "I thought it was a game of talent instead of a game of effort."

Froehling beat Arthur Ashe 6–4, 4–6, 6–3, 3–6, 8–6, saving a match point when Ashe was serving at 6–5 in a mighty fifth set. This was a tense, tempestuous and—eventually—highly dramatic match, briefly accompanied by the appropriate mood music of a thunderstorm. Froehling then came to grief against the exuberant virtuosity of Ilie Nastase, whose fast anticipation and reflexes blunted many of the American's most cutting blows. But it was a good match, all light and shade, with each in turn asserting a transient authority. They were vividly contrasted players.

A nice man called Bill Bowrey, who is not supposed to beat anybody in straight sets on clay, beat Ion Tiriac in straight sets. Bowrey said he volleyed and smashed well. Tom Gorman said he moved like a rabbit. Gorman is one of the men whose business affairs are handled by that tennis-playing lawyer, Donald Dell. Another is Charles Pasarell, who was beaten easily by Nicola Pietrangeli: Thirty-seven years old and looking slightly the worse for a lifetime of Italian food. Cliff Richey called out to Dell: "Hey, Donald! One of your boys is getting killed out there by an old gladiator."

Richey was beaten by our old friend Istvan Gulyas. "Richey is a bulldog," observed a French spectator. "But Gulyas is turning him into a lamb."

Gulyas is a craftsman and a runner. He seems to have dominated Hungarian tennis since the game was invented. He has the tired eyes, the lined face, and the bulky calf muscles of a man who has spent his life running. He always has a look of quiet suffering, as if he has just cantered five miles and suspects he has five more to go. Which is often true. He lost to Zeljko Franulovic, who calls me "Beny" because that is the shop where we buy our shirts in Rome. In the third set

Gulyas broke to 5–4 with a net cord. Then an obviously wrong call left him poised on set point. So he deliberately served a huge double fault.

It takes a special kind of man to do that. The crowd liked it. They liked it even more when Gulyas won the set anyway.

Franulovic had been two sets to one down against the well-muscled Pierre Barthes, who can roar through a match like a train unless his opponent tampers with the signals. Then Barthes goes off on a branch line. Jan Kodes had also been two sets to one down against a Frenchman, François Jauffret. But Kodes and Franulovic were now ready for a replay of the 1970 final. Kodes did not find it easy to reestablish his supremacy. They had a better match. But he effectively "long-and-shorted" the Yugoslav.

Still waspishly persistent, Kodes beat Nastase 8–6, 6–2, 2–6, 7–5 in the final. Kodes never let his concentration slip. Unflinchingly single-minded, he tends to be more solid, less flashy than Nastase—a child of nature, athletic and gloriously gifted, but sometimes a prey to the mood of the moment. You might choose Nastase to play for your delight. But on clay, you might choose Kodes to play for your life. When they are on court together, tennis can look the loveliest of games.

The seedings said the women's final would be between Margaret Court and Virginia Wade. But Miss Wade had to retire (a damaged wrist, prematurely returned to combat duty) after playing one set with Linda Tuero. Miss Tuero wore glasses and looked like some inscrutable archaeologist, roaming the desert for riches and ready to keep on roaming until she finds them.

Mrs. Court was beaten 6–3, 6–4 by the slim and fair Gail Chanfreau, who was born in Sydney, married a French Davis Cup player, and has represented both Australia and France in the Federation Cup competition. This was Mrs. Court's first defeat in a major tournament since Wimbledon two years earlier. She said she had a cold and felt lousy. She did not move well, failed to strike a length, and therefore could not get to the net. Mrs. Chanfreau's inelegant game is based on a heavily rolled, big-swinging forehand, a sliced backhand (sounder and more flexi-

ble than it used to be) and an enormous capacity for work. She is the kind who fight until they drop—and then jump up, throwing punches. That was the way it was now. She also played sensibly, and consistently well. "I decided I had to concentrate on every point and give everything I'd got, even if I died in the second set. If I'd lost the second, I'd have been gone in the third." This was a memorable triumph and the public were clinging to every available vantage point. They even turned the birds out of the trees.

All this left the doors to glory wide open. One of the players to step in was the winsome Helen Gourlay, a tough competitor with good credentials on clay. She had been winning hearts and matches for a few years but had never managed to break through to a big final. This time, in the early rounds, she went through all the fires of adversity, which can have a maturing effect on anyone strong enough to stand the heat. She came from behind to win thrilling matches with Christina Sandberg (who had done the same to her in 1970) and a jolly Japanese, Kazuko Sawamatsu, who had four match points at 5–2 in the third set. Then, again in three sets, she beat Mrs. Chanfreau. Miss Gourlay had so much trouble with her service that she tried serving underhand. But Mrs. Chanfreau, and anyone else alert to things that boom and flash in the sun, had good cause to respect her backhand drive and volley—and a forehand which Miss Gourlay often hit so hard that she seemed about to take off in pursuit of the ball.

Miss Gourlay was now playing as if all her Christmases had come at once. She played a dazzling match to beat Nancy Gunter, formerly Miss Richey, by the ringing margin of 6–2, 6–3 in a semifinal. There was some thrilling tennis, especially during the mounting drama of the last four games. Miss Gourlay ("I always take a while to get with it") lost eleven of the first thirteen points and served four double faults in her first three service games. But she then won seven successive games, the last three of them to love. The match was becoming one-sided. Mrs. Gunter was being made to look statuesque—her game disrupted by tennis that was cutely conceived, skillfully executed and illuminated by scorching winners. She was outmaneuvered, foxed into hesitance, by a lovely demonstration of clay-court tennis. Mrs. Gunter fought back, but she did not last much longer. "Maybe I'm growing up," said Miss Gourlay. "Nancy is so used to practicing with Cliff that you can't outpace her. You've got to break her up. At the start of the second set I had a mental lapse. But I thought that if I lost the second, she would probably have time to work something out—talk to Cliff, and so on. This will be my first experience of a final of this sort. I'm looking forward to it."

So were her two chums Winnie Shaw and Kerry Harris, who decided they might as well hang around a little longer to keep her game sharp and her nerves in tune. On the eve of the final, Miss Shaw and I had an early dinner with the Tasmanian—to make sure she did not go berserk with the chocolate sauce (if chocolate sauce is addictive, Miss Gourlay is in trouble).

By contrast, Evonne Goolagong was winning so smoothly and easily that we hardly noticed she was winning at all. She played great tennis to beat Francoise Durr 6–3, 6–0. It was an astonishing result. The highly experienced 1967 champion knows the game inside out. She was still at her peak. She was in form. She was playing before her own people. And she was a difficult test for a youngster because of her heterodoxy— her capacity for doing all the right things the wrong way.

This was quite a challenge. Miss Goolagong's response was always admirable and eventually breathtaking. From 3–all in the first set she lost only twenty more points and had only one game point against her. Her brilliance was such that there were gasps of disbelief from the crowd. Miss Durr was cute and tough. She tried everything, but it was all useless. Every card she played was trumped. Miss Goolagong played an attacking game from the back of the court, swooping on the ball so swiftly and fluently that she had time to turn Miss Durr's keenest thrusts to her own advantage. She drew Miss Durr forward and bamboozled her with a sparkling variety of shots. She took Miss Durr's game apart with a facile assurance that made it seem all the

experience was on Miss Goolagong's side of the net. It was a triumph of wits and concentration, as well as skill. Here was a contrast between two finely tuned tennis brains—Miss Durr's trained in the searching fires of experience, Miss Goolagong's instinctive.

"She's got something you can't teach anybody," said her coach, Vic Edwards. "You've either got it or you haven't."

Two of the most delightful people in the game gave us a final full of beautifully designed and firmly contested tennis. Miss Gourlay played every bit as well as she had done against Mrs. Gunter. She was brave and positive, went for her shots, and pushed in to the net whenever she could. She varied length and angle and pace, and kept Miss Goolagong on the move. But she was beaten 6–3, 7–5.

Sturdily athletic and unflappably serene, Miss Goolagong raced about at high speed, slid easily into her shots, and did it all so gracefully that she seldom seemed to be hurrying. "She's the fastest mover I've played," said Miss Gourlay. "So many shots that would have been winners just came back." Miss Goolagong's returns were shrewdly placed, many of them short and low so that Miss Gourlay's penchant for attack was inhibited. In the second set Miss Goolagong was 2–5 down but won five successive games— saving four set points on the way—to win the match. She began slow-balling, so that the ball came high to Miss Gourlay and had to be stroked rather than assaulted. Soon Miss Goolagong was playing flawlessly. "I was determined not to play three sets, and I find that when I'm down I can bring out my best tennis. I think, well, here goes, I might as well try something." This fine scrap had an appropriate finish, with the valiant Miss Gourlay in full stride as she cracked a forehand volley just too far across court. Nature designed this honey-blond for wine and candlelight and romantic music. But she had shown us the iron under the velvet.

Vic Edwards, a happy man jingling his francs in readiness, was waiting for Miss Goolagong ("I want a drink!") as she came bouncing and beaming down the dressing room steps. Miss Gourlay popped into the press room for a farewell beer with a couple of friends whose interest had exceeded its strictly professional requirements. The other was Mike Coward (Australian Associated Press).

It was a good year. We saw a lot of marvelous tennis, and some nice things happened to some nice people. Once again, first-time visitors from Britain were babbling with starry-eyed enthusiasm after their first sip of the wine that is tennis at Roland Garros.

"Why don't we see tennis like this at home?"

"Because we can't match these courts and this heat."

And again we felt that in many ways the season's peak was behind us.

Those are the French championships. We have used Roland Garros for a rendezvous with the tennis set. We have gone into the heat and dust of battle and met the troops. We have assimilated the nature of the game, and of the men and women who play it—because these championships bring out all the flowers of character. We have enjoyed the inimitable splendor of a major tournament on clay courts. The game has no shop windows that are more alluring.

The Wimbledon Centenary, 1977

by HERBERT WARREN WIND

Although he is renowned as the doyen of American golf writers, Herbert Warren Wind is conversant with many sports, about which he has written eloquently for over thirty years. His knowledge of tennis is commanding and, wedded to his command of English, produced his collection, Game, Set and Match. *Following is his account of the celebration of the first one hundred years of Wimbledon.*

EVERYONE wanted the tournament celebrating the first hundred years of Wimbledon to be a very fine one—Wimbledon deserved that. Besides, that summer the Queen was celebrating her Silver Jubilee, and Britain wanted something to cheer and to be proud about—such as a banner Wimbledon. As we all know, it is extremely rare when something devoutly wished for actually transpires. The centenary Wimbledon was one of them. It had more than its share of dappled sunshine and exciting matches, like Borg's semifinal against Gerulaitis and his final against Connors. But what really put the icing on the birthday cake was the victory in the ladies' singles by Virginia Wade. In her fifteen previous attempts to win at Wimbledon, Virginia, under the stress of the occasion, always found a way to lose. Now, at the perfect time, she found a way to win. London loved it, Britain loved it, the world loved it.

Of all the evocative place names in sport—such as St. Andrews, Green Bay, Madison Square Garden, Holmenkollen Hill, Pauley Pavilion, Fenway Park, the Restigouche, Ascot, Annapurna, Kooyong, Lord's, Old Town, Le Mans, Pebble Beach, Forest Hills, Churchill Downs, Bimini, Wembley, Cooperstown, Aintree, the Solent, Yale Bowl, Saratoga, Stade Roland Garros, Rugby, and Yankee Stadium, to list those that first rush to mind—I do not believe that any holds more significance or rings the bells of memory more loudly and clearly than Wimbledon, the site of the most famous tennis tournament in the world. When you look up Wimbledon in the *Encyclopaedia Britannica* you learn that Wimbledon is a suburb of London situated eight miles from Charing Cross; that Ceawlin, the King of Wessex, defeated Aethelbert, the King of Kent, in that neighborhood in A.D. 568; and that the district covers five square miles, including the thousand and more acres of Wimbledon Common. There is a passing reference to the All-England Club, which conducts the renowned annual tennis tournament—though, almost from the very beginning of the event, it has been the practice to refer to it by the name of its geographical site, much as it is the usual thing to refer to our national tennis championships as Forest Hills, after the village in Queens in which they take place and in which the host club, the West Side Tennis Club, has long been situated. Actually, Wimbledon's official name is The Lawn Tennis Championships, just as the golf competition that we call the British Open is known in Britain as The Open, there having been no other event of that kind in existence when it was inaugurated, in 1860.

The first Wimbledon was held in 1877, four years after the game of lawn tennis was invented, and, accordingly, early this summer Wimbledon celebrated its hundredth anniversary—or centeen'-ery, as the British like to say. It was no hollow occasion. The Wimbledon championships are still far and away the most important tennis event in the world. No other sports competition, not even the Masters or the Kentucky Derby, is so meticulously organized or so skillfully presented. Wimbledon is a little like Paris. When you walk down the cobblestone streets of the Ile de la Cité or the Ile St.-Louis and gaze across the Seine at the relatively small, exquisitely proportioned, time-yellowed buildings, some of them centuries old, that line the banks of the river, you are overwhelmed by the thought that man could have ever managed to create—and preserve—such a beautiful city. During the fortnight of the championships, when you walk around the grounds at Wimbledon—the Centre Court, surrounded by a dark-green twelve-sided structure, has seats for 10,651 people and standing room for about 3500; the number-one court has seats for 5500 and standing room for 1400; and there are thirteen other grass courts, three of which have fairly large stands—it strikes you, similarly, as almost too impressive to be true. Wimbledon has character as well as looks. It not only takes care of officials from all over the globe who carry the proper credentials and wear the right ties, as one expects it to do, it takes equally good care of the patrons whose only badge of distinction is a febrile addiction to tennis. Just as the nabobs can partake of that special Wimbledon treat, strawberries and heavy cream, in their large, ornate marquees, known as the Members Enclosure, so can the average spectator find

strawberries and cream of the same quality in good supply at the public refreshment stands. For me, the key to the fact that the people who run Wimbledon really mean to do the best possible job for everyone is the arrangement instituted many years ago for handling the tickets of patrons who cannot stay for the full day's schedule of matches. Since Wimbledon is regularly sold out months ahead (except for a relatively small number of tickets that are kept for sale to the public on each day of the tournament), holders of reserved-seat tickets who leave early are asked to put their tickets in special boxes at the gates, from which they are collected to be sold at a nominal price—around 50 cents—to tennis fans who have hurried from their offices to Wimbledon at the close of the working day and have queued up patiently outside.

So many enchanting players have trod the turf at Wimbledon and so many stirring matches have been fought there that it would take a book about the size of a *Britannica* volume to begin to cover the tournament's first century. In an article, one can only briefly mention a few of the heroes and heroines who loom largest as one looks back across the decades. For starters, there was that extremely successful brother act the Doherty (pronounced Do-hert'-ee) boys—R.F. (Reggie, also known as Big Do), who won the singles four years in a row (1897–1900), and H. L. (Lawrie, also known as Little Do), who after his older brother's physical stamina had been weakened by bouts of poor health, picked up the mantle and won the singles five straight years (1902–06). The Dohertys, handsome, chivalrous, graceful young upper-class Englishmen right out of "Beau Geste," won the doubles eight times. At the close of his reign in the singles, Little Do was succeeded by the first man from outside the British Isles to carry off the championship—Norman Brookes, an unflappable, saturnine left-hander from Australia, whose chief strengths were a sharp-breaking serve, a natural instinct for volleying, and a tough competitive temperament. Brooks won his second Wimbledon title in 1914, following four straight victories by Anthony Wilding, a tall, superbly conditioned New Zealander, whose sportsmanship and princely bearing on the court recalled the Dohertys. It was a sad day when the news arrived, in May 1915, that Wilding had been killed in action in Flanders.

When the championships were resumed after the First World War, it was all quite different. William Tatem Tilden II, the master of the cannonball service and the all-court game, became in 1920 the first American to capture the men's singles at Wimbledon. In 1930, at thirty-seven, he won his third, and last, title there, the oldest man in the modern era—since the First World War—to win the Wimbledon singles. The 1920's, of course, also saw the rise of the French Musketeers. Jean Borotra, René Lacoste and Henri Cochet each won the singles twice, with perhaps the most amazing feat being Cochet's comeback against Tilden in the semifinal round in 1927, when, down two sets and trailing 1–5 in the third, he turned the match around by sweeping seventeen consecutive points, and went on to win. In the 1930's, two players stood out. The first was Fred Perry, the last Englishman to win at Wimbledon. Champion in 1934, 1935 and 1936, Perry, a magnificent athlete, had possibly the finest running forehand of all time. When he turned professional, he was succeeded by Don Budge, one of a long line of superlative players from California—in his case, Oakland—and the possessor of one of the finest backhands of all time. Budge won back-to-back titles in 1937 and 1938, and then he, too, turned professional.

After the Second World War, the lure of the big money now available on the professional tour led two of the outstanding players of the immediate postwar period—Jack Kramer, from Los Angeles, and Frank Sedgman, from Australia—to go professional within a short time after they consolidated their reputations by winning at Wimbledon. Later on, Lew Hoad and Rod Laver, two more of the marvelous group of internationalists developed at this time in Australia—in full flight, both Hoad and Laver could be positively awesome—also took this step shortly after making successful defenses of their Wimbledon titles. With just about all the top talent now gathered in the professional ranks—Pancho Gonzales, from Los Angeles, had turned

pro after only one appearance at Wimbledon as a very young amateur, as had Ken Rosewall, from Australia, in the middle 1950's, after twice being an unsuccessful Wimbledon finalist—Wimbledon inevitably lost much of its meaning and luster. It did not recapture them until the arrival of open tennis—open to both amateurs and professionals—in 1968. The first open Wimbledon was carried off, fittingly, by Laver, then the best player in the world. The next year, Gonzales, by that time a graying forty-one, gave the Wimbledon regulars a long-delayed view of his ability and pertinacity when he defeated Charlie Pasarell, from Puerto Rico, then twenty-five, 22–24, 1–6, 16–14, 6–3, 11–9, in an early-round match that lasted five hours and twelve minutes—the longest match in Wimbledon history. As for the ageless Rosewall, in 1970 he reached his third Wimbledon final (against John Newcombe), and in 1974 his fourth (against Jimmy Connors), a full twenty years after his first.

Of the women champions, the first who bore the mark of greatness was a young English girl now almost totally forgotten—Charlotte Dod, known as Lottie or the Little Wonder. She was only fifteen in 1887, when she won the first of her five Wimbledon titles. When she retired, in 1894, Miss Dod turned to other sports, and became a skating champion, an international field-hockey star, a first-class archer, a prominent Alpinist, and the 1904 British Ladies Golf Champion. In 1905, another phenomenon appeared on the scene—an eighteen-year-old girl named May Sutton, the daughter of an English naval officer who had transplanted his family from Plymouth, England, to Pasadena upon his retirement. A powerfully built, combative young woman with a brutal topspin forehand (hit with a Western grip), Miss Sutton upset the defending champion, Dorothea Douglass, the daughter of an Ealing vicar, 6–3, 6–4, in the Challenge Round. (Until 1922, it was customary for the defending champions in the various divisions to "stand out" while those aspiring to their title played their way, round by round, through what was called the All Comers tournament; then the winner of the All Comers met the defender in the Challenge Round.) In 1906, Miss Douglass defeated Miss Sutton, 6–3, 9–7, but in their rubber match the following year it was Miss Sutton, 6–1, 6–4. After that, Miss Sutton never returned to Wimbledon during her prime, but in 1919, when the championships started up again after the war, Miss Douglass, who had by then become Mrs. Lambert Chambers—and who had accumulated seven singles titles in all—was still going strong at forty, and it was she who, as the defending champion, came up in the Challenge Round against the twenty-year-old French sensation Suzanne Lenglen. In three tremendously exciting sets, during which one player and then the other mounted courageous rallies when they stood on the edge of defeat, Mlle. Lenglen at length prevailed, 10–8, 4–6, 9–7. Thereafter, with the exception of 1924, when she was forced to default because of an attack of jaundice, Lenglen stood in a class apart from her competition, dropping a total of only thirteen games in winning her five final matches. She turned professional in 1926, and with her departure Helen Wills, later Mrs. Moody, became the new queen. Also a Californian (from Berkeley), she won the ladies' championship a record eight times between 1927 and 1938. The four other years, she didn't enter.

Among the women who won the singles at Wimbledon more than once in the years following the Second World War, in retrospect there is one surprise: Louise Brough. One is apt to forget that Miss Brough, yet another Californian (Beverly Hills), was a four-time champion. Her last victory was scored in 1955, after the enforced retirement, at nineteen, of the luckless Maureen Connolly, one of the most brilliant exponents ever of base-line play, who had won the first of her three straight Wimbledon titles at seventeen. Miss Connolly was a Californian from San Diego. Althea Gibson, a New Yorker, won two Wimbledons (1957 and 1958), and Maria Bueno, of Brazil, won three (1959, 1960, 1964). Margaret Smith, of Australia—she later became Mrs. Court—also won three Wimbledon singles, and the unpredictable Billie Jean King, no fewer than six. When she entered this year's championships, Mrs. King, a Californian from Long Beach who has also had great success as a doubles player,

needed to win only one more Wimbledon title (which she failed to do) to beat the record nineteen amassed by Elizabeth Ryan, that almost incomparable doubles specialist. Between 1914 and 1934 Miss Ryan—yet another native of Los Angeles—won the women's doubles twelve times and the mixed doubles seven times. The list of relatively recent multiple champions is completed by Chris Evert, the winner in 1974 and 1976. She, of course, is a Floridian.

In the opinion of many students of tennis history, two of the most magnetic figures in the long line of Wimbledon champions appeared on the scene even before the Dohertys—way back in the 1880's, when the game and the tournament were really in their infancy. These were the Renshaw brothers, Willie and Ernest, and the story of their careers—and especially their long rivalry with an implacable opponent named Herbert Lawford—reads less like fact than like something out of Thackeray with overtones of Kipling. However, before we get to the Renshaws, some even earlier contests and contenders are worth recalling. When the All-England Club was founded, in 1868, it was associated solely with croquet, but by 1875, about a year-and-a-half after the invention of lawn tennis, the club was feeling financial strain, and its officers, believing that the solution might well be to ally it with the new and more vigorous game, decided to install some courts. Lawn tennis not only caught on quickly at the club (and elsewhere) but created such interest that within the short space of two years the All-England Club decided to stage a lawn tennis championship. In his book *Fifty Years of Wimbledon,* published in 1926, A. Wallis Myers, the distinguished English tennis historian, declared that it was Wimbledon that "gave the new pastime a style and status." He added, "Wimbledon was the nursery of the game; it bred the giants of the past, men who, by the exercise of their art, the vigor of their physique, and the force of their personality, inspired countries beyond to accept and pursue the cult of lawn tennis."

Looking back at the first few Wimbledons, one is struck by the rapidity with which certain basic strokes and strategies of the modern game came into being. In the first Wimbledon, there were twenty-two entrants—men who had developed their hand-and-eye coordination at public school or the university by playing court tennis, that intricate medieval game, or racquets, which was an equally aristocratic game, despite its humble genesis, early in the nineteenth century, as a time killer for the inmates of the Fleet Prison, a debtors' prison. Most of these converts to lawn tennis served underhand, and the rest employed a soft, shoulder-high pat. Once the ball was put in play, they were content to exchange soft, looping forehands from the base line until an error was made. The first champion, Spencer Gore, had other ideas. A tall, agile man who had played racquets at Harrow—which, incidentally, was the first public school to adopt that game—Gore, disdaining the long, polite rallies, elected, whenever he had hit a good hard shot, to rush up to within a few feet of the net and volley the return out of reach of his opponent. In the final, Gore's adept volleying enabled him to defeat W.C. Marshall, a court tennis player, without much exertion: 6–1, 6–2, 6–4. Their match drew a gallery of two hundred people.

Gore was back the next year to defend his title. In the Challenge Round, he met another graduate of the racquets courts of Harrow—P. Frank Hadow, who was in England on a holiday after spending three years in Ceylon as a coffee planter. Hadow had been introduced to lawn tennis a few weeks before. He liked the game, found he had a gift for it, and sent in his entry for the championship. He won the All Comers by his solid backcourt play and moved on to face Gore in the Challenge Round. When Gore came in to net to volley, Hadow had the perfect antidote: He lobbed the ball over Gore's head for clean winners. After his holiday was over, he went back to Ceylon and his coffee plantations. He did not defend his title the next year, and, for that matter, never again returned to Wimbledon. Many years later, when he was asked how he had hit upon the lob as the riposte to Gore's volleying, Hadow said, "It was only natural enough, though, with a tall, long-legged, and long-armed man sprawling over the net."

Hadow's absence opened the door for J.T.

Hartley, a Yorkshire vicar, who had been a court tennis champion at Oxford. After overcoming an initial distaste for the new offshoot of his first love, Hartley began to play lawn tennis regularly, and at length he made up his mind to enter the championship. He was confident that he would acquit himself respectably, but he did not see himself surviving the quarterfinal round, scheduled for Saturday. When he did, he had a problem: He had made no provision for another minister to take over his Sunday duties. With his semifinal match scheduled for Monday afternoon, Hartley caught a train to Yorkshire on Saturday night, arrived in time to deliver his Sunday sermon, caught an early-morning train back to London on Monday, got in at two o'clock, changed trains, and hurried to Wimbledon. He reached the court just in time for his match, but the trip had tired him, and, moreover, in his rush he hadn't had time for lunch. Fortunately, a rain shower forced a temporary halt in play, and during this intermission Hartley had some tea and sandwiches. He returned to the court refreshed and recharged, and mopped up his opponent. He went on to win the final, from Vere St. Leger Gould, an idiosyncratic Irishman.

The following year, 1880, Hartley made a successful defense of the championship. Wimbledon was now beginning to look like Wimbledon. For the first time, two movable grandstands flanked the Centre Court, and there were eleven field courts. There was also a score board in the Centre Court, so that the patrons would be able to follow a match closely even if the umpire's voice was drowned out by the trains of the London & South-Western Railway, which rumbled down the tracks adjacent to the club's property. In the Challenge Round that year, Hartley's steady base-line game prevailed, but he did drop the third set to Herbert Lawford, a big, broad-shouldered physical-fitness fanatic who was to play a prominent role during these formative years of lawn tennis. Lawford had been deeply involved in sports at Repton, his public school, and at Edinburgh University. A top-level swimmer, runner, and cyclist, he was twenty-seven when he made his debut at Wimbledon, shortly after taking up tennis. He was rather slow in getting around the court, and extremely awkward playing his shots, but he had enormous energy and endless persistence, and, through long hours of practice, improved noticeably year by year. Besides, he possessed one magnificent stroke. This, essentially, was a topspin forehand, which he hit in a highly exaggerated manner: He let the ball drop very low on its bounce, and then, with his powerful right arm and wrist, whipped it up with his racket and came over the top of it, imparting immense speed to the ball and causing it to duck sharply after it had crossed the net. Few players could cope with this fearsome forehand—"the Lawford stroke," as it came to be called. Everyone in tennis attempted to copy it, but no one came close to matching the effectiveness of its originator. Lawford had one other thing going for him. He loved to compete, and, while he was basically a good sportsman, he was aware that his physical bulk, his strength, his stamina, his walrus mustache, and his fixed, sardonic expression on the court could often intimidate less determined players. In his secret heart, Lawford, in 1880, might have pictured himself defeating Hartley in their next confrontation and going on to enjoy a long and illustrious reign at Wimbledon, and he might well have achieved this had it not been for the Renshaws.

Willie and Ernest Renshaw were twins. They were born in Cheltenham, ninety miles west of London, in 1861, Willie entering the world fifteen minutes before Ernest. They learned their tennis on two courts in Cheltenham, an outdoor asphalt court and an indoor clay court. In 1879, deeming themselves ready for the big time, they sent in their entries for the championship. They got to Wimbledon all right, but at the last moment they decided not to report for their scheduled matches. The panache with which the championship was staged and the huge crowd—at least a thousand spectators were on hand—overawed them, and, remaining in their seats in the stands, they contented themselves with taking notes on the techniques of the players they watched. The next year, they really *were* ready. Members of a well-to-do family, they were able to devote all their time and thought to their tennis, and came on fast. They won the Oxford Dou-

bles Championship, which had been started the previous year and was regarded as the equivalent in doubles of what Wimbledon was in singles play. Then they traveled to Dublin for the Irish championships, which had also been established in 1879. They won the doubles, and Willie, who was a shade bigger than Ernest and hit the ball with more pace and aggressiveness, took the singles. Great things were expected of Willie at Wimbledon, but he lost in the third round to a good player, O.E. Woodhouse. It had rained all week, and Willie could not find anything like his usual form as he splashed around the waterlogged court. However, as someone must surely have pointed out at the time, Woodhouse had to put up with the same conditions. In the next round, Woodhouse eliminated Ernest. Back to the old practice court.

After practicing intensively that summer and fall, the Renshaws headed south to the Riviera early in 1881 and built themselves a hard sand court on the grounds of the Beausite Hotel, in Cannes. They worked diligently on their tennis that winter, and their successful spring campaign showed it. They won the Oxford Doubles and the Irish Doubles again. (The Renshaws practically invented doubles. They were the first team to use the formation in which one partner stations himself at net while the other serves. They learned to volley expertly and came to net whenever possible. When an opposing team tried to lob them, they were not disconcerted, for through practice they had mastered a revolutionary stroke, the overhead smash.) In Dublin, Willie again won the singles, and he finished his preparation for Wimbledon by carrying off the singles tournament at Prince's, in London. That year, there was no stopping him in the championship, although Lawford gave him all he could handle in their semifinal match before going down, 1–6, 6–3, 6–2, 5–6 (such a score was possible then), 6–3. The Challenge Round was an anticlimax. Hartley, who had not completely recovered from an attack of English cholera, could win only three games in the three sets.

In 1882, the Renshaws, the unbeatable doubles team, were beaten in both the Oxford and the Irish Doubles. An interesting circumstance underlay their defeats. For some time, the players who clung to the base-line game had been trying to persuade the governing body of lawn tennis to ban volleying as detrimental to the sport's best expression, but, although they failed to achieve this, their pressure forced a considerable concession; in 1882, the net, which had been four feet high at the sides, was lowered to three feet six inches, and this made it much easier for the base-liners to pass the volleyers down the alleys in doubles. That was what had happened to the Renshaws when they attempted to defend their doubles titles. In singles play, the lower net at the posts required greater agility and quicker reflexes of the players who loved to patrol the forecourt, as the Renshaws did, but the twins were equal to it. In fact, the period known as the Renshaw Era properly began in 1882. Ernest took the Irish All Comers. His forte was the accurate placement, and he had a finer touch than Willie. In addition, he was faster on his feet. In their informal matches, there was little to choose between them. However, Ernest declined to play Willie in the Challenge Round in Dublin. It was typical of Ernest to defer to his slightly older brother in nearly all matters, and he particularly disliked opposing him in tournaments. At Wimbledon, Ernest was again in splendid form. He outlasted Lawford, 6–4, 4–6, 6–2, 3–6, 6–0, in the fourth round and went on to capture the All Comers. This time, he was induced to meet Willie in the Challenge Round. E.C. (Ned) Potter, Jr., one of the leading authorities on the Renshaws, has written, "It was their first public meeting. Nothing else was talked of in the clubs and drawing rooms but their respective merits. Many bets were placed. In the afternoon, Wimbledon saw the first of the Renshaw crushes. Stately dowagers struggled for places at courtside where they might take a precarious stand on a folding chair. Courtly gentlemen forgot their manners as they elbowed their way among the clerks and shop girls for a better view." Two thousand fans attended the match. Willie won it in five sets—6–1, 2–6, 4–6, 6–2, 6–2—but many who were on hand left with the feeling that Ernest had possibly thrown the last two sets.

There was another all-Renshaw Challenge Round at Wimbledon the next year, 1883. Ernest's most difficult match in the All Comers had been in the first round, against his old, ever-hopeful rival Lawford. Playing in a heavy wind that bothered both men, Lawford was on the verge of a spectacular triumph when, with the match tied at two sets apiece, he moved to 5–0 in the fifth set. Down to his last gasp, Ernest decided to use a tricky underhand cut serve that he had often fooled with in practice. Not only did it enable him to hold serve but it disconcerted Lawford way out of reason, and his entire game began to unravel. Sticking with his underhand serve, Ernest pulled out the set to win the match. In the Challenge Round, he played just about as well as Willie but went down in five sets: 2–6, 6–3, 6–3, 4–6, 6–3. Some people, knowing how intransigent Ernest was about the importance of being Willie, were not a 100 percent certain that he had gone all out in the final set. Be that as it may, the tennis world was infatuated with the Renshaws. They were the first genuine Wimbledon heroes, and there is no question that their magnetism was a principal reason that the game underwent a stupendous boom at this time. When you study photos taken of the Renshaws in their prime, you can begin to understand their huge popularity. They were very attractive young men, handsome in a sensitive, delicate way. They parted their dark-brown hair on the side and had rather deep-set eyes, classically straight noses, light mustaches, and longish jaws. Whereas Lawford, the arrant individualist, sometimes showed up on the court wearing a porkpie hat, a striped jersey, tight knickers, and long stockings, the Renshaws favored conservative apparel: Long-sleeved white shirts, miniature four-in-hand ties that hung down only three or four inches, and white trousers. As you might imagine, their manners on the court were impeccable. Off the court, they differed somewhat in personality. Willie, who was far more outgoing, frequently appeared in amateur theatricals. Ernest had less self-confidence and stammered.

Beginning in 1884, there was a series of three exciting Challenge Round clashes between Willie and the unsinkable Lawford. Earlier in his career, Lawford had several times enunciated the dictum "Perfect back play will beat perfect volleying," but at this advanced stage of his career he buried his pride and, learning to volley, periodically came thumping into the forecourt after hitting one of his severe forehands. Willie, in top form for their meeting at Wimbledon in 1884, took the first two sets, 6–0, and 6–4. He then began to tire and had just enough left to win the third set, 9–7, and the match. The next year, scrutinized by a taut gallery of thirty-five hundred, who filled the new permanent stands, the two waged perhaps the best of all their duels. In the final of the All Comers, Lawford had defeated Ernest in five hard-fought sets. Against Willie, he dropped the first two sets, 7–5 and 6–2, but, summoning his extraordinary courage and pertinacity and his new adeptness at volleying, he battled his way back into the match. He won the third set, 6–4, and was ahead in the fourth set four games to none with double game point in the fifth when Willie mounted a gallant counteroffensive. He did this by suddenly altering his usual tactics. Volleying only rarely, he stayed patiently in the backcourt and traded ground strokes with Lawford. Gradually, he gained control of their exchanges, pulled up to 5–5, and then won the next two games and the match. In 1886, he started off in the Challenge Round as if he would make short work of Lawford. It took him only nine-and-a-half minutes to win the opening set, without the loss of a game. Lawford dug in and won the second, 7–5. Willie then lifted his game and ran out a very well-played match by taking the next two sets, 6–3 and 6–4. The most valuable result of this historic Challenge Round series—what with Lawford adding a new dimension to his tennis by learning to volley, and with Willie, in effect, doing the same by retreating at intervals to the base line and attacking from there—was that together the two enlarged the vocabulary of lawn tennis and laid the foundation for the all-court game, which is the game that nearly all the great champions of later eras have played. During the years of these encounters with Lawford, Willie Renshaw reached and then passed his peak. A little over a decade later, Herbert Chipp, a competent tournament player and a sound critic, paid Willie this

tribute: "The supreme advantage which, to my mind, William possessed over every other player, past or present, was his power of getting the ball back into his opponent's court with the least possible loss of time. The ball was taken at the top of the bound and forced across the net before the opposing player had well recovered his balance. . . . One never seemed to have any breathing time."

Early in the tournament season of 1887, the whole picture changed. While playing in the Scottish championships, Willie Renshaw came down with "tennis elbow"—one of the first cases on record. It was felt that it had probably been caused by the heavy overhead smashing that highlighted both his singles and his doubles play. Anyhow, Willie was out for the season. In his absence, Lawford, who was making his tenth appearance at Wimbledon, had his best chance ever to win the championship. One had to be sympathetic to this no longer young man—the "heavy" in the scenario—who had expended so much effort and had harvested so many disappointments in his quest for the championship trophy, which for him was the Holy Grail. But one found one's sympathy also going out to Ernest Renshaw, who had practically made a career of self-effacement. Realizing that perpetuating the Renshaw dynasty was now his responsibility, Ernest buckled down to business. He arrived at Wimbledon fit and serious, and made his way to the All Comers final that would decide the championship that year—with Willie hors de combat, there would be no Challenge Round. Across the net from Ernest in the final, glowering and purposeful, stood Lawford. A terrific match ensued. After Ernest had won the third set, to lead two sets to one, he appeared to be safely home. Then, as frequently happens to a player in any game who has moved out in front and is in sight of victory, Ernest began to play too conservatively. With his exceptional powers of recuperation, Lawford was able to take advantage of this lull to marshal his reserves of strength and to take command. He won the fourth set, 6–4, to draw even, and went on to win the crucial fifth set, 6–4. The old boy had done it—won Wimbledon. Well done indeed!

Lawford's reign lasted only one year. This was not due to the return of Willie Renshaw, although he was back in action at Wimbledon in 1888. Willie's elbow was better, but he was not yet his old self, and was ousted in an early round. No, it was Ernest—shy, stammering Ernest—who stopped Lawford. He really rose to the occasion in the Challenge Round, playing perhaps the most beautiful tennis of his life. From the backcourt he had perfect length off the heavy grass, and when he closed in he hit crisp, imaginative shots that Lawford could not deal with. This time, after Ernest had swept into the lead he did not let up. He dismissed Lawford 6–3, 7–5, 6–0. The Renshaws were back on top. As for Lawford, he was never again a factor in the championship. He had grown too old.

The story of the Renshaws, with its manifold twists and turns, reached its final big moment in 1889, when Willie came all the way back to win his seventh, and last, Wimbledon singles championship—no other man has won the singles more than five times—and when Willie and Ernest won their fifth, and last, Wimbledon doubles championship. (In 1884, the doubles were shifted to Wimbledon from Oxford, where the Renshaws had won them twice.) In the All Comers singles, after defeating Lawford in four sets, Willie, up against the young and promising H.S. Barlow, was within two points of losing in straight sets. He managed to reclaim the third set, 8–6. In the fourth set, Barlow held six match points. Willie fought them all off, and at length took the set, 10–8. In the final set, Barlow took the first five games. Willie refused to yield. He called on himself for everything he had, and, reeling off one game after another with dazzling play, capped his incredible comeback by winning the set, 8–6. In the Challenge Round, he faced Ernest, the defending champion, and once again Ernest produced the rather pale stuff he invariably produced when he was playing Willie. The first two sets went to Willie; Ernest took the third, and then subsided quietly in the fourth without winning a game. This marked the close of the Renshaw Era. In 1890, Willie defended his title but was defeated in the Challenge Round by a tall, thin Irishman, W.J. (Ghost) Hamilton.

After that, Willie played little competitive tennis, none of it notable. As for Ernest, in 1891, in the fourth round, he met Wilfred Baddeley, who was on his way to the first of his three Wimbledon titles. Ernest scratched out a paltry two games over the three sets. Ernest was then only thirty, yet, like Willie, was merely a tragic shade of his former self. With the Renshaws gone from the Centre Court, interest in lawn tennis entered a decline—some people felt that it had unquestionably seen its best days—but then other heroes came along and Wimbledon began to bloom again.

The Renshaws died young, and under unhappy circumstances. George E. Alexander, of Boise, Idaho, one of the leading scholars of the early years of lawn tennis, recently dug up, at the General Register Office in London, copies of the entries of death of the Renshaws. Ernest was thirty-eight when he died, of the "effects of carbolic acid but whether taken intentionally or not the evidence does not show." Five years later, Willie died of epileptic convulsions. In his will, the game's first great player bequeathed "the first Championship Lawn Tennis Cup won by me at Wimbledon to my sister Edith Ann Renshaw absolutely and without intending or implying any trust." Of course, no one who knows his Wimbledon has ever forgotten the Renshaws. It is wonderfully right that each year the winner of the men's singles receives not only replicas of the two Challenge Cups—the originals are kept permanently at the All-England Club—but also a special memorial trophy presented by the members of the Renshaw family.

The fortnight of the centenary Wimbledon started on Monday, June 20, and ended on Saturday, July 2. The first week of play, bringing us to the quarterfinals in both the men's and the women's singles, was rather uneven. There were a good many routine matches, a few bright matches, the usual percentage of upsets (the most surprising one being the expulsion in the third round of the third-seeded man, Guillermo Vilas—the Argentine who recently won the French championship—at the hands of Billy Martin, a twenty-year-old American, who has done very little since graduating from the ranks of the juniors), and the usual number of unexpected developments, controversial and otherwise. At the top of this last category was the failure of Jimmy Connors, the 1974 Wimbledon champion and the first-seeded player this year, to attend the parade of former Wimbledon champions on the Centre Court on the festive opening day—a ceremony that reached its emotional apex when Elizabeth Ryan, now eighty-five years old, hobbled out on crutches toward the Duke of Kent, the president of the All-England Club, and tossed her crutches away as she curtsied before the Duke and the Duchess. Connors, the *enfant terrible* of contemporary tennis, was practicing at the time about two hundred yards away, testing an injured thumb as he hit some shots with his buddy Ilie Nastase. The list of happier developments included the following: The successful debut of fourteen-year-old, ninety-pound Tracy Austin, of California—the youngest (and lightest) person ever accepted for Wimbledon—who won her opening match from Mrs. Elly Vessies-Appel, of the Netherlands, 6–3, 6–3, before succumbing in the next round to Chris Evert, 6–1, 6–1; an affecting performance by Maria Bueno, who, at thirty-seven, reached the third round and played patches of lovely tennis before losing her match with Billie Jean King; the sight of Stan Smith, the 1972 champion, looking more like his old self than he has in years, as he extended Connors to five sets in the fourth round; and some imaginative shotmaking on the part of the uncelebrated Tim Gullikson, the right-handed member of the Gullikson twins, from Onalaska, Wisconsin, who eliminated Raul Ramirez, the Mexican Davis Cup hero, and went on to reach the round of sixteen before losing to Phil Dent, of Australia, in five sets. (Tom, the left-handed twin, who is five minutes older than Tim, was put out by Nastase in the first round. The Gulliksons, the nearest thing to the Renshaws that tennis has seen in quite some time, entered the doubles but were defeated in their first match, in four sets, by the veteran American team of Stan Smith and Bob Lutz.) On Wednesday of the first week, a record crowd of more than thirty-seven thousand was in attendance. Wimbledon galleries are the most international attracted by any annual sports event, and as one makes one's way down the packed walks one hears a constant babble of strange languages and spots an unending assortment of blazers and insignia. I was seated, by the way, between Victor Vassiliev, the bearded representative of *Sovietski Sports,* and Gianni Clerici, the erudite tennis specialist of *Il Giorno,* of Milan.

By and large, the overall scene at Wimbledon is much the same as it has been for years and years. Outside the grounds, the traditional long queue of tennis enthusiasts lined up to buy standing-room tickets or general-admission tickets or tickets of any kind waits stoically for the gates to open. In the Tea Garden, the main relaxation area, which is filled with tables, chairs, and large umbrellas, there are numerous refreshment stands, offering sandwiches, salads, pies, cakes, strawberries and cream, and so on, and, along with those stands, the Champagne and Pimms Bar, the Wine Bar, the Wimbledon Long Bar, a bookstall, a souvenir shop, a post office, and, nearby, several Bon Bon Stands, where one fills one's own paper bag with a variety of hard candies from forty-five bins—20 new pence, or 34 cents, for a quarter of a pound. This year, there has been a splendid new addition— a tennis museum (naturally, it is called simply The Museum), which occupies part of a new building attached to the eastern rim of the Centre Court stadium. One noon, before the day's matches got underway, I spent a reflective and enjoyable hour inching through it. The museum, as you might expect, depicts the development of lawn tennis from court tennis and other early racquet games. It pays a proper tribute to Major Walter Clopton Wingfield, the inventor of lawn tennis, and then floods us with memorabilia, such as an exhibit of the intricate and voluminous dresses the women tennis players of earlier generations were encumbered by, a replica of an early-twentieth-century Wimbledon dressing room, and well-selected photographs of the standout champions, accompanied by descriptions of their deeds. In the center of the museum are two large glass cases, one filled with life-sized wax figures of Suzanne Lenglen, Fred Perry and Helen Wills Moody, the other with similar figures of Willie Renshaw, Dorothea Lambert

Chambers and William T. Tilden II. At Tilden's feet lies a scattering of the instruction books and the fiction he wrote, including two of his novels, *It's All in the Game* and *Glory's Net.* My favorite exhibit was a collection of early tennis post cards —in particular, one showing an auburn-haired beauty hitting a forehand drive, with the caption "Love to You from Harrogate." The only touch that rather disturbed me was that the recordings of snatches of the early radio broadcasts from Wimbledon, which are piped through the museum, seemed to contain only English triumphs, like Fred Perry's conquest of Jack Crawford and Dorothy Round's of Helen Jacobs. I mentioned this to an old friend, Lance Tingay, who is the tennis writer for the *London Daily Telegraph.* "Oh, I'm sure you're wrong about that," he told me, with a smile. "You must have been preoccupied when the feats of the American and the other foreign stars were described. I'm absolutely certain that one of Elizabeth Ryan's victories is given fitting attention."

During the second week, there was an abundance of interesting matches—far more than can be mentioned, unfortunately. However, the overriding fact was that this Wimbledon Centenary, which everyone hoped would be a tournament to remember, turned out to be exactly that. In the gentlemen's singles, the semifinal match between Bjorn Borg, of Sweden, the defending champion, and Vitas Gerulaitis, of the United States, which Borg won in five sets, proved to be an authentic classic. Don Budge said he thought that it was the best match he had ever seen, and Fred Perry, only a mite more conservative, said he could not remember seeing a better match. This was followed by a first-class final between Borg and Connors—their first meeting on grass. Played under a broiling sun on by far the hottest day of the championships, it consumed three hours and four minutes before Borg pulled it out, 3–6, 6–2, 6–1, 5–7, 6–4. Yet when tennis fans look back on the 1977 championships, what they will remember above all is that this was the year that Virgina Wade, the sweetheart of tennis-playing, tennis-talking, tennis-loving England, at last, in her sixteenth attempt, won the ladies' singles. Miss Wade has been one of the top

women players in the world for a decade—she won our championship at Forest Hills in 1968 and, later, the Italian and Australian championships—but year after year, instead of rising to the challenge of Wimbledon, she was the victim of attacks of nerves, and, playing miles below her usual standard, always found a way to lose to opponents who were not at all in her class. The knowledge of how keenly her compatriots wanted her to win at Wimbledon only served to impose an increasingly heavy burden on Our Ginny, as she is known in the popular press. What happened this year, consequently, was almost too good to be true. Just when nearly everyone had given up on her—Chris Evert was the odds-on favorite to win the ladies'—Our Ginny came through, and at the most appropriate time, for this, of course, is the year of Queen Elizabeth's Silver Jubilee, and the Queen herself, making her first visit to Wimbledon since 1962, was seated in the Royal Box.

Let us leave the women for a moment and turn to the men. In the upper half of the draw, Connors made his way to the semifinals, where he met one of the big surprises of the tournament—John McEnroe, of Douglaston, Long Island, a sturdy, athletic eighteen-year-old, who had had to earn a place in the championship field in the qualifying rounds at Roehampton and had then gone out and beaten such established players as Ismail El Shafei, Karl Meiler, Sandy Mayer, and Phil Dent on his way to becoming the youngest player ever to reach the last four of the men's singles. Connors vs. McEnroe, which Connors won in four sets, turned out to be a dullish match. McEnroe lacked his customary zest, and Connors played about the same stodgy, fragmented stuff he had got by with throughout the tournament. Connors, however, is respected for his ability to get himself up for a big match, and no one looked for Borg to have an easy time of it in the final, despite his inspired tennis against Gerulaitis in the other semifinal. Borg, who is now twenty-one, changes his game only slightly for Wimbledon: He concentrates on beefing up his serve, for on a skiddy surface like grass a potent serve pays off. At Wimbledon, as at other tournaments and on other surfaces, Borg only occasionally comes to net, preferring to stay at the base line and wear down his opponent with his heavy topspin forehand and his two-fisted topspin backhand, which are difficult to handle, and with his tireless ability to retrieve nearly everything hit across the net. Borg doesn't go for outright winners often, but when he spots an opening he can sting you with his cross-court backhand and his down-the-line forehand. Gerulaitis, who was born in Brooklyn and is now twenty-two, has recently improved his game immeasurably. In the preceding years, he was a good enough player to win sizable amounts of prize money, and this enabled him to buy a house, with tennis court, in Kings Point, on the North Shore of Long Island, and to acquire two Rolls-Royces, a Mercedes and a Porsche. During that period, he was content to embellish his image as a ranking playboy, but on a trip to Europe last year he noticed how zealously players like Borg practiced, and his attitude underwent a marked change. He became a devout practicer, and approached his career far more seriously. The improvement in his game has been sudden and astonishing. He has a stronger first serve now. His second serve, formerly one of his main weaknesses, has come along well. He has bolstered his forehand, though it still does not compare with his sliced backhand, which has always been his most dependable stroke. His forehand volley is surer, and so is his overhead. He now produces all these strokes with fluidity and rhythm, partly because he has practiced them faithfully, and partly because through practice he has sharpened his anticipation and refined his footwork. Today, he is a first-class player, not just an ambitious young man with a flair for the game. This was brought home this spring, when he won his first prestige championship, the Italian Open, and won it on clay, which is not his best surface. In contrast to Borg, he likes to attack whenever possible—to come into the forecourt behind a forcing approach shot. This contrast in the styles of Gerulaitis and Borg set up countless glistening sequences in which one player, seemingly beaten in a rat-tat-tat exchange, somehow got to the ball and improvised an apparent winner only to have the other player, acting purely on reflex, somehow get his racket on the ball and put it away with an unbelievable stroke. What made the Borg-Gerulaitis match the instant classic it was acclaimed? To begin with, both men were in top form, and that is a rarity. As the match moved on and individual points became more and more significant, both had the guts to play heroic shots in the clutch: Raffishly angled, high backhand volleys, soft little half-volleys, uncompromising overhead smashes, full-blooded drives that whistled through small openings, lots of deep lobs that had to be chased down—the whole book, in fact. Somehow or other, they sustained this level of play at top speed for the full five sets. Borg deserved to win, because he won the last two games, but Gerulaitis played just as superlatively as he did.

This was a hard act to follow, but the Borg-Connors final, particularly in view of the fact that most finals are anticlimactic, was a tough, bruising, superior match. From beginning to end, the pattern was one of strange fluctuations, with first one man and then the other dominating play. As many people had anticipated, Connors, that natural competitor, came on the court conspicuously abrim with a verve and intensity he had not previously shown in the championships. He was out to gain command of the match quickly, and he did. He won the first set at 6–3, hitting out ferociously, and came within a hair of breaking Borg's service in the third game of the second set. At this juncture, Borg, who may have been still feeling the effects of his battle with Gerulaitis two days before, began to increase the tempo of his play and to become more adventurous, and simultaneously Connors began to miss more frequently, especially with his forehand approach shots. The result was that Borg ran off four straight games, and with them the second set, 6–2. In the third set, with Connors still quiescent and erratic, Borg won five of the first six games, and eventually the set, 6–1, scoring with two blazing aces in the last game. During this stretch—indeed, throughout the final—Borg's serve was his chief strength; one cannot overstate its importance for him. Midway through the fourth set, there was another change. At 4–4,

Borg twice stood within a point of breaking Connors's serve for 5–4, but, almost as if he were psychologically unprepared at that moment to win the match, he faltered badly on both points. Following this, Borg began to look a little weary and to play a bit negatively, and Connors, who is never beaten until he *is* beaten, started to rip into his shots with a new surge of confidence. At 5–5, he won eight of the next nine points and took the set, 7–5, to square the match at two sets apiece. Now several other dramatic changes came swiftly. Borg, summoning his reserve strength, started to hit his drives with emphatic topspin again, and swept the first four games of the deciding set. In the fifth game, he was twice within a point of breaking Connors. Tired as he was, Connors fought back brilliantly, and not only saved that game but also carried off the next three games on the strength of some fine, deep approaches and remarkable put-away volleys. Now, just when it appeared that he would probably go on to win, he suffered a spasm of inexplicable carelessness in the critical ninth game, serving a double fault and banging two backhands far out of court. Borg to serve, leading 5–4. Revived by Connors's sudden loss of control—Connors may have simply run out of gas—Borg raced through his service game at love, ending the match with a flourish on an untouchable smash, a hard-hit drive that forced an error, a powerhouse serve that Connors barely got his racket on, and a backhand down the line, which Connors, who thought that Borg would be going cross-court, couldn't cope with. The score again: 3–6, 6–2, 6–1, 5–7, 6–4. An absorbing final, played with a most commendable spirit. Borg, by the way, now has a chance to become the first man to win Wimbledon three times in a row since Perry accomplished this in the middle 1930's.

Back to the ladies' singles: Virginia Wade, who is now thirty-one, grew up, and played her first tennis, in South Africa, where her father was the archdeacon of Durban. Aside from her exceptional athletic endowment—she is recognized as having the best service motion in women's tennis—she is highly intelligent, and took her degree at the University of Sussex in general science and physics. After deciding to make tennis her life, she rose quickly to the international level. Her style of play revealed a rigidly imperious attitude; in losing, as in winning, she insisted on dictating the structure of the match, not always wisely. The last few years, she has worked hard to overcome this tendency. She has tried to learn to make her game more flexible, and to understand that there are many different ways to win points if one thinks and perseveres. During the past year, she decided that, for all the raves she regularly received about her service, it was not doing all that it might for her, so she sought out two American teaching professionals, Ham Richardson and Jerry Teeguarden, to work with her on her toss. She also spent hours on end trying to correct the flaws in her vulnerable forehand. She came to Wimbledon in an uncharacteristically confident frame of mind. She felt that she was "by far the strongest person in the dressing room," and that this was meant to be her tournament.

Miss Wade's first real test came in the quarterfinals, against Rosemary Casals. Miss Casals has always been difficult for her to beat. An acrobatic scrambler, Miss Casals is very likely to cut off an apparently unreachable passing shot with a diving volley, then pick herself up just in time to hustle back and knock off with a leaping overhead smash the lob her opponent has thrown up. Losing points that had looked safely won was what had made Miss Wade's meetings with Miss Casals so exasperating for her. In their match at Wimbledon this year, Miss Wade was on the ropes several times in the first set, but she stayed in there and managed to win it, 7–5. Then, with games at 2–2 in the second set, she broke Miss Casals's serve twice in a row with a flurry of assertive placements, to take the set, 6–2, and the match. Miss Wade is often given to dithering and stumbling about when she is in sight of victory, and to see her play so effectively against Miss Casals when the chance to win presented itself made one wonder if this really was a "new Virginia." We knew for certain that it was after her semifinal with Chris Evert. In the quarterfinal round, Miss Evert had played an almost perfect match in devastating Billie Jean King with the loss of only three games. Theirs is a long and

The Wimbledon Centenary (1977) was a personal triumph for Britain's long-suffering Virginia Wade—at age thirty-one, her first victory at home. (Photo by Russ Adams)

animated rivalry, and Miss Evert was up for the clash. She displayed a diversity of shots we had never seen from her before, including things like sharply angled topspin forehands and a succession of defensive stab volleys in which she

guessed correctly each time just where Mrs. King, in charge of the forecourt, would be pasting her volley. Tennis can be an impossible game to understand. Two days later, facing Miss Wade in the semis, Miss Evert, unable to rouse herself from a deep lethargy, may have played the poorest match of her career, and Miss Wade, instead of being overcome by those old Centre Court jitters, was the one who played an almost perfect match. I will bother you with only one statistic: So complete was her control that in the three sets they played Miss Wade only twice hit ground strokes that carried beyond the base line. That night, the evening tabloids, instead of giving us the familiar front-page headline of "Wade Fails in Shock Defeat," featured variations on "Ginny K.O.s Champ." The score, incidentally, was 6–2, 4–6, 6–1. For a time, there was a prospect of an all-English women's final, for in the other semi Betty Stove, of the Netherlands, playing in her thirteenth Wimbledon, was up against Sue Barker, a charming young woman from Devon who has come on fast. It did not happen. Miss Stove—at six feet one, the tallest woman in tennis—was just too crushing with her serve-and-volley game: 6–4, 2–6, 6–4.

The first match each day at Wimbledon begins at two o'clock. At six minutes to two on the afternoon of the ladies' final, shortly after the military band in the Centre Court had concluded its rendition of "Land of Hope and Glory," the Queen arrived, wearing a pink-and-white outfit, and proceeded, amid exuberant applause, to the Royal Box. The band struck up "God Save the Queen," and halfway through the anthem the spectators began to sing it softly. Miss Wade and Miss Stove then came out on the court, made their curtsies, and warmed up. Miss Wade did not look nervous as she prepared to serve the opening game, but evidently she was. She did not move as fast or hit the ball as hard as she ordinarily does—a sure sign of tension. In fact, it soon became clear that, like Miss Evert, she was fated to follow a nearly perfect performance with an anguishingly mediocre one. After four deuce points, she did rescue the opening game. She was broken in the fifth game, broke back in the sixth against an equally tight opponent and was broken again in the ninth game at love. Miss Stove then held service. First set to Miss Stove, 6–4. Subdued groans from the fourteen thousand spectators in the Centre Court. Near the middle of the second set, Miss Wade began to

unwind a bit. Her agility improved, and she started to outguess and outmaneuver her opponent. This is essential against Miss Stove, who, once she has ensconced herself at net, is exceedingly hard to pass, because of her tremendous reach. In the eighth game, Miss Wade broke service, thanks in part to Miss Stove's eighth double fault, and then served out for the set, at 6–3. An explosive shout from the encouraged stands. The third set came more easily. Miss Wade won the first four games, mainly on her opponent's errors, for her own shotmaking remained somewhat inhibited. However, now that she had the match for the taking she seized her opportunity firmly and won the last two games with the loss of only two points. Wade, 4–6, 6–3, 6–1. It was a triumph less of flashing strokes and skillfully engineered points than of will, resolution and determination, but, in a way, this is close to quibbling. The fact of the matter was that Virginia Wade had actually won Wimbledon, and the roars and applause she was accorded by her ecstatic fans on the Centre Court as she was congratulated by the Queen and held aloft the golden salver, the ladies' championship trophy, could probably be heard as far away as Putney Bridge.

It was a lifting experience to hear Virginia Wade's thoughts on her triumph: "It was wonderful to win in front of the Queen, but the cheering was so loud it was difficult to hear what she said to me. All I heard her say was 'Well played. It must have been hard work.' I told her that it *was* hard work. . . . I felt I had more incentive this week than I ever had before. Everyone thought I was past it and that I couldn't do it. I wanted to prove that I deserved to be out there among the champions. I felt I belonged— that I was the best player who hadn't won Wimbledon so far. . . . I knew that the most important thing to do today was just to play the best I could and not to let any stray dreams distract me." She said later that she had got through the morning before the match by putting her pillow over her telephone and turning up the volume on a recording of Rachmaninoff's Second Symphony.

Earlier this year, when the spectacular program of events for the Queen's Silver Jubilee was being planned, many people held the view that, times being as parlous as they are today, the British public would hardly be in a mood for pomp and circumstance, reviews and tattoos, fireworks and festivities. These fears proved to be groundless. The Queen's great personal popularity carried the day, and the Silver Jubilee has been a colossal success. Then the Centenary Wimbledon came along, and Virginia Wade, with her victory, added that extra, unexpected contribution that really sets a celebration aglow. When the happy spectators in the Centre Court, following the presentation of the championship trophy to Our Ginny by Her Majesty, spontaneously began to sing "For She's a Jolly Good Fellow," I'm sure I wasn't the only American present who did not know for certain whether it was Virginia Wade or Queen Elizabeth II they had in mind.

Forest Hills: The Twelve-Day Week

by RICHARD SCHICKEL

Although Wimbledon remains the "world championship" of tennis, the United States Open Tennis tournament is the second most coveted title in tennis and was contested at Forest Hills until 1978, when it moved to Flushing Meadow. In his book The World of Tennis, *film critic Richard Schickel trained his cinematic eye on the multiple stories which made up the 1974 U.S. Open.*

FOREST Hills, or at least that portion of it where the West Side Tennis Club is located, has the slightly out-of-kilter look of the typical American compromise with other cultures—in this case a vision of an English village in something like Tudor times. One can imagine its attractions when it was set down in the semirural reaches of Queens early in this century, before megalopolis engulfed it. Offering the middle-class citizen solidity and comfort, it touched these virtues with a hint of the exotic, the distinctive, as well. One can see why, when the tennis club decided to move from crowded, expensive Manhattan in 1913, the setting struck the members' fancy. They were, after all, devoted to an English game that could, despite its comparatively recent origins as an outdoor sport, trace its antecedents at least as far as the local architecture could trace its stylistic influences.

In August 1974, I felt as I had before when invading these environs, that I was entering a region where time, though it had not stopped, had certainly congealed. What I was interested in discovering, after an absence of many years, was how much time had seemed to speed up in the small world that has taken root in this small world—the U.S. Open Tennis tournament, successor since 1968 to the closed, amateurs-only, national tournament for which, in the old days, it had generally been possible to buy a ticket—even for the final day—simply by strolling up to the ticket window a few minutes before the matches began. That I knew was now impossible, and I wanted to discover, by spending all day every day at the tournament, what else had become impossible now that tennis had become a big-time, big-money sport.

Inevitably, little changes have occurred with the passage of the years. The castlelike hotel which dominates the cool, leafy town square no longer takes in transients, and its restaurant has been converted to a brew-and-burger franchise. The darling little shops, complete with leaded windows in some cases, are mostly deserted, the commercial action having flowed a few blocks north, toward bustling, characterless Queens Boulevard. But the residential sections surrounding the old square (through which one must approach the tennis club) remain as well kept as ever, and every few feet signs warn intruders from the outside world of dire consequences should they leave their automobiles against these law-abiding curbs for any appreciable length of time. Happily, these injunctions are not enforced when the U.S. Open is in progress, but one gets the idea: Forest Hills, like its tennis club, which by playing host to this tournament since 1915 has made the town world-famous, feels embattled, slightly paranoid perhaps, about the way things keep changing, the way the world keeps intruding on what was once a well-ordered, parochial way of living.

The grounds of the club, as they are dressed for the big event, have an antique patina. The flags of many nations fly from the top of the half-century old, very well-designed stadium (I never found a really bad seat in it, except in the press box located in the marquee at its open end). Around it many tents are clustered, creating at first glance the impression that one has stumbled into an old-world bazaar or folk festival.

Such romantic fancies quickly disappear as one passes through the gates. The tents, it turns out, are mostly for the use of various corporate enterprises whose promotional "tie-ins" with the tournament include not only the right to flash messages from the electronic score board in the stadium (I'll never forget that 4711 was the "official" cologne of the 1974 U.S. Open), but the right to stage boozy lunches for clients under these canvases.

Indeed, almost everywhere you turn at the tournament, your eye is assaulted by some form of huckstering. Each and every court has an ice chest, bearing the strange device "Pepsi-Cola" and well stocked with same. God help the player—Arthur Ashe, for example—who has a tie-in with a rival soft drink (Coke in his case), or who in mid-match develops a craving for some other refreshment. (In 1973, Stan Smith decided that all that stood between him and victory was a shot of Gatorade and dispatched his fiancée, Marj Gengler, for that magic elixir. None was to be found anywhere on the grounds, its manufacturer not having contributed to the prize-money pool, and Ms. Gen-

gler had to run all the way to Waldbaum's supermarket on Queens Boulevard to obtain it.) It is a bazaar all right, but a very modern, hard-nosed, charmless sort of a bazaar.

Once the crowd begins to arrive one is quickly disabused of even the more modest fantasy that perhaps a note of fashionable elegance, something reminiscent of the teens or twenties of this century, will be struck here. To be sure, an elderly traditionalist or two will turn out in a blue blazer and club tie—and coats and ties are required of umpires and linesmen—but for the most part the crowd is tacky in a way that would distress an habitué of Wimbledon. Dress is strictly Central-Park-in-a-heat-wave, manners subway-in-a-rush-hour. This is the democratization of tennis in full, weedy flower.

The opening rounds, in particular, are a nightmare. For in addition to the stadium court and two courts in the smaller, wooden grandstand near that great concrete edifice (quite the nicest place to watch tennis on these grounds, by the way, since the permanent stands are shaded by fine old trees), seventeen other field courts must be used in the early going to accommodate all the matches required to reduce the huge player population to manageable proportions. For a great national tournament is actually a congeries of several tournaments: Men's and women's singles and doubles, mixed doubles, senior men's singles and doubles, junior tournaments for boys and girls and, in this case, something called the Grand Masters, which brings together older players who in previous years won, or at least were capable of winning, national tournaments. This means that some very good tennis, often involving seeded players, more often pitting well-matched competitors of the second flight, are in constant progress on the field courts. Narrow walkways separate these courts and there is a constant push and shove as spectators move from match to match, sampling the wares on display (again the bazaar analogy occurs), looking for upsets in the making or a match that has reached its moment of decision. Their attention span is very much that of the age of television (i.e., short), and the constant movement and chatter from the side lines must be one of the most difficult tests to which a player can submit his powers of concentration.

Nonetheless, until the men's singles field was reduced to approximately the round of sixteen, it was the field and grandstand courts I haunted. The theory was simple: Almost any tournament is going to be won by one of the top eight seeds. (The only unseeded player ever to win Forest Hills was Fred Stolle in 1966, and no unseeded player has ever won Wimbledon.) So there is plenty of time to see Connors or Newcombe or whoever among the favorites strikes your fancy. Indeed, most of them turn up at one time or another in the outlying precincts during the early days of play. Meantime, there is a great deal of attractive tennis being played in circumstances about as intimate as you'll find at your own club. If, for instance, you want to get a sense of what it is like to face Roscoe Tanner's famously powerful serve, the place to do so is when he is playing on a grandstand or field court. It is also a place to discover the human virtues (and the technical skills) of players who don't make many headlines. Out here, in the early going, one finds underdogs to root for.

Such a one, for me, was Mark Cox of Britain, whose chief claim to fame is that he was the first amateur to defeat a professional—Gonzales no less—at the world's first open tournament at Bournemouth in 1968. On the first day at Forest Hills he was playing young Jeff Austin of Rolling Hills, California, on the number-four court, hard by the stadium. Cox has curly blond hair, chunky legs and the dogged courage we like to think characteristic of the English. At thirty-one he was felling the sultry heat much more acutely than his younger, fleeter opponent, who has the look of an intense chipmunk, a tendency to foot fault, and a habit of talking to himself in a not altogether engaging manner.

Cox got off well, with 6–3, 7–6 victories in the first sets, then began to fade in the heat, losing 3–6, 1–6. He won my heart during this discouraging patch when he looked up at us railbirds during a changeover and inquired pleasantly, "Anyone want to stand in for a set?" He was to say later that part of his trouble was an inability to decide what to do once he had gained

his two-set advantage: Go for a quick kill in the third set or pace himself for a longer match. He compromised, neither going quite all out nor finding it in himself to totally tank the two sets, in the process permitting the momentum to pass to Austin. Now, in the final set he rallied and found himself—after an exchange of service breaks—involved in a tie breaker. Worse, he was down three match points in it. By this time, however, Austin's second serve was weakening and Cox began pouncing on it, at last bringing the match to a single point. He had the serve, followed it in and made one of the best shots of the tournament, a cross-court volley of tremendous daring. Austin may have had a chance at it, but he also saw that it was heading perilously close to the side line and decided to leave the decision in the lap of the gods. The ball landed in by inches and Cox dropped to his knees to salaam to those gods.

Afterwards, as I walked with him to the clubhouse, he had to reject autograph seekers because his hand was shaking too hard to hold a pen. "To win when you're down three match points," he cried in high excitement. "What are the odds on that? A million to one?" I asked him what had been going through his mind during the tie breaker. Mainly, it turned out, that the only time he had ever played Austin before, both sets had gone to tie breakers and that he, Cox, had won them both. If he remembered that, he reasoned, so did Austin, and that had to give Cox an edge. And what about that daring cross-court volley that ended the match? "I had a choice on that shot, where to aim, but I remembered making it against Ken Rosewall here a couple seasons ago. I remember thinking, 'Maybe it's a good shot for Forest Hills.' " Professional tennis players talk that way. They remember—their muscles remember—what ours do not. Like the rich, they *are* different from you and me, and I learned in brief exchanges like this one to resist tempting analogies between their game and ours.

At the time it seemed to me that Cox was too intelligent to spend his thirties as early-round cannon fodder for better players, also too nice a guy to ignore as he tried to move through this tournament. I watched him in an easy five-set win over Jiri Hrebec of Czechoslovakia in the next round, and a tough loss to the extraordinarily graceful and attractive Alex Metreveli of Russia in the third round. This was another five setter, featuring three tie breakers and eliciting from Tom Okker, sitting near me in the grandstand press section, an admiring "good stuff" as he reluctantly rose to leave for his own match while the issue was still in doubt. Since then, however, I have been pleased that Cox, after being used as Rod Laver's sparring partner in preparation for the $100,000 match against Jimmy Connors (Cox is left-handed, like Connors), went on a wonderful tear, winning three out of four WCT tournaments and proving himself capable of unsuspected heights.

Roscoe Tanner, another unseeded player, was beginning to prove the same thing right here and now. Indeed, he probably should have been seeded, because he has, by common consent, one of the six or eight best serves in the world and is thus a man to reckon with on grass. Unfortunately, on clay and other softer surfaces he has not done well, and so his overall record is not so impressive to tournament committees as it should be. Nor was his first-round victory over tiny Mike Estep, a Czech transplanted to Dallas, terribly impressive. That serve is Tanner's best weapon and it was not yet working at full efficiency.

Still, he lost only one set and, ironically, gained confidence from his performance, feeling that if he could win even when his serve was inconsistent, it was a good augury for the rest of the tournament, when he was sure it would return to full power. Today he was content to throw up a lot of lobs, partly because Estep is short, partly because he had lately played a lot of team tennis. "When I first come outdoors," he said, "those lobs look different as they come out of a clear sky."

For his part, Estep kept a cheery face in adversity. "Oh, he's so smart," he cried, when Tanner outdueled him at the net at one point. A little later he watched one of Tanner's amazing aces blaze past him and turned to the small gallery, shrugged, and said, "I just refuse to go for those."

By the end of the match, I had decided that Tanner was a man to keep an eye on. In part this was because in the last set he got his serve working and it struck me as perhaps the biggest one I had ever seen. In part it was because he was young and strong, and perhaps on the brink of seeing his game peak. I could imagine him sneaking quietly through a section of the draw that was not fraught with power and going a long way.

Meantime, there were Stan Smith and Arthur Ashe to worry about. They were the only Americans—other than Connors—among the top eight seeds, and since one of the subtexts of this tournament was the powerful desire of players and spectators alike to see the gauche Connors and his then-fiancée, Chris Evert, denied a repeat of their "love bird" double victory at Wimbledon earlier in the summer, it seemed only right to develop some sort of rooting interest in those of their countrymen who seemed to stand the best chance against them.

Neither had enjoyed especially good seasons. Smith had been co-ranked number one with Connors at the end of the previous year's competition, despite the fact that Connors had beaten him in the majority of their confrontations and had been outspoken in his insistence that Smith owed his ranking more to his ability to go along with, get along with, the tennis establishment than to his current skill with the racket. There was probably some truth in this, because Smith is nice to the point of blandness, while Connors is abrasive to the point that players as varied in temperament as Ashe, Laver and Okker have publicly been critical of him. There was no disputing the fact that as they came into Forest Hills, Connors was the better player, having won the Australian and English titles, as well as just about everything else he had set his hand to. (Had he not been barred from the French Open as the result of one of his many disputes with the power elite, he would almost surely have been working on a Grand Slam.) Smith, on the other hand, had won nothing of note and was having trouble with his serve, which is at once big and delicate, since he hits the ball not at the apex of his toss but precisely at the moment it drops six inches from that point—which means that small errors in timing can throw him off more than they do other players. Everyone was hoping he would start a comeback at Forest Hills.

As for Ashe, who is an excellent money player on the WCT circuit, but who has only a couple of major titles to his credit, he was saying that he thought this might be his last chance to win the U.S. title for a second time. He is aging, of course, but he is also a serve-and-volley player, which means he likes to play on grass. Since, after years of complaint about the turf, the West Side Tennis Club had finally decided to get rid of its grass after this tournament, Ashe felt that the slower surface of future years would further diminish his chances of winning.

Grass, and what might replace it, was indeed almost as powerful a concern in this tournament as the assault on the Connors-Evert axis. Since the press rarely ventures out of its air-conditioned lair in the stadium, and therefore has very little to ask the players when it confronts them in postmatch conferences, the newsmen were absolutely bewitched by the subject. There was universal agreement that the grass was, as usual at Forest Hills, terrible, but there was a lively controversy over what ought to replace it. The professionals, in meeting assembled, recommended what they believe to be the fastest of the new composition surfaces, Plexi-pave, but the club finally opted for clay, the surface least beloved by American and Australian pros. Partly, one suspected, this was the club's way of getting back at them for all the years they had bitched about the Forest Hills grass. Partly, one imagined, class considerations entered into the decision. Concrete, asphalt and variants thereof are public-court surfaces. Clay, which is not inexpensive to keep up, is very much a private-club —and eastern seaboard—surface.

Be that as it may, none of the people in whom I had developed an interest had an easy time of it in this tournament. Smith, for instance, drew the excellent Jaime Fillol of Chile as his first-round opponent, got tied up in a players' meeting in Manhattan, then in traffic on the way to the tournament. He arrived rattled and in lively fear that he might have to default. As a result he lost his first set to Fillol. Then, just as he started to settle down in the second set, rain settled down over Forest Hills and, since it was late in the day, play was suspended. The next day Smith closed out the set, but could not break Fillol in the next set and was himself broken in the twelfth game to lose 5-7.

I was sitting in the grandstand press section as it happened, next to Marj Gengler, who spent a good deal of the match covering her eyes and uttering fretful remarks. ("If he loses his serve now, I'll brain him.") She advised me that she is "not as bad as Sharon Lutz [wife of Smith's doubles partner, Bob Lutz]. "She throws up—and she cries when Bob loses." The next set is scarcely easier for Smith, though his serve has stiffened sufficiently so that he can advance confidently behind it, and his overheads are really crackling. Even so, he fails to capitalize on a service break at 4-3, being broken back immediately at 4-4, which means he has to go to a tie breaker just to stay alive in the first round.

This brings a lemminglike rush from the press box to the grandstand. Number-three seeds are rarely threatened in the first round of a tournament. Marj is putting a brave face on the situation: "His pattern is that when he struggles in the early rounds he does well in the tournament." Still, she cannot bring herself to watch when Smith, leading 4-2 in the tie breaker, serves for the match. It is a very good serve— perhaps his best of the day—and Fillol is not at all sure but what it might have missed the service line. However, linesman, umpire and Alan King, comedian and tennis fanatic, who had positioned himself along the fence that separates grandstand from court, all call it in. I have to tell Marj that her betrothed has won, and as we depart King is still showing anyone who is interested the exact point at which Smith's serve kicked up chalk.

Things will now ease off a bit for Smith, whose wins over Frew McMillan, Brian Teacher and Sid Ball in succeeding rounds will all be comfortable, but never, perhaps, so overpowering as they would have been a year or two earlier. He keeps telling people that, after all, this has not been "that bad a year," that the difference between it and an exceptional one comes down to a few key points that might have gone either way. Yet he is playing cautiously, tentatively, even as he slides through these early rounds. His aura is that of a man who can be had.

The same cannot be said of Ashe. They say of him what they say of Smith; that he spreads himself too thin, plays too much, has too many outside interests, although some of them are inevitable for the only black man playing world-class tennis. They also say he is streaky and, maybe, too gifted for his own good. His repertory of strokes is as extensive as that of anyone in the game, which means that he can, for example, choose between eight subtle variants on a backhand return of serve, which gives him too much to think about at moments when you would prefer instinct to take over.

In any event, he has an easy first-round match, and then a tough second-round match against Vitas Gerulaitis, a young player who, just a few months later, would begin to hit the first peak of his career. Even worse, the match is scheduled on the so-called clubhouse courts. These are the oldest patches of grass on the grounds—though in no better shape for the length of their history—and some players refuse to accept scheduling there. The problem is that the membership of the West Side Club foregathers on the terrace, glasses clinking in hand, gossip very much in mind, and they set up a frightful din. Club members are by no means universally in favor of the employment of their turf as a venue for the national championships—all those vulgar strangers tramping about—though the event contributes so much to their coffers that dues are lower than at any comparable club in the nation. Therefore, there is some pressure on the tournament's managers to stage at least a few choice matches near the sacred veranda, so the membership (which is admitted free to the tournament) can watch without bestirring themselves.

This is Ashe's second match here and his encounter with Gerulaitis can be regarded as typical of the worst that players have to contend with in the opening rounds at Forest Hills. The players appear on court at their appointed hour to find—unbelievably—no officials, no ball boys,

not even a can of balls to employ in a warm-up hit. After a while someone on the second-floor veranda—it is reached from the men's locker room—tosses down a can of balls so they can at least begin their hit. As they do, a child asks in a clear, piping voice, "Mommy, which one is the American?" Of course, both players are, and, indeed, Gerulaitis is a member of the West Side club. Mom, however, declares with complete confidence, "Mr. Ashe, sweetheart." The kid studies the black man for a moment and with equal confidence declares, "He doesn't look American," which perhaps says something about the progress of social awareness in a club that achieved a certain notoriety by denying a member of Ralph Bunche's family access to its courts two decades ago. "Well," the woman replies, "he's the most famous."

That vignette concluded, officialdom begins arriving on court. The match gets underway with one line judge missing. In due course he arrives —and strolls casually behind Ashe just as he is preparing to serve. Ashe glares, the umpire scolds, and, unbelievably, the man takes his seat at the midpoint of the side line—where he could not call any imaginable shot in or out. Ashe sets down ball and racket, walks over to the man, exchanges a few words with him, and then moves the chair to its proper position—where the man can see if a ball landing near the base line is in or out. Ashe then proceeds to the ad court for his next serve, only to perceive that an ancient LTA pensioner is sitting in the wrong position to call the service line to which Ashe will be addressing himself. Another halt, another rearrangement of the furniture by the tournament's number-eight seed. His work for the day is not yet finished, however, for yet a third official has drawn his chair up to the court as if it were a fire from which, despite the sweltering heat, he sought to draw warmth. In this position, of course, he may well interfere with play, and once again Ashe takes it upon himself to station the official properly. All of this Ashe performs with what one has come to think of as the modern American black man's customary manner: dignified patience covering, but not entirely disguising, disgust.

The first two sets are close, 7–6, 7–5, but

then Ashe closes out quickly, 6–2, and moves on into the third round, where thirteen of the tournament's sixteen seeds are still alive. Only Tom Gorman, a merry and graceful man, has gone out in the first round, and Bjorn Borg, the teenage idol, and Manuel Orantes have failed in the second.

Like Smith, Ashe will struggle through to the quarterfinals, and like Smith he will be pressed, but never with great firmness. After his easy third-round win over Australia's Geoff Masters he is asked if each new victory helps build confidence, and he snaps, "Well, my confidence is better than Geoff Masters's right now—and that's about all." Which indicates that his self-esteem is not in quite the sievelike condition of Smith's, but that the question of its strength is very much on his mind. Things are just not quite right with him. "I can't seem to fall back and regroup," he admits at one point.

Indeed, of the players I have chosen to follow closely in this early going, only Tanner seems actually to be growing in wisdom and in valor before my eyes. In his second-round match with Britain's Roger Taylor he drops the first two sets, though he seems to start grooving his serve late in the second set, and takes the next three sets with the kind of easily growing confidence that an older player would give anything to enjoy. At one point, I look up to see that Pancho Segura, Connors's coach, has joined the small gallery around the field court and I hear him say to a companion as Tanner whistles one of his aces past Taylor, "Jesus Christ, remember when you could do that?" He notes, as Tanner himself does in later interviews, that the effectiveness of this weapon derives in part from his low toss, which means the extraordinarily hard-hit ball skims the net at an extremely flat angle. The ball is thus harder for the receiver to track and it is likely to take a low bounce, too, when it hits the playing surface. It is an admirably unpretentious serve, and one does not imagine Tanner will ever have the trouble with it that Smith has with his more fussy stroke.

On the other hand, as Segura informs us, this weapon is so much the most powerful at Tanner's command that he tends to rely on it too

heavily, which could put him at a psychological disadvantage in certain tight situations. Suppose, for example, under the pressure of a tie breaker his nerve briefly falters; what does he have to fall back on?

Watching Taylor trying to contend with Tanner's heavy hitting (his ground strokes and volleys are brutes, too), Segura says, "If he's smart, he lob on heem"—in other words counterpunch. One then remembers that Segura is no idle spectator. He is Jimmy Connors's coach and he is present to scout a potential opponent. In time, one will see just how valuable this canny old pair of eyes is to Connors.

For me, at this point, Connors and the number-two seed, John Newcombe, might as well be playing in another tournament. It is simply impossible to take in everything that's going on in this huge sprawl of action. For example, the women, especially in the early rounds, are just simply not so interesting to watch as the men. Catching a glimpse of their matches here and there one begins to sympathize with the male players' opposition to prize parity with them. Their draw is half the size of the men's draw, meaning the winner has to play one less match than the male winner. But that's not where the real difference lies. The fact is that with Olga Morozova out of this tournament, and with Martina Navratilova not yet at the peak she achieved the following winter on the tour, there are only five or six good players on hand: King, Evert, Goolagong, maybe Casals, and Julie Heldman, who is having an exceptionally good tournament while Virginia Wade is having an exceptionally poor one. The result is a lot of boring tennis, many lopsided matches. The women's tournament, unlike the men's, does not really get interesting until the semifinal round.

As for events in the men's doubles and the mixed doubles, one can only afford to give them glancing attention, though perhaps the pleasantest experience of the tournament, for me, came late one afternoon as twilight fell on the nearly deserted grandstand court where Billie Jean and her longtime partner, Owen Davidson, were playing Estep and Navratilova in a second-round match. It was a surprisingly tough match for

King-Davidson. (They were seeded first, but did not win the title, which went to Geoff Masters and Pam Teeguarden.) Players do not take the "mixed" entirely seriously, and more than anything else I witnessed at Forest Hills there was about this encounter the air of a weekend match of the sort you and I are likely to find ourselves in. There was a lot more chatter back and forth across the net and between partners, much of it taking the form of mock anger. What developed was a sense of shared peril among all four contestants. They quickly discovered that they were all playing against the man in the umpire's chair, who persistently announced the wrong score and seemed, several times, to have nodded off up there on his perch. (The shortage of officials, especially of competent ones, is one of the minor scandals of the tournament, and since big money is now riding on their decisions something really ought to be done about it; perhaps they ought to be paid something more than an honorarium and a free lunch each day they work.) Anyway, this was a good match—King and Davidson pulling it out after losing the first set in the tie-breaker—loose and very human, in large part because chirpy little Estep was not intimidated by King. He was perfectly willing to engage her in chin-to-chin arguments across the net over disputed points, positively eager to test her by playing to her power. It was, one must imagine, a way of releasing tournament tensions, of having some fun in the midst of a scene that cannot offer the players much of that quality. Watching the match, I felt I had been allowed to witness a privileged, private moment.

Meantime, my little tournament was beginning to flow into the larger tournament—the tournament people were reading about in the papers and would shortly start seeing on national television. In the third round Tanner surprised the seventh-seeded Ilie Nastase, coming back from a two-set deficit to do so, squeaked by El Shafei to enter the quarters against Smith. We were in the stadium now, where it is impossible to determine the psychological flow of a match as you can in the grandstand or out in the field. But it seemed to me that when Tanner took the first set on a tie-breaker the match was, in effect, all over. Roscoe took the next set 6–2, relented to give Smith a set at 3–6, then crushed him 6–1 to move into the semifinals.

Ashe, too, was doing pretty well. Drawing Guillermo Vilas in the fourth round, he knew he was coming in against a good young player who was riding a winning streak. In a tentative mood, he lost the first set on a tie breaker, largely because he was being too cautious with his first serve. His return of service was never so authoritative as it might have been, and his volleying seemed to me to lack the crispness I had observed in it elsewhere. (Of course, he is notorious for his lack of faith in his forehand volley, a matter he talks about, according to the other players, almost obsessively.) Still, he had one of his strong streaks going for him in the second and third sets, and despite doing a sort of walkabout in the fourth set, he was able to break Vilas with both forehand and backhand passing shots in the twelfth game to take the deciding set without resort to a tie breaker. Later he told Vilas that "your serve got shorter and shorter as the match went on," that that was the major weakness he found to exploit.

So now he, too, was in the quarters, facing Newcombe in a premier match that was, for some reason, scheduled for the grandstand court (which Newcombe humorously imagined Raul Ramirez must have commandeered for a midnight bullfight, so bad was the surface). Needless to say, this was the kind of confrontation that draws a crowd and it could not be contained in the stands. It flowed out on to the grass of the unused second court and there was a certain raffishness about the atmosphere, in part because the spectators sprawled on the grass, so close to the court, felt less constrained than they would have sitting densely packed and upright in the hard wooden stands, in part because a lot of blacks turned out to cheer Ashe on. He is, as always, his cool, correct self on court, but his fans, though amiable and loose, feel free to urge him on in terms that are distinctly not approved by the USLTA. "Man, hustle. You gotta hustle for those," one youth shouts as Arthur chooses to conserve resources instead of pursuing a difficult get. "Hey Art. Just one more. Just one more,

John Newcombe bends to retrieve a low backhand at Forest Hills. His power game and cool nerves were perfect for grass court tennis. (Photo by Russ Adams)

babe," someone else cries as Arthur delivers an ace while fighting to hold serve. On the whole, it is hard to imagine a better match than this one. Newcombe, to be sure, wins, but in five of the toughest sets imaginable: 4–6, 6–3, 3–6, 7–6, 6–4. There was no "turning point" in the match. Ashe was in it right up to the final point, playing solid, yet imaginative tennis, as steady in his way as Newk was in his—nothing streaky or flaky about him today.

This was my first long look at Newcombe and, wearing his pink "lucky" shirt, he is a charmer. Yes, there is a wonderful ferocity about his game, but it is tempered by what I can only describe as a kind of existential humor, a great white-toothed grin flashing beneath his Key-stone Kop mustache as, after a rally, one of his desperation shots dribbles along the net cord and falls in for a winner, and he invites his opponent to join him in appreciating the absurdity of such a fine point being decided by pure chance. Similarly, when luck runs against him, he seems to find consoling humor in the notion that cosmic issues are decided by sheer luck.

So it is to be Newcombe against Rosewall in one semifinal, Tanner against Connors in the other, and my impression is that neither match is likely to be the walkover for the favorites that many seem to be predicting. Aside from Ashe and a hammering four-setter against his doubles partner Tony Roche, who is getting his game back after successfully submitting his crippled tennis elbow to a faith healer he found in the Philippines, Newcombe has not really been challenged in this tournament, while Rosewall, whom I have been sneaking off to watch whenever I could, has had a succession of tough tests to pass. Charlie Pasarell, Raul Ramirez and Vijay Amritraj have all extended him to four tough sets, and though he never looked flustered, he did give the impression of a man grateful for challenging practice rounds. "I wish he'd get old," Newcombe said before the match, and by the time it was over he had every reason to wish it even more.

Newcombe started off serving beautifully and had he kept it up, he would have blown his fellow citizen from Sydney off the court. Somehow, however, he seemed to lose confidence in the serve toward the end of the first set, got tangled up in a tie breaker which he won, but which seemed to hearten Rosewall, who in any event seems to like to use the first set as an opportunity to study his opponent. He is glad to win it, of course, but not sorry to lose it, and in this instance he seemed to sense that Newcombe's serve was not so domineering as it can be and he began working his guileful way to net behind his canny returns of serve and took the next three sets with—considering the round and his opponent—remarkable ease. Yet another of these sets went to a tie breaker, and this time Rosewall won it and received a standing ovation. One could not quite believe one's eyes, and one had the feeling that Newcombe shared that feeling, that at some point in the match he became a sort of spectator at his own defeat, entranced in some way by the miracle to which he was both

witness and victim. In any event, he was a befuddled and angry man when he left the court. Just hours later, he and Tony Roche managed to get themselves knocked out of the doubles competition, mostly because Newcombe was too down to care.

Now it was Connors's turn. I had watched him play only intermittently through the week, but I had attended a number of his press conferences and observed him in locker room and clubhouse, and had begun to feel an odd sort of pity for him. All athletes of championship caliber are, perforce, single-minded, which is another way of saying that they are narrow-minded, in their pursuit of excellence. Most, however, trouble to learn—or recall—a few modest graces to ease them through their inevitably trying encounters with press and public and, since those are somewhat less difficult to master than the intricacies of, say, a dropshot, they do well enough. Connors, I noted, was trying very hard to catch on to these tricks, but he was simply terrible at it. His compliments to his defeated opponents always struck a false note, his little flurries of humor generally fell flat. Like everyone else around the tournament I spent a good deal of time wondering what was wrong with him.

There are, of course, reasonable explanations for his isolation from the rest of the tennis world. These revolve largely around his choice of a mentor, who is a man named Bill Riordan. He is convinced that there is an informal conspiracy between ILTF, the WCT and the ATP (the touring pros' union) to exercise monopolistic control over world-class tennis. (Davis Cup competition is ruled by these groups, which is why his boy won't play in it.) Considering the quite violent conflicts and uneasy peace among these entities, this seems nonsensical. What one can say for certain is that for reasons impossible for an outsider to sort out, they have pretty much locked Riordan out, leaving him to run a small-time tournament tour, the chief—indeed, only—attraction of which is Connors. The latter claims that he is not legally bound to Riordan, that he can play anywhere, anytime he wants to. It is merely that he doesn't want to play as often as the WCT requires its players to do. And, of course, he is justifiably angry that the ILTF banned him from the French championships in the summer of 1974, costing him his shot at the Grand Slam, merely because he had played team tennis, the schedules of which conflict with the ILTF's spring schedule of European tournaments.

These, however, are justifications for Connors's isolation, not explanations of it. And one searches in vain through his brief biography for the sources of his attraction to the role of rebel without a discernible cause. His mother and grandmother—both strong players at the regional level in their day—taught him the rudiments of the game and found him an apt and eager pupil. Tennis was all he wanted to do and it is perhaps revealing that even as a child he claims he "never had time for friends or anything else. I didn't even *know* anybody in school. I was too busy. I used to leave class every day at noon to practice tennis." There he developed the greatest of his skills, his magnificent return of serve, by working out on the hardwood floor of an armory, which was faster than any surface a player is likely to encounter anywhere on the tour. It forced him to challenge every serve early, sweep it back before it could spin away from him. Still, he did not do remarkably well in national junior competitions. Finally, the Connors ladies moved with him to Los Angeles, where Segura—with a little help from Gonzales—took over his training, working particularly on his serve and volley, but making no dent in his crustaceous personality. He was a hungry player, but hungry only for wins, not popularity. And the former started coming his way in the early seventies. It may be—though this is the purest speculation—that Segura, who never won any major titles and who, with his comic Ecuadorian accent, may have been something of an odd man out in big-time tennis, saw in Connors an instrument for revenging past hurts and slights. Or not—who can say?

The important thing is that Connors has had, so far as an outsider can tell, a good, interesting, rewarding twenty-three seasons on earth. There is no visible wound that would account for the paranoid cloud that seems to hover over him, not even a history of the kind of adversity that,

say, Gonzales had to overcome en route to his status as a legend. Can it be that it is only the ineptitude of inexperience that so puts one off him, that he will outgrow all this?

I don't know. What I did observe in the Connors entourage was a distinct air of "us against them" and a singular absence of anyone to instruct him in the gentle art of public relations. All he really had going for him was a steadily growing reputation as a punishing tennis player, a reputation that had begun to build when he quit college in 1971, having observed that if he had been a professional instead of an amateur he could have earned some $50,000 for the performances he had turned in that year in tournaments. For a couple of seasons thereafter he had lurked around the fringes of the game, ambushing this and that star in this and that tournament, but never getting further than the quarterfinals of any great national tournament.

Then, in the summer of 1973 he won the National Professional title at Longwood and the Pacific Southwest, and things started coming together for him. He won the Grand Prix Masters tournament in December. (It is said that the very correct Stan Smith had tears in his eyes when Connors beat him in an earlier tournament, and it is a matter of record that Smith did not wait to walk off court with him, as tradition dictates, when Connors beat him in the Masters tournament.) He won the Australian title a month later. And after being banned from the French championships he swept through Wimbledon, crushing Rosewall in the final—which didn't add to Connors's popularity. Now he was the number-one seed, the man to beat, at Forest Hills. And still, seemingly, no one liked him. The galleries remained essentially hostile, the press difficult, his fellow players unaffectionately respectful. When he was not busy controlling his anger or trying lamely to ingratiate himself, Connors seemed honestly befuddled by the fact that all his victories had failed to win the hearts and minds of the tennis community.

Now as he appeared in the stadium with Tanner (their rackets borne by lovelies wearing tennis frocks fashioned of Kodel, "the fabric of American life," as the public-address announcer informed us to a smattering of bored boos), it finally came over me who Connors reminded me of: Richard M. Nixon.

By that I mean to say that he is a narrowly ambitious man, concentrating a furious energy on a narrowly defined goal—being a winner in his chosen field. To this end, he will sacrifice anything—the graceful presentation of self, the pursuit of pleasure whether it be cultural or merely idle, warming human relations. It accounts for that air of dark suspicion that hangs about him, his powerful feeling that everyone is out to make a fool of him. It is not necessarily so, but the fact is that he has no guile, no wit capable of turning attacks on him back on his attackers.

And there is irony in this, for that is the very basis of his style on court. "His countershots, returns, and passes are what beat people," Jack Kramer has said. "Longer rallies, more all-court, more lobs, and he runs around a lot." Quite literally, he steals his opponents' power and turns it against them. And he was to give a superb example of that in his match against Tanner. It may be, as Connors was to say later, that Tanner was tired from a succession of tough matches by the time he and Connors met. It may also be that Roscoe disobeyed tennis's basic dictum, which is not to change a winning game. For it seemed to me, at least in the early going, that he was not serving as hard to Connors as he had to the other men he had met, that in effect he came out trying to throw changeups at him. But that was a bad tactic, for Connors, besides being able to handle serves the rest of us can't even see, does have this dogged capacity to reach any ball and straighten out—with sheer power—any spin or slice. Then, too, Connors was throwing up a larger number of lobs than was customary, even for him, and I recalled Segura's courtside scouting report, indicating that Tanner was vulnerable to this shot, to soft stuff of all kinds for that matter. (It seemed to me Connors was employing the touch volley more than the usual amount, too.)

Now, on the score board the first two sets could not have been closer, 7–6, 7–6, with both players losing their serves twice in each set, but the first tie-breaker went easily to Connors (what

a wonderful weapon a fine return of serve is in this situation), and the next one went even more quickly to him 5–2. Again one recalled Segura's remark that a big serve can be a detriment in a tie-breaker if its possessor has nothing else to fall back on. Connors then ran out the match at 6–4 in the next set, having achieved psychological dominance through those tie-break victories. And, one must add, through his relentlessness. This was the first of his matches I had sat through from start to finish and it is that quality, finally, which seems to me to distinguish him from everyone else. There just doesn't seem to be any way to wear him down, discourage him. He runs for everything and he gets shots that no one else now playing the game does—not with his consistency, anyway.

So it was to be Wimbledon all over again in the finals—Connors vs. Rosewall. The only consolation for the determined Connors haters was that his fiancée, Chris Evert, had been put out in the semifinals by Evonne Goolagong. Play in that match had begun under threatening skies on the final Friday of the tournament and Ms. Goolagong, who likes grass, had whipped Chrissie, who does not, 6–0. She was leading in the second set 4–3 (and up a service break) when the rains came and play was suspended. It was the sort of luck that Evert seems to attract. (Lesley Hunt had had her on the ropes at Wimbledon earlier in the summer when rain forced suspension and gave Evert a chance to regroup and win.) And, indeed, after another day's suspension for wet grounds she came back to win the second set 7–6.

Standing at the base line, awaiting serve, there is something oddly complacent in her posture, her weight more on her heels than most players, looking somehow more demure than anyone else. And she plays like a ball machine—mechanically hitting the lines with her instruction-book ground strokes. When she misses, you don't feel that she has made a mistake. You feel the attendant has just slightly missed the proper setting on her control dial.

In the end, Evert cannot tame the delightful Goolagong. To borrow a phrase, Evonne floats like a butterfly and stings like a bee, and she is surely the most graceful player in women's tennis, combining a nicely tempered ferocity with a sweetness of spirit that communicates itself to the furthest reaches of the stadium. She came back to win the final set of the Evert match 6–3. It turned out that Evert was able to hold service only three times in the entire match.

This victory puts me in some conflict as the finals begin. Goolagong has won my heart, but Billie Jean is the kind of person I've liked ever since Howard Hawks started making women like her the heroines of his movies: Intelligent, straight-talking, asking no quarter and giving none in male company, and all the more attractive for being endowed with these allegedly "masculine" traits. In my mind anyway, the line from Katharine Hepburn, Rosalind Russell, Jean Arthur and Lauren Bacall to "the old lady," as Mrs. King now refers to herself, is entirely clear. One night as I was leaving the grounds she was walking down the road ahead of me, escorted by one of the male players. He said something that amused her, and the terror of the tennis world, the possessor of the fastest lip on the circuit, suddenly broke into a merry, girlish soft-shoe dance. Nice.

I tried, for a while, to preserve my neutrality in the King-Goolagong final. Evonne won the first set 6–3, then lost the second by the same score. She was up 3–0 in the deciding set, when King put on one of those gutty rallies that make her such an exciting performer. She broke Evonne's serve, was herself broken, then broke back again and again, finally taking the set and match 7–5. Somewhere in that run I started pulling hard for her. She is not, after all, getting any younger, but more to the point it is clear that tennis alone does not present enough of a challenge to her busy mind, that probably this would be the last Forest Hills at which she would be a fully committed contender.

The women's final, in any case, was a satisfying match and it salved some of the hurt one shared with Rosewall over his humiliation by Connors, who beat him 6–1, 6–0, 6–1 just before the women took the court. About this match, the less said the better. Connors made Rosewall look old and the rest of us feel old, in administering the worst defeat ever inflicted on anyone in this event's final. Rosewall won only nineteen points serving in a match that was over in just sixty-nine minutes, also a finals record. What can one say? Rosewall's game simply matches as badly as anyone's can with Connors's. Normally, of course, Rosewall compensates for his serve's lack of power with clever placement, but Connors's ability to retrieve anything anywhere on the court nullifies that skill, and his power on the return of serve is so shocking that Rosewall could simply not get the net away from him. One should not have to point it out at this late date, but for the record, Rosewall is not so bad a player as this score indicates. While we are at it, though, it should be firmly noted that Connors is as good a player as this score demonstrates.

It was that fact that the press was grappling with in the postmatch conference. They were trying at last to reconcile the fact that an unpleasant, or at least difficult, personality had somehow been joined with an indisputable talent. Once again, the Nixon analogy recurred, for he, too, had won most resoundingly at a moment when the leading edge of the culture, the opinion-makers, had decreed that his type, the inhumanly ambitious, win-at-any-cost public figure was done in America, when a sweeter image was deemed a prerequisite for any success.

Heavy stuff for the conclusion of a tennis tournament. And I was glad to put it out of my mind as, with a few others, I sought out Rosewall, that composed and sedate figure. A few desultory questions were put to him, but the purpose of the exercise, I think, was simply to gather consolingly about him, to suggest, wordlessly as it turned out, a sense of gratitude toward him and solidarity with him. Indeed, by this time, I had developed a powerful fellow feeling for quite a few of the personalities who had emerged from this twelve-day week. I thought back on the numerous Amritraj family, dark-complected Indians, the women dressed in saris, moving en masse through the crowds to watch one of their three sons play a match, as sweetly prideful as the family of a high-school valedictorian. I thought of Virginia Wade, whose feet kept getting into inextricable tangles in her second-round loss to Ann Kiyomura, and the burning anger that kept bursting through her English reserve—oh, Virginia, how often I've been there. I thought of a spectator standing next to me, and his startled, pleased exclamation when Roscoe Tanner blew an easy drop volley. "It's worth the price of admission to see one of these guys pull something like that," he said. I thought of Stan Smith trying to hide the pain of his struggle with himself and his out-of-kilter game, layering blandness over the shocking suddenness of his descent from number-one ranking. I flashed, finally, on a twilight scene after the semifinals. I was standing on the second-floor veranda of the clubhouse when my eye fell on a lone figure trudging across the now-deserted field courts. It was Roscoe Tanner, just defeated by Connors, taking the long, but crowdless way home—a small, lonely figure, alone with his mistakes, but, I hoped, consoled by the distance he had come from the unseeded pack to the semis. Beneath the commercial fandango, the media orgy, the human essence of the game as a naked confrontation of will and skill seemed to me very much intact, and here at the end I find myself as unwilling to say goodbye to this scene, to the people who had permitted me to share a little of their experience, as I have been, in the past, to leave an especially splendid cruise ship or to take my leave of the people with whom I had shared the camaraderie of making a film.

Finally, though, there were no more excuses to linger. The moment with Rosewall passed and it was time to go. But as we headed up toward the clubhouse along a path that borders the Har Tru courts that ring the grounds, we noticed a small crowd had collected. What to our wondering eyes should appear but Ilie Nastase and Vitas Gerulaitis, long-gone from competition, but in need of a tune-up for an upcoming tournament in New Jersey. They were not having a hit, they were having a match and they were going at it hammer and tongs, playing fierce and wonderful tennis (despite his reputation as a troublemaker, Nastase is an enormously graceful player and in many respects a pleasant fellow, capable of a wit as genuine as his buddy Connors's is false). They finished a point as Nastase, retrieving the ball, glanced up to see the gallery they had attracted. "Is all over," he said. "Why don't you go home and watch television? You have good television here." Doubtless it seems so to a Rumanian, and in any case we should by this time have been tennised out. Still there was something so pure about this action that we edged away from it slowly, returning reluctantly to the world where tennis occurs on weekends, and the things Nastase and the others do routinely are, for us, miracles.

The Australian Open

The Australian Open was once the first tournament of the year—the first leg of the Grand Slam. Now it is the last, a change that has not been a great disruption to the tennis calendar because the event is played over New Year's Day. In 1969 Rod Laver won his second Grand Slam, the first step of which was the Australian Open. In many ways the most important match of the year was his five-set victory over Tony Roche in the semifinals, which turned on a questionable call. What if that call had gone the other way? Would there have been a second Grand Slam? Would Roche have then gone on to win a multitude of major championships, as was predicted for him? The eternal if . . . . Here are Laver's thoughts.

THREE years had passed since I'd been home, and I was very anxious to see my parents. They're getting older—dad's over seventy—and there won't be too many more times when we're all together. Tennis means a big sacrifice in family life. More so if you're an Australian because almost everything is happening somewhere else. I left when I was fifteen to make tennis my career and have spent precious little time at home since.

You wonder, quite a lot in the beginning, if the loneliness and the being away from the family is worth it. I've really been a gypsy more than half my life. I've made good friends and enjoyed seeing the world and I believed I was doing the right thing to secure my future. But, remember, I've done extremely well. That fact helps combat the loneliness. I've known young Australians who seemed to have as much promise as I, who were my friends, but couldn't fight the homesickness. This kept them from being outstanding, and they had to find something else to go into.

During the Open, I learned that Mary was going to have the baby. Only that, and seeing my folks, made Brisbane bearable. The tournament was the most discouraging I've ever played in. There have been worse conditions while barnstorming as a pro, and fewer spectators. But when you come into Milton Courts, where your memories are so good, and then this long-awaited Open turns out as a terribly bush league production—well, it hurt.

Bill Edwards and several of his fellow officials snubbed the tournament one day to go to the races. We know Bill doesn't care for the pros and the idea of open tennis, but did he have to insult us by acting that way—to the detriment of an event that could have made money for Milton, his club? Australia's tennis old guard needs to be excused from the scene.

I arrived at Milton and walked out onto the stadium grass to look around and I thought back nine years. My first major title was the Australian in 1960, when I got that premature notion I could keep going through a Slam. It was a marvelous win for everybody, not just me, because by beating Neale Fraser of Melbourne in the five-set final I became only the second Queenslander to win the national championship since 1905.

Eight thousand were in the stands, among them a good-sized gathering of friends from Rockhampton, crowing for me every chance they got. Of course it was my crowd, considering the circumstances. Fraser was the number-one amateur in the world then and he had a match point on me in the fourth set. I slipped away and had seven of them on him at 7–6 in the fifth on my serve. He busted loose every time, but finally I held serve for the title.

A lot of people thought it was the most exciting match they'd ever seen. That was how I remembered Milton, for that struggling, unexpected triumph which had Australia talking, and started my collection of major championships. Others may have remembered it, too, but few bought tickets to witness the hero's return. Neale Fraser showed up, only as a spectator. And he was in on a free ticket.

A young Italian named Massimo di Domenico gets a mention as the first of twenty-six victims on the Slam. The grass wasn't as fast as usual at Milton, and I could experiment and get the feel in beating him, 6–2, 6–3, 6–3. Brisbane is always hot, but the heat seemed more blistering to me, though I'd grown up in the area. I wasn't used to it after years away from Queensland.

I knew it in my next match against Roy Emerson, and I'm happy we played at night. Dew makes night tennis on grass a bad, slippery idea. But we didn't miss the sun at all, and the crowds improved a little.

If there was one match that did revive some of the old tennis feeling in the town it was Emerson and Laver.

We were the local boys who had made it better than any Queenslanders. We'd played so many times that sometimes our matches seemed as familiar as summertime reruns on TV. No matter what happened, though, we became bet-

ter and better friends. We're doubles partners now, very close, but Emmo would cut out his heart to beat me. He's a tremendous competitor, unbelievable when it comes to fitness. I think he's the hardest-working athlete I've ever seen.

Emmo and I come from the same kind of background, out in the bush. He was brought up on a cattle ranch at a little place called Black Butt, and he got those really strong wrists by milking cows. I don't know whether he used the Continental grip on the cows, but they knew he was going to hang on until they produced their daily quota. He must have milked thousands of them. When Emmo began to show a high aptitude for tennis, his family sold the place and moved to Brisbane. They had a court on their ranch, but his father wanted Emmo to be able to get the best competition and instruction.

At first, in Brisbane, Emmo couldn't get used to taking a bath whenever he felt like it. "Out on the station, water was scarce and precious. It was almost rationed," he told his new friends. "I thought we were going to run out in Brisbane, and I never used much until I was certain we could have as much as we wanted."

Emmo has a very rigid code for himself, and we like to think this is the way of a dinkum (honest-to-God) Aussie. Although he has had numerous injuries during his career, one of them costing him his fourth Wimbledon title and the other possibly costing him a fifth—and making it easier on my Slam in 1962—he never, never talks about them or implies that an injury was the cause for defeat.

"Once you walk onto that court," says Emmo, "you're signifying that you're in perfect shape. Otherwise don't go on. Only two things happen. You win, or your opponent beats you. Injuries have nothing to do with it." Any talk of injury, as an excuse, grates on Emmo. He once snorted about the chronic moaner, Niki Pilic: "I never beat Niki when he was well." You'll never hear Emmo complain, but you will hear his footsteps all through a match as he charges the net incessantly, and sometimes you'll hear that piercing laugh of his, and be glad. That's Emmo's way of releasing the tension when he's bungled a shot he should have had.

Rod Laver, shown here at Wimbledon a decade ago, always seemed to find his best tennis when under the most pressure—the mark of a true champion. (Photo by Russ Adams)

Emmo gleams on a court, the sun or the lights glistening off his patent-leather hair and the gold fillings so prominent in his front teeth.

The sight of him is as much with me as anything else in the game because we've played each other so often in important matches. He has been my downfall, and I his. Titles of our own nation and numerous others have been at stake often when we've met, and we've meant a lot of disappointment for each other. During the two Slams, in eight tournaments, I've had to get past Emmo five times.

By 1960 Emmo and I were the rising players in Australia while Neale Fraser was briefly at the top. In the semis of the nationals at Brisbane, I somehow pulled up from 2–5 in the fifth to win five straight games and beat Emmo. Then I knocked off Fraser in that wild final. That delayed Emmo's winning his first Australian title, which he got a year later by going through me in the final. Later, in 1961, after winning Wimbledon, I was favored to win my first American championship. But there was Emmo in the final, winning his first instead, and me shaking his hand and saying, "Well played, Emmo."

Although Emerson has never won the Grand Slam, he's won more of the Slam titles than anybody else, a total of twelve—six Australian, two U.S., English, and French. At the close of 1969, I was one behind him with eleven, ready to pass. Emmo has lost just enough of his edge so that he's not likely to win one of the Big Four again, but he'll always be dangerous.

The grass was slick when we went on. Because of the slipshod scheduling it was after nine P.M. Emmo's a slow starter. So am I, but he was slower and I got the first set pretty quickly. And the second. But he took the third, and he had a break and was serving at 7–6 in the fourth, looking like he'd catch up. It was just about midnight now, the crowd excited. The year would be marked by patches like the one I struck then. I began hitting my returns harder, and they were buzzing with topspin. Emmo was charging in, but he missed a couple of volleys. I broke back, and kept going for a run of three straight games and the match, 6–2, 6–3, 3–6, 9–7.

There wasn't much time to have a beer and relax because after I'd showered and talked to the reporters it was one in the morning and I was due back to play Fred Stolle in ten hours. Hardly time for breakfast.

Stolle, a tall, slim blond, probably would have been a basketball player if he'd grown up in America instead of Sydney. He was quite a good cricketer, a wicket keeper, which corresponds to catcher in baseball, but he was always getting his hands banged up and his mother didn't like that. She encouraged him to play more tennis, and he had a talent for it. We're the same age, but Fred was a late developer and first made a name as a doubles player. I didn't consider him a rival when we were both amateurs but with his rifling serve, good volleys and backhand, he came along strongly in 1964 and won Forest Hills in 1966.

We had a terribly long second set, and I had to serve well to stave off a set point, but Fred couldn't get into the match after that and I won 6–4, 18–16, 6–2.

Like Emmo and me, Tony Roche is a country boy. He grew up in Tarcutta, a tiny New South Wales settlement surrounded by nothing and sheep, about two hundred miles from Sydney. His father, Andy Roche, is the town butcher, as my Dad had been briefly in Marlborough, and Tony has the strokes to do a splendid job with a cleaver. He prefers a racket, and is as threatening with that.

After pounding a ball against the side of his house so much that he nearly knocked it off the foundation, Tony decided he'd have to get out of Tarcutta if he was going to be a serious tennis player. He was missed. His departure cut the population noticeably, by almost 1 percent. Moving on to Sydney, he was quick to be noticed as an exceptional prospect.

All through 1969 Tony was trouble for me. The main trouble. He beat me five out of nine times, giving me my own medicine—a lot of left-handed spin—and making it clear that he thought my time was over and his had come. It seems strange with all the millions of tennis players in the world that two left-handers from the Australian Outback, from places called Rockhampton and Tarcutta, would be one-two for 1969.

One reason Tony got a jump on me, I think, is that he had more opportunity to play against left-handers. For years I was the only lefty among the touring pros. This was a decided edge for me because the only time my opponents encountered left-handed spin was against me, while I was well accustomed to the right-handed spin.

When Roche went pro with Dave Dixon's Handsome Eight, two other lefties went with him, Taylor and Pilic, so that he became well grooved in opposing his own kind. The abundance of left-handers in their troupe probably was a reason that Newcombe, Drysdale and Ralston were able to give me exceptional trouble.

I wish I had more time during a match to watch Tony, but I'm pretty busy following the ball. When he signed with the World Championship Tennis pro troupe, with seven others, they were called the Handsome Eight. Roger Taylor, John Newcombe, Niki Pilic, Pierre Barthes, Butch Buchholz, Cliff Drysdale, all have movie star looks, or what we used to think of that way, in the pre-antihero days. Denny Ralston has an all-American appearance, but Tony? Ask him where he ranked in beauty among the Handsome Eight, and he replies "fourteenth." The movie star he resembles is Victor McLaglen. He has a plastic face that he's always trying to rearrange with his right hand when he makes a bad shot. Tony's facial expressions are fantastic. He may not be pretty, but he does have a rugged Aussie look about him with his shocks of blond hair, his heavy jaw and sturdy chest. He could have been a fine boxer or football player, I think. Tennis was lucky to get him.

Just before we got to Brisbane, Tony beat me in the New South Wales final in Sydney, which was our country's first actual open. He took a lead on me that he never gave up over the year, but he couldn't beat me in the matches that mattered most—and paid best.

I brought three sun hats to the court that Saturday to play Tony in the semifinals, and each one was thoroughly soaked when we finished over four hours later. We started at noon. My brother Trevor was coming down from Rocky for the weekend, and since he keeps his sports goods shop open a half-day, he phoned me: "I won't be there till two. Try to keep it going so I can see something of it." We laughed about that later. Trevor got to see more than enough of me and Tony struggling away with the temperature at 105 and no shade anywhere. We kept towels in an icebox beside the court and draped ourselves with them every change game. It was only momentary relief. I kept taking glucose and salt pills, but I got groggy. It turned out to be the longest match I ever played—ninety games—and by far the hardest. Ten years back, at Wimbledon, I got by big Barry MacKay in eighty-seven games at Wimbledon, also a semifinal. But the London climate was a lot easier to take than Brisbane.

There wasn't much to choose between us after Tony got into the match. It looked like I had him when I won the first two sets, 7–5, 22–20, but I was getting tired. At that point of the season Tony was fitter than I, and when he grabbed the third set 11–9, you could see him begin to puff up with confidence. That brought merciful intermission with a shower in the dressing room, one of those showers you never want to leave. Too quickly we returned to the oven, and Tony came back eagerly to resume with the same heavy serves and stiff volleys. I was in a daze as he ran off five games. The set was gone. I conceded that much as I served the sixth game, but I wanted badly to hold serve so that I could lead off in the fifth set. It was hard to do because Tony was playing full-tilt now and felt he had me. He'd already beaten me in Sydney and he was going to do it again.

Confidence is the thing in tennis, as I'm sure it is in any sport. I hear other athletes talk that way. Confidence separates athletes of similar ability.

Tony had it . . . and in an instant during the decisive set he lost it, through no fault of his own, on what may have been a very bad break. I'll never be certain, but Tony Roche will go through life thinking he was bad-lucked out of that victory by a linesman's decision. Maybe he was.

We went to deuce in the sixth game of the fourth set but I worked to make sure I got the game. It was important to me, even though Tony

Tony Roche steps into a backhand volley, a shot judged by his peers to be the best in tennis during his prime. Roche was the heir apparent to Rod Laver . . . but it just didn't work out that way. (Photo by Russ Adams)

and I both saw that the set would be his. Maybe he didn't sense the importance. He served out in the next game for 6–1. We were even, and the momentum was his.

But serving first in the fifth set picked me up a bit. It's a psychological help to go into the lead every time you win your serve in a close match, and that's why I tried so hard for a seemingly meaningless game when I was down 0–5 in the fourth. I wanted to serve that lead-off game.

Naturally, now I had to hold my serve, and I hadn't been serving too well. Tony'd broken me three of the last four times. He was returning serve better than I was, and returning was tricky business on that court. It was freshly resodded and playing badly. Any time a ball landed on the court, hitting it was guesswork. That's unusual for Australian grass, but this was Brisbane 1969, with everything schemozzled. Bad courts were just one more factor in a general screw-up.

Now I knew I had to get my first serves in because Tony would be jumping all over the second ball. I tried to pull myself together and make sure the first serve was a good one and that I was up to the net in position to make a good volley. I figured one break of serve would decide the match, the condition we were in. Tony was stronger, but he'd never been in a fifth set with me, and he'd have just a little more pressure on him, serving second.

Every time I held, the situation would be just a little dicier for him. My serve began to work all right. His continued too. One–love for me, but he tied it. Two–one, and then 2–2. Three–two. I was feeling a little better. He wasn't blasting me off the court the way he had in the fourth set, and my confidence was beginning to come back. I've lost five-set matches, but not many, and I'd have to think hard to remember one. Three–all as Tony held, but his volleys didn't have quite the zip. I served to 4–3 and we changed courts. Slowly. The wet towels from the icebox felt good on my head. I wrung out my sun hat and it was like squeezing a sponge. One of the things I used to do on hot days was put a piece of wet cabbage inside my hat. That was a pretty good trick for keeping cool. Nothing like a green salad on your head, although I don't know if oil and vinegar does much for your scalp. I was tennis's answer to Mrs. Wiggs of the Cabbage Patch. But I had no greens this day, and Tony and I felt like the cabbage that lies alongside boiled corned beef.

It was his turn to serve and I screwed my mind into working for every point as though it were the last. If you do that when you come down the stretch in a tight match you'll be surprised how often a superhuman effort will come out of you. "It's 3–4 in the last set, and I'm going to hack and grub," I told myself. "Just do anything to get the ball over the net. It doesn't matter how you look. Form won't win this one."

You learn to hack, as we call it, when you join the pros. Get balls back, and the hell with trying to slap a winning shot that doesn't have too much chance. It looks great if you make it, but at this stage you can't give away points.

A big shot may look lovely, but anything that goes over the net now will look lovely. You still win matches by getting the ball over the net one more time than your opponent.

You face up to that when you leave the amateurs. You settle down. You can slam away when your opponent isn't too sound, or you clearly dominate him, but I was in with Tony Roche in the decisive set, and it was no time for pride and flamboyance. I was going to scratch and dig and bloop the ball over any way I could.

I was chipping my returns now, trying to squib them onto his feet. With the ball skipping erratically on those courts, the opportunities to hit full out were limited, and the best thing was just to meet the ball.

So Tony was serving at 3–4, and this was the place for me to do my utmost. He knew it; everybody who hadn't passed out from the heat in the stands knew it. Win this one and I'd be serving for the match at 5–3. This had to make it even a little more tense for Tony. We split the first two points: 15–all. Then he missed a volley. The 15–30 point is an awfully big one in this spot. He came in with a good serve, down the middle, spinning into my body. I sliced under it with my backhand to chip the ball cross-court with underspin. Tony looked relieved because he thought the ball was going out. He was sure it was out, but there was no sound. Tony turned around and looked at the side linesman sitting behind the court. The official held out his hands, parallel to the ground, like a baseball umpire signaling "safe." It meant my shot was good, and the umpire called: "Fifteen–forty!"

Tony was furious, and I can hold his hand and sympathize . . . now. It was such a big point, and the ball may have been out. I didn't have a good view, but I had the feeling when I hit the ball that it might be going wide. I wouldn't have been surprised if it had been called out because it was terribly close.

It was a judgment call. Nobody—and I know Tony agrees—can blame a linesman if he misses one on a day like that. He'd been sitting there broiling for more than four hours, trying to stay sharp and alert. And maybe the ball was good and the man was correct. No matter. It stands as good forever because the linesman said so.

"Fifteen–forty" was the best thing I'd heard all day. Two break points, and Tony was riled. Tony swung hard on his serve, and I knocked the ball back to him. He was at the net to make a backhand volley and sent the ball cross-court to my backhand. Now this was a shot I love—the backhand down the line. Tony realized it and began moving to his left to cover it. But in this situation—two points to break—I was going for it with everything. I got the racket back and drove at the ball, snapping my wrist to load the ball with topspin. Tony and I have been through all this before. But even though he anticipates me, he's going to have a hard time volleying that topspinning ball down his side line whenever I hit it that well. Out went his arm in the reach that failed. His racket probed for the ball and found it, but he couldn't control it. One of the most beautiful sights of 1969 was that ball clunking into the net.

Tony's game was knocked apart by that line call, and he couldn't get himself to function in the last game. He was mad and frustrated. He hadn't quit, but it all seemed so unfair to him. In that moment of his anguish I served through the game promptly, getting only token opposition.

Ninety games, the eighth longest singles match ever played: 7–5, 22–20, 9–11, 1–6, 6–3. It's a good thing that players customarily shake

hands at the end of a match. It was an effective way of holding each other up.

Even though Roche has been around, and at the highest level, he let himself get flapped out of that match like a novice, forgetting that you have to play the calls, as we say. Let's assume the decision that upset Tony was outrageously wrong, and everybody thought so.

You can ask the linesman if he's sure of his call. Sometimes he'll change it or ask the umpire's advice. But if he won't there's nothing you can do. You have to forget it, and make yourself work harder for the next point.

Serving on grass at 15–40, Tony still had something like an even chance of winning that game. When he didn't, he still had a shot at my serve. But by the time he pulled himself together the match was over. You mustn't let the worst call in the world fluster you. I'm glad to offer this advice to Tony today.

Physically, that was the toughest match of the year, certainly of the Slam. But the element of pressure wasn't there. Not for me. The Slam hadn't even begun. I'd won nothing, and there was nothing to be concerned about. It was only the second tournament of the year, and though I wanted the Slam, I really had no idea the year would turn out so incredibly well.

It could all have ended there as easily as not, on the center court at Milton. How many thousands of shots did I need to make the Slam? I don't know. Nobody counted. This isn't baseball. But that one shot, the questionable call, could have changed the whole thing. Roche, of course, is convinced that it did, and I can't argue with him. It's funny, the hours and hours you practice, the miles and time you put in, and maybe the whole thing hinged on a bloke sitting in a chair, looking down the side line, whose job it was to decide whether a ball was out or in. I like to think he was right, that he was wide awake and decisive and that my shot was a deftly hit winner. It reads better that way. But it doesn't matter. Over the years the calls even up, Tony, but that one will hurt even a century from now when you're playing mixed doubles against Bonnie and Clyde at the River Styx Sauna and Racket Club, won't it?

But it may have been more than just a point —15–40 instead of 30–all—for both of us. If Tony had won the game, he might have won the match. That would have given him three straight victories over me, and a substantial heightening of his confidence. It wouldn't have helped mine. I can still see that backhand return of mine streaking for the side line. Was a season for two men riding on that shot? That's one way to look at it, but maybe I'm getting too dramatic.

Nevertheless it's weird how a simple mistake can change not only a match but perhaps a career. To my mind the most fantastic example occurred in Brisbane during the Queensland championships of 1955. Nineteen-year-old Ashley Cooper, just out of the junior ranks, was playing and losing a first-round match to a local entry, tall Les Flanders. At match point, Flanders stood at the net about to crush a sitter. It was all over, Cooper was reconciled to that, and he didn't much care where Les put the ball. He was astonished when Les butchered the smash, knocking the ball way out of court.

The reprieve turned Coop into a tiger, and he went on to win the match. His confidence soared and he was the sensation of the tournament, beating Mal Anderson and Merv Rose (then number ten in the world) on the way to the final where he played well in losing to Rosewall.

Cooper never should have gotten to the second round, Flanders's carelessness let him live one more point, and somehow the spark he needed was kindled. Less than three years later Coop was Wimbledon champion, number-one man in the amateur world. Those wins over Anderson and Rose gave him faith in himself, put him in a position to-battle Rosewall impressively. But I wonder if Coop would have gone to the top if Les Flanders had finished off that easy shot properly.

The championship match in which I met Andres Gimeno was an anticlimax. Andres wasn't spirited, not strutting the way he usually does. He dislikes grass and extreme heat. Few Spaniards brought up on clay, care for grass, and for Andres, bad grass is more agonizing than eating dinner before ten P.M. Nevertheless he'd had a good tournament, beating Kenny Rosewall, Butch Buchholz and the amateur Ray Ruffels, without losing a set.

I think he felt he'd done enough, and he seemed pretty much resigned to defeat when he played me. I hadn't lost to Andres in a long time, and though he had several chances to break my serve in the third set, I took him pretty much as I knew I should, 6–3, 6–4, 7–5. I got my $5000 although the tournament went broke, and now the Slam was a definite possibility. I hoped my troublesome elbow would hold up, and I was pretty sure that there'd be no more 100-degree days along the way. Emerson and I won the doubles over Rosewall and Stolle, so we had a chance for a Slam there, too. One doubles Slam has been made, by Aussies Frank Sedgman and Ken McGregor in 1951.

I was so disgusted with the mismanagement of the tournament that I wanted to get out of Brisbane before I said some things I'd regret. The best part of it was seeing my family. We stayed together in a motel. Though it was pleasant, a reunion like that is spent mostly in talking about old times. You're not really a part of the family any more, and you aren't planning any future as a group. You talk about things you've done together, a lot of good times, but you know there won't be a lot of time together in the future. My life just isn't built that way. Maybe someday I'll go back to Australia to settle, but I don't know.

Diary Notes: Summer 1955

by GORDON FORBES

Lest we forget that tennis is played for fun, Gordon Forbes tells us how it really was—on the court and off —with the greatest cast of characters any sport would ever dare claim. This selection is an excerpt from Forbes's book, A Handful of Summers, *developed from the diary he kept during his time as a world-class competitor.*

Diary Notes: Rome

Today, Abie forgot to pack his tennis socks and jock-strap, for about the twentieth time this month, and borrowed mine. As usual, I received them back in a very dodgy condition—stretched to twice their size, for a start. In the dressing room, after his match, he dumped them in my lap, and while I was contemplating them, Roy Emerson began singing in the shower. Emerson has a singular showering technique. Thus:

1. Remove all clothing excepting tennis shorts.

2. Enter shower. Adjust temperature.

3. Cover body in soap suds from head to foot.

4. Scrub body.

5. Scrub tennis shorts.

6. Commence song of the week.

His delivery is enthusiastic, but inclined to drift off key. This week the song is one of the current hits:

"Many a tear has to fallllll

But it's allllll

In the game.

All in that wonderful game

That is know—."

"Shad up. Shad up. Shad up, bloody Emerson!"

It was Drobny. He had entered the dressing room, covered in the marks of a titanic struggle. Red dust, sweat, dirty shoes, fogged-up spectacles, tousled hair, generally unkempt. The singing stopped. Emerson's eyes appeared around the edge of the cubicle, then disappeared. Drobny dropped his rackets into the silence.

"That is known," came from the shower, "as LOVVVVE."

"Bloody Australians," said Drobny.

Another silence humming with prospects.

"Once in a while she may call-l-l-l,"

(came from the shower)

"But it's all-l-l-l

In the game

All in that mad, crazy game—."

"Emerson!" shouted Drobny. "Shad up singing or I'll get really mad."

Emerson's head reappeared from the shower. "What's up, Drob?" he asked, infinitely cheerful. "What's up? Did you play like a cunt, or what?"

Emerson is one of tennis's all-timers. An unbelievable disposition—perhaps the perfect combination of kindness, humor, determination and ruefulness. Tremendous lust for life—Emerson.

The tennis stadium in Rome, called Foro Italico, is a heavy marble affair, with sunken courts, red, wet surfaces, slow and soft as mozzarella cheese. Tennis in slow motion, under a Mediterranean sun, watched by statues and cypresses. Here the net-rushers curse and toil, and the ground-strokers adjust their grips, lick their lips and pound away at their topspins, with all the time in the world. The clubhouse, also marble, smells of capuccino and overlooks the outside courts. Arriving at Foro Italico on the opening day of the Italian championships, one is struck dumb by hundreds of ground strokes. Every young Italian player of any consequence sports immaculate forehands and backhands. Stand at the railings of the little cafeteria and look down over the sunken courts, and all you will see are the thousands of them, deep and heavy. Balls moving back and forth, carrying the marks of the wet, red clay. These were the hunting grounds of the great Italians—Cucelli, Del Bello, Gardini, Merlo, Pietrangeli, Sirola, Panatta.

Not Forbes and Segal.

In Rome, net-rushers were cannon fodder. On the way to net, one automatically had visions of the valley of death; the six hundred; the whistle of ball and shot, and danger to life and limb. Inevitably, we lost early on (though I once took Larsen to five sets) and so there was plenty of time for practice and sightseeing. The Colosseum, St. Peter's, the Catacombs, all the old places. In the Sistine Chapel Abie gazed upwards and said:

"Forbsey, would you believe that this whole roof was painted by a guy called Angelo. Old Michael. Goddamn, I bet he ended up with a chiropractor havin' to do one hell of a neck job to him!"

Diary Notes: Paris

The French foods sometimes confound Abie and me.

At the Racing Club where we practice, they have a fantastic al fresco lunch all laid out. You help yourself.

On the table are these huge artichokes which have fascinated us for some time. We always see the French carrying them about on trays.

"I'm going to give one of those green bastards a go," says Abe, and sticks the biggest one on his tray.

He can't wait. As we sit down he breaks off one of

the big outer leaves, sticks it into his mouth and begins chomping. Tremendous milling process inside his head, and then after a minute or two he gets a pained expression, and pushing a finger into his mouth, he pulls out this soggy wad of stuff that looks like jute fiber.

"Christ, Forbsey," he says, "these French must have tough jaws. How the hell do they eat these things?"

Later, Pierre Darmon came over and explained to us how you eat artichokes.

"This is the only thing in the world," said Abie, "that you end up havin' more left than you started out with."

Food for Abie was very important. To begin with, he needed a fair quantity to drive his fairly considerable plant and machinery. But there was more to it than that. More than anyone else I know, Abie loved, absolutely reveled in, the act of alleviating hunger. The hungrier he was, the faster he would eat. And, at such times, speed more than quantity seemed to be the essence. A fair-sized steak, for instance, would last about three gulps, while meat balls went down whole, like oysters in lemon juice. Somewhere in the primeval mists of Abie's breeding line, there must have been a canine strain. There was only one person whom I ever saw eat faster than Abie, and that was Orlando Sirola eating spaghetti. I mean, *all* Italians eat spaghetti twice as fast as anyone else, but Sirola simply annihilated it. A large bowlful would disappear in a flash. There seemed to be no question of it being chewed. Forkfuls would go into his mouth, like hay being loaded, and effortlessly slip down his throat.

In the Foro Italico restaurant once, we sat at a table beside Pietrangeli and Sirola, and Abie viewed the Sirola spaghetti assault with awe.

Here, at last, he must have decided, was a form of food that could be eaten even faster than steak.

The next day he ordered spaghetti for lunch, as a starter. When it arrived, he seized a fork, inserted it, wound it round until the spaghetti had reached the approximate dimensions of a tennis ball, then stuffed it into his mouth, and with a thoughtful faraway look on his face, he swallowed it. The experiment was apparently successful, for the rest of the plate got dumped in the same way: "Now I've figured out," he said happily, "how these Italians eat spaghetti as an hors d'oeuvre. If you eat it fast enough, you don't know you've eaten it, and then you can go on and have steak and salad!"

Later that afternoon, when I went into the dressing room to change for our doubles, I found Abie busy with a packet of Eno's Fruit Salts.

"Jesus, Forbsey," he said, "that spaghetti's hard to move. Maybe the steak's just sittin' there, waitin' to get by!" He downed a huge glass of foaming salts, and did up his shoes with a jerk.

Throughout our doubles match he retained an intense, anticipatory sort of look, as though he wasn't quite sure of his immediate future. Once or twice, as he passed me on his way to net after a big serve, I thought that I detected pressure leaks, and these suspicions were verified when we eventually led by two sets to love, 5–3 and my service to come. As I got ready to serve, Abie approached me and muttered with clenched teeth: "Better hold this one, buddy, or we may both never make it off the court. You've heard of being swallowed by an avalanche—well, just bear that in mind!"

With both of us, so to speak, under intense pressures, I held my service. Abie shook hands very briefly and then set off for the locker room at a sort of stiff-legged trot. No sooner had he disappeared inside, than I could swear that I felt a sort of distant rumble: A distinct tremor that would, without doubt, have shown up on the Richter Scale.

Diary Notes: Summer
Abie has taken up poker. He arranges his face into a slanted smile, narrows his eyes, and sardonically produces a pack of cards to practice his shuffling with. I think he thinks that if he can manage to shuffle extravagantly, the rest is easy. He's mad, of course. The poker school consists of a very tricky bunch of players. Mervyn Rose, Don Candy, Sven Davidson, Herbie Flam, Malcolm Fox, Hugh Stewart, and Warren Woodcock. Others occasionally sit in. They're very good, and know every trick and percentage backwards. Malcolm Fox is sup-

posed to have virtually cleaned out an entire troop ship on his way back from Korea. Warren Woodcock has an angelic face, and Mervyn Rose is evil, through and through. Abie, meanwhile, believes that there is nothing to it but shuffling and dealing. He absolutely relishes the way they look across at each other, eye to eye, adjust the stakes and say: "Your hundred, and another hundred." He'd like it even better if they could play in lire and he could say: "Your million, and another million!" He also likes the way they arrange themselves at a corner table surrounded by awe-stricken onlookers, who are riveted by the piles of money. Woodcock and Rose, apparently, have encouraged Abie to play. it's his own fault, of course, because he loves to act the big spender, and have everyone believe that if he is not already a millionaire, he's about to become one at any moment. He's been losing steadily for the last week. Twice I've caught him in the corner of the dressing room, doling out money.

But this afternoon, catastrophe struck. As usual, they were playing in the players' restaurant at Roland Garros, a dungeon of a place. The table was littered with "sandwich jambon," Cokes and ashtrays, with the air decidedly thick.

"Seven card stud," Abie says the game was called. A tremendous round developed and the pot grew and grew. By the time the stragglers had fallen out, at least three hundred dollars in French francs lay on the table, in carelessly crumpled notes, and only Abie and Mervyn Rose remained. A fortune was at stake.

By the time they had finished betting, the pile had grown to a thousand dollars, and then Abie's full house of aces and kings was pipped by Rose's four miserable nines. Gloom and tragedy, and frantic telephone calls to Abie's "shippers." Whatever they are. Whenever Abie runs out of money he phones up these mysterious "shippers." I asked him how one went about getting "shippers," and he told me that "good shippers are one hell-of-a-hard thing to find."

Just at that time tennis was weighed down with literally dozens of the most extraordinary characters. Colorful lunatics, one could almost say. To the extent, almost, that anyone young and unsuspecting coming on the scene might be excused if he thought that in order to reach the top in the game, one needed to be slightly touched.

Of course, Trabert and Seixas were reasonably sane, and so were Harry Hopman's squad of young Australians, Hoad, Rosewall, Hartwig *et al.* But as for the rest, virtually the whole lot were, to a greater or lesser extent, off their heads. Looking back at those tennis years, I find a whole list of names marching through my head. Art Larsen, Warren Woodcock, Herbie Flam, Torben Ulrich, Hugh Stewart, Gardner Mulloy, Mervyn Rose, Andre Hammersley, Fausto Gardini, Beppe Merlo, Pietrangeli and Sirola, George Worthington, Gil Shea, Don Candy, Freddie Huber. Abie Segal, of course. Even Drobny and Patty had their moments. As a newcomer I used to look on, amazed. Don Candy, for example. Now *he* had the charm of a truly funny man. His matches would always develop into critical situations and invariably, at such times, bad calls would occur, usually involving Continental umpires who spoke just enough English to intensify confusion. In any case, umpiring in Italy, Spain and almost all Latin countries was notoriously partisan, and chaos prevailed almost at the drop of a hat. Candy soon became keenly aware of the absurdity of such situations, and adopted a policy of countering chaos with chaos. Often we would watch his matches, eagerly awaiting incidents. Some of his better inventions bordered on lunacy.

During one particular match, for instance, linesmen's chairs were in position, but no linesmen. Drama was in the offing. Inevitably, at a critical deuce point, the bad call turned up and Candy pounced.

He began gesticulating and arguing in furious Spanish gibberish for a full two minutes with the empty chair on the offending line which he felt should contain a linesman. Then he suddenly stopped, walked to the umpire (who had made the call in the first place), pointed to the chair and said:

"I want that man removed!"

"There is-a no one there," said the umpire.

"Well, I want you to get someone," said Candy, "so that I can have him removed."

"But-a if-a you get-a someone, and then you remove-a him, then-a you would have no linesman," said the umpire, mopping his forehead.

"But we already have no linesman," said Candy.

"Then-a why-a you-a want to remove him if-a he comes?" asked the umpire.

"Because he made a bad call," said Candy.

"But-a he wasn't there," said the umpire.

"But if he had been, he would have," said Candy.

"Ah, then, if he had," said the umpire, "then-a you could remove him."

"But I couldn't," said Candy, "because there's no one there!"

"THAT-A-WHAT I SAY!" shouted the umpire. "There's no-a one there!"

"Instead," said Candy, "we play a let. If you play a let, I will not insist on removing that man," and he pointed again to the empty chair.

"All-a right!" said the umpire wearily. "We play a let. Mamma mia, a let, a let-a."

On another occasion, faced with an appalling decision by an Italian umpire who could speak no English at all, Candy approached the man, pulling faces, moving his lips, shaking his racket, tearing at his hair and generally going through all the motions of a furious diatribe, but silently, without uttering a sound. The umpire watched him with growing alarm. He put his finger in his ear and shook it, then clapped both hands to his ears and released them. This he repeated several times. Suddenly he descended from the chair and with a worried look on his face, he hurried off the court, probably to see a specialist. Candy watched him go then climbed into his chair and in a loud voice reversed the decision, immediately causing his Italian opponent, who had been watching the proceedings in a smug sort of way, to go into apoplexy.

Candy's methods were never vicious. Sometimes he would approach errant linesmen and whisper something to them in a very confidential way. This caused volatile opponents to rave about it being unfair to influence linesmen, to which Candy would reply:

"Relax. I was agreeing with him. There is no rule which says you can't agree with a linesman!"

He was what could be called an industrious player. No fabulous flights for him. he gave workmanlike performances, running around the backhands and hitting conservative topspin forehands from close to his ribs. His service was utilitarian, his backhand safely steered and his volleys sound. But he had a huge heart and a great deal of Australian cunning and resource and although he didn't win many big tournaments, he badly scared nearly all the top players a number of times.

Then there was always the possibility of overhearing snippets of conversations between Candy and Torben Ulrich, who at the time was busy inventing his remarkable world of meditation, profundity and dreams. Whenever Candy came upon Torben Ulrich in one of his profound moods, it seemed to trigger off within him an opposite reaction and he used to put on an air of excessive heartiness and good fellowship.

"Good morning, Torben!" he might say lustily, to which Torben would often reply, slowly and deliberately:

"Explain to me, Donald. What exactly is a 'good morning'?"

"Sunny!" Candy would say. "No rain!"

"Aha, then," Torben would reply, "perhaps it would be more accurate to say, 'Sunny morning, Torben,' because you see, for me, a sunny morning need not necessarily be a good morning."

"All right then. Sunny morning, Torben!"

"Yes, Donald. You are right. The sun is certainly shining."

Such exchanges took place in dozens of variations, always with a bland display of offhandedness, each treating the other with suitable indulgence of the kind with which fathers treat small children. Once in the midday heat of July in Athens, Candy came upon Torben sitting reflectively on a bench at the tennis club, with a wet towel on his head. Don sank down beside him.

"Hot," he said in a precise, firm voice.

"Yes," said Torben. "You could say that it is hot."

"Too hot to practice tennis," pursued Candy.

"I am not going to practice tennis," said Torben.

"I thought you were about to say to me, 'Let's practice tennis,' " said Candy.

"Even if it were cool," said Torben, "I would practically never say that to you. It would be much more likely that I would say to you: Donald, I think that it would be better for both of us if we *did not* practice tennis!"

"Then that's settled," said Candy firmly. "We are not going to practice tennis today."

"Yes," said Torben. "That's settled." Then he added: "In a way, you know, it was never really *not* settled."

On still another occasion (one of the rare ones when Candy and Ulrich *did* get to practice) they had been playing for some time when some eager club members approached the court. As usual during tournaments, practice courts were at a premium, and the members waited impatiently. At last one of them spoke to Ulrich.

"Have you been playing long?" he said.

"As long as I can remember," said Torben.

"How much longer will you play?" asked the member.

"We may go on for many years," said Torben. The member looked disgruntled. "You see," said Torben in a soothing way, "we hardly ever feel like ending our game exactly at the same time." Candy, who had been listening, now approached.

"He's mad," he said to the now puzzled member. He tapped his temple. "He believes that he is born blessed, but in actual fact, he's mad!"

"That," said Torben, "is a matter for discussion. Because, you see, it is hard to define who is mad and who is not." He fixed the club member with a penetrating stare and said: "What exactly is madness? Perhaps you can tell me!"

Torben was, and is, an extraordinary human being. With him in view one would automatically consider such phenomena as intellectualism, the power of the mind, mysticism, things deep, gurudom even. He had, for a start, long hair and a beard, which in those days were unheard of (we were busy imitating the crew-cuts of Trabert and Seixas) and which lent him the somewhat scary appearance of the son of some grave god. He moved in an aura of private contemplation which I, for one, was reluctant to interrupt. He explored thoroughly the fields of nearly all sensitivities, always distant and thoughtful behind his youthful, hirsute disguise. Pleasantries generally escaped him. All remarks addressed to him would make their way into his head for consideration. I once said to him as he left a court after a match,

"Torben, did you win?"

"No," he said.

"Then what happened?" I asked.

"I simply played in the usual way. It was my opponent who lost," he said.

His delivery was slow and deliberate, each word weighted with consideration. He played the clarinet and tenor sax (very well, when the time was right), immersed himself in the angular harmonies and oblique progressions of new jazz and carried, at all times, a record player and records—Miles Davis, Art Farmer, Mulligan, Terry, Bill Evans, Parker, Powell, John Coltrane. Complicated cadences always drifted out of Torben's quarters, sounds which greatly puzzled Don Candy. His music was more straightforward—a simple set of guitar chords and songs, about John Henry being a "Steel-Driving" man, "Muscles and Blood," "Whisky Bill" and "Home on the Range," which he did with a stetson and a Roy Rogers delivery, sometimes startling everyone with a yodel or two. After putting up with Torben's music for some time, he decided to remedy his taste and bought a record of marches. Armed with this, he broke in on Torben's contemplation of Thelonius Monk's "Round Midnight," turned off the player and presented Torben with the record.

"What," he asked, "do you think about this?"

Torben examined the record carefully, then handed it back.

"I would avoid thinking about it," he said.

"Try it," said Candy, unabashed. "Put it on."

"My machine," said Torben, "would not be able to reproduce it."

"Why not?" asked Candy in a challenging voice.

"Because," said Torben, "this is a machine which plays music. It cannot perform other functions."

"And this," said Candy haughtily, "is a musical recording. It cannot, for instance, be played through a washing machine."

"It would not surprise me," said Torben, "if it was not perhaps better to play that record through a washing machine."

"In any case," said Candy, "I did not come here with the intention of discussing the possibility of having laundry done. I came here to introduce to you a new kind of musical experience."

"I think, Donald," said Torben, "that I would find it more valuable if you told me how to get my laundry done."

A long wrangle ensued, involving the unlikely combination of laundry and music. At last, Candy's persistence won the day. Monk was removed, the marches installed. Suddenly the player began to emit stirring martial sounds. Candy marched up and down the room several times, delighted, saluting and giving Torben an exaggerated "eyes right"! Torben regarded the player with a puzzled expression, as though it had betrayed him. Abruptly the march ended and Candy came to a halt, gave a final salute and stood easy. Then he picked up his record and strode from the room, like someone who had done a trick. Torben was silent for some time, before he raised his eyes to me and said:

"It would be much better if people had never discovered the way to make war!"

Torben's tennis game, too, was heady and profound. He would sometimes become so engrossed in the science of the game, that the winning of it became incidental. At such times he might embark on a series of acutely angled volleys, each more fine than the last; or lob volleys or topspin lobs; or a round-arm sliced service which bit into the breeze, drifting across the net in a curve, light as thistledown, not bouncing but settling onto the grass with a soft sizzling sound. It was one of these services which had ended up in the water jug under the umpire's chair and left Teddy Tinling waiting with a forehand grip.

Somewhere in my diary I found a little description of a match which Torben had played against Manuel Santana.

What more unconventional, almost occult, tennis match could one want? For several games they try things out—their strokes, the flight of the ball, the quality of the court, the air movement, various slices and spins, like musicians tuning their instruments. Torben ponders immensely between points, strikes prodigious poses, thinks, listens, reflects. Manuel selects his strokes like a surgeon selecting his instruments—but it is Torben who leads 8–7 and 40–love. He loses the game and seven more set points before losing the set at 17–15. These situations bring to light a splendid bit of whimsical Ulrich logic. "You know, Gordon," he says to me in the change room, swathed to the eyes in towels: "Manuel is so good under pressure that it is a disadvantage to lead 40–love. You have a better chance leading 30–love, or 30–15. But 40–love is very dangerous!"

The Road to Nowhere

by **BARRY MCDERMOTT**

Not all tennis players make it to the big time. Most never get past the minor leagues, such as the Penn Circuit, a first-chance or last-chance series of events for players on the way up or the way down. Sports Illustrated *writer Barry McDermott distills all the pain and the hope of the competitors into the story of one player, Chip, who says it all in one final word.*

BEADS of sweat glistened on his eyebrows, and the ends of his hair were starting to turn damp as Chip whacked away furiously, like some demented woodchopper. "Topspin," he thought. "Hit the ball early. Follow through." His capering shadow was twenty feet tall on the wall as he swung his tennis racket up on the ball, sending it banging against the back of a supermarket. Behind him was a car, its front end pointed toward him its lights on, its motor idling. It was one-thirity A.M., and Chip was in an empty parking lot behind a closed Publix in Hialeah, Florida, practicing against a wall, trying to keep from going nowhere.

The night before, he had slept on three chairs outside a Holiday Inn. It was the high season in Florida, and the motel was overbooked. So he had put on three warm-up suits and a leather jacket, and he still froze. He had survived, though, and in the morning he had won his first-round match. Tonight he could sleep in the car he had borrowed—if his knee would let him. But first he would practice and get a little tired, perhaps too tired to remember who and where he was. Then maybe he could sleep. "Topspin," muttered Chip.

What he wanted to forget was that he was almost twenty-four years old, though he lied to most people and told them he was two years younger, that his knee hurt and that his father was waiting to hear from him back home in Texas. Most of all he wanted to forget about the Penn Circuit and that tomorrow would be only the second day of qualifying.

It was near the end of February, and Chip and more than three hundred other players were in Hialeah for the first stop of the USTA/Penn National Circuit, the satellite tour that is the underground and minor leagues of tennis. On the Penn Circuit one rarely hears applause, only the anguished cry of a player missing a shot because with each miss he gets closer to nowhere.

This is the circuit where one sees the game's fabric being woven—and sometimes unraveled; where a disgusted player will walk over to a garbage can and junk an armful of rackets only to have a solicitous girl friend retrieve them and hurry after him; where a young player can sit stock-still for an hour at a time staring at a tennis ball, hoping to improve his concentration; and where scores of players discuss why they lost matches and conclude it was not because they failed to hit the right shots, but because they were reluctant to cheat.

The Penn Circuit travels a purgatorial network of public parks and small private clubs where some of the locker rooms have no lockers and where the players never pass the pay phone without checking the coin-return box. But despite the poor facilities, each week pros from all over the world crowd around the tournament desk to sign in. In Hialeah fully 40 percent of the participants had foreign addresses, and thirteen of the top sixteen seeds were from overseas. The entries included talented youngsters such as Gabriel Urpi of Spain, who won the 1978 Orange Bowl juniors tournament; Ecuador's Raul Viver, the 1979 Orange Bowl champion; and Ben McKown, a three-time All-America and current NCAA doubles champion from Texas's Trinity University. Also on hand were veterans like thirty-three-year-old Ivan Molina, who once was ranked fifty-fourth in the world. And there was the group that included the likes of Chip, who is, in fact, not a real person, but a composite of a number of regulars on the Penn Circuit. These players are neither young nor old, and they are trying to live up to great but fading expectations. Rick Fagel, reputed to have one of the best forehands in the game, is one such pro. So is Van Winitsky, who, as a junior a few years back, was ranked on a par with John McEnroe. Neither of them, it must be said, contributed to the fictional Chip.

Chip came out of college three years ago as a two-time All-America and conference champion. He played the satellite circuit and did well right away, quickly moving up to the Grand Prix circuit, the high-priced habitat of Bjorn Borg and Jimmy Connors. But then he stopped winning. He went four months and won only two matches, and his computer ranking plummeted. His confidence was down, as was his game, so he decided to go back to school and finish the work for his degree in physical education while he still had the time and inclination.

At Hialeah he was embarking on another try

at pro tennis, only this time he had a greater seriousness of purpose, because he had seen the alternatives and hadn't liked them. For most of his life he had played tennis for the wrong reasons: Because his father wanted him to, because it was easy, because it meant he never had to work during the summers. Now he would play it for himself. He knew that if he failed this time, if he didn't play well enough on the Penn Circuit to get back up to the Grand Prix, it meant that he would turn out like his father: Teaching country-club ladies in dainty dresses, lying to them that their backhands looked improved. . . . In a few years he'd be a burned-out hack working fourteen hours a day and leaving a little piece of himself on the court each night when he walked away.

In tennis, computer points are what life's all about. Each week the latest results are fed into the Association of Tennis Professionals' computer, which then spews out the rankings of the world's top players. Pro tennis is a very exclusive club and the computer is its membership committee, and if you don't show it the proper credentials, the computer doesn't let you in.

The top 110 or so players in the world play the Grand Prix circuit, the multimillion-dollar series of tournaments sponsored by Volvo. The rest of the players work the Penn Circuit, a satellite tour of thirty or so $7,000 tournaments spread over the year, where they try to earn enough computer points to scramble up into the big time. It's a tough, unrelenting chase.

Until this season there was another level of competition between the Penn Circuit and the Grand Prix, the American Express Challengers Series, whose events were worth $25,000 apiece. In 1979 Vince Van Patten, the ATP Rookie of the Year, used this series to propel himself onto the Grand Prix tour. But American Express canceled the circuit this year. This means the competition on the Penn Circuit this season will be even more fierce, a crucible that will either turn a player into tempered steel or leave him on the slag heap.

The Penn Circuit is broken up into six segments of five tournaments each and a grand-finale tournament of champions. In each segment the top thirty-two players over the first four weeks meet in a masters event in the fifth week. If a player appears in a match in the masters tournament, he's assured one ATP computer point. One point is good for a ranking of about 68oth in the world, a position that some fifty or so players share.

There are other ways to show how tough the Penn Circuit is. Of the 345 entries in the Hialeah tournament, the large majority were excellent players, the kind that could give lessons to your teaching pro, and yet fewer than ninety of them had earned even one point on the ATP computer. Last year Bjorn Borg led the rankings with 1,497 points amassed in sixteen tournaments. He *averaged* ninety-three points per event. The 250th player in the world, John Hayes of the U.S., had thirty-four points.

The competition is so fierce that the Penn Circuit remains virtually the only route in the U.S. by which a player can break in. The last one who didn't have to come up the hard way was McEnroe, who, as an eighteen-year-old in 1977, worked his way through the qualifying rounds at Wimbledon and wound up in the semifinals before he lost to Connors, thereby earning enough computer points to be eligible for Grand Prix events.

But McEnroe's story is so unusual that it is the tennis equivalent of Lana Turner being discovered in Schwab's Drugstore. The usual road is the one taken by Andres Gomez of Ecuador, who last year showed up as an unknown for the first stop on the Penn Circuit. Gomez waded through the qualifying and the main draw, and won the tournament by sweeping eleven straight matches. He finished the year ranked sixty-fourth in the world and early in 1980 went to the finals of a $50,000 Grand Prix event in Sarasota, losing to Eddie Dibbs. Similarly, young John Sadri played against McEnroe in the finals of the NCAA tournament in 1978, losing a close match, and then went on the satellite circuit. It took him two years to work his way up in the standings, until at the end of 1979 he was a finalist at the Australian Open. In March, Sadri was ranked fifth in the Volvo standings. Many of the players in Hialeah thought that if they stood in the rain

long enough, they might catch the same sort of lightning.

The tournament was being played at the Goodlet Tennis Center, a public facility set among stark, empty fields of white limestone and coral. On the first afternoon of qualifying, Chip showed up early for his opening match, and while he waited he surveyed the players sitting in a covered patio area. Most of them had lost earlier, and they looked as if they had stepped out of one of those photographs of shocked and fatigued Vietnam combat troops, their heads drooping, eyes vacant. For a loser in the first round of qualifying, unless he had a high national ranking or was well fixed financially, the tour was in all probability over, because he couldn't enter qualifying for the rest of the circuit's Florida segment. Take the case of Khelil Lakdar of Belgium. Earlier in the week, while he slept in the Miami airport, his bag containing $3,000 in cash and traveler's checks had been stolen, he said. Now he was left with $850, but his airplane ticket home would cost $750. Lakdar's dilemma was that he would have to wait four weeks until the circuit began its next segment, in Louisiana, and he had only $100 on which to live until then. At that, he was better off than a doleful fellow from Panama who had stood in the tennis center parking lot earlier that morning, asking to borrow $7 so he would have enough money to pay his $10 entry fee.

There are a million sad or absurd stories on the Penn Circuit. One of the favorites is the tale of Charlie Owens and the telephone. The courtside phone began to ring during a match Owens was playing, and he hit a high lob, ran over, picked up the receiver and said, "Hold on." Then he scampered back to retrieve his opponent's return. Owens hit another high lob and ran to the phone. "I'll be right with you." This sequence was repeated several times before the other player finally smashed away one of Owens's lobs. The players laugh whenever the story is retold, but they most enjoy the kicker— that Owens is now on the Grand Prix circuit. He got off the street to nowhere, and that's the best part of all.

According to the players, none of them belongs on the Penn Circuit, or ever suspected he would be there. Each is waiting for his big break, getting together a portfolio and hoping for the day when his "look," or playing style, will come into vogue. Until then, each anticipates "a lucky draw," a succession of opponents so ineffectual that his ensuing series of wins will propel him upward. Borg hits with topspin, so Chip was trying to change his game from the classic, hard and flat shots his father taught him back at the country club. On the satellite trail, an inordinate number of players use oversized Prince rackets because, as with vitamins and religion, there is no evidence that they hurt you, and there remains the possibility they will help.

Because Hialeah was the opening tournament of the season, anyone with a racket, tennis shoes and a dream could enter. After five rounds, sixteen qualifiers would join the exempt players, those ranked about two-hundredth or better on the computer, in the sixty-four-man tournament the following week. Qualifiers would have to pay $10 to play the main event, and they'd be happy to pay it.

Money was of minor consideration for those entering the qualifying, perhaps because they generally had so little of it. Thus, fans who find the hyper-inflation of big-time tennis prize money disturbing should find solace in the Penn Circuit. No money is awarded for victories in the qualifying. In the main tournament at Hialeah, first-round losers were to be paid a piddling $28, and the winner of the tournament could count on only $1120, which, if he happened to have worked his way up through the qualifying, meant he would earn about $100 for each match won. "It's a one-way street for most guys," says one of the circuit's officials. "They think it leads somewhere, but it doesn't. All they do is keep going up and down the street."

From a distance, tennis appears to be a wonderful world of strawberries and cream, of royalty at courtside and Cheryl Tiegs on the disco floor. The satellite circuit offers a chance to sneak in the back door of this dreamworld, and John Lackey was representative of the players in Hialeah who thought they could crack the game's exclusivity—if only he could get past the security guard at the gate.

Lackey is thirty-five years old, and his most recent residence was Williamson, West Virginia, a small coal-mining town, where he worked for the federal government on a disaster-relief team. Lackey, a lawyer by profession, associates the times and places of his life with disasters. Louisville, 1974, tornado. Detroit, 1976, flood. He decided to take up tennis the year of the Detroit flood. He taught himself the game out of an instruction book.

He arrived in Hialeah driving a 1964 truck with, he said, about 120,000 miles on it. He was worried, not because he had to sleep in the truck each night, but because it had snowed in Williamson a month before, and he hadn't practiced since then. Lackey reckoned that he was the first touring professional Williamson had ever had, because there were only four courts in the town. "Five, if you count the one an accountant has in the back of his house," he said.

After a few days of practice in Florida, it became apparent to Lackey that the competition was tougher than he had expected, that the opposition had almost as many tennis miles on them as his truck's odometer. "I couldn't believe these young boys' legs," said Lackey. "They were so strong, a lot stronger than mine. So I started doing knee bends, and after two days I could hardly walk." He also developed a severe case of sunburn, and his forehead was blotched and peeling.

Lackey is a bearded, serious fellow with long hair that brushes his shoulders, and while playing he wears a thick hairnet to keep his locks in place. And that isn't his only idiosyncrasy. He employs a bizarre, self-taught grip in which the racket handle extends several inches up his wrist. "I learned on my own," he explained. "I figured I could make the racket an exact extension of my arm, so I could swing it like I swing my arm. It's just like I've grown the racket from my hand to my elbow."

Playing in his first-round qualifying match with a racket he had picked up for $19 at a local discount store, Lackey lost 6–0, 6–1. Later, he was philosophical about his plight. He had forsaken his girl friend and a job paying about $30,000 a year to play tennis. But losing in the first round meant he wouldn't even be eligible for qualifying during the rest of the circuit. For the rest of the week he slept in his truck, ate his meals in a cafeteria and hung around the courts, watching tennis and hoping for some practice time. For him the week was just another disaster, and, after all, he pointed out, he was accustomed to those.

Chip and the other players knew that to avoid disaster on the Penn Circuit you had to give to get, and so out in the parking lot of the Goodlet Tennis Center were an array of vans, campers and tents, many of them with extension cords connected to the main building's power supply so their inhabitants could cook on hot plates. And when they weren't eating, playing or resting, the players were working out, running wind sprints or doing leg kicks, stretching tight muscles. It was a Spartan existence. Every morning at eight o'clock Mike Jula, the tournament director, was confronted with a line of players, half of them waiting to charge onto the courts for a few minutes of practice, the others about to rush into the locker room for showers that would wash away the sweat of a three-mile dawn run.

The parking lot was the tournament's shantytown; the dilapidated state of many of the mobile homes made it look like something out of *Grapes of Wrath*. In fact, Brian Earley, the Penn Circuit tour director said he almost felt embarrassed to drive his Mercedes into the lot each morning. Even so, the players there were better off than those sleeping six to a room at motels for $9 a head per night, to say nothing of those who simply took their sleeping bags out into the surrounding fields and bedded down.

One of those traveling by van was Mark Rath, twenty-seven, who had a cottage industry going in the parking lot—stringing rackets. This is Rath's third year on tennis's back roads, and he admits the trip has been rough. He gauges his progress by noting that last year, "I missed getting an ATP point by one match in two different segments."

Rath, who is originally from Detroit, has curly black hair, a mustache and a thickening middle that he explains away by saying, "It isn't that my waist's so big but that my chest's so small." In his van are cartons of low-fat milk, peanut butter and strawberry jam, plus the obligatory book on concentration. He said he was holding his expenses to about $50 a week, partly by changing the oil in the van himself and making sure his engine was in tune. "There are a lot of players out here, and all of us are hungry," he said. "I lost today, but I shouldn't have. I had a 4–1 lead in the first set, then I let up a bit and he got a little confidence back. I blew it. Never give a sucker an even break. I gave him a break and it hurt me. Now I'm trying to decide whether to go back home and practice with my coach or stay here and string rackets. I do about three rackets a day. Any more, and I wouldn't have time to practice. And if I don't have time to practice, what's the use of being here? Right now one of my big problems is that I'm almost out of gut. When it goes, that's it. I just can't afford to buy more of it."

Many satellite players cannot afford to use gut, which gives a better "feel" than cheaper nylon stringing. To compensate, some of them string their rackets half with gut, half with nylon. These tend to be the same guys who put glue across the toes of their tennis shoes where they show wear, and at each tournament the first consideration of these impoverished players is picking up the free T-shirt to which they are entitled.

Chip has never wanted to learn how to string a racket or put on a new grip. Club pros like his father string rackets. Players like Borg have someone do it for them. And Chip doesn't have to worry about getting equipment, because he is a member of the ATP, his world ranking having once been better than two hundred. That means he still receives free clothing from Adidas, and manufacturers remain fairly generous with rackets and balls.

From his relatively exalted station, Chip cynically regarded the younger players milling around the tournament draw sheets posted outside the locker rooms in Hialeah. They were figuring the odds, which said that for every John Sadri who made it out of the parking lot, one thousand players didn't. And so they sifted through the draw sheets, checked the dog-eared computer standings and studied the entry lists for the next tournament. Circuit players sarcastically refer to this as "piling up indirect wins," figuring out that the player who beat them once beat someone else who beat, who beat someone else . . . In reality, they were searching for a shred of evidence that what they were doing made sense.

Chip thought back to his first pro tournament and how naive and unsuspecting he had been. He had changed. The Penn Circuit does that to you. Chip knew that good friends would cheat each other for a computer point. He had observed it, had seen buddies almost come to blows during a match. In qualifying, there are no umpires—except when a player requests one to arbitrate a disputed call—and the players call their own lines, which sometimes leads to cheating. Some players have even been known to sabotage an opponent's racket by pouring a soft drink on the strings just before a match.

Looking back, Chip could see how it was almost preordained that he would win in Hialeah on this particular week. Sure, his father had stuck the racket in his hand when he was five, but Chip realized now that he hadn't played only to please his father, though the old man certainly was proud he had. No, he had enjoyed it, loved the feeling of the ball coming cleanly off his strings. But he had never liked the competition, right from the time he played in his first tournament, a local ten-and-under event. He was seven years old, and after he won his match he felt like crying because he knew tomorrow he would have to play again. It was the fear of losing that bothered him. Winning never could erase tomorrow.

But he played because, after all, he was a natural. Anyone who knew anything about tennis saw that. He was always highly ranked as a junior, and he played well in college. So few people suspected what he knew—that he lacked the killer instinct. He didn't want to make the commitment to get out there and fight and scrap and, yes, even hate, to do whatever one had to do to make it to the top. Part of the reason he went to college was to delay the decision to turn pro for a few years. And when he did go on the circuit and moved up to the Grand Prix, he refused to let the subsequent losses bother him, because if he did, he knew he would have to change. He would have to make the game an obsession or give it up, and either way, he didn't know if he could live with himself. And so he'd come off the court and go to a telephone and call his father to tell him how he did. Week by week he could hear the disappointment growing at the other end of the line. And as his ranking continued to drop he came to realize that he wasn't good enough. So he went back to college, as much to hide as to finish the work for his degree.

It was while practicing with his old college team that his right knee started to bother him. At first he paid it no attention. But finally one morning he could barely walk. It was swollen. A doctor drained it and said that the cartilage was disintegrating and that he probably would need an operation. But that was the last thing he wanted. A knee operation would be the end of him. At his age, he couldn't afford to take a year off, and besides very few players fully recover from such an operation. With all of its cutting back and forth, the sport is simply too strenuous. So, just as he had disguised his fear of losing, he now hid his knee injury. No one knew about it. He didn't wear a brace on the court, and after matches he sneaked off by himself to ice the knee, because he knew that if the other players found out about his injury they would be like sharks around blood. They would work on this weakness, hitting dropshots and lobs, moving him around the court, hitting behind him when it meant he would have to plant his right foot solidly. The important thing was to get through the qualifying this week and into the main draw. The Hialeah tournament was being played on hard courts, the worst possible surface for his knee, but for the next two weeks the tournaments were scheduled for softer clay. If he could do well this week he was sure he would be all right on clay.

On the satellite circuit they say that you can check a player's wallet and predict whether he'll make it on the tour. If he doesn't have any kind of credit card, he's probably underfinanced and doesn't have a chance, because the nights of sleeping in his car will eventually wear him down. If he has an American Express card, his parents or a sponsor are funding him, and he won't be hungry enough to make it. The players to watch out for, this line of reasoning goes, are those with one bank charge card. They are sponsoring themselves. A bank card was the only one Chip had with him. And he was watching his expenses. In fact he had hit upon a scheme to get his meals half price, a proposition based upon the premise that, to busy waitresses, all tennis players look alike. Chip and another player of similar height and coloring used the scam at motel buffets. One would go into the dining room carrying a tennis bag and be seated. After finishing most of his food, he would walk out, leaving behind the tennis bag. Then the other player would sit in the same seat and go through the buffet line as if he were the first guy getting a second helping. The waitress wouldn't give him a second glance when he paid the bill.

The player who is probably the reigning authority on satellite-tour life is George Lea, a thirty-three-year-old pro from Vancouver, British Columbia who has played the circuit for seven years and never survived the qualifying, which means that he never has cashed a check. The other players regard a match with Lea as a workout on the light bag.

Lea doesn't much care how they feel. For him the circuit affords a chance to escape Canada's harsh winters, an opportunity for competition before he returns to a summer of lifeguarding or teaching tennis. He thinks many of the players ought to pack up their dreams. "There are only four or five guys here who are going to make any money," he says. "There's no circuit as tough as this one. Most of the guys aren't being realistic. If you haven't made it by eighteen in tennis, you don't have much hope of earning a living by playing. Down here, you're a little fish in a little pond." As he spoke, a fellow on a nearby court was losing a match 6–o, 6–o. After the player blew the final point, he walked over to a low mesh fence, smashed his racket on it and then stalked off, carrying the racket as if it were

a dead chicken with a broken neck. Bystanders could hear his girl friend running after him, yelling, "That was my racket. You owe me a racket." She didn't sound pleased.

Lea has witnessed two occasions when players fought on the court. "It's one on one, survival of the fittest," he says. "When it gets near the end of a segment and the matches are really important, a guy will try to help others beat someone ahead of him in the standings. He'll give them advice, or practice with them. And there are a lot of ways to intimidate players and get them uptight during matches. You can sit on the side lines and clap when the guy you're rooting against double faults. Stuff like that.

"When you're in a big match you can intimidate a guy easy. Every time the ball is close, give him a suspicious look when he makes his call. Then you make him feel like a heel for questioning one of your calls. Just keep him on the defensive the whole match. Don't talk to him at all. Just ignore him. Never call a ball 'out,' simply signal instead. And if you're going to cheat, do it late in the match. If you do it early, the guy will complain and call for an umpire. Or worse, he'll turn around and cheat you."

There is a theory that the amount of glamor attendant on a sporting event is in direct relation to the number of beautiful women in the stands. Using this formula, the Penn Circuit, especially during qualifying, is a no-glamor event. Despite the fact there were several hundred young, athletic and attractive men in the Hialeah tournament, there wasn't the slightest hint of perfume in the stands during the qualifying. In fact, except for a few travel-in girl friends, the only unattached female within miles was a poor creature who had been sentenced to sell hot dogs and soft drinks in the temporary concession stand outside the courts. And even she didn't pay the players much attention: After all, she was earning more selling hot dogs than they were playing pro tennis.

For the most part, the Penn Circuit attracts only the hard-core tennis wacko. The casual tennis enthusiast not only doesn't attend the tournaments, but doesn't know they're being played. At Hialeah there were few spectators. In fact, for the early days the only person on hand who wasn't a relative or close friend of a player was a tall, shirtless fellow who wandered around outside the courts, peering through the windscreens at the action. Asked his name, he said, "Have A Name. That's my last name. My first is, I Don't. Actually, you can call me 'Tennis.' Boy, this game keeps you alive. I play every day. I start playing at six or seven in the morning. Play here a lot, but I didn't enter the tournament because I don't want to interrupt my schedule. How old am I? It doesn't matter. I get up each morning and start over. I figure it's death when I go to sleep, and it's life when I wake up."

"Tennis" had picked an appropriate alias, because he could rattle off tournament results and recite statistics as if he had written the USTA handbook. Moreover, he knew many of the players at Hialeah by sight, a fact almost as odd as the balls of cotton stuck in his ears. These, he explained, were "to diffuse the sound waves. Too many sounds in this country. You don't need 'em. What we need are more tennis courts. I'd like to bulldoze that school over there and build one hundred tennis courts."

"Tennis" was interrupted by arguing voices. By looking through the windscreen it could be determined that there was a debate over the score of a match. Said one player to the tournament official who had arrived to mediate, "Someone's spaced out and it's not me."

That afternoon a reporter from a local newspaper came out to interview a player. Mike Sassano, the circuit's assistant tour director, suggested he speak with Chip, who had breezed through the first three rounds of qualifying and, almost as good, finally had found a motel room. Chip told the writer, "I hate this circuit, to put it mildly. It's so competitive that it'll either make you or break you. If I can't be in the upper echelons, I don't want to do this. I'll give it two good years, and if I'm not top fifty in the world, I'm going to bag it."

Just then a frustrated player sailed a racket over a fence. Chip and the reporter watched it windmill through the air. "See," said Chip. "That's what the tour will do to you."

It felt good to talk like this, to reaffirm, in his own mind at least, that for him it would never come down to throwing rackets. Chip had won his first three matches so easily that his bad knee felt as if it had undergone successful therapy. Of course, his opponents had been young and inexperienced. That would change the following day when Chip would play a tour veteran with a history of engaging in outrageous antics. Other players had given this fellow a wide berth ever since the time in Europe when he lost a match, took all six of his rackets and broke them over his knee, and then stood on his head for five minutes. At Hialeah, someone had asked this player what life on the Penn Circuit was like. He answered softly, his words punctuated with intermittent silences: "It's hard here to keep a conception of what reality is. . . . Sometimes you get a thought on this circuit and you think it has some context or relation with reality. . . . Then later you look back . . . and realize you were wrong and say to yourself: 'I was really out of touch with what reality is.' You realize . . . that you're not in reality at all."

Chip beat the eccentric easily, although throughout the match his opponent acted as if there were some alien being inside of him. After a missed shot he would yell, "Get out of me!" Later Chip told friends, "It was like something out of *The Exorcist.*"

The next day Chip faced a young player from a local college who had entered the tournament as a lark. Early in the match the younger player made several suspect calls, but Chip didn't protest. He was playing well, and as the match progressed, his opponent came to realize the inevitability of the result.

Chip rolled through the first set, and his confidence was mounting. Then it happened. He ran for a ball he should have let pass and managed to get his racket on it, at the same time making a sharp stop and scrambling to get back into position. His bum knee reacted as if it had been kicked. It didn't collapse, but it felt as if it might, and now with a 4–2 lead in the second set, Chip knew that the throbbing would only get worse.

Even more disturbing was the certainty that if he lost this set, he could kiss off any chance of winning the next one because in about forty minutes he was barely going to be able to walk. Indeed, Chip's opponent seemed to sense that something was wrong, and now he was jerking Chip around the court, hitting soft dinks and lobs, moving him up and back.

The only thing Chip could do was try to end each point as quickly as possible: Using this strategy he won one of the next three games, making the score 5–4. Now his knee was really hurting. In fact, he couldn't disguise his slight limp when the players changed sides. The only thing he had going for him was that he was serving for the match.

Playing aggressively, Chip quickly knocked off the first two points with sharp volleys, but then he netted a low return and, on the next point, got involved in a base-line rally that he lost. He won the next point, and now he could wrap up the match. He breathed deeply as he prepared to serve and, taking his time, carefully hit the ball down the middle, hoping to nick the service line. He was wide. On his second serve, Chip was startled to see his opponent take a cou-

ple of steps forward and catch the ball early. The return, powerful and flat, headed for the corner of the deuce court. And Chip's opponent was following the shot to the net. All of this happened, of course, in a second, but later it seemed to Chip as if time had slowed almost to the point of stopping. He remembered moving to his right and realizing that he could get to the ball, but to do so would mean hitting it off the wrong leg, his right one, and then trying to scramble back to the middle of the court. He knew his knee wouldn't let him do it.

As he went for the ball, all sorts of things flashed through his mind. Or maybe they really didn't, maybe he had been thinking of this moment for a long time, because he had changed. The shot was close, right on the edge of the side line, in fact, and Chip did the only thing he could, because he had been up this road before and back down, and now he was going up it for the last time. His father, and anyone else who played the game the way you had to play it, would understand. In a loud and clear voice, Chip yelled, "Out!"

Gladiators and Troubadours

by ARTHUR ASHE with FRANK DEFORD

During 1973 to 1974—from one Wimbledon to another—Arthur Ashe kept a diary of his tour life, later published as A Portrait in Motion. *The observant and articulate Ashe offers these vignettes as example of the peripatetic life-style tennis players enjoy—and endure.*

Tuesday, July 3, 1973—Toronto / New York

The life we lead in tennis is most unlike that in any other sport. Tennis knows no season now, and it is spectacularly international. I don't really live anywhere. Even some of the players who are married, and with young children, are on the road so much that it is merely a convention for them to call some place *home*. We come from somewhere, but we have no real home.

I've spent a year of my life in Australia, almost as much time in England and probably several months in airplanes. There has never been anything in sports like tennis today. I am not boasting that we are special, although we may be; but we are surely unique. The players are the modern hybrid of gladiators and troubadours. We entertain by combating each other all over the world. You try to beat a man's brains out on the court, take money out of his pocket, and then you return to the locker room with him, take a shower next to him, eat with him, drink with him, practice with him, chase women with him, maybe even play doubles with him, and two weeks or two months later, you draw him again, in Barcelona or Manila or Chicago, and all of a sudden you look across the net and it occurs to you that this is the same sonuvabitch who beat you in Vancouver the last time, and you give him no quarter, and ignore him when you pass next to each other between odd games, and then you shake his hand when you beat him or he beats you, and you have a beer together and share a cab back to the hotel.

To adjust to playing big-time tennis now, you must have some capacity for suspending time and place. You pretend that you are standing still, while it is the rest of the world that is moving. That's not so hard to do. After all, the same people I left in London will be in Boston when I get on to my next tournament. And we will play tennis and do the same things. The courts will be different, like the restaurants and the money and the spectators and the other incidentals, but the experience will be the same. It's like sitting in a room and changing TV channels.

Playing the tour is much different from being on a team. You must depend more on yourself, of course; and you must depend on the people you beat for friendship. This makes us a bit odd. Sociologists would have a field day with

118

the tennis tour . . . if we would let them get close enough. We are, however, a closed, proud elite, and we draw ourselves up whenever strangers seem to intrude. If four tennis players are having a conversation and they are joined by an outside acquaintance, the players will be likely to change the subject even if the topic is rather innocuous.

At Wimbledon, there is what is called the Players' Tea Room. If you are not a player, but some peripheral member of the tennis establishment—a promoter or a writer or a coach or a pretty girl or even just some hanger-on, a friend of a friend—it is easy to get into the Players' Tea Room. Either you give the old guard at the bottom of the stairs a pound or two the first day or you can climb over a little fence from a press balcony. But I have had friends—even former players—tell me that they feel uncomfortable in the Tea Room. None of the players is rude to the visitors, no one even says anything, but the outsiders tell me that they can sense being unwanted. There is a special irony for me in hearing that reaction, because it sounds exactly the way I often feel in gatherings where I am the only black.

Actually, the business of my belonging so strongly to the tour, of flaunting its territorial imperative, is really very foreign to the rest of me. I'm a loner by nature, and able to get along quite happily by myself. That's probably why I travel so well. I don't have to depend upon special tourist attractions and scenic overlooks; I can be quite happy anywhere with my books and my cassettes. I still want to do a lot more traveling in my life before I do what everybody always calls *settling down*.

I think of the Doral Country Club of Miami now as home more than anyplace else, but because of business I'm also forced to spend a lot of time in New York. I stay in an apartment on the East Side. But New York is mostly just a clearing-house for me, convenient to airports and the businesses I'm involved with. I almost feel like I'm on holiday when I'm in New York, because I seldom play any tennis there but mostly just go to night clubs and good restaurants and the theater, just like all the people who really do come to New York on their vacation.

Anyway, the reason I rushed back to New York today is because I have a date to play golf with Manny Parker. I stay in apartment A–1706. Manny and Ruth live in A–1606, right below. They are a couple of terrific people who don't have any children and have made me their surrogate son. We met because one night Ruth suddenly heard somebody making too much noise on her ceiling—which was me walking around A–1706 in my clogs. She inquired and found out who the noisy intruder was, sought me out down in the basement in the communal laundry room and told me to get some quieter shoes.

The Parkers always know I'm in New York, because they can hear me, so Ruth immediately gets on the building intercom and demands that I come down for a drink. It sounds like a pilot for a situation comedy: young black bachelor and his Jewish foster parents . . .

Wednesday, July 4—New York
No symbolism in the date—just a coincidence. I'm not much of a holiday guy anyway. Most blacks aren't. But I suppose that there is at least a benign significance in the fact that Independence Day was when I sat down and dictated letters to several friends, black and white, asking them for their views on any possible trip of mine to South Africa. I sincerely want to go, if only from a selfish point of view, out of curiosity, but I also am deeply concerned with how other blacks might take such a trip. So I wrote Julian Bond, and Congressman Andy Young; Congresswoman Barbara Jordan; Nikki Giovanni, the black poetess; Vernon Jordan, the head of the Urban League; Sargent Shriver; J.D. Morgan, the athletic director at UCLA, who had been my tennis coach; Bob Kelleher, the former head of the United States Lawn Tennis Association, who is now a federal judge; and Joe Cullman, the chairman of the board at Philip Morris.

There are two basic avenues used to approach the South African question. One is more a roadblock than an avenue, a militant, all-or-nothing policy, which maintains that nobody should have anything to do with the dreadful place: Boycott it, freeze it out, ignore it and wait for its millennium from a respectable distance. The United States wasted a generation on that philosophy toward China; it still operates its Cuban policy that way. The other avenue is a gradualist one—result-oriented. It assumes that progress can only come in small chunks, that you deal for your advances as you can. Surely, it is less emotionally satisfying this way, but, I'm certain, more realistic and more successful. It was the way Dr. King gained his advances—although it was hardly a new concept with him. Frederick Douglass wrote in the nineteenth century: "Power concedes nothing without a struggle— never has, never will."

So you must be prepared only to chip away at power and injustice. And let's face it: Sometimes you can't stand on your pride. I am terribly embarrassed now by some of the goings-on taking place in what is supposed to be free Africa. Amin's policies in Uganda seem no less despicable than South Africa's. The warfare among tribes in Burundi (and Nigeria before) is as murderous as anything whites have done to blacks anywhere in the world. When I was in the Ivory Coast last year I perceived a repression of freedom of expression that, surely, is only slightly exceeded in South Africa. None of this excuses things there, but all of it is important to keep in mind for the sake of perspective. The South Africans have not the only racist government in the world. I know that. Also, like it or not, it is all part of the general worldwide phenomenon of the lighter hues vs. the darker ones—and right now the lighter ones are winning.

I don't know whether I'm getting more pragmatic or merely jaded. I used to believe in Toynbee, in an eventual complete amalgamation of the races, but now I'm sure there will always be groups. It just seems to be the natural order for people to stay together with members of their own cultural stock. Race doesn't have to be the distinguishing factor either. On the tour, it is language which most determines how we separate ourselves. Anyway, if it is a bad thing to be prejudiced, it is a normal thing to express a preference. So now, after fifteen years of world travel, I must say that I am not for a nonracial approach, only for a multiracial one. Nonracial seems to me to be a concept against the natural laws of evolution.

Sunday, July 8—New York / San Juan / Palmas del Mar / San Juan / New York
I went down to Puerto Rico to play an exhibition at a new resort I'm involved with. I was booked on the ten o'clock Eastern flight Saturday night, but there were mechanical problems, and they kept setting the departure time back every few minutes. Finally, at ten-fifty, they stopped setting the departure time back. The reason they stopped setting the departure time back was because they canceled the whole flight.

Also, they only canceled in Spanish, so that just those who habla Espanol could then hustle over to Gate 16 and take up all the good remaining seats on the eleven-thirty flight. As an afterthought, they crammed me and the other poor English-speakers into the middle seats, and by one the eleven-thirty lifted off with the ten o'clock passengers. I got to sleep in the Sheraton in San Juan around five, or as you are supposed to say: It was *only* four New York time.

Palmas del Mar is about a forty-five minute drive from San Juan. I always think of it first as Charlie Pasarell's place, since he's the home boy. Naturally, he was my opponent in the exhibition. I was the bad guy—and I beat him 9–8, although that is no big deal since he has been down here helping put Palmas all together and is somewhat out of shape.

Charlie has never been the most mobile guy in the world to start with. It takes him about three weeks just to warm up for a practice match. A funny incident was at UCLA with Herbie Flam, who had been ranked as high as second in the country (in 1950). Since he'd gone to UCLA he'd come over sometimes and practice with us. He had a great touch, was very gifted with the racket. Herbie also had a very clever mind—he was one of the contestants on "The $64,000 Question"— although it could go off in all directions at once. Herbie would arrive at the UCLA courts wearing an old pair of Bermuda shorts and a faded T-shirt, with a floppy pair of Pete Maravich socks long before Pete Maravich thought of them, and

Arthur Ashe has his eye on the ball, a small fuzzy object players chase all over the world. (Photo by Russ Adams)

dragging an old racket without a cover on it. He had a high nasal pitch, and he'd get out on the court, hit one ball, one ball, and say, "Okay, serve 'em up." And here he is with Charlie, who needs a lifetime to get prepared to play.

So this one day, Herbie shows up, dressed in his usual outfit, and he hits one back to Charlie, and as always, he says, "Okay, serve 'em up," and just as Charlie tosses the first ball, Herbie calls over, "Wait a minute. I've got to put change in the parking meter." And he ran off the court and neither Charlie or I ever saw him again for about another five years. He was like the Judge Crater of tennis.

Anyway, Charlie really is a picture player. If he could have been just a bit quicker, I'm sure he could have been the best player in the world, because he does have the best strokes of anyone I've ever seen. If I had to teach someone to play tennis, the first thing I would do is, I would say, go watch Charlie Pasarell play and try to do what he does.

I first met Charlie when we played the fifteen-and-unders at the Orange Bowl in Miami. I'm eight months older than he is, so that would have been 1956 or '57. He beat me that day 2–6, 6–2, 6–2, but we saw each other all during the juniors and beat each other back and forth. He impressed me. He came from a lot of money, he was cultured and sure. And I was an insecure southern black kid out on my own. There were no blacks and no friends to speak of. And Charlie, I found out, was just always there. I don't know whether he did it out of sympathy, but when I did seek out his friendship, he never refused it.

It was at UCLA, where we played together and roomed together off campus for a year-and-a-half, that we really learned to understand each other. We alternated the number-one spot on the team there, just as we did for the country in 1967 and '68. Pasarell might have won that top ranking ahead of me in '67 because he beat me head-to-head in the finals of the National Indoors. To show you how close Charlie and I are, we watched that match together afterward over a delayed television broadcast, and sat there, each of us trying to point out to the other where

we had taken advantage and where he could improve.

Yet Charlie's a stubborn sonuvabitch. We used to argue religion constantly. He always give me the Catholic SOP, as if a never-ending barrage of Perpetuo Succuro will finally save me in the end. I happen to really like Charlie's wife too. When he and Shireen got married a couple of years ago, I made them a present of a hotel room on his wedding night. Charlie means a lot to me. He is as nice a guy and as loyal a friend as a man can know.

In 1968, when we won the Davis Cup back from Australia in Adelaide, I cost the U.S. a clean sweep by losing the last match to Bill Bowrey. Even though we had already clinched the cup, the Aussies were thrilled to escape a whitewash, and the crowd stood up and cheered Bowrey all the way off the court, while I left in despair. I felt like I'd let everybody down.

Charlie was standing by the players' gate, and when I raised my head up, I saw that tears were rolling down his cheeks. "It's okay," he said, "you're still the greatest." Then he put his arm around me, and I couldn't stop the tears either.

Because our set at Palmas ran on, they had to bring in the company plane to get me back to the airport at San Juan so I could get the six-thirty back to New York. I had originally intended to go to Miami, where the weather is nice and hot, and where I could practice at the Doral with Eddie Dibbs, but at the last minute I found out I had to return to New York. The reason was that the pictures we shot in May at Las Vegas for a booklet that goes with a cassette instructional I am doing turned out badly and we have to reshoot the whole act.

Monday, July 9—New York / Miami
They picked me up at my apartment at nine-fifteen to go out to Forest Hills to shoot the photographs, which everybody said looked fine, which is approximately what they had also said at Vegas in May.

Then I went directly to JFK, so that I could get to Miami and hit with Dibbs, but the plane got in at five-thirty, and poor Eddie had been just sitting there all the time. By then, it was too late to practice anyway, and I was too tired to go out so I went over to Rod Mandelstam's. He's South African, Jewish and used to be the teaching pro here at Doral. Strangely enough, some of my best friends are South Africans. Rod, his wife, Carol, and I just sat around and got pleasantly stoned.

Tuesday, July 10—Miami

It's my thirtieth birthday today. I was born in Richmond on July 10, 1943, the day General Patton's troops landed in Sicily. Actually, I don't feel too excited today; I don't get much worked up for birthdays.

It rained today too, so I called the office in Washington at Donald Dell's law firm and found out if they had any correspondence I had to catch up on. Unfortunately, they're predicting a 70 percent chance of rain tomorrow, so there's no sense staying around. The only reason I came down was to practice.

I really like Miami though. I've lived in a lot of places—Richmond, St. Louis, Los Angeles, New York—but I'm thinking about buying some property down here. I don't own any land. I'm a gypsy, downright un-American, since I don't even own a car.

Miami has a good smell to it. Torben Ulrich, our tour guru, the bearded tennis-playing philosopher from Denmark, pointed out to me once that we all place too much emphasis on the visual, that we should not reach judgments about a place simply from what we obtain from our sight. And he's right. Cities do smell quite different from one another. And they sound different too. Miami is especially nice because it's so tourist-conscious that they don't permit any industry to speak of, so there's almost no smog. And it seems to me there's still space to move around in here. Los Angeles is just becoming a warm-weather New York, plus it's spread out to even more disadvantage.

I don't miss L.A. or New York. I don't need that kind of go-go stuff. I've never been the life of the party. I'm not Tom Okker. I just don't crave the fast life that much any more. Maybe I sensed that I was burning myself out.

Wednesday, July 11—Miami / New York / Toronto

This is ridiculous. I came all the way up from Miami to practice, and I wasn't here for a half-hour before it started pouring. It's probably the 30 percent blue skies in Miami.

I have all my damn luggage I'm dragging around because I'm supposed to have been gone for a month, and it took a couple hours getting back to my apartment because some guy was holding up traffic, threatening to jump off the 59th Street bridge, and when I finally got in and called up Kathy, she wanted me to come up, so I went back to the airport and flew to Toronto. That's where I am now.

Thursday, July 12—Toronto / New York / Cincinnati

I flew back to New York this morning and went directly to the West Side Tennis Club, where at last I got a practice in. Between the weather, the airplanes business and Kathy, I have just flown six thousand miles in the last four days trying to get a chance to practice.

This was my last day in New York for some time, and it was so lovely that I set off on a walk down Fifth Avenue. When I passed Berlitz I got this uncontrollable urge to go in. It embarrasses me terribly that I can only speak English. I consider that the great failing of my life. I go bananas when I'm with somebody like Ion Tiriac, the big Rumanian, or Helga Schulte Hösl, the pretty German—both of whom can speak six languages fluently, switching back and forth. Almost none of the English-speaking players ever even make an effort to get along in another language. Julie Heldman is our best linguist, and Nailbags Carmichael, who moved from Australia to Paris, is another. The rest of the English-speaking players just barrel on in English and make everybody adjust to them, which, of course, they invariably do.

A lot of the foreign players join the tour

without any real comprehension of English, and they pretty much are forced to learn it if they want to get along outside their own language clique. Also, since so much of the tour is in the U.S. now, it is a handicap if a player doesn't pick it up. They learn by watching cartoons on TV or reading comic books. The language there is obvious and relates easily to the pictures. It really shames me that there are several players who knew virtually no English at all when I first met them, but who are now at ease with it: Orantes, François Jauffret of France, Alex Metreveli of Russia, Patricio Cornejo of Chile. Hell, Cornejo is getting to be a downright comedian in English, and he didn't know how to ask for the bathroom when I first met him.

So anyway, bugged by all of this, I stormed into Berlitz and signed up for a course which will guarantee me a working knowledge of twenty-five hundred words in French. I took three years of French in high school, and I do make an effort to speak it every time I'm in the country, and I honestly believe I'm very close to the barrier. I think if I *had* to talk it, I could break through. Since the whole thing will cost me $1019, now I have a great incentive.

The Catalina representative met me at the Cincinnati airport at quarter of eleven. I have to make some store appearances out here in Ohio for them in the next few days. We're in the pro-cess of negotiating a new contract with Catalina for the Arthur Ashe clothes line that will expand into international sales.

Sunday, July 15—Washington / New York / Boston

I caught this late flight from Columbus to Washington last night and was figuring spending the night there, but when I was at the baggage counter I heard them announcing an odd flight to New York—in from San Juan—so I made that, and I was so happy to be back to the apartment that I took a taxi and gave four stewardesses a ride into town with me.

This afternoon, Kathy came in from Toronto and met me at La Guardia and we flew up here for the U.S. Pro Championships. I got in a little practice tonight too, which I needed. I haven't played a whole lot of tennis lately, have I? I just looked at my schedule, and the last eleven days I've made twelve flights and I've only spent one full day in the same place. Here's what I've done: New York—Amherst—New York—San Juan—Palmas del Mar—San Juan—New York—Miami—New York—Toronto—New York—Cincinnati—Dayton—Columbus—Washington—Newark—New York—Boston.

It'll be nice just to stay in one place for a few days and try to make a living playing tennis.

PART II

THE COMPETITION: Champions and Challengers

"A person's tennis game begins with his nature and background and comes out through his motor mechanisms into shot patterns and characteristics of play. If he is deliberate, he is a deliberate tennis player; and if he is flamboyant, his game probably is, too. A tight, close match unmarred by error and representative of each player's game at its highest level will be primarily a psychological struggle, particularly when the players are so familiar with each other that there can be no technical surprises."

—from *Levels of the Game* by John McPhee

The California Comet

by AL LANEY

Hero worship is part of every sport and sports writers are no exception. Al Laney, who saw every great player of the twentieth century, recorded his impressions in a series of essays entitled Covering the Court. *The first chapter portrays the young Laney as he eagerly awaits the performance of Maurice McLoughlin, the first superstar of tennis.*

THE Hotel Bretton Hall still stands at Broadway and 86th Street, but surely it can never have been so luxurious as it seemed on the steaming August night of my first frightening contact with New York. No hotel, whether on the Champs Elysées, Park Lane, at Deauville, Biarritz, the Lido, San Moritz, or on Nob Hill in San Francisco, has ever appeared so elegant as this quite ordinary hostelry to a frightened schoolboy far away from home for the first time.

New York was in one of its heat waves, and the air was already hot and damp at six o'clock that Tuesday morning when, because of excitement and the heat itself, I was unable to sleep. The lobby was deserted and the breakfast room would not open for another hour. The tennis matches were to be played Thursday, Friday and Saturday, and I still had to decide how I should divide my days between Forest Hills and the Polo Grounds. A cruel decision for a boy to have to make and I decided to postpone it at least until I had read the morning papers.

Baseball exerted a strong pull because I could accompany a kind relative who had provided this wonderful opportunity, whereas I would have to go all alone to the tennis matches and have no one with whom to share the great adventure. The fear of being alone in the big city, which could rise to something like terror, is not easy to communicate, but I still can feel it a little so it must have been very strong at the time. I was very much afraid of losing my way in a place of such terrifying bigness. You could hardly get lost walking straight up the street and back so early in the morning, though, and it was a relief to be almost alone on a street from which last night's confusing bustle had departed.

At the 96th Street subway entrances men and boys were already selling papers, shouting the names in a confused chant that ran them all together. I bought the lot of them—*World, Times, Tribune, American, Herald, Sun*—and brought them back to the lobby. There I sat, a small, forlorn figure probing into his future and not knowing it. The headlines, big and black, spoke of the violation of Belgian neutrality and said that British mobilization was complete. They

126

meant nothing. The chain of tragic events set in motion by the shot fired at Sarajevo was beyond the understanding, beyond the interest even, of a schoolboy who was nonetheless to be caught up in them before attaining maturity.

I turned to the sports pages, and there for the first time was a small item that did make the war seem a little nearer. It said that the German Davis Cup team of Otto Froitzheim and Otto Kreuger, beaten by the Australians in Pittsburgh on the day England declared war on Germany, had been taken from a ship in mid-Atlantic by a British warship and would be interned.

The Tuesday papers already had long stories about the coming tennis matches, and after reading them I was so eager to get there I decided I could give up only one day to the Giants, although they were in first place and the "on-rushing Braves," as they were dubbed, already were close. It was a beautiful Polo Grounds experience on this day as the Giants beat St. Louis 8–2, marred only by the fact that Jeff Tesreau pitched instead of Matty. But Matty was there and all the others too—Larry Doyle, Red Murray, Art Fletcher, and Fred Merkle. There would be still one chance to come back for more if rain didn't extend the tennis program beyond the scheduled days.

The night clerk at the hotel, who knew nothing about it, had told me that I could easily get in to see the teams practice on the days before the matches, and this misinformation was what decided me to desert the Giants on Wednesday on the mere chance of seeing McLoughlin. I was impelled also by the necessity of making a trial run through that terra incognita of New York to where the matches were to be played so the way might be found easily when it would be so terribly important to be there in plenty of time.

With directions carefully memorized I set out into an already stifling day about eight o'clock, and my eventual arrival at Penn Station through those waves of frantic, inhuman rush-hour crowds, pushing into subway trains already too full, seemed a small miracle. I got somehow into the proper Long Island train and the relief was so great I did not mind the stifling heat so much. I had a new batch of papers to read and

now I slipped under the seat all but the sports sections.

Play, they said, would begin at two o'clock on Thursday with Tony Wilding, the New Zealander who had been Wimbledon champion for four years, against R. Norris Williams, described as "a young college boy from Harvard," a phrase which puzzled me since, from where I sat, a Harvard man was no young boy. The big match, McLoughlin vs. Brookes, the current Wimbledon champion, would follow and there would be doubles on Friday.

The experts were unanimous in the opinion that McLoughlin would have to beat both Brookes and Wilding if the United States, holder of the trophy, was to have any chance of retaining it. It seemed we had "only an outside chance" of winning the doubles, and so young Williams would have "to do his share by winning one of the singles."

I marveled at the assurance, the certainty with which these men wrote. How could they know? How could they be so sure? This week was to be my first encounter with the sports expert into whose ranks destiny was to lead me some years later; the first occasion on which I was able to read in the metropolitan papers reports of things actually seen by me and written by reporters presumed to be first rate. During this whole week all the New York papers, and there were about fifteen of them, were read carefully and the sports sections torn out and kept to be studied for a long time after. This was the only course of journalism then available, and the idea of trying to become a sports reporter myself was born at this time.

My knowledge of geography was slight, and I was still fearful of having got on the wrong train, but the sight from the train window of the wooden stands that had been erected in front of the West Side Tennis Clubhouse was reassuring. The club was surrounded by a sort of meadow-land on its side of the railway line, and there was a pleasant small-town atmosphere about the village. A few people got off the train, but it was hardly more than mid-morning yet, and only one or two walked down the path toward the club. The whole place seemed deserted and the courts

Maurice McLoughlin wallops his big Western forehand during his Davis Cup match against Norman Brookes at Forest Hills in 1914. (Photo Courtesy of the USTA)

that could be seen from outside the grounds were empty.

A walk around the whole place revealed little. The clubhouse and wooden stands enclosed and concealed everything that had to do with the coming matches. I longed to go inside but dared not try, even though there seemed to be no one guarding the entrance to the clubhouse. Fear of being spoken to sharply or asked my business by someone in uniform was a strong deterrent. I began to realize I had made a mistake.

Just to hang around outside all day seemed senseless, and I was considering trying to get back to the hotel in time to make the ball game when I saw through the wire fence at a corner of the grounds a couple of figures in white come out to one of the courts along the street and begin to hit a ball back and forth. In no time, then, the situation changed. The wait was not going to be futile after all. Here began the education of a tennis writer.

These players, whatever their proficiency at the game, were a revelation. This was not the game I and my companions had been playing, however much we admired one another's skill. This was the game I was to see at the top level tomorrow, for, looking back, I now believe these to have been very good players if not actually first-ten men. I had read about this game but had had no real conception of it. However ardent we had been back home, however faithfully we practiced to perfect strokes, we would never, I saw instantly, arrive at the game being played here. We were on the wrong road altogether. This kind of tennis was not known in our town in 1914.

The revelation was something of a shock. What now of those dreams of conquest? Never mind that, in the phrase of the day, ten years and a millionaire father were needed to acquire a ranking in the country's first ten. McLoughlin had no millionaire background and already, one thought, considerable progress had been made. Alas, for the dreams of youth and farewell to them. On the other hand, here, looking through the fence, fingers hooked into the wire netting, at players who were close to the heart of the game, began that close observation, that critical inspection of strokes that was to prove of value a decade or so later when my tennis reporting days finally arrived.

Here I saw a method of striking the ball very different from the strokes my boyhood opponents and I employed. This, I thought, must be the real thing, the way the great ones do it, and every single detail of it must be carefully observed and stored in memory to take home and put into practice.

I had not at this time read any tennis instruction books, which I rate a most fortunate circumstance, since I was able to observe without being misled by their fallacies and errors. Hour after hour I stood on tired legs outside the fence as groups of players came and went, trying to isolate the procedures which these men followed and which appeared to be fundamental, though the styles differed.

As the afternoon wore on, doubles players came, bringing still another revelation, other techniques to observe and remember, since a boy seldom has anything about his person on which to make notes, nor knows what notes to make if he does. It is the visual note that is most helpful in such matters, though, and very few have been really successful in reducing the techniques of games to words. This chance to see really good players from close up was valuable in preparing me for what was to come. During the big matches I was so wrapped up in the wonder of it all that little details could be observed and retained.

For some time, as I stood with fingers hooked into the wire of the fence, there had been signs of approaching rain, cooling the air. And the discomfort of standing so long was so great I decided to walk around a bit. I also was in great need of food, and thought there might be a place to buy a sandwich. An attendant barred the entrance to the clubhouse now, but I happened to arrive there simultaneously with a group of a dozen or more young men who promptly enveloped me. One of them announced that they were "from Columbia," and with an "all right, boys" they were passed in, I in their midst. It turned out presently that they were part of a contingent of Columbia University students who were to be ushers, and they were there to get their positions and instructions for next day and do a little rehearsing. I was still fearful of discovery but immensely pleased to be mistaken for a college man.

We all went through the clubhouse and out onto a terrace in some confusion, and while they stood about waiting for someone to come up and tell them what to do, I had enough presence of mind to slip off into the stands enclosing three sides of the court. A few dozen people were scattered about the stands, and there was some play going on below. I hardly dared look at the courts until I felt safe from discovery.

An expanse of green grass was enclosed by these towering wooden stands, and two courts were marked out with white lines. I did not at once notice that they were singles courts, so great was my surprise that the matches were going to be played on grass, showing how ill informed we were in the small towns in those days before radio. The courts that I had been watching from the street had been of clay, wonderful courts compared to ours at home, and it never had occurred to me that those inside would be different.

But it was beautiful, this perfect-looking green grass with the white lines upon it. It was just about the most beautiful sight I had ever seen. Two men were playing singles on one of the courts but obviously neither was the right one. I knew what my man looked like. These were lesser members of one of the teams, and it did not interest me much to know either which team or their names. Actually, I did learn many years later than one of them was Stanley Doust, an Australian player who became tennis correspondent for the *London Daily Mail* and a very good friend. But in August of 1914 if a tennis player was not Maurice McLoughlin he did not count for much.

After a while I got bold enough to get into conversation with a man sitting nearby. I wanted to ask if McLoughlin was going to practice and learned that all the principal actors in tomorrow's drama had finished and gone while I was outside watching lesser men through the fence. This friendly man seemed astonished to learn that I had come all the way from Florida to see the matches. He looked at me closely and said he knew a young man who had gone to Florida and never come back, giving the impression that it was rather a tremendous thing for a boy to do. Having established this, he then set me right on a budding misconception about court surfaces. I admired the wonderful-looking grass courts but remarked that they must be pretty slow compared with clay or other hard-surfaced courts. He said that was what most people thought who never had played on grass, and that was most people, I suppose. But grass was the fastest surface of all for playing tennis, he told me, except

the indoor board court. I did not really believe this at the time, but I remembered it, and when a year or so later I had the chance to play on grass, I saw it was true. In that way I avoided the mistake of ever writing the opposite, a mistake which some quite authoritative commentators in the so-called Golden Age were unable to avoid.

The drizzle had become more wetting now and I was dreadfully tired and hungry. I tried to find my way out without going back through the clubhouse, where I was sure I would be spotted for an interloper, but the gates for the public were not yet open. There was nothing for it, so I tried to look as though I belonged. I got safely through and onto the path to the station without being accosted, but I have thought of that slinking passage through the rooms many times while going back and forth in later years.

When I finally got back to Penn Station it seemed strangely quiet compared to the morning's stampede, so it must have been quite a while past the evening rush. A new batch of papers informed me both that "Braves Checked o–o by Red Ames; at Polo Grounds Tomorrow" and "First Great Battle Impending; Americans Fill West-Bound Liners."

The night of August 12–13, 1914, may be remembered by participants in and spectators of the Davis Cup Challenge Round of that year for other reasons, but for me, a subtropical visitor in New York, it stands out as the most uncomfortably hot night ever experienced. Unable to sleep, I indulged half a dozen times in the unaccustomed luxury of a shower, and was still a little groggy next morning when I set out, not later than nine o'clock, for Forest Hills and the great adventure.

This time I had missed most of the crush in the subway, although there still were plenty of them, and it was a wonderful feeling to know one's way about and not be so afraid. All of Long Island was already baking when I walked once more down the path from the station, drinking in the slow draft of anticipation. Near the entrance I stood in a spot of shade beside the railroad embankment for a long time contemplating the scene.

I saw again it had been a mistake to come

too early. There was no sign of life about the place, and the gates were not to open until noon. I had thrown away all the war news in the morning papers, retaining only the sports sections carefully folded and stuffed into a back pants pocket opposite the two sandwiches which the kind waiter at the hotel had got for me. There still were two hours to wait, and I was thinking of hunting a cooler place when more players came out, as on the day before. I could not leave then. This time it was all doubles and even more rewarding since I knew better now what to look for.

This also was a demonstration of a concept of the game I had not known, and I accepted without question that it was the correct manner of playing doubles. I had never known that the proper alignment of partners was parallel, not one up and one back, and was surprised to see that each pair sought the net together at every opportunity. Also that one always stood near the net even while his partner was serving. I had never seen the server rush to the net behind his serve. The Pensacola system of double plays was for both to stand at the base line while one served.

A maneuver that delighted me no end was employed now and then. Just as the ball was served, the man at the net—and how dangerously close in, it seemed to me, he stood—would move quickly across the court still close to the net, and the server would run in to replace him. This apparently was done on signal, but look as closely as I could, I never did discover when it might come.

I thought this must be standard practice that was no doubt employed by everyone who played the doubles game properly. It added to my store of learning, and I determined to try it out along with the other new things learned as soon as I could tell my friends back home about it. It also added to my store of amusement when, forty years later, I read that this trick was "invented" by one of our Davis Cup captains who had not even managed to get himself born in 1914 and was introduced into a Challenge Round doubles match in Australia. It was cited in the account of the match cabled back as a stroke of genius, and

the one thing that had ensured an American victory.

By that time, though, a score or more of Challenge Rounds and nearly as many Wimbledons and National Championships were behind me, and I had long since become accustomed to the foolish things people say and write about this game. I also had learned that the most one ought to permit oneself should be mild amusement, since one of the valuable lessons of experience is that you can so easily be caught out yourself.

The players left the courts a little before noon and the gates were opened. There was an entrance just where the wooden stands did not quite meet the clubhouse terrace, and you walked across another hard court to get there. I stopped on the way to examine the court carefully underfoot and marveled at its firmness and smoothness. We had nothing like it back home in spite of pulling a heavy roller back and forth interminably.

A small wooden house very like one of those outdoor privies so common at home had been set up for a ticket booth, but I had mine already. I had perhaps a hundred times made certain it still was there in my pocket. It was for a seat high up on the rim of the stands and in a corner diagonally opposite where I had entered. It was a good spot from which to view the surrounding country and no doubt was a bit cooler than down below, but the courts seemed disappointingly far away. Two courts were lined on the grass now, one directly below me, the other over by the terrace of the clubhouse. They had no nets yet, but presently two men came out to put them up. This was an interesting procedure, for they tightened the net cord with a little wheel attached to the post. A much better way, I thought, than trying to draw the net tight enough by hand, as was our way. For us it always seemed to slip, no matter what kind of sailor's knot we tied, and had to be pulled and tied over again every few games.

It was getting on toward one o'clock now and I began to realize I was hungry. So out came the sandwiches, made of bologna, a substance new to me. They are worth mentioning only because the wonderful taste of them is more easily recalled and more vividly remembered than more important impressions from that confusing day. Nothing since ever has seemed quite so good except the taste of the cold beef and ginger beer of a lost vintage consumed so often in later years on the terrace of the clubhouse at the Queens Club in London after a morning of play on those not always perfect grass courts.

People had begun to come in at the entrances now, first a trickle and then a flood. The line began to extend back down the path toward the station, and off to the right there was another line of motorcars going somewhere to park and raising great clouds of dust from the unpaved road. There were more automobiles than I had ever seen in one place, and a morning paper had reported that "a space has been marked off beginning at the Long Island railroad station and extending in an easterly direction to the grounds and no automobile will be allowed west of that line. So persons walking from the station need have no fear of the hundreds of automobiles that will be going to Forest Hills."

In a short time the stands were nearly full, and a few had taken their seats on the terrace, where the tiers rose almost to the second-floor balcony. Just above the balcony on the roof there were flags, and someone said the one with the six large stars was the Australian flag. The sun was fierce and a number of sunshades in bright colors began to be raised, especially on the terrace. The same two men who had fixed the net came out carrying the umpire's high seat and placed it beside the near court, its back to my side of the arena. Then they placed chairs on the extensions of every line of the court. I had never seen a match with umpires and linesmen.

I overheard a neighbor high on the rim volunteer the information that Teddy Roosevelt was supposed to come and probably already was in the clubhouse. All I knew about him was that he had something called a Tennis Cabinet while President, and had formed a Bull Moose party which had made possible the election of Woodrow Wilson, to the great joy of the owners of the *Pensacola Journal* and all good Democrats.

T.R. had reigned at a time when politics had not yet entered the consciousness of small boys, but only that morning on the way out I had read

The great Australian, Norman Brookes, as Al Laney remembered him, "long of face and solemn, wore long sleeves and had . . . a cap which he would wear throughout the match." (Photo Courtesy of the USTA)

an interview in one of the papers. Curiously, I cannot remember if I ever did see him, but the substance of the interview remains. Someone had remarked that the war would be over by Christmas, to which T.R. had replied, "Which Christmas?" adding that many might come and go before it was done.

The stands were really packed now and there did not seem to be vacant space anywhere. An odd impression of the crowd that remains is of a solid sea of hard straw hats of the kind we called the straw kady. Looking down from the rim you could see nothing but the tops of those hats. Many of the women in the crowd wore larger versions with pins sticking out. A great many things have passed from the memory but the picture of this ocean of straw remains. Every head among the fourteen thousand seemed to have one, except for the occasional soft Panama, and so, too, for that matter did mine.

A few people were still trying to find their places, and I was standing up to watch the snakelike progress of the automobiles in the distance, when there was a burst of applause and two white-clad figures appeared at the top of the steps leading down from the terrace to the court. Williams and Wilding. Since these were two of the finest players of the game I was to write millions of words about, it would be nice if I could recall something about their match. But I can find little, certainly nothing of importance. I can hardly remember what they looked like then without getting pictures from the files.

Undoubtedly I grew excited, cheered along with the others, and must have followed the play closely, since this was really the first tennis match I had ever seen, but practically everything I recall today about it I learned later by looking it up and reading about it in books. This would be the only time ever of seeing Wilding, and many times I have regretted the lost opportunity. I know that they came and played before my eyes and that Wilding won in straight sets, but I recall only that the defeat of Williams put a great burden on my man, and I carried away a faint resentment of Williams on that account. But I was there to see McLoughlin, not really to see tennis, and strictly speaking, I did not see tennis, because when McLoughlin came onto the stage the action, now magnified, became larger than life, so that no really reliable report of the match with Brookes ever could be made by me.

Nevertheless, the drama of it, often agonizing, can still be lived through a little. In that thirty-two-game service-governed first set, I lived and died with McLoughlin, and I never in the years since have witnessed what seemed to me so grim a fight or an athletic contest of any kind the winning or losing of which meant so much to me. I can well remember how these two looked as they came down the steps and stood for their pictures to be taken. Brookes, long of face and solemn, wore long sleeves and had in his hand a cap which he would wear throughout the match. McLoughlin's shirt was open at the neck and the sleeves were cut off at the elbows. He really did have that mop of hair I had read about, and altogether he was a most satisfactory-looking hero.

I had complete confidence in him and I watched every move during the preliminary hitting of balls back and forth. They were playing on the far court by the terrace, but we could still see from our seats that McLoughlin smiled a lot. Brookes seemed very dour. My confidence was shaken many times before that terribly long first set was over. Brookes gave the impression he would never yield no matter how many thunderbolts our man might hurl at him, blows one never could have imagined possible with a tennis racket. Several times a line from that poem of schoolboy recitation, "Horatius at the Bridge," came into my mind: "Will not the villain drown?" I said it over and over, and once I must have said it aloud, since a man alongside turned and said, "I beg your pardon?"

About halfway through, and after what seemed an eternity, Brookes, who had served first and thus was forcing McLoughlin to battle for his life every time the American served, was love–40 against the service. You would have to be a teenager again, I suppose, to suffer as I suffered then. But at this crisis, McLoughlin served three balls that Brookes could not even touch with his queer-shaped racket.

Other crises came later, near the end we could not know was near. Brookes again was within a point of winning the set, and each time the answer was the same, an unreturnable service. Was ever boyhood hero more worthy of worship? I have read and reread everything about this famous match that I could lay my hands on, and visual memory is all mixed up with other people's observations and opinions. Where the emotions are so terribly involved some details are blurred, others enlarged out of all proportion.

One picture, though, must be my very own. It is of McLoughlin, all fire and dash, leaping from the ground to smash a lob and, as the ball bit into the turf and bounded impossibly away, of Brookes dropping his racket, raising both hands above his head in despair and calling on high heaven to witness his misfortune. This happened several times near the end of that tense set, and whenever in the years that have run into memory's reservoir I have thought of this first exciting encounter with tennis of the highest class, this one picture repeats itself as if it actually were being seen again.

With McLoughlin winning this match for the United States 17–15, 6–3, 6–3, the series was tied and now would go, the experts said, the way they had predicted: Victory for Australia by three matches to two. And so it did. I do not remember about the doubles. I remember only McLoughlin in that match and the fact that Tom Bundy, his partner, wore a handkerchief around his head as though he had a splitting headache, but actually to keep the perspiration out of his eyes, a practice which I adopted myself a little later. Neither do I remember much of Brookes and Williams in the match that decided the issue, but of McLoughlin and Wilding there were things to note.

I was called upon to make a decision on a problem with the enormity of which no schoolboy should have to contend. I had to make up my mind whether I should go to Forest Hills on Saturday to see McLoughlin play again in a match the experts said would mean nothing after Brookes had beaten Williams, or go to the Polo Grounds to see the Giants play the Braves in the final game of their series. After wrestling with the problem overnight I returned to watch the tennis and so deprived myself of the right later to boast, and thereby acquire distinction in my set, that I had seen the fabulous Braves beat the immortal Matty.

McLoughlin vs. Wilding, where I watched my hero rather than carefully observing the match at the time, acquired a certain pathos and significance in later years, and I went over it care-fully in the papers I had saved. It was the last tennis match Wilding would play, and McLoughlin never won another important victory. Two weeks later McLoughlin was beaten by Williams in the final round of the National Championship at Newport, and before spring came round again Wilding was in a grave in Flanders Field, killed in action in the early months of the war.

Dame Mabel Brookes has written of the final meeting between Brookes and Wilding in her delightful book *Crowded Galleries*. They all left for England immediately after the Challenge Round, Wilding to join his regiment. They met for the last time in Boulogne, across the English Channel, in a small dockside hotel "that had that smell of new bread, tobacco, and lavatories that impregnates a certain type of French hostelry."

"Tony came," Dame Mabel recalled, "from nearby Belgium, where he was operating a trailer gun in the Westminster outfit. He was fit and full of energy. . . . he looked handsome in the fatigue cap and uniform that was something like an airman's. As usual, he was untidy, one button dangling by a thread. . . . He was leaving at dawn . . . and after a while bade a speechless, shoulder-holding farewell to him [Norman], for they were very close."

The account continues, "It was barely light when I threw back the shutters and the air came in sharp with a hint of autumn. . . . Tony strode out on the cobbled road, kicked his starter into action, contained, remote and lonely. He waved and wheeled out over the pavé to the bridge and, as he crossed and turned into the distance, he waved again. The smell of burning charcoal came up, mixed with the reek of exhaust from his bike, and drifted, ephemeral as the passing moment, leaving only memory. We never saw him again."

When I learned that Williams had beaten McLoughlin in the Nationals, I was back home working out a new forehand, studying the writing in the many sports sections I had saved, and dreaming of having a job on a New York paper. The shock of McLoughlin's defeat was great. I wondered at first if there could be some mistake. It was as if something had gone wrong with natural law, and it was difficult to forgive Williams when I knew it was true.

I could not, fortunately, foresee anything of this on those wonderful blistering days at Forest Hills, and there was nothing to mar the profound effect McLoughlin made on the individual as he had also caught and stirred the imagination of the millions. What remains to wonder at about that week of August is that I could have been so blissfully unaware and unconcerned about the war that was to change things so greatly in so short a time. The Challenge Round of 1914 was the last international tennis gathering for five years. For Tony Wilding, still in his twenties, it was the end of fun and games. For me, still in my teens, only the beginning.

William Tatem Tilden II

by PAUL GALLICO

Paul Gallico wrote superbly about sports. One of his special talents was relating athletes and their sport to a particular time and culture. In his book The Twenties: The Golden People *he explains the anomaly of Bill Tilden, who publicly made tennis a manly game while privately he led the life of a closet homosexual.*

O F all the changes in the world of sports that took place between the years 1920 and 1930 none was more astonishing or unpredictable than the emergence of lawn tennis as a spectator game and prime box office attraction.

For it was during that magic decade that the once-despised, girlish, and privately practiced game of tennis became a part of the exaggerated bonanza of those years, was compelled to build its own stadium and cast up upon the scene heroes and heroines who, through their skills and individualities, elevated the gates into the million-dollar class.

However, there are two prior dates to be noted which were of the greatest significance to this extraordinary flowering—1912 and 1913.

It was during the former that a young red-headed Californian of no particular social standing came out of the West to bludgeon his way through the up-to-that-time effete, sparsely at-tended and hardly noticed tournaments of the East. He produced a slashing, smashing, whirl-wind, attacking game of such speed and power that he swept the Eastern practitioners practi-cally off their courts and raised the eyebrows of the lifted pinkie set right up into their hatbands. His name was Maurice McLoughlin, and the ex-citement and novelty of his play drew the first real audiences to these matches and actually struck the initial blow which was to free the game forever from the stigmas imposed upon it by its supposedly effeminate nature.

McLoughlin, however, perhaps unfortu-nately for him, was ahead of his time; the pioneer who retired before he was able to reap the full rewards heaped upon his successors.

In 1913, a mixed doubles team consisting of Miss Mary K. Browne and William T. Tilden II appeared in the East and won the outdoor na-tional championship in that event and a long, lean shadow was cast ahead. For it was the first time the name of Tilden achieved national prom-inence. But it was not until seven years later, in 1920, when he won the men's outdoor national singles championship and then repeated for five successive years, that this sport came into its own.

This generation, the young people of today, can have no conception of the handicaps which the modern, taxing, violent, and wholly manly game of lawn tennis had to overcome to reach acceptance, and if you can spare a moment from the story of the man chiefly responsible for this change, I will try to give you an idea.

When I was growing up in New York, in the vicinity of Park Avenue and 60th Street, say around 1906 (Park Avenue at that time was an open cut through which the New York Central ran, belching smoke and soot into the neighborhood curtains), I had a friend whose parents, when he was naughty, punished him by dressing him up in girl's clothes for the day.

This, of course, was before the advent of Professor Freud. I never found out whether this popping of their son and heir into drag was their own sublimated wish for a daughter, nor am I able to tell you the result it had upon the unfortunate boy in later life. But I am prepared to say that psychologically the punishment was characteristic of the times.

There was no greater humiliation to which a youth could be exposed than to be made into a girl, or even thought of in that connection by his fellows. At that age I had never heard of such a thing as a homosexual, neither had my colleagues, but the smile-when-you-say-that-word among us was "sissy." When you were called that, you either put up your dukes and battled, or were forever labeled.

And I remember, too, that in our section it was worth your life to be caught walking anywhere east of Lexington Avenue carrying a tennis racket under your arm. And as for being clad in a pair of ice cream pants and blazer, this was sheerest suicide.

At the turn of the century you had only to be seen in any tough neighborhood bearing one of those bats thus accoutered, to bring out a swarm of young hoodlums, tagging one with mocking, falsetto shrieks of "Deuce, darling" or "Forty–love, dear." Whoever, in the early days of the invention of modern tennis in Great Britain around 1873, substituted the word "love" for the more sensible one of "nought" or "zero" to indicate "no score," imposed a staggering handicap upon it and was responsible, at least in the U.S.A., for a lot of black eyes and bloody noses.

Another encumbrance to a pastime which today is a symbol not only of skill and virility, but toughness and endurance as well (there are few sports more exhausting than a big-time five-set tennis match) was the juxtaposition of the word "lawn." There was nothing the matter with the word "tennis" itself, one of the most ancient games derived from the courts of the kings of France. Nor was there anything inherently upsetting in "lawn," a patch of grass connected with country or suburban houses which seemed to call for unending mowing and watering.

But put the two together to make "lawn tennis" and at once there arose a vision of prissy dudes in white flannel trousers, prancing about a greensward at Southampton, Newport, Bar Harbor, or Seabright, pitter-patting a ball across a sagging net to young ladies clad in long skirts, puff sleeves, and Gibson Girl hats. Serves were delivered underhand, and such a thing as an overhead kill, net play, or driving the ball straight for the refined countenance of your opponent would have brought shrieks of protest and, no doubt, expulsion from the club. It called up pictures of other cookie-pushers wearing chic, striped blazers and straw boaters with colored college headbands, idling on the sidelines, sipping tea with elegantly lifted pinkies, all on a summer's day. The whole business made for mockery.

Even as late as 1916 and 1917, when I made my first appearances as candidate for the Columbia University crew, I remember the stern warnings issued by our rough, tough, Canadian-born coach, the late Jim Rice, "Don't let me catch any of you fellows going out and playing that there long penis game." For on the crew we were supposed to be men and tennis was even then not considered for a man.

And one of the weirdest ironies in perhaps the entire history of modern sport is that the personality chiefly responsible for the metamorphosis of tennis from a game looked upon as effeminate to its present-day acceptance was himself, as he so honestly and tragically acknowledged in his own biography, a deviate.

Of all the colorful champions of that era, this man was far and away the oddest fish. As a player he dominated the decade at a period when there were more stars, national or international, to challenge him than ever before or since. As a box office attraction both amateur and professional, he lifted the gate from peanuts into the million-dollar class. As a person he was as strange, independent and controversial a figure as ever strutted across the sports scene.

He was a colossus! He was a tremendous athlete of unparalleled skill and inexhaustible endurance. And he was 100 percent ham.

It is astonishing how frequently the characters in this sport did not look like athletes, and it applies again to Bill Tilden. He stood six feet one inch in his tennis socks and never weighed more than 165 pounds. He was built, if you saw him stripped in the locker room, along the lines of a gibbon—the wide shoulders which always seemed somewhat hunched, long, prehensile arms, flat, narrow waist, and thin, caliperlike legs. His hair tended to sparseness on top, and he had a long nose and curiously heavy and prognathous jaw. But if you were designing a creature especially for the playing of big-league tennis, you could hardly improve upon Tilden's conformation—the elongated legs for covering the court in giant strides and the powerful shoulders and whiplash arms and wrists for flailing the ball.

Add to this one of the keenest game-analyzing brains of any of the champions, lightning reactions, the temperament of a prima donna, and his own personal tragedy of homosexuality, and one has little difficulty in regarding him as surely a most remarkable character.

At this time in our own development as a nation and a people emerging from war, our heated imaginations and the change from the excitement to the calmer days of peace necessitated the invention of different kinds of daily thrills. To provide these our sports heroes became *personae dramatis* of the great sports sagas. But Tilden was also his own dramatist.

Whereas fate and circumstances, and often the cagey manipulations of astute promoters, cast this or that famous sportsman as hero, heavy, or supporting role, Tilden wrote his own scripts. A total exhibitionist, stage-struck—he chewed up scenery in plays as a member of a number of road companies in the legitimate theater—he could not bear to be anything less than the leading man; Bayard, Cyrano, Galahad, Roland, d'Artagnan all lumped into one. If the spotlight ever wandered from him during his play on the tennis courts, he very quickly pulled it back onto himself. No top-dog or villain parts for Tilden; the sympathy of the audience had to be with him at all times.

You could almost always bet on the graph of the American public following the rise of any champion to his crown. Up and up and up it went with him, in pursuit of his fortunes until he reached the peak and then down it would plunge. Now that he was champ his fickle fans could hardly wait to see him knocked off. This should have been doubly operative in the case of Tilden, for he was not only outstanding and for a time unbeatable, but arrogant, with irritating court mannerisms, disputatious and supercilious. Yet, practically for all of his reign he had the crowd with him.

He achieved this by the very simple and rarely varying drama of the great master teetering on the brink of downfall or even a rout, then rallying and in a superb display of courage, stamina and often incredible shotmaking, snatching victory from what we liked to refer to as the jaws of defeat.

And how Tilden could teeter. If his antagonist could not produce the attack to make him temporarily look bad, or in danger—and there were plenty who could—Tilden would let down, appear off form, or develop a slight injury to handicap himself, until finally there he was, a lone and gallant figure on the courts, staring repulse in the face.

This was not crudely done, but deftly and subtly (Tilden could also throw a point to an opponent blatantly to show his contempt for a linesman's call, and reveal himself as one disdaining to accept an advantage he felt he had not earned)—and so skillfully that we were not conscious of anything but a champion momentarily off stride, until one looked at the score sheet and saw that he was five games down, set point

Big Bill's backhand: This top spin backhand was the missing element to Bill Tilden's all-court game. Once mastered, he began winning all the major titles that had eluded him. (Photo Courtesy of the USTA)

against him and in danger of blowing the tournament. And then the fun began.

But there was far more to it than just this kind of corny crowd appeal. The man did stir the emotions exactly as great actors do upon the stage, for at tennis he was more than just a champion and a top-notch technician, he was a genius and a superb artist. It was to this artistry that all of us inevitably reacted. It overcame every one of his handicaps, his little tantrums and gestures of pique, sulks, pets, glares, and *moues* and, believe it or not, cries of "Oh, sugar!" when he missed one. They simply did not matter in the light of the heights to which he was able to rise when he wished, or needed

to, and in rising would sweep us all out of ourselves and along with him.

It was, as noted, one of the maddest paradoxes of the age that the man who was responsible for bringing about acceptance of tennis as one of the most virile of men's competitive games was effeminate in his mannerisms and behavior. The paradox continued to hold good in that it didn't seem to matter, was hardly noticeable and rarely discussed. And I must confess that during the days I was covering Tilden's matches and writing about him, I didn't even know it, or think about it. His artistry was such that this was all one saw.

For if his personality was doubtful on the

male side, his tennis was not. It was as hard, manly and slashing a game as was ever seen on any court, and all the kids wanted to play and win like Tilden. His image was enormous, an international giant holding off the world. At his peak he beat the Americans, the British, the French, the Japanese, and the Australians. He was invincible *us.*

His strength was as the strength of ten, his blinding service unreturnable, his stamina inexhaustible, and his courage unquestionable. Then how could he be effeminate as well? There was no understanding whatsoever of homosexuality in America forty or fifty years ago. It was either an undercover whisper, or a dirty joke. It was not until World War II that the presence of some during commando raids revealed that they could be among the cruelest, bravest and toughest of men.

From the moment Tilden stepped onto the grass court, he dominated the scene to such an extent that there was no room in one's head for anything but the drama that was about to be unfolded.

He did it with a tennis racket, an oval bat strung with catgut, but it might have been a sword, a gun, a bow, or even a conductor's baton. It was not only the implement of the game, it was his instrument of creation. With it he could make us feel sad, thrilled, glad, worried, anxious, relieved, and even ecstatic, any mood that he desired to arouse; and frightened, too, for believe me the man was tough and the killer instinct was there when called upon, as brutal as that in any fighter or football player. To his opponents it was a contest; with Tilden it was an expression of his own tremendous and overweening ego, coupled with feminine vanity.

To this extraordinary spiritual, emotional and intellectual approach Tilden brought unusual physical mastery and technical skill. Like all great champions he was a student of every facet of his sport, a man with the interest and curiosity to pry into everything that had to do with producing winning tennis.

Lawn tennis as it had developed, from the time of Maurice McLoughlin, is a game of mathematics and angles, just as, let us say, baseball is

one of timing and judgment. Each calls for different equipment and the participants become dexterous in their use. But these play no more than a mechanical part in the basic concept of the pastime. With ball and bat, problems of judgment are created and the race is against time: Man arriving at base that split second before the throw. With the tennis racket, the speed of flight of the properly hit ball and the arbitrary confines of the court, angles are created which decide a point one way or another, either by forcing a bad return or setting the opponent the problem impossible of solution, i.e., the passing shot. But angles are mathematics, and Tilden was the master tennis mathematician.

The average player has to think about the components of making a proper shot, just as the average weekend golfer is not bothered about where he will hit the ball, but whether he will hit it at all, and how far and how straight. Players of modern tournament tennis, however, have their technique so perfected that their rackets are merely an implementation of their thoughts and strategic plans. Tilden had the stroke to meet every type of attack and the legs to get him to the spot for handling it. In aggression he was wholly formidable with a forehand and backhand drive which, for power hitting, have rarely been equaled, a booming cannonball service, cunning volley, and a smashing net game when he wanted to move up there. Further, he had the ability to turn what seemed like impossible gets, with his opponent already congratulating himself, into winning placements.

He was the perfect player and, as a result of this perfection, he won the American National Turf Court Championship seven times, the Wimbledon title three times, shared in the U.S. doubles five times (between 1918 and 1927), and in Davis Cup matches between 1920 and 1930 won seventeen and lost only five singles matches and shared in four doubles victories. From 1920 through 1929 inclusive, Tilden was ranked first in the U.S.A.

The difficulties in which Tilden often found himself embroiled during this brilliant period arose from the fact that he was not a snob, nor a socialite, nor a Mainliner. He came from a middle-class Philadelphia merchant family. And tennis was then still a snob game.

But there are snobs and snobs. The original tennis fathers (and moms) were ladies and gentlemen who did not look down upon those who did not play tennis. They were pleased with their own society and probably did not bother to look down at all.

But there were a great number of Americans shortly before and after World War I who were looking upward and dying to break into the closed circle of the charmed Four Hundred. The game of tennis was a means of entry to some, and those were the genuine copper-plated, triple-riveted, gold-rimmed snobs.

These were the new rich, the climbers and the pseudo-socialites who later were all lumped under the general heading of Café Society, and who thought that joining a tennis club would bestow upon them a large part of the standing they sought. The characteristics of the members of this class and their idea of comporting themselves in the manner of the *crème de la crème* was rudeness, arbitrary bullheadedness and stuffed-shirtism. Quietly, control of the game passed into their hands as the genuine aristocracy abandoned tennis in favor of polo, a pastime that demanded even more money and more space to be enjoyed. Their hero was Tommy Hitchcock and surrounding him was a crowd of tough, hard-drinking, well-mannered men. The Long Island polo set was authentic, but by this time the tennis crowd was as phony as a dime-store engagement ring.

How did the tennis snobs manage to keep their clammy hands upon the sport just as it was bursting from its chrysalis, ready for flight to its place in the sun? They were simply there. They ran the clubs, they had the only courts and the stadiums and thus were able to promote and hold the big tournaments.

They formed the backbone of the U.S. Lawn Tennis Association of forty years ago, stiffened by a few leftover antediluvian stuffed shirts of the previous generation. These climbers not only had no background for manners and genteel behavior themselves, but often by their conduct and superior airs succeeded in making amateur or assistant snobs out of many of the girls and boys who were attracted to the game.

The sudden shower of sports shekels of the twenties sent a shiver of surprise, shock and joy down the spines of the members of the committees of the important tennis clubs. After years when tennis was only a pay-out pastime, draining funds for upkeep of courts and damage to the locker rooms perpetrated by soused members, now, out of the blue, it was big box office.

And what was most marvelous, it was theirs, all theirs, and for free—well, almost for free. Theoretically the big money drawers were all amateurs who were not supposed to get a penny for their services beyond a cup that in those days could wholesale for $49.98.

With sell-out houses for the national championships, Davis and Wightman Cup matches and other invitation attractions, you can understand the anxiety of everyone connected with lawn tennis that the players should not sully their amateur standing by becoming a party to the transfer of hard cash. It was this attitude that so irritated Tilden and made him the gadfly of the USLTA. It was not so much the money involved but the impudence of the association's approach.

For three-quarters of a century now, the United States has been dogged by the amateur problem and all of the hypocrisy connected with it. But it really took the Russians and their simple, uncomplicated attitude to sports to show up the utter ridiculousness of our interpretation of an amateur vs. a professional in modern times.

From 1920 to 1930 it was tennis which provided the most strident battleground raised by this question, with foot running, golf and college football adding to the confusion as soon as they joined the big money earners.

Class-conscious Britain in the 1800's invented the distinction between the amateur and the professional and it was a simple one. The amateur was a gentleman and the professional wasn't. When the gentlemen consented to risk soiling their hands by meeting the professionals in a cricket match, the latter entered the clubhouse by the back door and through the kitchen. There was no financial problem connected at the beginning, since a gentleman did not make money; he *had* money. In modern times who is, or isn't a gentleman has become just as confused as to who is, or who isn't an amateur.

As social circles began to widen, so did these distinctions, and the dollar offered a convenient dividing line. A fellow who in any way, shape, form or manner permitted his connection with sport to be associated with the long green, was lumped as a professional, even if he had no more than sold sweat bands or tennis socks over the counter in a sporting goods shop during the Christmas holidays. An amateur played only for fun and recreation and was rich enough not to have to worry where his next dollar was coming from.

The trouble was that when an amateur sport, such as tennis, became big business, it was discovered that this type of simon-pure was unfortunately in very short supply.

When American tennis passed into the Golden Decade and the West Side Tennis Club-Forest Hills Stadium phase, what the U.S. Lawn Tennis Association required was amateur tennis players whose game reached professional standards. To acquire such proficiency meant they would have to devote practically all their time not only to practicing, but traveling on the tennis circuit and playing in tournaments the year round to keep sharp.

Their services, of course, were to be donated for free and under no circumstances were they to demand any part of the huge gates that their box-office personalities were attracting. They were to maintain themselves and be satisfied with travel and subsistence allowances about on a par with those given to a soldier or sailor.

Technically they got them, but from that moment on, of course, the genuine tennis amateur was as extinct as the dodo and everyone connected with the game, or who profited by it with the exception of the ball boys, was as crooked as the proverbial corkscrew, in the ethical if not the physical sense as well.

Many of the so-called amateurs were compelled to cheat in order to keep going, that is to say, take money under the table, and the phrase "tennis bum" joined the American language.

The officials knew they were cheating, but closed their eyes to it, otherwise there would not have been any stars to tone up the box office. As long as the cheating remained under cover, it was condoned. But let a player turn honest enough to try to make a few pennies with either personal or ghost-written newspaper articles, or a temporary job with a sporting-goods house, and he was immediately disbarred and banished into outer darkness, unless, as will be seen, his need was so great that the officials were compelled to backtrack on their own ruling and reinstate him.

If crooked seems a strong word to use in this context it is because there are simply no shades between honesty and twisting. A man cannot be a slight thief; he is or he isn't. And the absurd amateur rule and the constructions put upon it made dishonest men of everyone connected with amateur sport. This covers the ruling bodies of track meets, college football, golf, college baseball, or any other recreation in which amateurs were responsible for large gate receipts and where eye-closing was involved. It took only the merest droop of the eyelid and the whole affair was not on the level any more. It was in this atmosphere that an entire generation of young athletes grew up with a very early introduction to the double standard.

Where this state of affairs touched William Tatem Tilden II was the fact that he was no baby, but an intelligent, educated, sensitive man and hence a perpetual rebel against the hypocrisy of this system.

As well as their greatest star and box office attraction he was also the *enfant terrible* of the Lawn Tennis Association. Into this setup he fitted just like a hysterical bull in a china shop. An antisnob, he hated their guts, fought with them, ridiculed them, and rammed his weird personality down their throats for ten years. The great god Mazuma reigned and Bill Tilden was his profit. For this reason they had to put up with his mannerisms, umpire-baiting, refusal to conform, and an occasional shrewish offensiveness that matched their own. Tilden didn't give a damn for anyone or anything but the game and his own image.

Tilden's battles with the tennis greats of his

era—Little Bill Johnston, Vinny Richards, Dick Williams, Lacoste, Cochet, Borotra, Manuel Alonso from Spain, Patterson and Norman Brookes from Australia, Shimizu and Ichiya Kumagae from Japan, during those years were classics and, in the decade, drew more than a million dollars through the turnstiles. But they were mild compared to his rows with the Lawn Tennis Association which, at one time in 1928, reached the peak of international incident.

At that time the Davis Cup Committee of the U.S. Lawn Tennis Association had discovered that Tilden had been picking up some loose change for writing newspaper articles while traveling abroad. The idea of an amateur laying his hands on some cash into which the tennis body could not get its hooks was so depressing that Tilden was promptly suspended and barred from further amateur play.

But hold, the suspension came just at the time that Big Bill was due to meet the French Davis Cup team at Roland Garros Stadium in Paris, in the Challenge Round of the international competition.

The stadium was sold out, the French amateur body likewise being no dopes at cashing in, but the big attraction was, naturally, *le Grand Guillaume.* With Tilden blacklisted, a lot of people were going to ask for their money back. The French screamed loud and long. It was Tilden or else, if the two countries were to remain on the footing inaugurated by the Marquis de Lafayette. Myron T. Herrick, the United States ambassador to France, was compelled to telephone the chairman of the Davis Cup Committee in the United States to say that Tilden must be reinstated for the sake of international amity.

Sweetly cooperative at this point, the committee, which had barred Tilden as a professional, waved its wand over Big William and metamorphosed him back into an amateur once more for the Davis Cup matches in France. But, immediately upon his return to the United States, they magicked him back again into a professional and banned him from taking part in the United States singles championship. The French

won the Davis Cup that year by four matches to one, which may have had something to do with this waspish revenge, which was only exceeded in 1930 when, after Tilden won the world's championship at Wimbledon, the committee completely ignored him in its national ranking on the basis of a rumor that he was about to turn professional. And no single player ever did more for the USLTA than William Tatem Tilden II. In the meantime, lesser stars were picking up $500 at a clip for appearing at invitation tournaments at home and abroad, as well as their traveling tickets and more than generous expenses. The custom at that time was to collect total travel expenses from each tournament. When added up this made a nice little income. It was this kind of condoned dishonesty which was anathema to Tilden.

As a professional, Tilden racked up an even more amazing record than as an amateur, for he was thirty-eight when he relinquished his amateur status, and from 1931 through 1935 he compiled 340 wins to 147 losses, against such competition as Kozeluh, Nusslein, Richards, Hunter, Cochet, and Vines.

When he finished as an active professional player, Tilden's love for the game, a love far more generous and enduring than that of any tennis committee man, manifested itself in his teaching of the young, until the unfortunate deviate tragedy that brought his life tumbling down about his ears in 1946 and sent him to jail. He never really managed to fight his way back before his untimely death at the age of sixty in 1953.

But those of us who covered his matches between 1920 and 1929 and sat spellbound in the press marquee at the West Side Tennis Club's Forest Hills Stadium, on Long Island, or at the Germantown Cricket Club, outside Philadelphia, will remember him only as the great actor-dramatist, standing on the base line, pausing until every eye was on him and every lip stilled, to coil, uncoil, and release his thunder-and-lightning service, *obligato* to the theme of the ever-recurring melodrama, "Tilden Wins Again."

"I'll Play My Own Sweet Game"

by FRANK DEFORD

It wasn't until Bill Tilden was twenty-seven that he found the two things he most desperately wanted in his life—public admiration and the winning of a major singles championship. It all came together for him on Centre Court at Wimbledon in 1920. Frank Deford, a senior writer at Sports Illustrated, *describes Tilden's debut as the world's number-one player.*

WITH any artist who attains the ultimate in his craft, there must be one moment, an instant, when genius is first realized, when a confluence of God's natural gifts at last swirl together with the full powers of endeavor and devotion in the man to bear him to greatness. Virtually always, of course, that moment cannot be perceived, and it passes unnoticed, but with Big Bill Tilden it was isolated, forever frozen in time. He knew precisely when he had arrived, and, thoughtfully, he revealed it.

This happened on Centre Court at Wimbledon in 1920. Tilden was already twenty-seven, and although he had never won a major championship, he had reached the finals. It was his first trip abroad, and to his delight the British, unlike his own countrymen, had taken to him right away. Americans always only grudgingly granted Tilden recognition, never mind respect, largely because they were emotionally hung up on Big Bill's main rival, Bill Johnston, who was affectionately known as Little Bill, or even, in the soupiest moments, Wee Willie Winkie. Johnston was five feet eight, a wonderful cute doll-person from the California middle class, and all Americans (Tilden prominently included) were absolutely nuts about him: The little underdog with the big heart who cut larger fellows down to size.

By contrast, at six feet one-and-a-half inches tall, 155 pounds, angular and overbearing, a Philadelphia patrician of intellectual pretension, Big Bill was the perfect foil for Little Bill, and the great American villain. Until 1920 he had also cooperated by remaining a loser with a healthy reputation for choking in important matches. The year before, in the finals at Forest Hills, Johnston had defeated Tilden in straight sets, and so it was assumed that Wimbledon would serve as the stage where Johnston, the American champion, would duel Gerald Patterson, the Wimbledon defender, for the undisputed championship of the world.

Unfortunately for hopes for this classic confrontation, Johnston was waylaid in an early round by a steady English player named J.C. Parke. Not until the next day, when Tilden routed Parke, avenging Little Bill's defeat, did Big Bill move front and center as Patterson's most conspicuous challenger. Of course, from the moment Tilden strode upon their grass that summer, the British had been enchanted with him—his game, his manner, his idiosyncrasies: "This smiling youth, so different from other Americans." A woolly blue sweater Tilden wore seems to have positively enthralled the entire nation, and the *London Times* exclaimed that "his jumpers are the topic of the tea-table."

While little Johnston struck the British as just that, a pleasant little sort, the lean giant caused them admiration and wonder: "Of great stature, he is loosely built with slender hips and very broad shoulders . . . in figure, an ideal lawn tennis player." His game they found so arresting —"There is no stroke Mr. Tilden cannot do at full speed, and his is undoubtedly the fastest serve seen"—that one of the more poetic observers even rhapsodized, "His silhouette as he prepares to serve suggests an Egyptian pyramid king about to administer punishment."

Seeing Tilden for the first time, unprepared for that sight, was obviously a striking experience. Not so much in what exactly they said but in their evident astonishment and determined hyperbolic reach, do the British of 1920 best intimate what an extraordinary presence Big Bill Tilden must have been. Yet perhaps even more important, the British understood immediately that here was a different sort of athletic temperament. The Americans were not to fathom this in Tilden for years, if indeed many of them ever did. But Tilden had played only a handful of matches in England that summer before he was assessed perfectly in the sporting press: "He gives the impression that he regards lawn tennis as a game—a game which enables him to do fascinating things, but still a game. . . . When he has something in hand he indulges his taste for the varied at the expense of the commercial."

Pleased at the attention given him, even more gratified that his playing philosophy was appreciated, Tilden grew assured, and, boldly and not without some conceit, he began to enunciate his theories of the game. When not at the courts or attending the theater, he spent all his time writing in his hotel room, and within three weeks he had completed his first book, *The Art of Tennis.* "The primary object in match tennis is to break up the other man's game" was, significantly, the point he most emphasized.

Patterson, meanwhile, remained quite confident. An Australian, the nephew of the great opera star Nellie Melba, he was not only the defending Wimbledon champion but star of the team which held the Davis Cup. He was at his peak and generally recognized above Johnston as the ranking player in the world. At Wimbledon Patterson had only to bide his time scouting the opposition and practice at his leisure, for in those days the defender did not play in the regular tournament but was obliged only to meet the All Comers winner in a special Challenge Round.

Patterson's supremacy seemed all the more obvious after Tilden appeared to struggle in the All Comers final against the Japanese, Zenzo Shimizu. In each set Tilden fell far behind: 1–4 in the first, 2–4 in the second, 2–5 in the third. He won 6–4, 6–4, 13–11. Nobody realized it at the time, but it was one of Tilden's amusements, a favor to the crowd, to give lesser opponents a head start. Tilden had whipped Shimizu 6–1, 6–1 in a preliminary tournament the week before Wimbledon, and he certainly had no intention of cheating his Centre Court fans with that same sort of lopsided display. In the final set Big Bill tested himself and kept things going, largely just by hitting backhands and nothing much else.

"The player owes the gallery as much as an actor owes the audience," he wrote once; and Paul Gallico summed it up: "To his opponents it was a contest; with Tilden it was an expression of his own tremendous and overweening ego, coupled with feminine vanity." Big Bill never really creamed anybody unless he hated them or was in a particular hurry to get somewhere else.

Certainly he was not ever anxious to hastily depart Centre Court at Wimbledon, and he returned for the championship against Patterson on Saturday, July 3. Big Bill found this date especially felicitous; an obsessive patriot, he noted that, for an American, July 3 was the next best thing to July 4. He further buttressed this omen by somehow obtaining a four-leaf clover that he was assured had once grown under the chair that Abraham Lincoln used to sit in on the White

Bill Tilden on stage at Forest Hills. He didn't win his first major singles title until he was twenty-seven—it took him that long to build his "all court" game—but then he ruled tennis for a decade. (Photo Courtesy of the USTA)

House lawn. And so, with that talisman safely ensconced in his pocket, he set out to become the first American ever to win the Wimbledon men's championship.

Patterson had a strong serve and forehand, but his weakness was an odd corkscrew backhand that he hit sort of inside out. And so, curiously it seemed, Tilden began by playing to Patterson's powerful forehand. The champion ran off the first four games with dispatch and won the set 6–2. But then, as Tilden changed sides for the first time in the second set, he spotted a good

friend, the actress Peggy Wood, sitting in the first row with a ticket he had provided her, and he looked straight at Miss Wood, and with a reassuring nod, that kind delivered with lips screwed up in smug confidence, he signaled to her that all was quite well, that it was in the bag, that finally, at the age of twenty-seven, he was about to become the champion of the world.

Miss Wood, of course, had no notion that she would be used as a conduit for history; nor, for that matter, could she understand Tilden's cockiness. He had lost the first set 6–2; he was getting clobbered by the best player in the world. But down the five full decades, and more, that have passed, she cannot forget that expression of his, nor what followed. "Immediately," she says, as if magic were involved, "Bill proceeded to play."

In that instant he had solved Patterson's forehand, and the champion, his strength ravaged, had nothing but his weakness to fall back upon. *The primary object in match tennis is to break up the other man's game.* "A subtle change came over Patterson's game," the *Guardian* correspondent wrote in some evident confusion. "Things that looked easy went out, volleys that ought to have been crisply negotiated ended up in the net." Tilden swept the next three sets at his convenience, losing only nine games, and toward the end it was noted for the record that "the Philadelphian made rather an exhibition of his opponent."

Big Bill did not lose another match of any significance anywhere in the world until a knee injury cost him a victory more than six years later. Playing for himself, for his country, for posterity, he was invincible. No man ever bestrode his sport as Tilden did for those years. It was not just that he could not be beaten, it was nearly as if he had invented the sport he conquered. Babe Ruth, Jack Dempsey, Red Grange and the other fabled American sweat lords of the times stood at the head of more popular games, but Tilden simply was tennis in the public mind: *Tilden and tennis,* it was said, in that order. He ruled the game as much by force of his curious, contradictory, often abrasive personality as by his proficiency. But he was not merely eccentric.

He was the greatest irony in sport: To a game that then suffered a "fairy" reputation, Tilden gave a lithe, swashbuckling, athletic image—although he was in fact a homosexual, the only great male athlete we know to have been one.

Alone in the world of athletics, nearly friendless and, it seems, even ashamed of himself, there was seldom any joy for the man, even amidst his greatest tennis triumphs. It's quite likely that in his whole life Tilden never spent a night alone with an adult, man or woman. And his every day was shadowed by the bizarre and melancholy circumstances surrounding a childhood he tried to forget; certainly it is no coincidence that he did not blossom as a champion until just after he discarded the name of his youth.

He had been born on February 10, 1893, and christened William Tatem Tilden Jr., which he came to hate because everyone called him Junior or June. Finally, arbitrarily, around the time of his twenty-fifth birthday, he changed the Junior to the Second, II. That onus officially disposed of, June became Bill and then, even better, Big Bill.

He had been introduced to tennis early. It was an upper-class game, and the family he was born into was rich, of ascending social prominence, and even greater civic presence. The family mansion, Overleigh, was located in the wealthy Germantown section of Philadelphia, only a block or so from the Germantown Cricket Club. The Tildens belonged, of course, and the club was indeed to be the site of many Big Bill triumphs, but the family summered at a fashionable Catskill resort, Onteora, and it was there that young June learned the game of tennis, in the last year of the nineteenth century.

The first clear vision of him as a player does not arise, however, until about a decade later, when Tilden was playing, with little distinction, for the team at his small private school, Germantown Academy. This day he was struggling on the court, slugging everything, all cannonballs, when Frank Deacon, one of his younger friends, came by. Even then, as a schoolboy, Tilden was always closest to children years younger than he. At the end of a point, which, typically, Tilden had

violently overplayed, hitting way out, Deacon hollered to him in encouragement, "Hey, June, take it easy."

Tilden stopped dead, and with what became a characteristic gesture, he swirled to face the boy, placing his hands on his hips and glaring at him. "Deacon," he snapped, "I'll play my own sweet game."

And so he did, every day of his life. He was the proudest of men and the saddest, pitifully alone and shy, but never so happy as when he brought his armful of rackets into the limelight or walked into a crowded room and contentiously took it over. George Lott, a Davis Cup colleague and a man who actively disliked Tilden, was nonetheless this mesmerized by him: "When he came into the room it was like a bolt of electricity hit the place. Immediately, there was a feeling of awe, as though you were in the presence of royalty. You knew you were in contact with greatness, even if only remotely. The atmosphere became charged, and there was almost a sensation of lightness when he left. You felt completely dominated and breathed a sigh of relief for not having ventured an opinion of any sort."

Tilden himself said, "I can stand crowds only when I am working in front of them, but then I love them." Obviously the crowds and the game were his sex. For a large part of his life, the glory years, all the evidence suggests that he was primarily asexual; it was not until he began to fade as a player and there were not enough crowds to play to that his homosexual proclivities really took over. But ahh, when he was king, he would often appear to trap himself in defeat, as he had against Shimizu, so that he could play the better role, prolonging his afternoon as the cynosure in the sun, prancing and stalking upon his chalked stage, staring at officials, fuming at the crowd, now toying with his opponent, then saluting him grandly, spinning, floating, jumping, playing his own sweet game, reveling in the game.

And yet, for all these excesses of drama and melodrama, his passion for competition was itself even superseded by another higher sense: Sportsmanship. Tilden was utterly scrupulous, obsessed with honor, and he would throw points (albeit with grandeur, Pharisee more than Samaritan) if he felt that a linesman had cheated his opponent. Big Bill was the magistrate of every match he played, and the critic as well. "Peach!" he would cry in delight, lauding any opponent who beat him with a good shot. And, if inspired or mad enough at the crowd or at his rival, he would serve out the match by somehow holding five balls in one huge hand and then tossing four of them up, one after another, and pounding out four cannonball aces—bam, bam, bam, bam; 15–30–40–game—then throwing the fifth ball away with disdain. That was the style to it. Only the consummate showman would think of the extra ball as the closing fillip to the act.

"He is an artist," Franklin P. Adams wrote at Big Bill's peak. "He is more of an artist than nine-tenths of the artists I know. It is the beauty of the game that Tilden loves; it is the chase always, rather than the quarry."

Further, even more unlike almost all great champions in every sport, whose brilliance is early recognized, early achieved, Tilden was required to make himself great. Very nearly he created himself. Only a few years before he became champion of the world, he could not make the college varsity at the University of Pennsylvania. He taught himself, inspired himself, fashioning a whole new level for the game in the bargain.

Withal, it is probable that the very fact that he was homosexual was largely responsible for the real success he achieved in tennis; he had none elsewhere. Urbane, well-read, a master bridge player, a connoisseur of fine music, he held pretensions to writing and acting as well as tennis, but these gossamer vanities only cost him great amounts of stature and money, and even held him up to mockery. For all his intelligence, tennis was the only venture that June Tilden could ever succeed at, until the day he died in his cramped walk-up room near Hollywood and Vine, where he lived out his tragedy, a penniless ex-con, scorned or forgotten, alone as always, and desperately in need of love from a world that had tolerated him only for its amusement. "He felt things so very deeply," Peggy Wood says. "He was not a frivolous person, And yet, I never saw him with anybody who could have been his confidant. How must it be like that? There must have been so many things deep within him that he could never talk about. I suppose he died of a broken heart." It seems he did.

To the end, in the good times and the bad, he searched for one thing above all: A son. He could not have one, and so he would find one for himself, make one, as he made himself a great player to honor the dead mother he worshipped. But the boys he found, whom he loved and taught, would grow up and put away childish things, which is what any game is, what tennis is, and ultimately, what Big Bill Tilden was. He was the child of his own dreams, always, until the day he died, age sixty, his bags packed, ready once again to leave for a tennis tournament.

Lenglen vs. Wills

by JOHN TUNIS

Two of the greatest women who ever played were Suzanne Lenglen and Helen Wills. The two met but once during their careers, with Lenglen at her zenith and Wills's talent just beginning to crest. That match, played at Cannes, February 27, 1926, was simply called The Match. John Tunis, one of America's best sport journalists, remembers that historic moment in his autobiography, A Measure of Independence.

THERE was never a match of tennis like it, and I am convinced there will never be another like it again. Followers of sports today have long since forgotten the names of these two champions. But there were great men before Agamemnon.

Under the passionate sun of the *Midi* the two figures in white faced each other upon the red center court at Cannes, the American girl and the French woman, the Puritan and the *Parisienne,* the New World against the Old.

No match of tennis ever attracted such attention. France, suffering from the decisive defeat of her war hero, Georges Carpentier, by Jack Dempsey several years previously, had found in that black-haired, ugly girl, Suzanne Lenglen, a tennis champion able to beat both English and Americans at their own game. No one could hold her, no one could even take a set from her. She

was the queen. A peer without equal, she reigned supreme in Europe, and had won the French and Wimbledon titles half a dozen times each. Then that winter a fresh face and a real challenger appeared from the West.

The day Miss Helen Wills, a Californian with a concentrated seriousness upon the court that betrayed the essential warmth deep below, landed at Le Havre early in February, she was met by a battery of reporters and cameramen. The same scene was repeated in the railroad station at Cannes on the Riviera a few days later. Soon, up and down the coast there was but one topic of conversation: The Match. All France, even all Europe, watched and waited. When and where would they meet? There was a tournament along the littoral at a different club every week. Miss Wills entered—and won—several in which Suzanne Lenglen did not play. Finally both agreed to enter the Carlton Club meeting at Cannes in mid-February.

The organization for that historic finals, which took place on February 17, 1926, was not much worse than that for the Battles of Sedan (1870 and 1940), nor much better, either. The Carlton Club, a block from the blue Mediterranean, had six *en-tout-cas* type courts, bounded on both sides by narrow streets. The club was merely an adjunct of the grand palace

149

Suzanne Lenglen moves in to kill a high forehand (right). Helen Wills concentrates on her service toss (left). Lenglen was always dramatic, Wills always serious. (Photos Courtesy of the USTA)

hotel by that name across the road. Actually it was then pretty much owned by the Carlton and was a club in name only, with no facilities, no officers or members; in reality, a public tennis club.

Inasmuch as everyone along the coast wanted to see that match, and as the feverish publicity mounted daily, tickets were hard to secure at any price. The morning of the finals was a perfect Riviera day, cloudless, sunny, warm. Although the match was scheduled at eleven, I arrived an hour beforehand, knowing there would be a struggle to get inside. There certainly was. A line of ticket holders and persons wishing

to beg, borrow or buy a seat stretched five hundred yards back to the Croisette, or sea front. It took me half an hour to crowd through a tiny gate reserved for the press.

Inside they were still constructing the stands. Directly a plank was nailed down, someone placed a chair upon the plank and a seat holder grabbed it. Wandering beneath the structure I noticed its flimsy construction, and stopped a man on the tournament committee.

"Tell me, has this stand here been checked by your local building inspector?"

He was furious. *"Mais non, mon vieux,* do you not see it is only just being finished?"

"But if it collapses?" I glanced up nervously. The boards were sagging perceptibly.

"Ah . . . as for that . . . the club is assured." He hurried away, quite resigned to possible disaster.

Gingerly I climbed to my seat, the newly laid planking giving under me at every step. The sight of a tent and a Red Cross nurse below did not reassure me. I looked around. Along the street was a row of eucalyptus trees that stretched to the heavens. They furnished a perfect view of the stands and the entire center court, and every kid in Cannes plus a considerable number of agile adults climbed up. A gendarme strolled along, shouted at them and then shinnied up one tree. As he went up, the crowd went higher. When he reached his limit, they jeered down at him, calling him a *flic* and less pleasant names.

On the other street, a Frenchman with a large beard stood beside the front door of his villa and began selling places in his attic. Riviera roofs are made of red tiles placed upon beams. You took a chair to the attic, stood on it, removed a tile or several of them and stuck your head and shoulders out into the sun. Soon hundreds of faces spattered the roofs of all the villas in the vicinity. A young girl in a chic, white flannel sports costume tripped along the ridgepole of the garage just behind the court, others joined her and sat down. A painted white sign on the roof advertised in huge red letters that the garage did business at Cabourg in the summer; it was soon completely covered and the surface peppered with spectators. One could see the owner standing on the street below selling places at 100 francs apiece.

The stands filled; the general commanding the troops in the *Département*, the *préfet* of the Maritime Alps, the admiral commanding the French squadron in the harbor of Golfe Juan, the King of Sweden, the ex-King and Queen of Portugal, the Duke and Duchess of Westminster off their yacht in Monte Carlo, in fact half the peers and peeresses of the United Kingdom fought and argued for seats. The air became electric shortly after eleven when the two players took the court; Helen in a white middy blouse, a pleated white skirt and a rose-colored cardigan, Suzanne in a pleated tennis dress covered by a flimsy pink cashmere sweater. The one was stolid outwardly, sturdy, American; the other frail, emotional, effervescent, Latin.

The linesmen, all English because the English felt nobody else could be neutral and trustworthy, took their places. Commander Hillyard, tall, imposing, the president of the All-England Club and umpire at Wimbledon, climbed into his chair. Above, around me, workmen were still hammering boards into place; they continued throughout the match, with chairs handed up and people grabbing them. The streets around were black with hundreds standing, listening, unable to see, merely attentive to the sounds from the center court inside.

Helen, as the young challenger, was naturally nervous at the start, Lenglen winning the fourth and fifth games without the loss of a point, and taking the first set easily. Then the American brought up her heavy guns. That masterly forehand boomed into the corners or down the lines. She bored in to attack, something no player had ever dared against Suzanne. When lobbed, Helen went back on her toes and buried the ball. The crowd cheered as she led 3-1, then 5-4 in the second set.

This was the critical moment. Had Miss Wills been willing to hit out freely, been a trifle less discreet, a little less the disciple against the master at this point, she would surely have won the set and probably the match. But she hesitated. Suzanne's acute brain saw it. She shortened her length just when Helen needed speed to generate her pace. Soon the score was five games all.

In the twelfth game came the climacteric of the match. Suzanne had been drinking brandy handed by her mother each time they changed courts; she was visibly tiring, the strain was telling. She realized the challenge, put everything she had into every shot, led 6-5 and 40-15. Next came a long, nerve-racking rally. There was a silence over the court. Even the workmen stopped hammering to watch. Then Helen leaped at a forehand and powered it into the side line near the corner. A young British peer named

Lord Charles Hope was on the line. He said nothing, but Suzanne must have heard someone cry out, or felt certain the ball was out. She rushed to the umpire's chair and slumped upon a bench just below it.

Flowers, festoons, buckets, bouquets of flowers appeared from no place. Flashes shot from a dozen cameras surrounding her. Her little Peke in Madame Lenglen's lap barked furiously. Then, over the din, the confusion, the noise and the crowd, rose the giant figure of Charles Aeschliman, the Swiss singles champion and a *hôtelier* at Cannes.

That shot of Helen's had struck the line and was good. Consequently the score was now 40–30, the match was unfinished. Charlie waved the spectators back off the court. It was an awful moment for Suzanne. The contest, apparently won, was not over. Instantly she jumped to her feet.

"The ball was good? Then the match must go on."

Uncertainly she walked back to her place behind the service line to resume play again. It was like seeing a goddess in pain.

She lost the point, then the game. The score was now 6–all; obviously it was anyone's match. But Suzanne was a champion and champions react to a crisis. She did not fail nor falter before the challenge. Gathering herself together, using that fadeaway backhand, she teased Miss Wills with short-length shots, draining the Californian's strength and giving her no chance to attack. Helen lacked the experience to exploit the opportunity. When boldness was essential, she made the mistake of falling into defensive tactics. The next two games went to deuce, but Suzanne won both, finishing with a perfect smash of a deep lob. Only a champion could have made it. The ordeal was over, the toughest match of her career, also her greatest triumph. Even the ranks of Tuscany, the packed rows of English and Americans in the expensive seats, could scarce forbear to cheer.

Suzanne, that lithe and amazing woman, was not just a tennis player any more than Picasso is just a painter. She was above all a great human being. Her brains, her skills, her intelligence have never been equaled by any woman tennis player. She was an artist with ball control, and she seemed to bring the spirit of the ballet to the court; she made tennis a light and aerial dance in which her white silhouette moved from one phase of the contest to another without breaking a line. She was a fairy queen and her adversaries clumsy fumblers struggling to return her drives. Hazlitt put it best in his description of Cavanaugh, the Fives player: "There was not only nobody equal, but nobody second to him."

One thing about Suzanne was certain; only France could have produced her. A daughter of the Midi, she had coal-black hair, an olive complexion and no doubt Moorish, Jewish and Latin blood flowed in her veins. Her nose was large and her face lined even when young, for all her life she suffered from anemia, the disease which carried her away at forty. She had the gay seriousness of the Parisienne, and never forgot the importance of being feminine. Ugly she was, yet with such charm that I once saw her enter a Riviera drawing room full of exquisitely dressed women, and suddenly they all became commonplace and dowdy.

Born in Nice, tutored—and often bullied remorselessly—by her father, M. Charles Lenglen, the secretary of the Tennis Club de Nice, she had the same advantage as Californians, that is, year-round competition. During her best years she went through tournament after tournament and match after match, seldom losing more than a game a set. With a wrist of steel, remarkable coordination and footwork, she did not play, she commanded on the court. In the years ahead I saw many great players of her sex; Mrs. Hazel Wightman, Mrs. Molla Mallory, Mrs. Helen Wills Moody, Miss Helen Jacobs, Miss Alice Marble, Miss Maureen Connolly, but there was only one Suzanne. Along the Riviera, people who had never seen a tennis racket flocked to watch her as those who knew nothing of ballet went to see Ulanova or Margot Fonteyn. The day she competed several hundred spectators would stand in the hot sun of Provence when all seats were taken, waiting an hour or more for her match. The next afternoon perhaps twenty spectators paid to see ordinary mortals perform.

Suzanne had a French wit, so delicate that bores missed it. She also had a mind of her own. In 1926, when scheduled to play at Wimbledon, she reached the semifinals, with her singles match to be followed by a doubles. That afternoon the tournament committee came to her in distress. Queen Mary was visiting the championships, or, as the English call them, The Championships, and was not due to arrive until after tea. Could she, therefore, rearrange her schedule so she played the doubles first, and the singles later when the Queen had arrived?

Suzanne did not hesitate. No, she replied, the singles is important, later the light will be bad. If the Queen wants to watch it, she must arrive at the hour scheduled like everyone else. The committee stammered, stuttered, insisted. She remained firm. In the end they forced her to default, something against the rules of courtesy if not of tournament lawn tennis. She never played Wimbledon again, and there was much discussion in the London press of her strange French character, and what was termed her "temperament." Ah, Suzanne, in an epoch when champions were becoming neutral, colorless and insipid, you had character in life as in sports.

Her last years were spent teaching children.

I happened to be in Paris when she died, in the summer of the war, 1939. This woman who so loved flowers and sunshine was taken from her house submerged in roses in the full noontide. Two hearses packed with flowers followed. Behind stretched a throng all the way down the long Rue de l'Assumption. First were a dozen rows of small children crying as children cry when they have lost a friend. Then walked Léon Blum, a former premier of France, half a dozen cabinet ministers. Other friends followed, Georges Carpentier, the boxer; the Swedish ambassador; Lucien Gaudin, the fencing champion. Next came the Four Musketeers: Cochet, Lacoste, Borotra and Brugnon. After them hundreds of persons who never knew her but simply followed the cortege to show their respect for this woman.

Although she dominated European tennis for fifteen years, she never provoked jealousy or enmity. She was too far ahead of her rivals, she could beat them with ease, yet without arousing anything but their admiration. All her life was like that. All her life she hurried, never pausing for repose. That hot August morning in Paris she went slowly to her rest.

One for All

by TED TINLING

Four Frenchmen decisively ended Bill Tilden's reign in amateur tennis—the Four Musketeers: René Lacoste, Henri Cochet, Jacques Brugnon and Jean Borotra. They had planned it that way. Ted Tinling—who was later to come to fame as a fashion designer—remembers the emergence of these champions from the viewpoint of a friend, occasional tournament promoter and official, and would-be world-class player himself.

"ALL for one and one for all." A philosophy born from a motto, or was it more likely a motto born from a philosophy? Either way, this was the heart, soul and dedication of the four adventurous Gallic tennis characters, the French Musketeers.

Jacques ("Toto") Brugnon, Jean Borotra, Henri Cochet, and René Lacoste climbed individually, and side by side, to a summit of achievement unequaled by any one band of men before or after them in the world of tennis.

In their days, the most highly regarded tennis titles were the championships of France, Wimbledon and America. Above all, the team event of the Davis Cup stood highest in prestige.

In 1922–23 they won their own championships in Paris for the first time. In 1924–25 they won the French championships and Wimbledon. In 1926 they captured the French, Wimbledon and American titles.

In their peak period of 1927–28 France took every major tennis honor. The vertical red, white, and blue stripes of the Tricolor fluttered triumphantly over every championship court in the world, plus the Davis Cup.

Concurrently, their individual efforts were no less memorable than their team victories. In the period 1924–32 the Musketeers collected no fewer than nineteen major titles among them.

In the Davis Cup team event, after chipping away at the might of Australia, then America, their additional corporate triumph was to hold the Davis Cup from 1927 to 1933.

They gave a golden era to France. Together with Suzanne, they created joint legends never to be forgotten in world sport, and their struggles with the mighty Tilden will forever remain classics of the game.

There is only one possible comparison to the legend of the Musketeers, the Australian teams of the fifties and sixties, so carefully selected and nurtured by their captain and coach Harry Hopman. But even the Australian teams, spread over a much larger stable and also a longer time period, fell at times to the challenge of the Americans.

Harry achieved a comparable degree of national unity that resulted in four winning spells. Four, three, four, and four years respectively, were the magic numbers. But whereas the Australian teams needed the master chef, Hopman, to select and blend the ingredients, the Frenchmen were contrasting and individual personalities drawn together only by the common cause that was France.

The phenomenon of the French quartet was the span of a decade in their ages and the fact that all four emerged from quite different social backgrounds. Brugnon and Lacoste were Parisian, Cochet was from the provinces, while Borotra was from the Basque country, an area of southwestern France where the people have a pride of heritage comparable to Wales's independence in Britain.

As a team, each one of the Four Musketeers made so essential, yet individual, a contribution that it is difficult to give pride of place to any particular one.

On reflection, it is probably logical to think first of the oldest. This was Brugnon, though, of the four, he made the least impact in singles.

Brugnon's amenable personality made him the cornerstone of the Musketeers' success. He was "Mr. Dependable" in this mix-and-match, a model team member, always ready and willing to help iron out any problems with his friends on the practice court, as well as advise or comfort them.

Cochet, the most successful major tournament winner of them all, said, "In the victories of the French team, Toto had a role that surpassed all he had already done with his racket."

Brugnon was a master of doubles play, brilliant on the volley and remarkable on the return of serve. His only weakness was overhead, but he was able to cover this against most opponents with a high, round-arm "slap." Brugnon was the perfect foil for all his teammates in doubles, always encouraging whichever partner he might have, and apparently incapable of a moment of bad humor.

I remember calling a line for Toto when he played Gerald Patterson on Wimbledon's Centre Court in 1928. I infuriated Patterson by calling one of his cannonball services a fault when it was good. At the change of ends, he picked up a roll of adhesive tape from the umpire's chair and threw it at me. Brugnon was actually embarrassed for me. "I'm not going to dispute a pre-

sent," he said with a smile. "But that is not the way to behave and I apologize for him."

It was the combination of Toto's many charming characteristics that made Papa Lenglen decide he would be the ideal mixed doubles partner for Suzanne and together they were never beaten. And it was through this partnership that I had the pleasure of becoming a close friend of Toto's.

French tennis had been spearheaded by Maurice Germot, Max Decugis, Marguerite Broquedis, and Suzanne. Between the original elders of the men's game and the Musketeers, came André Gobert and a Belgian, William Laurentz, who became a Parisian by adoption. It was perhaps natural that Brugnon, being the oldest of the Musketeers, was the first to emerge internationally, with either Gobert or Laurentz as his partner.

Toto was awarded his initial French laurels in the 1920 Olympic games at Antwerp, then in a Davis Cup match against India in 1921. The next year saw the emergence of Borotra and Cochet, followed in 1923 by the "Crocodile," Lacoste.

Jean Borotra, a master showman, and a magnet of appeal in every country, could not have been more of a contrast to Brugnon. Charm was the mutual trait of all four Musketeers, but Borotra had his own unique expression that set him apart from his colleagues. He was an extrovert in both personality and tennis style.

Borotra did it his way. His effervescence on and off court was both astounding and exciting. The English loved all the things he represented in French chivalry, from his invariable hand-kissing to the unending flattery he bestowed on all.

Jean would always announce his arrival at Wimbledon by sending Norah Cleather, Dudley Larcombe's assistant, a gigantic basket of crystallized fruit. A pioneer of air travel, he would wing into London accompanied by his secretary, Suzanne Duboy, and his faithful chauffeur/valet, Albert, setting up residence at the old Carlton Hotel.

Wimbledon was a continual whirl of engagements for Jean, and Mlle. Duboy always had to be on hand to grapple with his personal business, shielding her boss from the admiring hostesses who deluged him with invitations for their parties and official functions.

He had an apparently endless succession of friends, business contacts and followers, and it became a full-time job arranging tickets for even a fraction of them to see his matches. Norah Cleather spent countless hours with Mlle. Duboy over Jean's ticket problems. "But Mees Clezair, M'sieu Borotra must 'ave ze tickettes, 'e 'as already promeesed zem." I was never quite sure which of the two girls had the final say in these discussions.

Typical of Borotra was his showering of gifts on those around him. Even after he lost to Cochet in the great 1927 Wimbledon final, he sent Norah a gold trinket with the very sporting inscription: "From Your Most Troublesome Runner-Up."

The corporate chivalry of the Musketeers made the perfect complement to Norah's own charm. She happened to be a very beautiful woman, and the setting in her office, much of which was provided by the Musketeers, made a perfect backdrop to her beauty. Borotra's six-foot-high centerpiece of crystallized fruit was most often surrounded by yard-square boxes of chocolates put on the floor because they were too big for the tables. And I remember on one occasion counting no fewer than eighteen floral offerings that almost muffled the incessantly ringing telephones.

It was also a typical Borotra gesture that, as early as my second year at Wimbledon, he should present me with an autographed gold fountain pen.

Albert, after parking the much-traveled Hispano-Suiza car, was always in attendance, carrying an armful of rackets and the huge tennis kit complete with a hatbox full of Jean's traditional berets.

Habitually, he took six berets with him when he had a long match in view. Changing berets as he changed ends (and sometimes when he was not changing ends) was a danger signal for his opponents because it meant he was really getting down to business.

Then, in between matches at Wimbledon, the busy Basque would fly back to Paris for the inevitable important business meeting, returning the following day to excite the crowds all over again.

It was one such return trip to Paris that still rankles Pat Hughes, a Wimbledon doubles champion and a member of Britain's four winning Davis Cup teams in the 1930's. Hughes played Borotra in the second round of the 1928 Wimbledon, and because the Frenchman had his rush, cross-Channel trip scheduled for that evening, the match was played on a soaking-wet court. By rights it should not have been played at all on that wet day.

Halfway through, one of Borotra's catgut strings snapped with the damp. Borotra called to the ever-watchful Albert. "Pass me racket number 6 B," he said. The gesture was typical of Borotra and still rankles Hughes to this day.

Borotra had a natural flair for tennis, with a flair for showmanship as well. He delighted the crowds, more often than not infuriating his opponents.

One such display of showmanship occurred in a Wimbledon doubles with Toto Brugnon in the early 1930's. In this game Borotra chased a wide ball that most players would have ignored, and finished the stroke in the laps of two startled female spectators in the second row of the stands. He managed to get the ball back into play. Then, helped to his feet, found time to kiss the ladies' hands while Brugnon kept the rally going, miraculously, for three shots. Seemingly from nowhere, Borotra then swooped from the stands to smash away a winning volley. One can imagine the reaction of the pro-Borotra crowd! I saw the incident nearly fifty years ago, and still find it difficult to understand how he managed it. It was vintage Borotra at its best!

This kind of dramatic escapade always annoyed Tilden intensely and produced another of the bitter feuds of tennis. Tilden thought that he alone should be master of every stage. Tilden once declared that he never lost to anyone he hated, and he certainly hated Borotra's "antics," as he called them. He once described Borotra as "the greatest faker in tennis history."

One might suppose that Borotra and Suzanne would have been involved in a comparable clash of personalities. They did not share any great affection for each other, but because they were both French and Tilden despised them equally, they fought for France as a common cause. It was the Tricolor vs. the Stars and Stripes. Fortunately for the Tricolor, Molla Mallory was never quite good enough to make her partnership with Tilden comparable to either Lenglen and Borotra or Lenglen and Brugnon.

When I visited Marguerite Broquedis in Orléans after the Wimbledon Centenary, she had some amusing memories of an amorous young Borotra. Marguerite was described to me as a "goddess" by Borotra, and he led a long line of men always anxious for the opportunity of flirting with her.

At one reception she was sitting between Borotra and Brugnon and Jean was making under-the-table advances with his hands. Marguerite told me she got bored with his constant passes at lunch time and told him to calm down. Borotra, of course, was only stimulated by the rebuff, so she told Brugnon to say nothing as she was going to play a trick. Marguerite moved slightly back. Pretending to use her compact as an excuse, she maneuvered her legs out of Borotra's reach and the groping Borotra then found himself stroking Brugnon's legs. Marguerite's still beautiful eyes laughed as she recalled the embarrassment she had caused him.

The effervescent smiles, the gallantry, and the hand-kissing routine made Borotra a hero in England. To the English he represented the actions, grace and charm that English women rarely received from their own men.

However, underneath the extrovert behavior, beat the heart of a real competitor, a man who never recognized Papa Lenglen's philosophy of giving up in the face of defeat. It was his enormously competitive spirit that made it possible for him to become the first-ever Frenchman, not only to reach the final at Wimbledon, but win it.

Borotra's rather ungainly tennis style derived from the game of pelota (*pelote basque*), a native game of Basque origin. In pelota, players use a "chistera," a sort of banana-shaped glove made from wicker, to project the ball against a wall. This results in an awkward gesture from the backhand side and needs a sharp twist of the wrist, which looks very unnatural when performed with a tennis racket. There certainly seemed to be a carry-over of pelota into Borotra's tennis. He chipped his forehand and stabbed at his backhand to such a degree that some people thought he used the same face of the racket for both shots. This was not so, but his style was very different from his contemporaries', particularly in an era when the classic Continental forehand was considered a basic hard-court technique.

However, Borotra's athleticism, his unique capacity to move laterally across the net (only comparable in my experience with Billie Jean King at her best) made Borotra almost impossible to pass. His knack of exploding from the starting blocks, enhanced by his already telescopic reach, fully justified the nickname the "Bounding Basque" that the English press was quick to give him. In French newspapers "Basque Bondissant" sounded equally appropriate and impressive.

Henri Cochet, from Lyon, was essentially the product of that industrial, hard-working city. He was the tough little "bantam-cock" of the four, a fighting mixture of aggressiveness and determination when the chips were down but with a dry wit that spilled over irresistibly whenever something unusual or incongruous caught his eye.

Henri's wit was based on keen observation and a sharply sarcastic mind, but his wisecracks were never delivered in a sarcastic way.

When I finished my first year as assistant director of the French championships in 1928, I marked the occasion with a gold identity bracelet. Bracelets for men were a novelty in those days, and on mine I had engraved what I thought a natural souvenir of some very happy days. The inscription read: "Championships of France, 1928," and I often looked at my wrist with pride.

As soon as I began wearing it, Henri observed the inscription without any appearance of noticing it at all. Quite innocently he asked, with his usual dry grin, "Which event did you win in the French championships, Ted?" No sarcasm, no put-down, such things were unknown to him. He was a true "copain," which is the closest the French language gets to the word "buddy."

As a buddy, he was always prepared to help out if possible. I was running one of the late 1920's Riviera tournaments in George Simond's absence and I hoped desperately for the status of Cochet's entry. However, with his forthcoming international schedule it seemed an impossibility. But when he understood how much his participation meant to me, he immediately agreed to rearrange his plans.

I remember one evening in that happy week when he even suggested we have a hit, and he concentrated on showing me the great tactical value of a cross-court forehand dink. I went around like a dog with six tails for the next two weeks thinking about my Cochet dink. I lost it all again because it had been learned too quickly. But in later years I did adapt it to my own game, and it served me a thousand times in doubles when I became a circuit player. For years I always remembered Henri whenever I heard my opponent bitching as the ball drifted sweetly across him into the right-court alley!

Cochet had that rare quality of being able to lift his game whenever a situation arose that triggered the necessary reflexes.

At Wimbledon in 1928 I was filling in for an absent linesman on Centre Court when Cochet was playing the semifinal singles against Christian Boussus. Boussus was heir apparent to the French Musketeers and was edging into world class. In this particular match Cochet had lost the second set and was well on the way to losing the third.

I had the outside line, the farthest removed from the umpire. This is a long way away at Wimbledon because of the unusual length of the runback. Cochet appeared totally bored with the whole proceeding, and at one point, ignoring the ball boys, he wandered aimlessly toward my corner to pick up some stray ball himself.

As he came toward me, I spoke to him in French. "Henri, you are a bore to take so long. I have seats for the theater tonight and really wanted to make it." His eyes lit up immediately. Some new and totally extraneous interest had

appeared that was the signal to rub the Aladdin's lamp of his genius. "Ah," he said. "You want to go to the theater?" He lost only three more games and turned to me from the umpire's chair with the wry grin I knew so well. "Will you make it now?" he asked, as I ran off the court like a scalded cat.

Another time, I was calling a line for a Riviera mixed doubles final in which his partner was Diddie Vlasto. They had a long lead in the final set, but only managed to clinch it at 13–11 nearly an hour later. Leaving the court, I found myself beside Diddie, saying how unnecessary it had been for them to take so long.

"Henri is always the same," Diddie said. "For him it is the impossible which is the easiest. Sometimes the easiest is the impossible." Diddie obviously shared my feelings that the match could have been won much earlier had Henri made a few bread-and-butter shots at the crucial points instead of attempting his favorite miracles.

Even against top-class players, Henri's miracles derived from his amazing capacity on the half-volley. Notoriously one of the most difficult shots in tennis, the half-volley was a natural reflex to Cochet on both wings. With this approach he reached his favorite net position without making any visible attempt to get there. He probably had the world's finest overhead, and once installed at the net, it was pretty much curtains for any opponent other than a Tilden, Borotra or Lacoste. Even Tilden went on record as saying, "Cochet plays a brand of tennis I shall never understand."

Henri had a very sharp eye for everything, including pretty girls. In mixed doubles he invariably partnered the prettiest of the good players in the tournament. Pretty girls were the only influence likely to subdue his determination to win. This is probably why Henri never won a mixed doubles title at Wimbledon and only two in Paris, in sharp contrast to Brugnon's seven.

The greatest contrast among the Four Musketeers was René Lacoste, a pale, studious, young man with soulful dark eyes, and a Semitic profile. He was the archetypal student of everything. Everything he did was prethought out and preplanned to the utmost detail.

He was a frail teenager, and at fifteen his father told him to give up sport altogether. It is a testimony to Lacoste's extraordinary dedication that, by the age of twenty, he was the Wimbledon champion and at twenty-one was also champion of the United States.

From the outset, René knew in his heart that he had the makings of world supremacy provided he was allowed enough time to study the mechanics and technique of tennis. Even the dimensions of different areas of the court always figured in his calculations and he would sit for hours taking copious notes on every player he was likely to meet in a match.

There was definitely something machinelike in his approach to the game. He was a dyed-in-the-wool base-liner, with the same abundant energy as Suzanne's to practice for long hours.

In fact, he gives credit to Suzanne for showing him the importance of "target grouping" his shots. One of my clearest memories of calling Suzanne's matches is of her ability to place three consecutive shots within an inch of each other, the marks being clearly visible on the red French clay courts.

Never satisfied he was getting enough practice, René was one of the first to conceive a ball machine against which he spent countless hours a day, working at whatever shot he thought needed strengthening or tuning, even after the longest matches. Tilden said he sometimes thought he was playing the ball machine and not Lacoste at all.

Then, after hours on the court, he would return home to practice his strokes in front of a full-length mirror. During a spell when he thought he had lost his service swing he saw a photograph of himself serving with a bent elbow. With his usual studiousness he traced the bent elbow. In practice in his bedroom he had been avoiding the chandelier. From then on his team captain, Pierre Gillou, always insisted on a room for Lacoste with no hanging lights.

In René's youth, and with this studious approach to the game, Tilden's unsurpassed knowledge made him Lacoste's idol, eventually

the man to beat at all costs. From the day at St. Cloud in 1921 when Lacoste first set eyes on Tilden, to beat Big Bill became the all-consuming passion of Lacoste's youthful life.

It took him five years to achieve this. The year 1926 saw the first fatal piercing of Tilden's armor. Borotra had already thrown down the French glove by beating Tilden indoors, but Tilden had never previously lost to a Frenchman on an outdoor court.

Lacoste, who had been in poor health in the spring, took three months away from tennis, to the point of foregoing Wimbledon, to tune up for the assault on America, even though he was the defending Wimbledon champion at the time.

Very appropriately, *The New York Times*, reporting Lacoste's comments on the Lenglen-Wills match at that same period, described Lacoste as "a young man who bears the weight of his twenty-one years very much more seriously than does Miss Wills the burden of her twenty."

Tennis always came first and last with Lacoste. During most Wimbledons the French team would be Lady Wavertrée's houseguests. However, Lacoste would separate himself as much as possible from the social round of her life. Wimbledon is a peak of the London season and the price he paid for being Sophie's guest was having to endure, on the way to Wimbledon in her car, an endless flow of socialite chatter, whereas his normal inclination before any match was for two hours' meditation or, at least, silence.

René was never an instinctive volleyer and rarely went in to volley unless forced to do so. I remember one telling point in his semifinal against Tilden at the 1928 Wimbledon. He had made one of his rare forward sallies, probably because it was set point to him, but he had to take three bites at the cherry before being able to put the ball away. Each time he put the ball almost onto Tilden's racket. Tilden told me he was so surprised himself that he could not manage to get the ball past Lacoste either. Eventually, out of sheer frustration, René let fly an almighty swat with both hands, falling flat on his back in the process. But he finally won the point and the set.

Lacoste's single-mindedness and his style of play made him the least flexible doubles player of the four Musketeers. He won one Wimbledon and two French doubles titles, with the mercurial Borotra compensating for his inflexibility, but while Lacoste's teammates revered him as a singles player, Cochet and Brugnon considered themselves the crack team and never thought they should lose to him in doubles.

I have an amusing memory of the relationship between these outstanding characters. I was walking back to the locker room with Henri some hours after the second French doubles title won by Lacoste and Borotra against Brugnon and Cochet. As Brugnon came toward us from the opposite direction and passed us, without a turn of the head or a change in expression, Brugnon's and Cochet's eyes met and they both said "Merde."

This single simultaneous utterance from them both illustrated their feelings about their loss more vividly than any argument or subsequent inquest could have done in hours.

It was in 1923, in a Davis Cup match against Ireland in Dublin, that the famous Musketeers conducted the first of their memorable campaigns as a foursome. Brugnon,* the eldest, was a month past his twenty-eighth birthday and Lacoste, the youngest, was still a month short of being nineteen.

During the Wimbledon Centenary I was already engaged in writing *Love and Faults*. Knowing full well the complexities of Jean Borotra's character, while at the same time remembering our half-century of friendship, I asked him, "Jean, from your long years in tennis, what do you now regard as the ultimate highlight which gave you the most pleasure?"

With his normally instant reflexes, I was surprised when he took quite a few moments before replying, "Of course, winning Wimbledon and being the first Frenchman to do so."

Then he dipped deeper into his memory. Fifty-five years had passed since his Davis Cup debut and an expression of great nostalgia crossed his face. "I think the most treasured

memory of all," he said, "is of the wonderful unity of spirit we evolved in the French team. In today's circumstances nothing comparable is even conceivable. Our winning the Davis Cup in Philadelphia was a crowning moment of national pride and emotion that has to be incomprehensible to those who never experienced it."

The team spirit and the crowning victory referred to by Jean derived from long-thought-out and preconcerted battle plans. The French boys had decided the beating of Tilden was the heart and soul of the affair. The Musketeers knew from previous experience that in the 1927 Philadelphia Challenge Round they would need more than one hero to achieve their dream.

They knew Tilden would be called upon to play all three matches: Two singles and the double. Tilden was then thirty-four, and the French plot was that by wearing him down in the first two days, they could conceivably deliver the fatal slingshot on the last day.

Little Bill Johnston had been called out of semiretirement because of Frank Hunter's previous failures against the Frenchmen and did not appear to pose any great threat. One falter by Tilden was all they needed for victory.

The French team was calm and deliberate in its preparation. Only the ultra-perfectionist Lacoste complained, first of losing his backhand, then his forehand, then both together. His teammates knew him well. He would be ready when the moment of truth came.

A tennis colleague of mine, called de Monteil, produced a very witty book of caricatures of these widely different personalities on their crusade. His drawing depicts the true scene on the eve of the match: Cochet forever on his toes, Brugnon cleaning his pipe and calmly reminiscing, Lacoste furbishing his weapons (in this case his crocodile), and Borotra telephoning agitatedly (probably to Mlle. Duboy).

In Philadelphia, chance gave them the draw they most hoped for: Tilden against Cochet on the first day, a fresh team of Borotra and Brugnon to play Tilden and partner on the second day, and the one Tilden feared most, the imperturbable Lacoste, for the showdown on the last day.

---

*Jacques ("Toto") Brugnon died in Paris, March 22, 1978, aged eighty-two.

In the opening match, Cochet played his preplanned part by running Tilden into the ground for four tough sets while Lacoste quickly disposed of Johnston in three.

Meanwhile Tilden was also being emotionally drained by his own selection committee being unable to make up their minds until five minutes before the doubles whether to pair Johnston or Hunter with Tilden. Eventually Hunter was chosen and Borotra-Brugnon further blunted Tilden's armor by keeping him on court for the full five sets. Rather tactlessly I mentioned this situation to one of the U.S. selection committee a few years later and his reply was, "You can't win a match when one of the team thinks he's God."

Big Bill, at loggerheads, again, with his own administrators, knew that he had to blast Lacoste off the court in quick sets if he were to survive the last singles. He played like a tornado in the opening set, but Lacoste, more than twelve years his junior, bided his time until Tilden had spent his all before moving in the for the *coup de grâce*.

Lacoste won in four sets. Cochet also beat Johnston in four sets. Thus the French Musketeers became the first and only team reared on slow hard courts ever to capture the Davis Cup from a home nation reared on turf. Brugnon dropped his pipe, Cochet grinned quizzically as usual, Borotra became his "Bounding Basque" self again, while Lacoste, allowing himself one brief moment of celebration, left immediately for some more practice.

The record says there were only thirteen French patriots in the Philadelphia crowd of thirteen thousand. But these thirteen included Suzanne Lenglen. She had been an integral part of the technical scheming and thus finally repaid Tilden for Molla Mallory's victory over her in which he played such a psychological part in 1926.

On May 20, 1927, Paris danced in the streets when Lindbergh landed after his historic first lone flight across the Atlantic. On September 10, 1927, Paris again danced in the streets, this time jubilant with its own national pride.

There was dancing in the streets a third time the following year. The USLTA did its best to hand the French the Davis Cup on its medallioned plinth by suspending its top player, Tilden, on the eve of the confrontation. This was not the first time Tilden controversies with the USLTA had reached the White House, and once again, as a result, Tilden was restored to the team at the last moment and at the personal instigation of the President.

He was supported only by Hunter and a newcomer, John Hennessy. His achievement in taking revenge on Lacoste was not enough and he succumbed to his old hex, Cochet, who led the French to their second victory.

That was the last Challenge Round for Lacoste. In his memoirs, Lacoste's close friend, Coco Gentien, recalls that almost immediately before the 1929 match in Paris, Lacoste was hospitalized with pneumonia. The French team captain, Pierre Gillou, visiting his sickbed and offering some would-be consolation, said, "Don't worry, your place in the team will always be waiting for you when you recover." In reply, Lacoste, who had just turned twenty-five, delivered one of the greatest-ever shocks to the French Federation, probably to the tennis world at large, when he replied, "I shall not be back. I am giving up tennis!"

Lacoste was the ultimate in single-mindedness. He achieved the goal set for himself as a boy, after five years of preparation beating Tilden and winning the Davis Cup for France. Now his thoughts could stray to other things, his health, his business future, both of new concern as he had recently fallen in love. The beautiful golf champion Simone Thion de la Chaume became his wife. It then took a great deal of persuasion for him to accept the captaincy of later Davis Cup teams.

With Lacoste in retirement, the Royal Flush of French Tennis was broken. Without Lacoste they needed the advantage of their home clay courts to retain the cup until 1933, when the British team of Fred Perry and "Bunny" Austin ended France's fourteen-year period of glory, which Suzanne had initiated.

The Greatest Match Ever Played at Forest Hills

by ALLISON DANZIG

Allison Danzig covered tournament tennis for more than forty years, developing a reputation as an astute critic of the game. He was the one reporter players would read to find out how they really *had played the day before. Here is his assessment of the greatest match he ever witnessed at Forest Hills—the downfall of Bill Tilden to René Lacoste in the 1927 final.*

IN calling the roll of the memorable matches played at Forest Hills in the sixty years since the West Side Tennis Club's opening production there—the Davis Cup Challenge Round with Australia in 1914—the two contests that remain indelibly in mind above all others involve the player I regard as the greatest who ever lived.

Strangely, it is the memory of his defeats that lingers on, rather than the triumphs that won him greater celebrity around the world than any other player had attained and recognition in his time as the greatest of all players.

The player: The late William T. Tilden II of Philadelphia. The two matches were played within the space of a year, in 1926 and 1927. His antagonists were not English, Australians or Americans, who among them ruled the courts for the first half-century of lawn tennis. The players who brought down the most autocratic, absolute

monarch of the lawn tennis racket were French—Henri Cochet and René Lacoste.

Cochet in 1926 administered Tilden's first defeat in the amateur championship of the United States since 1919, ending his six-year reign in the quarterfinal round. Lacoste, who had ended Tilden's perfect record for six years in Davis Cup singles, also in 1926, and beat him again in the 1927 Challenge Round, took on Tilden once more in the final round of the 1927 championship, in the role of defending title-holder. The biggest crowd to jam the four-year-old Forest Hills Stadium up to that time beheld what, to at least one press box tenant, was the greatest match ever played there—to that time and ever since.

This likely is the end of the line for the young clientele perusing here what to them probably amounts to idiocy—particularly those who are of the notion that modern tennis dates from the late 1940's when Jack Kramer and Ted Schroeder hit the Australians with what was called the "Big Game"—big serve and volley—and hit them so lustily that for four years the Aussies did not win a solitary match in singles. It's no use to explain to the young fry that the Big Game does not date from post World War II but, rather, was in use even before World War I. Specifically, Maurice (Red) McLoughlin was exploding cannonball serves in those days and following each and every one that wasn't an ace to the net to ram a volley down his opponents' throats.

Many matches could be nominated for "the greatest match ever played at Forest Hills." To be ultra-modern and completely bridge the gap of generations, what about the bruising, exhausting final no farther back than 1973, between John Newcombe, of the ponderous service and sledgehammer drive and poleax volley, and Jan Kodes of Czechoslovakia, undistinguished in his physical proportions but all muscle, whipcord, energy and intensified concentration.

Indeed, the Forest Hills panorama of sixty years is so vast, so starred with unforgettable drama involving heroes and heroines whose fame is legendary, that it would seem hopeless to undertake to invest any one match with distinction above all others. Nevertheless, I have forthwith singled out the two matches Tilden played against Cochet and Lacoste, and my problem is to choose between the two.

A consideration in settling upon these two is the fact that Tilden was the clear choice as the greatest player of all time in the vote taken as recently as 1969 by an international panel of tennis writers. Also, both Cochet and Lacoste were included in the top ten, at seven and eight, respectively.

So great is my personal respect for the three that in the 1969 vote I placed Tilden first, Cochet second and Lacoste fourth, behind Don Budge. If I regard Tilden as the greatest of all time—on strokes, physical attributes, intelligence, mastery of spin and tactics, fighting qualities, endurance and zest for the game—I regard Cochet as the greatest natural player, the player with the greatest flair, instinct and coordination to produce with the least effort and uncommon touch what Tilden and others had to strive for and persevere for years to achieve. His victory over Tilden in the 1926 quarterfinals was as great a sensation as the game had known.

A year following this epochal match, the equal of which I thought I would never see, came the one that stirred me more deeply in turn than has any other since—a match that transported fourteen thousand people into paroxysms of de-

lirious cheering and silenced them into chilling apprehension as Tilden fought the most ennobling fight of his career and won the hearts of a gallery in defeat as never he did in victory.

In this match, more than in any other I have seen, the apogee of attack was pitted against the epitome of defense. No one was more representative of the offensive player than Tilden, who had more weapons and resources for exploiting the weaknesses and overcoming the strength of his opponent.

The twenty-three-year-old Lacoste, phlegmatic and utterly expressionless, was the absolute master of defense. He was mechanically perfect, inexorable in the control and depth he maintained, impervious to fortune's fickleness, unshakeable in his concentration and in his alertness to the progress and changing pattern of the play and strategy. He stood as the greatest of all base-line players, a master of strategy who lobbed and passed with phenomenal accuracy.

For an hour and forty-five minutes, Tilden fought with desperation in one of the greatest matches of his career and one of the greatest ever played anywhere and yet he could not win a set—though he led 7–6 and 40–love in the first and stood at set point three times, led again at 3–1 in the second set and 5–2 in the third, holding set point three times more. He lost. Lacoste won, 11–9, 6–3, 11–9. I wrote in *The New York Times:*

"The spirit of Tilden was one thing that never broke. Long before the end of the match —yes, by the end of that agonizing first set which had the gallery cheering him madly and beseeching him to put over the one vital stroke that was lacking—those marvelous long legs of the Philadelphian were slowing up. By the second set, the fires of his wrathful forehanders were slumbering, and the third set found him a drooping figure, his head sunk forward, so utterly exhausted that not even the pitchers of ice water that he doused over himself could stimulate his frayed nerves, which must have ached painfully.

"It was a spectacle to have won the sympathy of even a French protagonist—the sight of this giant of the court, once the mightiest of the mighty, flogging on his tired body in the unequal battle between youth and age. If there were any French present, they did not make themselves known. One and all of those fourteen thousand spectators (it seemed) were heart and soul for Tilden as he made his heroic fight to prevent the last of the world's biggest crowns from going the way of all crowns.

". . . Late in the final set, the Philadelphian came back like a man from the grave to save himself from defeat twice by a single point in the fourteenth game. That game was the most agonizing a gallery ever sat through as a shell of a man stood off the inevitable in a classic exhibition of fighting entirely on nerve. . . . Lacoste reached 40–30, one point away from victory.

"The suspense was terrific as the next rally began, and when Tilden pulled up to deuce a sigh of relief went up. But the next moment Lacoste was again at match point. Again the French youth netted at the crucial point, and after deuce had been called five times, Lacoste drove out of court and Tilden whipped home a lightning drive down the line for the game.

"How they cheered Tilden! And when he won the fifteenth game quickly with his cannonball serve to lead 8–7 the crowd went wild with delight. Visions rose of victory for him, but they speedily vanished when Lacoste won the next two games. Once more Tilden had the gallery roaring when he broke through at love for 9–all. But that was the end. Dead on his feet, Tilden fought Lacoste tooth and nail in the nineteenth, which finally went to the younger player as he scored on three winners in a row, and then, utterly at the end of his rope, Tilden yielded quickly in the twentieth to bring the match to an end.

"It was a match the like of which will not be seen there again soon. . . . Both exponents of attack and defense were at their best, and the reaction of the gallery was that it had seen the best tennis can offer. As one spectator remarked: 'Everything else will seem stale after this match.' He had seen the zenith."

The Greatest Match

by DON BUDGE

On July 30, 1937, Don Budge of the U.S., the number-one-ranked player in the world, faced Baron Gottfried von Cramm of Germany, the second-ranked player, in the deciding match of the U.S.-Germany Davis Cup tie. Queen Mary was on hand and Adolf Hitler was listening intently to the radio. Play was spectacularly even through the first four sets, then von Cramm forged a 4–1 lead in the fifth . . . Budge recalls this as his greatest moment in tennis. Indeed, it was one of the greatest moments in of all sports.

HOWEVER hesitant I am to try to select the various "greatest" moments in my career—the best this, the most thrilling that, and so on—I certainly have no difficulty in naming the greatest match in which I ever played. It seemed to possess every element that could be called classic. The players, winner and loser alike, were only part of the whole scene. It was, simply, a supreme day for tennis and a triumph for all that the sport can mean.

There was high drama in every way. It was, first of all, crucial, a deciding Davis Cup match. It was competitive, long and close. It was fought hard but cleanly by two close friends. It was cast with the ultimate in rivals, the number-one-ranked amateur player in the world against the

number two. It was placed in the perfect setting, at Wimbledon, on the Centre Court, a piece of land that is revered in the game. There was a filled stadium. Queen Mary was on hand. Hitler listened intently to the play-by-play, and so did so many Americans that stock-market sales sagged during the action. There was so much that I think that day would have been well remembered even if the tennis had been pedestrian. There are other tennis legends that I have been involved in that are no more than that—legend, not truth—but I honestly do not think that anyone has ever had to embellish upon what actually happened when Baron Gottfried von Cramm of Germany and I played in the Interzone Finals of the Davis Cup on July 30, 1937.

As one of the participants, I have, of course, always found it impossible to evaluate objectively all that happened on the court that day and place everything in the right perspective. I do know, though, that I never played better and that I never played anyone as good as Cramm. Walter Pate, the United States team captain, said later, "No man, living or dead, could have beaten either man that day."

I realize too that a great many sports events get better and eventually find greatness with time and the retelling, but there was instant recognition of the quality of this match. It was, in

165

fact, Bill Tilden himself who I first heard declare that it was "the greatest tennis match ever played." He told me that, emotionally, clasping my hands, in the locker room only a few minutes after it was completed. The *London Times* correspondent wrote the next morning, "Certainly I have never seen a match that came nearer the heroic in its courage, as in its strokes, as this."

I suppose it was an hour or so after the match before I was at last able to dress and leave the locker room. I think it was almost nine o'clock by this time, but the midsummer sun wasn't down yet. I walked out and glanced up into the stands, and I was shocked because there were still thousands of people there, clustered together all over the stadium. It did not seem to me that they were talking much to each other or moving around. They did not seem to be ready to leave. It was as if they just wanted to stay there where they had watched the match. I've never seen anything like that, before or since, just all those people standing there and remembering, long after I had dressed and gone.

For weeks after the match I would often wake up in a sweat, dreaming of it again. In some way, it seemed to touch all of us who were part of it. So I know that the years have not honored the match as something better than it was. Obviously it is not for me to say whether it was truly the greatest match ever played, but I am sure of this, that however history will rank it, it was something very special.

It was already late in the afternoon, nearing four o'clock, when Gottfried and I at last moved out onto the court, to bow to Queen Mary and to play. Henner Henkel had just beaten Bitsy Grant in four sets to tie the score at 2–2 in the match between the United States and Germany. Gottfried and I, the two ranking amateurs in the world, were to play for it all.

The winner of the Interzone Final still would have to meet England, the defender, in the Challenge Round, but in just about everyone's view the winner of the 1937 Davis Cup would certainly be the survivor of the United States-Germany meeting. Fred Perry, who had led the English to victory in the competition for the previous four years, had turned pro, weakening the British team to a point where it would be a definite underdog against either of the challengers.

Thus it was, that if I won this one match the United States would almost certainly get the cup back across the Atlantic after a full decade in Europe. On the other hand, if Cramm beat me, the Germans looked just about as certain to win their first Davis Cup ever, a point not lost on Hitler himself, as it turned out. Perhaps he was still fretting about Jesse Owens.

Cramm was of the old German nobility. Whereas I had grown up learning tennis on the courts at Bushrod Park in Oakland, California, Gottfried had learned with such people as King Gustav of Sweden. But his real nobility was in his human qualities, rather than his lineage; he was one of the finest sportsmen in the world and perhaps the most popular of all the players. He also loved tennis. This match was to be one of his more than a hundred Davis Cup matches. As late as 1953 he was leading the West German team, and his strokes, like his honor, were so beautiful that he was always a threat, wherever he played.

As it turned out to be a match of such significance, it was only right that it should be staged at Wimbledon. I do not believe that any other sport possesses anything comparable to Wimbledon. It is a shrine and dripping with tradition, but the memories never dull the present. On the contrary, at Wimbledon the tradition seems to breathe life into the everyday and make it more significant. Besides, the courts are of the highest quality and the fans are the fairest and the most knowledgeable, so that it offers the finest in neutral surroundings, which was important this afternoon when a German and an American were playing.

I think that I realized early in the match that the crowd was slightly in favor of Cramm, but I could not be either surprised or disturbed at that reaction. The British fans had always been more than fair with me. Now, though, I was the only logical villain, for everyone loves the underdog and Gottfried was that even if he was number two in the world. I had beaten him in straight sets on this same Centre Court in the finals of the Wimbledon tournament only a couple of weeks ear-

Rough or smooth? Baron Gottfried von Cramm (left) and Don Budge pleasantly settle the issue of who will serve first. (Photo Courtesy of the USTA)

lier. Besides, and more to the point, the British team was supposed to have a slightly better chance against Germany than against the United States. Rooting for Cramm was sensible as well as sentimental. Maybe this was the last afternoon for a long time in which they cheered for a German in London. I never played Gottfried at Wimbledon again. Long before the next July the Nazis had trumped up some charges against him, rushed him through a kangaroo court, and put him in jail.

Of course I did have many English cheering for me, and I knew that I had a spirited American coterie rooting me on. Paul Lukas, the movie actor, had just about become an unofficial member of our team in the weeks before, and he had brought Jack Benny and Ed Sullivan along to the matches. I also had at least one American against me: Bill Tilden, who was the professional coach of the German team. Still, as the match wore on, I got the feeling that there was no one present who was really *against* either of us. It seemed that the longer we played, the more exciting and better the tennis became, the less the crowd really cared who won. The art of the match, and the competition, seemed to become much more important than the outcome. Here we were, the best two amateurs in the game, playing for both the individual and the national championships of the world, and playing on the most important court in the world, and yet somehow the magnificence of the game of tennis prevailed over all.

The ironic thing about the match was that right up to the time it started I had had hopes that it really wouldn't have to count for a thing. The matches with Germany had begun three days before, a Saturday. On this opening day Cramm whipped Grant in straight sets and I managed the same against Henkel. Then, after Sunday off, Gene Mako and I teamed up in the doubles Monday to beat Cramm and Henkel in four sets. We were very fortunate, for they had good leads in each of the three sets we won. But we won, so when I came into the locker room Tuesday before my match, I was hoping that Bitsy could beat Henkel, put us ahead 3–1, and make my match against Cramm relaxed and *pro forma*.

Unfortunately, however, Henkel defeated Bitsy easily, and before I really had time to console him, Teddy Tinling, the tennis-clothes designer, who was acting as sort of a sergeant-at-arms, was there in the American locker room, calling me. The main part of Teddy's job this day was to move things along at a brisk pace. The Royal Box was filled with Royal Family, and it was not to be kept waiting. In hardly any time at all, Tinling had me by one arm and Cramm by the other and was marching us off to play. Gottfried and I were bustled along so that we hardly had time to acknowledge each other, and Tinling had just about swept us out into the stadium when a phone rang. None of us paid any attention, but a locker-room man picked it up and called to Gottfried. "Mr. von Cramm," he said. "Long distance for you, sir."

"Come on, you can't keep Queen Mary waiting," Tinling said, tugging at Cramm, and myself, as well.

"But it might be an emergency," Cramm replied. I had to sympathize with Gottfried. As much as I would hate to get a long-distance call just before a match, I think it would be even worse to get a call but not take it and spend the whole match wondering who it was and what in the world it was all about. Tinling frowned but let Cramm pull free and go over and pick up the receiver. "Yes, hello," he said. "This is Gottfried Cramm." He spoke impeccable English, just as he did a half-dozen other languages. Teddy and I relaxed and did not pay much more attention until Gottfried finished speaking to the operator and suddenly switched to German. "Ja, mein Führer," was the first thing he said.

He said, in fact, little else but "Ja, mein Führer" for the rest of the conversation. He was firm throughout, though he spoke with respect. He showed no emotion. Teddy and I (and Hitler, for that matter) knew that Gottfried was less than enchanted with the Nazis. Finally, after a couple of minutes or so, Cramm hung up, turned sharply and walked over to Tinling. Teddy handed him his rackets back. "Excuse me, gentlemen," Gottfried said matter-of-factly. "It was Hitler. He wanted to wish me luck." That was all he offered, and there was time for no more. In a few steps we were marching into Centre Court, with the crowd rising and roaring all about us.

At this time, only a couple of weeks after I had beaten him to win my first Wimbledon, it was I who was clearly the favorite. Yet no matter how proud and confident you might feel—and I was, believe me—whenever you walked onto a court with Cramm, it was difficult not to feel that you were walking in his shadow.

I think the reason he irritated the Nazis so particularly was not so much just that he refused to go along with them, but that he looked and acted like the Nazis' propaganda said all Germans should. He was six feet tall, with blond hair, of course, cold blue eyes, and a face that was handsome to a fault. And more, Gottfried emitted a personal magnetism that dominated any scene he was a part of.

Later that year, in September of 1937, he came to Los Angeles to play in the Pacific Southwest Tournament. Most of the box-seat holders —I believe it was as much as 80 percent of them —got together in advance and agreed that in order to protest against the Nazi government, they would stand up and walk out of the stadium as soon as Cramm entered the court for the first time. Most of the movie people involved were enthusiastically behind the idea. So Cramm came out for his first match. They all looked at him, and even though they were all pledged to stand up and leave en masse, not one could make the first move.

They just looked at him and then at each other, and they suddenly found they could not do it to him. "When I saw that man, I just felt instant shame at what I was supposed to do," Groucho Marx told me later. And, of course, they were all relieved that they had not carried out the insult when they found out the next year that the Nazis had imprisoned Cramm. The Nazis eventually let him out, put him in the army, and sent him to the Russian front. At the time, the Germans desperately needed men of his training to be officers, but they sent Cramm to Russia as an enlisted man. He promptly won the Iron Cross for bravery. After the war Gottfried won another kind of fame for marrying Barbara Hutton. He also became a very successful cotton

broker in West Germany. In 1947 he was cleared by a special court of all the weird charges brought against him by the Nazis.

We still occasionally see each other. I can remember when I first met him, at Wimbledon in 1935 when I was nineteen years old and the ninth-ranked American, and suddenly found myself in the semis against Cramm, who was already second in the world to Perry. He sought me out on the players' porch and introduced himself as my next opponent. "Don," he said, as if I had no idea at all, "I'm Gottfried Cramm." He not only never used the "Baron," he never even used the "Von." The first thing we talked about was sportsmanship, which was appropriate, because he was, simply, the greatest sportsman I ever encountered. There was no one even close to him.

In 1935, for example, in the Davis Cup Interzone matches against the United States, Cramm and Kay Lund had Wilmer Allison and John Van Ryn at match point in the doubles. The Germans appeared to win the point and the match until Cramm volunteered that the ball had illegally nicked his racket. It cost Germany the match. But he was that way. From that first day I met him on the porch at Wimbledon he became one of the greatest influences upon my life. Gottfried Cramm's ideals bordered on being beautiful. I mean that.

This day in 1937 it was obvious to me as soon as the match began that his game this day was at a level with his demeanor. It was as if he was determined to make up for all his previous disappointments on this court, where, for three straight years he had lost in the Wimbledon finals—twice to Perry, this year to me. I realized very quickly that I would have to improve substantially on that last performance of mine were I to beat him again. Fortunately, I had no idea then how much I would have to improve.

Cramm had won the toss and elected to serve first, which as it worked out, was to be the case in each set. He held that first serve at love, I came back to win mine at 30, and we moved on that way, sharing service through the first eight games. In the ninth, I broke through. I didn't know it then, of course, but this was to be the longest game in the match—until the very last one. But then, at that time, ahead 5–4, I just felt pretty good. Hold my serve, take the set 6–4, and I'm winging.

There was no reason, either, why I shouldn't hold serve. It was moving well, I was getting it in deep, and Cramm had not been able to take more than two points off it in any game so far. Besides, I had fresh new balls. And the fact is that my reasoning was absolutely correct. I *did* serve well in the whole game. I held up the new balls and showed them to Cramm across the net. Right away, I smashed a beauty at him. It clicked right in. I never touched his return. I moved over and hit another beautiful first serve. I never touched his return. I hit another beautiful first serve. I never touched his return. I hit my fourth straight beautiful first serve. As a matter of fact, the only thing I hit in the game was beautiful first serves. And that was all he hit back. I never touched the fourth return either. Cramm had broken me back at love with four fantastic placements. I did not win the set at 6–4. He broke me again four games later, and *he* won the set 8–6.

The second set was much like the first, only now, increasingly, it was his serve that was dominant. I was holding my own and matching him, but with more difficulty. Tactically, we were both playing well, but he was having more success at getting to the net and staying there. He attacked incessantly, and kept me on the run and tried to exploit a bad patch of my forehand that showed up here.

For my part, as the set wore on, I found it more difficult to get to the net at all behind my serve. Eventually, I had to give up trying to do that altogether. Cramm was, as always, in such excellent condition that it was foolish of any opponent of his to introduce any waste motion into the game. By trying to rush the net after I served I was using many extra steps and a lot of extra energy every time I faulted and had to go back again for my second serve. And besides, the serves I hit that did go in—well, he was passing me with a lot of those anyway.

Therefore, I decided to put all the extra effort into the serve, hit it really hard, and lie back and try to take his return on the rise. Then I would attempt to come in to the net. This worked well, but I still had no defense for the placements he kept drilling past me no matter where I was. It was becoming a little discouraging. I was sure that I was playing tennis as well as I ever had before, but here I was one set down and struggling to stay even in the second. The fewer mistakes I made, the fewer still he made, and he held serve to 6–5.

Then in the twelfth game I roared right out to 40–love, but I let him off the hook and he took the next three points to catch me. We battled through two more advantages, and then for the first time, Gottfried got the advantage—and set point. He played to win it. He followed my serve in to the net and then took my return with a go-for-broke volley that swept past me and chipped the chalk off the back line. I was down two sets to none.

At this point I remember becoming more mad than analytical. Two things, in particular, kept going through my head. The first was that I was rapidly blowing what had been a very good chance to establish myself as the acknowledged number one in the world, the champion. Secondly, I knew I was doing what so many other Americans had done in past years: Come over to Europe, fare well at Wimbledon, and then play poorly in the Davis Cup. That was the one thing I had promised myself not to do, but I certainly was doing it. I called myself a lot of names.

At any rate, whatever I was thinking must have been right for me, for I promptly went out and broke his serve in the first game of the third set. For the second time in the match I was ahead, and I held on to 2–1. At this point I was serving, I had new balls, and I immediately fired off a beautiful batch of first serves. If all of this sounds slightly reminiscent of something else, it was. Exactly as in the first set, the last time I had been ahead, he blasted back four straight passing shots, broke me at love, and tied up the set. I was the unwitting pioneer of the instant replay, and to say it shook me up would be every bit of the truth. Happily, it was all so astounding, I think that it also shook up Cramm. I came right back in the next game and broke *him* at love. Touché.

I finished out the set at 6–4, and hurried off to the locker room for a welcome rest.

It was a warm, humid day, with just a touch of wind, the way warm days in England always are, and I was glad for the chance to take a quick shower and change into fresh clothes. Beyond that, there was little I could do. I don't remember talking to Captain Pate about much at all. How, after all, could I improve? Most matches, you know, are considered to be excellent technical performances if the number of winning placements equal the number of errors. In this match, both Gottfried and myself were to make *twice* as many placements as errors.

As a matter of fact, the only time in the whole match that one of us played poorly was when Cramm slacked off right after this rest period. I not only broke him at love in the first game, but I held my own serve and then broke him again to go ahead 3–0. Behind that much, Cramm then decided to junk the set and to try to save all he had for the final one. We went through the motions of playing it out to 6–2, and then he picked up the balls and began to serve in the fifth set, fifth match. The sun was still up and we would finish that night.

It was the first time I had ever played Cramm in a fifth set. I had a pretty good record in five-set matches, but his was unbelievable. He trained so hard and maintained such superb shape at all times that he often said that he figured that he had about a three-to-one advantage anytime a match entered a fifth set. If I had to be reminded of this fact, I knew that only a few days before he had won the key match against Czechoslovakia in the finals of the European Zone by the score of 3–6, 4–6, 6–4, 6–3, 6–2. Perhaps even more impressive than that, Cramm had won the French championships the previous year by lasting to five sets in almost all of his matches, and then finishing it off by beating Fred Perry 6–0 in the fifth set of the finals. This particular victory had, by itself, resulted in giving Cramm an almost mystical edge in long matches. Of course, he was a man of such tremendous bearing and presence that the other players seemed almost eager to present him with capabilities that possibly he did not truly possess. If you were the opponent,

however, coming into a fifth set it was not easy to ignore the mystique.

In this instance, while I could not be overcome by Cramm's fifth-set reputation, neither could I be deluded by his poor performance in the fourth set. I imagined that he was playing possum. Certainly, I never considered that he was tired. Perhaps Gottfried did become tired or hurt like the rest of us, but if he did he never showed it. The year before, in the finals at Wimbledon, I had seen Perry beat Gottfried 6–1, 6–1, 6–0. Obviously, something was terribly wrong with Cramm, but he never let on.

Afterwards, he admitted to the locker-room masseur that he had pulled a hamstring muscle in the second game of the first set. Instead of defaulting or asking for aid or seeking some solace in excuses, all he would do was apologize to Perry and the spectators for his poor performance. I pulled a hamstring once playing baseball, and it was all I could do to get out of a chair. Cramm didn't even seem to limp.

So now, as we entered our fifth set, I knew quite well that he would give no indication if he was tired. It didn't take me long to find out that that wasn't even worth speculating about. He took charge from the first, picked up momentum, broke my serve in the fourth game, and held his to move ahead 4–1. He had only to hold serve to run out the set easily.

In the stands there was a new, excited buzz, one of obvious anticipation. I did not notice it myself at the time, but in one section of the stadium, over where the other players were seated, there was an even livelier response. I was to hear about it in the greatest detail later.

It revolved about Tilden, who was the German coach. He had long been something of a private tutor to Cramm, and was close enough to him so that he often stayed in the Cramm family apartment when he was visiting Berlin. It was Tilden who had taught Gottfried to adjust his backhand grip in 1933, and the change had played a significant role in Cramm's rise to top world-class rank. Now Tilden was coach of the whole German team. It is, of course, not at all unusual for a pro in one country to coach another nation's Davis Cup team. But it is uncommon for a coach to maintain the post when it means working against his *own* nation. That is extraordinary, and a lot of people considered it, if not downright unpatriotic, at the least a little tactless of Bill.

But if his loyalties were divided, Tilden made it plain enough that his tennis allegiance was strictly with his employer. He was seated a few rows in front of our team's show-business friends—Benny, Sullivan and Lukas. They in turn were a few rows in front of Henner Henkel, who had come back to watch our match after beating Grant. Now, with Cramm ahead 4–1 in this last set, Tilden could not contain himself any longer.

He stood up in his seat and turned full around, looking up past Benny and Sullivan and Lukas to where Henkel was sitting. Tilden drew Henkel's attention, and then, without a word, but with only a large smug grin on his face, Tilden held up his hand, forming a circle with his thumb and forefinger—the traditional "it's in the bag" sign. Sullivan and the others saw it right away and were furious. Immediately, Sullivan leapt to his feet and began to try to tear his coat off. "Why, you dirty sonuvabitch," he hissed at Tilden. Lukas and Benny jumped up themselves and managed to pull Sullivan down and hold him. Tilden just smiled back and then sat down again, contented.

At this moment, out on the court, I was changing sides with Gottfried. I kept thinking: Is he really this invincible in the fifth set, am I going to go down just like all the others? Walter Pate threw me a towel, and I rubbed myself with it. "Don't count us out yet, Cap," I told him, perhaps with more courage than logic. "Look, I'm not tired and I feel great." And that was the truth. I won my serve at love and came back to 4–2.

I was at the net when I took the last point in the game, and in the walk back to receive serve I decided that it was time for me to try something new. The thought just struck me quickly that way; I really had no idea *what* I should try. But, after all, I could no longer take any solace in the hope that playing better than Cramm would reward me with the win. We were both playing too

well, and I was the one who was two games from extinction. I had to get lucky and I had to make my own luck. Okay, without thinking too much about the odds, I planned to play it half-safe and gamble on his second serve. I decided that if he missed the first one I would creep up several steps and attack his second serve, and then come to the net quickly behind it.

Looking back, I can't really consider this good strategy, because Cramm had such a controlled first serve that it was seldom that he did not get it in. Even when he missed, it was invariably off by only a hair. But if he missed—ah, *if*—well then I was in good shape because his second serve was pretty well typed for me. His second serve tended to be a high kicker. Against most players it was terribly effective, but in my case it just so happened that I had the type of backhand that made it possible for me to pick up the serve on the rise before the ball could take off on that big bounce. Also, moving up a couple of steps in advance of my usual position gave me that much better opportunity to hit the ball before it took the big hop. This also put me in better shape to rush the net afterwards. When I had been playing my normal, deeper receiving position, I couldn't force him enough to permit me to come rushing up and try to gain the net.

I have often wondered what happened to Gottfried at this point. Maybe I just got lucky with the law of averages. But I remember how anxious he was to get the balls to serve, and I think perhaps that he became just a little too impatient. The victory was so close now that perhaps for once in his life he lost the composure that he always guarded so well. But anyway, his first service, which had been so consistent throughout the match, failed him every time but one in this game, and that one serve was to be the only point he won. The other four times he served, he missed getting the ball in by just about the same slim margin each time. Each hit in almost the identical spot, at no more than two inches back.

And each time, of course, that gave me the chance to employ my new strategy. I moved up for that second serve. And located there, as I figured, I was able to catch his second serve be-

Don Budge feels that the greatest match he ever played was against Baron Gottfried von Cramm in the 1937 Davis Cup. Many feel it was just the greatest match ever. Period. (Photo Courtesy of the USTA)

proportions, we matched each other's serve to 6–all. Then, remarkably and suddenly, and without, really, any shots of distinction, I broke Cramm in the lucky thirteenth game and stood ahead for the first time in hours, 7–6.

Now, at last, I had only to hold my serve to win the match and the opportunity for the United States to play England in the Challenge Round. Clearly, after hours of play, I was now immune to pressure. This is why my first serve in the game went right smack into the *bottom* of the net. That either steadied me or embarrassed me, for I did manage to get the second serve in and even to win the point. He tied at 15–all, and then we repeated the sequence: 30–15, 30–all, and 40–30, the first match point of the long afternoon.

So, I guess, I played it too safe again. I was too tentative with both my serve and second shot. Cramm took the net easily, volleyed past me, and we were deuce. I came right back with a placement of my own for a second match point, but he took the net away from me again and once more tied the game. Moreover, when he was able to repeat the ploy on the next point, he moved ahead. Later, he also had one more game point, so that by the time I gained my fifth match point it was the eighteenth point of the game, and all of five minutes had passed since we had first played a match point way back there at 40–30. Five minutes under circumstances like these are like a month of 3–2 counts in baseball.

So once more I served. It was the 175th time that day I had made a first serve. What there had been of my cannonball had gone, but I managed to get enough on this one to clear the net and send it sufficiently deep so that Gottfried could not begin to move up and gain the net from me. But he made a beautiful long return that kept me far back in the court too. All I could do was trade long ground strokes with him. I hit a good backhand.

Cramm moved over to his right-hand corner, so that we were now both on the same side of the court, facing each other down my left-hand side. He caught my shot with a forehand and hit it cross-court. It was a beautiful shot, firmly hit, and it gave him the opening to move

fore it could bounce up and away. I hit each one back, hard and deep, putting Cramm on the defensive and myself at the net. Each of the four points that I won were made exactly the same way with a well-placed net volley on my second shot. I had the break I had to have, and I was back to 3–4.

He almost came right back and broke me in the next game, but twice in a row, as the score stood at his advantage, he punched backhands that went out, in the same spot, by inches. How many times in this match did these crazy things repeat themselves? After this sort of double jeopardy, I managed to hold and to tie the score at 4–4. As the tension grew to almost unbearable toward the net. He came up, crossing the court catty-cornered, following essentially the direction of his shot.

The ball was landing just inside my right side line, a bit deep of mid-court. I had hit my last shot far back on the other side of the court, and I had begun to move back toward the center as soon as I hit it. Now, however, when I saw Cramm place the ball so far over, I had to break into a dead run if I wanted to catch up to it. I could not worry about position at all any longer. In fact, as I neared the ball, just as it bounced in, I realized that my speed had brought my body too far forward. There was no way I could brace to hit the ball. As a matter of fact, there was suddenly no way I could keep from falling.

Instead, resigned to this indignity, I did the only thing I could. I kept going at full speed and just took a swipe at the ball. What did I have to lose? I was going to fall anyway. Then, immediately after I swung, I dived for the ground, preparing to break my fall. I could tell, though, as soon as I hit the ball that I had smacked it solidly, but only as I crashed onto the grass did I turn to look. The ball whipped down the line, just past Cramm's outstretched racket. He had come up fast and could cover all but about the last two feet on the right side of the net (his left). At my angle I could not have returned the shot crosscourt. I had been forced to try for a shot right down the line. Now I saw the ball slip past his reach.

By this point I was flat out on the ground, but so far outside the alley line that I could see around the net into much of the other side of the court. I could see the ball hit. I watched it kick up. But I had no perspective and no idea where the ball had landed. I waited for the call and then, suddenly, even before the linesman could begin to flatten out his hands in the "safe" sign, I could hear the cheers begin to swell. They were different cheers. The ball had landed, miraculously but perfectly, in the corner. I had hit the one possible winning shot. I was told later that the ball landed at a point less than six inches from being out *two* ways—to the side and long.

But now the roars were greater and more excited, and here I was, still lying flat out on the

ground. Gottfried, the noble loser, had to stand at the net, waiting patiently for me, the winner, to get up off the ground. I rose, finally, bewildered, and rushed toward him. I tried to hug him, but before I could he stopped me and took my hand. "Don," he said, evenly and with remarkable composure, "this was absolutely the finest match I have ever played in my life. I'm very happy that I could have played it against you, whom I like so much." And then he pumped my hand. "Congratulations." Only then was it, at once, that we threw our arms about each other. I think we both wanted to cry.

I know I was still in a daze in the locker room. It was as if everyone was trying to outdo each other in congratulating me. Tilden came in, and it was right then that he came over and told me it was the greatest tennis match ever played. Others had about the same thing to say as Tilden did—everyone, that is, except Jack Benny. He came in with Lukas and Sullivan, and while they were raving on at length, Benny just shook my hand and mumbled something like "nice match," as if I had won the second round of the mixed doubles at the club. I remember, Jack Benny was the only calm person in the whole locker room. The place was like a madhouse.

Finally, they were all gone and I was able to walk out into the night, out to where all those people still were, milling about their seats. Someone drove me back to the Hurlingham Club, where the team had its meals, but I was too excited to eat. I called my parents, but that only made me more excited still, so I finally just left everyone and took a walk. At last it was getting dark, but I don't remember much except that I left Hurlingham and walked all around Putney Bridge. Later, sometime, I came back and had a bowl of beef soup, and then I fell into bed.

We had to begin to prepare for playing the Challenge Round almost immediately. We managed well enough, I guess, because we beat the British 4–1, which was expected. But I don't think we were actually as well prepared as we might have been if it had not been for the excitement of the Cramm match. I know that I, anyway, could not put that match out of my mind for a long time. Even after we had played and beaten the English, there were still nights when I would wake up in a sweaty nightmare. It was always the same one. It was me behind 4–1 in the fifth set, and Gottfried was looking at me from across the net.

And even after the bad dreams ended, it was still worth speculating about what would have happened had I not pulled the match out. For one very obvious thing, it is likely that if we had not won the cup but would have had to challenge for it again the next year, 1938, I certainly would not have had the opportunity to try to win the Grand Slam of tennis. I probably would have been too busy working with the team for various preliminary zone matches to concentrate on individual play. Of greater importance, it is even possible to assume that the Germans would have had the Davis Cup when the war broke out and that it would have been in Nazi hands for many years. And if winning the greatest match ever meant the chance for the Grand Slam for me, losing it may have been the first step to jail for Gottfried. Would Hitler have dared to imprison him had Cramm brought the tennis supremacy of the world to the Third Reich?

But it was our team that brought the Davis Cup home to the United States a few weeks later. After I won at Forest Hills I went out to Los Angeles to play in the Pacific Southwest Tournament. After my first-round match there, which was a rather normal, unexciting one, I looked up from my locker, and who should be coming at me but Jack Benny. He was positively beside himself,

hardly pausing to say hello before he launched into a babbling, endless dissertation on how wonderful, how exciting, how fantastic the Cramm match had been. It was like one of those scenes from his show. I would keep trying to interrupt him, unsuccessfully. "But Jack—" I would try to start. And he would go right on.

"Magnificent, Don. It was just marvelous. Why when you—It was incredible. And then you —Why, I've told everybody about it." And on he went.

"But Jack—" I kept on, so that at last he stopped long enough to take that pose he is famous for, the palm cupped on his cheek, staring at me curiously. "Jack, I don't understand," I began. "At Wimbledon, after the Cramm match, you were the only person I met who was relaxed and calm. Now you carry on like this. The match was two months ago. Then you were unmoved. Now you're jumping around all excited. What is it?"

"Don," he said. "The truth is, that the Cramm match was the first tennis I ever saw. Now since then I've seen others, but at the time I thought all matches were more or less like that." I told him I was sorry, I would try to do better in the future when he was watching, but that it was a tough act to follow. I never again played in such a glorious match or had the thrill of coming out of the locker room and seeing people still standing there, refusing to leave, just savoring the experience and knowing they would never forget it.

The Grand Slam—
My Favorite Invention

by DON BUDGE

It's a fact that the first person to ever win the Grand Slam in tennis—the singles titles of France, Wimbledon, Forest Hills and Australia—was Don Budge. What's less well known is that the goal didn't exist until Budge set his mind to it, inventing the feat by accomplishing it. And this in the day of sea travel, when such an achievement required competition on three continents and a year-long, iron-nerved resolve.

EXCEPT for a fluke, I might not have been the first person to win the Grand Slam of tennis. Jack Crawford of Australia really deserved to have accomplished that in 1933, five years before I did. Of course, it is also another fact that when Crawford almost managed the feat in 1933, and even when I *was* successful in 1938, no one was really aware that there was such a thing as the Grand Slam. If that sounds like I am saying Crawford almost won something that didn't exist anyway, I am. I take a certain whimsical pride in not only having won the Grand Slam but, in a sense, having created it as well.

The Grand Slam (or what has become known as the Grand Slam) entails winning the national singles championships of Australia, France, Great Britain, and the United States, the four major titles in the world, in one year. This designation was not arrived at arbitrarily, for these four nations were in 1938, and still are, the only countries to have won the Davis Cup. Indeed, only six other nations have even reached the finals, the Challenge Round: Italy and Spain, twice each; and Belgium, Japan, Mexico, and India, one time apiece. Other national championships—the Italian, particularly—have come to possess considerable international prestige, but the greater stature and tradition continue to lie only with the championships of the four nations that have won the Davis Cup.

By 1938, however, no one had thought to lump the four titles together as a Grand Slam, or as anything, for that matter. In those prewar days of primitive air travel, no one could quite conceive of a cluster of championships that had to stretch more than ten thousand miles to find all its members. If you look back upon press accounts at the time when I won Forest Hills to complete this far-flung cycle, you will find no reference whatsoever to my having won a "Grand Slam." Indeed, there was only passing note made of the fact that I had also won three other major national titles that year. For further commentary on the accomplishment, I think it is interesting that I was *not* presented the Sullivan Award in 1938, although I had won it in 1937, when I had taken only half of the Grand Slam. (I did repeat as the American Sportswriters' Athlete of the Year, an accolade I still cherish particularly. Byron Nelson, who won it in 1944–45, and I remain the only back-to-back winners of this award, and I am the only tennis player ever to have been named for it.)

The fact that the Grand Slam was not recognized at the time is not unusual. Things of this sort tend to be accepted only with time and publicity. There was little special attention given when Babe Ruth hit sixty homers in 1927, and, similarly, the first horses to win the Kentucky Derby, Preakness and Belmont in the same year were not acclaimed as Triple Crown winners. Bobby Jones figured out his own Grand Slam in golf before me—the amateur and open championships of Britain and the United States.

Conceivably, the fact that there was no such acknowledged entity as the "Grand Slam" made it somewhat easier for me. I was certainly not faced with the cumulative pressure of the press and the fans that Rod Laver had forced upon him when he took the Grand Slam in 1962, or that Lew Hoad faced when he came within a set of winning the four titles in 1958. For the athlete, however, pressure more truly comes from within, and so I doubt that my feelings and fears were any less intense than Laver's or Hoad's were a quarter of a century later when the full glare of worldwide publicity was upon them.

I had set my goal to win those four titles in 1938, and the fact that only Gene Mako was also aware of this made the accomplishment no less easy for me. Whether or not anybody else knew what I was trying to do, *I* did, and that is all that matters once you are on the court or any competition begins. Mako happened to end up as my opponent in the finals at Forest Hills, and there is irony in that, perhaps, but I doubt that his presence across the net served to make the matter any more trying. The pressure within me was full and sufficient enough, and whoever I had played and whether the newspapers or the fans knew could not have increased the pressure any.

It is curious, though, that while I won the Grand Slam without acknowledgment, the feat eventually caught the public fancy, and it remains the one thing I am most remembered for.

I was delighted for Rod Laver when he too eventually won the Grand Slam, and I do hope that whatever developments tennis undergoes in the next important few years, the challenge and prestige of the Grand Slam will not be altered.

Of course, as I said, I should have been joining Crawford when I swept the four titles in 1938. Jack had come to Forest Hills with the three other championships already won. Furthermore, he then gained his way to the finals against Fred Perry, and just as Hoad was to do twenty-five years later against Ken Rosewall, Crawford took a 2–1 lead in sets. He, not Perry, was still the world's premier amateur, and since he was ahead and playing comfortably, he should have been expected to go on and take the last set, for the United States title and for the first Grand Slam.

As I have mentioned, though, Jack was asthmatic, and particularly on the hotter, muggier days—as this one was—the condition could begin to bother him. To help his breathing in these circumstances, Crawford would often take a bracing shot of brandy before a match, or, if conditions warranted it, even in the midst of one. Against Perry and, no doubt, also against a high autumnal pollen count, frankly, Crawford started hitting the brandy too hard. He had two or three ponies, and his coordination began to suffer. Fred, cold sober, lost only one game to Crawford in the last two sets, and thus ended his chances for the first Grand Slam.

So it was that no one had ever won the four major titles in a single year, when I set out on my quest in 1938. Even so, the Grand Slam was never more than an auxiliary goal for me. My prime target was the Davis Cup, which we had finally won in 1937 and were defending on our home soil for the first time since 1927. It was for this reason that I turned down the first substantial pro offer that I was tendered in 1937. Then, as something of an afterthought, the Grand Slam occurred to me. The defending Davis Cup titlist does not have to qualify for the Challenge Round —it wins the right to defense automatically. It left my schedule greatly reduced, so I decided to shoot for the Slam as a way of staying competitively fit.

As I said, I told no one of my aims except Mako. I was top-ranked in the world, so I was certainly not going to be able to surprise anyone wherever I played, but I realized that if I did shout my intentions abroad, it would just make everyone want to get me with even greater intensity.

Although I did not require any reinforcement to this reasoning, Ellie Vines provided it anyway. I did not tell Ellie of my full design, but I did let him know that I was going to play in Australia before that fact was released. Vines had played there himself as an amateur and was immediately appalled that I was going. Citing his own experience, he begged me not to make the trip. "Don, please," he said, "don't go down there. It's so very seldom that they get our top players, and with the novelty of having the number one in the U.S. *and* the world, they will absolutely play you to death. That's what they did to me. You may win the Australian title, but I promise you, you'll pay for it later. *I* did and I know. You'll be so tired for the Challenge Round and for Forest Hills and maybe even by Wimbledon that you'll be lucky to do half as well as you'd do otherwise."

Even if he had not been so emphatic, I recognized that Vines had a good point. Quite aside from the simple aesthetic value of winning the Davis Cup and Forest Hills was the obvious cold truth that poor performance late in the year stood to cost me a great deal of money if I decided to turn pro then. And if all went well, that was my hope, to turn pro.

It was difficult to argue with Ellie because I did not want to disclose to him that I was after the Australian title only as the first down card to a straight flush. But his advice was invaluable and convinced me that I could not poop myself out in matches that were mostly exhibitions to please the Aussie fans. I had to evaluate what I thought was important for myself in terms of my long-range goal, so I devised a strict battle plan, with intentions to point for only two tournaments—the Victorian, which was scheduled shortly after I arrived in December 1937, and the Australian National Championships themselves, about a month

later. In this regard too, I took only Mako into my confidence.

I realized that I had gotten a great psychological boost the first time that I beat Cramm and the first time that I beat Perry when they had slacked off against me in what seemed to them to be unimportant matches. I realized that some younger player who stood in awe of me now could turn into a confident and real contender if ever he beat me once and showed himself that he could do it. But I figured that was the risk I had to take. It was a matter of priorities, and I wanted the Slam.

Gene and I sailed from San Francisco in the winter and soon were in the summer of the South Pacific. We worked very hard on that cruise at doing nothing. It was a twenty-one-day trip (twenty-three coming back the wrong way over the International Date Line), and we were well rested and sunburned when we arrived in Sydney. We still had a week to get our tennis legs back before the Victorian championships began in Melbourne. When at last they opened, I was truly eager to play tennis. I swept the tournament without the loss of a set.

Then I fell into a comfortable possum posture. I had agreed to play several exhibitions and some test matches (with Gene) that were run along the Davis Cup format. I was beaten regularly in these matches. I approached every match as if it were practice. Physically, I did not extend myself, and rather than do what was strategically wisest, I often tried to work on the facets of my game that I felt needed most attention. The Australian press was at first encouraged that the local boys had begun to turn the tables on Budge, but the writers became, perhaps, a little suspicious of my repeated failures as time wore on. Besides, the issue of my health had to be inserted for a time, for I suddenly lost my voice and went for several days without being able to say a word. I felt fine otherwise, though, and the doctors were unable to locate any other signs of a more serious illness.

By the time the National Championships began, my speech had returned as mysteriously as it had gone, and I was so eager to play in earnest that I could hardly conceal the method in my madness. I was like a loosed tiger after the first ball that bounced. I was relaxed and tough, perfectly tuned for the action, and I swept through the field with ease. I played John Bromwich, who was the coming Australian player, in the finals, and I beat John badly—6–4, 6–2, 6–1. Then, as quickly as possible afterwards, barely after the trophies had been presented, Gene and I were on the boat home, lounging in the deck chairs and watching the southern hemisphere roll by.

France was next, in May. I had been there only once before, two years earlier, to play in an international match of no real significance, so Paris and all its beauty in that last peacetime year was really new to me. Gene and I stayed at the old Hotel Majestic, which is on the Avenue Kleber, just off the Champs Elysées near the Arc de Triomphe. The Majestic is a grand old Victorian hotel, a wonderful residence for us, though it has since become more of a political monument. The French Ministry of Information had its headquarters placed there after hostilities broke out, and when the Germans moved into Paris, the Gestapo became the new tenants. In 1968, of course, the Majestic became the site of the Vietnam peace talks.

This was all before us then, though, and Gene and I did not even have the time to concern ourselves with the usual temptations of Paris in the springtime, considerable as they were. Our main problem was something of a much more prosaic nature—adjusting to the *en-tout-cas* courts, which are surfaced with packed dust made of crushed red brick. The French championships at the Roland Garros courts is the only competition of the four Grand Slam titles that is not contested on grass.

We had begun preparing for the *en-tout-cas* back in the States by stopping off for a week or so in New York and practicing on the clay courts at Forest Hills before embarking for Europe. Before that I had rested at home for several weeks after returning from Australia, for I was wary of burning myself out, particularly as I had never played seriously so early in the year.

Truthfully, that concerned me more than the switch to clay, for the fact that I had won most of my recent important victories on grass was somewhat deceptive. Clay hardly frightened me. After all, I had learned the game on those gravel courts of Oakland that were much more similar to clay than to grass.

The French championship was the least memorable of the four in my Grand Slam. The tennis was not very exciting, and besides, I had terrible diarrhea during the whole tournament. My most pleasant memory was of Pablo Casals, whom I met and came to know so well during the tournament. I remember him much more than the tennis.

Despite my malady, I encountered serious competition only once, in the quarterfinals, when a Yugoslavian left-hander named Franjo Kukulevich took two sets from me. But he never gained the lead, and I never felt threatened seriously. I was fighting myself and my own very bad tennis that day more than I was the Yugoslav. I also have clear recollection of signaling to a friend in the stands, Russell Kingman, beckoning him to bring me something to eat. This went on throughout the tournament. I always came up hungry at the wrong time, and if Russell hadn't been on hand to smuggle candy bars and sandwiches out to me as I played, I might have collapsed at some point.

By the day of the finals, June 11, the diarrhea was almost gone and I was beginning to feel better. Roderich Menzel of Czechoslovakia was my opponent. He was a huge man, the tallest of my contemporaries. He stood about six four and weighed well over 200 pounds. (And remember, this was still a time when I, at six one-and-a-half, was considered quite tall. I had filled out some by now to about 155 pounds, though I was temporarily lighter because of my stomach problems at this particular time.) Menzel was a fine player, and I considered him the best clay-court player in the world after Cramm, and Gottfried, whom I had expected to be playing against this last day at Roland Garros, was now in a jail somewhere in Germany. We had said goodbye in Australia, but the Nazis arrested him upon his return on March 4, and just a few days before we docked at Cherbourg, on May 18, Cramm was convicted on outlandish charges and thrown in jail.

I was not surprised by then. It was obvious that they intended to embarrass and punish Cramm for his failure to turn Nazi. A few weeks before, early in May, I had headed an appeal that was directed in the form of an open letter addressed to the Nazi hierarchy. I had helped assemble twenty-five sports figures, including such people as DiMaggio and Alice Marble, and together we signed a message, entreating the Nazis to withdraw the false charges against Cramm and let him return to the tennis courts.

In the letter, we wrote that Baron Gottfried von Cramm was the "ideal sportsman, a perfect gentleman and decency personified. . . . No country could have wished for a finer representative—no sport for a more creditable exponent." The plea, as we all feared, was of no avail. He was in jail when I would surely have been playing him for the clay-court championship at Roland Garros in June; he was in jail until that October.

It was in Paris, on the clay, where I am sure Gottfried would have been at his formidable best. Menzel was the best on this surface after Cramm, but no fair substitute really, and he provided neither the drama nor the competition in the finals that Gottfried surely would have. I defeated Roderich without incident, 6–3, 6–2, 6–4, in less than an hour.

I remember that evening with much more clarity and pleasure than I do the afternoon. Russell Kingman had introduced me to Señor Casals earlier, and Pablo became a faithful visitor to the courts and a special fan of mine. "If you win, Don," he told me halfway through the tournament, "I would like to give a concert in your honor."

He did not forget the promise, and the party was held at Pablo's own apartment. It was a glorious setting, the city bright as ever below, the Eiffel Tower visible through the picture window, dominating the beautiful Paris night. As the songs say, we all remember Paris. I remember it that way, from Pablo's atelier, the night I won my French title. We assembled in the living room after dinner, and sat on large, magnificently ornate and comfortable cushions on the floor. Pablo and the pianist he had brought in to accompany him moved to their instruments. He

took his cello, and then, just before he began to play, he paused and said, very simply, "This concert is for my good friend Don Budge." That was all. I don't believe I was ever so flattered.

Mr. Casals played for me for almost two hours—considerably longer than I had been on the court that afternoon. I can remember recounting the incident later to a rather surprised Benny Goodman. "Don," he said at last, "do you know there are some people who would pay $50,000 for just such an evening?" I nodded humbly. By that standard, the French title was worth more than any other championship in tennis history. There was certainly no better way to leave Paris either, and the memory, however priceless, would have been worth even more to me had we known something of what was ahead. I would not be back in Paris until a war and a decade had passed over its streets. It was the eve of my twenty-third birthday when I left.

Wimbledon was next, and it was to be a curious tournament for me. I came to it after an easy triumph at Queens, a warm-up that helped me readjust to the grass. I was in good shape and top spirits—as it turned out, I was on my way to winning twenty-seven straight matches abroad—and I felt that my chances to repeat were excellent. By midway in the tournament, however, this buoyancy had been replaced by despair because for the first and only time in my career, my backhand was giving me trouble. It was inconsistent, and I had lost faith in it. I was becoming sure that, of all things, my backhand would cost me the Grand Slam.

Paradoxically, though, after falling to these depths, I was not only able to restore my backhand but to finish the tournament with a victory over Bunny Austin when I exhibited as fine a game of tennis as perhaps I ever showed as an amateur. And I owed it all to some grand old lady whose name I never knew, whom I never actually met, and whom I saw only once. But she was playing tennis then, and that old gal could hit a helluva dandy topspin backhand . . .

You can imagine, then, the utter despair I was thrown into at Wimbledon when I finally realized that my backhand had gone off for the first time. I knew it had to cost me a match soon.

I was also at a complete loss to understand why my best shot was suddenly so inconsistent. I would hit two or three pretty fair backhands in a row, and then I would get a chance to turn one into a real winner, and that's when my reliable backhand would leave me. The more this happened, the more I fretted, and the worse I became. Moreover, at just about this time I suddenly developed the curious throat difficulties I had experienced in Australia in January, and I began having trouble speaking again.

Altogether, I became quite convinced that I would lose my next match in the quarterfinals. Feeling sorry for myself, and also trying desperately to understand what was wrong with my game, I left the hurly-burly of the players' area late one afternoon and wandered off by myself. I had no idea where I was headed, and just meandered along, turning this way and that among the pathways that wind between the many outside courts.

At last I found myself far out, alongside something like court thirty-two. It was late in the day, the big matches had ended, and out here where I had ended up I was the gallery of one for what I think was a ladies' veterans' singles match. I was not really watching the two women play, just sort of staring at them absent-mindedly, seeing through them, really, to wherever my mind was. One of the ladies was dominating the match, though—that must have been obvious—and without knowing it I began to follow her more closely. Then I realized that I was concentrating on her. Slowly it began to dawn on me that some part of me quite below my conscious was being impressed. It was all curious, and I began to watch her more carefully.

Suddenly it was there. That old girl moved over and reached out and hit this gorgeous zinging topspin backhand. I kept watching. She did it again, and the rest just all fell into place for me. *She* was hitting a topspin backhand the way you are supposed to, stroking up; *I* had stopped hitting mine that way. I was trying to hit all my backhands with underspin. It was all, quickly, very, very plain before me. I saluted the lady, my benefactress, and dashed off to the clubhouse.

Bitsy Grant, the poor fellow, was just putting his clothes on when I arrived.

"Come on, Bitsy," I said, "you've got to give me a hit."

"Don," he protested. "Not now. It's late. We can get a good long one in tomorrow."

"Please," I said. "I've got to play right now with someone. I think I just found out what I've been doing wrong with my backhand, and I won't even be able to sleep tonight if I don't try it out now."

Grant cocked a tired eye at me, realized I was serious, and shook his head. He stopped buttoning his shirt in mid-button and began unbuttoning. I was in my tennis whites as quickly as I could rush into them, and I hustled Bitsy out to a sidecourt. "Just hit them all to my backhand," I yelled at him, and he started feeding ball after ball to my left. He was a good sport. I hope I remembered to buy him dinner.

It took hardly any time at all for me to see that my guess was right. I had not been hitting my offensive backhand. I had been using my defensive swing, stroking from high to low, on all my backhand shots. Not only that, but I believe I had been hitting that shot sloppily too by beveling the racket too much. I have no idea where I had lost the touch or how long it had taken to fade from me, but I know I was back in the groove within the few minutes I hit with Grant.

Once I had my backhand again, I was like Peter Pan getting his shadow back—a great deal more grateful for it than I had ever been before. I moved right back into peak form again and rushed through to a finals match against Austin. Except for the first two games there was little contest to it, which is unfortunate because it was the last time that Bunny and I ever met, and the scores of this final meeting—6–1, 6–0, 6–3—were certainly not representative of the closer matches we had usually played against each other.

It was just one of those days when I could do no wrong, and it was my good fortune that such a performance should fall in the finals of the most important tournament in the world. Bunny's best chance came in the opening game, which, as it turned out, was the longest and most thrilling of the match. He had three chances to break my serve, but lost each of the break points, and at last I held after five deuces. Bunny came right back to sweep me at love in the next game, so that it is possible to imagine such a lopsided match as this one having taken on a different flavor if Bunny, the underdog, had broken me in that first game and jumped off on top.

As it was, though, the competition was through after the first two games. I held my serve and broke him twice in a row to take the set 6–1. I won the next set at love and swept to a 3–0 lead in the last set before at last he broke me. I had won fourteen straight games, leading with my backhand, constantly attacking with it.

I broke Bunny seven consecutive games during this stretch, but each one of the breaks required a long game. He attained at least one deuce in each of the seven games, before at last I came through. On the other hand, I was holding my serve easily, and he was never able to win more than two points from me in any service game of mine during this skein. These results bear naturally on one another, for poor Bunny was constantly under pressure. He had to work hard in an effort to hold serve, but he never was able to force *me* to work hard when I was serving. I stayed upon the attack at all times.

At last Bunny did break the vicious circle when he closed to 3–2 in the third set, but the matter was all but concluded by then. Incidentally, this was yet another finals I played in that was upset by rain, but this postponement was the least bothersome of all I encountered, for it came so extremely late in the match. We were delayed for a full half-hour, but when at last Bunny and I came back on the court it took me only three minutes to conclude the action.

Bunny and I were presented to Queen Mary after the match, and she congratulated us both on our efforts. This time, I am glad to say, she neglected to make any more reference to that other match she saw us play—the one I "waved" in. Bunny himself was as gracious and warm a loser as we were friends. "I have never known such tennis as Don showed today," he told the press afterwards. I might add now in Bunny's behalf that his accomplishment of reaching the finals has grown more impressive as the years have passed, for it has turned out that his meeting with me that day remains till now the last time that an Englishman has played in his country's own men's finals.

I rounded out my last Wimbledon by sharing the men's doubles, or, as it is properly called, the four-handed championship, with Gene Mako and the mixed doubles with Alice Marble. With the same great partners helping me, I had managed to accomplish that hat trick for the first time the year before, but Bobby Riggs came right along after me and pulled the same thing off in 1939. Only Frank Sedgman (in 1952) has succeeded in winning the three titles in the same year since then.

There is even some feeling that the triple at Wimbledon is a more difficult feat than is winning the four Grand Slam singles titles. Certainly, at the time, winning the three Wimbledon championships was accorded a great deal more attention than the fact that I had now won Australia, France and Britain and had only the United States to go for a sweep of the major tournaments in singles alone. I took off happily for the Netherlands and Czechoslovakia to play in tournaments in those countries before I headed back to the States and the Challenge Round and the last of the Grand Slam.

I arrived in Prague for the first time in my life to play in the Czechoslovakian nationals only two months before some other gentlemen were to assemble in Munich to discuss other elements of the Czechoslovakian situation. Things were moving fast about us, as we journeyed about playing tennis that July of 1938. The Nazis were to be in Prague by the next March. The young player I beat after a long match in the first round of the Czechoslovakian championships was a local teenage prospect whom I had never heard of named Jaroslav Drobny. It was sixteen years later, 1954, when Jaroslav Drobny, now of England, became champion of Wimbledon.

I returned to the States early in August, with Forest Hills hardly a month away. For now, though, I was forced to divert my attentions from the Grand Slam and concentrate upon the Davis Cup. The defense of the cup was, after all, my prime goal for the year, and a defeat in it would leave the Grand Slam as a hollow achievement, even if I were able to finish it up at Forest Hills right afterwards.

The cup matches were scheduled again for Germantown, and as they had been the year before there, the Australians were the opposition. Last year we had met the Aussies for the Interzone title. This year they had fought through to meet us in the Challenge Round. It is significant that just as Austin was the last Englishman to play in the finals of Wimbledon in 1938, the Australians were beginning an unparalleled streak of another sort. Beginning in that signal tennis year of 1938, the Aussies have not failed to make the Challenge Round since. It is coincidental to my own career, but interesting nonetheless, that in my last year as an amateur the focus of United States competition turned from Europe—from Great Britain and France—and moved to Australia, where it remains to this day.

My opening match against the Aussies found me drawing John Bromwich, whom I had last defeated back in January for the Australian crown. I felt miserable. My throat was sore and parched, and my whole body was aching with flu. The sickness had burst over me in the hours before the tie began, and in those prehistoric times before antibiotics there was no effective way that my fever could be stilled even for a while. The flu peaked on that first day against Bromwich, and I was not in my best shape.

I won the first two sets, 6–2, 6–3, much as I had overpowered him in our Australian meeting, but he came back to take the next set from me 6–4, and I barely hung on to win the match 7–5 in the fourth. Had Bromwich won that set and extended me to five sets, the edge might have become his. I was weak with flu by this time. A tooth was beginning to hurt, and I ached all over my skinny body.

Mako and I had won the National Doubles at Brookline shortly after I had returned from Europe, but now, in the second day's play, Bromwich and Quist turned on us and upset Gene and me. That was a point we had counted on, so, as it turned out, had I not held on to beat Bromwich in the first day's play, the tie would have gone to

the Australians. We won only because Frankie Parker gave us a key point with a win over Adrian Quist, and then I gained the third and decisive tally with a straight-set win over Quist on the final day's play.

Somehow, ten thousand people had packed into Germantown for what was my last Davis Cup appearance, and it is ironic that while my final match was not a close contest (except for the first set, when Quist carried me to 8–6), it turned into something of a controversial imbroglio when the foot-fault arbiter, Harold Lebair, gained a certain notoriety and Quist's wrath by calling the Aussie repeatedly for foot faults. Lebair contended that Quist was dragging his back foot (the right one) over the service line and touching it in bounds before he hit his serve.

While I was, after all, the opponent and I had a rather high degree of interest in the proceedings, I still to this day can make no judgments on the calls. I was always at the other end of the court from all that action, and, crouched down waiting for Quist to serve, I no doubt had the worst location in the house for the purpose of seeing Adrian's feet.

The defense of the cup left me enormously elated, but I was tired, still not well, and my concern about my health returned to worry me as soon as our celebration ended. I had still felt ill playing Quist, although not as sick as I had against Bromwich two days before. The flu had begun to subside, but the pain in my tooth had developed into a ghastly full-scale toothache. What frightened me even more, though, was the fact that I was beginning to lose my voice once again. This problem was so recurrent that I could no longer pretend that it was not significant. It was now the eve of the United States championships, and though I was scared to learn the worst I knew that I had to be examined by a dentist immediately. Walter Pate recommended one in New York, and almost as soon as I checked into the Madison I reached him and he agreed to meet me in his office, even though it was late Sunday evening.

I catalogued all my recent ills to him, leading up to the toothache. I doubted that there could be any association between the loss of speech and the toothache, but I told the doctor about my repeated voice problems, and he nodded a more knowing response. When at last he peered into my mouth he seemed to quite expect what he found: a badly abscessed tooth. "Mr. Budge," he said. "The tooth has to come out immediately. I don't really understand how you've managed to get by with it for as long as you have." It was his opinion that the tooth had probably been worsening for a year or so, and that as long as eight months ago, when I was in Australia in January, it was responsible for my loss of speech. At other times throughout the year it had been acting to poison various parts of my system.

The doctor shot me full of novocain and yanked the offending fang out right there. Although my voice continued to fail and was actually lost completely for a while, I began to feel better almost immediately, and could almost feel the poison draining out of me. As a result, Forest Hills turned out to be a much less traumatic and a much more enjoyable exercise than I could have ever expected just a few days before. Aside from the rain delay, which Gene and I turned to our most beneficial social advantage anyway, the nationals were uneventful and almost anticlimactic.

Well, anyway, it seemed to me that they were anticlimactic, but no one quite believed me. I breezed to the finals without losing a set. Mako, unseeded, and burdened with the image of being strictly a doubles player, won his way through in the other bracket. He was the first unseeded player in fifty-seven years to make the finals, and as he went on the court to face me, this was the only fact that seemed to interest the fans. They forgot, first of all, that Mako had won his way there. A seeding is never more than a pleasant little honor and a promoter's simple device that manages to keep the luck of the draw controlled just enough so that all the supposedly best players do not happen to meet in the first round Tuesday afternoon when there is no one on hand to watch. Once a tournament begins, a seed means nothing more than yesterday's newspaper. Or: You are only as good as your last drop volley.

Also ignored was the fact that Mako *should* have been seeded in the first place. Perhaps it had already been forgotten that he had come within only two points of getting past Austin at Wimbledon in July—and Austin went on to become a finalist. Gene was playing the best singles of his life, and was probably overlooked in the seeding because he was unfairly typed as strictly a doubles player. I knew, though, that he was a much better player than some of those who had been seeded in his place. And I also knew he was hot.

To the fans, though, the fact of his being an unseeded interloper preempted all other consideration. Mako was to be a patsy for Budge and even a willing public sacrifice, since the two opponents were such good friends.

Oh well, this was Munich's month, and I guess myopia was catching. Gene Mako was as likely to roll over and play dead for me as peace was to come in our time. I do not recall ever sitting down with Gene and discussing the matter. There was no more need to delineate such thinking as there was for him to inscribe his intention of defeating me on our bathroom mirror with toothpaste. We both knew that our mutual compassion halted the instant that one of us threw a racket down and the other called out "rough" or "smooth." And that is the way it went in the finals.

I was a better player than Gene that day. Indeed, I usually was, for I had too much power for him. But Mako and I played together for a lot of years under all sorts of conditions, on most continents, on all surfaces, and it was unusual only when he did *not* give me a tough game. It was not an exception when he took a set from me. And this is all that happened on this occasion, for although I won the match without a great struggle, Gene made me work all the way, and he took the second set from me, 8–6. So it was that there was hardly a person on hand or anyone I have met since who does not believe that I threw that set to Gene as a token of our friendship.

The suggestion is patently ridiculous and altogether specious. First of all, whoever the opponent, such an idea was in direct opposition to my philosophy of play—keep the pressure on, never let up. Secondly, in the finals of a tournament of the stature of Forest Hills, I cannot imagine anyone taking the chance of willingly losing a set. The longer a match goes, the greater the chance of injury. In the third place, this was *this* Forest Hills, the fourth to my Grand Slam set, and under those special circumstances I would not even have *mused* on the possibility of giving up a single point to anyone, even if I were ahead 6–0, 6–0, 5–0, 40–love. Fourth, I had too much respect and affection for Gene to treat him as if he were an inferior player who could be given a set for his troubles, rather like a condescending pat on the head.

Fifth, forget all the first four logical reasons and turn to the sixth and seventh, which are founded in the same cynicism that forces the point to begin with. To be blunt, no one throws a *second* set. If you are really up to that sort of thing, you at least have the good sense to wait till the third set when you have a 2–0 lead. And no one ever throws a set at 8–6. Be sensible about it—lose a set at love or a comfortable 6–2 or 6–3, but for goodness sake, don't wear yourself out to a frazzle playing fourteen hard games when you have no intention of winning the thing anyway.

Gene Mako beat me 8–6 in the second set of our finals. It was the only set I lost in the tournament, but I dropped it squarely. And once I had won the match, I doubt if it mattered to me one way or the other that Mako had taken a set from me. But I do know what did matter, and that is that because Gene was my last opponent, I enjoyed the warmest, most appropriate possible conclusion for my Grand Slam. When at last I hit the shot that won Forest Hills and the Grand Slam, when I rushed to the net, the man who was there to take my hand and congratulate me and smile at my triumph, was the only other man in the world who knew what I had really accomplished and how much I cared.

The Short and Happy Life of Maureen Connolly

by GIANNI CLERICI

Gianni Clerici, an Italian tennis writer and former top-level player, is recognized by his peers as one of the finest prose stylists covering the game. Perhaps being the product of another culture gives him a special insight into the development of an American woman champion. It seems so in this translation of his succinct essay on the career of Maureen Connolly, to whom great success and ultimate tragedy came so young.

"MISS Connolly," the reporter asked, "what was your most amusing experience in the sport?" "I have never had one," Miss Connolly replied.

In 1951, Maureen Connolly won Forest Hills when she was only sixteen, won Wimbledon in 1952, and then, the first to do so in the annals of the sport, won the Grand Slam in 1953. In 1954, while she was mounting the horse given her by her home town, an accident deformed her leg and ruined her career as an athlete. She later died of cancer at the age of thirty-five.

Maureen's father, a sailor, deserted the family when she was only three years old. Her mother's hands were too short for her to become a concert pianist, and she began again as organist in a church in San Diego. Abandoning all hopes of personal fulfillment, she concentrated all her dreams on her chubby, stubborn and will-

ful little daughter. Maureen's mother unwisely pushed her into ballet and then directed her into singing. When a badly performed tonsillectomy ruined her chances in that direction, her mother encouraged her to write, to draw and in general to act like a child prodigy. The small girl really had no special talent and did not hold her own in these endeavors. She spent hours on end dreaming of a horse, for horseback riding was her real interest. The family's modest means denied her the chance to succeed as a horsewoman, however.

The three Connollys, mother, aunt and daughter, lived very near to three cement courts. One day Maureen stopped short to see playing there, not the usual unfriendly neighborhood children or elderly couples, but Gene Garret, a tennis player gifted with a rigorous style. Tennis suddenly seemed to her the perfect substitute for riding, and she became ball girl for the teacher Wilbur Folsom, who hobbled around on a wooden leg. Maureen wrote with her left hand, but Folsom was aware that there had never been a truly successful left-handed woman player and encouraged her to hold the racket with her right hand. For once, using her right hand did not seem to bother her.

Thanks to the good offices of a dancing teacher, she quickly found herself in the presence of Teach Tennant, the enthusiast who had transformed Alice Marble. Teach had parted company with her first protégée after some stormy sessions, and Pauline Betz had slipped away from her authority too quickly. Teach must have realized that she was in the presence of greatness, but she made no indication of it to the girl. She said simply: "Well, let's see what you can do. Go ahead and play!" Maureen, who was then twelve years old, quickly decided that she wanted Teach Tennant to give her lessons more than anything else in the world. Teach did, and along with the instruction came the gradual rise to success that her mother had longed for so fervently.

At first, Teach could not imagine that a future world champion could be different from Alice Marble, who, though ungrateful to her, had still been greater than any of the others, including Wills and Lenglen. Although Maureen was totally unsuited for it, her teacher made her try the big game, rushing the net, thereby abandoning the backcourt where her real strength and potential lay. "I was upset by her authoritarian voice, by her dominating ways," Maureen wrote. Only after crying in secret on many occasions and many sleepless nights, did she dare confess that the nightmare of another smash hitting her, as had happened on the first days of play, paralyzed her every time she ventured to the net. Maureen played for hours on end, studied and breathed tennis. She had over Alice the advantage of excellent physical health and an iron will. Teach was content and spent her time modifying her student's strokes and her thoughts, selecting her food and her clothing. "I adored her. Her opinions were commands, and her dislikes controlled mine as well," Maureen wrote.

Teach had always been the teacher preferred by the stars. When she saw that Maureen was becoming interested in John Garfield and Cornell Wilde, she told her never to play with them, so as not to ruin her own game. Maureen refused to obey the order and was caught red-handed rallying with Gilbert Roland. An implacable Teach sent her home. "My world fell in pieces," Maureen wrote. She was also upset because her mother had remarried. She begged

Teach to take her to live with her, but her Pygmalion refused to do so and socialized with her only on the court.

At the age of thirteen, Maureen went on her first tour and collected her first victories as well as a defeat. The public, which attended her match with Laura Lou Jahn in a jovial and unattentive mood, seemed a court of tyrannical judges. "They hate me now because I lost," she said. "If I had won, they would love me." One of the newspapermen called her "the killer in curls," alluding to her rigid, tight-lipped stance as she attacked her unknown opponents with ferocious tenacity. "Teach thinks that you can't be friends with your opponents. You have to stay alone," she commented sadly. Before every match, that girl, who "needed to hate, to detest each of her opponents," sought asylum for hours in the churches of these unknown cities where she was playing.

A close friend of Bishop Charles Buddy of San Diego, Maureen must have paraphrased him in her thoughtful observation that "tennis is a gift of God." "Losing therefore is an offense, a sign of ingratitude," the poor child reasoned, clutching with her chubby fingers her ring, upon which two dragons guarded a tennis ball. Without that talisman, without her devotions, Maureen was not only in no condition to win, but not even to go out on the court. Once she refused to compete for a half-hour until an out-of-breath referee finally turned up her ring for her.

At the age of fourteen, the youngest to do so in the history of U.S. tennis, Maureen won the junior championships, and both Tilden and Kramer came to congratulate her, unaware that, according to her own words, "no fame or immortality could compensate for the price that I paid for the victory." At the age of sixteen, she confronted Forest Hills for the second time, filled with anguish over the thought of survival on the court. Teach was far away trying to save the life of her dear sister Gwen, her only living relative. Perhaps Maureen was not aware of that fact, or perhaps she did not think that Gwen's drama was any more terrible than her own. She insisted on help, and Teach finally left Gwen to sustain her pupil as far as the semifinals with Doris Hart.

No woman—not even Chris Evert or Tracy Austin—won as many major titles so young as did Maureen "Little Mo" Connolly. (Photo Courtesy of the USTA)

Doris was a delightful person and the year before in the same stadium she had done all she could to praise and encourage the young girl during the breaks in their match. Teach confided to Sophie Fisher that Doris really disliked Mau-reen, had called her a little brat and was only waiting for the chance to teach her a lesson on the court. Sophie told Maureen the lie, and she in turn rushed for confirmation to Teach, who played the role of Iago very well. The little dervish vented her rage on Doris, inflicting a 6–0 victory in the first set and beating her in a truly impressive second. Mervyn Rose said that he had never seen such an expression on a player's face, and everyone agreed with Nelson Fisher, the San Diego reporter, when he baptized her "Little Mo," from the name of the battleship bristling with cannons, the famous *Missouri*.

Maureen still had to defeat Shirley Fry, Doris's dearest friend. Shirley came out on the court ready for anything, and when she returned to the dressing room for the rest period before the decisive set, she was not the only one to believe that she might actually take the match. Little Mo felt terribly worn and incapable of will-power, but Teach was there to hold her up and to communicate her great drive. "You have to win this set, even if you kill yourself doing so," she said slowly, looking at the girl with her enormous burning eyes. Maureen suddenly got up, like one possessed. "I'll take care of her," she promised.

Not since the days of the tennis goddess had such a crowd of photographers been on the scene as those who greeted Little Mo, her mother and Teach, when they arrived in London in June 1952. The English reporters tried in vain to interview Maureen. They were able to observe her practice sessions and finally got her to talk to them. Was this quiet, submissive young lady really the student of the greatest coach in the world? they asked themselves in amazement. Not only did Little Mo treat her mother like a simpleton, but she lost no opportunity to go against the wishes of Teach as well, and even made fun of her on occasion.

The misunderstandings and the arguments among the three women reached colossal proportions during the Queens Club Tournament. When Little Mo suddenly suffered a terrible pain in her shoulder, Teach could think of nothing better than to seclude her in the dressing room and answered the curiosity of the public with a stony silence. A reporter thought that this might very well be an indication of Little Mo's withdrawing from Wimbledon, and began to telephone the story. He had barely had time to get the first sentence out, when Little Mo came dash-

ing up, half-dressed, to snatch the telephone out of his hand. She had heard him from within.

The story made the day for the newspapers, and the doubts of the fans over whether or not she would be able to play were so many that even bookmakers began to phone the women asking for information. Both Dr. Hugh Dempster and Teach were of the opinion that Mo had pulled a muscle. Her teacher furiously opposed her playing Wimbledon, fearful of compromising her entire career. Encouraged by the diagnosis of a second doctor, Little Mo refused to listen to her. On Monday, the opening day, Teach declared that Little Mo would be foolish to play.

On Tuesday Maureen defeated Mrs. Moeller by sheer grit and immediately announced a press conference. The reporters were amazed to hear her say in measured tones, as if she were reading a prepared statement, that Miss Tennant did not represent her, and that her decisions did not express the views of Little Mo, who was determined to finish the tournament. Perry Jones was called from Los Angeles to help Mo's confused and anxious mother decide whether or not her underage offspring could risk her health this way. He agreed with Mo's doctor and decided that the one procured by Teach had been in error.

Maureen Connolly felt fine. She had no trouble playing. Suddenly, incredibly, she seemed near defeat at the hands of the beautiful but very little known Susan Partridge. In the nightmare of an anguished third set, she looked for and failed to find the suntanned face and the sparkling eyes of her beloved Teach. Perhaps it was the call of encouragement from a young American sailor, in marked contrast to the English crowd, that saved her from defeat. That evening, all alone, beyond the wall that divided her from Teach's room, Maureen suddenly felt a tremendous surge of power and freedom. She would win Wimbledon, she would win Forest Hills, she would win everything. And then perhaps, one day, tennis would no longer loom in her mind as some sort of wild aggression that seemed to consume her very heart. Perhaps one day, she sighed wistfully, she would find peace.

Lone Wolf of Tennis

by DICK SCHAAP

Before open tennis in 1968, the pros labored in a series of one-night stands, burned out cars driving back and forth and across the country, wondered if the pro game would ever pay off . . . and were beaten regularly by Richard "Pancho" Gonzales. Schaap traveled with Pancho during one of these seemingly endless tours to produce this piece, which won the Best Sports Story Award for magazines in 1958.

WHEN Richard Alonzo Gonzales stretches to the top of his toes, whips his right arm high in the air and serves a tennis ball at 112 miles an hour, he is doing more than simply powering the swiftest shot in tennis history. He is swinging at every Southern Californian who ever called a Mexican "Pancho," flailing at every tennis official who ever barred a youngster from a tournament, and whacking at every father who ever ordered his daughter to stop dating the kid from the wrong side of the tracks.

Richard Gonzales is the greatest tennis player in the world today. He has considerable wealth and prestige, plus an incredible amount of ability—almost everything a man could want. But on his strong right shoulder sits the same chip that marks so many men who have overcome odds not of their own making. It is the chip that has made him the fiercest competitor in tennis, a relentless champion who must prove again and again that in all the world there is no one else so skillful. But it also has had a deeper, more significant effect. It has shaped Gonzales into the lone wolf of tennis, a dark, brooding figure silhouetted against a rococo backdrop of fame, fortune and talent.

Gonzales is a loner in the strictest sense of the word. While he was winning the most recent pro tennis tour, he did not travel with Lew Hoad, Tony Trabert and Pancho Segura in the spacious station wagons provided by promoter Jack Kramer. He drove alone in his own car, a souped-up Ford Thunderbird, picking his own routes and his own way stations. When the rest of the troupe checked in at one hotel he generally stayed at another. Usually he ate by himself, away from the bright lights and the noise. He rarely attended social functions, and when he did, he seemed to generate electric tension.

Once, the night before the tour made its annual stop in Madison Square Garden, Gonzales went to a party on New York City's swank East End Avenue. Among the other guests was Gina Lollobrigida, the Italian movie actress who has been described as the most tempting seven syllables since "Come up and see me sometime." At the party, a press photographer suggested, quite logically, that Gina and Pancho pose for a picture together. Gina warmly agreed. Gonzales seemed somewhat cooler. While the subjects waited, the photographer carefully adjusted his camera.

"Come on," Gonzales snapped. "Let's get this over with."

Gina took a deep breath—and smiled.

The photographer checked his flash attachment.

"What are you waiting for?" Gonzales demanded.

Gina smoothed her dress, wet her lips and laughed lightly.

"Stand a little closer together," the cameraman said. "Would you please smile, Pancho?"

Gonzales scowled. "Take the damn picture," he said, and then delivered a brief lecture on the social and technological failings of press photographers. A short while later, Gina was still smiling and Gonzales was still fuming. He left the party.

Yet the same man who verbally dissected the photographer can be genuinely pleasant and cooperative. It is one of the paradoxes of Gonzales that he deeply wants to be friendly, but he instinctively fears anyone who might hurt or misuse him. On his most recent tour, he seems to have relaxed a little bit, but not much.

The genial, relaxed Gonzales appears at strange times. Late one evening not long ago, he stopped in a restaurant for a light snack. It was after midnight and the match with Hoad, which had ended only thirty minutes earlier, had lasted more than two hours. He was thoroughly exhausted. Blisters seared his feet. He could easily have been curt and irascible.

As he entered the restaurant, Gonzales spotted men seated around a table in a corner, all sipping tall glasses of white milk. "What's this," he asked, "the local milk club?" One of the men grinned. "No," he said. "We saw you play tonight and decided it was about time we got in shape."

For the first time all night, Gonzales cracked a broad smile. He walked over to the milk table, postponing his own meal, and chatted for several minutes about tennis, conditioning and sports in general. When he was finished, he had won five lifelong fans.

His fellow professionals recognize Gonzales's aloofness and changeability, but, for the most part, they can neither predict nor explain his moods. Even Segura, the little Ecuadorian who is closer to Gonzales than any other tennis player, admits that he is often puzzled by the champion. "Gorg's a funny guy," Segura says. "He's independent. He likes to be alone. I don't know why."

(The nickname of Gorg, or Gorgo, has stuck with Gonzales since he won the 1948 U.S. Singles Championship and promptly lost half a dozen matches in a row to Ted Schroeder. Tennis writer Jim Burchard called Pancho "The Cheese Champ" which inevitably became Gorgonzales—from gorgonzola, an Italian cheese—and eventually Gorgo.)

Lew Hoad found Pancho's outward coolness no easier to handle than his service. "I guess," Hoad says, "that Gorg feels he can't be friendly with a fellow he has to try to beat every night. Maybe he's right. He does rather well, you know."

The only pro who advances a definite theory about Gonzales is Tony Trabert. "He's got a persecution complex," Trabert insists. "I don't blame him for having had it originally. He was persecuted. Even his nickname was a form of persecution. In California, many prejudiced people call all persons of Mexican descent 'Pancho.' But things have changed since he was a kid. When people call him 'Pancho' now, they say it admiringly. It's time he got over his complex."

But as any psychiatrist will confirm, it is not easy to erase a feeling that has deep roots in childhood and adolescence. The first of Carmen and Manuel Gonzales's seven children, Richard was born in Los Angeles on May 9, 1928. His father was a house painter and, although the family was never destitute, there was no extra money for luxuries. The Gonzaleses lived in a section of the south side of Los Angeles where a boy was considered an unqualified success if he grew up to become an auto mechanic.

One day, when Richard was seven years old, his father reluctantly gave him permission to cross the street alone and visit South Park, a local playground. The youngster set out on a scooter he had built from two-by-fours and rollerskate wheels. When he reached the intersection, he did not stop or look or listen. He barreled into the street just as an automobile was approaching. The driver braked hard, but before the car could stop, its door handle hooked Richard's cheek. The accident left a scar several inches long. Today Pancho scarcely notices it. "Sometimes I forget which side it's on," he says.

But later there were less violent incidents that left more serious scars. Gonzales suffered one particularly depressing setback when he was fifteen. By then he was the best tennis player his age in Southern California. An above-average student, he decided his future was not in the classroom. He quit high school to spend all his spare time on the tennis court. As soon as Perry Jones, the czar of Southern California tennis, learned that Gonzales had left school, he called the boy into his office.

"Richard," Jones began, evenly, "it isn't fair for you to play anybody who goes to school all day while you practice tennis."

"But Mr. Jones," Gonzales said, "I don't want to go to school any more. I want to play tennis."

Jones paused and leaned forward. "Until you return to school," he said, "I must bar you from all tournaments."

Gonzales was crushed. He had embraced tennis, and tennis, in turn, had spurned him. Rumors spread that Jones barred Gonzales because he was Mexican. This was not true, but by repetition, it became a popular theory. Even now, although Pancho concedes that the ban was justified, he still seems to think that somehow he should have been eligible for the junior tournaments.

Not until after four years had elapsed, including fifteen months spent swabbing decks in the Navy, was Gonzales reinstated. Then, suddenly, he received another emotional slap in the face. He had been dating an attractive blond tennis player from the Los Angeles area. Everyone who saw them agreed that the dark, handsome Gonzales and the pale, beautiful girl made a stunning couple. Everyone, that is, except her father. He told her to stop seeing Pancho. For a while the girl tried deception. She took her school books, said she was going to the library and, instead, met Pancho. But, finally, the subterfuge proved too burdensome. They stopped dating.

No sensitive adolescent could experience such difficulties without absorbing considerable pain, and Richard Gonzales was a sensitive boy. His hands were sensitive to the feel of a tennis racket and his mind was sensitive to the sting of an antagonistic society. He reacted naturally; he withdrew into himself.

"I remember Pancho at the first tournament he ever played away from home," says Gussie Moran, the former Wimbledon sensation. "He was a quiet, shy boy who sat alone in the clubhouse. He had a forlorn look on his face and a chip on his shoulder. But when he stepped onto the tennis court, he was someone else. He was a god, patrolling his personal heaven."

Gonzales, basically, is not much different today. He is a far better tennis player. He has sharpened his strokes to the point of perfection. Yet he still sits by himself in the locker room, his head sunk in his hands, the sweat dripping from his brow.

Until one night recently, I had seen Gonzales play as a pro only in big cities where a sizable press corps, an army of tennis stars and the attendant fanfare always acted as a buffer against reality. The best way to understand and appreciate Richard Alonzo Gonzales, I decided, was to see him on tour in small towns, winning most matches, living alone, traveling alone, eating alone. Late one rainy and foggy afternoon, after a quick stop at the insurance vending machine, I boarded a DC–3 and flew from Newark to join the pro tour in Corning, New York.

Corning is an industrial town on the southern tier of upstate New York, nestled near the Finger Lakes. It is known for producing Steuben crystal, the finest glass in the country, and Ted Atkinson, one of the finest jockeys. In Corning everything revolves around the glass works, and there, in a modern gymnasium, Pancho Gonzales and Lew Hoad played the sixty-seventh match of their current series.

The picture of Gonzales in action is unforgettable. For pure artistry, it rates with Musial, coiled and ready to strike; Cousy, flipping a backhanded pass; Snead, at the height of his backswing; and Arcaro, whipping a horse through the stretch. When he serves, Gonzales strains, rears back and fires. Despite his size, he rushes catlike to the net, defying an opponent to return service. His long, light strides carry him to shots that lesser men never reach. On an overhead smash, he kicks up and follows through with frightening force. His nervous energy is never wasted. It is stacked up into a huge pile until the sheer weight of Pancho's ability falls upon an opponent, startling him at first, then bewildering him and, finally, crushing him.

For thirty-two games in the first set at Corning, Hoad refused to crack. Then Gonzales broke service, held his own and won, 18–16. He also took the second set, 7–5, and stretched his series lead to five matches, 36–31. After the final point, champion and challenger shook hands perfunctorily, posed for several photographs and retired to the dressing room.

Hoad entered first, shuffled to his locker in the far corner and sat down. Gonzales slumped onto a bench five feet away. For fully three minutes, neither said a word. The tension slowly ebbed from their faces. Then Gonzales spoke. "Give me a towel, will you," he said to Hoad. The taut, hard lines that striped both men's brows began to disappear. Gonzales drained half a Coke with one swallow. "I was lucky," he said. "I hit two shots I never saw."

They changed their shirts and socks and walked back to the court for a doubles match. Just as Hoad's right arm swept up for the first serve, Gonzales dropped his racket loudly to the floor. "Excuse me, Lew," he said. "Did I disturb you?" The doubles served as an escape valve and, throughout the match, Gonzales clowned openly, hitting balls behind his back and swinging vainly at shots ten feet beyond his reach. On one serve he tossed up three balls and smacked two of them. As the crowd laughed, Pancho relaxed.

Afterward, in the locker room, he stripped off his shoes and socks and poked at huge callouses beneath the large toe of each foot. "Look at this one," he said. "Full of fluid." A trace of fatigue darkened his face. "This is the toughest sport of all," he said. "Even in pro basketball, they don't play every night. Besides, when they're tired, they get a substitute. We don't. We play even when we're hurt. I've played with a sprained ankle. Lew finished a match one night after colliding with a wall and being knocked unconscious."

Gonzales showered and put on a pair of slacks and a red polo shirt. Then he turned to me. "I'm going to get something to eat," he said. "Want to come along?" It was a stunning reversal in mood. Only six hours earlier, I had asked Gonzales if I might ride with him. His answer had been pointed. "No," he had said. "I don't have any room."

As we walked from the locker room, a spectator shouted, "Good exhibition, Pancho." Gonzales frowned. "It was not an exhibition," he said. "If it had been, it would not have gone on so long."

Outside, in a parking lot behind the glass works, Gonzales unlocked his Thunderbird. Even in the dark, its yellow body and white top shimmered brightly. He switched on the electric ignition and a modified Cadillac engine roared mightily.

For Gonzales, there is only one object more fascinating and more challenging than a tennis racket. It is a hot rod. The tennis champion of the world owns four automobiles that are constantly being tuned for drag-strip racing in California. Usually Pancho works as a mechanic, adjusting the steering, changing the gear ratio, pampering the engine. But sometimes he puts on crash helmet and goggles, settles into the driver's seat and hurtles down an old, abandoned air strip at speeds of more than 150 miles an hour.

Gonzales let the motor idle for several minutes before he slipped into gear. Then he pulled out of the parking lot, turned right, crossed a bridge over the Chemung River and turned right again on Market Street. A few blocks down, he parked at the Athens Restaurant. He walked in and sat down on a stool by the counter. "Give me a rare hamburger steak," he told the waitress, "and a cup of coffee."

Gonzales leaned forward, resting his elbows on the counter. "When I gain extra weight," he said, "I eat nothing but meat and liquids for a week to ten days. Then I get an awful hunger. It is something you cannot imagine. I see a piece of pie and I want it terribly."

While he ate, Gonzales said nothing. After a second cup of coffee and a glass of milk, he smoked a cigarette and went out to the Thunderbird. By one A.M. he was back in his single room at the Centerway Motel. At five, he fell asleep. "I replayed the match in my mind," he explained the next day. "I tried to figure out what I did right, why I won. Then I tried to decide how I would play the next match."

The next morning, while Hoad, Trabert and Segura toured the museum at the Corning Glass Works, Gonzales tried to sleep. At eleven-thirty, a steady, driving rain fell as I walked to the motel to meet Pancho. He was standing outside, conspicuous in his red polo shirt and a yellow sleeveless sweater, bent over the motor of his car. While the rain drenched him, he changed spark plugs. "You have to have two sets of spark plugs," he said, "one for the city and one for the open road."

For fifteen minutes he fastened, checked and adjusted. Then he went into the motel's restaurant and ordered a bowl of Wheaties, two three-and-a-half-minute soft-boiled eggs, two cups of coffee and a glass of milk. After breakfast he returned to the car, checked it once more and packed his clothes and equipment. At twelve-fifteen, he climbed into the driver's seat and I got in beside him. We pulled away from the motel on Route 414 and started toward the next town on the tour—Clinton, New York, some 160 miles from Corning. Gonzales began to relax. His hands slipped easily into the ten o'clock and four o'clock positions favored by race drivers. Two miles outside Corning, the motor suddenly sputtered, coughed and died. Despite Pancho's checks and double-checks, we were out of gas.

The road from Corning to Watkins Glen,

roughly thirty miles away, is a bumpy one, but after we refueled, Gonzales cruised along at sixty to seventy miles an hour. It was fast, but not dangerous driving. "I don't open it up," he said. "The T-Bird can do 145 miles an hour if I let it out. I'll go from zero to 115 in fifteen seconds."

Then, abruptly, we headed into a sharp curve. I braked, involuntarily, where there was no brake. Gonzales did not even take his foot off the accelerator. We whipped around the bend into a straightaway. "That's how I make up time," he said. "I don't slow down on the curves."

After we passed Watkins Glen, bounced through a long stretch of highway under construction and picked up Route 14, Lake Seneca glimmered in the rain on our right. Gonzales ignored the scenery and concentrated on the road. "I like to travel alone," he said. "I can leave when I want. I don't have to wait for the others and they don't have to wait for me. When I want to stop and rest, I can."

Water leaked slowly through the windshield on the driver's side. "Is the feud between you and Kramer really bitter?" I asked.

"You're damn right it is," Gonzales said. "The main reason I don't like Kramer is simple. Money."

He lit a cigarette and continued. "I'm the best player and I deserve the most money. Kramer has me over a barrel now. He's got me under contract and I can't do a thing about it. After it runs out, we'll see. Some people have suggested that I start my own tour, but that's not my idea. I'll probably stick with this. I want a better deal, though. Somebody's going to get hurt and it's not going to be me."

Under his contract, Gonzales earns 20 per cent of the gross receipts, an income of close to $75,000 a year.

Gonzales once dragged Kramer into court, seeking to have the contract changed. The judge threw out the case. Pancho had no legal complaint, he ruled; the contract was binding. Since then, even when they played gin rummy together at a nickel a point, Gonzales and Kramer have not spoken. "Pancho never says a social word to me," Kramer says.

Still the Lone Wolf—Pancho Gonzales on the prowl at age forty during the dawn of open tennis. (Photo by Russ Adams)

Gonzales passed three cars easily, pulled into the right lane and began to talk about his family. "I've got three boys," he said, "Richard, Michael and Danny. Richard, the oldest, is ten and looks like he's going to be a good tennis player."

He leaned back and rubbed the scar on his left cheek. He might have been thinking about his personal troubles. He is divorced from his wife, Henrietta, and was planning to marry Madelyn Darrow, a former Miss Rheingold.

We passed Syracuse and the sun threatened to break through the heavy rain clouds. "Pro tennis is a funny game," Gonzales said. "It's hard not to relax when you get far ahead. That's what Hoad did when he had me, 18–9. That's what I did when I had him, 32–23. He almost caught up and I had to bear down. I had to diet, practice, sleep, train. I'm training harder this year than I ever did before. I'm in the best shape of my life."

A few miles before Utica, we turned onto a side road that led into Clinton. On the outskirts of Clinton, we stopped at a service station. "Change the oil and fill it up," Gonzales told the attendant. We ran down the road, dodging puddles, to a small restaurant. It was almost three-thirty and Pancho wanted a large meal before the night's matches. He finished off a bowl of soup, a sirloin steak, a lettuce and tomato salad, and a bottle of 7-Up. Then he hesitated. "I'll have a piece of apple pie," he said.

While he ate Gonzales read the Utica newspaper. Next to a story announcing the arrival of the tour, there was an AP dispatch praising Jack Kramer for his work in training young Barry MacKay for the Davis Cup matches with Australia.

"Kramer's always taking the credit," Gonzales mumbled. "I don't think he played once with the kid. We did all the work."

We hurried back to the service station and, after Pancho supervised the changing of his oil filter and bought a new set of spark plugs, we drove to the Clinton Arena, a barnlike construction that serves as home for the Clinton Comets in the Eastern Hockey League. We got out of the car, walked inside and shivered. It felt cold enough for a hockey game.

Jerry Dashe and Don Westergard, the tour's equipment managers, were installing the tour's portable canvas tennis court. "When's it going to be ready?" Gonzales asked. "I want to get some practice."

"Not before five," Westergard called back. "You might as well go out until then."

We went back to the car and drove to a nearby hardware store. Gonzales bought a set of wrenches, then visited the local Mercury agency. "I want some floor mats for a T-Bird," he said. "Have any?"

The owner picked out two black mats and handed them to Gonzales. He started to fill out a sales slip. "Could you give me your name sir?" he said.

"Sure," Pancho answered. "Gonzales."

"How do you spell that?"

"G-O-N-Z-A-L-E-S."

"Oh," said the proprietor, "like the tennis player."

"Same guy," said Gonzales.

"You're Pancho Gonzales," the owner said, with considerable awe. "I've read about you."

Gonzales turned his head away, slightly embarrassed. He didn't say a word, took his change and brought the mats out to the car. We returned to the arena, but the court still was not ready. Gonzales stepped outside and, with his new wrenches, began working on the car. Shortly after five, he went inside, dressed and went on the court for a practice session with Segura. For half an hour, Big Pancho and Little Pancho volleyed back and forth, concentrating on lobs and backhands. Then they went into the locker room. Trabert and Hoad had just arrived. "Hey, Gorg," Trabert said, "what's that big bubble sticking out of the hood on your car?"

"That's an air filter," Gonzales said, seriously. "I found that particles of dirt were getting into the motor and causing . . ."

"Okay, okay," said Trabert. "That's enough. You start to lose me when you get technical."

Before the preliminary match between Segura and Trabert began, Gonzales walked outside and climbed into one of the Kramer station wagons. He tried to sleep, but had no success.

Spectators, waiting in line for tickets, approached the station wagon and stared at Pancho as though he were the firing unit in a NIKE display. Children banged on the windows and asked for autographs.

Gonzales gave up and went back into the locker room. In a few minutes, Trabert and Segura came through the door. "How'd it go, Segoo?" Gonzales asked.

"No good, Gorg," Segura said. "He beat me again. He was really serving the ball tonight."

"How are the lights?"

"Not bad," Segura said. "Sometimes you lose the ball in them."

About fifteen minutes before match time, the lines in Gonzales's face started to harden again. By the time he ran onto the court, he was wearing his mean face, the one that he reserves for frightening opponents and reporters. But in the first set, Hoad refused to be frightened. His serve boomed across the net and skidded past Gonzales. His passing shots and net game were superb. He easily polished off the champion, 6–2.

Then Pancho loosened up and, in forty minutes, swept two sets, 6–3, 6–1, extending his tour lead to six matches.

When the match was finished, Gonzales dressed quickly. The next day's match was scheduled in New Castle, Pennsylvania almost four hundred miles away. There was a good deal of driving to be done and not much time for pleasantries. "I'll try to reach at least Buffalo tonight," he said. "Maybe I'll drive all the way." Then he climbed into the Thunderbird, switched on the ignition and, delicately, patiently, let the motor warm up. Alone in the small car, away from the crowds, the dark night enveloping him, Richard Gonzales looked like a traveling salesman, a Willie Loman without samples. He shifted into reverse, backed out of his parking spot and started off, alone, on a four hundred-mile trip to a tennis match. He intended to win it.

Levels of the Game: Arthur Ashe vs. Clark Graebner

by JOHN MCPHEE

One of the most brilliant pieces of tennis writing ever done is John McPhee's Levels of the Game, *a story about the Arthur Ashe-Clark Graebner 1968 U.S. Open semifinal, which Ashe won. McPhee, a writer for the* New Yorker, *was intrigued by the possibility of doing a double profile—telling the life stories of two individuals interlocked in one event—where A plus B would equal far more than just C. He found a suitable milieu in the first U.S. Open Championships at Forest Hills. This excerpt is merely the opening of the book-length piece, but if it inspires readers to seek out the original, its inclusion here will have served its purpose.*

ARTHUR Ashe, his feet apart, his knees slightly bent, lifts a tennis ball into the air. The toss is high and forward. If the ball were allowed to drop, it would, in Ashe's words, "make a parabola drop to the grass three feet in front of the base line." He has practiced tossing a tennis ball just so thousands of times. But he is going to hit this one. His feet draw together. His body straightens and tilts forward far beyond the point of balance. He is falling. The force of gravity and a muscular momentum from legs to arm compound as he whips his racket up and over the ball. He weighs 155 pounds; he is six feet tall, and right-handed. His build is barely full enough not to be describable as frail, but his coordination is so extraordinary that the ball comes off his racket at furious speed. With a step forward that stops his fall, he moves to follow.

On the other side of the net, the serve hits the grass and, taking off in a fast skid, is intercepted by the backhand of Clark Graebner. Graebner has a plan for this match. He does not intend to "hit out" much. Even if he sees the moon, he may decide not to shoot it. He will, in his words, "play the ball in the court and make Arthur play it, because Arthur blows his percentages by always trying a difficult or acute shot. Arthur sometimes tends to miss easy shots more often than he makes hard shots. The only way to get his confidence down is to get every shot into the court and let him make mistakes." Graebner, standing straight up, pulls his racket across and then away from the ball as if he had touched something hot, and with this gesture he blocks back Ashe's serve.

Ashe has crossed no man's land and is already astride the line between the service boxes, waiting to volley. Only an extraordinarily fast human being could make a move of that distance so quickly. Graebner's return is a good one. It comes low over the net and descends toward Ashe's backhand. Ashe will not be able to hit the ball with power from down there. Having no choice, he hits it up, and weakly—but deep—to Graebner's backhand.

Graebner is mindful of his strategy: Just hit the ball in the court, Clark. Just hit the ball in the court. But Graebner happens to be as powerful as anyone who plays tennis. He is six feet two inches tall; he weighs 175 pounds. The firmly structured muscles of his legs stand out in symmetrical perfection. His frame is large, but his reactions are instant and there is nothing sluggish about him. He is right-handed, and his right forearm is more than a foot in circumference. His game is built on power. His backswing is short, his strokes are compact; nonetheless, the result is explosive. There have to be exceptions to any general strategy. Surely this particular shot is a set-up, a sitter, hanging there soft and helpless in the air. With a vicious backhand drive, Graebner tries to blow the ball cross-court, past Ashe. But it goes into the net. Fifteen–love.

Graebner is nervous. He looks down at his feet somberly. This is Forest Hills, and this is one of the semifinal matches in the first United States Open Championships. Graebner and Ashe are both Americans. The other semifinalists are a Dutchman and an Australian. It has been thirteen years since an American won the men's singles final at Forest Hills, and this match will determine whether Ashe or Graebner is to have a chance to be the first American since Tony Trabert to win it all. Ashe and Graebner are still amateurs, and it was imagined that in this tournament, playing against professionals, they wouldn't have much of a chance. But they are here, close to the finish, playing each other. For Graebner to look across a net and see Ashe—and the reverse—is not in itself unusual. They were both born in 1943, they have known each other since they were thirteen, and they have played tournaments and exhibitions and have practiced together in so many countries and seasons that details blur. They are members of the United States Davis Cup Team and, as such, travel together throughout the year, playing for the United States—and also entering general tournaments less as individuals than en bloc, with the team.

A person's tennis game begins with his na-ture and background and comes out through his motor mechanisms into shot patterns and charactieristics of play. If he is deliberate, he is a deliberate tennis player; and if he is flamboyant, his game probably is, too. A tight, close match unmarred by error and representative of each player's game at its highest level will be primarily a psychological struggle, particularly when the players are so familiar with each other that there can be no technical surprises. There is nothing about Ashe's game that Graebner does not know, and Ashe says that he knows Graebner's game "like a favorite tune." Ashe feels that Graebner plays the way he does because he is a middle-class white conservative. Graebner feels that Ashe plays the way he does because he is black. Ashe, at this moment, is nervous. He is famous for what journalists have called his "majestic cool," his "towering calm," his "icy elegance." But he is scared stiff, and other tennis players who know him well can see this, because it is literally true. His legs are stiff. Now, like a mechanical soldier, he walks into position to serve again. He lifts the ball, and hits it down the middle.

Ashe's principal problem in tennis has been consistency. He has brilliance to squander, but steadiness has not been characteristic of him. He shows this, woodenly hitting three volleys into the net in this first game, letting Graebner almost break him, then shooting his way out of trouble with two serves hit so hard that Graebner cannot touch them. Ashe wins the first game. Graebner shrugs and tells himself, "He really snuck out of that one."

Ashe and Graebner walk to the umpire's chair to towel off and wipe their glasses before exchanging ends of the court. Both wear untinted, black-rimmed, shatterproof glasses, and neither uses any kind of strap to hold them on. "They just stay on," Ashe will say, shoving them with his forefinger back to the bridge of his nose. Graebner's glasses have extra-long temples that curl around his ears like ram's horns. The sun is really fierce. The temperature is in the eighties. Fourteen thousand people are in the stadium. Graebner is mumbling. One of Ashe's winning serves came as a result of confusion among the officials, who delayed the action while discussing some recondite point, and, because of the delay, awarded Ashe, in accordance with the rules of the game, an extra first serve. Ashe, who seldom says much to Graebner during visits to the umpire's chair, does use the occasion now to tell Graebner that he believes the officials' decision was fair and correct. Graebner glares but says nothing. Graebner's memory for lost points and adverse calls is nothing short of perfect, and months later he will still be talking about that extra serve that turned into an ace, for he can't help thinking what an advantage he might have had if he had been able to crack Ashe open in the very first game, as he almost did anyway. Ashe, for his part, believes that it is a law of sport that everything that happens affects everything that happens thereafter, and that Graebner can simply have no idea what patterns might have followed if he had won the debated point. Having so indicated, Ashe returns to the court. It is now Graebner's turn to serve.

To the question, Who has a bigger serve than Arthur Ashe? the answer is Clark Graebner. The word most frequently used by tennis players describing Graebner's serve is "crunch": "He just tosses the ball up and crunches it." Graebner's big frame rocks backward over his right leg, then rocks forward over his left as he lifts the ball for his first serve of the match. Crunch. Ace. Right down the middle at 130 miles an hour. Ashe is ten feet from the ball when it crosses the base line. His racket is only about halfway back when the ball hits the wall behind him. His face showing no expression, Ashe marches to the opposite side of the court and turns to receive the next serve. At any given moment of action, some thoughts that cross the mind of an athlete are quite conscious and others are just there, beneath the surface. Ashe will remember later on that at this particular moment in this match he is thinking, "Jesus, Graebner really hits the hell out of that first serve. He starts fast. He served nine aces in the first set against Stolle at Wimbledon, and it was over in no time." Graebner serves again—crunch, ace, right down the middle. Graebner is buoyant with sudden confidence. Ashe marches stiff-legged back

across the court. The second game is Graebner's quickly. Games are 1–all, first set.

Ashe lifts the ball and leans in to serve. Graebner sways and crouches as he waits. It must have cost at least $200,000 to produce this scene —to develop the two young men and to give them the equipment, the travel and the experience necessary for a rise to this level. The expense has been shared by parents, sponsors, tournament committees, the Davis Cup Team, and the United States Lawn Tennis Association, and by resort hotels, sporting-goods companies, Coca-Cola, and other interested commercial supporters. The players themselves paid their way to Forest Hills for this match, though—20 cents apiece, on the subway. Graebner lives in an apartment on East 86th Street with his wife, Carole; their one-year-old daughter, Cameron; and their infant son, Clark. Graebner spends much of his time selling high-grade printing papers, as assistant to the president of the Hobson Miller division of Saxon Industries, and he is in love with his work. He knows the exact height and tensile strength of the corporate ladder. His boss likes tennis very much, so Graebner's present rung is the handle of a racket. Ashe is an Army lieutenant, working in the office of the adjutant general at the United States Military Academy. He is a bachelor, and during tournament time at Forest Hills he stays at the Hotel Roosevelt. The Army is almost as tennis-minded as Graebner's boss, and Ashe has been given ample time for the game. But tennis is not, in any traditional sense, a game to him. "I get my kicks away from the tennis court," he will say. With accumulated leave time, he plans to go on safari in Kenya. It will be his first trip to Africa. In 1735, the Doddington, a square-rigger of eighty tons and Liverpool registry, sailed into the York River in Virginia carrying a cargo of 167 West African blacks. In or near Yorktown, the ship's captain, James Copland, traded the blacks for tobacco. One young woman, known only by a number, was acquired by Robert Blackwell, a tobacco grower from Lunenburg County. Blackwell gave her to his son as a wedding present—in the records of the county, she was listed only as "a Negur girl." According to custom, she took the

Reflections in a silver high: Arthur Ashe holds the first U.S. Open trophy, which he won by beating Tom Okker, 14–12, 5–7, 6–3, 3–6, 6–3. Ashe, an amateur at the time, had bested Clark Graebner in the semifinals for the right to face pro Okker. (Photo Courtesy of the USTA)

name of her owner. She married a man who, having the same owner, was also named Blackwell, and they had a daughter, Lucy, whose value is given in her owner's will at $50. Lucy Blackwell married Moses Blackwell, and their daughter Peggy Blackwell had a daughter named Peggy Blackwell, who married her cousin Tony Blackwell. Their daughter Jinney married Mike, an otherwise nameless Indian of the Sauk tribe who was a blood relative of Chief Black Hawk. The preacher who married them told Mike to call himself Mike Blackwell forevermore. Jinney and Mike had a son named Hammett, who, in this

chain of beings, was the last slave. Hammett was born in 1839. In 1856, he married Julia Tucker. They had twenty-three children. When he became free, he should have been given forty acres and a mule, of course, but no one gave them to him, so he bought his forty acres, in Dundas, Virginia. On the Blackwell plantation, where Hammett had lived, the plantation house—white frame, with columns—still stands, vacant and moldering. The slave cabin is there, too, its roof half-peeled away. Hammett's daughter Sadie married Willie Johnson, and their daughter Amelia married Pinkney Avery Ashe. His family line reached back, in analogous fashion, to the ownership of Samuel Ashe, an early governor of the State of North Carolina, whose name, until now, has been kept alive largely by the continuing existence of Asheville. Pinkney and Amelia had a son named Arthur, who, in 1938, married Mattie Cunningham, of Richmond. Their son Arthur Junior was born in 1943.

All these names are presented on separate leaves or limbs of an enormous family tree—six by seven feet, and painted on canvas—that is kept in the home of Thelma Doswell, a cousin of Arthur Ashe. Mrs. Doswell, who lives in the District of Columbia and is a teacher of children who have specific learning disabilities, did much of the research that produced the tree, using vacation time to travel to courthouses and libraries in southern Virginia. There are fifteen hundred leaves on the tree, and one leaf—Arthur Ashe, Jr.'s—is painted gold. Matrilineal in nature, the tree was made for display at annual reunions of the family, which have been held in various cities —Washington, Bridgeport, Philadelphia, Pittsburgh—and have drawn above three hundred people. The family has a crest, in crimson, black and gold. A central chevron in this escutcheon bears a black chain with a broken link, symbolizing the broken bonds of slavery. Below the broken chain is a black well. And in the upper corners, where the crest of a Norman family might have fleurs-de-lis, this one has tobacco leaves, in trifoliate clusters. Graebner has no idea whatever when his forebears first came to this country.

Graebner has the sun behind him now, and he means to use it. He runs around Ashe's serve, takes it on his forehand, and drives the ball up the middle. Graebner's favorite stroke is his forehand, and Ashe thinks that Graebner sometimes hits his forehands about twice as hard as he needs to, for pure Teutonic pleasure. Ashe punches back a deep volley, and Graebner throws a lob into the sun. Ashe moves back lightly, looking for the ball. In a characteristic that is pretty much his own, he prepares for overheads by pointing at the ball as it arcs down from the sky. He is like an antiaircraft installation. Left arm up, fist closed, index finger extended, he continues to point at the ball until he has all but caught it. His racket meanwhile dangles behind his back. Then it whips upward in the same motion as for a serve. He picks the ball out of the sun this time, but not well enough, and his shot goes into the net. Graebner plays on according to plan, forcing Ashe into another error, then finding a chance to send another lob into the sun. Ashe drops back, points, smashes—into the net. The score is now 15–40. All Graebner needs is one more point to break Ashe's serve. Ashe maintains his cool appearance, but he is thinking, "My God, what's happening? Here he goes. He's going to get the first set. And if he does, my confidence is going right down the tube. Graebner is a frontrunner, very tough when he's ahead. Someday he's going to get the lead on me and he's not going to give it up." In this game, Ashe's first serve has not once been successful. Perhaps enlivened by his fears, the next one goes in, hard and wide, drawing Graebner off balance, but Graebner reaches the ball and sends it low over the net and down the line. Ashe picks it up with a half-volley and tries to flick it cross-court at an acute angle, far from Graebner's reach—a fantastic shot, unbelievable. Other tennis players wonder who in his right mind would attempt something like that, but this is the way Ashe plays the game—the all but impossible shot at the tensest moment. As it happens, the shot goes out. Graebner wins the game. His strategy pays off. Ashe's serve is broken. If this were a wrestling match, Graebner could be said to have thrown his man.

Behind every tennis player there is another tennis player, and in Graebner's case the other player is his father. Clark grew up in Lakewood, Ohio, and played tennis as a boy in Lakewood Park, at Lakewood High School, and at clubs in Cleveland and Shaker Heights. Paul Graebner, Clark's father, grew up in Lakewood, and played tennis as a boy in Lakewood Park, at Lakewood High School, and at clubs in Cleveland and Shaker Heights. He was the state high-school tennis champion—a title his son would win three times. He was on the tennis team at Kenyon College and played briefly on the tournament circuit in the Middle West. He went to dental school at

Western Reserve University and then went into practice with his own father, Clark's grandfather. From then until now, the major diversion of Dr. Graebner's life has continued to be tennis. His week revolves around Wednesday afternoon and Saturday doubles games. When Clark was a beginner, however, Dr. Graebner completely gave up his own tennis for five years, and every Wednesday and Saturday and at all other practicable times he took Clark to a tennis court and patiently taught him the game. Clark was an only child, as Dr. Graebner himself had been. Clark's mother, Janet Clark Graebner, was an only child, too. Clark was seven when the formal instruction began, but he had regularly hit ground strokes with a squash racket against a basement wall when he was three years old. Within a short time, his absolutely favorite activity was smashing tennis balls, with a proper racket, against the door of the family garage. His mother would say to friends, "My one great big weapon over his head is 'If you don't take a nap, you can't hit the tennis ball against the garage door.'" The door happened to have windows in it, and little Clark's already Wagnerian forehand had a tendency to penetrate the glass. That was all right. Dr. Graebner covered the windows with Masonite.

When Dr. Graebner first hit strokes back and forth with Clark, they did not use a net. Dr. Graebner wanted Clark to hit a good flat stroke with follow-through, and not to worry about its altitude. When the foundation was grooved, they began to hit across a net, and to build Clark's game, shot by shot, through sheer repetition—backhands cross-court, forehands cross-court, forehands down the line, backhands down the line, lobs. Gradually, he just grew up into his overhead. "Every shot I hit now is built on the rudiments of my father's strokes," Clark acknowledges. "He taught me everything. I don't think he wanted to make me a champion. He just wanted to make me as good as I wanted to be. He hit balls at me for hundreds of thousands of hours, as if he were a Ball-Boy machine."

There are in tennis any number of devices that are used as teaching aids, the Ball-Boy machine, a $400 mortar that belches tennis balls, being one. The Graebners used none. "I was the only device. I was the only device," Dr. Graebner says. "I wasn't trying to build a champion. I was trying to get him interested in something he could do all his life."

"We did not push Clark into tennis." (Mrs. Graebner is talking.) "It was Clark's idea. No one pushed him. He was good at baseball. He might have been a baseball player. When he was nine and ready for the Little League, his father pointed out to him that he really couldn't do both baseball and tennis, and said, 'It's your decision.' Clark said, 'There is no decision,' and he gave up baseball."

Dr. Graebner did step in unequivocally when Clark showed an interest in ice hockey. "You have too much at stake, with all that you enjoy so much, to have it stopped by someone with one blow of a hockey stick," he said.

When Clark was first learning his tennis, Dr. Graebner in winter rented a junior-high-school gymnasium on Saturdays, and, later, took him to the indoor courts at the Cleveland Skating Club. "He hit and hit and hit," Dr. Graebner says. "He never got tired of it. You couldn't get him to stop." Dr. Graebner did what he could to keep Clark on the base line and force him to learn ground strokes—"Get back! Get back! You're edging up again. Get back! Get your fanny around. You're not getting your hips into it"—but Clark showed considerable precocity in his desire to get to the net. Most junior players tap ground strokes at one another for four hours a match, but Graebner, even when he was ten, was playing the Big Game—going for the net, trying for the sudden kill. "From a little tyke on, he had a lot of coordination," his father says. "He had it. He was a natural."

When Dr. Graebner and Clark were not on a tennis court together, they hit badminton cocks in their back yard or played ping-pong in the basement—anything that would improve the relationship between hand and eye. Clark shot pool with his mother. Asked what the family did for vacations, Mrs. Graebner says, "Vacations? You're kidding. We went to Florida so Clark could play tennis." Lakewood is just west of Cleveland, and almost every summer afternoon in his early playing years Clark went to Lake-

Clark Graebner was nicknamed "Clark Kent." He was the master of Crunch Tennis—he hit the ball so hard it didn't come back much and opponents would complain that they "didn't get enough tennis." (Photo Courtesy of the USTA)

wood Park—about eighteen acres under big elm and buckeye trees, with a bandstand, bowling greens, horseshoe pitches, and eight cement tennis courts. If his father was not with him, he played with older children, or firemen, policemen, doctors. When he was ten years old, he traveled across Cleveland to a tournament in

Shaker Heights, and this was his first appearance on the East Side. A boy who lived there was Warren Danne, eleven years old at the time and so much in love with tennis that he had decided he wanted to be the best tennis player in the world. Danne would eventually be the captain of the Princeton tennis team, and in the years of early adolescence he would be the doubles partner and inseparable friend of Clark Graebner. But now, as a child, watching Clark for the first time, Warren quietly took in all the grace and power that Clark already had and decided at that moment that he was going to try to become the second-best tennis player in the world.

Graebner is now planing along through the balance of the first set, unstoppable. He hits the ball six times and wins another game. He steps aside and lets Ashe's service games go by him like fast-moving cars; then he bears down some more. Both players talk to themselves. Tennis players are forever talking to themselves, sometimes out loud, and not infrequently at a volume high enough to be heard in the upper stands.

"I should be trying something bold," Ashe says. "He's just booming his serves in there."

Graebner hits a forehand down the line. *"Get* in there," he says.

An Ashe backhand drops eight feet inside the base line. "Don't be chicken. *Hit* the ball."

"Go *through* the ball. Don't come straight up." . . . "I don't believe it." . . . "I didn't move through that one. I was all arms on that shot." . . . "Turn your shoulder." . . . "Jesus, that was close." . . . "That's too tough." . . . "Graebner's saving himself for the next game." . . . "I've got that shot down pretty well now, that slicing backhand cross-court." . . . "Unbelievable!" . . . "Too tough." . . . "Arthur hasn't hit a return in the court."

Graebner is almost correct. In the entire first set, Ashe returns only three of Graebner's big first serves. Points are over quickly. Only one game goes as far as deuce. The longest point played in the set consists of six shots. The average number of strokes per point is two and a half.

Ashe and Graebner play tennis with an efficiency that is thought by some to diminish tennis itself. Modern power tennis—the so-called Big

Game (overwhelming serves followed by savage attacks at the net)—has now had many years in which to evolve, and Ashe and Graebner are among the ultimate refinements of it in the United States. Statistics of tennis published half a dozen years ago gave twenty-four hundred strokes as the expectable number that would be hit by two players playing serve-and-volley tennis in a match of average length (faulted serves excluded). If a spectator closes his eyes while Ashe and Graebner are playing, he is impressed by the cumulative silence. The stretches between points are long compared to the points themselves—sudden detonations quickly over, sporadic fire on a quiet front. This match between Ashe and Graebner will be of average length, and when it is over they will have hit the ball—all faulted serves *included*—821 times. After matches with Ashe or Graebner, some players have complained that they "didn't get enough tennis."

Reformers who remember the Old Game and think something should be done about this one have suggested eliminating the first serve or making the server serve from several feet behind the base line. Possibly the best suggestion is that the serve be left intact—for the sheer spectacle of it—but that the server not play his next shot without first letting the ball bounce. This would tend to keep the server back near the base line and remove the homicide from his following shot. Breaking serve would not so routinely be tantamount to breaking open a set. However,

there are plenty of people who like tennis the way Ashe and Graebner play it. It is the megagame. It has the spectral charm of a Joe Louis stalking a Billy Conn in silence and then dropping him with a few echoing thuds.

Both Ashe and Graebner have a great deal of finesse in reserve behind their uncomplicated power, but it surfaces once or twice a game rather than once or twice a point. Ashe is a master of dropshots, of drop half-volleys, of miscellaneous dinks and chips. He is, in the idiom of tennis, very tough at cat-and-mouse—the texture of the game in which both players, near the net, exchange light, flippy shots, acutely angled and designed for inaccessibility. Graebner is a deft volleyer, reacting quickly and dangerously at the net, but in general—although the two players technically have the same sort of game—Graebner does not have the variety of shots or the versatility that Ashe has. Ashe says that Graebner "could use a little more junk in his game."

Junk is the last thing Graebner needs at this moment. He is hitting so hard and so accurately that there is very little Ashe can do. Graebner says to himself, "Look at him. He's just slapping at my serves." Graebner is closing out the set. He is serving, and he leads five games to four and 40–15. He lifts the ball. Crunch. Ace. Right down the middle. Set to Graebner. He wins the first set, six games to four. For the second time in a quarter of an hour, Ashe feels his confidence going right down the tube.

The Intersexual Saga of Tennis

by BUD COLLINS

It was mixed singles, the biggest media event of the year, the greatest hype job in the history of tennis, the most watched match ever. It was Billie Jean King vs. Bobby Riggs. No one knew more how much—and how little—was really at stake than Bud Collins.

Riggs Ruining Mother's Day

A Dirty Old Man named Riggs is Geritoling himself up to spoil Mother's Day for Margaret Court, which may be the meanest thing a guy has done since a Greek named Oedipus got carried away as mama's little helper.

But Margaret Court isn't Bobby Riggs's mother. She's younger, bigger, stronger, faster than this fifty-five-year-old tennis hustler, who has set himself up as the Great Chauvinist Hope by challenging the world's number-one broad to a friendly little game—for $10,000.

Just a few friends in to observe, at San Diego Estates—plus the millions who'll be watching an international telecast, watching over Margaret's powerful right shoulder to see if she can shut up and shut off the little pest.

Boy and man, Robert Larimore Riggs—Wimbledon champ in 1939, U.S. champ in 1939–41—has been scheming and scuffling, contriving this kind of come-on: Where it looks like he's loaded himself with too much of a handicap. That's where the action begins, and Bobby al-

ways suggests there ought to be an amicable bet to keep the interest up.

Action is what Riggs lives for, like that Greek named Nick. Bobby will play anybody for money. Anybody. You . . . me . . . your mother-in-law . . . Stan Smith . . . Rod Laver. "We can set things up to make it interesting," says Bobby, who has handicapped himself by giving away huge point-spots; carrying fully-packed suitcase throughout a match; holding a dog on a leash.

"Riggs stories get exaggerated," he laughed over the phone. "It's not true that I played while holding a baby elephant on a rope. Even a baby elephant's too damn big. But I have tied myself to a poodle, which can make it tough to move. You can trip on that leash. It's even worse if the dog ain't housebroke.

"Now for you . . . uh," he mused, "I'll give you the two chairs. For a grand, okay?"

What's the two chairs, Bobby?

"You can put two chairs anywhere in my court, and we'll play a match. Naturally, you hit the chairs, or maneuver me into them, I lose the points. I can't beat you, but it'll be fun."

No thanks, Bobby.

"Tell Laver I'll play him that way—only I put the chairs in his court," Riggs said.

Margaret Court, who has won more major titles than anybody to play the game—male or female—isn't betting with Riggs, though. Not money anyway. It will be a straight match. No gimmicks—except, obviously the whole thing is a gigantic promotional gimmick grabbing the imagination of us all involved in the perennial war of the sexes. All three TV networks fought to cop the program. CBS won.

Although it's being billed as "winner-take-all" for ten grand, the Mother's Day Melee will mean much more to the women's movement in tennis. If Margaret loses, the money might not be enough consolation. "I'm not worried about it," she says, but—silly as it is—what she's betting may be the newly established prestige of women's tennis. This is what Bobby challenged: "I don't know why those dames are making big money, and complaining that they should get as much as the men. They're not as good. A broken down old guy like me can beat the best of them."

That started it. His verbal challenge went out along with I-dare-you telegrams to Court, Billie Jean King, Nancy Gunter and Chris Evert. Margaret accepted, saying, "I've beaten better men than Bobby in practice matches."

This isn't practice. Yet it isn't anything. Any really decent male player can beat the finest females at tennis. You could quickly name four or five guys in Boston who'd take Margaret apart: Paul Sullivan, Ned Weld, Jerry Cromwell, Ferdi Taygan, Chum Steele. There are several hundred across the country.

But the brashness of the aging con man in short pants—the fact that he was a "name"—has made it a classic of hype and ballyhoo, something like a big fight between boxers of contrasting styles. Probably the match itself won't compare with the buildup. Bobby loves it. His name is alive again, and he's giving the foe the kind of edge that makes talk and betting inevitable: Can Margaret, with physical and chronological superiority, outgun the crafty ancient?

Billie Jean King worries, "Our (the female pros) reputation is at stake, and I'm afraid Bobby will win. His nerves are too tough for Margaret, and Margaret wasn't too well at Sea Pines last week. Here's an old jerk, who dyes his hair, waddles like a duck, and has trouble seeing. Everybody knows the good men are better than the good women—but if a guy like Bobby can beat our best . . . well, that has to hurt us. We have nothing to gain. If Margaret beats an old guy, so what?"

When money's involved, look out for Riggs. He carries his own bookmaker (posing as a spectator) to lay on and lay off bets in the grandstand. Bobby made $100,000 betting on himself to win all three events (singles, doubles and mixed) at Wimbledon thirty-four years ago. "It was legal, with a bookie," he recalls. "I just let 100 pounds ride (worth about $500 then) at three-to-one for the singles, six-to-one for the doubles and twelve-to-one for the mixed. Of course if I lost in any of the three I lost my dough. Five hundred bucks was a lot of money in 1939 . . . for an amateur tennis player," he laughs. So was 100 grand. "I've still got a bank account in England," he says.

Tennis isn't a betting sport in this country, but for one day, Riggs will change that. He'll have thousands going in side bets himself, the way he always has. He reveals in that nervous atmosphere. It's new to Margaret.

People who've watched Riggs's action matches wonder, though, as Rod Laver puts it: "If Bobby has bet on Margaret and will go into the tank?"

Or maybe she'll rise to the bait magnificently. Maybe, as Rosie Casals hopes, "Margaret will run him to a coronary." So do Susan B. Anthony, Amelia Bloomer, Victoria Woodhull and the Libbers of Bobby's vintage who'll be looking down from that great court in the sky. Plus Margaret's contemporaries such as Gloria Steinem, Germaine Greer and Betty Friedan, who'll audit TV.

Porcine instincts have led me to put my money on Bobby, who has all angles, on court and off. But my heart's with Margaret. I mean, how can I cheer against a big mama on Mother's Day?

Bobby the Wolf and Little Red Riding Hood
When he poses nude for the centerfold of *Geriatrics Digest,* what shade should Bobby Riggs dye his hair?

Will he accept an offer from Bertolucci to

play the lead in a musical of "Last Tango in Paris"?

Can he maneuver himself into a best-of-three challenge from Linda Lovelace?

Is it time for him to begin peddling "You've Come a Long Way, Bobby!" bumper stickers?

Or marketing his "Oldie but Goodie" superiority complex vitamins for senile swingers?

Must tiny Bobby fight a duel with six-foot-five-inch Barry Court for dishonoring—and devaluing—Barry's wife and meal ticket? And if so, will it be the Australian's choice of weapons: Beer cans and boomerangs at thirty paces?

These are among the problems of sudden fame for Robert Larimore Riggs, who has come up with a new schtick: Mugging young ladies with a wooden club in broad daylight—on international TV yet. Instead of being arrested, he is hailed as a defender of the faith in faded fathers.

That tells you what's happened to law and order. In the old days they'd have strung up this dirty old man for molesting an innocent who didn't know any better. Today he gets celebrity rating, and acclaim as the greatest sex symbol for the aged since Strom Thurmond.

Bobby never got this much attention when he was playing straight tennis. But papa's got a brand new bag. In fact he'd like to find one every week. If he could only pass, Riggs would make a million on the Virginia Slims circuit. No chance there. Judge Bookman of Houston, an official of the women's pro tour, says, "We won't accept Bobby in our tournaments. Not even in drag. The only way we'll let him enter is if he gets the operation and the silicone treatments."

Is that reverse discrimination?

But you're wrong if you think I'm gloating. Or pleased because I advised you to refinance the house and put it on Bobby. True I'm dining out handsomely on numerous bets I collected, but I'm only just catching up. Remember me: I'm the guy who picked Dewey over Truman; Liston over Ali; Poland to win World War II; and Westmoreland over the Viet Cong.

Sure, Bobby gave a boost to the Social Security set. You had to admire his gall and ability, and put him up there in your pantheon alongside Ponzi, Billy Sol Estes, Willie Sutton, John Mitch-

ell and the rest of the quick-fingered and flim-flamming. It was the old carny gig, and Bobby was playing the shell game with the rube from the Outback.

Yet only a sadist could have enjoyed watching. It was one of those things you have to see, like a bull fight or a geek eating broken glass. A spectacle, a happening, a public execution. But what was poor Margaret doing there? This wasn't her milieu and she found out quick. This wasn't Mrs. Muscle slugging out the less quick and strong on the lawn at tea-time while hushed worshippers watch appreciatively in a cathedral called Wimbledon. It was Little Red Riding Hood walking into the poolroom to test Wolf Bobby at eight-ball.

Even Wimbledon turned on her once, in 1971. They were tired of Margaret winning everything by then. When fresh-faced Evonne Goolagong appeared to captivate London, the hostility of the crowd—yes those mannered Limies—made her choke. It was quiet, subtle hostility, but the evil messages got to her then. England cried out for Goolagong, just as mankind prayed for Riggs. Anybody who witnessed Court's collapse marked her nerves as suspect in any confrontation at the climax of a publicity buildup.

So why did she stray? "Money," says Billie Jean King. "Margaret couldn't resist a guaranteed $10,000."

Could you, B.J.?

"I did," says Billie Jean, who appears next in line to try to vindicate womankind against St. Bobby, patron saint of dirty old men everywhere. Six weeks ago, amidst furious negotiations involving the three networks, Billie Jean said, "if I'm going to risk my reputation, it won't be for ten grand." Her price was somewhere between $25,000 and $50,000, and the networks said no-thanks.

"I didn't think Margaret's nerves would hold up," King said, "but I didn't think she'd play so awful either. This hurts us. This is why I'm challenging Bobby. Somebody's got to shut him up, and show the public what's happening. I don't mean we can beat top men—but we can play well and fight. Margaret was awful. It wasn't a real indication of our tennis." B.J. at least has the style, combativeness and chutzpah to beat him.

As challenger, she wants men's rules (three of five sets), and her own court in Sea Pines, South Carolina. The resort she represents there will put up $10,000 for the winner. Of course there'll be added TV revenue, and the challenger, King, will want a big chunk of that.

So there may be another sideshow. Riggs has to hope so. He could become more famous than Bluebeard for pushing chickies around. And if he runs out of opponents, it's either silicone, or back to backgammon hustling.

Nuts, Shekels in Astrodome

"I want you to shuffle off to Houston," said the boss.

"Houston?"

"That's right," he said. "The Astrodome..."

"Football game? Ali fighting again?"

"Nope. Tennis. Some old guy's playing a broad, and people are buying tickets. The honor of old guys and broads is supposed to be at stake..."

"Come off it, boss... you got to be kidding ... a tennis game in the Astrodome?"

And that's how I wound up in the middle of a pecan grove on the outskirts of Houston, Texas. It seemed appropriate with all those nuts around that a tennis court had been built here only yesterday morning and carpenters were hammering away in the completion of grandstands as The Broad in question, Billie Jean King, skipped onto this court in her blue suede sneakers.

Promptly she beat up in succession Cynthia Doerner (6–0, 6–4) and Kristien Kemmer (6–0, 6–2). Only these weren't sparring partners, and this wasn't a hideaway in the wilds as the heavyweight champ of the tennis branch of the women's movement got ready for the champion of the dirty old men, Bobby Riggs.

It was the $30,000 Virginia Slims of Houston Tournament at the Net Set Club which is attached to a housing development, and Billie Jean was playing and winning her first two rounds—"be back Friday for the quarterfinals, after I get through with Bobby," she promised the promoter, Hugh Sweeney.

What was she doing out there on that steaming asphalt court playing real, live matches with all that alleged honor and genuine money at stake two nights later in the Dome? "Well, I committed myself to this tournament before I signed for Riggs," said Billie Jean, who could take away as much as $190,000 if she wins, and will settle for about $120,000 otherwise. "Besides I needed the work."

It seemed like Muhammad Ali taking on a couple of minor contenders for pocket money the week of a title fight. Not even Ali would do that. Suppose she broke a leg or pulled a muscle or had her head split open by an aggrieved opponent. "I'm not worried about my health now," said Billie Jean, who had gone groggy in her last two big matches, losing to Julie Heldman at Forest Hills and Chris Evert at Hilton Head, South Carolina, and had hurt her knee less than a month ago. "I'm stronger than ever."

That seems to be the King theme. "My vibes are good, and I feel like Helen Reddy singing, 'I Am Woman.'" Which Ms. Reddy, who's appearing in Houston, may do in a serenade to Billie Jean prior to the match. It sounds like the sort of hype Bundini would pull for Ali.

As you can gather, the promotion evokes the heavyweight brouhahas of Ali in the Dome. I keep looking for Big Cat Williams or Buster Mathis to show up in the umpire's chair.

Larry King, watching his infrequent roommate put away two opponents in less than two hours, seems to have it in perspective: "Little and big," said Ms. King's Mr. King. "Little meaning, but big attention. Good for the game." Better for his bank account, since attorney King is also Billie Jean's agent.

"It's show biz, of course it is," said Billie Jean. "That's what sports is today. But," she narrowed her blue eyes, "when the match starts the BS is over and Bobby better believe it. He isn't BS-ing me when it begins because that's when I start hitting shots. He better not try giving me flowers like he did Margaret Court. I told him I'm giving him a subscription to *Ms.* magazine, and he didn't know what I was talking about. No awareness, that man. But I like him. He's made this match take off. I don't think he's the chauvinist he says he is. He talks so chauvinist that some of the chauvinists can't take him.

"He said he'd jump off a bridge if he loses. Well, man, I'll be out there selling tickets for the bridge-jumping. He says I can't take the pressure. Tell me this—has he ever played this big a money-pressure match?"

"Who has the most to lose in this?" she paused for a moment. "Heck, he does. If I win, Bobby's through. Who'd pay to watch him against a top old guy? Pancho Gonzales would kill him.

"Bobby needs us!"

So he does, the clever little piggy. Where would Bobby be without women, indeed? "I hope all his women keep him up for this," said B.J. "He'll need all the help he can get.

"He doesn't turn me on with those legs of his. I can be sexist, too. I know a couple of sportswriters with legs better than Bobby's." Bless you, dear.

I never heard Buster Mathis knock Ali's legs, but Billie Jean is starting to talk tougher than any of the fighters who've come into the Dome. "I can go the distance (best-of-five sets for the first time in her career) with any old guy even if he's in as good shape as Bobby."

That was all she had to say about Robert Larimore Riggs, the white, middle-aged, hard-of-hearing Muhammad Ali. "Now I'm going to practice against men, rest, and talk to nobody," said Billie Jean, leaving me where I belonged—in the middle of a pecan grove with the rest of the nuts.

Riggs Serves Pure Schlock

Little Bobby Riggs was up past his bedtime, and his big brother, John Riggs, at sixty-three, was pouting and muttering, "Sure he was a fresh punk when he was a kid—but he wasn't this bad. Come on, Bobby, you got to get your rest. You got to take this thing seriously . . ."

Bobby Riggs, who has done more to advance the cause of womanhood than anybody

since Jack the Ripper, was scrunched up in an easy chair in green-and-gold ski pajamas. His eager Koala bear face was dominated by an open mouth as he talked and gorged on vitamin capsules. You may have your daily glass of orange juice, but Riggs daily has two thousand oranges —"that's the equivalent in the amount of vitamin C he takes," said his nutrition engineer, Rheo H. Blair, who lounged at Bobby's elbow, ingesting pills himself.

It was about one in the morning, and Bobby was feeling very good. Earlier in the evening, at his workout across the street from his motel, he'd lifted $1000 from a local banker named Sanders, a joyous holdup with racket—joyous for both. "These Texans are big sports all right. They come from all over to play me and lose. They love it. A hundred bucks is the minimum," said Bobby. Another contributor to the Riggs campaign fund was a Congressman, Rep. Bill Archer (R-Texas). "He flew in from Washington just to play, paid his hundred, and flew off again with his button and his purple heart.

"They all want to be hustled by the Happy Hustler. When I beat them I give them a button that says 'I've Been Hustled by Bobby Riggs.' And a little purple heart pin."

Another of the hustled was Dr. Denton Cooley. "You know, the heart guy. He told me a man my age, fifty-five shouldn't play singles. Then he examined me and said I've got the heart of a forty-year-old." A forty-year-old lion.

The phones were ringing. Lorne Kuhle—Riggs's top sparring partner was acting as a buffer. But Bobby was on two calls at once. And on, on, on continually in person. A masterful social juggler. "Yeah, Jim Welch . . . how are you Jim . . . how are things in Boston?" Bobby spoke into a phone. "Don't forget you're bringing down that sixteen-pound all-day sucker for me to give to Billie Jean. What a lollipop!" Riggs said to the candy manufacturer. "Just another surprise for her . . ."

The pill man, Rheo Blair, passed a plate containing twenty-or-so capsules to Bobby. "Time for more," Blair said. "Bobby takes more than five hundred a day, but some days he can't get down more than three hundred . . ."

Bobby grimaced and said in a low voice, "Who the hell knows if they do any good . . . but it's psychological. He's got me believing they've rejuvenated me. And if you believe . . . but I think all these pill are giving me a glass stomach."

"It's the ortho-molecular approach of mega-doses," Blair was saying. "These pills, among other things give him the equivalent of six pounds of beef and two pounds of liver a day. Liver's very important for stamina. You know," said Blair, a wavy-haired, youthful Californian. "They did some tests on rats with these liver doses. They had two rats. One they gave the massive doses, and the other, nothing. Then they threw the rats in freezing water. Of course they died. But the one that took all the liver lasted for hours; the other was gone in a few minutes . . ."

Munching away like an experimental rodent himself, Bobby screeched, "but I'm not playing this match with Billie Jean in ice water, Rheo. This is a tennis match, not a swimming meet."

Supposedly it is a tennis match that Bobby will indulge in with Billie Jean King at the Astrodome, but it's become more than that. No matter how you feel about the young libber against the old libertine, Bobby has turned it into Schlock 'Round the Clock.

And reveling in every second of it. Riggs is no Walter Mitty. He was a great player once, the best in the world in 1946 when he took the pro tour away from Don Budge. But in those days he never sucked up as much glory as he wallows in now. No magazine covers. No TV. No universal celebrity. "I was big with people who followed tennis, but that was a minority. It was nothing like today, and I love it. Maybe I'm a gladiator against Women's Lib, but a lot of women love me. More than ever.

"But," he said, pleading celibacy during his last days of half-hearted training, "all I'm doing with my bosom buddies (as he calls his female friends) is shaking hands.

"Hey," he jumped up, "look at these costumes people want me to wear for the match." He began to model creations that had come in from designers across the country. One, baby blue with stars and "Bobby Riggs—Men's Lib-

ber" on the back, was decorated by probably the first codpiece to adorn a pair of tennis shorts.

"Look at this." He slipped on a T-shirt with cutouts, baring his breasts.

His white-haired big brother, John, snapped, "Take that off, Bobby, and don't wear it. It's nauseous in the extreme. Bobby was never this bad as a kid. Go to bed. You need your rest. Billie Jean's resting."

"But not sleeping," Bobby says. "She's got to be worrying about me. But, okay, John. My brother's had four heart attacks and I don't want to upset him."

Little Bobby Riggs finally did as he was told. The monologue ended momentarily, and he went to bed and dreams of sugar plum hustles danced in his head.

Wrinkled Tiger Tests the Lady

The lady or the wrinkled tiger?

The goddess of the tennis auxiliary of Women's Lib or the sex god of the Geritol Generation?

Billie Jean or Bobby?

Who knows or who cares?

Apparently an awful lot of men and women across this Watergate-crashed country, who are debating and betting on the subject of Billie Jean in Wonderland against Mad Hatter Riggs. Curiouser and curiouser gets the spectacle which may be the best floated issue since the South Sea Bubble gang was watering stocks in 1711.

But your curiosity should be satisfied when through the looking glass of TV Billie Jean King and Robert Larimore Riggs—"born the same year as her father, 1918"—will perform in the living rooms of America.

Opposite them on another channel will be that other lovable couple, "Bonnie and Clyde," who had their own racket: Robbing banks. It wasn't nearly as profitable, but it may have been more honorable than a fresh old man picking on a fresh-faced young woman. Or vice versa.

If you're silly-rich and curious, of course you're right here at the gates of the Astrodome, paying $100 a seat for the right to be close enough to sniff the athletes, who will have doused themselves in cosmetics they've endorsed. You can get in for $6, too, but those seats are as far away as East Boston. It will mostly be the more expensive seats swelling the crowd to as many as thirty-five thousand.

Never have so many people witnessed in person a game of tennis, if that's what is it.

"It's more, much more—the battle of the sexes," trumpeted Bobby Riggs for the 2,081,917th time. "Man against woman; sex against sex; an old one-foot-in-the-grave champion against the current Wimbledon champion. People can identify. Husbands argue with wives, bosses with secretaries. Everybody wants to bet." (The odds are two-and-a-half to one Riggs, according to Jimmy-the-Greek Snyder who arrived from Las Vegas.) "It's great for the game—and it isn't bad for Riggs and King." Hardly: The winner will take at least $200,000, the loser half that amount.

Seldom has a champion been so overconfident as Riggs, the self-proclaimed monarch of women's tennis by virtue of his 6–2, 6–1 molesting of Margaret Court in May.

"Are you sure you can win, dad?" asked his sixteen-year-old son, Billy.

"Son, no broad is gonna beat me."

Regretfully, that's my feeling. Riggs in four sets is my sexist, piggy guess, but I wouldn't go into mourning if Billie Jean shoved the little con man's other foot into that grave he keeps citing. Could it be Miami Beach 1964 all over again: The speed and youth of Billie Jean overcoming the fearsome, elder Riggs, as Muhammad Ali did Sonny Liston? The comparison isn't quite apt since Riggs in spirit out-Ali's Ali. "That man talks better'n Ali," said George Foreman, imported to present the winner's check.

"I'll tell you why I'll win," says Riggs. "She's a woman, and they just don't have the emotional stability. She'll choke just like Margaret Court did."

That infuriates King, who's been a big-match player. "That creep runs down women, that's why my feeling is like—hate. I like him for many things, but I hate him putting down women, not giving us credit as competitors."

"Please don't call me a creep," Bobby asked her at a joint press conference. "You don't mean it."

"Creep . . . that stands," said B.J.

Lorne Kuhle, Riggs's sparring partner, worried, "he's exhausting himself having a ball. Look at that . . ."

Riggs was leading his buxom cheerleaders in Riggs cheers at a Riggs pep rally in his hotel ballroom. He's been as accessible as a Combat Zone hooker, while Billie Jean has pretty much secluded herself—"psyching myself up."

Both are driven winners, and somewhere in the midst of a super-hype that would make P.T. Barnum weep in envy, they will play a tennis match to the hilt. Billie Jean is okay at Wimbledon. How will she be in Wonderland?

"If I lose, it's not the end. I know where I stand in women's tennis," she says. "If Bobby loses, he can go back to his booze and broads in Beverly Hills—but that's it in tennis."

"If I lose?" mused Riggs. "I guess I'll be marked the biggest talking bum of all time. I'll head for that bridge to jump off."

"Suicide Bridge in Pasadena?" somebody asked, remembering Bobby had mentioned the notorious structure.

"Hell, no," replied Riggs. "I'll go to Lake Havasu in Arizona and leap from London Bridge that they've put up there. It's about ten feet. I've got too much money in the bank, and I'm having too much fun to go jumping off serious bridges."

Love at Last Sight . . .

Susan B. Anthony, Elizabeth Cady Stanton, Joan of Arc, Amelia Bloomer, Emmaline Pankhurst, Carrie Nation, Molly Pitcher and a lot of other bygone heroines must have been rocking on that great court in the sky when their spiritual descendant, Billie Jean King, landed on Bobby Riggs like a ton of mascara.

"How did Bobby play?" Billie Jean was answering questions following her emotionally uplifting 6–4, 6–3, 6–3 triumph over the Voice of Chauvinism in the tumult amidst the tumult created by 30,472 customers at the Astrodome. "Well," she giggled, "he played like a woman, Uh, like a lot of women I beat on our tour."

Billie Jean, a swooping volleyer who made Bobby a drooping follower, had never been accused of "playing like a woman" before Riggs began chiding her. Her attacking style is that of the leading male pros. Her competitive verve is second to none in any game. But Riggs had said that underneath it all she was "still a woman," which from his lips was a put-down. "She'll choke like they all do. No matter how good they are in their league, they can't even beat an old man like me with one foot in the grave."

As Billie Jean came on like thunder, Bobby Riggs was duck-waddling around the Astrodome with both feet in the grave, a guest of honor at Waterman's.

"Just one night—him or me—that's the kind of challenge I like," Billie had said. "If I have to play five sets, even though I never have, my psyche will drive me to do it."

Anything he could do, she could do better. Why not? She was twenty-six years younger. But most of us believed he could out-cute her, drive her nutty with lobs, and that his own time-tested competitiveness would break her down. The odds were two-and-a-half to one on him for The Big Scrape-off (each had boasted "they'll have to scrape [the loser] off the Astrodome floor").

"Well, she never let me do what I wanted to do. She was all over me," sighed Bobby, who had only nice things to say as a loser. "I'd like a rematch, but that's up to Billie. She didn't beat me that bad."

Bad enough, as far as B.J. was concerned, and it appears the Super Schlock of mixed singles is over. "I was upset with Margaret Court for accepting his challenge in the first place," said Billie Jean of Bobby's 6–2, 6–1 conquest of Court, the foremost female of this season. "We've got enough problems trying to build all women's sports without getting into something like this. But once Margaret had lost—and played so badly, nervously—in losing, I felt it was up to me to prove that we women pros can play a lot better than that. It wasn't Margaret's kind of scene—but I love this, all the noise and ballyhoo. I can handle it."

With the band playing, the dancing girls jiggling, the crowd screaming, Billie handled Bobby like a starlet hustling a sugar daddy, such as he proclaimed himself to be.

The hustler got hustled, muscled and bustled out of the joint. So inspired and invincible was she that Bobby was forced to say, "I guess the women are too tough for a fifty-five-year-old."

She beamed and whispered, "he's okay."

They had both hustled the public and the media into producing unprecedented monies and headlines for tennis. "My dreams for tennis came true tonight," said Billie whose $100,000 purse put her over the 100-grand mark for the third successive year. "Everybody was watching. Everybody talked about it. That was a first for tennis. It was good from that viewpoint."

"I've said all that women are good for is the bedroom, but," Bobby smiled wanly, "Billie's pretty good elsewhere, too. She was great." Billie Jean smiled again, then went off to "celebrate with a couple of beers."

Early the next morning workmen were cleaning up the empty Astrodome. The Preposterous Panorama was over, the MCP's had gone home to nightcaps and nightmares, and the workmen were scraping something off the floor. It may have been Robert Larimore Riggs.

Pig and Riggs Share Sorrow
"What is the pig called?" somebody asked.

"Pig . . . just Pig," answered a tall young man who was holding Bobby Riggs's pig while it nuzzled and nibbled in a bowl of fried shrimp, declining the offer of a scotch and soda from a woman whose neckline plunged to the floor.

Pig was a gift to Riggs from Billie Jean King, before she turned little piggy Bobby into a boiled ham at the Astrodome. It was about two A.M. at the party following that phantasmagoria advertised as a tennis game, and Riggs and Pig were exchanging occasional soulful looks over the drink in Bobby's hands. Bobby, who said he'd had nothing to drink for a month but fruit juices, water, and protein elixir stirred by his nutritionist, Rheo Blair, was now going at the booze the way Chris Evert goes after a backhand—with both hands.

He deserved it. A blond actress, Sandra Giles—one of Bobby's Bosom Buddies—was stroking his back, and other assortedly handsome females were sliding up for a kiss and a coo: "I still love you, Bobby . . ."

Pig munched on a slice of roast beef rare, and Bobby murmured, "Do you think anybody will want to talk to me now I'm a loser? I can't get over how quick Billie Jean was . . . I hit balls past her, but she'd flick them back with unbelievable half-volleys . . . I wasn't my best . . . but no alibis . . . she made the action . . . she pushed me . . . sure I'd like a rematch . . ."

Across the penthouse barroom of the Astroworld Motel, Jackie Barnett, a show-biz slicker from Hollywood who got it all started by promoting the Riggs conquest of Margaret Court, was saying, "Listen, there's a rematch clause." He sounded like a fight promoter, and there was nothing the atmosphere of King-Riggs resembled more than a heavyweight title fight. Except there's never been a fight duded up like this bout at which the principals arrived like empress and mandarin—she on a sedan chair borne by Central Casting-style Adonises, he in a rickshaw pulled by an array of chickies who can be described only as the greatest mass of breastworks since the fortification of Bunker Hill.

"Oh, Bobby can have a rematch . . . it's in the contract," Jackie Barnett was assuring his listeners. Only Billie Jean won't have it. "It wouldn't be as big next time, but you could do it in Madison Square Garden," Barnett was fantasizing.

"No amount of money," Billie Jean said earlier when she looked in on the party briefly. "I proved what I had to prove. We women did enough for Bobby Riggs. He became a big man long after his day. A nice man, though. Maybe he can play better . . ."

Possibly Riggs can take his act out of the country for one more shot: A rematch with Margaret Court in a male chauvinist bastion called Australia.

"What was wrong with Bobby? Was he sick?" the diehards kept asking, unwilling to concede that Billie Jean—higher on emotion than you can get on pills—had played him off his duck-walking feet. "Do you suppose Bobby tanked—bet against himself?"

"No way," interjected an associate of Billie Jean's from Philadelphia. And he produced a $10,000 check decorated by Riggs's signature: The fruits of a wager with Bobby. Riggs wouldn't say how much he'd lost. It was plenty, but he could afford it. "It still hurts, though," he said.

Not far from Riggs, Gracie Lichtenstein, a journalist who'd predicted Billie Jean's victory in *The New York Times*, was yipping, "we're rich!" She and the brilliant feminist writer, Nora Ephron, had just collected their women's lib communal bet from Bobby. They'd hustled the *Ms.* magazine crowd and other friends to raise $500 to bet against $800 of Bobby's in a head-to-head gamble: The Movement against the monster. "It was a spiritual thing," Ephron had explained two days before when she arrived at Bobby's hotel room with the $500 in fives, tens and twenties.

"Money down the drain, Nora," Bobby had said whipping out eight hundred-dollar bills as his end, and giving the $1300 to a holder. "I know," Ephron said. "But we have to back Billie Jean. This came from a lot of people. A shrink put up $50."

"You mean a smart guy like a shrink, a guy with a psychiatric degree, would bet against me?" chortled Riggs.

"It was a she," Ephron said.

"You broads use she-shrinks?" he was amazed. "I'll be damned. You're really with the outfit."

But the outfit had beaten Riggs out of his money just as their avenging angel had beaten him out of his jock. Lichtenstein and Ephron were counting the money. "Thirteen hundred we made, Nora," Grace was ecstatic.

"Please, Grace," said Larry Merchant, whose new book, *The National Football Lottery* pertains to gambling. "You put up $500, so you only won $800. Not $1300."

"Thirteen hundred sounds better," she said.

Everything sounded better to Billie Jean's people, and tasted better. She'd taken the broads off the hook Margaret Court had left them dangling from. "So it was a circus, and so what?"

said another writer, Neil Amdur. "But I think Billie Jean's win really did mean a lot to all women athletes. It was an inspiration. They don't play against men, but they get put down by men. Their games are good and interesting, and they play as hard, but they don't get much attention. Billie Jean has got to mean a lot to them."

Bobby was leaving the party, double-teamed by drinks and blonds. "Nice try, Bobby," people were saying and meaning it. "You made the show . . . You built it . . . it was your night as much as hers."

So it was. Bobby shook his dyed head in appreciation. "I gotta go jump off London Bridge into Lake Havasu . . ." You haven't heard the last of Riggs's ballyhoo.

"I wish I'd seen him in his prime," said an alleged blond writer from *Family Circle.*

"Hell," I said. "This is his prime. Who knew or cared who Bobby Riggs was in 1939 when he only won Wimbledon and 100-grand betting on himself to win? He's a magazine cover, a genuine piece of American Present and maybe Future Schlock. Maybe it tells you how sick our country is, but Bobby Riggs is a prime cultural hero." This is the kind of speeches I make at three A.M.

Pig wasn't listening. Pig didn't give a sow's ear about me, Bobby Riggs or Billie Jean King, maybe a sign of stability. Pig had become a item of Americana, too, a little red body on nationwide TV, acknowledged by Howard Cosell, applauded by 30,472 customers, framed by hundreds of cameras. Pig had even slept through all the noise of the occasion—the music, the cheers, the boos, the general tumult and ragtime. Very stable.

And now Pig was into the free shrimp, enjoying until that day when—like his master—Pig, too, would become a boiled ham.

The Man Who Has to Win

by AL BARKOW

Becoming a champion is one thing, but staying at the top is quite another—an impossible, lonely obsession. Jimmy Connors reached the top and like every other champion before and since couldn't stay there. This was never more evident than in his defeat by Guillermo Vilas in the 1977 U.S. Open final. Al Barkow, veteran observer of golf greats, in addition to other sports interests, followed Connors during that tournament seeking answers to what drives a champion on to constantly keep winning.

FOR angrily leaving the West Side Tennis Club within minutes after being defeated in the 1977 U.S. Open singles final, Jimmy Connors was roundly booed; bad form, his not shaking the winner's hand or appearing at the presentation ceremony. From this quarter, though, Connors's behavior after that match gets a measure of understanding. The way the match itself concluded was rather bad form, considering its importance. The last, decisive line call that sank Connors came so late it seemed the result of a judge intimidated by the vigorous and highly vocal pro-Vilas crowd, which mobbed the court too soon after the call was finally made to further shabby the finish. Then too, that Connors was a thoroughly whipped athlete, and one who in any case is prone to truculence, makes it

not surprising he would pass up end-of-match formalities. The handshake, at least, was impossible for the crush of press and fans surrounding Guillermo Vilas.

More difficult to understand about Connors, though, is his behavior only a few days earlier, after he beat Manuel Orantes in a quarterfinal match. Against Orantes, Connors was at his most formidable, a blitzkrieg in short pants driving one perfectly aimed yellow bomb after another into his opponent's tennis factory. Orantes at his finessing finest would have trouble stopping Connors that night, and the Spaniard was a bit off; Connors's exceptional force may have been the reason. So dynamically good was Jimmy, even those who detest his public personality could not help but admire his talent for his game.

For Connors himself, the Orantes match had to be a tremendously satisfying athletic "hour." But one could hardly believe that when following him closely and listening to him as he walked back to the clubhouse. Connors was stiff with fury, his face hard-set, his normally narrow, shrouded eyes slitted tighter still. He was growling curses, their focus defined only when his mother, walking close at his side, asked if he was upset by "that woman." Apparently, a woman in a courtside seat had heckled Jimmy. "Yeah,"

216

Connors answered his mother, "she said f———
you, to me. I told her I'd f——— her, see me
after the match."

Then, one of Connors' retinue—the sturdy
young men who protect him at his four corners
going to and from competition—said, "There
was some guy who said. . . . you, too." "Yeah?"
Jimmy, said, "Then I'll do him, too. Bring him
around." The bodyguards laughed. Mrs. Connors was expressionless, staring straight ahead
with the same taut intensity she maintains when
watching Jimmy on court. If she had any qualms
or reservations about her son's language and
sexual allusions, they did not show.

As the Connors group strode on, Jimmy
continued to spew a stream of hard curses, although not to any specific target now. It was
more the guttering of an animal still in the throes
of conquering violence. In all, a strange scene,
made eerier by the illumination of the few spot-
lights that quarter-lit the area between stadium
and clubhouse. It was on the one hand something one might see and hear at a small-time fight
club, on the other a grotesque tableau from the
imagination of a sportswriting Franz Kafka.

Twenty minutes later, after a massage and
shower, Connors met the press. He was calmed
down now and as he entered the room and noticed the close-packed bunch of journalists
awaiting him, he murmured, "Ah, this is more
like it." His earlier press conferences had been
sparsely attended owing to more tennis to
cover and Connors's previous victories being
relatively unspectacular. Obviously pleased with
maximum attention now, Connors took a seat
at the table, on which stood a microphone. His
first act was to fondle the microphone irradica-
bly with his hand.

What to make of this young man, Jimmy
Connors? He refuses all requests, even polite
ones, for private, one-on-one interviews; "You'll
get all you want at the press conferences," he
tells you, implying that what is seen and heard of
him in those crowded circumstances is either all
there is or all he wants to be shown or known.
Yet in these appearances he is often smug or
arrogant in victory, peevish in defeat and crudely
obscene in either case. He is displeased when he

gets bad press, but he leaves little choice. Jimmy
Connors makes himself easy to dislike.

But what if that easy way is not taken? What
if we try to see Connors symbolically? In the
process we might find a way to at least better
comprehend him, if not like him. Why bother?
Because one way or another Connors makes an
impact on us, in particular dredging up some of
our less attractive emotions. For example, isn't it
cruel, even sadistic, for an audience that has
shown a clear aversion to an athlete to want that
athlete to stand defeated before it at Forest
Hills?

And of what is Jimmy Connors symbolic?
Enough is known of his personal history and
what that tends to produce, to fairly say the Connors we know is the quintessential distillation of
stage parenthood. Stage parenthood? A mother
or father (or both) take an all-consuming interest
in their child's development into a top-flight
competitor/performer beginning just past toilet
training; maybe even during. Through strict discipline and single-minded control of play and
practice schedules, the child's tennis (in this
case) is firmly made to come first. Anything else
—toys, tree-climbing and extra-tennis compan-
ionships—comes after, time allowing, which it
seldom does. By way of compensation, what
might be called the sugar-cube gambit, the child
is allowed a wide latitude in his or her social
behavior, especially as to displays of temperament and articulation of it. That latitude, combined with the overall excessive attention received, develops kids who, not unexpectedly,
believe they are the center of the universe. They
of course act accordingly and become "brats."
As they get older, if they are successful in their
main pursuit, brats could become neurotics. If
they fail, or through the normal attrition of their
talent can no longer win, they could become
psychotics.

With the enormous rise of interest in sports
in the past fifty years, and especially big money
on the professional side, there has been much
hectoring of athletically talented, and even
worse, untalented youths by parents. Little
League baseball is notorious for its mothers and
fathers rabidly urging their kids to win. There

Jimmy Connors slides into position to intercept a volley with his two-handed backhand. (Photo by Russ Adams)

are examples from many other sports—youth football, age-group swimming, figure skating and even the soap box derby.

Perhaps the first of the notable "cases" in tennis was Suzanne Lenglen, the French "Maid Marvel" of the game in the 1920's.

An only child, and with a prominent aquiline nose, sallow complexion and quite short stature, Suzanne was not at all pretty, and her father set out to make something of his ugly duckling. Picking up on her excellent physical coordination, M. Lenglen drilled his daughter exhaustively in tennis stroke production beginning when she was a tot; Suzanne knew no dolls, only drills. M. Lenglen's technique of spreading handkerchiefs on one half of the court, to be hit by Suzanne's shots from the other half, became famous. Shots that found the mark were rewarded with franc notes and a kiss on the cheek of "Bebe Peugeot." Failure brought stern admonition and more practice.

It worked. But whether it was worth it is another matter. Suzanne became a faultless base-line player (she once won sixty straight games), won her first championship at age eleven, and eventually became the undisputed high priestess of tennis. At the same time, when not playing the haughty *prima ballerina* (Lenglen was famed for her leaps and bounds around the court), Suzanne was invariably high-strung and given to emotional tantrums, suffered neuritis, palpitations of the heart and asthma, the last considered by many to be in no little part psychosomatic. Her need to win, or her fear of losing, was so great that if the latter seemed at all possible she began to cough badly, suffer shortness of breath and depressing fatigue. At such times, Papa Lenglen, always at courtside to signal advice to "Bebe," would remind her to drink a "precious vial" of brandy and water; sometimes he threw her ice cubes loaded with the liquor.

M. Lenglen had inherited a small-town bus concession that brought him a moderate income. This was considerably increased, however, as was his family's social scope, when Suzanne became the toast of France. In the winters the Lenglens lived in a villa in Nice "donated to her father by admirers for his having developed tennis locally." That is, hotels on the Côte d'Azur sponsoring tennis tournaments to attract guests were guaranteed handsome profits if Suzanne played. Her appearances were assured by M. Lenglen, who for his efforts in this enjoyed the under-the-table fees Suzanne took in and the well-paid position of manager of one of the best tennis clubs on the Riviera. As for Suzanne, after her ground-breaking 1926 professional tour of the U.S. for C.C. Pyle, which of course ended her "amateur" career, she ran a Paris dress shop for a while and some tennis schools. She never married and at age thirty-nine she died of pernicious anemia, a gradually degenerative disease that if it is to be fought off at all requires the kind of physical and emotional rest her driven tennis career never allowed.

While the details are of course different, there are some striking parallels between the careers of Suzanne Lenglen and Jimmy Connors. Both were originally from moderate- to low-income backgrounds, were put into tennis at very young ages and were dominated by a parent of the opposite gender; in Connors's case, his grandmother, his mother Gloria's mother, was an added strong factor. Lenglen put on regal airs, including *haute couture* and limousines. While Connors dresses in denim, and for all his money worried over his purchase of an expensive Porsche, Jimmy, when told that comedian Alan King wanted to say hello, remarked that it was one King meeting another. Ironically, just as Connors was castigated for not attending the 1977 Parade of Champions at Wimbledon and thereby snubbing the Duke of Kent, Lenglen caused a furor when she failed to appear for a 1926 match at Wimbledon that Queen Mary had come to see. There were more extenuating circumstances in Lenglen's "snub," but the thrust in both instances was essentially the same— spoiled bratness. As if the narrow range of their initial training left them without the ability to grow, to improvise or to adjust to new or different exigencies, Lenglen was, and Connors is, a basically one-dimensional player, albeit brilliant in that. Lenglen rarely came to net, Connors is a line-drive power hitter.

Finally, Connors has had more physical problems than ever since Arthur Ashe shattered his mystique in the 1975 Wimbledon singles final. His thumb injury and back problems have been quite real hurts (he has curvature of the spine aggravated by his excessive twisting at service, a style he has not altered). And in two years Connors has defaulted with injuries nine times, a record of fragility unmatched by anyone among the world top ten.

Grooming Jimmy Connors for championship tennis began when he was around five years old. Actually, it was Jimmy's older brother (by twenty-two months) who was to be the champion, but in his teens Johnny Connors opted out. As Gloria Connors has put it, Johnny didn't "have the guts" for the grind. That Jimmy obviously did have the "guts" is to say that he is what he is by the luck of the gene draw. Still, genes are much influenced by external forces. Jimmy Connors became, in effect, an only child, the sole focus of his mother and grandmother to their exclusion of all else including, it appears, his father, who was around but not there, who was written out of the act.

"I think the loss of his father (who died in 1977) has had a deeper effect on Jimmy than anyone knows," says Bill Riordan, Connors's manager from 1972 through 1976, one of the longer close associations Jimmy has had outside his family. "He realizes what he missed and has guilt feelings," Riordan concludes.

It can be dangerous playing amateur psychologist, but with all that has been made available to the public in this field, along with simple common sense, it doesn't take any professional expertise to conceive that Jimmy's relationship, or lack of one with his father during his most formative years, a void filled by two aggressively doting women, has probably been the single-most shaper of the Jimmy Connors personality we are shown. Neither is it too much to speculate on that central fact of his life.

Connors's pugnacity, the jaw-jutting and hard glares at opponents after he cracks a winner, the flaunting of tennis's traditional niceties, the general tough-guy stance he takes can surely be attributed to one aspect of his upbringing. As Bill Riordan reminds, Jimmy was very early on instilled with the idea by his mother and grandmother that he was a poor kid from the other side of the tracks (river). "It's you and I against the world," Gloria would tell her son repeatedly. The no-money, no-place Connors of Belleville, Illinois, were out to rub the noses of the tennis snobs in St. Louis, just across the Mississippi. "How long can he win on hate?" a player once asked Riordan, who responded, "It's the way he was taught, and his nature."

Connors's belligerence is not simply focused on his opponent—it spills over, in-

fluencing his every public gesture. What to make of the manner of Connors's obscene gestures? What of the suggestive phrases, or the finger, or the forward thrusting pelvis, or the answering of hecklers by poking a racket between his legs? It almost never amuses, but it does infuriate. It is all part of the antiestablishment positioning that Connors seems to need to spur on his competitive drive. It's as if he *wants* the crowd against him, to fight them too. An example of this was Connors's actions in his semifinal match against Italian Corrado Barazzutti. At a critical point in the match, Barazzutti disputed a call and Connors ran over and ended the dispute by rubbing out the ball mark in question with his toe. Whatever Connors may have thought he had in mind, what he achieved was turning the crowd solidly against him. (Ilie Nastase, by contrast, has the ability to charm and alienate in equal measures; Connors tries Nastaselike gestures and only alienates. As a comedian, Connors lacks the essential ingredient of timing.) Later in the final match against Vilas the Forest Hills crowd was behind Vilas—this was due in no small measure to Connors's treatment of Barazzutti, which most had found offensive.

After a relatively brief period of living on his own in California, and his hurtfully overpublicized romance with Chris Evert, at an age, twenty-five, when young persons strike out and at least take their own apartment, Connors has returned to his mother's fold. Gloria now looks after the business affairs and Jimmy is once again making his base of operation in Belleville, where he lives with Gloria. As Gloria said to me, with a decided emphasis, "This *is* Jimmy's *home.*"

A renewed closeness to his mother could signal Jimmy's sense of declining powers as a player, however subtle that decline may appear to the casual viewer. When I asked Jimmy at a Forest Hills press conference how he gets out of slumps, he referred to his not having played well in Boston two weeks earlier while he was alone, but when his mother joined him, he felt fine again. "When mom's with me I've got it made both ways, my mom and my coach." At the same time, he can be disturbingly defensive about this dependence and can be easily upset about his relationship with his mother. Once, when kidded that he lost a match because of the women in his life, Connors, according to Bud Collins, "went crazy" and said, "Mom is the dearest person in my life."

With or without his mother, Connors's need to win seems to be growing. (His mother's *needs* in all this are by no means unimportant, but beyond the scope of this article.) You might think that with all Jimmy has accomplished already, anything he wins from here on would be a bonus and he would be at some ease with himself and he would have come to terms with old goals. But it doesn't always work that way, and for various complex psychological reasons. In a new book, *The Champions, The Secret Motives in Games and Sports,* author Peter Fuller deals at great and fascinating length with the need to continue winning among professional athletes. Except to say that when someone has dedicated a life to winning, not merely to win a game but to displace more elemental anxieties and conflict (emasculation?) the fear of losing becomes almost unbearable. Fuller's study is too deep to capsulize here. Instead, let's go back to the conclusion of the Connors-Vilas match at Forest Hills.

At courtside, beneath the judge's chair, Connors was nudged by one of the mob seeking to photograph or touch Vilas. Jimmy reportedly shoved the offender and asked with a snarl who was next. After that almost obligatory, image-retaining act, Connors was quiet; smoldering, but quiet. He put on his Aetna Cup U.S. team warm-up suit, and stalked out of the arena. His guards cleared the way and Gloria joined him in the marquee. No words were uttered by anyone in his entourage. At the patio below the men's locker room, Jimmy harshly ordered that Gloria be taken to the waiting car and said he would be down in a minute. His tone seemed a guard against breaking down. He ran up the stairs to the locker room and was back down in a minute with his belongings in a bag; he had not changed clothes. As he passed through the outer courtyard leading to the street, Connors spit hard at a tree. It was not a random expectoration. By its force it seemed a defiant statement, made to and for himself for he was not aware of anyone near him, a Connors goodbye forever to Forest Hills and to all it stood for in his mind. But as Connors hastily stuffed his gear into the plain, old-model Ford, its engine running, one saw in his left hand a small white tissue or handkerchief. When someone's flash camera lit up the Connors's car, Gloria quickly turned down the sun visors. And then the young man who has been characterized as "the loneliest guy on the pro tennis scene," rode off into the dark of the New York evening.

Dr. Jekyll and Mr. Hyde

by RICHARD EVANS

There's a special raw-nerved excitement whenever Ilie Nastase steps on a tennis court because no one knows what might happen next . . . least of all, Nastase himself. During one period in 1975 to 1976 Nastase was involved in several of the most infamous incidents in the history of tennis, and Richard Evans was there.

"WHERE'S Ramirez?" It was mid-afternoon on the Saturday of the Italian championships 1975 and suddenly the question was being asked all over the elegant restaurants, bars, administrative offices and locker rooms of the Foro Italico.

"Anyone seen Raul?" No one had. The sense of acute urgency with which that question was being asked centered on the fact that the Mexican was due to play Ilie Nastase in the day's second semifinal like . . . NOW. Ramirez wasn't there.

Someone in the referee's office put through a frantic phone call to the Holiday Inn, which has become the headquarters for most of the players in Rome. One of the desk clerks, a lovely Eritrean girl called Doris, who, like most of the staff, knew the players personally, confirmed that Ramirez had rushed out just a couple of minutes before. Taking into account the unpredictable flow of Roman traffic, that

would mean he would be between twenty and thirty minutes late.

In the locker room Nastase started to fume. Although Ilie has transgressed against most of the rules in tennis at one time or another, I cannot think of a single instance when I have known him to be late for a match. He had every right to be angry. Ramirez had absolutely no excuse. The day's schedule was posted every night in the lobby of the Holiday Inn and, although he had checked it, he had committed the naive and unacceptable error of *assuming* that the women's final and the first men's semifinal—which were scheduled before his match with Nastase—would take a "normal" amount of time. But there is no such thing as "normal" when predicting the length of a tennis match. It can take three hours, or a player can pull a muscle in the first game and default. There is only one thing to do. Play safe. Get there early.

Ramirez was unlucky in that both matches had taken an inordinately short length of time. Chris Evert had destroyed Martina Navratilova 6–1, 6–0, and Manolo Orantes, making the game look so easy, as he always does when in top form, had outclassed Guillermo Vilas 6–2, 6–2, 6–2. So by playing so well Chrissie and Manolo had caught Raul on the hop.

"So you give me walkover? When do I get

walkover? Rule says fifteen minutes and he's scratched, right? So now it's twelve minutes. He has three to go." By this time Nastase was pacing up and down the spacious locker room like a caged lion. As usual he was exaggerating a bit. It was only about eight minutes since the match had been called, but nonetheless the time was fast approaching when a decision on whether or not to default Ramirez would have to be taken. Ostensibly that responsibility lay solely with the referee but, as European director of the ATP, I knew I would get dragged into the issue, at least in an advisory capacity. During the two years in which I ran the ATP's Paris office, I found myself frequently acting as a sort of joint tournament director-cum-referee at many tournaments I attended, purely because harassed local officials felt that players were more likely to accept rulings and judgments made by one of their own directors.

Nastase had gone one further than that by assuming that I was going to make the decision as to when to default Ramirez on my own. In deference to the tournament committee, that I could not do, but I was certainly prepared to weigh in with an opinion if the situation demanded it. Actually, the referee and I saw things in much the same light. As soon as it was verified that Ramirez was on his way, I agreed with him that the match should go on. I came to that conclusion with a clear understanding that in doing so I was allowing the ATP rules—as they stood at the time—to be broken and was therefore being unfair to Nastase. For the rules clearly stated that if a player was not ready to play fifteen minutes after the match had been called to court, he should be fined and defaulted.

As I explained to the ATP board of directors later, that looks like a very fair and reasonable rule when it is written in the peace and quiet of a conference room in a hotel in London, Paris or Palm Springs. It is the sort of rule that would work perfectly in Palm Springs. One would just walk up to the microphone and announce that, on account of one player arriving sixteen-and-a-half minutes late, there would be no further tennis that day. Assuming that the match was not being nationally televised—in which case the

ATP rule book would be torn up and thrown in the referee's face—everyone would boo and hiss for a couple of minutes, and then climb elegantly into their Cadillacs and Thunderbirds and drive away.

But try implementing it on a hot Saturday afternoon in Rome with six thousand Italians already restless over the fact that their money has been spent on two matches that barely warrant the name. Instead of a rout, they are now wanting a contest—some value for their money. Try telling a crowd like that they have seen all the tennis they are going to see, and it is quite possible you will have a riot on your hands. Not a very big riot by today's standards, perhaps—just big enough to get a child trampled to death by angry spectators as they jump down from the marbled terracing and charge across the court. Then what do you tell the child's mother? Do you hold up your little ATP rule book and say, "Well, I'm terribly sorry but you see it says here under Section Three, sub-clause fifteen. . . ."

You give the crowd a tennis match, that's what you do. And if you want to call that mob rule, that's quite all right with me. At least it's peaceful. No matter how carefully we write the rules, nor how much we want to see them implemented in a uniform and impartial manner, blindly to ignore special circumstances and situations is merely abdicating one's responsibility as a human being. Computers might do otherwise, but when it comes to the crunch, I'd rather bend a rule than a limb. So Ilie got screwed. Sorry, Ilie. But, in similar circumstances, I would advise the referee to do exactly the same thing.

With due deference to Raul, who had simply made an honest mistake, it would have been more just if Nastase had managed to keep calm about the whole thing and gained his revenge on court. But that would be like expecting Muhammad Ali to become a Trappist monk two weeks before a world title fight. For the first twenty minutes that we waited for the errant Ramirez, Ilie was in a state of near hysteria. He shouted at me; he shouted at the referee; and he shouted at the Italian Federation general secretary, Gianfranco Cameli.

Then, as the fifteen-minute mark came and

went and there was still no sign of Ramirez, he fell silent and seemed to become reconciled to the fact that he was going to have to play the match. I think Cameli might have had something to do with Ilie's sudden change in mood. Gianfranco had reminded Ilie that he was to receive a presentation on court before the match to mark his appearance in every Italian championship since 1966, apart from the one year in 1971 when it had been primarily a WCT event. Either Ilie did not want to let Cameli down, or he rather liked the idea of receiving a presentation. Probably it was both. At any rate, when Ramirez finally swept in half an hour late, Nastase never said a word and calmly waited for the Mexican, who looked slightly embarrassed but otherwise unruffled, to change.

Ilie duly received his presentation and then proceeded to go to pieces once the match got underway. He had no feel, no touch and the harder he tried, the less he seemed able to time the ball. Ramirez, playing cool, steady tennis, moved swiftly to 6–2, 5–2 and, at the changeover, Nastase picked up his rackets and stormed off court amidst a barrage of boos and high-pitched whistles.

"I'm too nervous, I can't play. I don't concentrate. Shit, I shouldn't be playing anyway. I should have had walkover." Ilie, shaking with a combination of nerves, anger and frustration, babbled away as he made the long walk down the tunnel to the locker room. Barging his way through a rapidly growing bunch of reporters crowding the doorway, he eventually slumped down on the locker-room bench. He looked exhausted.

"It's your fault," he suddenly screamed at me. "You're the bloody ATP. You should have defaulted him. That's what you're here for. Why should I have to wait forty minutes to play my match?"

He needed a target and at that moment I was as good a one as any. There was no point in arguing about it. He wasn't rational and, in any case, looking at it strictly from his point of view, I wouldn't have had much ammunition with which to argue. The rules, as written, were in his favor, and they hadn't been obeyed for reasons that I have tried to explain. It had been the referee's decision more than mine, but there was no point in pretending I hadn't backed him up. If Nastase wanted to blame me, so be it. Frankly I felt sorry for him.

So by June 1975, Nastase had already been involved in three highly publicized furors and was already becoming guilty by association. No matter what the facts of any particular rumpus might be, if Nastase was in any way involved then, in the mind of the public, he tended to be considered the cause of it. That, of course, was not always fair, but at the Canadian Open Championships in Toronto in August there were no excuses. Nastase was guilty.

He was playing Orantes in the final, and an excellently fought first set had reached three points to one for Nastase in the tie-break when Ilie hit a first serve that seemed to clip the line. But it was called out. So Nastase went into his rant-and-rave routine which achieved nothing. The linesman refused to change his call. So, quite inexcusably, Nastase went into a major sulk. He didn't stop playing, he didn't even stop running. There were points when he actually looked as if he might be trying . . . a little. He hadn't switched the engine off. But from overdrive, he had simply changed down to let it idle. Not even when your name is Nastase do you win championship matches that way, and Orantes, looking faintly embarrassed, walked off with the title 7–6, 6–0, 6–1.

It was not difficult to fathom what was going through Ilie's mind. "So they screw me again," he was thinking. "So, okay, I screw them. I don't care any more. If they want Orantes to win, he can win." It was the classic, petulant reaction of a sulky little boy. But Nastase was supposed to be a great tennis champion with a responsibility toward the crowd, the sponsors and the game. And he had let them all down. As Bud Collins wrote in the BP *World of Tennis Yearbook*, "Ilie insulted his opponent, Orantes, as well as a sell-out crowd of six thousand and nationwide television audiences in Canada and the U.S. . . . even his staunchest admirers were saddened by the episode of August 17 at the Toronto Skating, Curling and Cricket Club."

CBS sportscaster Don Chevrier voiced the opinion of many Canadian sports fans when he told me, "That was the most disgraceful exhibition by a top athlete I have ever seen in any sport. If Nastase is not thrown out of the game for a long time as a result, I shall lose all respect for pro tennis."

During the match Ilie's language had also been a disgrace. I was sitting on the side of the court taking photos when something caught his eye in the crowd and he yelled over my head, "Go f——— yourself!" Apart from being vulgar and embarrassing, it was unnecessary. But such was his state of mind that he didn't care. Inside, he was threshing about with his own emotions— scared, angry, unhappy and, as a result, vindictive. He wanted to strike back at a world he was rapidly losing faith in. Pressures he often didn't understand and could rarely control were becoming too much for him to handle. The more he struggled, the tighter the web of disaster clung to him and although there were times when he was innocent, it was he who had spun that web. Ilie was his own spider.

When I interviewed him for John Chanin's "World of Sports" radio program on the ABC network that evening, Ilie denied having thrown the match, just as he continued to deny it to everyone else.

But there was something he had said to me the instant he walked off court that made it clear he had not tried. I will not attempt to quote his exact words here because I cannot remember them with any precision. But the impression they left was absolutely clear. In my mind, there was no doubt at all that he had not cared whether he won or lost. That makes the whole thing a charade, and I firmly believe it is the worst sin a professional athlete can commit.

As Marty Riessen said in his book *Match Point*, "As a paid performer, be it boxer, singer, juggler or tennis player, there is no way you should be allowed to cheat the public and get away with it."

Some people will feel that Nastase's foul-mouthed outbursts of anger are as bad. In an article written for *World Tennis*, the comedian, Bill Cosby, who is a good player himself, made the following valid point. "There are millions like me who want to see the game executed as beautifully as Ilie Nastase can, but when he goes off into one of his tirades, our minds are clouded by his arguing; no longer is his chipped backhand down the line a thing of beauty. . . . He must stop because, in truth, he is wasting the time of the people who have paid to see a great tennis player play great tennis."

I take Cosby's point which, basically, I agree with. But in response I would just say this. When Nastase goes off into one of his tirades at least he is interested. At least he is trying. It is, in fact, because he cares so much that he is spitting fire. One should not condone it nor hold it up as an example of how a young player should behave. But a man who behaves like Nastase has to be competing with every fiber of his being and as long as he is doing that, professional sports retains its one magic ingredient—its unpredictability.

Of course people pay to see professional sport so that they may marvel at the precision of Ken Rosewall's backhand; or swoon over Pele's goal-scoring magic; or gasp at Jack Nicklaus's power off the tee. But it is the fact that you never know when or how those incredible moments are going to happen that gives sport its extra magic. As a form of entertainment, it is what separates sport from art. The thrill of watching Nureyev dance or listening to Olivier speak such lines as "He which hath no stomach to this fight,/Let him depart . . ." is just as mesmerizing for the connoisseur of the classics. Yet the lover of Shakespeare has not gone to find out what happened to Henry V. The verse and the way it is spoken is reward enough.

But sport is unrehearsed. That might make it less perfect art, but it gives it the edge in raw excitement. Yet as soon as one competitor ceases to compete, the whole enterprise becomes meaningless. The public are cheated as surely as they would be if, unannounced, Laurence Olivier was replaced by an incompetent understudy.

In tennis, no one in their right mind would stage an exhibition match between Nastase and Borg in London or Paris. Exhibition matches are only worthwhile in places where the local fans

Ilie Nastase, wronged yet again, pleads his point to an unsympathetic Wimbledon umpire.
(Photo by Russ Adams)

have never had a chance to see either man in the flesh. Then, and only then, will curiosity overcome the absence of the competitive ingredient from which all exhibitions suffer. The final of the Canadian Open was no exhibition, and that is why Nastase's insult to his audience was so great. By having no stomach for the fight, he deprived them of what they had paid to see—namely a competitive match.

The scene in the referee's tent after the debacle against Orantes was chaotic. The sponsors, Rothmans, whose loyalty to tennis over the years is deserving of special thanks, wanted to prevent Nastase from playing in the doubles final.

At first Nastase himself seemed too distraught and belligerent to want to play. But Jan Kodes, his partner that week, talked him into it after a blazing row with the tournament director, Don Fontana.

"I blew my stack at him which wasn't too smart," Fontana admitted when we talked about the unhappy episode some time later. "But I couldn't agree to Rothmans' request to put on an exhibition doubles instead of the final. I felt that would have been cheating the public still further."

Typically, Nastase's mood changed completely when he got back on court, and large sections of the crowd were ready to forgive and forget by the time he and Kodes lost a thrilling match 7–6 in the third set to Cliff Drysdale and Ray Moore.

But quite rightly, that was not the end of it. Fontana filed a report on Nastase as well as on Bjorn Borg and Kodes, both of whom had been involved in other incidents during a troublestrewn week. After a series of hearings held by the Pro Council during the U.S. Open in New York a couple of weeks later, Nastase was fined $8,000—the equivalent of his runner-up money in the singles.

The Rumanian authorities were beginning to be concerned over Nastase's problems, and it was at about this time that Mitch Oprea was called in to act as troubleshooter.

"The situation with McCormack at the hearings in New York was a little absurd," said Oprea. "They were not only Ilie's agents, but they were also representing the Canadian Lawn Tennis Association. How could they plead in front of the Pro Council for parties on both sides of the arguments? They should have disqualified themselves."

To amend this situation, Oprea called in New York lawyer Fred Sherman who immediately appealed against the council's decision, complaining of "procedural defects" at the hearing. So a second hearing was set up in London later in the year, this time with a panel of independent arbitrators consisting of two former Wimbledon champions, Jaroslav Drobny and Lew Hoad, and an eminent British judge, Sir Carl Aarvold, who was also president of the British Lawn Tennis Association. After listening to Sherman and considering reams of written evidence, the arbitration panel decided to reduce the fine from $8,000 to $6,000, having found the allegation of swearing proven, but dismissing the suggestion that Nastase had thrown the match. It was, I admit, a difficult charge to prove, and apparently Sir Carl was loath to uphold it because of what he described as the inadequate and legally worthless constitution with which the Pro Council was trying to govern tennis at that time.

"A lot of people in the game wanted to see Nastase suspended," Hoad told me. "But Sir Carl said there was no way we could legally suspend the guy. Apparently there were just too many loopholes for Nastase's lawyer to wriggle through."

So a check was sent to the Canadian LTA for $6,000—a contribution, according to Nastase's lawyers, to the development of Canadian junior tennis. In my opinion he got off lightly.

Despite a great deal of heavy criticism in the Canadian press, Ilie returned to Toronto the following February to play in a WCT event and went a long way to silencing his critics.

"There was no personal animosity on my part," said Fontana, "although Ilie was, quite understandably, a little wary of me to start with. But he accepted my invitation to attend the Ontario Sports Celebrities Dinner at the Royal York Hotel one night, and helped us out on another occasion by agreeing to play an exhibition with Vitas Gerulaitis when we were short of a match.

On the whole he couldn't have been more co-operative. He's really a pretty harmless guy and it's hard to dislike him."

In other words, it was the same old story. Once Dr. Jekyll reemerges, one wonders how on earth Mr. Hyde can exist in the same soul.

Arthur Ashe was left pondering the enigma that is Nastase after the Commercial Union Masters in Stockholm at this end of the year—a year that for Ilie had become a series of running battles with officialdom all over the world. The night before their memorable encounter at the Kunglihallen. Nastase had staged a little scene-setter for Ashe's benefit in the bar of the Grand Hotel. That the preview turned out to be a lot funnier than the main act was unintentional, but perhaps predictable. Off court few people mind if Nastase gets a little outrageous. On court, especially against a man like Ashe, it is different. At any rate, when Arthur strode into the bar for a nightcap, Ilie was already holding forth. Perched on a bar stool, he was chattering away with a whole group of people from the tennis world including Spence Conley, then with Commercial Union's Boston office; Susie Trees from San Francisco and the *World Tennis* editor Ron Bookman.

"Ah, Negroni," exclaimed Ilie, addressing Arthur in his customary manner. "How you feeling? Good, I hope. Tomorrow night you will need to feel good."

Ashe, who genuinely enjoys Nastase in this kind of mood, smiled and sat down next to the Rumanian. Without saying much, but laughing heartily at times, Arthur sipped a drink and let Ilie rattle on.

"Such a good serve you have, Negroni. Such a pity for you they put Supreme Court over the tiles. The tiles they are so much better for your serve, no? But it does not matter because I beat you anyway. Tomorrow night I do things to you that will make you turn white. Then you will be a white Negroni."

Although most of the people in the bar were falling about by this stage, it was nothing new for Ashe. He had heard it all before. He also knew how to handle it. Pushing his drink tab toward Nastase, he leaned across and with an air of quiet

authority, said to the barman, "That'll be on Mr. Nastase's check." With that he slipped gently off his stool; tapped Ilie on the shoulder by way of recognition and, with a satisfied grin on his face, walked out. It was the kind of exit only Arthur Ashe could have pulled off with quite so much dignity and timing.

Twenty-four hours later the contrast was total. From the serene, understated, imperturbable human being I had always known, Ashe had been reduced to a screaming, nerve-ruined wreck. I have never seen him like it before or since. And the cause of it was, of course, Nastase.

It had started in a drearily familiar way. Ashe was leading 1–6, 7–5, 4–1 and seemed set for victory. Then Ilie started arguing over a line call, and a heckler in the crowd began baiting him. Almost invariably that triggers a response in Ilie which I do believe is instinctive and compulsive. He shouts back. A lifetime's training might have made him able to ignore the lone loudmouth, but it is too late for that now. He just has to answer back. And so it started. Every time Nastase would bounce the ball and begin his service action, the man would call out. Each time Ilie stopped, turned and shouted back. This happened four or five times. The umpire repeatedly warned Ilie that play must be continuous, but Ashe suddenly decided there would be no play at all.

Striding up to the umpire's chair, simultaneously shaking his head and waving his arms in front of him to signal termination, Ashe's high-pitched voice cut through the sudden buzz of the crowd. "That's it," he said. "I'm not putting up with it any longer. He's contravening the rules and I'm not taking it any more."

With that Ashe picked up his rackets and was off the court before the West German referee, Horst Klosterkemper, could reach the courtside and activate the decision he had taken seconds before the American's dramatic exit—namely to disqualify Nastase.

When I got down to the locker room a few minutes later, confusion reigned. Klosterkemper, the umpire, John Beddington of Commercial Union and Hans-Ake Sturen of the Stockholm Open were milling round trying to decide what should be done. All that would have been normal under the less than normal circumstances had it not been for the condition of Arthur Ashe. I have known Arthur a long time. I have seen him in dire situations on court and even tougher situations off it, as when he faced a militant group of black students in South Africa. I have seen him angry, sometimes very angry. But never before had I seen him lose control of himself.

"I'm not taking any more of that crap," he screamed, his voice a whole octave higher than normal. "There's no goddamn way you're getting me back on that court. He's broken the rules, goddamn it. I helped write them. I ought to know."

Ripping off his damp shirt he flung it down on the bench, his whole lithe body trembling with emotion. "That sonuvabitch isn't going to get away with it any more. I'll damn well see him run out of the game before he tries that kind of stunt with me again."

The subject of this tirade was sitting somewhat sheepishly behind a row of clothes and towels that almost completely hid him from Ashe's view. It was not difficult to see that he had been shocked by Ashe's sudden flare-up. "What you go so crazy for?" he asked plaintively a couple of times in between long bouts of brooding silence. "Shit, what you want me to do, say I'm sorry? I'm sorry. But that guy kept yelling at me, what could I do?"

But Ashe was not about to get drawn into a verbal slanging match with his antagonist. He knew his emotions were running wild in a manner that was quite foreign to him, and he thought he had better try and channel his anger as best he could. So he ignored Nastase and confined his attention to the various officials who were trying desperately to come up with a solution. The problem was that Ashe, by walking off court, had committed an offense just as grave as Nastase's. The fact that Klosterkemper was on the point of defaulting Ilie when Ashe made his move was, technically, of no consequence. Instead of remaining on the court and demanding that the referee implement the rules, he had taken the law into his own hands and left the arena. And,

even some fifteen minutes later, as the argument raged on, it was still Ashe, not Nastase, who was refusing to continue the match.

But no one wanted to default Ashe and give the match to the Rumanian. The fact that Arthur had been provoked also had to be taken into consideration. It was also impossible to overlook the fact that he was not merely president of the ATP, but one of the most orderly and respected players ever to grace a tennis court. Orderly, however, did not quite describe him at this point. Half-naked, dripping with sweat and still taut with rage, he caught the gist of several half-whispered discussions between Klosterkemper, Beddington, Sturen, myself and others and quickly interjected, "Don't think you're getting me back on that court—there's no way. I've quit and it's his fault. You guys work it out any way you like but I'll tell you this—if you penalize me, I'm walking straight out of this tournament right this minute."

We all stared at him like men hit with a sudden attack of migraine. He was not making it any easier. As the Masters is partially played under a round-robin format—two groups of four play round robin to produce two semifinals that are then played off on a knock-out basis—any player walking out on the first day would leave a nasty hole in the scheduling. But the round-robin format also offered Klosterkemper the possibility of a compromise solution. I don't know whether I was the first to suggest it to him or whether he had already thought of it himself, but I remember whispering the suggestion to him as he talked on the locker-room phone with the ILTF president, Derek Hardwick, who was back at the Grand Hotel, having left the Kunglihallen half an hour before the incident occurred.

The solution was to default them both. In a knock-out format this would, I agree, have been too hard on Ashe. But in round-robin play, it is quite possible for someone who loses his first match to go on and win the whole tournament. Nastase himself had done it in Boston two years before and, as it turned out, was destined to repeat the feat that week in Stockholm.

By simply depriving both men of the point one of them would normally have gained for a victory, they would be left joint bottom of the White group after the first round of matches—a handicap certainly, but not an insurmountable one. Klosterkemper liked the idea and initially Hardwick agreed. "It's your decision, Horst," the ILTF president told him on the phone. And so indeed it was. One of the younger and more progressive members of the European tennis hierarchy, Klosterkemper had made his reputation in the game by organizing the Grand Prix event in Düsseldorf each year—a tournament considered by most of the players to be one of the best-run in the world.

But nothing he had had to face in Düsseldorf had posed as many delicate problems as the situation facing him now. Emotionally he wanted to overlook Ashe's indiscretion because he knew how genuine Arthur was in wanting to make a stand against the kind of behavior he felt was intolerable. But his teutonic respect for rules could not allow him totally to ignore the fact that Ashe had committed a serious offense by leaving the court. So Klosterkemper finally decided on the double default solution and, rather bravely, considering the American's frame of mind, walked over to Arthur to tell him.

"I'll appeal against that," Ashe retorted. "You won't get away with it."

Incredibly, he was right. In one of the stranger decisions professional tennis has witnessed over the past decade, a tournament committee, consisting of Hardwick, Klosterkemper, Beddington and his Commercial Union boss, Geoff Mullis, voted to overturn Horst's original decision and award the match to Ashe.

It was an enormous compliment to Ashe's standing and reputation in the game that he was able to convince the committee that this was the correct course of action. I understand how important it was to him to be officially exonerated from blame. And to an extent I sympathize. But I cannot honestly say that I consider it to have been a good thing for the game. For an ATP president to use his position and his influence to have an official decision overturned on his own behalf throws up too many ethical question marks. But he got away with it and if one views it as a somewhat unorthodox bonus for all the

esteem he has brought to his sport over the years, then one should not complain too loudly. During the particular match in question he had, if not technically, then in essence, been more sinned against than sinning and, to his credit, Nastase was the first to admit as much. Even now he looks back on the incident and says, "That time I think I go too far. It was not intentional. Arthur had such a big lead I think he would have won the match anyway, but this guy keeps talking to me as I try to serve and what could I do?" He still does not have the answer.

He did, however, find an immediate method of soothing the last remnants of Ashe's anger. Having practiced after the committee meeting in the morning, Arthur was having a late lunch by himself in the Grand Hotel dining room, gazing out at the panoramic view of the steamers and fishing boats riding at anchor in front of the Royal Palace. There weren't many other people in the room, but even those unconnected with tennis could not have missed the significance of the little scene that was about to be enacted. Appearing at the doorway half-hidden by a huge bunch of flowers. Nastase almost tiptoed his way across the room and then, with the half-scared look of a child who is trying to make it up with his father, laid the flowers across Ashe's table.

"Please forgive me," he said with a smile.

Of course everyone laughed but in many ways it was an action, as Oscar Wilde once said, "so sweet and simple as to hush us to silence." Certainly he knew how and in what spirit he should approach his rival and as he flitted away as silently as he had come, Arthur lifted his hands in a gesture of despair and smilingly shook his head. "That was so typical of Nastase," he said when we talked about it later. "You can't be mad at the guy for long." Ashe also maintained that he was angrier at the officials than he was at Ilie. "Nastase was just being Nastase," Arthur said. "I was just furious that everyone was letting him get away with it."

Yet, incongruous as it may seem, I think Arthur helped Ilie reclaim his Masters title. If he had lost that opening match in the normal way, he would have fiddled and footled his way through the rest of the week, bemoaning his luck, complaining about his lack of form and getting himself into more and more trouble. But the intensity of the row with Ashe both shocked him and knocked him into shape. Even he realized he had gone one step too far and he suddenly became desperately keen to make amends. And in doing so he played some of the most brilliant tennis in his career.

It is a sad but seemingly inescapable fact of life for Nastase that he needs one good blowout before he can settle down to play serious tennis. In a normal tournament this means he needs to survive one gigantic row without disqualification or defeat—otherwise, of course, it is all over. But in the Masters, the round-robin format allows him that one early setback without putting him completely out of the tournament. As he proved both in Boston and Stockholm, he can overcome any penalty or handicap just so long as he is still allowed to play.

At the Kunglihallen, in front of the knowledgeable Swedish crowd who were already inclined to forgive him his trespasses because he was working diligently with their Davis Cup squad, Ilie battled his way back to form and favor. But he still required Ashe's assistance to reach the semifinals. Ilie produced two workmanlike victories to beat Manolo Orantes and Adriano Panatta, and then had to sit and wait while Ashe played Orantes in the last of the round-robin matches. If Ashe had lost, the Spaniard would have advanced to the semifinals in Ilie's place. But Arthur was in commanding form and won 6–4, 6–1.

From then on Nastase needed no further assistance. John Barrett, editor of the *World of Tennis Yearbook* and an important figure in the British tennis scene, described Ilie's semifinal like this: "Nastase, wielding his racket like a wand, conjured pure magic from the ball in destroying Vilas 6–0, 6–3, 6–4. The young bull of the Pampas was reduced to impotence—every charge was parried; every attack blunted until the despairing Vilas was executed at last by the flashing Rumanian rapier."

Borg stopped Ashe in the other semifinal, but then discovered that Nastase, on this form, was an altogether different proposition. Disap-

pointingly for the crowd, the final lasted only sixty-five minutes. Shrugging with despair and obviously embarrassed by his inability to match magic with magic. Borg found himself served, volleyed and dropshotted into a 6–2, 6–2, 6–1 defeat. Ilie was ecstatic. A fraught and worrying year had finally produced a ray of sunshine minutes before the Nordic night closed in on a chill November afternoon. But no matter how brilliant the finale, it could not obscure the sour memories of the past months. Fined in Tucson and Toronto, disqualified in Bournemouth, Washington, D.C. and Stockholm—it was not a happy record.

I did not witness the incident at the *Washington Star* event but, in his customarily erudite style, Barry Lorge of the *Washington Post* described it thus:

"The disqualification episode was filled with low comedy. Down match point at 30–40 on his serve, Nastase was called for a foot fault which some people thought he committed intentionally to start a furor. He argued at length and eventually took off his shoe and flipped it in the direction of the foot-fault judge.

"At the other end, Cliff Richey—who had said the day before that his long-running feud with Nastase was over—was steaming. Finally he walked off court, packed his gear, and departed. As the crowd howled and confusion reigned, an official sought out Richey and told him he would be defaulted if he didn't return to the court. Eyes bulging and his complexion the color of a tomato, he stomped back like a man possessed. Nastase asked for two serves, and when the umpire ruled he should only have one, he began to argue again. Off went Richey a second time, shoving an official as he went. Once more he was coaxed back on court and the umpire told Nastase he had fifteen seconds to serve. The Rumanian kept arguing as the crowd counted down, and at the stroke of fifteen he was defaulted.

"Nastase has pulled that crap forty-nine thousand times," Richey said afterward. "It was time to stand up to him. He'll go on intimidating officials, ruining his opponent's rhythm and concentration until his bluff is called. Otherwise there's no telling how far he'll go. Maybe next time he'll pull off both his shoes and drop his pants."

Although the hot-tempered Texan was not perhaps the ideal person to start lecturing Nastase on how to behave, he was voicing an opinion shared by many players, not to mention the public. Yet, in America especially, the difference between the public's attitude toward Nastase and those who knew him personally was considerable. The players understood that Ilie was a very different character off court from on, and the majority of them were prepared to accept this, often liking and enjoying Jekyll while hating Hyde. But the average American tennis fan never got close enough to recognize the difference. And watching him at his worst moments on court many true-blue citizens from the great American middle class were mortally offended by what they saw. To a far greater extent than in Europe, a deep puritanical streak still runs through the core of the American psyche and often Nastase's behavior simply blew its collective mind.

The cables that poured in after the match against Rosewall at the American Airlines Tennis Games showed how easily people could be roused to righteous indignation. It took Ilie some time to realize this, but by the time he did I think he was past caring. He had, by then, been the victim of so many bad line calls and been abused so frequently by spectators using language every bit as abusive as his own, that he saw no reason to spare anyone's feelings. The more vicious the criticism, the more outrageously he reacted and by the end of 1975 he was, on the sports scene at least, public enemy number one.

He had his problems in Europe, too, but somehow they never reached the same intensity. Even when crowds in Rome or Madrid turned against him, he never felt as threatened or as alienated as he did in the States where the culture gap between the emotional Latin and Mr. Middle America is wider than the Grand Canyon.

Even in Britain, where the stiff-upper-lip syndrome is supposed to abhor an excessive display of emotion, Nastase has always been much more warmly received than in the United States. In fact there is probably no country in the world that has taken Ilie to its heart as Britain has. This is not so strange as it may seem. As a nation, the British not merely tolerate but actively enjoy eccentrics. Acutely aware of the primness of their society, a sizeable minority of British people are forever seeking ways of expressing themselves in an extravagant manner, either by deed or dress. In tennis no one provides a better example of this than the inimitable designer, Teddy Tinling. And even little old ladies who have spent a lifetime in twin sets and pearls seem to get a kick out of those who have trodden a more daring path. After watching Nastase behave in a manner that would induce heart failure if copied by their sons or family friends, I have heard them talk of Ilie being "terribly naughty" but "such a dear boy." The American matron tends to take a less tolerant view.

Of course, Ilie does ask for it. There is no quicker way to stir up a hornet's nest in the States than by making racial remarks in public and before 1976 was halfway through, Nastase had done it twice.

The first incident occurred in January at the indoor event in Baltimore. Nastase was involved in a close match with that gritty little fighter Harold Solomon, whose home town of Silver Spring, Maryland, is a mere thirty miles away. Both players had received a few bad calls and when Nastase began reacting in his usual manner, some of Solly's numerous fans in the crowd started heckling him. So, true to form, Ilie decided to hit back. And, of course he went straight for the jugular. "Not only do I have to play you here," he said to Solomon across the net. "But I have to play two thousand Jews as well."

Harold returned the compliment by calling him a Rumanian commie bastard and all hell broke loose. Solomon couldn't help smiling when he looked back on the incident some time later.

"Jewish people were going nuts all over the country," Solly told me. "They're very defensive about things like that. You should have seen some of the letters written about him in the papers. He knows what he's saying, of course, but I think he just wants to strike back. He's not really a racist. Actually I enjoy him a bit. Off court I don't mind him at all but on court he's an asshole."

A few months after he had alienated the most influential ethnic minority in America, Ilie turned his attention to the most populous—the blacks. If ever a politician with a death wish is looking for ways of how not to get elected, he should ask Nastase to write a pamphlet for him. He makes Spiro Agnew look like a beginner.

This time it was in the final of the WCT Challenge Cup in Hawaii and once again Arthur Ashe was the player involved. Having won the first set, Ilie was trailing 1–5 in the second when he began muttering away to himself as he so often does when he loses his grip on a match. During the course of a long monologue, the sensitive NBC microphones at courtside picked up the inflammatory phrase "bloody nigger." Few spectators heard it—merely a few million television viewers across America. Again the complaints started flooding in. Ashe never heard the remark and even when he was told about it afterward, he kept his cool. Nastase's stalling tactics in Stockholm might have roused his ire, but Arthur was not going to get upset over the names Ilie calls him or anyone else. He had heard them too often. Echoing Solomon, Arthur commented, "Whatever he said, I don't think he's a racist."

For anyone heavily into horror shows, Nastase's second-round match with Hans-Jurgen Pohmann at the 1976 U.S. Open was a classic. Vesuvius erupting would have been hard put to challenge the sheer ferocity that Nastase's temper spewed forth. The linesman who refused to go and check the mark after a call against Ilie was either incredibly brave or turned instantly to stone by the piercing glare of the Rumanian's eyes. Along with Dominique and Mitch, I was sitting in a little group of seats to one side of the base line in the stadium court and was not more than eight feet away when Nastase's first temper tantrum rent the air. The veins pulsating in his forehead; his whole body jerking in rhythm to the epithets that were pouring out of his mouth, he swung round on the linesman and yelled at him like a man possessed. It was really quite a frightening sight. But that was only for openers.

Pohmann, a little blond Berliner with an awkward but effective style, is also a showman at heart and, as the match headed for a dramatic third set tie-break finale, he was not beyond milking the situation to a point where Nastase was in danger of being upstaged.

Having reached match point twice and twice been thwarted on the brink of victory, Pohmann eventually collapsed with cramp, and after that it was cabaret time. There was no doubt at all that Hans did get hit with a bad attack of cramp in his thigh. But, equally, there was no doubt that he made the most of it. Writhing in agony at the net, Pohmann let out a half-stifled scream of pain as he clutched his leg. Quite contrary to the rules, the umpire allowed a doctor to attend to Pohmann on court and for a minute or two, Nastase merely paced up and down on his side of the net. But soon he could stand it no longer.

"That's not allowed," he yelled at the umpire. "You should give me default."

Nastase was right. But the doctor continued to treat Pohmann; the umpire continued to ignore Nastase, whose language was becoming more obscene by the minute; and the crowd was as loud and as abusive as a New York crowd can be.

Finally Pohmann staggered to his feet, hobbled about in dramatic fashion and managed to wince his way through a few more points before collapsing once more. Nastase ranted; the crowd yelled; Pohmann writhed—the din was ear-splitting, the atmosphere electric. But the shrillest crescendo of noise was reserved for the end when Nastase, having squeaked through to a 7–6, 4–6, 7–6 victory, not only refused to shake Pohmann's hand, but spat in the German's face. It was all very unpleasant.

As usual Nastase received 99 percent of the blame—a bit more that he probably deserved. In the *World of Tennis Yearbook*, Bud Collins's summary put it in perspective:

"The Bucharest Buffoon appeared to set new standards of bad taste. . . . With victory came a $1,000 fine and, eventually, a twenty-one-day suspension because Nastase had exceeded $3,000 in penalties for the calendar year. Yet Ilie had been treated unfairly, too, in that Pohmann was permitted too much time to recover from cramp and was even examined on court by a physician, wrongly summoned by the umpire. More offensive even than Nastase was the audience of 12,553 who, like the worst of hockey or football nuts baited and taunted him viciously. He felt cornered."

Collins was correct in his indictment of the crowd. That particular year they were as bad as any tennis crowd I have known. True to form, Nastase's behavior did a 180-degree turn after he had drained it of all the vitriol against Pohmann, but the crowd, if anything, became worse.

Both Marty Riessen and Roscoe Tanner, who lost to Nastase in subsequent rounds, expressed sympathy for Ilie after they heard some of the things spectators were yelling at him.

"They were on him before we had hit a ball," Riessen said. "I have never had any great problem with him personally and, just as I expected, we had a perfectly normal match. But it couldn't have been easy for him to ignore that crowd."

After beating Dick Stockton in the quarterfinals, Nastase once again seemed to have exhausted his supply of nervous energy when he faced up to another meeting with Borg. Right from the start the Swede never let go of the firm grip he took on the match and won in straight sets. But two days later, Connors thwarted Bjorn's hopes of adding the U.S. Open title to his Wimbledon crown.

The twenty-one-day suspension to which Collins referred did not begin immediately. It was not that simple. All sorts of legal ramifications were involved, and for a while no one seemed able to decide precisely when the suspension should or could begin. Mitch Oprea, who had a few lucrative deals set up for Nastase in Venezuela and Norway, wanted it to start as soon as possible. However the Pro Council informed Oprea that the suspension could not begin until Nastase knowingly waived the right to appeal.

"So I quickly sent them a cable saying that Ilie 'knowingly' waived that right," said Oprea. "I have a certain amount of sympathy with the Pro Council. It is necessary that there should be such a body, but the current composition of the council is entirely [unjust]. It is supposed to be split into three groups . . . three from the ITF, three from the ATP and three tournament directors. Yet at one stage no less than seven members of a nine-man council were responsible for running tournaments. Everybody seems to represent everything on that council and they all appear to work in cahoots—or at least a majority do."*

By chance more than design, the delay in starting Ilie's suspension did help one council member, Jack Kramer, whose Pacific Southwest Championships in Los Angeles follow Forest Hills two weeks later. Kramer badly needed a big foreign name for the tournament and as they don't come any bigger than Nastase he was delighted to secure Ilie's services. It was a close thing. The final council decision was that the suspension should start as soon as Ilie was beaten in the Pacific Southwest.

The real farce lay in the fact that there was no law to prevent Nastase from earning a fortune through exhibition matches during the period of his suspension. Oprea reckons he picked up about $80,000 in the three weeks he was supposedly banned from the game. But as Fred Sherman was quick to point out, the Pro Council only had the right to ban him from Grand Prix tournaments. They would have been leaving themselves open to a lawsuit under American law if they had tried to prevent Nastase from earning a living on a tennis court. After all that happened, it was ironic that Nastase should end up helping Kramer's tournament even though Jack had voted for his suspension, not merely in this most recent instance where the $3,000 limit on fines gave him little choice, but also a year earlier following the Toronto fracas.

"I had it in my mind that he tanked against

---

*The Pro Council at that stage consisted of Bob Briner, Pierre Darmon and Cliff Drysdale (ATP), Philippe Chatrier, Paolo Angeli and Stan Malless (ITF) and Jack Kramer, Owen Williams and Lars Myhrman (tournament directors). As president of the ITF, Derek Hardwick acted as council chairman. Although it would be a little difficult to find six qualified people totally divorced from any involvement in tournaments, Oprea makes a valid point. Only Drysdale and Angeli were not involved with the organization of a tournament somewhere in the world.

Orantes," Kramer told me. "And as a member of the Pro Council I was prepared to be as difficult as possible, in an attempt to try and cut out that kind of crap which is so bad for the game."

Evidently Kramer's attitude did not go unnoticed by Nastase. It resulted in an incident at the U.S. Open in 1975 which Jack laughs about now, but which could not have been too amusing at the time.

"It was just after he had lost in the quarterfinals at Forest Hills and Ilie was walking back to the clubhouse over the grass courts," Kramer recalled. "I happened to be walking parallel with him along the pathway. There was a small fence and about twenty-five yards separating us. Suddenly Ilie starts yelling at me. 'You did it' he screams. 'You went after me, you dirty sonuvabitch.' He was swearing away at me in English and Rumanian and soon a lot of people started yelling back in my defense. I remember thinking that if I was half a man, I should climb the fence and go after him. But I suppose it would have been a bit undignified. Eventually he just goes in one side of the clubhouse and I go in the other and that's the end of it. Neither of us mentioned it again. Frankly I feel sorry for the guy. I have always felt that if he could learn to handle himself better and try to emulate some of the great champions like Don Budge or Fred Perry, he could amass the record of an outstanding player. With his super ability, he hasn't won as much as he should have."

The balance of the $3,000 fines had been accumulated at the American Airlines Tennis Games and, ironically considering his general deportment during the fortnight, at Wimbledon. Apparently Connors and Nastase had damaged the court during their rather overboisterous doubles, and for that Ilie was docked $500.

The American Airlines incident was more serious. Even though the tournament had been moved from Tucson to the Mission Hills Country Club at Palm Springs, it was all the same desert as far as Nastase's fortunes were concerned. It was obviously not an event at which he was destined to enhance his reputation.

After an ill-tempered match with Dick Stockton which ended with the American standing pointedly at the net with his arm outstretched while Ilie ignored the customary postmatch handshake, Roscoe Tanner came on court to face Nastase in the next round with his ATP rule book tucked under his arm. It had been the general opinion of the players that Ilie had got away with murder against Stockton and Tanner was determined not to let it happen to him.

In fact, he need not have bothered. Charlie Hare, the former British Davis Cup player who twice reached the Wimbledon doubles final, had decided to emulate Mike Gibson in his role as tournament referee and keep a close eye on the whole match. In view of Nastase's behavior earlier in the week, it was a perfectly reasonable decision for Hare to make but, in fact, the sight of the referee sitting next to the umpire's chair probably ruined whatever chance there had been of Ilie playing through the match without incident. His reaction was typical, and it is not difficult to interpret what went through his mind. So if you come expecting trouble, I'll give you trouble, was Ilie's belligerent response to the sight of encroaching officialdom. And, inevitably, there was trouble. The details become repetitious, but I seem to remember that at one stage he responded to a provocative remark from a spectator by climbing into one of the courtside boxes and unzipping his shorts.

"Some woman made a remark about my underwear, so I thought maybe she ought to have a look at it," Ilie explained mischievously afterward. Other ladies present, who kept their fantasies to themselves, were justifiably disgusted.

With Ilie in that kind of mood, the outcome was a foregone conclusion. Before Tanner had a chance to start waving his rule book around, Hare disqualified the rebellious Rumanian. After the various misdemeanors Nastase had committed throughout the week had been toted up— $250 for hitting a ball out of court, $500 for abusing an umpire, etc.,—the grand total was judged to amount to $4,100.

"That would have meant immediate suspension and with the Davis Cup coming up it would have caused serious problems with the Rumanian Federation," Oprea explained. "So after long negotiations with the ATP and the

236 • *The Tennis Book*

tournament officials, we managed to get it reduced to $2,200."

The $500 at Wimbledon increased it to $2,700, and the $1,000 levied at Forest Hills as a result of the Pohmann affair put Nastase over the top.

Even after the farcical—and highly profitable—suspension period was over, an unrepentant Nastase was not finished for the year. There was a bad scene at the end of his final against Ken Rosewall in Hong Kong and more disruptive incidents when he played Wojtek Fibak in the Benson & Hedges Championships at Wembley the following week.

But if 1976 showed no improvement in Nastase's record of behavior over the previous year, at least the tantrums had been punctuated with some worthy title-winning achievements. Apart from triumphs in the Avis Challenge Cup and the Pepsi Grand Slam, he had won singles titles at Atlanta, Salisbury and La Costa while reserving some of his best tennis for two of the most important events of the year, Wimbledon and Forest Hills. By December he had moved back up to number three on the ATP computer, behind Connors and Borg.

But at no time was Nastase—or Jimmy Connors for that matter—seen in better light than during the rain-afflicted John Player Tournament at Nottingham the week before Wimbledon. There is no more treacherous surface to play on than wet grass and the footing on a tennis court has seldom been worse than it was when Ilie and Jimmy elected to play their singles final after a long delay because of the rain. They were both taking a considerable risk which would have been bad enough at any time of year, let alone on the eve of Wimbledon. Yet not only did they play, they played with such zest and flair that one would have marveled at many of their strokes had they been playing in the most perfect conditions. Eventually after Connors won the first set and Nastase the second, the grass had become so slippery that the odds against injury were no longer reasonable. So they asked the umpire to abandon the match. Deservedly, the crowd gave them a rousing ovation.

"We had to do something for the people," said Ilie afterward. "The place was full; three thousand people getting wet and cold hoping to see some tennis. So we have to try."

That was a side of Ilie Nastase that the Nottingham tournament director, Tony Pickard, had seldom seen before. In 1975 Nastase had refused to play the John Player event because of some injudicious remarks Pickard had made about what Nastase might or might not do, and until he proved himself a real trouper in the 1976 final, their relationship had been a little strained. Now Pickard, who had worked hard to bring top-class tennis to the Midlands, had discovered an unlikely ally in his bid to make professionalism a respectable word amongst the somewhat old-fashioned local tennis hierarchy. Not for the first time, Ilie had turned an enemy into a friend.

For that alone he could look back on the year with a modicum of satisfaction.

Vilas Tries Harder

by PHILIP TAUBMAN

Can a champion be made? Take the case of Guillermo Vilas, a strong, patient player, with the temperament of a poet. His coach, Ion Tiriac, believed that a lot of sweat and the infusion of his own iron will would turn the reflective player into the properly competitive killer. Philip Taubman studied the reconstruction project and wrote this status report.

THE midday sun beats down on the red clay courts of the Buenos Aires Lawn Tennis Club, scorching everything it touches. The only sensible place to be is under a large tree with a cool drink. Guillermo Vilas knows that but ignores it. Sweat is streaming down his body, small rivulets feeding larger tributaries that flow into rivers of perspiration running down his chest and back. Clouds of red dust swirl around his feet as the races back and forth across the base line, skidding through the loose clay to hit a forehand, driving back to the right corner to stroke a backhand, pivoting to head for another forehand. The balls keep coming, Vilas keeps moving until he is gasping for breath. He stops, walks up to the net, and leans on it for support, resting his arms and head on the net cord like a marathoner drained of all energy at the end of a race. Ion Tiriac, Vilas's coach, collects the balls from around the court

and orders his student back to work. Vilas swallows deeply from a bottle of mineral water, adjusts his soaking wristband, and steps back to the base line to resume the drill.

The basic training of Guillermo Vilas is underway. It is a rite of physical and mental conditioning unlike anything in tennis. Its objective: The alteration of a personality, the transformation of a romantic Latin poet into a disciplined Prussian tennis machine. Tiriac is the sorcerer, Vilas the base metal to be changed to gold, and the alchemy includes the transplantation of will and concentration from Tiriac to Vilas. The ultimate goal is victory in the finals of the French championship in June, Wimbledon in July, the U.S. Open in September, and undisputed ranking as the number-one player in the world. Last year, working under Tiriac's full-time guidance for the first time, Vilas won more money and matches than anyone in the sport, joining Bjorn Borg and Jimmy Connors at the top of the tennis pyramid.

They dominate the sport, playing at a level above the rest of the tennis world. Their matches against one another are the great rivalries of the game and the great gate attractions. When Connors and Vilas met in the Masters Tournament last January in New York, the match drew eighteen thousand people to Madison Square Garden, the biggest crowd ever to attend a tennis contest. It was like a heavyweight fight, with fans cheering after every point. The biggest controversy in tennis is the debate over who is number one: Connors, because he reached the finals of both Wimbledon and Forest Hills and regularly defeats Borg; Borg, because he won Wimbledon and seems to psyche out Vilas whenever they play; or Vilas, because he was the victor at Forest Hills and the French Open and defeated Connors the last two times they met, both dramatic tennis battles.

Vilas is the least known of the three, by far the most interesting. Unlike Borg and Connors, he got to the top by *not* being himself. Borg's game is a reflection of his personality and Swedish blood: Cool and steady. His patience is limitless; his strategy, to wear down opponents with endless rallies from the base line. Connors throws himself into every shot the way he throws himself at life. His strategy is to make every shot a winner, to attack every ball. He was born spunky. Vilas's game lies in between. He is more patient than Connors, stronger and more aggressive than Borg. But his game is not his life. He was born reflective and sensitive. His profession is tennis, but his heart belongs to art.

It is written all over his face: the shaggy shoulder-length hair that spills down over his forehead; the easy, friendly smile; and the eyes, incredible eyes—large, soft, soulful hazel eyes that women find irresistibly sexy and men find trusting and relaxing. The eyes are the man. They speak of distant, secret places, of dreams and andante tempos, of ripples silently spreading across a still pond. They soothe and caress. It is not the face of a driven, methodical tennis champion. It is the face of a poet, which is what Vilas longs to be.

Tiriac was born intimidating, impatient, churlish—he has no time for poetry. His profession is tennis, and his heart belongs to his work. It is written all over his face. Tiriac wears a permanent scowl. With dark, tangled hair covering his head like an overgrown bush and a thick, drooping mustache complemented by equally dense sideburns, the Rumanian native looks as if

he stepped from the pages of Grimms' Fairy Tales—or from a Transylvanian nightmare. On the tennis circuit he is known as Count Dracula.

When seen together, the faces of Vilas and Tiriac are so powerfully opposed that they seem unreal. Only an artist free to let his hand follow his imagination could create such absolute opposites. Good and evil, trust and cynicism, innocence and experience: Vilas and Tiriac look like characters in a medieval morality play.

In a way, they are. While neither Vilas nor Tiriac is entirely what he appears to be—Vilas can be calculating and tough; Tiriac, sentimental and whimsical—the basic training of Vilas boils down to a struggle between freedom and servitude: Freedom for Vilas to be whatever he feels—a poet, writer, lyricist, lover, and, sometimes, a tennis player—vs. servitude to a demanding, unforgiving master called professional tennis. Vilas's instincts draw him to the freedom. Tiriac's job is to tie him to tennis.

Even when they are both focused on tennis, the tug-of-war is evident. One day during lunch break at the Buenos Aires Tennis Club, I asked Vilas why, with all his other interests, he plays tennis. "I like the way the game is," he replied. "It's an individual game. You're always in motion. No two shots are ever the same, and you must constantly think about strategy. It's a lot like chess, no? You have to be an artist. You are creating all the time."

Tiriac dropped his fork. "Now, my friend," he said to me, "you see my problem. You ask him about tennis and you get motion, flowers, trees, and birds singing in their nest. Instead, it should be, 'I like to kill that sonuvabitch on the other side of the net.' " Tiriac threw up his arms and shook his head. "Now you see my problem."

The room at the top of the steep, narrow stairway is tiny and oppressively hot, like a sauna. Egg cartons are pasted on the walls to soundproof the makeshift studio. A single, bare fluorescent bulb casts an unflattering glow on five young Argentine musicians crammed, shirtless, in the room amid a clutter of instruments, speakers, and a tangle of wires on the floor.

"Uno, dos, tres." The lead guitarist snaps his fingers to the beat, and the band shakes the room

Ground stroke power—the key to Guillermo Vilas' game, mastered through strength, sweat and top spin. Here he hits a forehand just after having placed his first serve in play. (Photo by Russ Adams)

with the opening chords of a Latin jazz-rock number. Guillermo Vilas, sitting cross-legged on the floor, closes his eyes and starts tapping his feet to the rhythm.

We have come here, driving over the cobblestone streets of Buenos Aires in the fading light of a South American summer day, to hear Vilas's friends perform. The group, named Spinetta after its lead guitarist and organizer, Luis Alberto Spinetta, is an important part of Vilas's life. He likes their music. Better, they like his lyrics and are rehearsing a piece for which he wrote the words.

The band stops. The players wipe their brows, and Vilas shifts his position on the floor. Dressed in Vilas tennis shorts and Vilas sneakers, coiled up in front of an electronic organ and a large Acoustic speaker, he looks like an athlete who has wandered far from his arena. In one way, he has. Yet he hasn't. "Play some more," he suggests. Spinetta picks a tune, and soon the room is again reverberating to the heavy Latin beat.

"He can't hit the damn ball on the court. I can't get into Uruguay until the last minute because they don't want any Rumanians, so he gets no good practice. We started training ten days ago, but now we have to start all over again." Tiriac is pacing around the patio of the Buenos Aires Lawn Tennis Club. He and Vilas returned from Punta del Este early in the morning after a disastrous tournament. Vilas, who had not played for a month after injuring his ankle in New York in January, lost to two South American rivals, neither in his class. "I don't give a damn if he lose," says Tiriac. "But the way he's playing, it's crap. We start, now, to get him in shape." Vilas jogs around the patio, listening to the outburst, picks up his rackets, and follows Tiriac down the steps to the courts.

It rained last night, and the courts are still slightly soggy. Tiriac leads Vilas onto court number three and pops open two cans of white Dunlop balls. He removes his shirt and unzips the cover on one of five Prince rackets. Vilas sheds his shirt and pulls on his trademark, a three-inch-wide elastic headband that keeps his hair and sweat out of his eyes. He does a few waist bends and stretching exercises, then tests a grip on several of his Vilas-model Head rackets. He helped design the black-and-tan rackets, made from ash, graphite and fiberglass, and earns a hefty income from Head for endorsing them. Vilas bounces his palm on the gut and holds the racket up to his ear as if it were a string instrument, concentrating on the tone of the ping he hears. Satisfied the racket is strung at the fifty-three pounds he likes for hitting topspins, he walks out on the court.

It is noon. They are about to begin six hours of practice, a routine they follow seven days a week during training. Vilas, twenty-six, has classic athletic proportions: Muscular arms and chest, taut stomach, and powerful, tapered legs. Tiriac, who has just turned forty, has stooped shoulders and a developing paunch. He is top- and bottom-heavy, his hair dominating the top, his thick legs the bottom. They begin with some easy ground strokes. Vilas is left-handed, Tiriac right. The chatter is in Italian. Tiriac speaks good Spanish, and Vilas can get by with some Rumanian, and they both speak fluent English plus some French, but they prefer a mixture of Spanish and Italian. *"Perdón,"* Tiriac shouts to Vilas when he hits a ball astray.

After fifteen minutes of warm-up rallying, Tiriac starts feeding ball after ball to Vilas's forehand. Vilas slides into each shot, then dashes back to the middle of the court. Tiriac shouts out instructions. *"Recupera, recupera,"* he yells, telling Vilas to recover back to the middle of the court and be ready to move either to his backhand or forehand side. *"Bene, bene.* When you keep running it is good." Enrique Caviglia, one of Argentina's top-ranked players, comes on the court and joins Tiriac, creating a two-on-one drill. The balls are now coming faster to Vilas's forehand. Again, and again, and again, he runs to the left, brings back his racket, and slaps a topspin forehand over the net. After twenty minutes, Tiriac stops the drill and lectures Vilas about his form. "You're hitting the forehand square," he says. "You have an open stance. You must turn into the shot." It is a sight to make any hacker happy: The best player in the world is going to tennis camp.

At one o'clock, Tiriac switches to overhead

and volley practice. By now, a dozen club members have gathered around the court, peering through the fence at the national hero in their midst. Vilas says the people are distracting him. Tiriac tells him to forget the spectators and keep playing. Vilas sets up a few feet in front of the service line, at mid-court. Tiriac hits a lob over Vilas's left shoulder. Vilas races back and smashes the ball back toward Tiriac's feet. Tiriac lofts it back, this time to Vilas's backhand side. He spins, turns his shoulder to the net, and pounds the ball again. After a few minutes, Tiriac and Caviglia mix low, hard volleys with the lobs. Vilas looks like a figure in a speeded-up film: He runs to hit a forehand smash, barely looks up before he must intercept a knee-level volley, then lunges to his right for another volley before digging back to blast another lob. It is a killing drill.

From volley and overhead, Tiriac moves Vilas back to the base line to hit serves for thirty minutes. A brooding tutor, Tiriac stands behind Vilas, watching every movement. Vilas's serve, good enough to handcuff 99 percent of the players in the world, has not been satisfactory to him or Tiriac recently, so they have developed a new motion. Instead of starting from a stationary position just behind the base line, Vilas now begins a yard back and takes two steps forward before tossing the ball. "New serve, isn't it?" I ask. "Yes," replies Vilas, "What's the advantage?" Vilas: "It goes in."

The time is now two P.M. Tiriac looks over at one of the spectators, an attractive girl whose loose shirt hangs to her thighs. "Does she have any pants on?" he asks Vilas. The girl laughs and lifts her shirt, revealing a pair of tight tennis shorts. On that rare note of comic relief, Tiriac and student break for lunch. Vilas eats creamed spinach topped with two fried eggs and drinks several pitchers of ice water mixed with grenadine. He greets friends and plays with some of the young children gathered in the club dining room. He clearly is not in any rush to get back to the courts. "Come on," orders Tiriac eventually, "time to go." Vilas lingers. "If I let him," says Tiriac, "he would go out under some tree and write poetry." (Two days later, Vilas does just

that, settling in the shade of a eucalyptus tree after lunch to write and listen to music.)

Practice resumes at three-thirty, beginning with a volley drill, Tiriac and Caviglia at the service line on one side, hitting volleys to Vilas stationed at mid-court on the other. Balls fly back and forth across the net in a white blur. It is like a rapid volley exchange in championship doubles, except Vilas is doing the work of two men. After thirty minutes, he moves back, and backhand practice starts. Balls streak into the backhand corner. Time after time, Vilas launches them back, hitting blistering shots straight down the line, each a rehearsal for the next time he passes Jimmy Connors with a backhand winner.

At four-thirty, Vilas drops on the bench next to me, exhausted. He pours cool water down his throat. "This is like the meal before they kill you," he says. "Now comes the tough part." Vilas heads back to the base line. This time, Tiriac moves up to the net. The drill will be forehand and backhand ground strokes, but Vilas will not have the extra second to cover ground while the ball is returned from the opposite base line. It will come back at him instantly as a volley. The drill commences. Vilas looks like a man trapped on a runaway treadmill, running from corner to corner. Low balls, high balls, spinning, flat; he sends them all back. Finally, his breath nearly gone, he murders one right at Tiriac's head. The ball rockets across the net like a cannon shot. Instinctively, Tiriac blinks and ducks. The ball knocks the racket loose from his hand. He picks it up, a broad smile crossing his face. "Bravo, bravo, Guillermo," he beams. "Now you play doubles for two hours."

Two dozen color photographs are spread on the purple blanket. Vilas's pictures of sunsets and trees silhouetted against the blue sky. A stereo system is set up next to the bed, some plants are set by the window. Vilas, in jeans and a red shirt, is curled up on the bed, leafing through an album of photos and poems. "Here's the one," he says, pulling another sunset picture from the collection. "How do you like?" Ken Regan, a professional photographer, examines the print. "Pretty good," he says. "How could it be better?" asks Vilas. Regan points out that a larger magnification lens would have allowed Vilas to focus in on a bird flying near the setting sun. Vilas nods and inquires about the shutter speed, f-stop, and the best film for different lighting.

A few minutes earlier we had finished lunch in Vilas's apartment, a comfortable but not lavish ninth-floor layout overlooking the Plata River in Olivos, just outside Buenos Aires. (He owns several others in the same building, one in Punta del Este, another in Monte Carlo, and plans to buy yet another in Paris.) His cook and housekeeper served roast chicken, cold cuts, and hearts of palm, while Vilas talked about photography, music and death. He is fascinated by death and writes many poems about it. His ideas are not elegant or terribly sophisticated, but not many professional tennis players spend their lunch hour ruminating about death. "Death is so perfect," he says. "In life you can find so many problems. Life is so imperfect. But death. Boom, that's it. It's so simple."

I ask about a screenplay he has been working on for two years. "It's, how do you say, a psychodrama. It is about two friends, how they split up and discover themselves as individuals, then come back together again. I know it is not great, but I enjoy writing it and will keep working on it." A blue notebook rests on the arm of a couch, open to a page half-covered with script. Whenever he has a spare moment, Vilas likes to write. He has published, at his own expense, a book of his poetry, much of it about death. What attracts him to poetry? "I like it. I can't explain. I started when I was fourteen. My teacher read my first poem and said it was very bad and threw it away. I know I still do not write well, but someday maybe I will."

One of his favorite authors is J. Krishnamurti, an Indian philosopher-cum-guru whose writing stresses understanding oneself, freeing the individual from the conditioning of society. The idea appeals to Vilas. "He wants to make you live withinside yourself," says Vilas. "Most people think, talk, behave like their parents, friends and the place where they live. They adopt things without thinking. From Krishnamurti, I started knowing why I do things. I became more alert to myself."

As we talk over lunch, framed by two giant elephant tusks that Vilas brought back from an African trip, I ask him about his relationship to the Argentine government, a repressive military junta. I wonder whether, with all his wealth and fame, he is concerned about human rights. Argentine professors had told me about militia in the classrooms, about the government's ban on teaching about Freud. Newspapers that break censorship codes are shut. People, with terror in their eyes, told me about friends arrested in the middle of the night and never heard from again. Just under the busy pace of Buenos Aires life, there is real fear.

Vilas is wary of the question. His answer is short. "I am not political. If I win a big tournament, the government may congratulate me, but I am not political." Friends later explain that Vilas has no choice but to remain silent. If he spoke out against the regime, he would be banned from his homeland. A rationalization, perhaps, but for Vilas, one not easily dismissed.

The discussion turns to the relationship between Vilas's artistic and athletic temperaments. I asked where they intersect. "I think a tennis player can be a great artist *as* a tennis player, but he has a serious problem. Nothing lasts. If he plays a match that is a masterpiece, it is so fast forgotten. When I played Connors at Madison Square Garden in January, everyone says that is one of the great matches of all time. But by next year they forget. When Jack Kramer was playing, everyone said he was the greatest. Now, they say Vilas, Borg or Connors, we are better. You cannot hang a perfect tennis shot in a museum for everyone to see. A tennis player who wants to play the game like an artist, he must paint the Mona Lisa two or three times a year."

The matches on surrounding courts have stopped, the players abandoning their games to watch the contest on court number ten. Vilas is playing Tiriac, best two out of three. The teacher is taking on the student. Several days of drills have drained Vilas and bored him. Tiriac has switched to more realistic practice to keep Vilas's mind on the job. Vilas wins the toss and serves first. He hits a bullet to Tiriac's forehand. The Rumanian lunges for the ball and hits it into the net. He slaps his racket against his leg. It is clear this is no good-natured afternoon set. Vilas has a look of concentration on his face I haven't seen before.

Tiriac evens the score at deuce. Vilas serves, moves up to hit a volley, and knocks it into the net. He curses and kicks the ball toward the fence. He wins the next point on a cross-court forehand. Ad Vilas. He bounces the ball behind the base line, takes the two steps he worked on in practice, and serves. The spin serve lands in the backhand corner of the service box and twists away from Tiriac. He reaches out and hits a backhand cross-court. Vilas races over and returns the ball to Tiriac's backhand. Tiriac rifles it back down the line. It looks like a sure winner. Vilas sprints over the court, and just before the ball passes beyond his racket, he connects. The ball flashes across the net, kicking up red clay in the cross-court corner. Tiriac cannot touch it. Game to Vilas.

The older man is no match for his young protégé. The first set goes to Vilas, 6–1. But the intensity of the struggle is palpable. After one close line call by Tiriac, Vilas rushes up to the net to take a closer look at the mark left by the ball. Later, he throws his racket to the ground in disgust after Tiriac calls a ball out. Tiriac keeps cursing his own slowness and poor play. Usually, when Vilas needs to replace the gauze he uses on his racket grip. Tiriac does the job. Not now. During the match, Vilas receives no assistance. Perhaps it is the competitiveness of the two, but the match also seems to be a release for the undercurrent of tension between Vilas and Tiriac that is built up during the endless hours of drill. Tiriac pushed him hard, harder than you would expect the premier player in the world to be pushed. The match seems to be a catharsis for Vilas.

Vilas ends the match with a booming overhead. Tiriac kicks the clay. "I play terrible today," he says. "I can't hit anything." I ask if he ever defeats Vilas. In the background, Vilas is already starting another match with an Argentine Davis Cup player. Tiriac turns and gives Vilas some instructions. The coach is back in command. "Oh sure, I win," he finally answers. "I usually win."

They met eight years ago. At the time, Vilas was a promising young player on the rise, Tiriac a veteran in the final years of his competitive career. A close friendship did not seem likely. Tiriac was a fanatic about athletics. Before sharpening his tennis skills and joining the pro tour, he had played ice hockey, competing on the Rumanian national team as a defenseman in the Olympics. When he and Vilas met, Tiriac was busy coaching fellow Rumanian Ilie Nastase, polishing both Nastase's tennis and temper tantrums. The two Rumanians were Davis Cup teammates and doubles partners, cultivating an image as the bad boys of tennis.

Vilas, meanwhile, was a quiet, enigmatic newcomer. He was still training with his hometown coach in Mar del Plata, a coastal resort city 225 miles from Buenos Aires. Vilas had taken up tennis when he was six. His father, a lawyer, was president of the local tennis club, and the younger Vilas grew up on the courts. At nine, he started practicing all day, quickly developing into a top young competitor. By the time he discovered his interest in intellectual and artistic activities, he was already launched in a tennis career. His talent was so obvious he could not ignore it. Love it or not, he was wedded to tennis. He was a poet trapped in an athlete. Not the kind of personality anyone expected to mesh, with Tiriac's.

But in uncommon ways they had a great deal in common. Neither was a big winner on the tennis circuit. Tiriac had won the French championship, but never Wimbledon or Forest Hills. Vilas, even at seventeen, was already showing signs of choking in big matches. There was more. Tiriac was looking for a son. "Ion has a need to be a father," says his wife, Mikette. Vilas needed someone to order his life and enforce concentration on tennis.

Slowly, the two men got together. It started with Tiriac giving Vilas tips. A change in grip, a recommendation about shot selection. The advice helped. The exchanges increased until last spring, at the French Open in Paris, Tiriac announced that Vilas would win the tournament if he followed Tiriac's instructions. Vilas was hungry for a big win. He had won plenty of tournaments, enough to lead the Grand Prix point standings in 1974 and 1975, but of all the major players he was the only one without a Grand Slam tournament title. He accepted Tiriac's offer: "I will tell you everything, what to do, what to think, how to play."

Vilas lost only one set in six matches, winning the French title by destroying Brian Gottfried in the finals, 6–0, 6–3, 6–0, the most impressive margin of victory since 1925. From then on, Vilas turned his tennis life—and a percentage of his winnings (some say 20 percent)—over to Tiriac. Tiriac wasted no time taking charge. He reformed Vilas's practice routine, making him work out for six hours every day, even during tournaments. Vilas became the strongest, best-conditioned player on the circuit. Meanwhile, Tiriac refined Vilas's powerful topspin ground strokes and worked on improving his net game. They spent hours discussing strategy: When to lob, when to attack, when to hit topspin, when to use underspin. During matches, Tiriac started flashing signs to Vilas like a third-base coach in baseball signaling the batter. A lift of an eyebrow or an arm might mean Vilas should throw his service toss higher, a glance toward the net would be a signal to serve and volley rather than play a base-line game. Between points, Vilas would glance over for advice. It is now a habit.

Soon Tiriac was helping in other ways. When reporters pressed around Vilas, Tiriac shepherded him away. When business offers came in, Tiriac handled the negotiating. Though new to the business world, he learned fast. He incorporated Vilas-Tiriac International, with offices in Buenos Aires, Paris and Bucharest. Like a magazine offering regional editions for advertisers, he signed Vilas up to one brand of shirt in Argentina, another in the United States. Shrewdly, he kept count of the number of hours Vilas appeared on TV last year: Twenty in France, seventy in the States. When companies asked to advertise on Vilas's headband, Tiriac was ready. Fine, he said, you want your product on the most visible headband in the world? you want it live and in color on TV every time the

camera zooms in on Vilas? You can have it—for $1 million a year. He may get it. Even without it, Vilas earned better than $2 million last year, about half in prize money, half in endorsements.

The results of Tiriac's presence were dramatic. Vilas, after stumbling at Wimbledon, went on to win fifty-seven matches in a row on clay. That streak included forty-four consecutive tournament victories on all surfaces, the longest winning skein in tennis since 1968. Along the way, he won the championship at Forest Hills last summer.

An unrivaled record. And an unrivaled relationship between player and coach. Connors got help from Pancho Segura, and Borg calls on fellow Swede Lennart Bergelin, but no one in tennis depends on a coach as heavily as Vilas does on Tiriac. They appear to be a tennis hybrid, the body of Vilas playing with the mind of Tiriac; two men who could not win big alone becoming unbeatable together. Some call it Faust revisited, with Vilas as Dr. Faustus, Tiriac as Mephistopheles, and the bargain: One romantic soul in exchange for ranking as number one.

The price Vilas pays is unmistakable. It is the loss of independence. The curious thing is that while Vilas resists that sacrifice instinctively, while he reflexively clings to his personal passions, forcing Tiriac at times to drag him into fighting trim, intellectually he accepts and embraces the dependence. "If Tiriac should leave me," says Vilas frankly, "I would be lost. I lean on him. I put myself completely in his hands and do whatever he tells me. He say come out at noon, I come out at noon. He say get up at nine, I get up at nine. This is not easy," he says. "It is not easy to go out and practice so hard. These drills are not nice. Tiriac only understands his way. It is difficult to stay with a guy like that." Tiriac does not always enjoy the relationship either. "I have to push him," he says. "I have to split his attention from all other things, make him concentrate on one thing."

Yet Vilas understands why he stays with Tiriac. "It is difficult for me to concentrate on tennis. I love the game, but not to live twenty-four hours a day. It is hard for me to make the adjustment from other things to tennis. When I am writing, the feeling is so different from playing tennis. When you write, you have to live, you cannot be a stranger to the world. When you play tennis, you have to cut off the world. You must be a stranger then. You must think of tennis only. I would like to write books, short stories, screenplays. I would like to be a great philosopher, a great poet, but I am not one now. I am now a tennis player. In tennis, I can do great things now. Ion never lets me forget that."

Three Verses by Vilas
(Translation by Jerome Williams)

TIME

For an hour I have been meaning to sit down.
For an hour I have been waiting to be alone.
For an hour I have been defiling people.
For an hour I have been thinking about writing to you.
I have been writing about this vile hour for five minutes.
Damned watch, you even measure my love.
My love,
pardon me for having wasted a minute speaking about my watch.

THE FLY

It is night.
A restless fly stole into my room.
It flew about nervously.
More and more, the heat of the blankets lulled me to sleep.
The fly would alight on my naked body and awaken me each time.
It did not make me angry.
The warmth of the room and the bed was so enchanting that I did not want
to lose such pleasure without possessing it.
The fly awoke me a thousand times,
and a thousand times I enjoyed that instant, thanks to the fly.
To think that in another moment I would have killed it!
The fly awoke me all night long, and in the morning I killed it.

TO LIFE AND TO DEATH

But what fault is it of yours, death,
if yours is but a moment.
Life merely saddens me,

my eternal companion,
because I'll have to leave her to her fate
when I cross your border.
It saddens me to go with you,
as a lover, to your bed,
because I'll be nothing but a moment,
leaving without witnesses,
without my life and without my death,
alone, as I was born.

What must be at least the twentieth bottle of wine arrives at the table. The meal started with sausages, followed by sweetbreads and cow's stomach, an Argentine specialty. The coals under the fire are still red hot, and smoke rises from beef ribs dripping fat into the fire. The southern heavens are clear and bright over the tennis club patio, and the mood is light. Vilas and Tiriac have played the directors of the club in a casual pro-am match before dinner, and now the club officials and their families are hosting an *asado,* or Argentine barbecue.

Vilas sits at one end of the row of circular tables, a glass of wine in one hand, his other hand resting on the shoulder of his girl friend, Gabriela Blondeau. She is only sixteen but appears mature beyond her years. Her face, like those of Vilas and Tiriac, is rare. The features are simple but striking. In the candlelight, she looks like a Botticelli madonna. She says she and Vilas are in love.

Tiriac is holding court at the middle of the table, a large cigar jutting from his jaw. The wine has loosened his tongue, and he has not stopped talking since the first glass was filled. As the cigar smoke drifts up past his mustache, he looks more sinister than ever, but all the gruffness is gone. Wisecracks that came so sparingly during the workouts with Vilas have suddenly expanded into a sentimental warmth and affection. Tiriac lifts his glass in a toast to the club president and roars with laughter. It is possible now to imagine Vilas calling Tiriac "Papito" and "Papanitsch," as he sometimes does, Italian and Rumanian for "father." Tiriac starts another story. The party rumbles with laughter, and Vilas nearly knocks his glass off the table.

By the time the last bottle is drained, it is after midnight. Tiriac hugs the club president. Vilas, his arm around Gabriela, picks up his rackets and starts toward the door. As is his habit, he might well be headed out for a night of dancing, followed by breakfast at dawn. "Guillermo," cries out Tiriac, "we start tomorrow at ten-thirty." Vilas nods unenthusiastically and departs with Gabriela. "Christ," says Tiriac, to no one in particular, "we still have another month of training before he is ready."

The Basic Borg

by BARRY LORGE

If Bjorn Borg had been born American he might have been Gary Cooper—the strong silent type, answering virtually every question with a "Yep" or "Nope." But Borg's Swedish—he says "For sure" or "No." This makes him your basic tough interview, but Barry Lorge, the sports editor of the San Diego Union *and a contributing editor to* World Tennis *magazine, has gotten past the glacial exterior.*

WE live in a society that teaches us early that it is important to be a well-rounded individual. From grade school on, the virtues of a liberal education are extolled. The student of literature should know something of geometry, the better to figure out life's acute angles. The historian should be familiar with logarithms and trigonometric functions, in case the batteries of his pocket calculator run down before he can figure out the square root of his income tax. The chemist should know a bit about rhyming couplets as well as balancing equations. In an age when jobs require specialization, the Renaissance Man is looked upon with a certain romantic fascination.

In sports, too, we like our highly paid heroes to do something more than throw or hit the ball further and more accurately. We know Jack Nicklaus as businessman and course architect as well as golfer, Muhammed Ali as crusading orator as well as boxer, Guillermo Vilas as poet and philosopher as well as tennis player. We prefer, if possible, that our sporting figures have other talents and dimensions, interesting lives and personalities off the field or the court. We love it if they are characters of substance, with a bit of wit, wisdom and color.

Bjorn Borg does not sing, dance, tell hilarious jokes, paint, study archaeology, play the flute, manage a chain of Swedish massage parlors, recite Ibsen, or say much that is terribly absorbing. He will not win a Nobel Prize unless they start giving one for topspin. He has an agreeable temperament and a certain savvy for dealing readily with life on the run, but he is not cultivated or particularly insightful. As a conversationalist, he is a rhinestone in the rough.

What he does is play tennis—extraordinarily well, in a style that is unorthodox and perhaps revolutionary. Another generation will testify as to whether his exaggerated topspin is the technique of the future. For now, Borg has accomplished far more than any previous twenty-one-year-old in the history of the game. Two Wimbledon titles. Two French Opens. One Italian. Three U.S. Pro titles. One WCT championship. And in 1975, at age nineteen, he led Sweden to its first possession of the Davis Cup.

Last year Borg earned $424,420 on the

court, plus more than an additional half a million for endorsements, exhibitions and appearances. This year, including his World Team Tennis contract with the Cleveland-Pittsburgh-and-Points-Beyond Nets, reportedly worth $350,000 for four months, he could make between $1.5 and $2 million. His is the kind of success and accomplishment, material and otherwise, that can only come from intense specialization. In this case, from an almost single-minded obsession with tennis.

When Bjorn was nine years old, his father, a salesman in a clothing store, won a table tennis tournament. The prize was a tennis racket, which Rune Borg gave to his only child.

Bjorn promptly decided that he preferred tennis to table tennis, which his father played often and well, and could never seem to get enough of the game. Within a year he caught the eye of Percy Rosburg, a respected coach of the Swedish Tennis Federation, who was impressed with young Borg's tireless enthusiasm and determination, and with the pace and accuracy with which he hit his unconventional strokes. Despite pressure to do so, Rosburg did not change his protégé's extreme Western forehand or two-fisted backhand. He built upon them, helping Borg develop his own natural inclinations. He taught Borg a great deal about technique and tactics, but recognized and did not tamper with a great gift for the game.

Borg chose to devote himself to tennis at age thirteen, to the exclusion of his other sporting passion, ice hockey. "I won two national junior tournaments in Sweden. That was fun. I never won a big tournament in ice hockey. Then I thought I could be a very good tennis player and I stopped playing hockey, football (soccer), things like that and just concentrate on my tennis," he recalls.

At fifteen, he chose tennis over school, with the concurrence of his doting parents. He was never happy in a classroom anyway. He always preferred comics to any other kind of books, and still does. He was not good at sitting still and despised homework. He discussed his future with his parents and Lennart Bergelin, the one-time Wimbledon quarterfinalist and Swedish Davis Cup captain who had become his coach-advisor-confidant, and decided to leave school midway through the ninth grade.

"If I should continue in the school, I couldn't travel so much and play tournaments," he reasoned. "My parents said, 'It is worth a try. If you don't like the tennis, you can go back to school.' But I think I never go back. I didn't like so much sitting for one hour in a chair, listening to the teacher."

Nowadays, when he is not playing tennis, which is not very often, Borg likes to do some of the things he had little time for in his abbreviated formative years. He enjoys going to the movies or the beach, swimming, lying in the sun, listening to pop music, and idling away hours with his fiancée, Rumanian player Marianna Simionescu. He watches TV and reads about the adventures of Kalle Anka (Donald Duck), Pluto and Goofy. His favorite pastime, he says earnestly, is "just relaxing—you know, resting and not do anything."

He most likes to do this at his adopted homes: Hilton Head Island, South Carolina and Monte Carlo. At the former, he can play house with Marianna at his condominium amid the Spanish moss, pleasantly isolated from an intruding world; at the latter he blends easily into a tranquil, lovely landscape peopled by celebrities living tax free and relatively unbothered.

"My parents are in Monte Carlo now, that's our home. We feel very comfortable there," he says, though some rumors insist that Rune and Margaretha Borg feel alienated and uprooted in idyllic Monaco, and long to go home to Sweden.

"When I have time off, I prefer to go there more than Sweden. In Sweden, it is impossible to be alone and have a rest for a couple of weeks because everyone will bother me," Bjorn says. "It is the same when Nastase goes to Rumania or Vilas to Argentina. But there is so many famous people in Monte Carlo, no one cares down there. It's a good climate, no one is bothering you, everything is nice there."

Borg likes his private life sedate and uncomplicated. He does not have much to say. He is noncontroversial, without much in the way of causes or concerns beyond whether to go cross-court or down the line on the backhand. If he has deep feelings or profound thoughts about anything, he does not choose to share them with the world at large.

His interviews are pleasant enough, but dull. He gives them because, as he learned early, they are part of his job. "When I was fifteen or sixteen, Lennart Bergelin was with me. He told me all kind of things what's going to happen in the future if I'm very successful," Borg remembers. "He said, 'There's going to be a lot of press, radio, TV, they're going to bother you a lot, but that's part of the life, part of the game, and if you want to be very good in something you have to accept it.' I understood, so it wasn't that big a surprise."

Most of his fellow pros like Borg, but do not know him well. "He's a very personable guy. He'll do anything for you. He's considerate. But he likes his privacy, he likes to do what he wants to do and to plan the day the way he wants it," says Vitas Gerulaitis, who practiced four to six hours a day with Borg the week before and during Wimbledon, then lost to him 8–6 in the fifth set in the finest match of the Centenary Championships, one of the great Centre Court classics.

"I really didn't spend that much time with him except to practice, and we did the same thing every day—just work, work, work, break for lunch, then go back and play," Gerulaitis went on. "He's a great worker, a very hard worker. Otherwise, I don't really know him. He's polite. He'll talk to anybody, but he doesn't socialize much. He's not what I'd call an outgoing guy."

"You don't see him very much," adds colleague Roscoe Tanner. "The times I've talked to him, I like him. I think he's a very good guy. You never used to see him at all; now that he's older, he's more relaxed on the circuit. He's found his place, and maybe that's one of the reasons he's playing so well. But he still keeps to himself."

In short, except on the tennis court, where everyone agrees he is an absolute marvel, Bjorn Borg is a thoroughly unremarkable young man. We tend to find this disappointing, which is unfair.

"It's the same as if you go to Van Gogh and say, 'Oh, but you know, Mr. Van Gogh, yours are the best paintings in the world, but why don't you play soccer?'" suggests Vilas, Borg's good friend and neighbor in the tax haven of Monte Carlo.

"It is enough that Bjorn is the best in what he is doing. I don't think he has a lot of time to do other things," insists Vilas. "To be number one, to win Wimbledon at his age, he has never had free time. When I was his age I had a lot of free time because I was losing quite early in tournaments. I started writing because I was feeling lonely and depressed. Maybe he didn't pass such a time, so that's why I write poems and he reads comics."

Attempts to spice up a rather bland dish undoubtedly account for the fact that so much of what has been written about Borg has been fabrication or embellishment. There has been little that is meaty or perceptive or revealing.

You pore over files of newspaper and magazine features, and it is astounding how often the same old stories, anecdotes, misinformation, and manufactured quotes, which usually sound nothing like Borg, are repeated, often becoming more distorted and less timely in the retelling. Borg has been the subject of more shallow movie-magazine-style trash reporting than practically any other tennis player. It seems that his biographer should not be Boswell, but Rona Barrett.

A *People* magazine cover story last March is a good case in point. It was embarrassingly full of inaccuracies, distortions, and rehashes of similarly shoddy work—a collection of lint, as it were, from unverified dirty linen. Borg portrayed as the erstwhile "golden boy and resident Lothario of men's tennis," who "quickly acquired a reputation for disappointing as few of his young admirers as possible. In a sport known for its gallants, Borg was the top seed in the Groupie Open."

That is nonsense. Borg was always a bit bewildered, turned off, even frightened by the hordes of pubescent teeny-boppers who engulfed him, making him a pop idol, turning Wimbledon and other staid tennis settings into reasonable facsimiles of backstage at a Donny Osmond concert.

People referred to Borg being "photographed indelicately pulling up his pants after a romantic interlude in London's Hyde Park." That stemmed, apparently, from a regrettable incident a couple of years ago when a photographer followed Borg and his then girl friend, the sensitive Swedish player, Helena Anliot, as they went for a stroll at Wimbledon Common (not Hyde Park). Unknown to Bjorn and Helena, he took photos with a long lens as they strolled hand in hand and lounged on the grass. One of the sensational London dailies took a photo of Borg tying a sweater around his waist and cropped and captioned it suggestively. In fact, he was not pulling up his pants, indelicately or otherwise. The photo and the episode, if not the newspaper layout, were totally innocent.

"It bothers me if they write I'm a playboy because I've never been a playboy and I never want to be a playboy," shrugs Borg. "I think maybe I'm the same guy I was when I was in school at fifteen. The only thing that has changed is that I'm playing better tennis, and that has led to a lot of things. But I always want to be the same guy."

People repeated, as has been written so often, that Borg's parents were grocers in the little town of Sodertalje. In fact, his father sold clothes and his mother was a housewife; Sodertalje is a not-so-little town of eighty thousand, ten miles from Stockholm. Bjorn bought a grocery store for his parents in 1973, but they now live in Monte Carlo and operate the Bjorn Borg Sports Shop, a sporting-goods boutique there.

"Sometimes these articles disappoint me, but what can you do?" asks Borg, who has been the target of more than his share of vitriolic, unflattering prose in the Swedish press. He is under more or less constant fire since forsaking Sweden for Monte Carlo, and because, on the advice of his agents, International Management Group, he has made a practice of going where the money is, not necessarily where a sense of responsibility to the game would dictate.

Some of the criticism has been valid, some unfounded and hysterical. When he won the Davis Cup for Sweden, Borg was hailed as a national treasure. But by depositing himself else-where, where he would not have to pay the severe Swedish taxes, he embittered some of his countrymen. His absence from important Swedish tournaments when there were golden exhibitions to be played elsewhere incensed others. But despite the sad estrangement—Borg has not been to Sweden since November 1976—he says, "I am still a Swede . . . I miss the Swedish people, for sure." Nor are the ties cut. Borg still has many friends and supporters, not to mention lucrative contracts with a number of Swedish firms, including Scandinavian Airlines and Saab automobiles. He can go home again.

Still, he has been stung sharply enough that he says flatly that his fear and loathing of the Swedish press is the reason he did not play Davis Cup or any tournaments in Sweden this year.

"For the last three or four years, they've been pretty bad to me. They write a lot of bad things about my private life, my parents, Lennart, Marianna. They put a lot of stuff in the papers that is not true. When the Swedish people read this, they believe these things and I get very disappointed," Borg says.

"One thing that was unbelievable was when I won Wimbledon last year, they wrote that we shouldn't be happy Bjorn won because he is not Swedish any more. He is from Monaco. Those kind of things, that's not too nice. That's why I decided not to play in Sweden this year, to have a rest for one year. Probably next year I will play. But if I go to Sweden, I want to feel comfortable, to look forward to going there."

Despite these problems, Borg says convincingly that he has never been happier. He is in love with Marianna. His goal of achieving the number-one world ranking, which narrowly eluded him last year, is within sight. He beat his archrival, Jimmy Connors, in a brutally tough Wimbledon final. His game and his life-style are in reassuringly top form. Bjorn, Marianna and Lennart travel the world as a trio.

"I think that's the most important thing, to be happy off the court," Borg says. "I remember before, when I was by myself, sometimes I'd lose matches and get very disappointed. Since I met Marianna I am always happy. We are always together. I think I'm very different now because

Once upon a time Bjorn Borg didn't care to hit volleys, but he learned—Oh, did he learn!
—well enough to win five consecutive Wimbledon titles. (Photo by Russ Adams)

I'm a much more happy person than I was before, and I think that has helped my game, too."

And what about Bergelin, the balding, raw-boned, shrewd but good-natured man who is known around the tennis circuit as "Kojak"?

"He is like a big brother for me," says Borg. "We've been doing so much together, I know him so well, he knows me so well, we are very close. He's such a big help to me because he's been playing tennis himself. He knows exactly what's going on. If I lose matches, he knows exactly how I feel. He give me good advice because all these things happen to me now that happened to him when he was playing. It's such a big help to have someone who understands you on the court as well as off the court.

"At tournaments he takes all the telephone calls and makes the arrangements for practice courts, rackets, transportation, all these things. That's something that is unbelievable tough, because there's so many people calling every day. He takes every call to his room, he is asking what they want and then telling me. If I have to do all these things myself, I would be so tired, I could not play well."

The year could scarcely have started better for him than at Boca Raton, Florida, where he beat Connors in the final of the four-man, $200,000, made-for-television Pepsi Grand Slam tournament. Connors had beaten him seven times in a row since Borg's victory in their first encounter at Stockholm in November 1973.

"I thought that I had a good chance to be number one last year, but I played Jimmy four times and he beat me four times. So he was ranked number one, even though I won WCT and Wimbledon. Boca Raton was very important because last year I lost to Jimmy in the finals at Forest Hills, very close match, and I thought I could have a good chance to win that one. So I was thinking to myself, okay, next time I look really forward to playing him because I know I can beat him, even if I don't play exactly my best, best game.

"I remember when he played Orantes in the first match at Boca Raton, I was hoping that he will beat Orantes because I wanted to play him in the finals very bad," Borg says. "So we played,

and I won the match. It is very important to beat a guy who has been beating you all the time. It was a very important win for me."

So was the encore at this year's Wimbledon.

You do not even have to watch him play to realize that Bjorn Borg's tennis is different from that of most players; you can *hear* it. He has a special set of sound effects. Because his rackets are strung so tightly, and he hits with so much topspin, the "ping" of ball against gut has a kind of shrill, space-age pitch and resonance. Borg also mis-hits more shots than any other world-class player, so if his timing is a fraction off, you hear the sound of the ball hitting off-center and ricocheting off the frame.

Borg likes his rackets strung at eighty pounds tension, which some stringers say is physically impossible. Jack Kramer has commented that if the average player used Borg's racket for any length of time, his arm would fall off. Although other players may use the same racket for weeks or longer, Borg goes through ten or fifteen a week. He regularly travels with thirty or forty rackets.

Bergelin, who is in charge of the care and transportation of this arsenal of equipment, says that sometimes a string will break in the middle of the night "with a big noise, like a gun going off. Then I have to take off all the covers to find the one and cut the strings, or the frame goes out of shape." Bergelin is the bane of racket stringers around the globe. He is not easily satisfied. "We need so many rackets, because most places we can not get them restrung properly," he says.

Some people consider Borg's game futuristic tennis. "He hits every shot hard, about six feet over the net, and it lands six feet inside the base line because he puts so much topspin on the ball," says Barry Phillips-Moore, the veteran Australian left-hander who is a keen student of the game. "Although he doesn't really think about it, Borg's game is a case of advanced technique."

Slender and broad-shouldered, with the muscular, tapered build of a fullback, Borg is exceedingly strong for a five-foot-eleven, 165-pounder. He can simply outlast and overpower other persistent backcourt players such as Eddie

Dibbs and Harold Solomon. The only current players who have shown evidence of being able to stay with him in torrid base-line rallies are Connors and Vilas, and Borg has a much better serve than both of them.

Borg is so swift afoot, and has such good anticipation, that it is difficult to knock outright winners off rallies against him, even though he hits quite a few short balls. His overhead is devastating. He has beefed up his serve considerably the last two years and now wins a number of points with it, especially on fast surfaces.

The weakest part of his game is the volley, especially on the backhand. His two-fisted style limits his reach, and his grip makes it difficult for him to get much penetration, especially on low volleys. His passing shots are superb, but opponents have to gamble because the best way to beat him is to take command of the net.

He feasts on pace, so the players who fare well against him usually do so with finesse, cleverly mixing speed and spin, giving him enough dinks and soft balls to keep him from finding a groove, establishing a rhythm on his thumping ground strokes.

Having grown up on clay, Borg has always been formidable on slow surfaces. What amazed most people, including himself, were his back-to-back triumphs on the fast, skiddy grass of Wimbledon.

"I thought Borg might be vulnerable on fast surfaces like grass until I watched him during Wimbledon in 1976," comments Kramer in his recent book, *How to Play Your Best Tennis All the Time*. "He made two adjustments in particular that impressed me with his adaptability and his dangerousness on all surfaces. He flattened out his stroking motion somewhat, reducing that extreme vertical lift of his, and so got better depth off the ground. And he improved his serve when he had to."

"When a guy stays back as much as he does, he should be more vulnerable on grass," says Roscoe Tanner. "Looking at him, you wouldn't say his game is suited to grass. But he plays well on all surfaces, and that's what you've got to do to be number one.

"Technically, he's one of the toughest guys to play against. A lot of times he hits a return off-center, and the ball just pops high, with nothing on it, but carries deep so you have to turn around and come back to the base line. It works out perfect, and that's kind of irritating, because you figure there's no way he could plan that shot. I'm sure he doesn't practice mis-hits. But that's the way he plays and it works.

"Otherwise, he hits with so much topspin that the ball comes over and dips, which makes it difficult to handle. His shots are tough to volley. You can't establish a good, clean rhythm against him the way you sometimes can against Connors," Tanner continues. "His passing shots are good because he takes a little of the topspin off. You can get more penetration, more forward movement and speed through the air when the ball has less topspin. On a passing shot, you want the ball to dip, but you also want to get it past the guy. Borg does that.

"He just picks a shot and hits it. It may be completely the wrong shot to hit, but he makes it work. He doesn't think, 'Should I go crosscourt or down the line?' He just picks a shot and goes for it. Boom. That's confidence. He hits it so well that it comes off."

Gerulaitis agrees: "I think he's pretty instinctive," he says. "He's quite machinelike in the way he plays. I don't think it really requires too much thinking. Not that he couldn't think, or doesn't sometimes have to, but he always plays his game. His style is dominating, like Connors's, so most of the time he is dictating the pattern."

If you listen to Borg's postmatch interviews, or read verbatim transcripts, they become repetitious and monotonous, full of the same superficial analyses, tired cliches about playing the big points better, and comments that miss the mark as consistently as his shots are on target. He can make the most dramatic matches sound humdrum, the most bizarre episodes commonplace. He does not articulate his feelings, emotions or the subtleties of the game well. A language barrier, perhaps? No, we are assured by Swedish colleagues, his comments do not lose anything in the translation. The lack of incisive insights is bilingual.

But one should not conclude that he does

not have a nimble brain. "He may not communicate things so well, but he is thinking all the time," says Vilas. "Tennis was not invented the last day; tennis has been played for a long time. You can do some things without being 100 percent concentrative, but you cannot do great.

"Maybe he has such a good game that he doesn't have to think about the other guy, he thinks only about himself. That is a good approach also. But let's put it this way: You cannot be stupid if you are the best in the world in something. You have to be very intelligent, very bright, to have that kind of concentration, that kind of feeling, to be in that good shape physically.

"Bjorn has a very strong mind. On the court, he's playing with one mind. Off the court, he is very good about getting away from his fame, relaxing, preparing properly. He's a very good worker. I think he won Wimbledon because he was the strongest mentally."

Borg has an uncommon grasp of the complexities of tennis, a mind that absorbs and stores information readily. He has superb instincts for the game and what Kramer aptly calls "a wonderful feel for the dynamics of match play." Some would call this innate genius.

Stolid, unflappable, with an extraordinary pulse rate of thirty-five, Borg has always had terrific powers of concentration and fighting spirit on the court. He won the Junior Wimbledon title over Buster Mottram from 2–5 down in the final set. In his first Davis Cup match, against the experienced New Zealander Onny Parun at age fifteen, he won from two sets down, displaying the quality that Swedes call *is i magen*—"ice in the stomach." After Borg beat Manuel Orantes from two sets down to win his first French Open title in 1974, Bergelin summed it up nicely: "Bjorn

has the right kind of courage. This is a gift. It cannot be learned."

That is not to say that Borg cannot be distracted. He has been known to quit in matches, too, especially after blowing a commanding position, though he has pretty much erased that tendency. Though usually icy and imperturbable on the court, he occasionally becomes obstinate or pouty on court.

This is particularly true when some extraneous problem is dwelling on his mind. Last winter, for example, shortly after World Championship Tennis Inc. decided to file a $5-million suit against its defending champion for alleged breach of an agreement to play its circuit this year, Borg was involved in a couple of testy episodes on court. At the National Indoors in Memphis, which he won, he threatened to walk off court in one match unless a linesman was removed, claiming the man had not only made bad calls, but laughed when he protested. He prevailed, and when the public-address announcer made mention of the fact in introducing Borg the next night, saying he had whipped not only Jeff Borowiak but also the offending linesman to reach this round, Borg again threw a tantrum, insisting that the man with the microphone be fired.

At a World Team Tennis match this summer, Borg went up to a heckler and silenced him by quietly but forcefully asserting in a face-to-face confrontation that the man's mouth resembled a part of the female anatomy, and that he should go home and do something pleasurable with it. From all accounts, this brief lecture was delivered with great skill and effectiveness.

Which just goes to prove that maybe Borg is more well-rounded and verbally accomplished than we give him credit for.

True Chris

by GERRI HIRSHEY

Gerri Hirshey, a staff editor at Family Circle, *came to sportswriting through her husband, David, a sports reporter for the* New York Daily News. *She brought a fresh approach to this 1978 profile of Chris Evert.*

T HE afternoon sun had fried the Har Tru to cracklin's, and even the persistent honeybees had curled up inside the bougainvillea for a midday siesta. The morning doubles set had retreated to the air conditioned din of the Sea Pines pro shop, jockeying for court time and a five P.M. game. It was an afternoon for only mad dogs and tennis players.

"Get the lead out, cutie," Rosie Casals bellowed across court six and Chris Evert, having a little hit before her semifinal match in the Family Circle Cup, scurried to oblige. Chris and Rosie were practicing together, as they do wherever the tour goes, and the reigning monopoly was brooking a lot of tough talk.

"Are you *kidding* with that overhead, Evert? You wanna seeing eye dog?" Chris swatted a half-volley into the net and draped herself over the tape.

"I surrender," Evert croaked, and groped for a Diet Rite. By normal standards, she was a mess, unpressed and untucked in warm-up shorts and a bright red T-shirt that bore the lightning bolt logo of the movie "Network," and a white block-lettered message: "I'm mad as hell. And I'm not going to take it any more." It clung to her back in the wet Carolina heat. Chris Evert was sweating and she said it felt good.

She headed for the showers, and forty-five minutes later, she emerged from her stuccoed waterfront villa as the other Chris Evert, in a crisp white halter dress, with just the faintest hint of gold lamé and with a gold-and-diamond bracelet to complement the glow. To her match, she carried three Chris Evert autograph rackets, a stick of insect repellent and a pair of oversize, mauve-tinted sunglasses.

"To make it as a celebrity in America," said designer Ted Tinling, "you've got to have an image. If you don't have one, they'll make you one, and stitch you a soul in the bargain. If it fits, that's nice. If it doesn't, we'll buy it anyway."

Christine Marie Evert was sanforized at sweet sixteen, swathed in pastels and suspended in the public mind's eye like the slumbering Snow White. She looked better under glass where we could get a fix on her and italicize her soul. *Miss American Pie. Miss Cool. The Ice Dolly.* Chris Evert is a figment of our none-too-active imaginations and only she can tell you what it's like.

"I hate the word 'image,' " she said, making an uncharacteristically horrid face. "You can't believe how much." Chris finds the idea of an image almost as distasteful as losing. But, being a pragmatist, she understands how the two are all bound up. If you're a winner, you've got to pose with the trophy. If you're the best woman tennis player in the world, you've got to sit through a lot of interviews. And if it makes them happy, then let them compare you to the girl next door, even though you haven't lived there in years. For Chris Evert, accommodation is not one of the seven deadly sins as it is for Billie Jean King and Chris's good friend Rosie Casals.

"They (the press) can say whatever they want," said Chris, smiling. "As long as I know who I am."

There was a time when Chris Evert would have read about who she was and believed it. Or at least worried about it. But that was before she knew better. Before she started to win every tournament she entered. Before Jimmy. Now she says she knows better and can put it all in perspective. She's got a better grip on life and on her serve. And she can look a television reporter right in the lens and say, "Yeah, sure. It's always been my dream to play doubles with Billy Carter," when tennis hype landed her in the Plains Peanut Classic.

On the media starship that once threatened to run away with her, Chris Evert is now charting her own course. Like many of the famous, she has learned to compartmentalize her life, into what's Hers, and into what's Theirs.

"Otherwise," she said, "there would be nothing left for me."

Chris Evert remembers herself as an obedient, tractable child, raised in a Fort Lauderdale tract ranch with the standard equipment—firm, but loving parents, a two-wheeler, two siblings of each sex, party dresses with crinoline slips, a best friend named Laurie, a good Catholic education and scratchy wool uniforms that made it a blessed relief to burst out of school at three and head for nearby Holiday Park. In class, she was just one of the girls. Never stood out, never did anything rash like raise her hand first.

It was on the tennis court that Chrissie began to pull away from the pack, and further into herself. "It happened when I started to win," said Chris. "That's when things started to change inside. When I was six or ten, I could lose matches at love and love and I didn't care at all. I don't know if I was just too young to be fierce about it, but I didn't feel a thing, then."

That changed at age twelve, when Chris began to feel that ineffable thing that moves her now—pressure. "Once I started winning," she said, "it was simply taken for granted that I should win most of my matches. I felt compelled to do it. It was expected."

Expected by whom, she's not exactly sure. Certainly Jimmy Evert never told his daughter, as he tossed her one hundred forehands a day, that he expected her to become the darling of tennis and the savior of Forest Hills at sixteen. And later, though it was expected for an engaged girl to think about her silver pattern, nobody suggested she fill her hope chest with the jumbo silver fruit bowls and trays from Wimbledon and Forest Hills wins. The only person who expected all this was Chris Evert. By the time she was twenty-one, most of the world was fervently hoping Chris Evert would *lose* a match, or at least a set. They had also learned not to expect it.

"I don't like to disappoint people," Chris said. "So I always try and give them a good match. That means playing the best I can. If it means I keep winning, I can't help that. What they don't understand is that I enjoy a good, tough match more than anybody in the stands. I want what's best for women's tennis."

Women's tennis. It's an organism now, a living, breathing corporate entity with ups, downs and tax problems, like everyone else. Women's tennis. Billie Jean King wields the phrase like an avenging sword. Chris Evert talks about women's tennis in almost reverential tones, as though it were some mystical covenant that bound her, body and soul. It has helped her define her values, strengthen her resolve and zero in on her goals: Women's tennis has given

Deep in the backcourt, Chris Evert moves to hit a backhand, changing her grip as she watches her opponent's shot. (Photo by Russ Adams)

Chris Evert a place in the world and right now she is very happy to be there.

It wasn't always that way.

Like many adolescents, Chris had her small problems. Once she was plunged into the tour, with its tendency to magnify highs and lows, she began having trouble balancing those peak experiences with everyday relationships. She traveled with her mother and spent most of her days in hotel rooms, holed up with a chicken salad platter and "The Edge of Night." A grim mask of concentration was acceptable on the court; indeed, it was an effective weapon. Elsewhere it was interpreted as unfriendly and aloof.

"I was just scared to death," Chris says now. "And terribly shy. I used to dread the tour when I first started. The girls were not very friendly toward me. I can remember a time when I'd have nobody, no friends to stay and watch my matches. It really hurt me and I felt nobody cared."

Trouble was, the women cared too much. Though women's tennis and the women's movement may have come of age shoulder to shoulder, the early years were hardly harmonious. The psychological warfare often carried into the locker room and beyond. In 1971, when all women athletes were considered "jocks," and two-thirds of the women were still mortgaging their spare rackets for a plane ticket, nobody needed an ingénue to skip off with the money and smile cutely. The fans were delighted with Chris, and they came out to see her. Women's tennis needed a Chris Evert, but the women did not. Chris says she knows that now and she doesn't blame them a bit.

"The women had fought a tough battle, and they were just protecting themselves," she said. "It was a natural reflex back then. They had been working hard, fighting for every inch and then I came along and I was getting everything easy."

The winning has always been easy for Chris. Coping with it has not. For Chris Evert and Evonne Goolagong, the pair of teenage whiz kids that brought women's tennis a youthful, exciting dynamism, there were growing pains and dangerous slumps those early years. Their lifetime record stands at 18–11, their lives and games at opposite poles. Examining their careers, it's pos-

sible to distill the pure essences that have kept Chris on top of the game and Evonne on top of the world. Watch them play, listen to them talk, and you'll find it—joy vs. satisfaction; abandon versus concentration; Chrissie and Evonne. It was a delicious contrast. Without it, women's tennis could have had all the glamor of Bowling for Dollars.

Remember how it was? Remember how they electrified Wimbledon in that incredible semifinal match when Chris was seventeen, and Evonne twenty? On the crisp English grass they were as similar as passion flowers and daisies, the uncola and Coke, and in the upstairs tea room, it was the same. Goolagong's carefree, outgoing nature made her instantly popular among the women; Chris was tentative and alone. The only thing that bound them was their youth and their stormy confrontations with the fragile emotions of adolescence.

For both, the rites of passage into adulthood and the top seedings were painful and public. Evonne, chafing under the fatherly harness of coach/guardian Vic Edwards, saw her game stall out and her concentration evaporate. Chris, feeling stifled under the motherly wing of Colette Evert, began to lose for the first time since she was twelve.

"The one real slump I've had in my professional life came during the summer I was eighteen," she said. "I lost the French and Italian, and at Cincinnati, all on clay, and then Wimbledon. It really was an emotional slump.

"I was very unhappy, I wanted to be on my own. I would go everywhere with my mother, and at first it was security. But by the time I was eighteen, I realized she was doing too much for me, and I wasn't really growing. It got so bad—the losing—that I wasn't sure I wanted to keep playing," Chris said.

Then, at nineteen, in a move she knows hurt her mother at the time, Chris asked Colette Evert to leave the tour. Jimmy Evert had already begun to avoid tournaments. His job as teaching pro, high blood pressure and the resolve to keep Chris's business affairs in family hands kept him home. Colette, too, returned to the nest and set her hand to another motherly task. Her eldest daughter was to be married to James Scott Connors on the second Saturday in November 1974, and there was plenty to do.

As any cognizant American with at least a passing acquaintance to a television can tell you, it never came off, and Chris was to suffer the most painful slings and arrows yet—a fishbowl romance, a breakup and the excruciating humiliation of being told, on prime time TV, that her ex-intended was making time with Dodge car hustler Mean Mary Jean. Chris cried later, off camera. But this time, it didn't affect her game.

"I'd love to say—I mean it would be easier to explain—that when things are going badly off the court, my tennis is bad," she said. "But I started playing my best tennis ever after I broke up with Jimmy. I think that my strength is that once I'm on the court, I can pretty much block half my life out of my mind."

Lately, however, Chris has no reason to block out the off-court half. She's having the time of her life. There have been dinners with Jack Ford and Burt Reynolds. There's theater, ballet and when there's time, a little horseback riding in La Jolla. Chris has starred in player burlesques, with the aid of a Groucho Marx false nose and a lot of bad jokes. Instead of room service, the girls go out. Chris is always the first to leave those gatherings, but it's not because she's having a bad time.

"I'm a sleep fanatic," she said. "If I lived on four hours like Rosie, they'd have buried me long ago." Rosie will eat the hot fudge sundae, have the extra glass of wine. Chris will demur, with the next day in mind. "Rosie and I are as different as night and day," Chris said. "The way we play, the way we live our lives is miles apart. There was a time when we might not be such friends. But the women are all closer now, and we accept each other for what we are."

Of the few good friends Chris says she "would do anything for," the closest is Kristien Shaw, who talked Chris into cutting off her ponytail and growing her nails. "Kristien made a real effort to be Chris's friend," said Jeanie Brinkman, Virginia Slims' publicity director. "She really had to pursue Chris, since she was so gunshy at first. It's done a lot for Chris, in the way she feels and the way she looks. She used to see photos of herself and say, 'Ugh, I look awful.' Kristien is very into fashion and makeup, and she helped her with those things."

In rare weekends off the tour, Chris visits Kristien Shaw and her lawyer husband in their Manhattan apartment and they do the town—Gucci, Cartier, Elizabeth Arden, Bloomie's. And, if time permits, they'll squeeze in a short practice at the Lincoln Tower courts, high on the roof above the West Side apartment of another acquaintance, Billie Jean King.

With the Old Lady off the circuit, Chris has grown closer to Billie Jean's puckish sidekick, Rosie Casals. The Evert/Casals roadshow goes everywhere, performing impromptu vaudeville routines in airports and in locker rooms. It was Rosie who bought a dozen kazoos for the newly formed Kazoological Society Band, a group of young women seen startling the patrons of better restaurants on this continent with stirring renditions of "Oklahoma" and other kitsch classics. Chris admits she can't carry a tune, but it does feel good to be a member of the band.

"It took me three years to belong," she said, laughing. "Now my closest friends are on the tour. It's amazing. Unless you live it, you can't comprehend the comradeship, the loyal feelings women have towards each other. It makes living on the tour a pleasure."

Pressure, not pleasure, though, is what the tour's about. And depending on the amount of pressure, her friends can see two different Chris Everts, indistinguishable on the court, but prone to flights into the old Chris Evert before big matches. It depends on where she is, who she's playing and how close she feels to losing.

"There's a story about Chris," said rookie player Mary Carillo. "She had discovered she was about to meet an old friend in a match, someone from Florida she hadn't seen for years. She sent Kristien over to tell her, 'Chris told me to tell you she'd talk to you after the match.' Once Chris had beaten her, they got together and had a great time."

Old friends, new friends, it doesn't matter. Friendship does not stand in the way of a two-fisted backhand, though it can complicate things.

When Chris plays Kristien Shaw, she annihilates her, love and love. The same goes for Chris's sister Jeannie.

"It's almost as though she works extra hard to prove something," said Mary Carillo, "to prove she can keep those parts of her life separate, and not let it affect her game."

"Chris'll never drop a point out of sympathy," said Rosie Casals after being crushed, 6–1, 6–0 in the Virginia Slims in New York. "I wouldn't want her to. But losing like this is humiliating as hell." Chris, sitting next to Rosie at the interview, fiddled with her jewelry, looking uncomfortable.

"Rosie's helped my game tremendously in practice," Chris offered. "She runs me around, makes me work on my serve."

"Aw, Chris, cut it out," Rosie muttered. Her smile was feeble.

That week in the New York media crucible had been enough to test the closest of friends. Pressure took its jangling toll, and for a few days, Chris and Kristien Shaw were not even speaking. "Chris is a dear, dear friend of mine," said Jeanie Brinkman on the second day. "But I told her last night, 'Chris, I'll talk to you next week.'"

By the final, the locker room beneath Madison Square Garden was oddly silent—no radios, no backgammon games, no jokes, no kazoos. Even the players' dogs were intimidated, preferring to curl up beneath a table and forgo the usual hijinks. "All the girls were really wired," Brinkman said. "I mean, this was Madison Square Garden. They'd worked for this for years. It was the Big Time."

So big, that anything seemed possible. Navratilova had won four tournaments, and the largest share of prize money; Sue Barker had come off a month's intense training strong and very eager. And there were the little personal pressures. Chris's occasional dinner partner Burt Reynolds was in the stands. No one needed to ask him whom he'd come to watch. Chris was tense, almost irritable as she fielded a barrage of inane questions that ignored her tennis and probed the supposed new love match.

"Of course it's justified," snapped one reporter who had engaged Chris in some verbal

volleying. "It's the only thing about Chris Evert that's interesting any more."

Five days later came the Family Circle Cup, a week-long idyll in the Hilton Head sun, that offered the dusty, down-home security of clay. Chris had settled in on the pro shop veranda to watch Rosie Casals's match. She was relaxed, but firm, as she explained her concept of privacy.

"I understand that in my position I have to expect those questions," she said. "But I tell people every time, and I mean it—it's the only private thing I have. My family, and my relationships with special people. That's mine, and I intend to keep it that way."

"Theirs" is her public life, her game and the biggest chunk of her time. "Theirs" are the fulfilled obligations, the term as president of the WTA, the cocktail parties. The interviews. "I feel I have to spread myself pretty thin," said Chris. "But I can't be selfish and play these tournaments, then take the money and run. I have more responsibility and I can't take it too lightly."

Some of those responsibilities she would rather avoid altogether and it was over the questions of "sacred duty" that a rift developed between Chris and her one-time mentor, Billie Jean King. A magazine article quoted Billie Jean as saying Chris didn't give a hoot about women's tennis. Billie Jean insisted she was misquoted. Chris countered by saying that King's entry into an obscure Texas tournament with Renée Richards was "very disappointing."

"Chris was really very hurt," Brinkman said. "Regardless of how Billie Jean meant it, Chris took it personally since they had been such good friends." When the two women faced each other in the Family Circle final, Chris pounded Billie Jean, 6–0, 6–1, just as she would any old friend.

"The fundamental difference between Chris at the top, and Billie Jean at the top, is that Chris just doesn't want to be a spokeswoman," Brinkman said. "Chris does her speaking quietly, through image. Billie Jean had to talk about the future of women's tennis, but Chris is content to *be* women's tennis and let her behavior speak for her."

"The way I feel," said Chris, "is that since I'm no longer president of the WTA, my opinion should have as much weight as any other, no more. I don't feel anything I say is gospel. I'm just one of the girls."

The girls, of course, include the best of the best. There is a core group—Chris, Rosie, Virginia Wade, Betty Stove, Frankie Durr—that sets the tone on the tour. They pick the restaurants, they arrange the nights out. And though their limited budgets might exclude them from the little dinners at 21 or the Rainbow Grill, the younger players have found Chris and most of her friends accessible and friendly.

"Some people say Chris has this personal space around her that no one dares violate," Carillo said. "I think that's contrived. There's no unwritten law that says a rookie doesn't talk to Chris. If there is one, she doesn't know about it."

A talented nineteen-year-old whose enthusiasm moved Billie Jean King to nickname her "Bright Eyes," Mary is part of the younger wave that hopes to move up and someday, challenge Chris. Mary has held Chris in awe since junior high, and she remembers, very well, the day she joined the tour and met her idol. "She was just sitting there chewing on a piece of cheese," said Mary. "She said, 'Hiya, Mary,' and I thought, wow, she's a regular person."

Yes, Chris Evert eats cheese and drinks diet cola. She has to have nine hours sleep, absolutely, and no, she doesn't do anything special to psyche up for a match. Maybe she'll have Rosie warm her up, but she is not above practicing with the likes of Mary Carillo, or at least offering an encouraging word.

"I only wish," Chris said, "That someone had done that for me. I'm glad to give them my time. After all, I may learn something. My game isn't perfect."

She doesn't think it ever will be. And, as she's said on many occasions, "If I were perfect, it would be boring."

"Cheez," Carillo said. "It drives me crazy when people say they get bored watching Chris. I find it dazzling. It's beautiful. What in the world is boring about perfection?"

Even Secretariat would have become a bore beyond the Triple Crown, if he had thundered through race after race and made the others eat

mud. Only a few diehard purists would still vaunt the poetry of thoroughbred sinew and the strength of his stride. But the smart money would come to rest on the noses of place and show. In the eyes of a bettor, there's no thrill in a favorite, and little joy in his art.

Chris Evert, looking for the Triple Crown this year, is prone to the same damning disinterest. Her skill is largely neglected; the beautiful efficiency of her wins has just become the mirror of the women's failure to produce an heir. They're piling the chips behind Sue Barker one week; Navratilova the next. There's no "start money" in women's tennis except on Chris and nobody cares about even money.

If you can't count the thrills, you can count the accomplishments. And you'd need a Bowmar Brain to compute the purses. As tennis's first millionairess, she has won more than $252,000 this year as of May 24, and at the end of 1976, she had compiled a 445–40 lifetime match record. That includes two Wimbledons, two U.S. Opens, four Virginia Slims, a pair each of French and Italian Opens, and 106–plus successive wins on clay. She has been the best in the world since 1974, no contest.

"You just have to play Chris once," Billie Jean King said, "to know exactly where you stand in women's tennis."

If this is so, why, then, do fans and experts alike consistently downgrade Chris's game? Why is it that every magazine survey and every self-proclaimed scholar will award best backhand to Evonne Goolagong, and best serve to Wade? Even Chris Evert refuses to credit herself with a complete, rounded game. Just what is it that gives her that mile-wide edge?

"I want it," she says simply. "Every time I step out on that court, I want to win. I like it. I need it. The winning keeps me going, and the successive wins give me momentum."

At the suggestion that the big bucks might add some incentive, she shrugged. "I know my image is probably money-oriented. It's the most obvious thing, and it's always emphasized. Money is a visible thing, with all the cars and the prizes. Of course I enjoy it. I like being able to buy nice things and to dress the way I want. But it's titles I'm after. The wins. I just love it."

For this reason, she is never satisfied, never content to rest. There are still the personal challenges, still flaws to be exorcised. Though she's learned to have fun, Chris still works at her game.

"I don't think I can improve my ground strokes much more," she said. "But I think I can gain a little more self-confidence at the net. Rosie's helped me with that, and with my serve. I think it's starting to be a weapon, instead of just something to start off a point with. I think I've played matches where I don't believe I can get much better, but those matches don't occur every day."

Since most of those matches involved Goolagong, it may be some time, then, before Chris Evert peaks again. Unless, of course, another wunderkind arises overnight. Chris assesses any opponent's chances by the degree of confidence she brings to a match.

"Martina has beaten me, so I feel she can do it again," she said. Evonne has always made me nervous. Sue Barker got a set in the Slims, and she was very tough. I'm not nearly as confident as I used to be about Sue."

And what of Billie Jean, with her reconstructed knee, and her new lease on life? Chris smiled. "She's in great physical shape, but she's not match tough. She needs a few more tournaments before she's a threat mentally."

Mental threats. That's what opponents have become to Chris Evert. Bring on the best backhand in the world. Pit her against the toughest serve. Chris will out-guts them, out-grit and out-grunt them. Even pit vipers can be hypnotized into submission, if the power of concentration is strong enough.

But enough of this. Enough about the fabled psyche that can bend spoons at twenty paces. To attribute Evert's greatness to her powers of concentration is simplistic and lazy.

"People forget that I've worked hard," said Chris. "They can't see it, but I have callouses on my heels." She also has a set of ground strokes as streamlined and well tempered as a set of surgical curettes. She can anesthetize an opponent with a long, temperate rally, then stun her with one deft cross-court cut.

Watching her play those long points, you cn see the exacting connection as she meets a ball and directs it with one clean, economic motion. As easily as she can point with her finger, she can send a ball over the net in a perfect series of concentric arcs. The arcs grow wider, and wider still as she moves her victim to the base line. Or they'll grow shorter, before she chips one, glancing off the line. Sometimes an opponent will simply make a mistake. But more often, the opponent is caught in the wrong place, mesmerized by Chris's smooth, hard geometry, then done in by one clean stroke.

"You can think you're doing great when you hold up your end of a long rally with Chris," said Mary Carillo. "Then suddenly, you blow it, and for the next fifteen minutes, you're still wondering why."

The skill, then, and the determination form an invincible alloy. But there is a chink in Chris's dazzling armor, one little-known way to beat her and it has nothing to do with her backhand, or her second serve. It has to do with her jewelry.

"You're not going to believe this," she said. "But I'm very conscious of my jewelry for good luck. I always wear the same pieces to a match." Those pieces always include two delicate gold chains, the gold and diamond bracelet and the gold necklace that says "Athlete," a gift from Rosie Casals when Chris was chosen *Sports Illustrated* Athlete of the Year.

"I always wore the Athlete necklace, but one day I took it off, just for a diversion, and wore something else. I lost that match, and I *knew*. I knew right away that was why. I thought about it the whole match. Why, Chris? Why did you take it off? While I was thinking about it, the points, and the match slipped away," she said.

Anyone harboring thoughts of hiring a cat burglar to snatch the glittering object can forget that tack. Chris handles her superstitions with the same steely logic she applies to tennis. She just never takes the necklace off.

This being the case, you'll probably see a flash of gold at her throat during the rest of her season for the WTT Phoenix Triangles, and at

Forest Hills. Probably, you'll see her carry off a few more armfuls of precious metals hammered into little tennis figurines, and sterling tennis balls, if things go as scheduled. "I have my itinerary made up through October," Chris said. "Beyond that, I'll just have to see."

It's not that she is harboring any notion of laying down her weapons and retreating into domestic life, or corporate finance. It's just that the new Chris Evert believes in keeping her options open.

"I'm living a lot looser now," she said. "I mean, in terms of tennis. There are so many things I'd like to do, and can't find time for. They'll just have to wait, though." On her itinerary for "someday" are skiing, softball, basketball, learning to cook and quitting tennis. Someday. For now she sticks to rooting for the favorites in spectator sports ("I can't cheer for underdogs"), making salads ("You can't burn them"), and trying not to think about thinking of quitting.

"What would it take to make me quit? Ooooh. Gosh." She pushed her sunglasses up onto her hair, and stared up at the sky. "I just don't know. When people ask me what I'll do after tennis, it's easy to say I'll play it by ear. But *when* to stop . . . that's a question I haven't had to ask myself. I think all athletes put it off until it becomes pressing. I can see myself quitting if I'm just tired of the life, but I love it right now."

Would she love it if she stops winning? "Ugh. Don't ask me about that now. It's not in my nature to keep losing, and coping with it. I couldn't live with losing. I think if I ever had a slump again, I couldn't just keep playing to get it out of my system. I've come too far for that. I'd probably quit, rather than be number two."

Like she said, Chris really doesn't have to think about that now, or for the rest of the 1970's. Coping with being number two will probably end up as Chris Evert's mid-life crisis. "I think I have a few great years yet," she said. "I've got a lot of time to come to grips with that decision, and when I do, it will be my decision alone. I don't have to try and meet other people's expectations any more, or worry about their criticisms. I feel good about myself, my friends and my game, and that's what counts."

Yes, at last she's made it clear. She no longer worries about an image dogging her rubber-soled heels. Chris Evert is confident as hell. And she doesn't have to take it any more.

The Last Tennis Rogue

by MIKE LUPICA

Bill Riordan was more than just Jimmy Connors's manager, he was a world-class character himself, someone out of a Dickens novel as rewritten by Damon Runyon. Mike Lupica, a sports columnist for the New York Daily News, *understands Riordan better than most—which is to say, he enjoys him, as shown by this profile.*

HE sat in the semidarkness of the New York saloon, and after all the years of running hard, Bill Riordan looked to be at peace. He was chasing no one, no one was chasing him. Candlelight hit the craggy, character actor's face like a smile, and was kind to the face. From the front room came the sweet tinkling of a piano, and a singer gently took apart "Angel Eyes" and tried to sound like Sinatra. The peaceful setting in the night was perfect for the stories he told. The stories were about tennis.

Riordan grinned across all the years of action and told about tennis, which he loved and lost. You kept expecting Jimmy Connors to walk into the saloon, so that Riordan, like Bogart in the movie "Casablanca," could look up and say, "Of all the gin joints in all the world, why'd he have to walk into this one?" It was that kind of night.

Riordan managed Connors once and made

Connors millions. Riordan had all the funny lines and told outrageous lies, and when he ran out of lines and lies he sued someone. He brought this thing called the winner-take-all match to tennis; well, it wasn't *exactly* winner-take-all, which he neglected to tell a television network. The winner-take-all matches left tennis, but took with them the highest ratings in the history of the sport. Riordan left tennis shortly thereafter; the sport still has no idea how much it misses him.

He was the last tennis rogue—an original. The big guys today wear suits and make dirty deals and take no pleasure in what is still a wonderful game. You never see them at a tennis match. Riordan was a con man, a glorious con man. You couldn't take all of *his* deals home to mother. But he always watched the matches, and he knew how to laugh. Riordan was the last big guy who knew how to laugh.

Tennis does not laugh any more. The sport has no sense of humor. The players especially act like the first trace of a smile might cost them money. Bill Riordan was up and he was down, and he was always playing for big stakes at the end. He never took it all too seriously.

And, in his glib Irish way, he loved tennis more than anyone. He loved it, and he sold it better than anyone who ever lived. Those who hated him—hate him still—never really saw how much Riordan loved the damn game. He loved it when he was the president of the Maryland Tennis Association in the early 1960's; loved it when he ran the first indoor circuit in this country out of his pocket; when he'd never heard of Jimmy Connors. Bill Riordan always liked hanging around. Crazy notion.

"I was around," he says, "before all the boys got uptight."

Bill Riordan is rich. He has inherited well, he has invested better, he has saved best of all. He sells skate-boarding shows to television as a hobby, and the shows win Emmy Awards. But Riordan misses tennis. He will never be totally comfortable away from tennis. And he is still at his best when he reminisces about the wild run he had over the last twenty years, like one of his skate-boarding kids careening down a steep hill.

There were the Salisbury, Maryland, years, then the Connors years. Riordan has not forgotten much of it. In a time when tennis grows more stern by the day, Bill Riordan's stories are a treasure. Most of them are probably true.

"By 1962," he says, "I was calling my tournament the Salisbury *International.* Had a nice sound to it. *International.* Of course, the closest thing I had to an international player was this guy named John Sharpe, a transplanted Aussie. Lived in Canada, I think.

"That year, we housed the players at this place called Cherry Hill, an executive house for a company called Wayne Pump. Donald Dell was in the tournament that year, and he was one of the guys staying at Cherry Hill."

For those who don't know, Donald Dell is a Washington lawyer who basically runs tennis on this planet. When Riordan was still in the sport, he and Dell were mortal enemies. They hated each other. This is all understatement. Riordan grins a mean, nasty grin and continues his story.

"When I dropped Donald off, I told Donald there was only one condition on him staying there: He had to stay away from the east wing. I told him that the finalists for the Miss Maryland contest would be staying on the third floor, and I'd given the Miss Maryland committee my word of honor that none of the players would bother the girls. Donald swears to me he won't go anywhere near the third floor.

"Of course, there's no girls, and the third floor is an attic, and Donald was the only player I told. About one o'clock in the morning, the rest of the players hear this terrible ruckus from upstairs. Here's Donald on his hands and knees with a flashlight, looking for Miss Maryland. The other players break up. Donald yells, 'That sonuvabitch Riordan!' "

Riordan pauses.

"See, even then I couldn't trust the ___ ___ ___ ___," he says. Nor could Donald Dell trust him.

He laughs.

He started out with something called the Middle Atlantic Indoor Tennis Tournament in 1960 and 1961. In 1962, he called it the Salisbury *International* and could afford to bring in better players. He decided it might be feasible to branch out. He got together with some friends named Leif Beck and Carl Bruhns. They decided that if they could split the cost of bringing in big-name amateurs, maybe they could all make some money.

"Even then," Bill Riordan says, "I was believing my own material."

In 1963, there was the Salisbury International and the Philadelphia Indoor at St. Joseph's Fieldhouse. By 1964, there were three tournaments: Salisbury, Philadelphia, Richmond. Macon was added in 1965. The top amateur players began to hear about this crazy man from Maryland named Riordan. Not only did he pay expenses . . . he gave bonuses! Yeah, bonuses. He thought Chuck McKinley put on a good show in the finals at Salisbury, and gave him $100 out of his own pocket. A hundred bucks, really? Yeah. What's this guy's name again? Riordan. Bill Riordan.

"Imagine," says Riordan, who would later make million-dollar television deals with a wink, "imagine the goodwill I could buy in those days with a hundred bucks. I'd say to the kids, 'Well, I've met with the committee, and the crowd response was so great last night that they've decided to give you an extra hundred.' They'd go crazy. They didn't know that *I* was always the committee."

He had a crazy vision about an indoor circuit. He would fly around to various cities in the fall, selling tennis door-to-door. He was his own

PR man, his own front man. One day in the mid-1960's, he flew into Macon, Georgia, to meet with a promoter named George Peake. Riordan had convinced George Peake that Macon was ready for indoor tennis.

But they could not find a tournament site in Macon. Finally, they found themselves at Mercer College—specifically at the Mercer College gym.

Riordan pauses in his story and points to the low ceiling of the saloon. He nearly sends a tray of drinks toward the East River. Riordan has always loved grand gestures.

"See this ceiling here," he said. "That's how high the ceiling was in the Mercer College gym. Place looked like it could hold six hundred people, tops, I figured. No way they could play doubles. No lobs.

"But I figure if I didn't do something, I was gonna blow Macon. The local people were all getting nervous. I swept a hand across the place like it was Madison Square Garden. 'Gentlemen,' I said, *'this* is the new site of the Macon *International.'* "

According to Riordan, the Macon International grossed $22,000 in 1965, its first year of operation.

He went from city to city like this, beating his own drum, fanning his own flames, telling people that the future of indoor tennis was right here in Macon . . . or Birmingham . . . or Richmond.

"I always liked Macon," he says. "Macon was where Nastase wore the polka dot pajamas."

This was on one of Nastase's first trips to the U.S. Most of the players were still wearing white. Adidas had not yet invented the stripe; Ted Tinling had not invented purple. But Brazil's Thomas Koch liked wearing colored shirts; his favorite was one that had sunflowers all over it.

Nastase liked the idea of being colorful on the court, even in dress. He liked Koch's sunflower shirt. He liked it so much that he told his friend Ion Tiriac that the next day he would wear his polka dot pajamas for his match. Tiriac bet Nastase $50 that he wouldn't do it. Nastase told him that he had a bet.

The next night, Nastase took off his warmups and, sure enough, he was wearing polka dot pajamas. The Mercer College gym became fairly excited. Reporters went looking for Riordan, wanting to know if Nastase would be fined.

This is the kind of moment that Riordan has always seized. When Connors would come off the court after winning the U.S. Open in 1974, Riordan grabbed him and told him to say "Get me Laver" at his press conference when asked what was next for him. Connors was asked "What's next?" at the press conference. "Get me Laver," he growled. Challenge matches were thus born. Jimmy Connors made about $2 million from challenge matches, and Bill Riordan didn't do so bad, either.

But in Macon, in 1965, publicity was money to Riordan.

"Fine Nastase?" he growled. "Absolutely."

Riordan fined Nastase $50, since he knew Nastase had won that much from Tiriac. And the next day, in *The New York Times,* a box appeared explaining that international star Ilie Nastase had been fined in Macon. It was the first tennis fine anyone knew about. It was publicity.

"I was big news in Macon," Riordan grins. "I decided I liked fining. Later in the tournament, I fined Nasty another $50 for hitting a ball at a linesman. The writers wanted to know how I was arriving at the figure. I told them it was easy: $50 if he hits the linesman, $25 if he misses. They bought it. Amazing."

Riordan sips some soda water.

"I was the top indoor promoter in the world in those days," he says. "Of course, there wasn't anybody else."

He remembered more about those days: a six-and-a-half-hour doubles match between the team of Bobby Wilson and Mark Cox and Charlie Pasarell–Ron Holmberg in 1968 (Wilson and Cox won 28–26, 19–21, 30–28); a legendary figure in Salisbury named Bob the Barber, who threw legendary parties and kept the players stocked with legendary girls; a midnight match one year in Hampton, Virginia, Coliseum, one in which Nastase beat Zeljko Franulovic, after saving nine match points, one that Riordan calls "as great an indoor match as I've ever seen."

He remembered more: Giving a player (still prominent today) $8,000 one year as a bonus, and twenty minutes later having the same player demand $11 in bus fare for his girl friend; that first bonus, on a whim, to Chuck McKinley in 1963; getting Manuel Santana, the number-one amateur player in the world, for $400 in 1964, then giving him a $200 bonus.

"That money," Riordan says, "produced some fantastic tennis."

Money came into tennis in 1968: The open era. Riordan did not stop. He ran his tour. He kept adding cities; he lost one occasionally, but there was always a Roanoke or Washington or Baltimore to take its place. He tried a tournament with both men and women in New York in 1968, and got murdered.

"They'd just opened the new Garden," he says. "The matches would be going on and all you could hear was hammering. There were pigeons flying around, too."

Then, in the 1970's, came the kid, Connors. Junior, Riordan called him. Jimbo. Riordan stepped out of the shadows, took his place next to the dynamic kid from Belleville, and the spotlight hit them. Riordan never blinked. And the sport would never be the same.

The colorful, stormy history of their relationship has been told and retold. They were together until a few years ago; they broke up; the parting was not amicable; there have been—surprise!—lawsuits between them, proving that neither teacher nor student has forgotten the lessons.

But there are stories, too . . .

"Junior's first match on Centre Court (Wimbledon) was against Bob Hewitt in 1972," Riordan says. "Gloria (Jimmy's mother) and I were sitting in the International Box, front and center. It became kind of, uh, a famous match because every time the kid would hit a good shot, Gloria would yell out, 'C'mon, Jimbo!' or 'Way to go, Jimbo!' And every time she'd yell out, there'd be this ghastly silence all around us. Occasionally, somebody would do a little throat clearing, if you know what I mean. She kept yelling. They kept clearing their throat."

Gloria Connors was hammered in the English press the next day. There were front page caricatures of her in the newspapers, one of which was captioned, "Go home, mum." Gloria and Jimmy were in a panic. By the time Riordan got to their London hotel, the place was crawling with reporters, looking for reactions from mother and son, particularly the mother.

"Junior, go practice," Riordan recalls telling Connors. To the mother, he said, "Gloria, just shut up and listen. In a few minutes, we're gonna play meet the press, and you're going to be asked your reaction to the press, and, believe me, your answers are gonna be important to our future."

They went downstairs to the bar at the Westbury Hotel, and a British writer walked up to Gloria Connors and asked, "What was Jimmy's reaction to all the negative press about his mum this morning?"

Gloria laughed and said, "Oh, he *loved* it. He teased me about it all through breakfast." Riordan stood off to the side, smiling the way he always did when his material was delivered properly.

"That's how it was before they both forgot the lines," he says.

The big breakthrough for Connors, Riordan feels, came at the U.S. Pro at Longwood in 1973. Connors was twenty. Stan Smith was the number-one player in the world. Connors was gunning for him, but had had a bad summer. He lost to Alex Metreveli at Wimbledon, then flew to Bstaad, Sweden, and threw out his back. Didn't want to play, see.

"Of course, that was no big deal for Junior," says Riordan. "He's double-jointed; he can throw out his back any time he wants to."

Jimmy Connors then went to Boston, where he started his run as a great player. He beat Stan Smith easily in the first round, 6–3, 6–3. He beat Arthur Ashe in the finals. He and Riordan were off.

"That was the start," Riordan says. "The Old Guard would never be the same after that."

Riordan is asked what the highlight for him was in the Connors years.

"Laver," he says promptly.

Really?

"It was Laver," he says. "I'll remember every detail of that day as long as I live. You think the adrenalin was pumping for the kid that day? I thought I was gonna have a heart attack."

This was the first challenge match. Caesar's Palace. The old left-hander against the kid left-hander. Forget about where all the money went. This was the best television show tennis ever produced, the first time the sport produced a heavyweight fight.

"The suite was like a fight dressing room a half-hour before the match," Riordan says, excited at the memory, the pictures vivid. "A tape recorder was blaring. Jimmy was bouncing up and down, screaming obscenities at the top of his lungs. Pancho Segura was sitting there like a fight trainer yelling, 'Keel him, keel him.' Jeezus, it was something.

"By the time we got down to the court, the adrenalin was really going. It was like the lions and the Christians. The kid was the enemy. The whole crowd was for Laver, loud. So here comes the kid bouncing up the aisle in his London Fog raincoat, the people are going crazy, and he's cursing them out! F——— you. F——— you, too. Top of his voice. Always was a class kid.

"It was everything I had planned, everything I had hoped for—until the kid fell behind in the fourth set. The script was going perfectly until then. I never thought the kid could lose. 'He's gonna blow it,' I thought. 'My God, Laver's gonna win the goddamn match.' I'd never even considered that. Then the kid came back and saved everybody."

After a while, the kid went away, and then Bill Riordan went away.

It was a mighty love affair, though, the one between Bill Riordan and tennis. It had big ups and big downs, and it always had laughter. Like most love affairs, the two of them did not know how much they needed each other until they lost each other. But they never could make the damn thing work after they both hit the big money. They were probably happiest in Salisbury.

Summer 1980: Borg vs. McEnroe

by NEIL AMDUR

How do you know when you have seen a really great match, an all-time classic? That's like asking how you know when you've fallen in love. If you have to ask, you haven't. Thus, all those who saw the Borg-McEnroe 1980 Wimbledon final knew immediately that this was about as good as tennis gets. And so too with their return engagement two months later at Flushing Meadow, where McEnroe turned the tables, frustrating Borg's Grand Slam bid. Neil Amdur, tennis reporter for The New York Times, *tells what made these two matches the great events that they were. Borg vs. McEnroe . . . indeed, this is the tennis rivalry of the 1980's, and beyond—into the record books.*

WIMBLEDON, England, July 5—Bjorn Borg posted a five-set victory over John McEnroe today that not only gave the Swede his fifth consecutive Wimbledon singles title but also gave tennis followers something to cherish long after both players have left the sport.

Like well-conditioned fighters, they traded shots for three hours fifty-three minutes on the Centre Court of the All-England Lawn Tennis and Croquet Club. The top-seeded Borg won, 1–6, 7–5, 6–3, 6–7, 8–6, only after the determined second-seeded McEnroe had saved seven match points in the fourth set, including five in a dramatic thirty-four-point tie-breaker that will stand by itself as a patch of excellence in the game's history.

"Electrifying," said Fred Stolle, a former Australian great, of the tie-breaker that the twenty-one-year-old McEnroe finally won, eighteen points to sixteen, to deadlock the match, after Borg had earlier lost two match points on serve at 5–4, 40–15.

If this marathon was not the greatest major championship final ever played—and tennis historians treasure the past with reverence—it ranked as one of the most exciting. Lance Tingay of *The London Daily Telegraph*, who was watching his forty-third final here, put it at the top of his Wimbledon list.

"For sure, it is the best match I have ever played at Wimbledon," said the twenty-four-year-old Borg, who now has won a record thirty-five singles matches in a row here, including five-set finals from Jimmy Connors in 1977 and Roscoe Tanner last year. Connors and Tanner, like McEnroe, are left-handers.

This one was more a struggle of indomitable wills that would not buckle, even under the normally strenuous circumstances of a championship final. Heightening the drama were the contrasting playing styles and personalities of the participants—Borg, the stolid, silent man of movement, and McEnroe, the brash, aggressive serve-and-volleyer, dubbed by one Fleet Street tabloid as "Mr. Volcano" for his outbursts during yesterday's stormy four-set triumph over Connors in the semifinals.

McEnroe spoke only with his racket and spirit today, flooring Borg with his kicking serve and deep first volleys for almost two sets and then defying the Swede's attempt to close out the match in the fourth set.

That Borg lost the fourth set and then played one of the best sets of his career, losing only three points in seven service games, reaffirmed the notion that he must be ranked alongside Rod Laver and Bill Tilden among the sport's greatest champions.

"He's gone through every kind of testing," Roger Taylor, a British player during Laver's reign, said of Borg. "If you were going to find any chinks, this would have been it today."

Borg found the winning weapons in his serve and two-handed backhand. Both spoke with authority at different stages.

Until he broke McEnroe for the first time in the twelfth game of the second set, the Swede had never even held a 30–15 lead. At 3–all in the second set, fourteen of McEnroe's first forty-one points on serve, or one in three, were won by aces, service winners or errant returns. However, Borg made the one brilliant shot that shifted the tempo. It was a backhand service-return winner down the line that gave him a double set point in the twelfth game.

Throughout the rain-delayed fortnight, even in winning his first six matches comfortably, Borg had been frustrated on his two-handed backhand because of soft grass courts that yielded low bounces. For two-handed players, who must scoop and lift, the low bounce is a curse.

However, dry weather in recent days had hardened the turf. "In the semifinal against Brian," Borg said of his four-set victory over the unseeded Brian Gottfried, "I started to play the shot well."

Borg and McEnroe served well enough, getting in more than 60 percent of their first balls, to minimize the chance of breaks. Borg broke for a 2–0 lead in the third set by running around a second serve and hammering a cross-court forehand. He held for 5–2 after a twenty-point game in which McEnroe had five break points.

An offspeed cross-court backhand, which McEnroe volleyed into the net, and another backhand cross-court service return gave Borg another break for 5–4 in the fourth set. The match seemed over, but Borg proved that he, like Laver and others, was still only human.

Sensing the second leg of the Grand Slam (he won the French Open for the fifth time last month without dropping a set) in his grasp, the Swede succumbed to nerves. The pace suddenly went off his flat first serve, he volleyed tentatively and McEnroe climbed back from double match point to 5–all with a backhand cross-court service-return winner.

The tie-breaker took twenty-two minutes, only five less than the entire first set. It was fiercely contested, with both lunging, stretching and sometimes sprawling onto the scarred turf for shots.

Borg had his third match point, with McEnroe serving at 5–6. Although playing in his first Wimbledon final, the left-hander from Douglaston, Queens, saved himself with a forehand volley that died on the grass, after Borg had made a thunderous forehand return of his second serve.

McEnroe finally got his first set point at 8–7. This time Borg drove a forehand return of serve down the line. McEnroe dived in vain, tumbling to the ground.

Match points and set points were played on almost every succeeding point, in a blur of brilliance. That they had already struggled for three hours was of little consequence: They hammered first serves, attacked, scrambled, sometimes missing the lines by inches, other times splattering chalk.

"How the guy got up to serve those match points I don't know," Stolle said in a tribute to McEnroe's courage.

McEnroe took the advantage in the tie-breaker, 17–16, when Borg, apparently still thinking about the lost match points in the tenth game, drove a forehand service return wide by inches. The American then deadlocked the

John McEnroe's shotmaking talent is matched only by his temper. A perfectionist, he demands more of himself—and of umpires, linesman and officials—than seems humanly possible. (Photo by Russ Adams)

match on his seventh set point, when Borg, attacking off serve, netted a forehand volley.

Under such strain, a less-composed player might have let the match slip away. More than any other single factor, however, concentration is the key that unlocks Borg's treasures. The fifth set showed his genius.

Although losing the first two points, Borg continued to tell himself, "Don't give up, don't get tight." He did not lose another point on serve until the tenth game, an incredible string of nineteen points in a row.

Meanwhile, McEnroe had to battle to hold serve from love–40 in the second game and again from love–40 to reach 4–all. The strain of yesterday's match with Connors and the following doubles match that he and Peter Fleming admittedly gave away to avoid further physical strain on McEnroe apparently was taking its toll.

The end came swiftly. From 15–all, Borg again ran around McEnroe's second serve and drove a forehand return down the line, inches inside. McEnroe anticipated Borg's flicking backhand cross-court at 15–30, but hurriedly netted a forehand volley.

The match wound up, perhaps almost fittingly, with the two throwing their favorite punches. McEnroe, attacking off a second serve, punched a forehand volley into the corner. Borg countered with the backhand cross-court winner.

Borg collected $50,000 and made his score eighty-two victories in his last eighty-four singles matches since last year's Wimbledon final. His only losses have been to Tanner at the United States Open, which McEnroe won last September, and to Guillermo Vilas in the recent Nations Cup.

His goal, he says, is to leave the sport as number one of all time. He already has achieved that distinction at Wimbledon.

The records show that H. Laurie Doherty won five titles between 1902 and 1906 and William Renshaw took six from 1881 to 1886. But those crowns were won during an era when defending champions played fewer matches.

FLUSHING MEADOW, N.Y., September 8—What an encore!

John McEnroe beat Bjorn Borg in five sets yesterday for his second consecutive singles title at the United States Open tennis championships.

Two months after their five-set Wimbledon classic, which might have been the best men's final ever, the sport's top two pros traded firepower for four hours thirteen minutes at the National Tennis Center. This time McEnroe won, 7–6, 6–1, 6–7, 5–7, 6–4, frustrating Borg's bid for his first Open crown and a Grand Slam sweep of the four major championships.

The match may have lacked Wimbledon's fourth-set tie breaker intensity and fifth-set drama in the minds of the players. But it had the same number of total games, fifty-five; two tense tie breakers and was especially noteworthy for McEnroe's amazing stamina. He had struggled to a five-set semifinal victory over Jimmy Connors on Saturday night that lasted four hours sixteen minutes and went to a decisive tie-breaker.

Few athletes have been subjected to such stress under championship conditions. That McEnroe survived, after admitting that "I thought my body was going to fall off" after the fourth set, was the strongest tribute to credentials often lost in his courtside conduct.

McEnroe won $46,000. But the top prize seemed almost secondary to a situation that saw the top-seeded Borg beaten in the fifth set for the first time in fourteen matches, a span that had covered four years. It capped a tournament that, like Wimbledon, began slowly with the early emphasis on weather, but wound up in a blaze of glorious matches.

Borg had fought back from deficits earlier in the tournament and won five-set matches against Roscoe Tanner in the quarterfinals and Johan Kriek in the semifinals. But he did not serve with the consistency or force that had helped him win nineteen points in a row on serve against McEnroe in the fifth set of their Wimbledon final, which Borg won, 1–6, 7–5, 6–3, 6–7, 8–6.

Borg twice served for the first set, at 5–4 and 6–5, but was broken each time, the second time at love. After he had lost the first-set tie-breaker, seven points to four, with McEnroe attacking his serve and putting away forehand volleys, Borg's mind, spirit and first serves drifted.

"I don't know what happened in the second

set," he said of the span in which McEnroe ran off thirteen points between the first and fourth games. "I didn't have any feel for the ball."

Ahead, two sets to love, McEnroe was aware of his good fortune. But as Borg struggled and held serve from love–30 to 1–all in the third set and from 15–30 to 2–all, the Douglaston, Queens, left-hander knew that Borg was down, but not out.

"He gets you in that lull," McEnroe said of Borg's ability to rebound when it appeared that he had given up. "Then you start going around slower and he wins a set. You don't think he's trying, but he's trying to find a way to get his game back together."

Borg found a way with backhand winners down the line that opened and closed the third-set tie-breaker, which he won, 7–5. When McEnroe, serving at 5–6 in the fourth set, started guessing that Borg would try to hit down the line, Borg instead went cross-court with the backhand, broke for the only time in the set and evened the match.

"I thought I had a good chance, especially when it came to the fifth set," Borg said.

The fifth set has been Borg's sanctuary, in which he has had some of his most majestic moments as a five-time Wimbledon and French Open champion. The last time he lost a match in the fifth set, after having dropped the opening two sets, was six years ago. Ironically, that defeat came against Vijay Armitraj in the second round of the 1974 Open, a tournament that has frustrated Borg since 1972.

"That's going to be my biggest ambition in the future," Borg said of his pursuit of the Open title, after his third runner-up showing.

It may have been only coincidence that the decisive set was contested under the lights, a situation in which Borg has never felt comfortable, particularly on service returns. McEnroe's first-serve percentage in the fifth set was 70, which allowed him to move in for decisive first volleys. By contrast, Borg faulted fourteen of his twenty-nine first serves and double faulted twice in the seventh game, which he lost from deuce on McEnroe's backhand lob and his own netted forehand volley.

"I think I lost the match because I wasn't serving well," Borg said, unable to determine whether his problem came from the toss or a lack of rhythm. The thought of McEnroe ready and eager to rush the net could not have helped Borg's concentration.

Both carved the lines like surgeons, creating several controversial points for the five linesmen, half the number utilized at Wimbledon. In the final few games, however, McEnroe's wide-sweeping southpaw serve was the dominant weapon, extending the reign of left-handed men's champions in the world's richest tournament to seven consecutive years.

Serving at 4–3, McEnroe held at fifteen. Three of the points were won on serves, the fourth on a backhand volley placement.

Borg held at love, thus forcing McEnroe to serve out the match, in the tradition of a champion. On Saturday night, Connors had broken McEnroe's serve at 5–4 in the fifth set to send the match into the decisive tie-breaker, which McEnroe won, seven points to three.

At 5–4, McEnroe won the first point when Borg's short cross-court backhand dropped inches wide. McEnroe drove a high forehand volley long, but reached 30–15 with a service winner deep to the backhand that Borg could only lift straight in the air. Two forehand volleys clinched the match.

"The intensity was higher at Wimbledon," McEnroe said afterward, calling the title he had won the most satisfying of his career. "There was consistency today, but I don't think Bjorn played that well through the whole match."

"The Wimbledon match was much better," Borg said. "John can play better, I can play better."

Perhaps. But McEnroe's achievement reflected his ability to sustain an extraordinary level of excellence over a demanding stretch. On Thursday night, he ousted Ivan Lendl of Czechoslovakia, one of the tour's hottest players, in a long four-set battle. On Friday, he was back on the court in the men's doubles final and lost in five sets. Then came Connors and Borg.

"I felt better here than at Wimbledon in the fifth set," he said.

PART III

THE SECRET:
Strokes and Strategies

"Cut out the fancy thinking and just concentrate on mastering the basic fundamentals. Learn to hit the same old boring shot and you'll beat most of the people who now beat you."
—from *Tennis for the Future*
by Vic Braden and Bill Bruns

Power Tennis and the Forehand

by **MAURICE McLOUGHLIN**

"The California Comet" was the man who intro-duced punch to tennis and excitement to tennis galleries. Here he explains how, plus the secret of his much-copied Western forehand, a stroke not unlike that employed currently by Bjorn Borg.

I have always felt very happy and proud to be associated in the minds of many with the introduction of a new era in tennis. Whether deserved or not it might be of interest, in the light of your request for some data from my rusty pen, to have some observations on the development of the game my association with it would seem to suggest.

In one word it might be described as "punch." Enlarging on that word leads me to suggest some of the "whys and wherefores." The principal reason probably was the hard courts in California which produce a livelier, faster acting ball. Our cement and asphalt courts yield dividends on a hard-hit ball. It remained for someone like myself, who by nature derives more pleasure out of the game by hitting, to bring a certain measure of control into the joyful abandon of "socking the pill." Obviously one of the best ways to control point-winning shots is to shorten them and get your opponent to "play up" to you as often as possible,

so you can "hit down." Wherefore the faster service and following same to the net. Wherefore the predominance of net play, more offensive type of volleying, particularly on all "down shots."

I think when we Californians first brought a more or less highly developed hard-court game on to grass, we brought a faster pace or tempo which to us seemed natural as the air we breathe, which to many in the East at the time seemed a revelation.

Our early experience on turf entailed adaptations in our play both difficult and interesting. The bounce of the ball is less uniform on turf than on the hard courts. The ball itself, in the course of play, tends to pick up weight on turf, whereas with us it grows lighter. The totally different "feel" under foot, plus the spiked shoes contrasted with the light sneakers we were used to, made a very marked change in footwork to become accustomed to. After all was said and done, we grew to feel at home on turf, and I think you'll find most Californians would prefer a good turf court to their own if the choice were an equal one. After thus adapting ourselves we still retained all the outstanding characteristics of a game developed exclusively on hard courts, thereby proving it could be done, and as a result did our part to inject much needed zest into the

McLoughlin poses his forehand and explains that this photo was "meant to show my forehand drive at the moment of impact . . . When the racket was drawn back, the left shoulder was pointed in the general direction the ball was to take. As the racket came through to the position shown here, the body rotated at the waist so that the chest is now almost where the left shoulder was at the start of the stroke."

Compare the previous photo of McLoughlin to this shot of Bjorn Borg preparing to hit his forehand, some seventy years later. Note the similar Western grip, arm and shoulder position. Borg is hitting from an open stance (right foot advanced) while McLoughlin's stance is closed (left foot forward), but McLoughlin often hit from an open stance as other photos indicate. Actually, Borg's photo could be the first shot in McLoughlin's posed sequence. (Photo by Russ Adams)

tennis appetites of Easterners which at the time of our advent had all the appearance of having become a bit jaded.

The average player is naturally stronger on his forehand than on his backhand. In both strokes the position is *sidewise* to the net, and the ball should not be played too close—preferably near arm's length. At the end of your reach you can make a full swing. Cramped action is fatal. Poor form in general is caused by the player falling into cramped positions. The ball should also

be played a little in advance of the body. This does not mean, however, that you should reach forward before the ball is hit, as such a move would naturally ruin your swing. Neither should you allow the ball to get past your body before hitting it. It should be fairly opposite your body, but a trifle in advance. You should have your left shoulder pointed down the line of flight along which the ball is coming. In other words, the body, edge-forward, should be parallel to the line of flight of the ball. The swing should be free and natural, the weight at first evenly distributed on the balls of the feet. In your swing back your right foot will bear most of it. This foot will be about parallel to the net; the left foot in advance and at somewhat of an angle. The feet are about eighteen inches apart as a general rule. The weight will be transferred from the rear foot to the foot in front as the stroke is made, and a good player will be found "advancing on the ball." Your feet do not necessarily have to be perfectly stationary, but it is essential that the stroke be "timed" accurately so that it gets the advantage of some body-weight and the proper loin rotation. It is well to have the forearm as much in line with the racket handle as possible when racket meets ball, but there is no hard and fast rule.

I put a varying amount of "top" on all forehand strokes, depending entirely on the speed and depth I want the ball to have. The forearm principally imparts this spin to the ball, which is, of course, sent away rotating forward or "top first" from the striker. This makes the shot "dip" or "dive" rather suddenly, and when it bounds it goes faster than a straight drive. But exaggerated top will slow its flight. The drive is more of a sweep than a hit, as in golf, and the finish should be well after the ball and not primarily across the body. My attention was once called to a lady player at ————, a very good forehand shot, but her position was directly facing the coming ball, and in her swing she did not turn her body at all, *striking directly against herself.* Needless to say this is a "horrible example" of what to avoid.

The steps to learning how to apply top are, first the vertical upward movement of the racket from below the ball and across it; then the combination of this motion with a general forward movement of racket and arm; third, whatever additional wrist-work comes naturally and effectively. By a slight lifting of the racket at the moment of impact more or less top is imparted, and its use certainly makes one's stroke easier to control. Wilding says that he likes to "feel the ball on his racket" before imparting this overspin. Personally, I think the correct "feel" of the stroke has much to do with its success, but the racket must of necessity be at the same time moving forward and upward across the ball.

In this connection the remarkable forehand grip of May Sutton (Mrs. T.C. Bundy) comes to mind. I should describe it as follows: In the case of the various great players I know, if, when holding their racket for a forehand drive, they should extend their arm as though to show you their grip, the head of the racket would be seen to be either edge up, or with the upper edge slightly inclined toward the ball. In the case of Mrs. Bundy's grip, on extending the arm in the same manner, the upper edge of the racket is so far inclined toward the ball that it virtually amounts to holding the racket face-up. In order to lay the face of the racket back so as to allow impact with the ball, her wrist is turned back and under. As the stroke goes through, and at the moment of impact, the wrist flicks around into its natural position. In this manner the excessive overspin is imparted. I do not know of any other great players who use this extreme hold. Many, however, use its modifications. William Johnston, whose forehand commands a great deal of respect, is among these. My own forehand grip is of the same nature.

What is known as the English forehand ground stroke is like a sliced drive in golf, that is, instead of top being applied at the moment of impact, the racket is drawn across the ball, imparting slice. For this stroke it is especially important to be at a proper distance from the ball in order not to be hampered. The ordinary ground stroke does not impart either top or slice, and is a perfectly straightforward underhand swing, the racket being started back at about shoulder-height; the weight at first (as in the other strokes) being on the right foot, and shifted as the swing goes through with a straightforward finish. In the ordinary forehand drive the finish is somewhat more across the body, and, naturally, the more horizontal the stroke is the more exaggerated such a finish becomes. Horizontal drives do not get as effective a lift.

Most emphatically one should always follow through. I said I should enlarge upon this point, and certainly in these few words lies one of the most fundamental principles of the game. In almost every game of science this principle must be mastered in order to attain big results. In

McLoughlin says: "This illustrates my follow through on a forehand drive, such as shown in (previous accompanying photo) . . . Note here that the body has completed its rotation at the waist, thus imparting a certain amount of body weight to the ball by this rotary movement of the back muscle."

McLoughlin hits a forehand drive at Wimbledon in 1913. He says: "Quite an idea can be gained from this picture of the tenseness, concentration and power that must be put into a stroke of this sort . . . The racket here has completed its follow through and with it the body has rotated at the waist. For ideal driving position the left foot might be a little further advanced and the feet not quite so far apart, but it must be remembered that this is a return of serve during a match of vital importance, and more often than not at such times you are not permitted the time or opportunity to perfectly set yourself up for the stroke." (McLoughlin photos reprinted from Tennis As I Play It, *courtesy of the William M. Fischer Lawn Tennis Collection)* tennis it consists of the ability to let the racket go through to the natural completion of the stroke, and not to hold it up during any stage of the swing immediately after impact of ball and racket, a common and fatal tendency. Some call it "letting the racket do the work." Throughout all the strokes in tennis, variations of the same principle are ever present. One exception is in the stop-volley, when you employ methods directly opposite to the follow-through with a view to deadening the ball's flight, like the bunt in baseball. But the follow-through exists in all other volleys, and is of primary importance. It is this fact that a great many net players fail to realize. If they think at all about the follow-through, they associate it only with strokes that require a full arm swing. The follow-through on the volley is only a matter of inches, yet in just this small, but important, feature hundreds of volleyers fail. Their volley stroke is in the manner of a poke—quick stabs here and there at the ball, that carry no weight behind them because the racket is checked immediately on impact instead of the head being allowed to go through in line with the ball's flight for the smallest fraction of a second after it is struck. I shall recall this to your mind when I treat of the volley itself, but it illustrates the great importance of "following through."

Another very important point in the mastering of ground strokes is the concealment of direction; that is, being able to make a shot straight down or across-court, as the case may be, so that it is not perfectly obvious to your opponent which you intend. The most common method of concealing direction is the slight turn of the wrist a fraction of a second before, and during, the impact of the ball and racket. This wrist variation is so slight and delicate that it is difficult to adequately describe. In fact, it is one of those finer points of finish in stroke technique that generally only come in advanced stages of development.

"Good length" in ground strokes is worth cultivation, but when playing against sound, aggressive net players, one never gives very much thought to his length; then it is placement and keeping the ball low that figure most prominently. Length is only important when your opponent is in the backcourt. However, the average player, when developing his ground strokes, should first give his attention to the length he is getting, as the short angle game is considerably easier to acquire. In general, swing easily and naturally and do not attempt too much at first. Watch your position and train your eye to take the ball at the right distance. As in the serve do not try for top and pace too soon, and, when you acquire these, keep them well in control. Your forehand might be called your most natural stroke, and a trained eye and timing sense will work wonders.

The Spin of the Ball

by BILL TILDEN

Bill Tilden was the first player to combine attack and defense, building what he called the "all court" game. He credits his development to understanding the spin of the ball—how to make the tennis ball do his bidding to break up his opponent's game.

MOST tennis players look upon the ball that is used as merely something to hit. It is not an individual, separate factor in their play, like their opponent. They use it as a means to an end. Let me suggest the ball for a moment as an individual. It is a third party in the match. Will this third party be on your side or against you? It is up to you.

The ball will do as it is told. Suggest (with your racket, not your tongue) that the ball curve this way or that and it obeys. It is the power of your suggestion that determines how well your wishes are carried out.

Every ball has an outside and inside edge every time it comes to you. I admit it is round, yet to the player the side nearest you is its inside edge and that away from you its outside edge; and the edge you hit determines the curve and spin of the ball on your return. Why should we curve or spin the ball?

1. We do it to gain control of our shot.
2. We do it to fool our opponent.
3. We do it by accident.

Let me recommend that you confine your activities to the first two of these, for the third will happen anyway.

Curve and bound will be affected not only intentionally by your shot but quite unintentionally by wind, air friction and poor court surface. Tennis matches are often won by conditions, and the man who is sufficiently master of his game to turn conditions to his account is the one who will usually win. The factor in the game most affected by external conditions of wind, heat and playing surface is the ball. Its weight, bounce, flight, and even size, vary with varying conditions. It is for this reason that the mastery and complete knowledge of spin and curve of the ball is of paramount importance to a tennis player. I prefer to make the ball follow my suggestions, rather than chase it around at those of my opponent.

Let me open this discussion by a sound tennis maxim:

"Never give your opponent a chance to make a shot he likes."

281

The whole object of putting twist, spin, cut, curve, or whatever term you prefer to describe your control of your stroke, on the ball is to force your opponent into error.

I may sound unsporting when I claim that the primary object of tennis is to break up your opponent's game, but it is my honest belief that no man is defeated until his game is crushed, or at least weakened. Nothing so upsets a man's mental and physical poise as to be continually led into error. I have often seen players collapse in a match after they have netted or driven out a crucial point which they should have won. It is with a view not only to your own stroke but to the effect on your opponent that leads me to say, "never make any stroke without imparting a conscious, deliberate and intentional spin to the ball."

There are two fundamental facts as to spin:

1. *The more spin the less pace, and vice versa.*
2. *Topspin tends to drop; slice or cut spin tends to rise.*

Spin may be imparted either by a long follow-through, which, in my opinion, is the soundest method for all ground strokes, drives or slices; and by a wrist movement, which is preferable in volleying. This latter is essentially a slice or undercut spin.

Remember, that where a shot is designed to defend the spin should tend to bring the ball toward the center of the court; when a shot is used for attack, the spin can be used to curve the ball either way, according to the direction of your passing shot.

Slice shots tend to curve toward the side line closest to the point from which the stroke is made, and are thus apt to go out over the side. Topspin tends to curve the ball toward the center of the court.

The slice is a right-hand baseball pitcher's "in-curve," while the topspin is analogous to the "out-drop." In hitting a slice or undercut shot the racket passes under the ball and inside (closer to the body). The topspin shot is hit with the racket head outside the ball and passing up and slightly over it.

Every player who desires to attain championship heights must understand the value of spin on the ball. Spin means control. Knowledge of how to use it assures a player of a versatile defense and attack.

The most useful, and, in the main, the most used service carries slice spin. The rotation of the ball causes it to curve and bounce from the server's right to his left, or, in other words, toward his opponent's forehand.

The object of this service spin is to force your opponent to reach for his return, causing his shot to either slide off his racket or to pop weakly in the air. The spin will tend to make his shot travel down the backhand side line of the server's court unless he acutely pulls his stroke across court, a difficult and dangerous shot. To offset the natural tend out of the return of this slice service I advocate meeting the service with a flat racket and imparting topspin by a long follow-through, thus neutralizing the twist of the serve.

The reverse twist, so popular among beginners as something unique in their experience, is not a sound service.

This reverse twist is imparted by hitting the ball from *below* and behind and carrying the racket up sharply from right to left, with a sharp lifting motion. The ball travels in a high, looping parabola, with a fast shooting drop, which, on hitting the ground hops high to the forehand of the receiver.

The first few meetings with this freakish delivery are apt to be disastrous until the receiver recognizes the hop and the excessive twist away from the curve of the ball—the reason for its name, reverse twist. Once that is gauged, all one needs to do to handle the service is to advance on the ball, meet it at the top of the bound with a firm, fast stroke and a flat racket face. The twist, still on the ball as it leaves the ground, again reverses and, acting as topspin, holds the receiver's drive in court. I know of no service so ideal to drive hard as the reverse twist.

The American twist, also a reverse as to curve and bound, but far more effective and useful, is one of the greatest assets to a player. It is the service which made Maurice E. McLoughlin famous. It is used by R.N. Williams, Watson Washburn and myself as the foundation of our delivery, although we all mix it up with the slice.

The ball is struck behind the head with the racket traveling from left to right and up over the ball, imparting a distinct "out-drop" topspin. The ball curves from the server's right to left and bounces from his left to right and high or, in other words, to your opponent's backhand, generally his weakest point. The great twist with which it hops from the ground tends to pull his stroke out over the side line. For this reason the receiver should always strive to pull an American twist service into court and allow a large margin of safety at the side line.

I am discussing twists in service in detail because, in service, twist rather than speed is the essential point. It is by twist and placement, rather than by speed, that you can force your opponent on the defensive at the opening of the point. Speed alone is easy to handle. It must beat the other man clean or his return will force *you* on the defensive by your own speed turned back on you. The cannonball service, a delivery of which I am supposed to be a leading exponent, is almost without twist, hit with a flat racket face and quite incapable of control or placement except by accident. Richards, Johnston and Williams, if they can put their racket on the ball at all, and they usually can, all handle my cannonball flat service more easily than either of my spin deliveries. So I strongly urge, from personal experience, base your service on a twist of some sort.

Let me turn to the use of spin in actual play, once the service has been delivered. Remember that, as a general rule, topspin or a flat, twistless shot is offensive, the basis for attack; while a slice, or undercut, backspin shot is defensive. Topspin carries control, speed and pace. Undercut carries control and direction but no speed.

Against the net man, who is storming the barrier, all passing shots should be hit with topspin. In the first place, topspin will drop more quickly and force him to volley up from below the top of the net. Secondly, the shot carries more speed and as much control as a slice. The reverse of the spin of a top shot when it is vol-

leyed tends to cause it to rise up in the air unless the volley is perfectly hit, while a slice, when volleyed, pulls down off the racket, often for a kill. There can be no two views about the advantage of topspin over chop or slice against a net attack when striving for a passing shot.

Let us consider the defensive lob for a moment—the attempt to gain time when you are forced off your feet by your opponent's attack. Here the undercut lob is the better choice. The undercut tends to hold the ball longer in the air, as the friction of its spin reacts. Also, when struck, it comes down rapidly, often forcing the net man to hit into the net. The slight gain in time itself may give you time to recover your position, even if your opponent makes his kill. Topspin lobs, or the so-called loop drive, are useful only as a surprise, never as a sound defense.

Admitting the foregoing, the question arises as to spin from the base line when both players remain in the backcourt. Here is where the undercut shot, with its tantalizing hesitation of bound, advances to almost equal footing with the topspin. The topspin will win outright more often than the undercut, owing to its greater speed and severity, but I am of the opinion that the undercut shot is more apt to force your opponent into error. There is less labor involved in making the slice shot, while its irregularity of twist is greater than that of the topspin shot, and therefore harder to judge accurately.

The ideal combination is a mixture of the two. Personally, I study my man and lay my attack accordingly. I form the basis of my game on a topspin drive, using the slice shot to mix pace, speed and depth.

Certain players are peculiarly susceptible to error from certain twists. A sliding chop to the forehand of Johnston or Williams is fairly effective, while against Wallace Johnson or Vincent Richards it is a waste of time; yet this shot will almost alone defeat Shimizu or Kumagae.

If I were to lay down a general principle to follow, I would advise slicing to a player who prefers a high bounding ball to drive, and topspin driving to the man who likes to slice or chop his return.

My Backhand

by DON BUDGE

Budge was the first strong backhand player, and thus almost invulnerable to attack. His is still rated by most as the best backhand ever, a simple stroke he developed from the baseball swing.

MY own backhand was derived naturally from baseball. I had a free, easy swing, and depending on the situation, it was as accommodating for me to hit up on the ball as down under it. It was just natural, and so I imagine the facility must have come from learning to swing a baseball bat differently according to where a ball was pitched.

Today, few players even try to hit different types of backhands. The backhand appears to have been relegated to being a strictly defensive shot. The backhand is almost invariably now hit with underspin, the stroke beginning high and finishing low. If we continue the tennis-baseball analogy this is comparable to the kind of swing a ballplayer makes when he is trying to punch an outside pitch for a single, or just to move the runner along with a ground ball. Try it with a bat and a racket, and you will see.

When I was playing, there were many more of us who hit an offensive backhand, the stroke beginning down low, ending up high, with topspin and the flourish of a home-run hitter. There is nothing very tricky to this. Since you hit the ball with a squared-up face and don't have to concern yourself with beveling it, it may, in fact, be an *easier* backhand to hit than the underspin variety. I certainly cannot suggest that it is all a vanishing art. It just seems to me that confidence in the backhand is gone. Players today have so little faith in their backhand that they would rather hit down under it and use it to parry. They figure they can thrust later with a forehand or a volley.

Of all the modern players, I think Manuel Santana of Spain and Arthur Ashe hit the most devastating offensive topspin backhands. Of the pros, Rosewall hits the best backhand, but he always uses underspin, beginning the stroke high. Although Ken uses only that one type of backhand, he has the amazing ability to hit the ball so hard that he can regularly turn on terrific power (they call the little fellow "Muscles") and change a normally defensive shot into an offensive one. Two other professionals, Laver and Dennis Ralston, employ topspin, unlike Rosewall, but neither does it so well as either Ashe or Santana, in my opinion.

Of my contemporaries, Don McNeill hit perhaps the best offensive topspin backhand. It was a prime reason for his upset victory in the finals of Forest Hills in 1940, when he beat Bobby

Riggs. That defeat cost Riggs the honor of being the only player in the twentieth century besides Tilden to win the United States title three straight times. Riggs had a pretty fair topspin backhand himself, although it was not the equal of McNeill's, or of Frank Kovacs's or Parker's. Tony Trabert was one player who had a reliable attacking backhand in the 1950's. Even by then, though, the stroke was becoming almost exclusively a defensive instrument, and the usage of the topspin backhand was fading rapidly.

Despite all those superb backhands, from Parker to Ashe, I would settle for none but my own. I state that unequivocally, not because I think mine was necessarily better but because I am sure that it was a more natural shot than anyone else's. Tom Stow changed various parts of every other aspect of my game, but he never tampered with the backhand. He has always taught his students to swing as I did. I still hear people comment that my backhand looks so different. It is, I suppose. It is just so simple.

Indeed, in the case of explaining how to hit a backhand as I do, I do not want to go into a long involved polemic on exactly how and when to pivot your hips and turn your shoulders and swivel your neck and furrow your brow and so forth and so on. If you will hit the easy baseball-style backhand that I do, about all I must tell you is to stand sideways, feet spaced comfortably apart, and then stroke through the ball—that is, do not flail at it like a .050-hitting pitcher. If you follow my suggestions, the rest of your body, the legs and the shoulders and the arms and the back, will all take care of themselves. You will be surprised how easy it is to hit a really good backhand.

For the best backhand grip, I advise turning the hand about a one-eighth turn farther behind the racket than with the forehand—and remember the forehand is the shake-hands, flat part of the hand upon the flat part of the racket. Turn your hand the one-eighth turn and you are ready for the backhand.

My backhand grip is, incidentally, exactly the same one as the Continental *forehand* that was used by such players as Perry, Cochet, and Drobny, except that I put my thumb diagonally up behind the back of the handle. The Continental forehand is turned the other way from the Western, and is thus best for reaching low balls, and is most vulnerable to high bounces. I always felt that the reason Fred Perry could manage so well with the Continental forehand grip was because he had such a strong, massive wrist. He could handle stress in reaching for high balls that other players could not.

The backhand shot should begin with your elbow in tight to your body—which is, again, the example of most sound baseball batters. When you move up on your toes in preparation to swing, the elbow will move out from your body, so that you will be uncoiling with power. Follow through directly and without waste motion. The left arm should be brought back with the racket. Remember, I began as a two-handed hitter, and I actually gripped the racket handle with my left hand. The motion is the same with the proper one-hand swing. As the racket goes forward to hit the ball, you "release" your left hand and let it go out naturally behind you. You should look a bit as though you are trying to fly as you go into the follow-through.

Although I would be delighted to see the topspin backhand return to fashion, I want to repeat that I often had occasion to hit the defensive underspin backhand (high to low) when strategy dictated. The swing is the same, except that you are bringing the racket down, and you must bevel it slightly—about the angle of a three- or four-iron, if you are familiar with golf—for you are swinging down, in league with gravity, and you simply must hit somewhat under the ball if it is to clear the net.

If you also want to hit an offensive backhand —and I hope that you do—you will discover that you can make the shot by hitting it with a flat racket face, starting your backswing low and finishing up high. Remember, the offensive backhand is up, the defensive down. Swinging up on the offensive backhand imparts sufficient topspin, I have found, so that the ball can clear the net by quite a bit and still have the spin on it to fall inside the base line.

The player with the telling offensive backhand is always a special threat simply because his talents have become so rare. Tennis strategy on so many levels now consists almost entirely of the one ploy: *Play to the backhand.* I'll bet that every time you face a new opponent, and whatever your caliber of play, your first thought is to work to his backhand. And he is just as quick to start working on yours. The player who develops a respectable backhand that can actually make points has a dual advantage.

First, a backhand gives you an all-court game. How many players are really vulnerable for a whole *half* of the court? It is like failing to bring a putter along when you play a round of golf. But further, the extra dividend a good backhand supplies is the element of shock. The assumption that it is always safe to play to the backhand is so widely held and is also so generally accurate that when a player runs into an opponent who renders that bias false, he is thrown into confusion and obstinacy. The play-his-backhand strategy is so ingrained that people will continue to try it long after they actually realize that their opponent really is strong on that side.

It was rare, too, that my backhand ever disappointed me. When I was good, it was very good; when I was bad, it was still good.

Pressure Tennis

by JACK KRAMER

Big Jake invented the Big Game and everybody started banging big serves and dashing to the net. It wasn't what Kramer had in mind . . . here is what he did have in mind.

ATTACK! That one word, in my estimation, sums up the best execution of championship tennis. Never go on the defensive if you can help it, for that gives your opponent a physical and mental respite that lets him regain control of the pace. A player who switches from offense to defense is admitting that he is getting beaten.

They say I play the "Big Game." I play that way because it is the best method for winning. Notre Dame, Michigan, and the Chicago Bears win football games because they go out to score. The Yankees are a great baseball team because they have built up an offense that is unequaled. All champions believe in the adage that a good offense is the best defense.

Most critics consider me a hard hitter and somewhat of an erratic slugger. Instead, I try to pace my game as Joe Louis or Jack Dempsey boxed; I keep moving and employing my natural power. I play tennis much the same way Bob Feller pitches—finding that the tremendous speed used offsets the disadvantages of occa-

sional wildness. Since coming into my own as a singles player, I have learned to play cautiously without sacrificing my attack. Naturally, you won't win by being erratic, but there is a difference between an offensive game and an erratic one.

As soon as you learn to hit the ball in, which should come first, learn how to hit it hard. After you get control, you can master power.

At times, however, you will have to take chances. This is true in any sport. A football team gambles with a run on fourth down or on a pass deep in its own territory. A runner on first base attempts to steal second. In tennis you occasionally have to gamble on pet shots, on more power, or on slackening pace. First, know your opponent. Feel him out. Then take chances. Most of the time you will have watched your opponent play and will know what he can and can't do. Try to use his own weaknesses against him.

When you beat an opponent by taking advantage of his weaknesses, you are conserving your valuable energy and keeping your own strengths and weaknesses under cover.

I try to take a match in stride, playing naturally and deviating from my usual style only as much as is necessary to take advantage of any flaws I detect in my opponent's attack. I hit the ball hard and deep, continually pressing, and

287

coming in to the net as often as possible. The net is the best spot for a kill and I have found that if I go to the net ten times, the percentage always is in my favor. I don't play so well if I try to vary my game, though there are players who find great utility in a change of pace. These players generally are strong in several departments and sacrifice nothing by switching their style occasionally. They may play the first set with demonstration of a powerful base-line game. In the second set they will come in and volley. These changes, of course, are part of the strategy they have planned in advance or the result of mental notations they have made during the match. If they think the opponent is beginning to solve their base-line tactics, they suddenly cross him up with volleys.

Don Budge and Ellsworth Vines also played the "Big Game." I patterned my methods on their style. The success they enjoyed vouches for the soundness of the "Big Game."

Riggs is the greatest strategist active in tennis today. He can master almost any shot and has the uncanny knack of knowing when to employ it. He always is prepared when he uncovers a flaw in his opponent's game. Bobby spars with you like a light boxer in the ring against a heavy slugger. He is a bit cautious, feinting around for an opening. When he works into the advantage, he knows what to do, and acts with lightning thrusts. Bobby can beat more powerful players for the same reason that Gene Tunney twice defeated Jack Dempsey for the heavyweight championship. He uses every advantage he can draw on. He has been required to resort to brilliant strategy because he has lacked size and power. You can learn a lesson from Riggs—he became a champion despite the odds. You can, too. And, if you have the tremendous physique and power that Riggs lacks, you might be even better than Bobby. Though Tunney wasn't small and did have great physical advantages, imagine what a great champion he would have been if all his skill could have been combined with the ability to deliver powerful punches possessed by Dempsey or Joe Louis!

A good little man can beat a big man, and a skillful player can beat a powerful one. But one who is able to combine power and skill should beat them all.

In 1947, when I played Frankie Parker in the national singles finals, Parker almost came up with a system to beat me after I had whipped him in straightaway tennis play in many previous matches.

Going into the match, I expected to encounter Parker's usual game, but he crossed me up, hitting nothing but slow balls and dew droppers. The first few times he did it, I let the balls bounce, then moved back to hit them, but I couldn't get any speed on my returns. Instead, I was setting up openings for Parker.

Then, I stepped in close to the balls and tried to chop, but still I wasn't able to get Frankie out of position.

Finally, I started taking his returns in the air. I was able to volley the balls back at him with added speed. This broke up his attack and by that time I knew I had the pace and went on to win. My victory was accomplished chiefly because I shifted to offense and was in excellent physical condition, which enabled me to withstand the rigors of the grueling match.

When you are running toward the ball, going into the net, never hit it down the line unless you are trying for an ace. It is best to hit it cross-court. If you are playing a base-line performer like Riggs or Bitsy Grant, it is best to drive the ball deep.

After you have learned to master certain shots, you then must learn when to employ them. You must calculate the risks and percentages for each stroke. You know that the angle is in your favor when you take an overhead shot close to the net. You scarcely can miss with a killing smash. But, in taking an overhead shot back near your base line, you know that you have to be more careful. You can't utilize the angles to any great extent and you know you are going to have to drive the ball deeper.

One of your biggest problems will be on return of the service, for this is one time when you will have to be on the defensive. If your opponent has a powerful, accurate service, he can place you at a disadvantage. This he will attempt to follow up quickly to win the point.

Jack Kramer believed in "pressure tennis," and that the net position was the most effective place to apply pressure. Typically, he would hit his forehand down the line to his opponent's backhand and come to the net to pick off the weak reply with a volley. (Photo Courtesy of the USTA)

Watch the server's stance and how he tosses the ball on the service. This may give you an inkling of what is coming. You may anticipate that if you have a flaw in your game, your opponent will attempt to take advantage of it on his service.

If the opponent is pressing, you scarcely can take the attack away from him on your return. Your concern, then, should be in making a return that will force him back and give you adequate time for recovery. If you sense that he is going to come into the net on the service, try for a short return that will have to be picked up low, perhaps a return that he will have to half-volley.

*Rod Laver's top spin backhand was the perfect reply to a net rusher playing "pressure tennis."
Laver could hit the ball violently and still keep it in bounds as the top spin made it dip as
it crossed the net. Laver was the first left-hander whose backhand was a strength. (Photo by
Russ Adams)*

Don't give him a deep ball that he can take in the air and stroke back decisively.

Otherwise, if you conclude there is little chance of the server coming to the net, make your return deep and try to keep the ball away from him. This will enable you to recover and get in the waiting stance.

We already have discussed the advisability of hitting the ball cross-court when rushing into the net. Now you are going to ask, "When do I go in?"

Because the advantages of being at the net are so tremendous, I try to go in on any forcing shot. I also go in when I get a short return within the service line. If I anticipate that my opponent plans to rush to the net, I try to beat him in. To do this I generally hit a forcing shot, usually down the line, and go in on the same side. I already have explained the advantages of this. I am guarding my own line and, unless he lobs (and I may smash his lob), his only other alternative is to try to return cross-court. In this, I have the advantage of the angle with me.

Now that you have an idea about the proper procedure for running in, apply the knowledge conversely. What do you do when your opponent comes to the net and is pressing you?

If he isn't guarding one side of the net, you

may attempt to pass him down the line. If he is in close, your best bet is the lob. If he is far enough back so that he might smash your lob, then you must try for a return close to his feet. Avoid hitting a ball that he can take on the rise. Try to give him a return that will make him stroke up.

On any shot, whether you are forced or forcing, take your time. Remember that most balls are hit too soon rather than too late. This error may be attributed to your attention to the ball in flight. A player watching the flight of the ball gauges its speed in the air. Too frequently he fails to allow for its slowing up after it bounces. This demonstrates another advantage of volleying—you seldom will miscalculate the speed of the ball.

During a game, your immediate concern will be to attempt to keep the ball in play until you decide on the strategy necessary to win the point. That is an important rule—keep the ball in play. Do your best to cause your opponent whatever inconvenience is possible in making his return. If you notice that he plays an habitual base-line game, you will attempt to draw him into the forecourt for volleys. The backcourt play he demonstrates may indicate he is weak at the net. If so, experiment and find out. Lure him in, then force him back. Gradually, you will discover how to handle him.

If you are playing an opponent who is a strong volleyer, think the matter over. Remember that a football team, facing an impenetrable line, doesn't knock itself out by continually smashing against the rugged wall. Instead, it passes and circles the ends, trying to go over or around. Do this in your tennis game. You can go over—and you can go around. Don't knock yourself out by batting your head against a wall.

Frequently, in watching other players, you will notice that the player who is on the defensive wins the point by taking a forcing shot and scoring a spectacular placement. These remarkable recoveries always astound the galleries. Actually, they shouldn't. The placement was premeditated. When you take a forcing shot, particularly one that sends you way out of position, you know that your return may be weak and, even though you get the ball back, you will be unable to return to position. One alternative is a high lob, which will send or keep your opponent in the backcourt. The other is a spectacular recovery; you gamble everything on trying to kill the ball. You use every effort to "put it away," knowing that you probably will lose the point anyway, and the chance of winning it with a spectacular shot is worth the effort. The chances against your success are not as great as you might expect, for you actually do not need an excellent shot. You only need a well-placed one. Your opponent, who has forced you out and who is anticipating a lob or weak return, may be caught flat-footed if you surprise him with a placement.

There are many ways of winning a point in tennis. The two cardinal ones, however, are: (1) Run your opponent out of position; (2) force your opponent into an error.

The Serve and How to Vary It

by PANCHO GONZALES

Everybody remembers Pancho's big serve—what they may forget is that he was too crafty to use it all the time. He would conserve his strength and vary the speed and spin.

PICTURE in your mind a chain reaction in which the body moves into the ball, the shoulder moves into the ball, the elbow extends and the wrist snaps through the ball. There, simplified, you have the service action. The power comes from the coordinated speed of the action.

In modern lawn tennis the emphasis has shifted increasingly on to big serving, and it is not easy to recall a champion in recent years who got by without a powerful service weapon. The advantage of having a big service is in the pressure it puts on one's opponent. As the match progresses he begins to fear that if he loses his own service it will cost him the set. The strong server may also be able to conserve more energy than his opponent by winning his service games more easily. He should be more confident of his condition lasting in a long set or a long match.

In all these years of lawn tennis, years in which I have managed to beat off many players' challenges, I have never become overconfident with my service. I have practiced my serve just as much as, if not more than, any of my other strokes. Sure, you have to practice on your weaknesses. But you mustn't overlook practicing your strength. Your game will always be built around your strength.

Let me tell you how I serve. My grip, which is orthodox, is very important. It's almost the backhand grip, but perhaps not quite all the way.

In singles I stand about six inches from the center line when serving into the deuce court, and about two feet away from the center line when serving into the advantage court.

The stance for each service is exactly the same, thus increasing the deception. One of the big secrets in serving is in disguising the delivery in order to keep the opponent off balance.

The flat serve is hit by snapping the wrist and opening the face of the racket just as the ball is hit. I aim the flat serve primarily to the backhand corner, and, being right-handed, I follow through on my left side.

For the slice serve I swing the racket away from my body, hitting around the ball and again following through on my left side. The ball is thrown up about nine inches in front of my forehead (though higher, of course) and into the court, so that I have room to hit around it. The slice is used for drawing the opponent out of court, especially if he has a weak forehand, and

292

it is effective on grass on which the ball stays rather low. It is an offensive shot, used in the top company almost as much as the flat serve.

The twist serve is hit by dropping the head of the racket behind the back, then swinging up and over the ball. For this serve the ball must be thrown behind the head, and the follow-through of the racket is high and to the right of the player's body. The twist, or American twist, as it is often called, is mostly a consistent serve used as a second serve, because it clears the net comfortably and cuts back into the court with a greater margin of safety.

Incorrect tossing up of the ball in serving causes as many errors as any other one factor. You must practice and practice and then practice still more to synchronize the toss of the ball and the swing of the racket.

The position of the ball in the air varies by two, three or maybe four inches between the first serve and the second serve. You throw it to a height about an inch or two beyond the point you can reach with your racket. At the ball's zenith you go up on the toes of your left foot, stretching as far as you can in striking it.

On the first serve you should hit the ball just at the moment it starts to fall. On the second serve the ball can be allowed to drop two or three inches before you go up to meet it. From this position you will be able to impart the spin which will bring the ball into the court. Because the back has to be arched in order to get spin on the ball, the twist serve is the most tiring of all. Otherwise, I have found that big serving doesn't necessarily use up undue energy.

Whether a player should go flat out for a cannonball on his first serve depends largely on the quality of his opponent. A flat serve bothers some players more than the spin serve. You must react very much like a baseball pitcher, varying your serves to keep the other guy off guard and off balance, but serving mostly to his weakness, whether it be the forehand or the backhand. Sometimes the court surfaces are inferior and it may pay, therefore, to make sure your first ball goes into play by sending over your second spin serve first. Then you can hurry in and command the net position.

While the second serve cannot be quite as server a weapon as the first serve, it can be more aggressive than most players make it. Practice the second serve by hitting it deep and to the corners. That will give you confidence. Your first serve will be as good as your second serve allows it to be. If you are sure that you can hit a second serve without double faulting, you will get more of your first serves into play. But the knowledge that your second serve is poor will make you miss more first serves through fear of double faulting. You have to work on that second serve to make it as consistent as it possibly can be.

Before serving you should stand relaxed behind the base line, bouncing the ball once prior to beginning your wind-up. The left foot ought to be planted firmly by the base line, two to three inches behind it, with the left shoulder pointing toward the net.

Your body must move freely as you transfer the weight from the ball of your left foot onto all of the toes, which bear most of the strain as you reach up for the ball.

Do not hesitate on your forward motion. The tendency to fall into the court is perfectly natural and is part of a good service. As you fall forward you regain balance and are ready to move off in any direction for the return. Normally, in regaining balance you take one step into the court, occasionally two, and these steps ought to be made quickly to prevent being caught in the middle of the court on a deep shot.

Rhythm comes with practice. The service is a continuous motion from start to finish, and if you relax and swing freely you ultimately will fall into a rhythm.

I like to see players taking their time with their service, analyzing their action and trying to do something extra with the ball. Outwardly, they should go through some ritual of approaching the base line and bouncing the ball in the same way each time. That will help them to get into a groove.

But while they go through this drill they must be thinking. They must put thought into their second serve, using their first serve as a guide. If the first ball was too long, the racket must be brought into the ball sooner to pull the second serve down. And if the first serve finished in the net, the racket has to be swung farther out to carry the second ball deeper.

Most of the time when I'm serving I try to penetrate my opponent's weakness. Normally, the more his weakness is attacked the more errors he will make. Once in a while, however, I will serve to his strength in an attempt to stop him from getting set for one particular shot. I do this especially on my second serve.

People can remember that over the years Pancho Segura was devastating with his forehand, and yet, throughout my career, I felt I won many points serving to his forehand, simply because he crowded his backhand, opening up the whole of his forehand court. It was a calculated risk which a lot of players wouldn't have taken. It is very dangerous playing into as great a shot as Segura's forehand.

Too many players follow their serves into the net irrespective of some factors that should discourage them. You must assess your serve and your opponent's ground strokes before gambling everything on a rush to the net. If your serves are falling short it is suicidal to follow them in. You must wait for the ball on which you can be more offensive.

The other guy's return of service may be extremely accurate. In that case you'll have to wait longer and try to maneuver yourself into a more aggressive position. Of course, you may have no ground strokes at all. Then you haven't much choice: You are safest at the net.

Wind and sun can pose problems for players of all standards. I wish I knew the answers. The only attitude to take on a windy day is to concentrate harder and make allowance for the strength of the wind. In serving into the wind, naturally you have to hit harder to get the ball deeper. Hitting with the wind, you ease up on your shot, allowing the wind to carry the ball to a good depth. It's not a bad idea to shorten the service action. There will be less risk then of mistiming.

As for finding yourself looking directly into the sun when serving, all I can suggest is that you adjust your stance to the right or the left. The fact is that the wind and the sun, and all other weather conditions, affect both players. Accept

this from the start. Try to use the conditions to the best of your ability, and don't allow them to upset you. What it really comes down to is strength of character.

Some players feel that confidence in the whole of their game hinges mainly on their serving. I don't know why this should necessarily be so, unless all they have is a big service. Confidence, to my mind, comes from hitting the ball in the middle of the racket and executing winning shots.

But I agree that a bad spell of serving in the middle of a match can break a player's morale. If he can't get his first serve into play he becomes that much more apprehensive. What ought he to do?

Well, he must concentrate more and look more intensely at the ball. Sometimes a player will take his eyes off the ball before it is struck; this is the cause of numerous faults. He must stretch up for the ball at its highest point as he swings. And, if necessary, he must ease up on the power. It sounds obvious, but many players don't seem to realize that you must get the serve in to have a chance. A slower serve is better than a cannonball that never goes in.

Be careful of foot faults, which occur more frequently in club tennis than is generally realized. The most common foot faults are usually caused by lack of concentration—perhaps by a player unthinkingly walking up and stepping on the line as he serves. If you form a habit of deliberately placing your left foot two or three inches behind the base line you will avoid this.

Other foot faults are caused by the left big toe, as it bears the weight, turning onto the line; by the left foot creeping onto the line; and by taking a small, steadying step onto the line. These faults can be eliminated if you step back as much as four to six inches behind the base line before serving.

I doubt whether I have been foot faulted more than a dozen times during my career. My left foot is very firm. I know that I can place it within half an inch of the line without risking a foot fault.

When I started playing the game the rules forbade the back foot from crossing the line before impact, and I must have been foot faulted about a half-dozen times on this clause. I solved the problem by stepping back six inches. Now, of course, the rule doesn't operate.

Height is a great advantage in serving, for it allows a player to hit the ball with greater angle. A tall man has this extra angle and he can hit the ball harder with a greater margin of safety.

The smaller man has to put spin on the ball to get it to hook into the court. He thereby loses power. Two small men who've developed great serves are Rod Laver and a player of the past, Bobby Riggs. Jaroslav Drobny, wasn't too tall, either. Lew Hoad, who has a fine serve, is five feet eleven inches, but most of the best servers are at least six feet. I stand a little over six feet three inches and Barry MacKay is about six feet four inches.

Change of pace in serving is often worth a few points. The receiver may be standing a foot or two behind the base line waiting for the fast first serve. A slower, spinning ball may catch him by surprise and give you a little more time to close in on the net. If, however, he has quick reflexes and a strong return of service you are taking a risk. He will be away ahead of the ball, unworried by the change of pace.

One of the curious aspects in many long sets between two good servers is that finally, when there's a break, the other player breaks back immediately. Although it causes excitement in the gallery, it shouldn't really happen. The player who has the set in his grip by breaking through first either relaxes from overconfidence or suffers a mild letdown. The pressure has built up while the games were going with service and when, after sustained effort, he takes his opponent's service, he has a nervous reaction, missing volleys that up till then he's been putting away. The answer is to concentrate harder, move in more quickly to a volley and watch the ball like a hawk.

When you get into this position of having victory within your grasp you must call on all your "killer" instinct and try to close out the match without the loss of a point. Don't relax on the first point when you are serving at 5–4, 9–8 or whatever the score is. Move in immediately

and close out the set as quickly as you can. Then concentrate even harder in the second set, because overconfidence and lack of concentration will automatically become a hazard, causing you to drop service early in the set.

So often your strategy in serving must be governed by the state of the game and the ability of your opponent. At 5–4, for instance, you might feel that it's important to get to the net more quickly, so you serve a little more slowly, providing yourself with more time in which to go forward and make a sound volley.

It pays always to be offensive with the first service, because an attacking delivery gives you two chances of winning the point. But in a tough match, when I can see my opponent is tired, I may try to conserve my energy by discarding my cannonball and making sure my first serve goes in. The fact that he is weary means that my opponent will have just as much trouble returning a consistent first service—even though it lacks my full power.

A number of present-day players have developed the habit of holding only one ball when they serve. I cannot see any merit in it. Most players can hold two balls in one hand quite comfortably, and with practice, it becomes easy to retain one ball while throwing the other into the air.

Those who keep one ball in the pocket of their shorts may be creating a pressure on a leg muscle, causing them to get cramp or tire that particular muscle much faster than muscles in other parts of the body.

As for throwing one ball aside when the first ball is good, I don't know that it is fair to the opponent. Some umpires rightly have ruled interference when this has been done.

New balls in a match, or balls that become wet and heavy, demand added concentration. It is an advantage to have new balls to serve, because they travel about one-tenth faster. A wet, heavier ball will drop as much as five or six feet shorter than a dry ball. One has to concentrate on hitting through it with the center of the racket in order to get it deeper.

It shouldn't be beyond anyone to develop a strong service as long as he sets out observing the right principles. Women have more difficulty because they are not as strong physically. A little girl is more content playing with dolls and dresses and helping round the house than in building up her muscles. Boys meanwhile play sports such as baseball, basketball and, in Britain, cricket, in which they use a motion that can be incorporated later into a tennis service. Consequently, when they start playing tennis, boys find it more natural to serve than girls. And, of course, they have stronger forearms anyway. Wrist action, as I have said, is important in generating service power.

All of us in trying to improve our service will occasionally serve double faults. They needn't be discouraging. I have served many in my time, not because of a fault in my swing or any nervousness, but through aiming for the lines and the corners. I have great confidence in my service and I figure that going for the lines pays off. Don't, therefore, be distracted by double faults, if you are trying to play boldly.

Finally, never serve in a lazy manner when practicing. Serving hard over the years will develop those muscles that are used in serving. Practice as often as you can, hitting your serves to the corners and lines, and slicing the ball off short to the forehand. Have confidence in this and every other serve so that in a match you know exactly what you can do with each ball. Your game will grow accordingly.

The Hoodoo Shot: A Left-hander's Backhand

by ROD LAVER

It was a truism in tennis that left-handers had weak backhands—that they couldn't hit out with topspin—until Rod Laver came along. Here is how Rocket Rod and his coach, Charlie Hollis, developed the backhand that broke down the serve and volley specialists.

CHARLIE Hollis always taught the backhand before the forehand, the volley, the lob, or the smash because he said it was an easier shot to learn than any of these. Charlie, a keen student of young boys, saw that the sequence in which you progressed from stroke to stroke was important. He aimed to produce a master tennis player, but the parts had to be assembled in a certain order or the whole machine would fall apart.

He used to say that it was nonsense for beginners to be afraid of the backhand, as 90 percent of ordinary players were. In the beginning, both right-handers and left-handers have difficulties with the shot, and it often remains suspect long after all the other strokes have been mastered. Novices try to run round the ball to play it on the forehand rather than take it on the backhand, but to Charlie the forehand is a much harder stroke to control than the backhand.

"It is true that there has never been a left-hander with a really strong backhand," he said. "Norman Brookes, Jaroslav Drobny, Neale Fraser, and all the others failed to make their backhand reliable enough to withstand sustained pressure on it. None of them used it as a shot to hit outright winners. There has never been one left-hander in the whole history of the game whose backhand was not suspect. We're going to work and work and work and make you the first left-hander whose backhand is completely invulnerable to attack. Are you with me? Good."

At the start, my backhand didn't appeal to Charlie at all. The foundation on which he rebuilt my backhand began with the ready position he outlined in one of his first lessons. Next came footwork, getting the opposite foot across the body and a little in front of it so that you turned sideways on to the net. In my case, this meant thrusting my left foot across, but to right-handers it meant that the shot was played off the right foot. "Why defend on the backhand when you can attack?" he said, and he would support this by hammering away a great backhand.

By the time the foot was across, knee bent, weight switched to this side, the top hand had pushed the racket down to the backhand side from the ready position and the fingers were starting to close on the handle in the backhand grip.

297

Today, to give more control, I use a backhand grip which is a quarter turn round the handle from the Eastern grip, about midway between the Eastern and the Continental grips. This places my palm on top of the handle of the racket instead of against its side. My wrist is not on top of the racket as it would be in the true Continental grip, but is slightly behind it. To brace the shot, I move the thumb up along the back of the racket: there is no question that this improves my control.

Charlie stood out in front of the class, with all of us in the ready position. At his call of "backhand," we would step to our backhand side, knees bent, and as we took the racket back we would slip the grip from the Eastern so that the thumb came up the back. The racket would swung back low down between our knees and the ground, with the racket arm rigid.

Then Charlie would walk down the class, checking each of our grips to make sure we had made the switch from the true Eastern grip. In two lessons the whole class mastered the change in grip. Nevertheless, any time our backhand missed, the first thing Charlie looked for was whether we had the right grip for the shot.

The crucial stage of the backhand after you have learned the right grip is the backswing. In fact, the backswing causes more errors than any other factor. The backswing puts the racket on the various levels of the ball and also supplies the power. Take the racket back properly and you are well on the way to executing the shot fluently. But you cannot take the racket back at the correct level unless you have your feet in the correct position.

At the top of the backswing for the backhand, open the face of the racket so that you can take a full swing at the ball without discomfort. Don't try to block your backhand shots; hit them.

Immediately we reached the stage where we were ready to hit the ball, Charlie introduced us to spin, despite the fact that up to now we had not had lessons on the forehand, smash, lob, or volley. There are three basic ways of hitting a tennis ball: (a) flat, which is straight ahead with the racket face; (b) topspin or overspin, which is hitting from under the ball, rolling the strings over the top on impact; and (c) backspin, which is achieved by chopping under the ball. Right from the start Charlie advocated topspin.

"Mugs hit over the ball; champions hit from under it," he said. "The secret of the champion is his command of spin."

Then he made sure all of the class was comfortably seated, and proceeded to explain how the ball bounces with the three types of spin. A flat shot bounces straight through. Topspin forces the ball to dip low over the net and keep low on impact, making your opponent hit up with his return. Backspin makes the ball lift after bouncing. The amount of spin you can get on the ball depends mostly on the strength of your wrist. Keep squeezing that squash ball!

Once we understood how the ball reacted to the three methods of applying the racket head to it, we were allowed to hit the ball with our first ground shot, taking the racket through to complete the backhand. We had to hit through the ball and not chip at it as many beginners do.

The wrist is bent for the backswing, but at the moment of impact the entire racket arm forms a straight line, with the wrist tightly locked. Your weight is on the back foot for the backswing but shifts to the front foot as you strike the ball and follow through with a smooth, flowing swing.

Left-handers and most women tend to make contact with the ball with a slightly inclined (or tilted) racket face.

When we Laver boys were not on the court learning these things, we went swimming or fishing or kangaroo shooting with our dad or our uncle. I must admit I did not have much interest in school; all I lived for was the open-air life of sport and Charlie Hollis's coaching sessions. Spearfishing as a sport had just been discovered, and we boys used to go in off the reefs after the big fish that abound in that part of the Pacific.

The strange thing was that although we all loved the sun on our backs, we all suffered badly from sunburn because we were so fair-skinned. For years I tried all sorts of creams and lotions to try and protect my face while I was out on the court practicing. One or two of the creams were torture because you could not sweat inside them and your face baked inside the skin it formed. Finally I discovered a cream which enabled me to perspire freely without burning up, but even now every time I play in a strong sun I have to apply it carefully.

There were dozens of Lavers all over North Queensland, and they were all tireless, freckle-faced tennis fanatics. At weekends dad and mum and all the family would drive to friends' properties for a game, and I got used to people playing to my backhand every chance they got. A weak backhand is, of course, the first thing tennis players the world over look for in a strange opponent.

Dad was very pleased with the progress all the pupils in Charlie Hollis's Rockhampton tennis school were making, because he was the one who had instigated the formation of the school and had got Charlie appointed as coach. Before he came to Rockhampton, Charlie had coached all over northern New South Wales and at Theodore in northern Queensland, where he taught Mal Anderson. It must have been very satisfying for him years later when Mal and I were in the Australian Davis Cup team at the same time.

After he had taught me the basic backhand swing, the next step was to get me hitting a flat backhand, taking the racket head through the ball instead of chipping it. I had a little trouble for a while finding the grip with the thumb up the back, but because of his army-style drills I finally found it automatically whenever I switched to the backhand side.

"Now this is how Donald Budge played the backhand," he would say, and then demonstrate a lovely, smooth-flowing swing. He had studied Budge and all the other great players who visited Australian from grandstands in Sydney and Melbourne. Years later when I played against Budge his backhand was identical to the one Charlie had showed us.

I have always been described as a wristy tennis player, probably because Charlie taught us topspin shots almost from the start. But as I am a comparatively short, wiry player I must have something to match the power of the big fellows. My spin does just this for me.

To give my backhand speed and power

Charlie showed me how to take the ball on the rise—before it reached the top of its bounce—so that I could use some of the speed imparted to the ball by my opponent. I loved to experiment, to try new shots, even if this meant losing control of the ball.

Not to brag, I really enjoyed learning the variations of the backhand, whacking it across court or down the side line as Charlie called the shots. I had been playing to the very natural strategy of hitting the ball as far away from my opponent as possible, but now I started on something a little more subtle: Tricking the character on the other side of the net to go the wrong way.

To smack a backhand down the line, you delay your swing and hit the ball just a fraction behind the hip. For cross-court shots, you hit the ball a trifle ahead of the front foot, hitting up from under the ball in a brushing motion if you want topspin. In competition, you often have to hit cross-court backhands as your opponent drives deep into the corner. You have to hit the ball on the run, and you have to hit it hard to make sure that you pass him and that he does not put away the volley he has followed in to the net to make. Don't let it worry you, though, because the cross-court shot is the most natural of the backhand shots. The down-the-line variety is hardest, because you have to let the ball get a little past you for it.

Some of those little fellows whose parents burden them with the leaden rackets I told you about find they can't swing the racket with one hand on the backhand side. This is why the old maestro John Bromwich and fellows like Pancho Segura took to the two-handed stroke. They got amazing control with it, but I don't recommend it for youngsters. Segura reckons he was such an undernourished, spindly kid he just had to use two fists to get the ball back. Never scold or punish a kid for using two hands; he is doing it from an instinctive desire to get more control over the racket. Instead, give him a lighter racket that he can swing with one hand.

When I was thirteen Charlie entered me in the Under-Fourteen State Championships at Brisbane. The week before the tournament started he sent me to Bundaberg to let me get my eye in and my strokes grooved in an under-nineteen tournament.

"Don't come back to Rockhampton without that State title, Rodney," he said, as I left for Brisbane. "Whoever beats you will be the winner."

"All right, Mr. Hollis."

Thanks to the warm-up at Bundaberg I was lucky enough to win the State Championship, and when I got home Charlie was the happiest man in town.

"How'd you play, Rodney?" he asked.

"My backhand was really bad, Mr. Hollis. It let me down. If the other kids hadn't been so bad I'd never have won."

"We'll start work on it first thing in the morning. We're going to get you the best backhand in the world."

That's how it was with Charles. No sooner had you learned a shot than you had to pull it apart and start all over again.

The Inner Game

by TIM GALLWEY

It's debatable who was more surprised when Inner Tennis *became the bestselling tennis book of all time— author Tim Gallwey or the tennis teaching establishment. Gallwey, a teaching pro, never made it as a top player and always wondered why. Here he tells of how he discovered the answer . . . the Inner Game.*

ONE day when I was teaching a group of men at John Gardiner's Tennis Ranch in Carmel Valley, California, a businessman realized how much more power and control he got on his backhand when his racket was taken back below the level of the ball. He was so enthusiastic about his "new" stroke that he rushed to tell his friend Jack about it as if some kind of miracle had occurred. Jack, who considered his erratic backhand one of the major problems of his life, came rushing up to me during the lunch hour, exclaiming, "I've always had a terrible backhand. Maybe you can help me."

I asked, "What's so terrible about your backhand?"

"I take my racket back too high on my backswing."

"How do you know?"

"Because at least five different pros have told me so. I just haven't been able to correct it."

For a brief moment I was aware of the absurdity of the situation. Here was a business executive who controlled large commercial enterprises of great complexity asking me for help as if he had no control over his own right arm. Why wouldn't it be possible, I wondered, to give him the simple reply, "Sure, I can help you. L–o–w–e–r y–o–u–r r–a–c–k–e–t!"

But complaints such as Jack's are common among people of all levels of intelligence and proficiency. Besides, it was clear that at least five other pros had told him to lower his racket without much effect. What was keeping him from doing it I wondered.

I asked Jack to take a few swings on the patio where we were standing. His backswing started back very low, but then, sure enough, just before swinging forward it lifted to the level of his shoulder and swung down into the imagined ball. The five pros were right. I asked him to swing several more times without making any comment. "Isn't that better?" he asked. "I tried to keep it low." But each time just before swinging forward, his racket lifted; it was obvious that had he been hitting an actual ball, the underspin imparted by the downward swing would have caused it to sail out.

"Your backhand is all right," I said reassuringly. "It's just going through some changes.

301

Why don't you take a closer look at it." We walked over to a large windowpane and there I asked him to swing again while watching his reflection. He did so, again taking his characteristic hitch at the back of his swing, but this time he was astounded. "Hey, I really do take my racket back high! It goes up above my shoulder!" There was no judgment in his voice; he was just reporting with amazement what his eyes had seen.

What surprised me was Jack's surprise. Hadn't he said that five pros had told him his racket was too high? I was certain that if I had told him the same thing after his first swing, he would have replied, "Yes, I know." But what was now clear was that he didn't *really* know, since no one is ever surprised at seeing something they already know. Despite all those lessons, he had never *directly* experienced his racket going back high. His mind had been so absorbed in the process of judgment and trying to change this "bad" stroke that he had never perceived the stroke itself.

Looking in the glass which mirrored his stroke as it was, Jack was able to keep his racket low quite effortlessly as he swung again. "That feels entirely different than any backhand I've ever swung," he declared. By now he was swinging up through the ball over and over again. Interestingly, he wasn't congratulating himself for doing it right; he was simply absorbed in how different it *felt*.

After lunch I threw Jack a few balls and he was able to remember how the stroke felt and to repeat the action. This time he just felt where his racket was going, letting his sense of feel replace the visual image offered by the mirror. It was a new experience for him. Soon he was consistently hitting topspin backhands into the court with an effortlessness that made it appear this was his natural swing. In ten minutes he was feeling "in the groove," and he paused to express his gratitude. "I can't tell you how much I appreciate what you've done for me. I've learned more in ten minutes from you than in twenty hours of lessons I've taken on my backhand." I could feel something inside me begin to puff up as it absorbed these "good" words. At the same time, I didn't know quite how to handle this lavish compliment, and found myself hemming and hawing, trying to come up with an appropriately modest reply. Then, for a moment, my mind turned off and I realized that I hadn't given Jack a single instruction on his backhand! I thanked him for his praise, and then asked, "But what did I teach you?" He was quiet for a full half-minute, trying to remember what I had told him. Finally he said, "I can't remember your telling me anything! You were just watching me, but I sure learned a lot." He had learned without being taught.

I can't describe how good I felt at that moment, or why. Tears even began to come to my eyes. I had learned and he had learned, but there was no one there to take credit. There was only the glimmer of a realization that we were both participating in a wonderful process.

The key that unlocked Jack's new backhand —which was really there all the time just waiting to be let out—was that in the instant he stopped trying to change his backhand, he saw it as it was. At first, with the aid of the mirror, he directly *experienced* his backswing. Without thinking or analyzing, he increased his awareness of that part of his swing. When the mind is free of any thought or judgment, it is still and acts like a perfect mirror. Then and only then can we know things as they are. In the game of tennis there are two important things to know. The first is where the ball is. The second is where the racket head is. From the time anyone begins to learn tennis, he is told the importance of watching the ball. It's very simple: You come to know where the ball is by looking at it. You don't have to think, "Oh, here comes the ball; it's clearing the net by about one foot and coming pretty fast. It should bounce near the base line, and I'd better hit it on the rise." No, you simply watch the ball and let the proper response take place.

In the same way, you don't have to think about where your racket head *should* be, but you should realize the importance of being aware of where the racket head *is* at all times. You can't look at it to know where it is because you're watching the ball. You must *feel* it. Feeling it gives you the knowledge of where it is. Knowing where it *should be* isn't feeling where it is. Knowing what your racket *didn't do* isn't feeling where it is. *Feeling* where it is is *knowing* where it is.

No matter what a person's complaint when he has a lesson with me, I have found that the most beneficial first step is to encourage him to *see* and *feel* what he is doing—that is, to increase his awareness of *what actually is.* I follow the same process when my own strokes get out of their groove. But to see things as they are, we must take off our judgmental glasses, whether they're dark or rose-tinted. This action unlocks a process of natural development which is as surprising as it is beautiful.

For example, suppose that a player complains that the timing on his forehand is off. I wouldn't give him an analysis of what is wrong and then instruct him, "Take your racket back sooner," or "Hit the ball farther out in front of you." Instead I might simply ask him to put his attention on where his racket head is at the moment the ball bounces on his side of the net. Since this is not a common instruction, it is likely that the player will never have been told anything about where his racket should or shouldn't be at that particular moment. If his judgmental mind is engaged, he is likely to become a little nervous, since Self 1 likes to try to do things "right" and is nervous when he doesn't know the rightness or wrongness of a particular action. So at once the player may ask where his racket should be when the ball is bouncing. But I decline to say, asking him only to observe where his racket *is* at that moment.

After he hits a few balls, I ask him to tell me where his racket was at the moment in question. The typical reply is, "I'm taking my racket back too late. I know what I'm doing wrong, but I can't stop it." This is a common response of players of all sports, and is the cause of a great deal of frustration.

"Forget about right and wrong for now," I suggest. "Just observe your racket at the moment of bounce." After five or ten more balls are hit to him, the player is likely to reply, "I'm doing better; I'm getting it back earlier."

"Yes, and where was your racket?" I ask.

"I don't know, but I think I was getting it back on time . . . wasn't I?"

Uncomfortable without a standard for right and wrong, the judgmental mind makes up standards of its own. Meanwhile, attention is taken off what *is* and placed on the process of trying to do things right. Even though he may be getting his racket back earlier and is hitting the ball more solidly, he is still in the dark about where his racket is. (If the player is left in this state, thinking that he has found the "secret" to his problem —that is, getting his racket back earlier—he will be momentarily pleased. He will go out eagerly to play and repeat to himself before hitting every forehand, "Get it back early, get it back early, get it back early . . ." For a while this magic phrase will seem to produce "good" results. But after a while, he will start missing again in spite of his self-reminder, will wonder what's going "wrong" and will come back to the pro for another tip.)

So instead of stopping the process at the point where the player is judging positively, I again ask him to observe his racket and to tell me exactly where it is at the moment of bounce. As the player finally lets himself observe his racket with detachment and interest, he can feel what it is actually doing and his awareness increases. Then, without any effort to correct, he will discover that his swing has begun to develop a natural rhythm. In fact, he will find the perfect rhythm for himself, which may be slightly different from what might be dictated by some universal standard called "correct." Then when he goes out to play, he has no magic phrase that must be repeated, and can concentrate without thinking.

What I have tried to illustrate is that there is a natural learning process which operates within everyone—if it is allowed to. This process is waiting to be discovered by all those who do not know of its existence. There is no need to take my word for it; it can be discovered for yourself if it hasn't been already. If it has been experienced, trust it. To discover this natural learning process, it is necessary to let go of the old process of *correcting* faults; that is, it is necessary to let go of judgment and see what happens. Will your strokes develop under the effect of noncritical attention or won't they? Test this.

Before finishing with the subject of the judgmental mind, something needs to be said about "positive thinking." The "bad" effects of negative thinking are frequently discussed these days. Books and articles advise readers to replace negative thinking with positive thinking. People are advised to stop telling themselves they are ugly, uncoordinated, unhappy, or whatever, and to repeat to themselves that they are attractive, well coordinated and happy. The substituting of a kind of "positive hypnotism" for a previous habit of "negative hypnotism" may appear at least to have short-range benefits, but I have always found that the honeymoon ends all too soon.

One of the first lessons I learned as a teaching pro was not to find fault with any pupil or even his strokes. So I stopped criticizing either. Instead, I would compliment the pupil when I could, and make only positive suggestions about how to correct his strokes. Some time later, I found myself no longer complimenting my students. The realization that preceded this change occurred one day when I was giving a group of women a lesson on footwork.

I had made a few introductory remarks about self-criticism when Clare, one of the women, asked, "I can understand that negative thinking is harmful, but what about complimenting yourself when you do well? What about positive thinking?" My answer to her was vague— "Well, I don't think positive thinking is as harmful as negative thinking"—but during the lesson that followed, I came to see the issue more clearly.

At the beginning of the lesson, I told the women that I was going to hit each of them six running forehands, and that I wanted them simply to become aware of their feet. "Get in touch with how your feet move getting into position, and whether there is any transfer of weight as you hit the ball." I told them that there was no right and wrong to think about; they were only to observe their own footwork with full attention. While I hit the balls to them, I made no comments. I watched intently what was happening before my eyes, but expressed no judgment either positive or negative. Similarly, the women

were quiet, watching each other without comment. They each seemed absorbed in the simple process of experiencing the movement of their feet.

After the series of thirty balls, I noticed that there were no balls at the net; they were all bunched together in the cross-court area on my side. "Look," I said, "all the balls are together in the corner, and not one at the net." Although semantically this remark was simply an observation of fact, my tone of voice revealed that I was pleased with what I saw. I was complimenting them, and indirectly I was complimenting myself as their instructor.

To my surprise, the girl who was due to hit next said, "Oh, you would have to say that just before my turn!" Though she was half-kidding, I could see that she was a little nervous. I repeated the same instructions as before and hit thirty more balls without comment. This time there were frowns appearing on the women's faces and their footwork seemed a little more awkward than before. After the thirtieth ball, there were eight balls at the net and the balls behind me were quit scattered.

Inwardly I criticized myself for having spoiled the magic. Then Clare, the girl who had originally asked me about positive thinking, exclaimed, "Oh, I ruined it for everyone. I was the first to hit a ball into the net, and I hit four of them." I was amazed, as were the others, because it wasn't true. It was another person who had netted the first ball, and Clare had hit only two balls into the net. Her judgmental mind had distorted her perception of what had actually happened.

Then I asked the women if they were aware of something different going through their minds during the second series of balls. Each of them reported being less aware of their feet and more intent on trying to keep from hitting balls into the net. They were trying to live up to an expectation, a standard of right and wrong, which they felt had been set before them. This was exactly what had been missing during the first set of balls. I began to see that my compliment had engaged their judgmental minds. Self 1, the ego-mind, had gotten into the act.

Through this experience, I began to see how Self 1 operated. Always looking for approval and wanting to avoid disapproval, this subtle ego-mind sees a compliment as a potential criticism. He reasons, "If the pro is pleased with one kind of performance, he will be displeased by the opposite. If he likes me for doing well, he will dislike me for not doing well." The standard of good and bad had been established, and the inevitable result was divided concentration and ego-interference.

The women also began to realize the cause of their tightness on the third round of balls. Then Clare seemed to light up like a thousand-watt bulb. "Oh, I see!" she exclaimed, slapping her hand to her forehead. "Compliments are criticisms in disguise! Both are used to manipulate behavior, and compliments are just more socially acceptable!" Whereupon she ran off the court saying she had to find her husband. Evidently she had seen the connection between what she had learned on the tennis court and some other aspect of her life which was important to her, for an hour later I saw her with her husband, still absorbed in intense conversation.

Clearly, positive and negative evaluations are relative to each other. It is impossible to judge one event as positive without seeing other events as not positive or as negative. There is no way to stop just the negative side of the judgmental process. To see your strokes as they are, there is no need to attribute goodness or badness to them. The same goes for the results of your strokes. You can notice exactly how far out a ball lands without labeling it a "bad" event. By ending judgment, you do not avoid seeing what is. Ending judgment means you neither add nor subtract from the facts before your eyes. Things appear as they are—undistorted. In this way, the mind becomes more calm.

"But," protests Self 1, "if I see my ball going out and I don't evaluate it as bad, I won't have any incentive to change it. If I don't dislike what I'm doing wrong, how am I going to change it?" Self 1, the ego-mind, wants to take responsibility for making things "better." He wants the credit for playing an important role in things. He also

worries and suffers a lot when things don't go his way.

Before concluding, read this profound but deceptively simple story told me by a much respected friend of mine named Bill.

Three men in a car are driving down a city street early one morning. For the sake of analogy, suppose that each man represents a different kind of tennis player. The man sitting on the right is a positive thinker who believes that his game is great and is full of self-esteem because his tennis is so superior. He's also a self-admitted playboy who enjoys all the good things of life. The man sitting in the middle is a negative thinker who is constantly analyzing what is wrong with himself and his game. He is always involved in some kind of self-improvement program. The third man, who is driving, is in the process of letting go of value judgments altogether. He plays the Inner Game, enjoying things as they are and doing what seems sensible at the moment.

The car pulls up at a stop light, and crossing the street in front of the car is a beautiful young lady who catches the attention of all three men. Her beauty is particularly apparent because she is wearing no clothes.

The man on the right becomes engrossed in thoughts of how nice it would be to be with this lady under other circumstances. His mind races through past memories and future fantasies of sensual pleasures. As he reminds himself what a great lover he is, he breathes heavily, causing fog to form on the windshield and slightly dimming the view for the others.

The man sitting in the middle is seeing an example of modern decadence. He's not sure that he should be looking closely at the girl. First miniskirts, he thinks, then topless dancers, then bottomless dancers, and now they're out on the streets in broad daylight! Something must be done to stop all this! He thinks that he should begin by straightening out the playboy on his right.

The driver is seeing the same girl that the others are observing, but is simply watching what is before his eyes. Since his ego is uninvolved, he sees neither good nor bad, and as a result, a detail comes to his attention which was not noticed by either of his companions: The girl's eyes are shut. He realizes that the lady is sleepwalking, and his response is immediate and uncalculating. He stops the car, steps out and puts his coat over the woman's shoulders. He gently wakes her and explains to her that she must have been sleepwalking and offers to take her home.

My friend Bill used to end the story with a twinkle in his eye, saying, "There he received the rewards of his action," leaving each listener to hear what he would.

The first inner skill to be developed in the Inner Game is that of nonjudgmental awareness. When we "unlearn" judgment we discover, usually with some surprise, that we don't need the motivation of a reformer to change our "bad" habits. There is a more natural process of learning and performing waiting to be discovered.

Common Myths and Key Fundamentals

by VIC BRADEN and BILL BRUNS

Vic Braden is not your average teaching pro—he has more than twenty years of experience, a doctorate in pyschology and a sense of humor. Somehow that all adds up to a common-sense approach to tennis that makes the game both more fun and more easily learned for players at all levels. Here are some of his "secrets."

IF you're like many tennis players, the chances are good that you can't control the shots you brag about in the locker room, nor are you likely to master those shots you see the pros try to hit—sharply angled cross-court drives, topspin lobs, underspin dropshots, service returns at your opponent's feet. So let's be honest. Cut out the fancy thinking and just concentrate on mastering the basic fundamentals. *Learn to hit the same old boring shot and you'll beat most of the people who now beat you.*

If you can learn to hit the ball deep and down the middle—and keep it in play—that's all the strategy you'll need to know to beat 99 percent of the players in the world. Trying to play this way may sound a little dull—"I want to do something *big* out there"—but believe me, you'll never get bored with winning. I've never heard anyone complain, "Nuts, I won again."

Before I delve into specific stroke production, I feel it's important to provide an overview of the game that will help make my approach to these strokes—and strategy—more meaningful. First, I will explore some of the physiological and psychological reasons why people don't improve. Second, I will try to refute entrenched myths that keep people from playing better tennis. And third, I will present the fundamentals that I regard as crucial to a sound tennis game.

Learning Blocks

Parents often ask me how competitive they should be when they play tennis against their children. I tell them, "Beat their brains out because in two or three years they'll be murdering you and you'll want to have something nice to remember." Most youngsters who get hooked on tennis are not afraid to make changes that will improve their games. But adults are thinking, "Gee, I've only got about thirty years left— maybe I'd better not mess around with my swing." They work desperately *not to look bad* by sticking with what is comfortable, rather than pushing through that awkward, frustrating period of making corrections that will eventually help them look good *and* win.

Thus, when you begin to work on a different grip or a new stroke, you will learn to play a much better game of tennis if you can remember

307

one thing: *Try to feel good about feeling crummy* because the crummy feeling that accompanies new and accurate strokes is going to make you famous.

No matter how uniquely you may swing, making changes in that swing is always painful because you must break muscle-memory patterns; you're going against what has become comfortable for you to do and what is ingrained, even if you've only played the game five or six months. We have people at the tennis college who give us 185 moves on their forehand, but when we try to make one basic correction that cuts off 110 extraneous moves, they say, "Boy, that is really awkward." Yet that uncomfortable feeling that accompanies the correct swing is what you must adopt if you hope to correct a bad habit. Even a slight grip change requires a whole new set of muscles. A person will come to the tennis college who has played for twenty-five years, but when we alter his grip an eighth of an inch he gets blisters.

Believe me, I know how grooved a habit can become. When I was giving lessons at the Toledo Tennis Club, one of my adult students had a bad habit of stepping forward with the wrong foot as he swung. I had only been teaching about a year but I figured I knew it all. So I nailed an old tennis shoe to a piece of wood, and pounded through eight-inch spikes to anchor it into the clay court. Then I had the fellow put his back foot in the shoe and take a swing. I wanted him to get the sensation of leaving that foot stationary as he stepped forward with the other. Well, he took one swing and yanked the board right out of the clay court. He also pulled every ligament in his right leg. He was in a cast for a long time and it just about ruined his tennis game. But both of us learned how strong muscle-memory really is. Fortunately he didn't sue me.

Interference by your ego is another hindrance to effecting important changes in your swing. When the pro starts tinkering with what you feel is comfortable, the natural tendency is to think there's something wrong in his method rather than in your swing. Furthermore, every good teaching pro has heard the complaint, "Jeez, I was better before I took lessons." Very

often this is true. No matter what the sport, when you are trying to make corrections, there's always a force trying to bring you back to your old comfort levels. Dr. Joe Sheehan, the UCLA psychologist and speech therapist whose research work related to stutterers, has termed this phenomenon the Approach-Avoidance Conflict: You want to do something the new way but you want to maintain some of the old, and thus you get caught in the middle, vacillating between the two. This can be murder on your tennis game.

For instance, people will spend a week at the tennis college and try hard to solve basic problems in their swing. But when they return home to play their old rival, they may lose 6–0, 6–0, whereas before they lost 6–3, 6–3. It's only natural for them to think, "Boy, I can't wait to get back to my old form and lose 6–3, 6–3." Their ego takes such a beating over the next couple of weeks that unless they have patience and really work hard at grooving these new stroking sensations, they will soon retreat to their same old comfortable swing. The reason they get worse before they get better is that by working on new things, they no longer have a good handle on their old game nor do they have control of their new, and thus they have very spotty performances.

What it really comes down to is this: *If the pain you are suffering in losing to people is greater than the pain of making changes, then you'll try like heck to make the changes.* You'll experiment, you'll have an open mind, you'll concentrate, you won't try to avoid your weaknesses as you polish your strengths—and you'll have a much better future in this game than the average person. Believe me, most people tend to stay the same once they reach a certain level of performance, and you'll be amazed at how quickly you move up to higher playing levels if you can hang in there long enough to get the kinesthetic feeling for your new strokes.

Another deterrent to acquiring good strokes is the myth in tennis that you should "Do what feels natural," since everything that's right feels comfortable. On the contrary, my experience with thousands of students has been that *nearly everything that's natural in tennis turns out to be less desirable.* I can't think of any change in your swing, or even your grip, that will feel natural to begin with. In fact, if I ask a relative beginner to try something new, and he or she does it right on the first or second try, I'm absolutely shocked, for I've only seen this happen two or three times in a thirty-year career of coaching. (This doesn't mean, however, that you can't take a much more relaxed attitude toward a game that's unnatural.)

The reason tennis is such a difficult game to master is that it's natural to roll your wrist over on the forehand instead of keeping it fixed; it's natural to swing on a horizontal plane rather than from low to high; it's natural to play people instead of the ball; it's natural to watch your opponent's shot and to try to confirm your decision about which direction the ball is going rather than react instinctively the instant the ball leaves his racket. If tennis were a natural game, we would have far more people swinging correctly, right from the beginning. Instead, people are flocking to teaching pros because the accurate movements in tennis, in my opinion, are not natural; they have to be learned, and muscle-memory patterns have to be broken down.

Of course, this doesn't mean that if you're unnatural in the beginning you will be awkward in the end. You can learn to play the game with fluid, easy strokes when at first you were stiff and uncomfortable. Yet when somebody tells me immediately after the first trial, "Hey, I tried your stroke—it's fantastic," I know that person probably hasn't really made a change, because if it feels good, it's usually what that person has been doing all along. That's why good pros won't teach "comfort." They won't keep telling you, "If it feels good, keep doing it," unless what you're doing is correct.

Myths and Misconceptions

Nearly everybody brings to the tennis court a great many incorrect impressions about how the game is played—and how well they play. But don't think lightly of these impressions, for they have everything to do with your attitude about the game, your future progress, and even the internal battle with your subconscious.

Believing the Court Is Gigantic

When you stand on the base line, it's only natural to envision the court as a gigantic expanse, with plenty of leeway for your wrap-around follow-through. Instead, you should try to visualize playing on a long, narrow sidewalk with a follow-through that takes your racket out toward your target. Stand on the right base line/side line corner and see for yourself how little you can vary your follow-through when hitting from the base line. Point your racket down the singles side line to a righthander's backhand corner, and then to his forehand corner, and you have moved the direction of your follow-through only 19.1 degrees. From the center stripe, pointing from corner to corner, you still have just 19.6 degrees to play with.

Unfortunately, even though the follow-through for a shot down the line (passing shot) must virtually resemble the follow-through for a cross-court drive, this isn't the way most people swing. When they get their opponent in one corner they think, "Now I've got him!" and they proceed to take a 180-degree swing that pulls the ball ten feet wide. I try to tell them, "You seldom get a chance to play your opponent on the next court."

The Concept of the "Low" Net

People love to talk about the low net. Yet you always see them going up to the net and retrieving their last shot with the cry, "One more inch, Bertha, and I would have killed you." What they don't understand is that in terms of hitting a tennis ball on a horizontal plane, the net is actually very high. When you stand at the base line you must be at least six feet seven inches tall in order to look over the net and see your opponent's base line. This means that 99 percent of us never really see our opponent's court when playing from the base line; we spend our lives looking through those little squares in the net in order to see the ball land.

Therefore, to play this game correctly you must think about *lifting* the ball up over a high barrier. Picture a volleyball net rather than a tennis net, and concentrate on elevating your shots

—with a degree of topspin—so that the ball lands deep in your opponent's court rather than always catching the tape. I've found that an interesting thing happens, psychologically, when you put up a solid net. People suddenly start bending their knees and elevating the ball because they can't even see their opponent's feet, let alone the court. But when you put up the regular net again, they say, "That's better," and they go back to their old horizontal swing. Pretty soon they start taking that thirty-nine-foot trip to the net to pick up the ball.

The Fallacy of Believing in "Net-Skimmers"

Players who continue to visualize a low net simply reinforce one of the most prevalent myths destroying good tennis everywhere: The concept that tennis balls should be hit on a horizontal plane, with hard, line-drive shots the ideal. Interestingly, the pros have an entirely different approach. They know that tennis is not just a driving game, but a lifting game; that to hit the ball hard and still make it come down inside their opponent's court, they must develop an ability to hit topspin while elevating the ball four to six feet over the net when both players are at the base line. The pros also know that balls hit on a horizontal plane also begin to drop sooner than balls hit at the same speed but elevated with topspin.

Thus I'm always amused by the paradox illustrated by the average player who says, "I can't wait to play like a pro and hit those nice low net-skimmers," and the pro who goes into the locker room after a match and moans, "Jeez, I'm playing so crummy. My ball's going so close to the net it's a joke."

The Theory of the Fallible Racket

I've always stressed the point that a tennis ball is really your pal, not your enemy: Most tennis balls are round and they go exactly where you hit them. Unfortunately, if you take the ball on as a pal your ego needs an out, and so your racket becomes the target for all your frustrations and excuses. Tell me it's not true that often when you

hit a truly lousy shot your first instinct is to blame your racket? You pluck the strings or give it the knee test, while muttering, "That doggone guy really sold me a lemon." Sporting-goods dealers have told me that people actually come in and complain, "I'm returning this racket because it has no backhands in it at all."

Let's be realistic. Even at the pro level, it doesn't matter whether you use wood or metal, gut or nylon—the racket will go well beyond your ability level. I've seen Bobby Riggs beat a good player with a broom, and if there's that much resiliency in straw, then gut or nylon is not your problem. In fact, all the great players I've known have only talked about their inability to effect the right stroke pattern. They've never said, "I failed to win the tournament because I had a crummy racket." Sure a $120 racket may give you a little extra juice and make you feel good, but it's not going to help you win matches if you continue to swing improperly. Almost any racket will do what you ask of it if you place it in the right position at the right time. Yet most people place the racket in the wrong position at impact and expect it to produce a winning shot.

"I'm Not Smart Enough to Play Good Tennis"

In talking about the intricacies of technique and tactics for the more advanced player, I sometimes unintentionally scare people off. They start thinking, "I'm not smart enough to do all that. I just want to stay at the base line and try to get a suntan." Thus I always try to assure my students that it doesn't require any exceptional intellect to grasp the basic concepts that can help them beat 95 percent of the tennis population.

I once gave a battery of personality and psychological tests to twenty successful tournament players, hoping I could isolate some of the psychological variables that help make a champion. I thought, for instance, that tennis demanded a lot of high-level intellectual functioning and that the top players were really smarter than we normals. But when my test results came in, IQs ranged from 88 to 144—from educable mentally retarded to gifted. So I start with the assumption that nearly all the readers of this book are in that range, and that you have the ability to understand the most complex, but logical, theory ever promulgated about the game of tennis.

In my view, sophisticated theories about technique and strategy normally have little relevance in tennis. The game ultimately comes down to the basic question: *Do you have the weapons?* If you are at the base line and the ball is hit to your backhand and your opponent rushes the net, you normally have only four options—lob over his head, drive a passing shot down the line, hit the ball cross-court, or try to give him a new navel. You don't need a Ph.D. in tennis to know that whatever option you choose, the real question is: Can you hit a backhand?

Furthermore, physical laws dictate where the ball goes, not your IQ or a coach's "unique" approach. To hit the ball hard and make it land in a particular zone with a certain speed, you must hit with the same speed and ball rotation as everyone else, whether you are Rod Laver or Bertha Finkenbaum. If the racket is placed perfectly and contacts the ball properly, then the ball is going to be on target regardless of your IQ. Better to have quick reactions and an ability to coordinate body movements. For you can be the smartest person in your club, but if you're at the net and the ball is screaming at you a hundred miles an hour, you can forget your swing, your name, everything.

"Okay, Then, I'm Too Uncoordinated"

One of the most common fears in tennis is the feeling by some people that they can't play the game, or they'll never be very good, because they don't have the coordination or an athletic background. Thus I tell all my students, "If you can walk to the drinking fountain without falling over, you have the physical ability to play this game pretty well." I'm always honest about the difficulty everybody will encounter with this game, but I point out that enjoyment and "success" certainly don't need to be measured by how many matches you win or lose. Taking part in a physical activity and striving to improve your strokes—that's what counts. The list of the relatively uncoordinated people who have become fine players simply because they had the desire and the hunger to learn to play the game properly is endless.

Adults are always coming to the tennis college who claim they have no athletic ability whatsoever, and who give us the impression they're going to buy an ice cream cone and stick it against their forehead on the way to their mouth. But when they get out on the court they are terrifically coordinated and they have tons of fun. When we talk to them about this we usually discover that ever since high school they have been suffering from a delusion that they were athletic failures. "I never made the high school team," they will say, almost apologetically. But they've been comparing themselves with the super jocks—the upper 2 percent of the population—when they should have compared themselves to the average person.

It's tragic to see people who live in mortal fear of looking bad athletically, who think that nobody can have fun playing with them, or that they have to hit the ball well in order to really enjoy the game. I try to tell these people, "So you lose? So you don't play as well as you want to play? So what—you're still running around, you're getting some sun, you're meeting new people, you're having fun. That's what the game is all about."

PART IV
THE IMAGINARY GAME

"Maybe for the first time in my life, I guess, I found out that it was only a game we were playing—only that and no more. And I began to realize what my old man and I had done to that game. All that time, all those years, I had only been trying to grow up and he had been trying to keep young, and we'd both done it on the tennis court."

—from *Tennis* by Roger Angell

The Tennis Court

by PAUL THEROUX

The tennis court can be a war ground and, as some club members learn, the vanquished often return to be victorious.

EVERYONE hated Shimura; but no one really knew him: Shimura was Japanese. He was not a member of the club. About every two weeks he would stop one night in Ayer Hitam on his way to Singapore. He spent the day in Singapore and stopped again on the way back. Using us—which was how Evans put it—he was avoiding two nights at an expensive hotel. I say he wasn't in our club; yet he had full use of the facilities, because he was a member of the Selangor Club in Kuala Lumpur and we had reciprocal privileges. Seeing his blue Toyota appear in the driveway, Evans always said, "Here comes the freeloader."

Squibb said, "I say, there's a nip in the air."

And Alec said, "Shoot him down."

I didn't join them in their bigoted litany. I liked Shimura. I was ashamed of myself for not actively defending him, but I was sure he didn't need my help.

That year there were hundreds of Japanese businessmen in Kuala Lumpur selling transistor radios to the Malays. It seemed a harmless enough activity, but the English resented them

and saw them as poaching on what they considered an exclusively British preserve. Evans said, "I didn't fight the war so that those people could tell us how to run our club."

Shimura was a tennis player. On his fifth or sixth visit he had suggested, in a way his stuttering English had blunted into a tactless complaint, that the ball boys moved around too much.

"They must stand quiet."

It was the only thing he had ever said, and it damned him. Typical Japanese attitude, people said, treating our ball boys like prisoners of war. Tony Evans, chairman of the tennis committee, found it unforgivable. He said to Shimura, "There are courts in Singapore," but Shimura only laughed.

He seemed not to notice that he was hated. His composure was perfect. He was a small dark man, fairly young, with ropes of muscle knotted on his arms and legs, and his crouch on the court made him seem four-legged. He played a hard darting game with a towel wound around his neck like a scarf; he barked loudly when he hit the ball.

He always arrived late in the afternoon, and before dinner played several sets with anyone who happened to be around. Alec had played him, so had Eliot and Strang; he had won every match. Evans, the best player in the club, refused to meet him on the tennis court. If there was no one to play, Shimura hit balls against the wooden backboard, barking at the hard ones, and he practiced with such determination you could hear his grunts as far as the reading room. He ate alone and went to bed early. He spoke to no one; he didn't drink. I sometimes used to think that if he had spent some time in the bar, like the other temporary members who passed through Ayer Hitam, Shimura would have no difficulty.

Alec said, "Not very clubbable."

"Ten to one he's fiddling his expenses," said Squibb.

Evans criticized his lob.

He could not have been hated more. His nationality, his size, his stinginess, his laugh, his choice of tennis partners (once he had played Eliot's sexually browsing wife)—everything told against him. He was aloof, one of the worst social crimes in Malaysia; he was identified as a parasite, and worst of all he seemed to hold everyone in contempt. Offenses were invented: He bullied the ball boys, he parked his car the wrong way, he made noises when he ate.

It may be hard to be an American—I sometimes thought so when I remembered our beleaguered Peace Corps teachers—but I believe it was even harder to be a Japanese in that place. They had lost the war and gained the world; they were unreadable, impossible to know; more courtly than the Chinese, they used this courtliness to conceal. The Chinese were secretive bumblers and their silences could be hysterical; the Japanese gave nothing away; they never betrayed their frenzy. This contempt they were supposed to have: It wasn't contempt, it was a total absence of trust in anyone who was not Japanese. And what was perhaps more to the point, they were the opposite to the English in every way I could name.

The war did not destroy the English—it fixed them in fatal attitudes. The Japanese were destroyed and out of that destruction came different men; only the loyalties were old—the rest was new. Shimura, who could not have been much more than thirty, was one of these new men, a postwar instrument, the perfectly cali-

brated Japanese. In spite of what everyone said, Shimura was an excellent tennis player.

So was Evans, and it was he who organized the club game: How to get rid of Shimura?

Squibb had a sentimental tolerance for Malays and a grudging respect for the Chinese, but like the rest of the club members he had an absolute loathing for the Japanese. When Alec said, "I suppose we could always debag him," Squibb replied fiercely, "I'd like to stick a *kukri* in his guts."

"We could get him for an infraction," said Strang.

"That's the trouble with the obnoxious little sod," said Squibb. "He doesn't break the rules. We're lumbered with him for life."

The hatred was old. The word "Changi" was associated with Shimura. Changi was the jail in Singapore where the British were imprisoned during the war, after the fall of the city, and Shimura was held personally responsible for what had gone on there: The water torture, the *rotan* floggings, the bamboo rack, the starvation and casual violence the Japanese inflicted on people they despised because they had surrendered.

"I know what we ought to do," said Alec. "He wants his tennis. We won't give him his tennis. If we kept him off the courts we'd never see his face here again."

"That's a rather low trick," said Evans.

"Have you got a better one?" said Squibb.

"Yes," said Evans. "Play him."

"I wouldn't play him for anything," said Squibb.

"He'd beat you in any case," said Alec.

Squibb said, "But he wouldn't beat Tony."

"Not me—I'm not playing him. I suggest we get someone else to beat him," said Evans. "These Japs can't stand humiliation. If he was really beaten badly we'd be well rid of him."

I said, "This is despicable. You don't know Shimura—you have no reason to dislike that man. I want no part of this."

"Then bugger off!" shouted Squibb, turning his red face on me. "We don't need a bloody Yank to tell us—"

"Calm yourself," said Alec. "There's ladies in the bar."

"Listen," I said to Squibb, "I'm a member of this club. I'm staying right here."

"What about Shimura?" said Alec.

"It's just as I say, if he was beaten badly he'd be humiliated," said Evans.

Squibb was looking at me as he said, "There are some little fuckers you can't humiliate."

But Evans was smiling.

The following week Shimura showed up late one afternoon, full of beans. He changed, had tea alone, and then appeared on the court with the towel around his neck and holding his racket like a sword. He chopped the air with it and looked around for a partner.

The court was still except for Shimura's busy shadow, and at the far end two ball boys crouched with their sarongs folded between their knees. Shimura hit a few practice shots on the backboard.

We watched him from the rear veranda, sitting well back from the railing: Evans, Strang, Alec, Squibb, and myself. Shimura glanced up and bounced the racket against his palm. A ball boy stood and yawned and drew out a battered racket. He walked toward Shimura, and though Shimura could not possibly have heard it there were four grunts of approval from the veranda.

Raziah, the ball boy, was slender; his flapping blue sports shirt and faded wax-print sarong made him look careless and almost comic. He was taller than Shimura and, as Shimura turned and walked to the net to meet him, the contrast was marked—the loose-limbed gait of the Malay in his rubber flip-flops, the compact movements of the Japanese who made his prowl forward into a swift bow of salutation.

Raziah said, "You can play me."

Shimura hesitated and before he replied he looked around in disappointment and resignation, as if he suspected he might be accused of something shameful. Then he said, "Okay, let's go."

"Now watch him run," said Evans, raising his glass of beer.

Raziah went to the base line and dropped his sarong. He was wearing a pair of tennis shorts.

He kicked off his flip-flops and put on white sneakers—new ones that looked large and dazzling in the sunlight. Raziah laughed out loud; he knew he had been transformed.

Squibb said, "Tony, you're a bloody genius."

Raziah won the toss and served. Raziah was seventeen; for seven of those years he had been a ball boy, and he had learned the game by watching members play. Later, with a cast-off racket, he began playing in the early morning, before anyone was up. Evans had seen him in one of these six o'clock matches and, impressed by Raziah's speed and backhand, taught him to serve and showed him the fine points of the game. He inspired in him the psychic alertness and confidence that makes tennis champions. Evans, unmarried, had used his bachelor's idleness as a charitable pledge and gave this energy and optimism to Raziah, who became his pet and student and finally his partner. And Evans promised that he would, one of these years, put Raziah up for membership if he proved himself; he had so far withheld club membership from the Malay, although the boy had beaten him a number of times.

Raziah played a deceptively awkward game; the length of his arms made him appear to swing wildly; he was fast, but he often stumbled trying to stop. After the first set it was clear that everyone had underestimated Shimura. Raziah smashed serves at him, Shimura returned them forcefully, without apparent effort, and Shimura won the first two sets 6–love. Changing ends, Raziah shrugged at the veranda as if to say, "I'm doing the best I can."

Evans said, "Raziah's a slow starter. He needs to win a few games to get his confidence up."

But he lost the first three games of the third set. Then Shimura, eager to finish him off, rushed the net and saw two of Raziah's dropshots land out of reach. When Raziah won that game, and the next—breaking Shimura's serve—there was a triumphant howl from the veranda. Raziah waved, and Shimura, who had been smiling, turned to see four men at the rail, the Chinese waiters on the steps, and crouching just under the veranda, two Tamil gardeners—everyone gazing with the intensity of jurors.

Shimura must have guessed that something was up. He reacted by playing angrily, slicing vicious shots at Raziah, or else lifting slow balls just over the net to drop hardly without a bounce at Raziah's feet. The pretense of the casual match was abandoned; the kitchen staff gathered along the side lines and others—mostly Malay— stood at the hedge, cheering. There was laughter when Shimura slipped, applause when the towel fell from his neck.

What a good story a victory would have made! But nothing in Ayer Hitam was ever so neat. It would have been perfect revenge, a kind of romantic battle—the lanky local boy with his old racket, making a stand against the intruder; the drama of vindicating not only his own reputation as a potentially great tennis player, but indeed the dignity of the entire club. The match had its charms: Raziah had a way of chewing and swallowing and working his Adam's apple at Shimura when the Japanese lost a point; Raziah talked as he played, a muttering narration that was meant to unnerve his opponent; and he took his time serving, shrugging his shoulders and bouncing the ball. But it was a very short contest, for as Evans and the others watched with hopeful and judging solemnity, Raziah lost.

The astonishing thing was that none of the club staff, and none of Raziah's friends, seemed to realize that he had lost. They were still laughing and cheering and congratulating themselves long after Shimura had aced his last serve past Raziah's knees; and not for the longest time did the festive mood change.

Evans jumped to the court. Shimura was clamping his press to his racket, mopping his face. Seeing Evans he started to walk away.

"I'd like a word with you," said Evans.

Shimura looked downcast; sweat and effort had plastered his hair close to his head, and his fatigue was curiously like sadness, as if he had been beaten. He had missed the hatred before, hadn't noticed us; but the laughter, the sudden crowd, the charade of the challenge match had showed him how much he was hated and how much trouble we had gone to in order to prove it. He said, "So."

Evans was purple. "You come to the club quite a bit, I see."

"Yes."

"I think you ought to be acquainted with the rules."

"I have not broken any rules."

Evans said curtly, "You didn't sign in your guest."

Shimura bowed and walked to the clubhouse. Evans glared at Raziah; Raziah shook his head, then went for his sarong, and putting it on he became again a Malay of the town, one of numerous idlers who'd never be members of the Ayer Hitam Club.

The following day Shimura left. We never saw him again. For a month Evans claimed it as a personal victory. But that was short-lived, for the next news was of Raziah's defection. Shimura had invited him to Kuala Lumpur and entered him in the Federation Championship, and the jersey Raziah wore when he won a respectable third prize had the name of Shimura's company on it, an electronics firm. And there was to be more. Shimura put him up for membership in the Selangor Club, and so we knew that it was only a matter of time before Raziah returned to Ayer Hitam to claim reciprocal privileges as a guest member. And even those who hated Shimura and criticized his lob were forced to admire the cleverness of his Oriental revenge.

Mixed Doubles

by **IRWIN SHAW**

As a potential four-cornered Freudian drama, there is nothing quite like mixed doubles. In this version, Irwin Shaw leads us to a poignant moment of recognition.

AS Jane Collins walked out onto the court behind her husband, she felt once more the private, strong thrill of pride that had moved her again and again in the time she had known him. Jane and Stewart had been married six years, but even so, as she watched him stride before her in that curious upright, individual, half-proud, half-comic walk, like a Prussian drill sergeant on his Sunday off, Jane felt the same mixture of amusement and delight in him that had touched her so strongly when they first met. Stewart was tall and broad and his face was moody and good-humored and original, and Jane felt that even at a distance of five hundred yards and surrounded by a crowd of people, she could pick him out unerringly. Now, in well-cut white trousers and a long-sleeved Oxford shirt, he seemed elegant and a little old-fashioned among the other players, and he looked graceful and debonair as he hit the first few shots in the preliminary rallying.

Jane was sensibly dressed, in shorts and tennis shirt, and her hair was imprisoned in a bandanna, so that it wouldn't get into her eyes. She knew that the shorts made her look a little dumpy and that the handkerchief around her head gave her a rather skinned and severe appearance, and she had a slight twinge of female regret when she looked across the net and saw Eleanor Burns soft and attractive in a prettily cut tennis dress and with a red ribbon in her hair, but she fought it down and concentrated on keeping her eye on the ball as Mr. Croker, Eleanor's partner, sliced it back methodically at her.

Mr. Croker, a vague, round, serious little man, was a neighbor of the Collinses' hosts. His shorts were too tight for him, and Jane knew, from having watched him on previous occasions, that his face would get more serious and more purple as the afternoon wore on, but he played a steady, dependable game and he was useful when other guests were too lazy or had drunk too much at lunch to play in the afternoon.

Two large oak trees shaded part of the court, and the balls flashed back and forth, in light and shadow, making guitarlike chords as they hit the rackets, and on the small terrace above the court, where the other guests were lounging, there was the watery music of ice in glasses and the bright flash of summer colors as people moved about.

How pleasant this was, Jane thought—to get

away from the city on a weekend, to this cool, tree-shaded spot, to slip all the stiff bonds of business and city living and run swiftly on the springy surface of the court, feeling the country wind against her bare skin, feeling youth in her legs, feeling, for this short Sunday hour at least, free of desks and doors and weekday concrete.

Stewart hit a tremendous overhead smash, whipping all the strength of his long body into it, and the ball struck the ground at Eleanor's feet and slammed high in the air. He grinned. "I'm ready," he said.

"You're not going to do that to me in the game, are you?" Eleanor asked.

"I certainly am," Stewart said. "No mercy for women. The ancient motto of the Collins family."

They tossed for service, and Stewart won. He served and aced Eleanor with a twisting, ferocious shot that spun off at a sharp angle.

"Jane, darling," he said, grinning, as he walked to the other side, "we're going to be sensational today."

They won the first set with no trouble. Stewart played very well. He moved around the court swiftly and easily, hitting the ball hard in loose, well-coached strokes, with an almost exaggerated grace. Again and again, the people watching applauded or called out after one of his shots, and he waved his racket, smiling at them, and said, "Oh, we're murderous today." He kept humming between shots—a tuneless, happy composition of his own—like a little boy who is completely satisfied with himself, and Jane couldn't help smiling and adoring him as he light-heartedly dominated the game and the spectators and the afternoon, brown and dashing and handsome in his white clothes, with the sun flooding around him like a spotlight on an actor in the middle of the stage.

Occasionally, when Stewart missed a shot, he would stand, betrayed and tragic, and stare up at the sky and ask with mock despair, "Collins, why don't you just go home?" And then he would turn to Jane and say, "Janie, darling, forgive me. Your husband's just no good."

And even as she smiled at him and said, "You're so right," she could sense the other

women, up on the terrace, looking down at him, their eyes speculative and veiled and lit with invitation as they watched.

Jane played her usual game, steady, unheroic, getting almost everything back quite sharply, keeping the ball in play until Stewart could get his racket on it and kill it. They were a good team. Jane let Stewart poach on her territory for spectacular kills, and twice Stewart patted her approvingly on the behind after she had made difficult saves, and there were appreciative chuckles from the spectators at the small domestic vulgarity.

Stewart made the last point of the set on a slamming deep backhand that passed Eleanor at the net. Eleanor shook her head and said, "Collins, you're an impossible man," and Croker said stolidly, "Splendid. Splendid," and Stewart said, grinning, "Something I've been saving for this point, old man."

They walked off and sat down on a bench in the shade between sets, and Croker and Jane had to wipe their faces with towels and Croker's alarming purple died a little from his cheeks.

"That overhead!" Eleanor said to Stewart. "It's absolutely frightening. When I see you winding up, I'm just tempted to throw away my poor little racket and run for my life."

Jane lifted her head and glanced swiftly at Stewart to see how he was taking it. He was taking it badly, smiling a little too widely at Eleanor, being boyish and charming. "It's nothing," he said. "Something I picked up on Omaha Beach."

That, too, Jane thought bitterly. Foxhole time, too. She ducked her head into her towel to keep from saying something wifely. This is the last time, she thought, feeling the towel sticky against her sweaty forehead, the last time I am coming to any of these weekend things, always loaded with unattached or semiattached, man-hungry, half-naked, honey-mouthed girls. She composed her face, so that when she looked up from the towel she would look like a nice, serene woman who merely was interested in the next set of tennis.

Eleanor, who had wide green eyes, was staring soberly and unambiguously over the head of her racket at Stewart, and Stewart, fascinated, as always, and a little embarrassed, was staring back. Oh, God, Jane thought, the long stare, too.

"Well," she said briskly, "I'm ready for one more set."

"What do you say," Stewart asked, "we divide up differently this time? Might make it more even. Croker and you, Jane, and the young lady and me."

"Oh," said Eleanor, "I'd be a terrible drag to you, Stewart. And besides, I'm sure your wife loves playing on your side."

"Not at all," Jane said stiffly. The young lady! How obvious could a man be?

"No," said Croker surprisingly. "Let's stay the way we are." Jane wanted to kiss the round purple face, a bleak, thankful kiss. "I think we'll do better this time. I've been sort of figuring out what to do with you, Collins."

Stewart looked at him briefly and unpleasantly, then smiled charmingly. "Anything you say, old man. I just thought . . ."

"I'm sure we'll do better," Croker said firmly. He stood up. "Come on, Eleanor."

Eleanor stood up, lithe and graceful in her short dress, which whipped around her brown legs in the summer wind. Never again, Jane thought, will I wear shorts. Dresses like that, even if they cost $50 apiece, and soft false bosoms to put in them, too, and no bandanna, even if I'm blinded on each shot.

Stewart watched Eleanor follow Croker onto the court, and Jane could have brained him for the buried, measuring glint in his eye.

"Let's go," Stewart said, and under his breath, as they walked to their positions on the base line. He added, "Let's really show the old idiot this time, Jane."

"Yes, dear," Jane said, and pulled her bandanna straight and tight around her hair.

The first three games were ludicrously one-sided. Stewart stormed the net, made sizzling, malicious shots to Croker's feet, and purposely made him run, so that he panted pitifully and grew more purple than ever, and from time to time muttered to Jane, "Ridiculous old windbag," and "I thought he had me figured out," and "Don't let up, Janie, don't let up."

Jane played as usual, steady, undeviating, as

predictably and sensibly as she always played. She was serving in the fourth game and was at 40–15 when Stewart dropped a shot just over the net, grinning as Croker galloped heavily in and barely got his racket on it. Croker's return wobbled over Stewart's head and landed three inches beyond the base line.

"Nice shot," she heard Stewart say. "Just in."

She looked at him in surprise. He was nodding his head emphatically at Croker.

Eleanor was at the net on the other side, looking at Stewart. "It looked out to me," she said.

"Not at all," Stewart said. "Beautiful shot. Serve them up, Janie."

Oh, Lord, Jane thought, now he's being sporting.

Jane made an error on the next point and Croker made a placement for advantage and Stewart hit into the net for the last point, and it was Croker's and Eleanor's game. Stewart came back to receive the service, not humming any more, his face irritable and dark.

Croker suddenly began to play very well, making sharp, sliding, slicing shots that again and again forced Stewart and Jane into errors. As they played, even as she swung at the ball, Jane kept remembering the shot that Stewart had called in, that had become the turning point of the set. He had not been able to resist the gallant gesture, especially when Eleanor had been standing so close, watching it all. It was just like Stewart. Jane shook her head determinedly, trying to concentrate on the game. This was no time to start dissecting her husband. They had had a lovely weekend till now and Stewart had been wonderful, gay and funny and loving, and criticism could at least be reserved for weekdays, when everything else was dreary, too. But it *was* just like Stewart. It was awful how everything he did was all of a piece. His whole life was crowded with gestures. Hitting his boss that time in the boss's own office with three secretaries watching, because the boss had bawled him out. Giving up his ROTC commission and going into the Army as a private, in 1942. Giving $5000, just about the last of their savings, to Harry Mather, for

Mather's business, just because they had gone to school together, when everyone knew Mather had become a hopeless drunk and none of his other friends would chip in. To an outsider, all these might seem the acts of a generous and rather noble character, but to a wife, caught in the consequences . . .

"Damn these pants," Stewart was muttering after hitting a ball into the net. "I keep tripping over them all the time."

"You ought to wear shorts, like everyone else," Jane said.

"I will. Buy me some this week," Stewart said, taking time out and rolling his cuffs up slowly and obviously. Jane had bought him three pairs of shorts a month before, but he always pretended he couldn't find them, and wore the long trousers. His legs are surprisingly skinny, Jane thought, hating herself for thinking it, and they're hairy, and his vanity won't let him. . . . She started to go for a ball, then stopped when she saw Stewart going for it.

He hit it out to the backstop. "Janie, darling," he said, "at least stay out of my way."

"Sorry," she said. Stewie, darling, she thought, Stewie, be careful. Don't lay it on. You're not really like this. I know you're not. Even for a moment, don't make it look as though you are.

Stewart ended the next rally by hitting the ball into the net. He stared unhappily at the ground. "The least they might do," he said in a low voice to Jane, "is roll the court if they invite people to play on it."

Please, Stewie, Jane begged within herself, don't do it. The alibis. The time he forgot to sign the lease for the apartment and they were put out and he blamed it on the lawyer, and the time he lost the job in Chicago and it was because he had gone to the wrong college, and the time. . . . By a rigorous act of will, Jane froze her eyes on the ball, kept her mind blank as she hit it back methodically again and again.

Eleanor and Croker kept winning points. Croker had begun to chop every ball, spinning soft, deceptive shots that landed in mid-court and hardly bounced before they fell a second time. The only way that Jane could return them

was to hit them carefully, softly, just getting them back. But Stewart kept going in on them furiously, taking his full, beautiful swing, sending the ball whistling into the net or over the court into the backstop. He looked as pretty and expert as ever as he played, but he lost point after point.

"What a way to play tennis," he grumbled, with his back to his opponents. "Why doesn't he play ping-pong or jacks?"

"You can't slam those dinky little shots like that," Janie said. "You have to get them back soft."

"You play your game," Stewart said, "and I'll play mine."

"Sorry," Jane said. Oh, Stewart, she mourned within her.

Stewart went after two more of Croker's soft chops, each time whipping his backhand around in his usual, slightly exaggerated, beautiful stroke, and each time knocking the ball into the net.

I can't help it, Jane thought. That *is* the way he is. Form above everything. If he were hanging over a cliff, he'd let himself fall to the rocks below rather than risk being ungraceful climbing to safety to save his life. He always has to pick up the check in bars and restaurants, no matter whom he is with or how many guests there are at the table, always with the same lordly, laughing, slightly derisive manner, even if we are down to our last $50. And when they had people in to dinner, there had to be two maids to wait on table, and French wines, and there always had to be those special bottles of brandy that cost as much as a vacation in the country. And he became so cold and remote when Jane argued with him about it, reminding him they were not rich and there was no sense in pretending they were. And his shoes. She blinked her eyes painfully, getting a sudden vision, there in the sun and shadow, of the long row of exquisite shoes, at $70 a pair, that he insisted upon having made to his order. How ridiculous, she thought, to allow yourself to be unnerved at your husband's taste in shoes, and she loyally reminded herself how much a part of his attraction it had been in the beginning that he was always so beautifully dressed and so easy and graceful and careless of money.

The score was 4–3 in favor of Eleanor and Croker. Stewart's shots suddenly began to work again, and he and Jane took the next game with ease. Stewart's grin came back then, and he cheerfully reassured Jane, "Now we're going to take them." But after winning the first two points of the next game he had a wild streak and missed the base line by a few inches three times in a row, and they eventually lost the game.

I will make no deductions from this, Jane told herself stonily as she went up to the net for Stewart's serve. Anybody is liable to miss a few shots like that—anybody. And yet, how like Stewart! Just when it was most important to be steady and dependable. . . . The time she'd been so sick and the maid had quit, and Jane lay, broken and miserable, in bed for three weeks, with no one to take care of her except Stewart. . . . He had been charming and thoughtful for the first week, fixing her meals, reading to her, sitting at her side for hours on end, cheerful and obliging, making her illness gently tolerable. And then he had suddenly grown nervous and abrupt, made vague excuses to leave her alone, and vanished for hours at a time, only to come back and hastily attend her for a few moments and vanish again, leaving her there in the rumpled bed, staring, lonely and shaken, at the ceiling as dusk faded into night and night into morning. She had been sure there was another girl then and she had resolved that when she was well and able to move around again, she would come to some decision with him, but as unpredictably as his absences had begun, they stopped. Once more he was tender and helpful, once more he sat at her side and nursed her and cheered her, and out of gratitude and love she had remained quiet and pushed her doubts deep to the back of her mind. And here they were again, in the middle of a holiday afternoon, foolishly, in this most unlikely place, during this mild, pointless game, with half a dozen people lazily watching, laughing and friendly, over their drinks.

She looked at him a few moments later, handsome and dear and familiar at her side, and he grinned back at her, and she was ashamed of herself for the thoughts that had been flooding through her brain. It was that silly girl on the other side of the net who had started it all, she thought. That practiced, obvious, almost automatic technique of flattering the male sex. That meaningless, rather pitiful flirtatiousness. It was foolish to allow it to throw her into the bitter waters of reflection. Marriage, after all, was an up-and-down affair and in many ways a fragile and devious thing, and was not to be examined too closely. Marriage was not a bank statement or a foreign policy or an X-ray photograph in a doctor's hand. You took it and lived through it, and maybe, a long time later—perhaps the day before you died—you totalled up the accounts, if you were of that turn of mind, but not before. And if you were a reasonable, sensible, mature woman, you certainly didn't do your additions and subtractions on a tennis court every time your husband hit a ball into the net. Jane smiled at herself and shook her head.

"Nice shot," she said warmly to Stewart as he swept a forehand across court, past Croker, for a point.

But it was still set point. Croker placed himself to receive Stewart's service, tense and determined and a little funny-looking, with his purple face and his serious round body a little too tight under his clothes. The spectators had fallen silent, and the wind had died, and there was a sense of stillness and expectancy as Stewart reared up and served.

Jane was at the net and she heard the sharp twang of Stewart's racket hitting the ball behind her and the riflelike report as it hit the tape and fell away. He had just missed his first service.

Jane didn't dare look around. She could feel Stewart walking into place, in that stiff-backed, pleasant way of his, and feel him shuffling around nervously, and she couldn't look back. Please, she thought, please get this one in. Helplessly, she thought of all the times when, just at the crucial moment, he had failed. Oh, God, this is silly, she thought. I mustn't do this. The time he had old man Sawyer's account practically in his hands and he got drunk. On the sporting pages, they called it coming through in the clutch. There were some players who did and some players who didn't, and after a while you got to know which was which. If you looked at it coldly, you had to admit that until now Stewart had been one of those who didn't. The time her father died, just after her sister had run off with the vocalist in that band, and if there had been a man around, taking hold of things, her father's partner wouldn't've been able to get away with most of the estate the way he did, and the vocalist could have been frightened off. One day's strength and determination, one day of making the right move at the right time . . . But after the funeral, Stewart had pulled out and gone to Seattle on what he had said was absolutely imperative business, but that had never amounted to anything anyway, and Jane's mother and sister, and Jane, too, were still paying for that day of failure.

She could sense Stewart winding up for his service behind her back. Somewhere in her spine she felt a sense of disaster. It was going to be a double fault. She knew it. No, she thought, I mustn't. He isn't really like that. He's so intelligent and talented and good, he can go so far. She must not make this terrible judgment on her husband just because of the way he played tennis. And yet, his tennis was so much like his life. Gifted, graceful, powerful, showy, flawed, erratic . . .

Please, she thought, make this one good. Childishly, she felt, If this one is good it will be a turning point, a symbol, his whole life will be different. She hated herself for her thoughts and stared blankly at Eleanor, self-consciously alert and desirable in her pretty dress.

Why the hell did she have to come here this Sunday? Jane thought despairingly.

She heard the crack of the racket behind her. The ball whistled past her, hit the tape, rolled undecidedly on top of the net for a moment, then fell back at her feet for a double fault and the set.

"Too bad." She turned and smiled at Stewart, helplessly feeling herself beginning to wonder how she would manage to find the six weeks it would take in Reno. She shook her head, knowing that she wasn't going to Reno, but knowing, too, that the word would pass through her thoughts again and again, more and more frequently, with growing insistence, as the days went by.

She walked off the court with Stewart, holding his hand.

"The shadows," Stewart was saying. "Late in the afternoon, like this. It's impossible to see the service line."

"Yes, dear," Jane said.

Tennis

by **ROGER ANGELL**

Part of becoming an adult is taking the measure—in a game like tennis—of our own parents. Sometimes the process, as captured by Roger Angell, is a combination of admiration, confrontation and, finally, illumination.

THE thing you ought to know about my father is that he plays a lovely game of tennis. Or rather, he used to, up to last year, when all of a sudden he had to give the game up for good. But even last summer, when he was fifty-five years of age, his game was something to see. He wasn't playing any of your middle-aged tennis, even then. None of that cute stuff, with lots of cuts and dropshots and getting everything back, that most older men play when they're beginning to carry a little fat and don't like to run so much. That wasn't for him. He still played all or nothing—the big game with a hard serve and coming right in behind it to the net. Lots of running in that kind of game, but he could still do it. Of course, he'd begun to make more errors in the last few years and that would annoy the hell out of him. But still he wouldn't change—not him. At that, his game was something to see when he was on. Everybody talked about it. There was always quite a little crowd around his court on the weekends, and when he and the other men would come off the court after a set of doubles, the wives would see their husbands all red and puffing. And then they'd look at my old man and see him grinning and not even breathing hard after *he'd* been doing all the running back after the lobs and putting away those overheads, and they'd say to him, "Honestly, Hugh, I just don't see how you do it, not at your age. It's *amazing!* I'm going to take my Steve [or Bill or Tom] off cigarettes and put him on a diet. He's ten years younger and just look at him." Then my old man would light up a cigarette and smile and shake his head and say, "Well, you know how it is. I just play a lot." And then a minute later he'd look around at everybody lying on the lawn there in the sun and pick out me or one of the other younger fellows and say, "Feel like a set of singles?"

If you know north Jersey at all, chances are you know my father. He's Hugh Minot—the Montclair one, not the fellow out in New Brunswick. Just about the biggest realty man in the whole section, I guess. He and my mother have this place in Montclair, thirty-five acres, with a swimming pool and a big vegetable garden and this *en-tout-cas* court. A lovely home. My father got a little name for himself playing football at

Rutgers, and that helped him when he went into business, I guess. He never played tennis in college, but after getting out he wanted something to sort of fill in for the football—something he could do well, or do better than the next man. You know how people are. So he took the game up. Of course, I was too little to remember his tennis game when he was still young, but friends of his have told me that it was really hot. He picked the game up like nothing at all, and a couple of pros told him if he'd only started earlier he might have gotten up there in the big time —maybe even with a national ranking, like number eighteen or so. Anyhow, he kept playing and I guess in the last twenty years there hasn't been a season where he missed more than a couple of weekends of tennis in the summertime. A few years back, he even joined one of these fancy clubs in New York with indoor courts, and he'd take a couple of days off from work and go in there just so that he could play in the wintertime. Once, I remember, he played doubles in there with Alice Marble and I think Sidney Wood. He told my mother about that game lots of times, but it didn't mean much to her. She used to play tennis years ago, just for fun, but she wasn't too good and gave it up. Now the garden is the big thing with her, and she hardly ever comes out to their court, even to watch.

I play a game of tennis just like my father's. Oh, not as good. Not nearly as good, because I haven't had the experience. But it's the same game, really. I've had people tell me that when they saw us playing together—that we both made the same shot the same way. Maybe my backhand was a little better (when it was on), and I used to think that my old man didn't get down low enough on a soft return to his forehand. But mostly we played the same game. Which isn't surprising, seeing that he taught me the game. He started way back when I was about nine or ten. He used to spend whole mornings with me, teaching me a single shot. I guess it was good for me and he did teach me a good, all-round game, but even now I can remember that those morning lessons would somehow discourage both of us. I couldn't seem to learn fast enough to suit

him, and he'd get upset and shout across at me, "Straight arm! Straight arm!" and then *I'd* get jumpy and do the shot even worse. We'd both be glad when the lesson ended.

I don't mean to say that he was so *much* better than I was. We got so we played pretty close a lot of the time. I can still remember the day I first beat him at singles. It was in June of 1937. I'd been playing quite a lot at school and this was my first weekend home after school ended. We went out in the morning, no one else there, and, as usual, he walked right through me the first set—about 6–1 or so. I played much worse than my regular game then, just like I always did against him for some reason. But the next set I aced him in the second game and that set me up and I went on and took him, 7–5. It was a wonderful set of tennis and I was right on top of the world when it ended. I remember running all the way back to the house to tell mother about it. The old man came in and sort of smiled at her and said something like "Well, I guess I'm old now, Amy."

But don't get the idea I started beating him then. That was the whole trouble. There I was, fifteen, sixteen years old and getting my size, and I began to think, Well, it's about time you took him. He wasn't a young man any more. But he went right on beating me. Somehow I never played well against him and I knew it, and I'd start pressing and getting sore and of course my game would go blooey.

I remember one weekend when I was in college, a whole bunch of us drove down to Montclair in May for a weekend—my two roommates and three girls we knew. It was going to be a lot of fun. But then we went out for some tennis and of course my father was there. We all played some mixed doubles, just fooling around, and then he asked me if I wanted some singles. In that casual way of his. And of course it was 6–2, 6–3, or some such thing. The second set we were really hitting out against each other and the kids watching got real quiet, just as if it was Forest Hills. And then when we came off, Alice, my date, said something to me. About him, I mean. "I think your father is a remarkable man," she

326 • *The Tennis Book*

said. "Simply remarkable. Don't you think so?" Maybe she wanted to make me feel better about losing, but it was a dumb question. What could I say except yes?

It was while I was in college that I began to play golf a little. I liked the game and I even bought clubs and took a couple of lessons. I broke ninety one day and wrote home to my father about it. He'd never played golf and he wrote back with some little gag about its being an old man's game. Just kidding, you know, and I guess I should have expected it, but I was embarrassed to talk about golf at home after that. I wasn't really very good at it, anyway.

I played some squash in college, too, and even made the B team, but I didn't try out for the tennis team. That disappointed my father, I think, because I wasn't any good at football, and I think he wanted to see me make some team. So he could come and see me play and tell his friends about it, I guess. Still, we did play squash a few times and I could beat him, though I saw that with time he probably would have caught up with me.

I don't want you to get the idea from this that I didn't have a good time playing tennis with him. I can remember the good days very well— lots of days where we'd played some doubles with friends or even a set of singles where my game was holding up or maybe even where I'd taken one set. Afterward we'd walk back together through the orchard, with my father knocking the green apples off the path with his racket the way he always did and the two of us hot and sweaty while we smoked cigarettes and talked about lots of things. Then we'd sit on the veranda and drink a can of beer before taking a dip in the pool. We'd be very close then, I felt.

And I keep remembering a funny thing that happened years ago—oh, away back when I was thirteen or fourteen. We'd gone away, the three of us, for a month in New Hampshire in the summer. We played a lot of tennis that month and my game was coming along pretty fast, but of course my father would beat me every single time we played. Then he and I both entered the little town championship there the last week in August. Of course, I was put out in the first round

(I was only a kid), but my old man went on into the finals. There was quite a big crowd that came to watch that day, and they had a referee and everything. My father was playing a young fellow —about twenty or twenty-one, I guess he was. I remember that I sat by myself, right down beside the court, to watch, and while they were warming up I looked at this man playing my father and whispered to myself, but almost out loud, "Take him! Take him!" I don't know why, but I just wanted him to beat my father in those finals, and it sort of scared me when I found that out. I wanted him to give him a real shellacking. Then they began to play and it was a very close match for a few games. But this young fellow was good, really good. He played a very controlled game, waiting for errors and only hitting out for winners when it was a sure thing. And he went on and won the first set, and in the next my father began to hit into the net and it was pretty plain that it wasn't even going to be close in the second set. I kept watching and pretty soon I felt very funny sitting there. Then the man won a love game off my father and I began to shake. I jumped up and ran all the way up the road to our cabin and into my room and lay down on my bed and cried hard. I kept thinking how I'd wanted to have the man win, and I knew it was about the first time I'd ever seen my father lose a love game. I never felt so ashamed. Of course, that was years and years ago.

I don't think any of this would have bothered me except for one thing—I've always *liked* my father. Except for this game, we've always gotten along fine. He's never wanted a junior-partner son, either in his office or at home. No Judge Hardy stuff or "Let me light your cigar, sir." And no backslapping, either. There have been times where I didn't see much of him for a year or so, but when we got together (at a ball game, say, or during a long trip in a car), we've always found we could talk and argue and have a lot of laughs, too. When I came back on my last furlough before I went overseas during the war, I found that he'd chartered a sloop. The two of us went off for a week's cruise along the Maine coast, and it was swell. Early-morning swims and trying to cook over charcoal and the wonderful quiet that comes over those little coves after you've anchored for the night and the wind has dropped and perhaps you're getting ready to shake up some cocktails. One night there, when we were sitting on deck and smoking cigarettes in the dark, he told me something that he never even told my mother—that he'd tried to get into the Army and had been turned down. He just said it and we let it drop, but I've always been glad he told me. Somehow it made me feel better about going overseas.

Naturally, during the war I didn't play any tennis at all. And when I came back I got married and all, and I was older, so of course the game didn't mean as much to me. But still, the first weekend we played at my father's—the very first time I'd played him in four years—it was the same as ever. And I'd have sworn I had outgrown the damn thing. But Janet, my wife, had never seen me play the old man before and *she* spotted something. She came up to our room when I was changing afterward. "What's the matter with you?" she asked me. "Why does it mean so much to you? It's just a game, isn't it? I can see that it's a big thing for your father. That's why he plays so much and that's why he's so good at it. But why you?" She was half-kidding, but I could see that it upset her. "This isn't a contest," she said. "We're not voting for Best Athlete in the County, are we?" I took her up on that and tried to explain the thing a little, but she wouldn't try to understand. "I just don't like a sorehead," she told me as she went out of the room.

I guess that brings me down to last summer and what happened. It was late in September, one of those wonderful weekends where it begins to get a little cool and the air is so bright. Father had played maybe six or seven sets of doubles Saturday, and then Sunday I came out with Janet, and he had his regular tennis gang there—Eddie Earnshaw and Mark O'Connor and that Mr. Lacy. I guess we men had played three sets of doubles, changing around, and we were sitting there catching our breath. I was waiting for father to ask me for our singles. But he'd told me earlier that he hadn't been able to get much sleep the night before, so I'd decided that he was too tired for singles. Of course, I didn't even

mention that out loud in front of the others—it would have embarrassed him. Then I looked around and noticed that my father was sitting in one of those canvas chairs instead of standing up, the way he usually did between sets. He looked awfully pale, even under his tan, and while I was looking at him he suddenly leaned over and grabbed his stomach and was sick on the grass. We all knew it was pretty bad, and we laid him down and put his cap over his eyes, and I ran back to the house to tell mother and phone up the doctor. Father didn't say a word when we carried him into the house in the chair, and then Dr. Stockton came and said it was a heart attack and that Father had played his last game of tennis.

You would have thought after that and after all those months in bed that my father would just give up his tennis court—have it plowed over or let it go to grass. But Janet and I went out there for the weekend just last month and I was surprised to find that the court was in good shape, and father said that he had asked the gang to come over, just so I could have some good men's doubles. He'd even had a chair set up in the orchard, halfway out to the court, so he could walk out there by himself. He walked out slow, the way he has to, and then sat down in the chair and rested for a couple of minutes, and then made it the rest of the way.

I haven't been playing much tennis this year, but I was really on my game there that day at my father's. I don't think I've ever played better on that court. I hardly made an error and I was relaxed and I felt good about my game. The others even spoke about how well I played.

But somehow it wasn't much fun. It just didn't seem like a real contest to me, and I didn't really care that I was holding my serve right along and winning my sets no matter who my partner was. Maybe for the first time in my life, I guess, I found out that it was only a game we were playing—only that and no more. And I began to realize what my old man and I had done to that game. All that time, all those years, I had only been trying to grow up and he had been trying to keep young, and we'd both done it on the tennis court. And now our struggle was over.

I found that out that day, and when I did I suddenly wanted to tell my father about it. But then I looked over at him, sitting in a chair with a straw hat on his head, and I decided not to. I noticed that he didn't seem to be watching us at all. I had the feeling, instead, that he was *listening* to us play tennis and perhaps imagining a game to himself or remembering how he would play the point—the big, high-bouncing serve and the rush to the net for the volley, and then going back for the lob and looking up at it and the wonderful feeling as you uncoil on the smash and put the ball away.

PART V

THE RECORD OF THE GAME

"Are today's stars superior to those of yesteryear? In that endless, monotonous argument, the imponderables are large."
—from *Tennis: Game of Motion* by Gene Scott

The 20 Greatest Matches of All Time

as picked by *TENNIS MAGAZINE*

A great match needs top-ranked competitors playing at the height of their abilities with something of import at stake . . . and something else harder to define. Tennis Magazine *assembled a panel of experts who picked the following matches as the best ever.*

1 **Don Budge (U.S.) d. Gottfried von Cramm (Germany) 6–8, 5–7, 6–4, 6–2, 8–6; 1937 Davis Cup Interzone Final, Wimbledon.** In this spectacular exhibition of shotmaking, Budge recovered from a 1–4 deficit in the fifth set to clinch a U.S. victory over Germany. Von Cramm saved four match points before Budge hit a running forehand winner on the fifth. Budge then led the U.S. to its first Davis Cup victory in ten years, over Great Britain, in the Challenge Round one week later.

2 **Suzanne Lenglen (France) d. Helen Wills (U.S.) 6–3, 8–6; 1926 final of the Carlton Club tournament, Cannes, France.** The only match between two of the greatest women players ever, it received worldwide attention. Lenglen was nearing the end of a brilliant amateur career, and had never lost a match in

France. Wills was just twenty and destined for future greatness. Playing before her most ardent fans, Lenglen fell behind 1–3 in the second set, but came back to win.

3 **Henri Cochet (France) d. Bill Tilden (U.S.) 2–6, 4–6, 7–5, 6–4, 6–3; 1927 Wimbledon semifinals.** The most celebrated turnabout in Wimbledon history. Tilden led 5–1 in the third set, but Cochet won seventeen consecutive points to reverse the tide. Twice Tilden served for the match and didn't win a point. No satisfactory explanation was ever offered for Tilden's mysterious collapse. To a charge that he tried to prolong the contest when Spain's King Alfonso entered the Royal Box at 5–1 in the third, Tilden snapped: "Rubbish. I didn't even know he was there."

4 **Jack Crawford (Australia) d. Ellsworth Vines (U.S.) 4–6, 11–9, 6–2, 2–6, 6–4; 1933 Wimbledon final.** The precision of Crawford and the power of Vines produced what many have called the best-played Wimbledon final ever. Crawford, wearing a long-sleeved shirt and wielding a flat-topped racket, hit a brilliant lob and two superb backhands to reach match point in the fifty-sixth game. Then, Vines missed a backhand and it was over.

5 Ken Rosewall (Australia) d. Rod Laver (Australia) 4–6, 6–0, 6–3, 6–7, 7–6; 1972 WCT Finals final, Dallas, Texas. A three-hour, thirty-four minute masterpiece that gave tennis its first great boost on TV. After losing the fourth-set tie breaker Rosewall had match point in the tenth game of the fifth. He then fell behind 3–5 in the final tie breaker, but two brilliant backhand service returns helped him to win four points in a row and the match.

6 Suzanne Lenglen (France) d. Dorothea Lambert-Chambers (Great Britain) 10–8, 4–6, 9–7; 1919 Wimbledon Challenge Round. Lambert-Chambers was forty and seven times a Wimbledon champion. Lenglen was twenty and playing on grass for the first time. Suzanne saved two set points in the first set, and two match points when Lambert-Chambers served at 6–5 in the third. Lenglen never lost a singles match in eight Wimbledon appearances, although she defaulted twice.

7 Fred Perry (Great Britain) d. Don Budge (U.S.) 2–6, 6–2, 8–6, 1–6, 10–8; 1936 U.S. Championship final. In a contest that lasted two hours and forty-five minutes, including two rain delays, Perry became the only foreigner ever to win the men's singles at Forest Hills three times. Twice he stood only two points from defeat, but he recovered and closed out the match with an ace.

8 Margaret Court (Australia) d. Billie Jean King (U.S.) 14–12, 11–9; 1970 Wimbledon final. For two hours and twenty-seven minutes, Court and King stretched each other to the limit in a dazzling display of offen-

sive and defensive tennis. It is still the longest women's final in Wimbledon history. Court finally won on her sixth match point. Later that year, she completed only the second Grand Slam in women's tennis.

9 Arthur Ashe (U.S.) d. Jimmy Connors (U.S.) 6–1, 6–1, 5–7, 6–4; 1975 Wimbledon final. Ashe planned and flawlessly executed a tactical masterpiece in what was considered a stunning upset. He effectively blunted Connors's power by consistently changing the pace, angle and spin of his shots, which was totally out of character with his usual slam-bang style.

10 Pancho Gonzales (U.S.) d. Charlie Pasarell (U.S.) 22–24, 1–6, 16–14, 6–3, 11–9; 1969 Wimbledon first round. At 112 games, it is the longest match ever played at Wimbledon. It consumed five hours and twelve minutes, over two days. When the temperamental, forty-one-year-old Gonzales left Centre Court two sets to love behind as darkness fell the first day, he was booed. The next afternoon he was cheered. He saved seven match points in the fifth set, twice coming back from love–40 down on his serve.

11 Pancho Gonzales (U.S.) d. Ted Schroe- der (U.S.) 16–18, 2–6, 6–1, 6–2, 6–4; 1949 U.S. Championship final. Gonzales, twenty-one, lost a heartbreaking first set after an hour and thirteen minutes, and then surrendered the second tamely. But he then summoned all his competitive fury and won the next three sets for his second U.S. title.

12 Bjorn Borg (Sweden) d. Vitas Gerulai- tis (U.S.) 6–4, 8–6, 6–3, 3–6, 8–6; 1977 Wimbledon semifinals. A three-hour struggle of breathtaking shots and lightning quickness about the court by both men.

13 René Lacoste (France) d. Bill Tilden (U.S.) 11–9, 6–3, 11–9; 1927 U.S. Championships final. Tilden led in all three sets but France's Crocodile wouldn't be denied victory.

14 Maureen Connolly (U.S.) d. Doris Hart (U.S.) 8–6, 7–5; 1953 Wimbledon final. This technical gem was the centerpiece of Connolly's Grand Slam and "the best tennis I ever played in my life," she said.

15 René Lacoste (France) d. Bill Tilden (U.S.) 6–3, 4–6, 6–3, 6–2; 1927 Davis Cup Challenge Round, Philadelphia. Lacoste's disciplined defense under supreme pressure won the match and spearheaded France's first Davis Cup victory.

16 Lew Hoad (Australia) d. Tony Trabert (U.S.) 13–11, 6–3, 2–6, 3–6, 7–5; 1953 Davis Cup Challenge Round, Melbourne, Australia. An epic battle between two power players that was contested in a chilling drizzle. Hoad seemed on the ropes in the fifth set, but broke through for victory in the sixty-second game.

17 Bill Tilden d. René Lacoste (France) 1–6, 6–4, 6–4, 2–6, 6–3; 1928 Davis Cup Challenge Round, Paris. Tilden exacted revenge on Lacoste for two previous Davis Cup defeats with a masterful exhibition of clay-court tennis. Said Lacoste of Tilden afterward: "Is he not the greatest player of all?"

18 Jaroslav Drobny (Czechoslovakia) d. Budge Patty (U.S.) 8–6, 16–18, 3–6, 8–6, 12–10; 1953 Wimbledon third round. Drobny fended off three match points in the fourth set and three more in the fifth before winning in the ninety-third game.

19 Billie Jean King (U.S.) d. Bobby Riggs (U.S.) 6–4, 6–3, 6–3; 1973 Battle of the Sexes, Houston, Texas. King's superb play dashed male chauvinists' hopes and put women's tennis on the sporting map.

20 Helen Wills Moody (U.S.) d. Helen Jacobs (U.S.) 6–3, 3–6, 7–5; 1935 Wimbledon final. Moody trailed her great rival 2–5 in the third set, but came back to win her seventh of eight Wimbledon singles titles.

The Way It Wasn't

The great tragedy of tennis was that the world's best players, once they had turned professional, were barred from the world's major events. This finally changed in 1968 when tennis began to allow open competition, but things would have been very different—the record book rewritten—had that change been allowed much earlier. Here Jack Kramer gives his list of who would have won what, if everybody had been allowed to play.

TO my mind the real "fix" in tennis was in the championships, so-called because the real champions, the professionals, couldn't get in. Wimbledon, Forest Hills, all the big amateur championships were frauds. It was like running the high-jump championship of the world, barring all the kids who could jump seven feet, and then calling the guy who did six-eleven the champion.

From 1931, when Tilden turned pro at the age of thirty-seven, until 1968, when the game finally went open, virtually every player who won both Wimbledon and Forest Hills turned pro. The only amateurs who won the two major titles and didn't sign were Schroeder, Vic Seixas, Neale Fraser and Manolo Santana. Schroeder, as we know, passed up the opportunity. Seixas, Fraser and Santana were smart enough to realize that the only reason they won in the amateurs

was because the best players had turned pro. As the 1950's wore on, it was possible for very average players to become great amateur champions. Ashley Cooper was another who won Wimbledon and Forest Hills, but when he joined the tour he had a great deal of difficulty holding his own. The same applied to kids like Mal Anderson, who won Forest Hills, or to Alex Olmedo, who won Wimbledon.

Anyone with any intelligence knew this situation existed. Olmedo was not only a Wimbledon champion but had also received an inordinate amount of publicity as the Peruvian who won the Davis Cup for the United States; but when he signed with me, I couldn't even get Madison Square Garden to give us a date to debut him. They knew it would be no contest if he played Gonzales; they knew that the "champion," Olmedo, was really only the tenth or eleventh best player, and they knew that the fans knew this too.

I've often wondered how the history books of this era would look if the real champions had been allowed to play in the championships. They say you can't rewrite history, but just this one time for the sake of justice, that's exactly what I'm going to do. In the two left-hand columns, I'm listing the players who did win Wimbledon and Forest Hills. In the two right-hand columns,

I'm listing those players I think are most likely to have won if the competition had been opened to all players. This is dream stuff, and it is impossible for me to imagine when the upsets would have occurred. Somewhere along the line, players like Schroeder, Segura, Trabert, Emerson, possibly even Santana would have sprung a surprise and taken a Wimbledon or Forest Hills or two. But let me make up my history strictly on the basis of form.

Basically what I've done here is list the probable winners of Wimbledon and Forest Hills if they'd been open to pros and amateurs, next to the amateurs who actually won. When I've felt that a player was absolutely dominant—as I was, say, in 1949—then I've given that player both titles. If there was some question as to who was the best, I've given one title to one player and the second to the other (arbitrarily assigning Wimbledon to one, Forest Hills to the other—they could be reversed). So here it is: On your left, history as it was, unfairly. On your right, history rewritten the way it probably would have happened.

	AMATEUR CHAMPIONS		KRAMERS "OPEN" CHAMPIONS	
	Wimbledon	Forest Hills	Wimbledon	Forest Hills
1931	Wood	Vines	Tilden	Vines
1932	Vines	Vines	Vines	Vines
1933	Crawford	Perry	Crawford	Perry
1934	Perry	Perry	Vines	Vines
1935	Perry	Allison	Vines	Vines
1936	Perry	Perry	Perry	Vines
1937	Budge	Budge	Vines	Budge
1938	Budge	Budge	Budge	Vines
1939	Riggs	Riggs	Vines	Budge
1940	NOT HELD	McNeill	NOT HELD	Budge
1941	NOT HELD	Riggs	NOT HELD	Budge
1942	NOT HELD	Schroeder	NOT HELD	Budge
1943	NOT HELD	Hunt	NOT HELD	Budge
1944	NOT HELD	Parker	NOT HELD	Budge
1945	NOT HELD	Parker	NOT HELD	Riggs
1946	Petra	Kramer	Budge	Riggs
1947	Kramer	Kramer	Riggs	Kramer
1948	Falkenberg	Gonzales	Kramer	Kramer
1949	Schroeder	Gonzales	Kramer	Kramer
1950	Patty	Larsen	Kramer	Kramer
1951	Savitt	Sedgman	Kramer	Gonzales
1952	Sedgman	Sedgman	Gonzales	Kramer
1953	Seixas	Trabert	Kramer	Gonzales
1954	Drobny	Seixas	Sedgman	Gonzales
1955	Trabert	Trabert	Sedgman	Gonzales
1956	Hoad	Rosewall	Gonzales	Sedgman
1957	Hoad	Anderson	Hoad	Gonzales
1958	Cooper	Cooper	Gonzales	Hoad
1959	Olmedo	Fraser	Gonzales	Gonzales
1960	Fraser	Fraser	Rosewall	Gonzales
1961	Laver	Emerson	Gonzales	Rosewall
1962	Laver	Laver	Rosewall	Gonzales
1963	McKinley	Osuna	Gonzales	Laver
1964	Emerson	Emerson	Laver	Rosewall
1965	Emerson	Santana	Rosewall	Laver
1966	Santana	Stolle	Rosewall	Laver
1967	Newcombe	Newcombe	Laver	Rosewall

In some cases, I have had to be very arbitrary in selecting the winners, because there were years when three players were so close. In 1938 and 1939, for example, Perry could have been better than both Vines and Budge. In 1957 Sedgman could have been as good as Hoad and Gonzales, and in 1963 Gonzales, Laver and Rosewall were all very close.

As you can see, a lot of things happened quite differently. Fred Perry would have won only one Wimbledon, and so I, not Fred, would have been the first modern player to win three Wimbledons in a row (in fact I would have won four straight, 1948–51 before Gonzales beat me 6–4, 6–7, 13–11, 6–8, 7–5 in the famous long final in 1952). Budge would have won six straight Forest Hills and would have made it seven but for Riggs's comeback victory in 1945, when Don was serving for the match at 5–3 in the fourth and then lost 7–5, 6–4. Gonzales also would have won seven Forest Hills and six Wimbledons too, giving him the modern record of thirteen. And little Rosewall—not only did he get a Wimbledon title, he would have gotten four to go with his five Forest Hills.

Oh it would have been very different. . . .

The Greatest Doubles Teams and Players

by GEORGE LOTT

George Lott was five times a U.S. doubles title holder and twice a winner at Wimbledon . . . he has modestly omitted his own name from the lists of all-time teams and players.

MY friend Hot Horse Harry and I were having lunch at Chicago's Pump Room recently and, as usual when we get together, world affairs and sporting events got a thorough going over. It took us only a short time to dispose of such matters as civil rights, Vietnam and welfare. Long before the meat course arrived, we were on our favorite subjects, tennis and horse racing.

Hot Horse Harry is a gent who swims with the tide and, since tennis is at a high tide these days, he has become an avid tennis fan. For my part, I have improved the breed more than a little in the past.

Soon our talk turned to tennis doubles and since I have played them a bit in my time, H.H.H. asked: "What was the greatest doubles team in the history of tennis?"

A good question, I thought, and a difficult one, considering all the superior doubles teams that have played the game in different eras and with different styles. The more I thought about it, the more it struck me that the great teams had one thing in common besides teamwork, experience and ability. That was friendship. To play at the top in doubles, it's important for the players to get along and to think along the same lines. The Australians, especially, have been good at this; they like to pal around together off the court.

As Hot Horse Harry pressed me for an answer, I reminded him that I would give him only a personal opinion, based on both participation and observation. Then I plunged ahead with the following all-time doubles ranking.

1—John Newcombe and Tony Roche who are, I think, certainly the top doubles team in history. Their record in the Big Four tournaments speaks for itself; it includes four Wimbledon titles, three Australian, two French and one American. That's ten major wins by one team! Both men are, of course, complete tennis players. But above all, they had the intelligence and the patience not to try for winners on every shot. They carefully led up to the winning point.

2—R. Norris Williams and Vincent Richards who were almost unbeatable during a brief partnership in the mid-1920's when they captured two straight U.S. titles. They complemented each other perfectly. Williams was a daring player, one who would go for an outright winner on a service return. Richards was the

335

George Lott (left) and Les Stoefen pose with one of their many doubles championship trophies. (Photo Courtesy of the USTA)

steady one and probably the best low volleyer ever to play the game.

3—Bill Talbert and Gardner Mulloy, two very sharp, wily tacticians who won four U.S. championships in the 1940's. Both were remarkably consistent players who concentrated on creating openings for each other and who had enough power to put away winners when necessary.

4—Frank Sedgman and Ken McGregor who in the early 1950's won the Wimbledon, French and Australian titles twice each and the U.S. championship once. In fact, they swept all four of the major titles in 1951. McGregor had a skillful power game while Sedgman was the quickest man at the net I've ever seen.

5—Adrian Quist and John Bromwich, two superb doubles players who, like Newcombe and Roche, took ten major championships between 1938 and 1950. Eight of them, though, were Australian titles; they won the Wimbledon and U.S. crowns once each. Bromwich, to my mind, was the greatest doubles player in history.

6—Roy Emerson and Rod Laver, a courtwise team with victories in the Wimbledon, French and Australian tournaments in recent years. Despite Laver's brilliant overall record, Emerson is actually the better doubles player. He's particularly adept at the preparatory shots designed to set up winners by his partner.

7—William Tilden and Vincent Richards who won the U.S. championship three times just after World War I. This team is ranked below the Williams-Richards duo because Tilden, although he was a great singles player, was not Williams's equal at doubles. Tilden, for one thing, could be maneuvered out of position more easily.

8—Jacques Brugnon and Henri Cochet, the victors in two Wimbledon and three French championships in the late 1920's and early 1930's. They weren't spectacular, but they were steady.

9—Wilmer Allison and John Van Ryn who took the U.S. and Wimbledon titles twice each between 1929 and 1935. Again, here were two tough players whose games meshed nicely. Van Ryn was slow but steady, while Allison was a streak player who, when he was good, was very, very good.

10—Lew Hoad and Ken Rosewall, winners of six of the big four championships. Their most memorable feat was gaining the Wimbledon crown when they were each just eighteen. Their great strength was Hoad's all-around game, and their weakness was Rosewall's mediocre serve.

This list leaves out quite a few really great teams such as Budge and Mako, Kramer and Schroeder, Seixas and Trabert, and Smith and Lutz. These teams could quite possibly beat any team on my list, but their records do not indicate that they could. Reissen and Okker are also a fine team but have never won a major event.

It is frequently said that a doubles team is as good as its weakest link. I differ a bit from the norm in that I believe a really great doubles player can solidify that weak link. My list of great doubles players (with ties indicated at several positions) would read like this:

1. John Bromwich
1. Jack Kramer
1. Don Budge
4. Frank Sedgman
4. Adrian Quist
4. Roy Emerson
7. Rod Laver
8. Vincent Richards
9. Jacques Brugnon
10. Marty Riessen
10. Bill Talbert
10. Gardner Mulloy

What a pleasure it would have been to have any one of these men for a partner, I told Hot Horse Harry. He nodded a little limply and excused himself, muttering something about already being late for the fifth race.

Some of the Greatest Marathons of History

by BUD COLLINS

Because of the scoring system in tennis, a match could go on indefinitely . . . and indeed, some matches seem to have taken a run at just that. Here Bud Collins presents the best and longest of the legendary marathons, the matches that prompted the creation of the tie breaker scoring system. These are records that will never be broken.

THEORETICALLY, a tennis match could last forever, but that theory has given way under the presistent assault of Big Daddy VASSS, Jimmy Van Alen. Perhaps it is fitting that the longest match ever—one that seemed destined never to end—was perpetrated on the lawn of Van Alen's club, the Newport, Rhode Island Casino in 1967.

Because of Jimmy Van Alen, the imaginative "Newport Bolshevik," who radicalized America's major tournaments in 1970, "sudden death" (or some form of tie-breaker) is here to stay. If adopted universally, Van Alen's set scoring scheme to eliminate long deuce sets will remove the possibility of 147-game matches.

That is the record: 147 games. A doubles match consuming more than six hours! Halted by darkness one evening, finished the next morning. The winners: Dick Dell of Bethesda, Maryland, and Dick Leach, Arcadia, California, coach

and schoolteacher. "Only because I hit a lucky shot off the wood did it end," laughs Leach. "Golly, we might still be playing."

But it did end, a second rounder in the Newport Invitation—Dell and Leach over Len Schloss of Baltimore and Tom Mozur of Sweetwater, Tennessee, 3–6, 49–47, 22–20. Suppose it had been a best-of-five sets match?

Jimmy Van Alen, another cocktail hour ruined, sat through the whole "blasted thing." In 1958, he had begun plotting to overthrow "such an idiotic system" by devising a new scoring. Tennis wasn't ready for him until 1970, however, and Jimmy had to be content to fiddle with his antideuce methods in nonsanctioned tournaments.

Under Jimmy's sudden-death solution, at 6–all in each set, a best–of–nine points sequence is played, and the first to get five points wins the set, 7–6. Period. That's it. No more 49–47 sets. It was a smash hit—with the spectators and on TV, anyway—at the U.S. Pro Championships in Boston and the U.S. Open of 1970 at Forest Hills, and was well received elsewhere, too.

So well did it go over that Herman David, the guiding hand at Wimbledon, said his tournament would adopt a tie-breaker. It was almost as startling as Wimbledon's announcement in 1967 that the world championship was going open.

David isn't, of course, a leftist on the Van Alen scale. "We start our tie breaker at 8–all in games; 6–all is too soon," David said. The fact that Wimbledon added a tie breaker was shocking news. Especially, since it probably meant the end of matches such as Pancho Gonzales's 112–game victory over Charlie Pasarell in 1969, perhaps Wimbledon's most dramatic. There is something incredibly gripping about matches like that. Twice old Pancho lashed back from love–40–triple match point both times—and finally won it on an eleven–point rush, carried by waves of applause and cheers in Centre Court. The score: 22–24, 1–6, 16–14, 6–3, 11–9.

If a tie-breaker had been in force, that match couldn't have lasted more than seventy games. (Wimbledon, with its own form of tie-breaker, does not invoke it for a men's fifth set or a women's third.) Some of the beauty would have been missing. But so would some of the boredom. Depends on how you look at it.

Jerry Scheuer, tennis's eighty-five-year-old mnemonic wizard from Boston—he can recall the style of every fine player since Harold Hackett in 1905—cherishes the memory of the longest match in American championship play. "Fascinating throughout," says Scheuer of a quarterfinal doubles in the National Indoors of 1968 at Salisbury, Maryland. "I got cramps," remembers Bobby Wilson, the Englishman who nevertheless hit a blistering forehand return off Ron Holmberg's serve to conclude the 144-game struggle after six-and-a-half hours.

Holmberg and Pasarell were beaten by Wilson and countryman Mark Cox, 26–24, 17–19, 30–28, stopping three games short of the Leach-Dell vs. Schloss-Mozur record set in Newport five months before.

"I know Scheuer liked the match, but it was an awful long time to stay on one court," says Holmberg. "We saved six or seven match points, and at times, it was very exciting. But we spoiled the day for a lot of people, too, including the tournament director, Bill Riordan, and my partner, Pasarell.

"We were the last match of the afternoon program, going on the one court in the Wicomico Center at four-thirty. We played . . . and played . . . and

"People missed cocktails, then supper . . . then bedtime," Holmberg laughs, "and we're still playing, as the clock moves toward eleven P.M. The evening program can't start till we get off. I think Arthur Ashe and Stan Smith started their singles—which was supposed to be the feature—at twelve-forty-five A.M.

"A funny thing was, a guy called from Salt Lake City in the afternoon to ask if he could get there in time to see Arthur and Stan play. It was doubtful. He got on a plane anyway, changed planes in Chicago, flew to Washington and rented a car and drove down to Salisbury. He walked in and we're playing doubles. 'I thought this was on the afternoon program,' the guy said. It was. He arrived in plenty of time for Arthur and Stan.

"But poor Charlie was so pooped from our match that Clark Graebner beat him easy the next day. That was too bad because Charlie had won the Indoors in 1966 and 1967, and might have become only the second player to win it three straight years."

Scheduling headaches prompted Van Alen to invent VASSS, and most tournament directors and referees inwardly bless Jimmy even if they honor tradition and call him a nut. "Our tournament runs like a dream, like clockwork. You know, pretty closely, when matches will start and end," said Bob Smith, referee of the Pennsylvania Grass Open at Merion, which uses and approves sudden death.

Sudden death meant Vic Seixas's record for that tournament is safe. Nobody will surpass Vic's startling ninety-four-game victory over Bill Bowrey in 1966. The young Aussie (twenty-three then) must have been astonished—and chagrined—when forty-three-year-old Vic lasted through the second longest singles set on record while winning, 32–34, 6–4, 10–8.

Fortunately, or unfortunately, according to your tastes, tennis has never kept records as meticulously as baseball or various other organized sports. When Wilson-Cox vs. Holmberg-Pasarell came within three games of Dell-Leach vs. Schloss-Mozur's longevity mark, I'm sure nobody was aware of it. Nor did the Browns—tall Bill of Omaha and short John of Melbourne—realize they had engaged in the longest *set* of singles after John beat Bill, 36–34, 6–1, in the Heart of America Tournament at Kansas City in 1968.

Such matches are called "marathons" in the newspapers. An accompanying line usually says: "Believed to be one of the longest matches ever played." But nobody is sure. That has always bothered me. In editing the 1969 *USLTA Yearbook and Guide,* I listed the results of a good deal of research: The sets and matches I had discovered to be the longest, in point of games, in tennis history. Certainly there could be some I have overlooked or missed. I haven't scanned every draw sheet of every tournament played, and I would welcome any corrections or additions. (A partial list, reprinted from the *Guide* accompanies this article.)

With tie-breakers coming in, these lists of the longest will likely stand inviolate. Another factor reducing length of matches is the disappearance of grass. In a few years, grass will doubtless be gone from the American tournament scene, and quite possibly the Australian. Eventually, even Wimbledon will no doubt give way to a slower, surer, less expensive surface. Of the 15 "centuries"—matches that have reached one hundred games—ten were played on grass; three were played indoors on wood or canvas; two on cement—all fast surfaces, where serve rules and deuce sets are common. I have no idea what the longest clay-court match of all might be. Maybe it was Brown vs. Brown, seventy-seven games in Kansas City.

There is some feeling that a tie-breaker isn't necessary on slower surfaces, except indoors where courts are limited (usually to one) and the customers prefer to get to bed sometime before breakfast.

King of the marathoners is the left-handed Yorkshireman, Roger Taylor, who played three of the longest sets on two of his coldest nights in Warsaw in 1966. They were during the King's Cup, an indoor competition along Davis Cup lines. With Britain playing Poland, Taylor beat both Wieslaw Gasiorek, 27–29, 31–29, 6–1, and

Taddeus Nowicki, 33–31, 6–1. Taylor vs. Gasiorek, at 126 games, outdistances Gonzales-Pasarell by fourteen for the singles record. Roger's set with Nowicki was the third longest, and those with Gasiorek fifth and sixth. And what would have happened if those matches were best of five!

"Crikey, we'd have grown old together, Gasiorek and I, if it had been five sets," Taylor says. "I couldn't see how we were going to get to bed at all. It was five hours and twenty-seven minutes, I believe, and went past one in the morning. It was in a sports hall with all kinds of lines on the fast wood floor for basketball, volleyball, tennis. Pretty confusing. Then there'd been some sort of meeting or party there during the day, and the place was filled with smoke. They couldn't open the windows to get rid of it because it was below zero outside. It was like playing in a dream. Returning serve was impossible.

"But when I broke Gasiorek in the seventieth game of the second set, he lost heart a little, and I didn't have much trouble in the third. Hardly anybody was left from the crowd when we finished. When we went outside, the streets were completely deserted and cold as anything. No transportation. Had to walk to the hotel. We froze. One hundred and twenty-six games. It's something to have gone through," Taylor smiles in retrospect.

It's something most people don't want to go through, least of all Jimmy Van Alen. But sudden death wouldn't have helped Taylor too much that frigid night in Warsaw. A tie breaker can lower the score, but can it keep you warm?

Men's Singles

126 games—Roger Taylor, England, d. Wieslaw Gasiorek, Poland, 27–29, 31–29, 6–4. King's Cup match, Warsaw, 1966.

112 games—Pancho Gonzales, Los Angeles, d. Charlie Pasarell, Santurce, Puerto Rico, 22–24, 1–6, 16–14, 6–3, 11–9. First round, Wimbledon, 1969.

107 games—Dick Knight, Seattle, d. Mike Sprengelmeyer, Dubuque, Iowa, 32–30, 3–6, 19–

17. Qualifying round, Meadow Club Invitation. Southampton, New York, 1967.

100 games—F. D. Robbins, Salt Lake City, d. Dick Dell, Bethesda, Maryland, 22–20, 9–7, 6–8, 8–10, 6–4. First round, U.S. Open, Forest Hills, 1969.

100 games—(not completed) Jaroslav Drobny, Czechoslovakia, tied with Budge Patty, France, 21–19, 8–10, 21–21. Lyons Covered Courts Invitation, Lyons, France, 1955.

94 games—Vic Seixas, Philadelphia, d. Bill Bowrey, Australia, 32–34, 6–4, 10–8. Third round, Pennsylvania Grass Championships, Merion Cricket Club, Philadelphia, 1966.

93 games—Jaroslav Drobny d. Budge Patty, 8–6, 16–18, 3–6, 8–6, 2–10. Third round, Wimbledon, 1953.

93 games—Dennis Ralston, Bakersfield, California, d. John Newcombe, Australia, 19–17, 20–18, 4–6, 6–4. Quarterfinal, Australian Open, Sydney, 1970.

92 games—Allan Stone, Australia, d. Phil Dent, Australia, 6–3, 20–22, 6–1, 8–10, 9–7. First round, Victorian Championships, Melbourne, 1968.

90 games—Rod Laver, Australia, d. Tony Roche, Australia, 7–5, 22–20, 9–11, 1–6, 6–3. Semifinal, Australian Open, Brisbane, 1969.

Men's Doubles
147 games—Dick Leach, Arcadia, California, and Dick Dell, Bethesda, Maryland, d. Len Schloss, Baltimore, and Tom Mozur, Sweetwater, Tennessee, 3–6, 49–47, 22–20. Second round, Newport Casino, Newport, Rhode Island, 1967.

144 games—Bobby Wilson and Mark Cox, both England, d. Ron Holmberg, Highland Falls, New York, and Charlie Pasarell, Santurce, Puerto Rico, 26–24, 17–19, 30–28. Quarterfinal, National Indoors, Salisbury, Maryland, 1968.

135 games—Ted Schroeder, La Crescenta, California, and Bob Falkenberg, Los Angeles, d. Pancho Gonzales, Los Angeles, and Hugh Stewart, San Marino, California, 36–34, 2–6, 4–6, 6–4, 19–17. Final, Southern California Championships, Los Angeles, 1949.

106 games—Len Schloss and Tom Mozur d. Chris Bovett, England, and Butch Seewagen, Bayside, New York, 7–5, 48–46. Second round, Meadow Club, 1967.

105 games—Cliff Drysdale and Ray Moore, both South Africa, d. Roy Emerson, Australia, and Ron Barnes, Brazil, 29–31, 8–6, 3–6, 8–6, 6–2. Quarterfinal, National Doubles, Longwood Cricket Club, Boston, 1967.

105 games—Jim Osborne, Honolulu, and Bill Bowrey, Australia, d. Terry Addison and Ray Keldie, both Australia, 3–6, 43–41, 7–5. Semifinal, Pennsylvania Grass, Merion Cricket Club, Philadelphia, 1969.

105 games—Joaquin Loyo-Mayo and Marcelo Lara, both Mexico, d. Manolo Santana, Spain, and Luis Garcia, Mexico, 10–12, 24–22, 11–9, 3–6, 6–2. Third round, National Doubles, Longwood, 1966.

102 games—Don White, Coronado, California, and Bob Galloway, La Jolla, California, d. Hugh Sweeney and Lamar Roemer, both Houston, 6–4, 17–15, 4–6, 18–20, 7–5. First round, National Doubles, Longwood, 1964.

102 games—Russell Bobbitt and Bitsy Grant, both Atlanta, d. Ed Amark, San Francisco, and Robin Hippenstiel, San Bernardino, California, 14–12, 15–17, 6–4, 4–6, 13–1. Second round, National Doubles, Longwood, 1941.

100 games—Bob Lutz, Los Angeles, Joaquin Loyo-Mayo, Mexico, d. Bill Bond, La Jolla, California, and Dick Leach, 19–17, 33–31. Quarterfinal, Thunderbird, Phoenix, 1969.

Women's Singles
62 games—Kathy Blake, Pacific Palisades, California, d. Elena Subirats, Mexico, 12–10, 6–8, 14–12. First round, Piping Rock, Locust Valley, New York, 1966.

60 games—Kristy Pigeon, Danville, California, d. Karen Krantzcke, Australia, 17–15, 2–6, 11–9. First round, Kingston Invitation, Kingston, Jamaica, 1969.

56 games—Helen Jacobs, Berkeley, California, d. Ellen Whittingstall, England, 9–11, 6–2, 15–13. Quarterfinal, British Hard Courts, Bournemouth, 1933.

64 games—A. Weiwers, France, d. Mrs. O. Anderson, U.S.A., 8–10, 14–12, 6–4. Second round, Wimbledon, 1948.

53 games—Mary Ann Eisel, St. Louis, d. Karen Krantzcke, Australia, 3–6, 16–14, 8–6. Final, Piping Rock, 1968.

53 games—Corinne Molesworth, England, d. Pam Teeguarden, Los Angeles, 3–6, 7–5, 17–15. Third round, Palace Indoor, Torquay, England, 1968.

51 games—Juliette Atkinson d. Marion Jones, 6–3, 5–7, 6–4, 2–6, 7–5 (best of five sets!). Final, National Singles, Philadelphia Cricket Club, Philadelphia, 1898.

50 games—Molly Hannas, Kansas City, Missouri, d. Lourdes Diaz, Mexico, 9–7, 13–15, 6–4. First round, National Girls 18 Championships, Philadelphia Cricket Club, Philadelphia, 1969.

49 games—Mabel Cahill d. Elizabeth Moore, 5–7, 6–3, 6–4, 4–6, 6–2 (best of five sets). Final, National Singles, Philadelphia, 1891.

48 games—Mrs. Margaret Osborne Du-Pont, Wilmington, Delaware, d. Louise Brough, Beverly Hills, California, 4–6, 6–4, 15–13. Final, National Singles, West Side Tennis Club, Forest Hills, 1948.

48 games—Janet Hopps, Seattle, d. Mary Ann Mitchell, San Leandro, California, 4–6, 6–4, 15–13. Seattle Championships, Seattle, 1956.

Women's Doubles

81 games—Nancy Richey, San Angelo, Texas, and Mrs. Carole Caldwell Graebner, New York, d. Justina Bricka and Carol Hanks, both St. Louis, 31–33, 6–1, 6–4. Semifinal, Eastern Grass, Orange Lawn Tennis Club, South Orange, New Jersey, 1964.

48 games—Pat Brazier and Christabel Wheatcroft, both England, d. Mildred Nonweiller and Betty Soames, both England, 11–9, 5–7, 9–7. First round, Wimbledon, 1933.

48 games—Mrs. Billie Jean Moffitt King, Long Beach, California, and Rosie Casals, San Francisco, d. Mrs. Ann Haydon Jones, England, and Françoise Durr, France, 6–8, 8–6, 11–9. Final Pacific Southwest Open, Los Angeles, 1969.

Mixed Doubles

71 games—Mrs. Margaret Osborne duPont, Wilmington, Delaware, and Bill Talbert, New York, d. Gussie Moran, Santa Monica, California, and Bob Falkenburg, Los Angeles, 27–25, 5–7, 6–1. Semifinal, National Mixed, West Side Tennis Club, Forest Hills, 1948.

59 games—Jane Albert, Pebble Beach, California, and Dave Reed, Glendale, California, d. Kathy Blake, Pacific Palisades, California, and Gene Scott, New York, 6–3, 7–9, 19–17. Semifinal, Thunderbird, Phoenix, Arizona, 1965.

58 games—Virginia Wade, England, and Dick Crealy, Australia, d. Mrs. Joyce Barclay Williams and Bob Howe, both England, 7–5, 17–19, 6–4. Third round, U.S. Open, Forest Hills, 1969.

52 games—C. Lyon and W. Dixon, both England, d. Ann Barclay, Canada, and O.K. French, Australia, 2–6, 9–7, 15–13. Second round, Wimbledon, 1963.

Suppose They Gave a Tournament and Everybody Came

by GENE SCOTT

One way—maybe the best—to decide who was the top player of all time is to have an imaginary tournament, playing the matches in one's mind. Gene Scott did just that in his 1974 book, Tennis: Game of Motion, *and if his interpretation seems a bit dated, well, that's the fun of it—that's your own imaginary tournament. Play on.*

ARE today's stars superior to those of yesteryear? In that endless, monotonous argument, the imponderables are large.

What surface would be chosen? Would modern equipment be used by old-timers, or would Arthur Ashe have to serve with a spoon-shaped wooden relic? Would Bill Tilden alter his serving and volleying style? Could Helen Wills handle Billie Jean King's bustle about the court?

Such absurd conjecture might be stilled if thirty-two of the best men and sixteen of the best women in tennis history were to come together in the same tournament. And the tourney's outcome might be dictated by the draw.

In every championship tennis event, the tournament committee selects at least eight of the best players, a selection based on the players' recent performance. These elite players are called "seeds" and are separated in the draw so that they will not meet, if form holds true, until the quarterfinals. (The reason for seeding is obvious. It would be disastrous if the best players were to eliminate each other in the opening rounds, leaving one good player and seven rabbits in the quarterfinals.)

After the seeds are placed in the draw, the names of the remaining players are picked by chance to determine pairings. To give tradition its due, the names in our super championship were paired by drawing them from the Davis Cup itself, before it was sent into sacred storage in Tiffany's vaults. We trust the more stringent traditionalists will not be disconcerted by the thought of tennis generations united in the great urn.

When people attempt to rate the all-time great players, they usually fail to realize that tennis is a game of distinct match-ups in which the pairings are as important as an accurate first serve. Rod Laver has beaten Arthur Ashe twelve times without losing. With almost as much regularity, Ashe defeats Marty Riessen, yet Riessen gives fits to Laver. He has won at least half their meetings.

Match-ups can present psychological subplots, which have nothing to do with tactics or skill but which can affect the outcome of the contest just as much. Ashe, for example, rose through the junior ranks considering Riessen, though only sixteen months older, a journeyman player with solid but not exceptional skills. In later years, Ashe could not alter his original impression, even after Riessen radically supercharged his game. With such confidence, Ashe dominated their meetings.

When players have similar or offsetting skills, as they do on the top professional level, confidence is crucial. Any super championship, therefore, will be affected by the draw, which can determine match-ups that psychologically unhinge one player or arouse confidence in another.

Stan Smith would have had an excellent chance of upsetting Bill Tilden, so mechanically perfect and basic are Smith's serve and volley. But Smith would have been baffled by the athleticism of Tony Trabert, who, in turn, would have been bedeviled by Henri Cochet's guile.

Unmindful of such psychological factors, many Davis Cup captains choose their teams in challenge matches with little regard for who the opposition will be. Smith might lose to Tom Gorman in intrasquad competition, but Gorman, having never beaten Ilie Nastase, would be a poor choice to face the agile Rumanian.

The surface is also important. In the championship, we envisioned a surface with enough traction to help the fleet and one that produced the ideal bounces—fast enough to give a premium for boldness, true enough to ensure errorless rallies. In short, we assumed the ideal surface. We picked Pancho Gonzales to win. As often as not, Lew Hoad might beat Gonzales, but we picked Pancho to prevail in an arduous tournament.

The best match of the first round was Ilie Nastase against Jean Borotra, a pairing of fidgety, high-strung temperaments. Nastase won when his bustle bewildered the frenetic Frenchman.

Ashe defeated Maurice McLaughlin, his first opponent, in a battle of whistling serves. Cochet outlasted Manuel Santana, in a triumph of cunning over artistry. John Newcombe's firepower overwhelmed Dick Sears. Smith's basic speed of service offset Frank Sedgman's quickness at net,

and Gonzales, though outshot by the talented Ellsworth Vines, was the more resolute competitor.

In the second round, the Tilden-Ashe affair was the most intriguing as "Big Bill" dropped the first two sets, as was his custom, but accelerated dramatically to win the next three, by identical scores, 6–4. Trabert performed with customary, all-American heroics before bowing to Laver. Fred Perry taunted Smith for his implacable seriousness, making Smith a sentimental choice, but Perry's athletic facility conquered Smith, whose concentration was nonetheless exemplary, particularly when he won both sudden-death sets. In a match of service bombardments, Gonzales won over Hoad with competitive brilliance at crisis.

In the quarterfinals, Gonzales's toughness was the proper riposte to Perry's raw tongue and raw talent, but Tilden's win over René LaCoste came only with a flicker of luck—he served the last of the sudden-death points. Laver's powerful wrists produced mighty topspin on both forehand and backhand, and dispirited Cochet. Don Budge and Kramer, unluckily placed in the same sector of the draw, resolved the issue when Budge bludgeoned a winning backhand return of Kramer's second serve in the final point of the tie-breaker.

In the semifinals, the most dramatic play came when Gonzales coldly and professionally executed Tilden, the performer. Meanwhile, double Grand Slam winner Laver battled single Grand Slam winner Budge. Laver won not with his slam but because Budge's awesome backhand drove naturally cross-court to Laver's strength— his southpaw forehand. In the final, Gonzales triumphed when he made one stroke, his fearful serve, dominate a match as no other weapon could. Laver's skills remain unsurpassed, but a single lightning shot can defuse the most versatile arsenal. The Gonzales serve did.

The women presented a difficult problem because Billie Jean King, Maria Bueno, Maureen Connolly, Margaret Court, Suzanne Lenglen, and Helen Wills were so evenly matched. We confess weakness in choosing legend over icy statistics, but we chose Lenglen as champion.

The first round showed no surprises, though the Evert-Connolly encounter was entrancing. The score was short, but the rallies were long, as Maureen won, stolid and businesslike over Chris, stylish and graceful. Connolly won over Bueno in the quarters because the Brazilian's artistry could not overcome Connolly's smoothly churning ground strokes. Court's physical conditioning wore down even such a staunch advocate of fitness as Wills.

In the semifinals, King persevered over the meteoric Connolly. Court's loss to Lenglen and Lenglen's ultimate triumph over King are our irrepressible but improbable hope that the supreme artist would overcome the supreme athlete.

NAME

SEEDED PLAYERS
1. Tilden
2. Laver
3. Budge
4. Gonzales
5. Kramer
6. Lacoste
7. Perry
8. Cochet

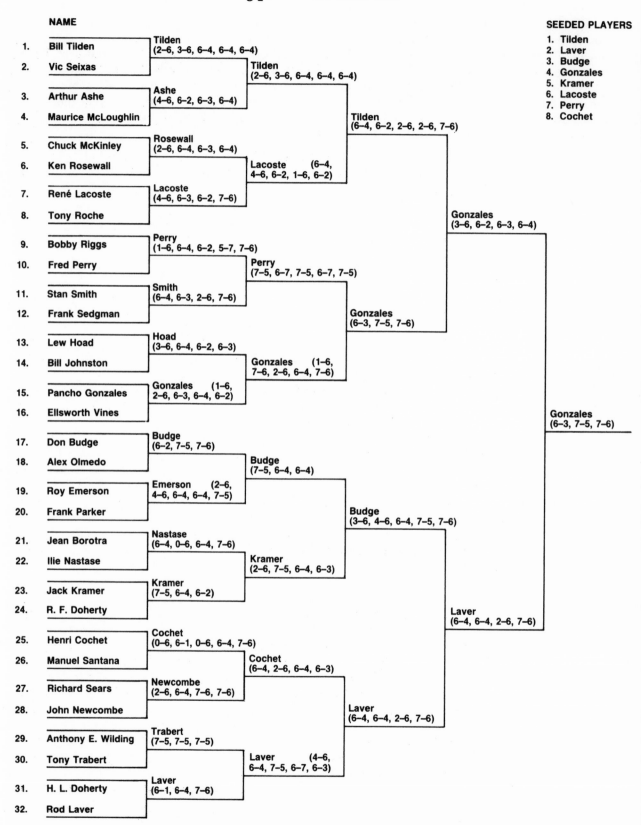

1. Bill Tilden

Tilden
(2–6, 3–6, 6–4, 6–4, 6–4)

2. Vic Seixas

Tilden
(2–6, 3–6, 6–4, 6–4, 6–4)

3. Arthur Ashe

Ashe
(4–6, 6–2, 6–3, 6–4)

4. Maurice McLoughlin

Tilden
(6–4, 6–2, 2–6, 2–6, 7–6)

5. Chuck McKinley

Rosewall
(2–6, 6–4, 6–3, 6–4)

6. Ken Rosewall

Lacoste (6–4,
4–6, 6–2, 1–6, 6–2)

7. René Lacoste

Lacoste
(4–6, 6–3, 6–2, 7–6)

8. Tony Roche

Gonzales
(3–6, 6–2, 6–3, 6–4)

9. Bobby Riggs

Perry
(1–6, 6–4, 6–2, 5–7, 7–6)

10. Fred Perry

Perry
(7–5, 6–7, 7–5, 6–7, 7–5)

11. Stan Smith

Smith
(6–4, 6–3, 2–6, 7–6)

12. Frank Sedgman

Gonzales
(6–3, 7–5, 7–6)

13. Lew Hoad

Hoad
(3–6, 6–4, 6–2, 6–3)

14. Bill Johnston

Gonzales (1–6,
7–6, 2–6, 6–4, 7–6)

15. Pancho Gonzales

Gonzales (1–6,
2–6, 6–3, 6–4, 6–2)

16. Ellsworth Vines

Gonzales
(6–3, 7–5, 7–6)

17. Don Budge

Budge
(6–2, 7–5, 7–6)

18. Alex Olmedo

Budge
(7–5, 6–4, 6–4)

19. Roy Emerson

Emerson (2–6,
4–6, 6–4, 6–4, 7–5)

20. Frank Parker

Budge
(3–6, 4–6, 6–4, 7–5, 7–6)

21. Jean Borotra

Nastase
(6–4, 0–6, 6–4, 7–6)

22. Ilie Nastase

Kramer
(2–6, 7–5, 6–4, 6–3)

23. Jack Kramer

Kramer
(7–5, 6–4, 6–2)

24. R. F. Doherty

Laver
(6–4, 6–4, 2–6, 7–6)

25. Henri Cochet

Cochet
(0–6, 6–1, 0–6, 6–4, 7–6)

26. Manuel Santana

Cochet
(6–4, 2–6, 6–4, 6–3)

27. Richard Sears

Newcombe
(2–6, 6–4, 7–6, 7–6)

28. John Newcombe

Laver
(6–4, 6–4, 2–6, 7–6)

29. Anthony E. Wilding

Trabert
(7–5, 7–5, 7–5)

30. Tony Trabert

Laver (4–6,
6–4, 7–5, 6–7, 6–3)

31. H. L. Doherty

Laver
(6–1, 6–4, 7–6)

32. Rod Laver

NAME

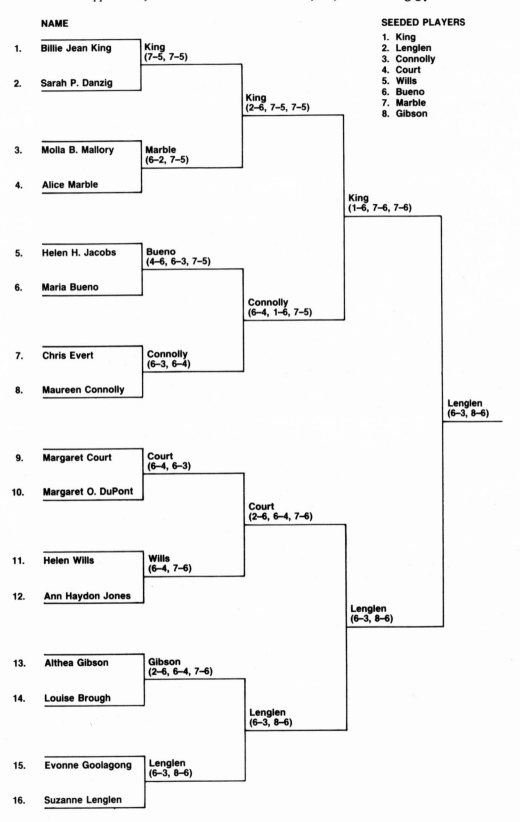

1. Billie Jean King
    King
    (7–5, 7–5)

2. Sarah P. Danzig

    King
    (2–6, 7–5, 7–5)

3. Molla B. Mallory
    Marble
    (6–2, 7–5)

4. Alice Marble

    King
    (1–6, 7–6, 7–6)

5. Helen H. Jacobs
    Bueno
    (4–6, 6–3, 7–5)

6. Maria Bueno

    Connolly
    (6–4, 1–6, 7–5)

7. Chris Evert
    Connolly
    (6–3, 6–4)

8. Maureen Connolly

    Lenglen
    (6–3, 8–6)

9. Margaret Court
    Court
    (6–4, 6–3)

10. Margaret O. DuPont

    Court
    (2–6, 6–4, 7–6)

11. Helen Wills
    Wills
    (6–4, 7–6)

12. Ann Haydon Jones

    Lenglen
    (6–3, 8–6)

13. Althea Gibson
    Gibson
    (2–6, 6–4, 7–6)

14. Louise Brough

    Lenglen
    (6–3, 8–6)

15. Evonne Goolagong
    Lenglen
    (6–3, 8–6)

16. Suzanne Lenglen

The All-Time Tournament

by GIANNI CLERICI

The great players of tennis are linked, by their continued participation in the game's traditional events, and by their matches through the years against each other. Here Gianni Clerici has assembled real re-sults to form an all-time draw sheet. Of course the final match was never played, and the final question—who was the best?—remains unanswered.

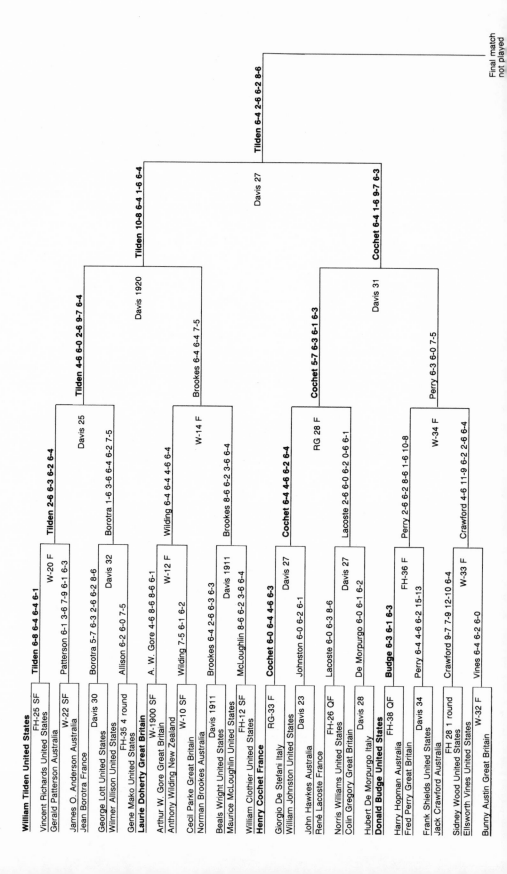

Final match
not played

Tilden 6-4 2-6 6-2 8-6

Davis 27

Tilden 10-8 6-4 1-6 6-4

Cochet 6-4 1-6 9-7 6-3

Davis 1920

Davis 31

Tilden 4-6 6-0 2-6 9-7 6-4

Cochet 5-7 6-3 6-1 6-3

Brookes 6-4 6-4 7-5

Perry 6-3 6-0 7-5

Davis 25

W-14 F

RG 28 F

W-34 F

Tilden 2-6 6-3 6-2 6-4

Wilding 6-4 6-4 4-6 6-4

Cochet 4-6 6-2 6-4

Lacoste 2-6 6-0 6-2 0-6 6-1

Perry 2-6 6-2 8-6 1-6 10-8

Crawford 4-6 11-9 6-2 2-6 6-4

W-20 F

Davis 32

W-12 F

Davis 1911

Davis 27

Davis 27

FH-36 F

W-33 F

Patterson 6-1 3-6 7-9 6-1 6-3

Borotra 1-6 3-6 6-4 6-2 7-5

Brookes 8-6 6-2 3-6 6-4

Johnston 6-0 6-2 6-1

De Morpurgo 6-0 6-1 6-2

Perry 6-4 4-6 6-2 15-13

Vines 6-4 6-2 6-0

Tilden 6-8 6-4 6-4 6-1

Borotra 5-7 6-3 2-6 6-2 8-6

A. W. Gore 4-6 8-6 8-6 6-1

Brookes 6-4 2-6 6-3 6-3

Cochet 6-0 6-4 4-6 6-3

Lacoste 6-0 6-3 8-6

Budge 6-3 6-1 6-3

Crawford 9-7 7-9 12-10 6-4

Allison 6-2 6-0 7-5

Wilding 7-5 6-1 6-2

McLoughlin 8-6 6-2 3-6 6-4

FH-25 SF

W-22 SF

Davis 30

FH-35 4 round

W-1900 SF

W-10 SF

Davis 1911

FH-12 SF

RG-33 F

Davis 23

FH-26 QF

Davis 28

FH-38 QF

Davis 34

FH 28 1 round

W-32 F

William Tilden United States
Vincent Richards United States
Gerald Patterson Australia
James O. Anderson Australia
Jean Borotra France
George Lott United States
Wilmer Allison United States
Gene Mako United States
Laurie Doherty Great Britain
Arthur W. Gore Great Britain
Anthony Wilding New Zealand
Cecil Parke Great Britain
Norman Brookes Australia
Beals Wright United States
Maurice McLoughlin United States
William Clothier United States
Henry Cochet France
Giorgio De Stefani Italy
William Johnston United States
John Hawkes Australia
René Lacoste France
Norris Williams United States
Colin Gregory Great Britain
Hubert De Morpurgo Italy
Donald Budge United States
Harry Hopman Australia
Fred Perry Great Britain
Frank Shields United States
Jack Crawford Australia
Sidney Wood United States
Ellsworth Vines United States
Bunny Austin Great Britain

Laver 7-5 14-16 7-5 6-2

MSG 67 F

Gonzales 7-5 6-3 6-4   Laver 6-4 5-7 6-4 6-4

Phil.-50 F   RG-69 F

Gonzales 16-18 2-6 6-1 6-2 6-4   Kramer 3-6 6-3 6-0 6-1   Rosewall 4-6 6-2 6-3 6-3   Laver 6-4 6-3 6-4

FH-49 F   FH-47 SF   FH-56 F   W-69 F

Schroeder 8-6 7-5 3-6 4-6 6-2   Gonzales 8-6 6-4 9-7   Drobny 6-3 6-4 6-4   Kramer 6-0 6-4 6-4   Hoad 4-6 6-3 6-3 8-6   Rosewall 6-2 2-6 6-3 6-4   Newcombe 6-3 5-7 2-6 6-4 6-4   Laver 4-6 6-3 8-10 6-2 6-4

FH-42 F   Davis 49   Hmb-50 F   FH-46 SF   Davis 55   Davis 53   W-71 F   W-60 SF

Parker 6-3 6-4 1-6 7-5   Schroeder 3-6 7-5 5-7 6-1 6-2   Sedgman 6-3 6-4 4-6 6-1   Gonzales 6-0 6-2 6-4   von Cramm 0-6 8-6 6-8 6-3 6-2   Drobny 8-6 16-18 3-6 8-6 12-10   Falkenburg 7-5 0-6 6-2 3-6 7-5   Kramer 6-3 6-2 1-6 6-2   Trabert 6-4 7-5 6-1   Hoad 6-2 6-1 6-2   Seixas 6-4 10-12 9-11 6-4 6-3   Rosewall 6-4 6-4 6-3   Smith 4-6 6-3 6-3 4-6 7-5   Newcombe 6-4 1-6 4-6 6-2 6-3   Pietrangeli 11-9 6-3 1-6 6-2   Laver 14-16 9-7 6-2 6-2

Davis 39   W-49 SF   Aus.-50 F   Las Vegas-69 F   FH-37 SF   W-53 3 round   W-48 F   FH-46 QF   RG-55 F   W-57 F   W-53 SF   Aus.-71 QF   W-72 F   FH-73 F   Davis 60   W-62 QF

Adrian Quist Australia
Frank Parker United States
Eric Sturgess South Africa
Ted Schroeder United States
Ken McGregor Australia
Frank Sedgman Australia
Arthur Ashe United States
Pancho Gonzales United States
Bobby Riggs United States
Gottfried von Cramm Germany
Budge Patty United States
Jaroslav Drobny Czechoslovakia
John Bromwich Australia
Bob Falkenburg United States
Don McNeill United States
Jack Kramer United States
Sven Davidson Sweden
Tony Trabert United States
Ashley Cooper Australia
Lewis Hoad Australia
Mervyn Rose Australia
Vic Seixas United States
Roy Emerson Australia
Ken Rosewall Australia
Ilie Nastase Rumania
Stanley Smith United States
Jan Kodes Czechoslovakia
John Newcombe Australia
Neale Fraser Australia
Nicola Pietrangeli Italy
Manolo Santana Spain
Rod Laver Australia

Aus. = Australian Champion
Davis = Davis Cup
FH = Forest Hills
Hmb. = Hamburg
MSG = Madison Square Garden
Phil. = Philadelphia
RG = Roland Garros
W = Wimbledon
WC = Wightman Cup
QF = Quarterfinals
SF = Semifinals
F = Finals
1 = 1st round
3 = 3rd round
4 = 4th round

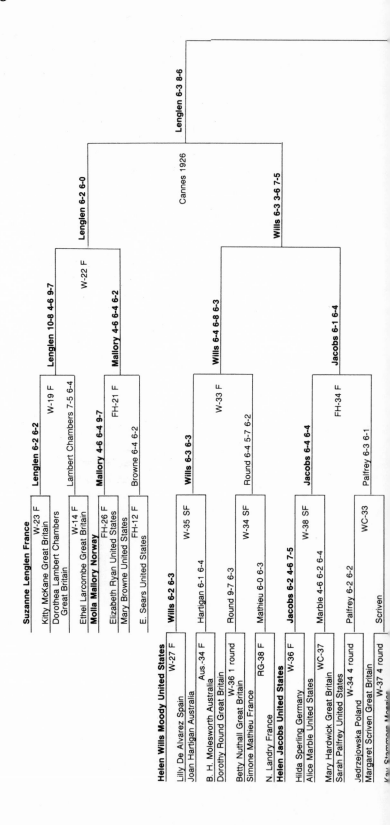

Suzanne Lenglen France

W-23 F	
Kitty McKane Great Britain	
Dorothea Lambert Chambers Great Britain	
W-14 F	
Ethel Larcombe Great Britain	

Lenglen 6-2 6-2

W-19 F

Lambert Chambers 7-5 6-4

Lenglen 10-8 4-6 9-7

W-22 F

Lenglen 6-2 6-0

Cannes 1926

Lenglen 6-3 8-6

Molla Mallory Norway

FH-26 F	
Elizabeth Ryan United States	
Mary Browne United States	
FH-12 F	
E. Sears United States	

Mallory 4-6 6-4 9-7

FH-21 F

Browne 6-4 6-2

Mallory 4-6 6-4 6-2

Helen Wills Moody United States

W-27 F	
Lilly De Alvarez Spain	
Joan Hartigan Australia	
Aus.-34 F	
B. H. Molesworth Australia	
Dorothy Round Great Britain	

Wills 6-2 6-3

W-35 SF

Hartigan 6-1 6-4

Wills 6-3 6-3

W-33 F

Wills 6-4 6-8 6-3

Wills 6-3 3-6 7-5

W-36 1 round	
Betty Nuthall Great Britain	
Simone Mathieu France	
RG-38 F	
N. Landry France	

Round 9-7 6-3

W-34 SF

Mathieu 6-0 6-3

Round 6-4 5-7 6-2

Helen Jacobs United States

W-36 F	
Hilda Sperling Germany	
Alice Marble United States	
WC-37	
Mary Hardwick Great Britain	
Sarah Palfrey United States	

Jacobs 6-2 4-6 7-5

W-38 SF

Marble 4-6 6-2 6-4

Jacobs 6-4 6-4

FH-34 F

Jacobs 6-1 6-4

W-34 4 round	
Jedrzejowska Poland	
Margaret Scriven Great Britain	
W-37 4 round	
Kay Stammers Magazine	

Palfrey 6-2 6-2

WC-33

Palfrey 6-3 6-1

Scriven

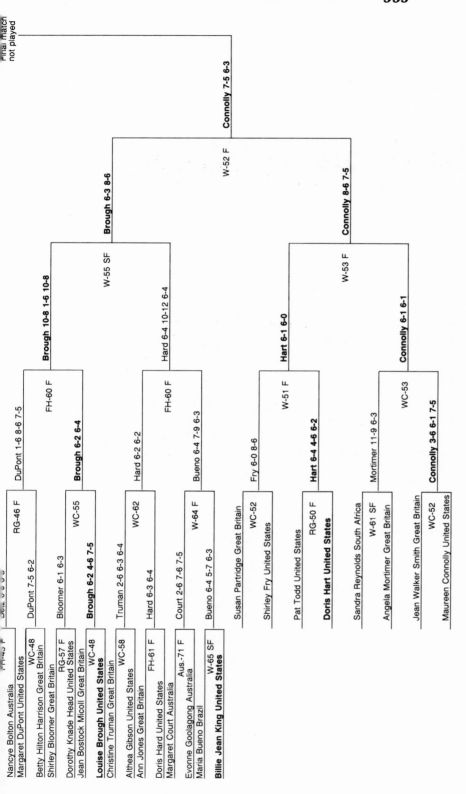

Final match
not played

Connolly 7-5 6-3

W-52 F

Brough 6-3 8-6

Connolly 8-6 7-5

W-55 SF

W-53 F

Brough 10-8 1-6 10-8

Hart 6-1 6-0

Connolly 6-1 6-1

FH-60 F

W-51 F

WC-53

DuPont 1-6 8-6 7-5

Brough 6-2 6-4

Hard 6-2 6-2

Bueno 6-4 7-9 6-3

Fry 6-0 8-6

Hart 6-4 4-6 6-2

Mortimer 11-9 6-3

Connolly 3-6 6-1 7-5

FH-60 F

RG-46 F

WC-55

WC-62

W-64 F

WC-52

RG-50 F

W-61 SF

WC-52

DuPont 7-5 6-2

Bloomer 6-1 6-3

Brough 6-2 4-6 7-5

Truman 2-6 6-3 6-4

Hard 6-3 6-4

Court 2-6 7-6 7-5

Bueno 6-4 5-7 6-3

Susan Partridge Great Britain

Shirley Fry United States

Pat Todd United States

Doris Hart United States

Sandra Reynolds South Africa

Angela Mortimer Great Britain

Jean Walker Smith Great Britain

Maureen Connolly United States

Nancye Bolton Australia

Margaret DuPont United States

Betty Hilton Harrison Great Britain

Shirley Bloomer Great Britain

Dorothy Knade Head United States

Jean Bostock Micoll Great Britain

Louise Brough United States

Christine Truman Great Britain

Althea Gibson United States

Ann Jones Great Britain

Doris Hard United States

Margaret Court Australia

Evonne Goolagong Australia

Maria Bueno Brazil

Billie Jean King United States

WC-48

RG-57 F

WC-48

WC-58

FH-61 F

Aus.-71 F

W-65 SF

The Championships

ALL-ENGLAND CHAMPIONSHIPS
Wimbledon Championships

From 1877 to 1921 the men's singles was decided on a Challenge Round system, the previous year's winner standing out until a winner of the so called All Comers event qualified to challenge. The same system applied in the women's singles from 1886 to 1921 and in the men's doubles from 1886 to 1921. It never applied in the women's and mixed doubles.

The championships were staged at the All-England Club, Worple Road, Wimbledon, from 1877 to 1921 when the club moved to Church Road, Wimbledon.

Wimbledon became "Open" in 1968.

English Championships—Men's Singles

1877	Spencer W. Gore
1878	P. Frank Hadow
1879	John T. Hartley
1880	John T. Hartley
1881	William Renshaw
1882	William Renshaw
1883	William Renshaw
1884	William Renshaw
1885	William Renshaw
1886	William Renshaw
1887	Herbert F. Lawford
1888	Ernest Renshaw
1889	William Renshaw
1890	William J. Hamilton
1891	Wilfred Baddeley
1892	Wilfred Baddeley
1893	Joshua Pim
1894	Joshua Pim
1895	Wilfred Baddeley
1896	H.S. Mahoney
1897	Reggie F. Doherty
1898	Reggie F. Doherty
1899	Reggie F. Doherty
1900	Reggie F. Doherty
1901	Arthur W. Gore
1902	H. Laurie Doherty
1903	H. Laurie Doherty
1904	H. Laurie Doherty
1905	H. Laurie Doherty
1906	H. Laurie Doherty
1907	Norman E. Brookes
1908	Arthur W. Gore
1909	Arthur W. Gore
1910	Anthony F. Wilding
1911	Anthony F. Wilding
1912	Anthony F. Wilding
1913	Anthony F. Wilding
1914	Norman E. Brookes
1915–18	Not held
1919	Gerald L. Patterson
1920	William T. Tilden
1921	William T. Tilden
1922	Gerald L. Patterson
1923	William M. Johnston
1924	Jean Borotra
1925	René Lacoste
1926	Jean Borotra
1927	Henri Cochet
1928	René Lacoste
1929	Henri Cochet
1930	William T. Tilden
1931	Sidney Wood
1932	Ellsworth Vines
1933	Jack Crawford
1934	Fred J. Perry
1935	Fred J. Perry
1936	Fred J. Perry

1937	Don Budge
1938	Don Budge
1939	Bobby Riggs
1940–45	Not held
1946	Yvon Petra
1947	Jack Kramer
1948	Bob Falkenburg
1949	Ted Schroeder
1950	Budge Patty
1951	Dick Savitt
1952	Frank Sedgman
1953	Vic Seixas
1954	Jaroslav Drobny
1955	Tony Trabert
1956	Lew Hoad
1957	Lew Hoad
1958	Ashley Cooper
1959	Alex Olmedo
1960	Neale Fraser
1961	Rod Laver
1962	Rod Laver
1963	Chuck McKinley
1964	Roy Emerson
1965	Roy Emerson
1966	Manuel Santana
1967	John Newcombe
*1968	Rod Laver
*1969	Rod Laver
*1970	John Newcombe
*1971	John Newcombe
*1972	Stan Smith
*1973	Jan Kodes
*1974	Jimmy Connors
*1975	Arthur Ashe
*1976	Bjorn Borg
*1977	Bjorn Borg
*1978	Bjorn Borg
*1979	Bjorn Borg
*1980	Bjorn Borg

English Championships—Men's Doubles

1879	L.R. Erskine—Herbert F. Lawford
1880	William Renshaw—Ernest Renshaw
1881	William Renshaw—Ernest Renshaw
1882	John T. Hartley—R.T. Richardson
1883	C.W. Grinstead—C.E. Welldon
1884	William Renshaw—Ernest Renshaw
1885	William Renshaw—Ernest Renshaw
1886	William Renshaw—Ernest Renshaw
1887	Herbert W. Wiberforce—P.B. Lyon
1888	William Renshaw—Ernest Renshaw
1889	William Renshaw—Ernest Renshaw
1890	Joshua Pim—F.O. Stoker
1891	Wilfred Baddeley—Herbert Baddeley
1892	E.W. Lewis—H.S. Barlow
1893	Joshua Pim—F.O. Stoker
1894	Wilfred Baddeley—Herbert Baddeley
1895	Wilfred Baddeley—Herbert Baddeley
1896	Wilfred Baddeley—Herbert Baddeley
1897	Reggie F. Doherty—H. Laurie Doherty
1898	Reggie F. Doherty—H. Laurie Doherty
1899	Reggie F. Doherty—H. Laurie Doherty
1900	Reggie F. Doherty—H. Laurie Doherty

1901	Reggie F. Doherty—H. Laurie Doherty
1902	Sidney H. Smith—Frank Riseley
1903	Reggie F. Doherty—H. Laurie Doherty
1904	Reggie F. Doherty—H. Laurie Doherty
1905	Reggie F. Doherty—H. Laurie Doherty
1906	Sidney H. Smith—Frank Riseley
1907	Norman E. Brookes—Anthony F. Wilding
1908	Anthony F. Wilding—M.J.G. Ritchie
1909	Arthur W. Gore—H. Roper Barrett
1910	Anthony F. Wilding—M.J.G. Ritchie
1911	Andre Gobert—Max Decugis
1912	H. Roper Barrett—Charles P. Dixon
1913	H. Roper Barrett—Charles P. Dixon
1914	Norman E. Brookes—Anthony F. Wilding
1915–18	Not held
1919	R.V. Thomas—Pat O'Hara Wood
1920	R. Norris Williams—Chuck S. Garland
1921	Randolph Lycett—Max Woosnam
1922	James O. Anderson—Randolph Lycett
1923	Leslie A. Godfree—Randolph Lycett
1924	Frank Hunter—Vincent Richards
1925	Jean Borotra—René Lacoste
1926	Jacques Brugnon—Henri Cochet
1927	Frank Hunter—William T. Tilden
1928	Jacques Brugnon—Henri Cochet
1929	Wilmer Allison—John Van Ryn
1930	Wilmer Allison—John Van Ryn
1931	George M. Lott—John Van Ryn
1932	Jean Borotra—Jacques Brugnon
1933	Jean Borotra—Jacques Brugnon
1934	George M. Lott—Lester R. Stoefen
1935	Jack Crawford—Adrian Quist
1936	G. Pat Hughes—Raymond Tuckey
1937	Don Budge—Gene Mako
1938	Don Budge—Gene Mako
1939	Ellwood Cooke—Bobby Riggs
1940–45	Not held
1946	Tom Brown—Jack Kramer
1947	Bob Falkenburg—Jack Kramer
1948	John Bromwich—Frank Sedgman
1949	Richard Gonzales—Frank Parker
1950	John Bromwich—Adrian Quist
1951	Ken McGregor—Frank Sedgman
1952	Ken McGregor—Frank Sedgman
1953	Lew Hoad—Ken Rosewall
1954	Rex Hartwig—Mervyn Rose
1955	Rex Hartwig—Lew Hoad
1956	Lew Hoad—Ken Rosewall
1957	Budge Patty—Gardnar Mulloy
1958	Sven Davidson—Ulf Schmidt
1959	Roy Emerson—Neale Fraser
1960	Rafael Osuna—Dennis Ralston
1961	Roy Emerson—Neale Fraser
1962	Bob Hewitt—Fred Stolle
1963	Rafael Osuna—Antonio Palafox
1964	Bob Hewitt—Fred Stolle
1965	John Newcombe—Tony Roche
1966	Ken Fletcher—John Newcombe
1967	Bob Hewitt—Frew McMillan
*1968	John Newcombe—Tony Roche
*1969	John Newcombe—Tony Roche
*1970	John Newcombe—Tony Roche
*1971	Roy Emerson—Rod Laver

*1972	Bob Hewitt—Frew McMillan	
*1973	Jimmy Connors—Ilie Nastase	
*1974	John Newcombe—Tony Roche	
*1975	Vitas Gerulaitis—Alex Mayer	
*1976	Brian Gottfried—Raul Ramirez	
*1977	Geoff Masters—Ross Case	
*1978	Bob Hewitt—Frew McMillan	
*1979	John McEnroe—Peter Fleming	
*1980	Peter McNamara—Paul McNamee	

English Championships—Women's Singles

1884	Maud Watson
1885	Maud Watson
1886	Blanche Bingley
1887	Lottie Dod
1888	Lottie Dod
1889	Blanche Bingley Hillyard
1890	L. Rice
1891	Lottie Dod
1892	Lottie Dod
1893	Lottie Dod
1894	Blanche Bingley Hillyard
1895	Charlotte Cooper
1896	Charlotte Cooper
1897	Blanche Bingley Hillyard
1898	Charlotte Cooper
1899	Blanche Bingley Hillyard
1900	Blanche Bingley Hillyard
1901	Charlotte Cooper Sterry
1902	Muriel E. Robb
1903	Dorothea Douglass
1904	Dorothea Douglass
1905	May Sutton
1906	Dorothea Douglass
1907	May Sutton
1908	Charlotte Cooper Sterry
1909	Dora Boothby
1910	Dorothea D. Chambers
1911	Dorothea D. Chambers
1912	Ethel W. Thomson Larcombe
1913	Dorothea D. Chambers
1914	Dorothea D. Chambers
1915–18	Not held
1919	Suzanne Lenglen
1920	Suzanne Lenglen
1921	Suzanne Lenglen
1922	Suzanne Lenglen
1923	Suzanne Lenglen
1924	Kitty McKane
1925	Suzanne Lenglen
1926	Kitty McKane Godfree
1927	Helen Wills
1928	Helen Wills
1929	Helen Wills
1930	Helen Wills Moody
1931	Cilly Aussem
1932	Helen Wills Moody
1933	Helen Wills Moody
1934	Dorothy Round
1935	Helen Wills Moody
1936	Helen Jacobs
1937	Dorothy Round
1938	Helen Wills Moody

1939	Alice Marble
1940–45	Not held
1946	Pauline Betz
1947	Margaret Osborne
1948	Louise Brough
1949	Louise Brough
1950	Louise Brough
1951	Doris Hart
1952	Maureen Connolly
1953	Maureen Connolly
1954	Maureen Connolly
1955	Louise Brough
1956	Shirley Fry
1957	Althea Gibson
1958	Althea Gibson
1959	Maria Bueno
1960	Maria Bueno
1961	Angela Mortimer
1962	Karen Hantze Susman
1963	Margaret Smith
1964	Maria Bueno
1965	Margaret Smith
1966	Billie Jean Moffitt King
1967	Billie Jean Moffitt King
*1968	Billie Jean Moffitt King
*1969	Ann Haydon Jones
*1970	Margaret Smith Court
*1971	Evonne Goolagong
*1972	Billie Jean Moffitt King
*1973	Billie Jean Moffitt King
*1974	Chris Evert
*1975	Billie Jean Moffitt King
*1976	Chris Evert
*1977	Virginia Wade
*1978	Martina Navratilova
*1979	Martina Navratilova
*1980	Evonne Goolagong Cawley

English Championships—Women's Doubles

1913	Mrs. R.J. McNair—Dora Boothby
1914	A.M. Morton—Elizabeth Ryan
1915–18	Not held
1919	Suzanne Lenglen—Elizabeth Ryan
1920	Suzanne Lenglen—Elizabeth Ryan
1921	Suzanne Lenglen—Elizabeth Ryan
1922	Suzanne Lenglen—Elizabeth Ryan
1923	Suzanne Lenglen—Elizabeth Ryan
1924	Hazel Wightman—Helen Wills
1925	Suzanne Lenglen—Elizabeth Ryan
1926	Mary K. Browne—Elizabeth Ryan
1927	Helen Wills—Elizabeth Ryan
1928	Peggy Saunders—Phoebe Watson
1929	Peggy Michell—Phoebe Watson
1930	Helen Wills-Moody—Elizabeth Ryan
1931	Phyllis Mudford—Dorothy Shepherd-Barron
1932	Doris Metaxa—Josane Sigart
1933	Simone Mathieu—Elizabeth Ryan
1934	Simone Mathieu—Elizabeth Ryan
1935	Freda James—Kay Stammers
1936	Freda James—Kay Stammers
1937	Simone Mathieu—Billy Yorke
1938	Sarah Palfrey-Fabyan—Alice Marble
1939	Sarah Palfrey-Fabyan—Alice Marble

1940–45	Not held
1946	Louise Brough—Margaret Osborne
1947	Pat Todd—Doris Hart
1948	Louise Brough—Margaret Osborne-DuPont
1949	Louise Brough—Margaret Osborne-DuPont
1950	Louise Brough—Margaret Osborne-DuPont
1951	Doris Hart—Shirley Fry
1952	Doris Hart—Shirley Fry
1953	Doris Hart—Shirley Fry
1954	Louise Brough—Margaret Osborne-DuPont
1955	Angela Mortimer—Anne Shilcock
1956	Angela Buxton—Althea Gibson
1957	Althea Gibson—Darlene Hard
1958	Maria Bueno—Althea Gibson
1959	Jeanne Arth—Darlene Hard
1960	Maria Bueno—Darlene Hard
1961	Karen Hantze—Billie Jean Moffitt
1962	Billie Jean Moffitt—Karen Hantze-Susman
1963	Maria Bueno—Darlene Hard
1964	Margaret Smith—Lesley Turner
1965	Maria Bueno—Billie Jean Moffitt
1966	Maria Bueno—Nancy Richey
1967	Rosemary Casals—Billie Jean Moffitt-King
*1968	Rosemary Casals—Billie Jean Moffitt-King
*1969	Margaret Smith-Court—Judy Tegart
*1970	Rosemary Casals—Billie Jean Moffitt-King
*1971	Rosemary Casals—Billie Jean Moffitt-King
*1972	Billie Jean Moffitt-King—Betty Stove
*1973	Rosemary Casals—Billie Jean Moffitt King
*1974	Evonne Goolagong—Margaret Michel
*1975	Ann Kiyomura—Kazuko Sawamatsu
*1976	Chris Evert—Martina Navratilova
*1977	Helen Gourlay—Jo Anne Russell
*1978	Kerry Reid—Wendy Turnbull
*1979	Billie Jean Moffitt-King—Martina Navratilova
*1980	Kathy Jordan—Anne Smith

English Championships—Mixed Doubles

1913	J. Hope Crisp—C.O. Tuckey
1914	J.C. Parke—Ethel T. Larcombe
1915–18	Not held
1919	Randolph Lycett—Elizabeth Ryan
1920	Gerald Patterson—Suzanne Lenglen
1921	Randolph Lycett—Elizabeth Ryan
1922	Pat O'Hara Wood—Suzanne Lenglen
1923	Randolph Lycett—Elizabeth Ryan
1924	J. Brian Gilbert—Kitty McKane
1925	Jean Borotra—Suzanne Lenglen
1926	Leslie Godfree—Kitty McKane-Godfree
1927	Francis T. Hunter—Elizabeth Ryan
1928	Pat Spence—Elizabeth Ryan
1929	Francis T. Hunter—Helen Wills
1930	Jack Crawford—Elizabeth Ryan
1931	George M. Lott—Mrs. L.A. Harper
1932	Enrique Maier—Elizabeth Ryan
1933	Gottfried von Cramm—Hilda Krahwinkel
1934	Mike Ryuki—Dorothy Round
1935	Fred J. Perry—Dorothy Round
1936	Fred J. Perry—Dorothy Round
1937	Don Budge—Alice Marble
1938	Don Budge—Alice Marble
1939	Bobby Riggs—Alice Marble
1940–45	Not held

1946	Tom Brown—Louise Brough
1947	John Bromwich—Louise Brough
1948	John Bromwich—Louise Brough
1949	Eric Sturgess—Sheila Summers
1950	Eric Sturgess—Louise Brough
1951	Frank Sedgman—Doris Hart
1952	Frank Sedgman—Doris Hart
1953	Vic Seixas—Doris Hart
1954	Vic Seixas—Doris Hart
1955	Vic Seixas—Doris Hart
1956	Vic Seixas—Shirley Fry
1957	Mervyn Rose—Darlene Hard
1958	Bob Howe—Loraine Coghlan
1959	Rod Laver—Darlene Hard
1960	Rod Laver—Darlene Hard
1961	Fred Stolle—Lesley Turner
1962	Neale Fraser—Margaret Osborne-DuPont
1963	Ken Fletcher—Margaret Smith
1964	Fred Stolle—Lesley Turner
1965	Ken Fletcher—Margaret Smith
1966	Ken Fletcher—Margaret Smith
1967	Owen Davidson—Billie Jean Moffitt-King
*1968	Ken Fletcher—Margaret Smith-Court
*1969	Fred Stolle—Ann Jones
*1970	Ilie Nastase—Rosemary Casals
*1971	Owen Davidson—Billie Jean Moffitt-King
*1972	Ilie Nastase—Rosemary Casals
*1973	Owen Davidson—Billie Jean Moffitt-King
*1974	Owen Davidson—Billie Jean Moffitt-King
*1975	Marty Riessen—Margaret Court
*1976	Tony Roche—Françoise Durr
*1977	Bob Hewitt—Greer Stevens
*1978	Frew McMillan—Betty Stove
*1979	Bob Hewitt—Greer Stevens
*1980	John Austin—Tracy Austin

UNITED STATES CHAMPIONSHIPS
USTA Champions—Men's Singles

National Champions of the United States Tennis Association were provided for when that body was organized, May 21, 1881. Prior to that time so-called national championships had been held, in some cases several being contested in one year, but conditions varied at each tournament and the implements and equipment of the game had not become standardized. The first championship of the United States under uniform conditions, open to all comers and sanctioned by the National Association, was held at The Casino, Newport, Rhode Island, in August 1881, and for thirty-four years without interruption the championship was held there. From 1915 to 1920 the West Side Tennis Club staged the tournament at Forest Hills, Long Island, New York, and from 1921 to 1923 it was held at the Germantown Cricket Club, Philadelphia. In 1924, after the completion of the West Side Tennis Club Stadium, the championship returned to Forest Hills, and was held there until 1978, when it moved to the USTA's brand new tennis complex at Flushing Meadow, New York. Championships have been held each year since 1881 with the exception of 1917. In that year only Patriotic tournaments were sanctioned by the National Association, because of the participation of the United States in the World War. The Challenge Round was instituted in 1884 and abandoned after the 1911 championship. During those years the champion "stood out"—did not play through the tournament—meeting the winner of All Comers in a Challenge Round for the championship.

1881	R.D. Sears
1882	R.D. Sears
1883	R.D. Sears
1884	R.D. Sears
1885	R.D. Sears
1886	R.D. Sears
1887	R.D. Sears
†1888	H.W. Slocum, Jr.
1889	H.W. Slocum, Jr.
1890	O.S. Campbell
1891	O.S. Campbell
1892	O.S. Campbell
†1893	R.D. Wrenn
1894	R.D. Wrenn
1895	F.H. Hovey
1896	R.D. Wrenn
1897	R.D. Wrenn
†1898	M.D. Whitman
1899	M.D. Whitman
1900	M.D. Whitman
†1901	W.A. Larned
1902	W.A. Larned
1903	H. Laurie Doherty
†1904	Holcombe Ward
1905	B.C. Wright
1906	W.J. Clothier
†1907	W.A. Larned
1908	W.A. Larned
1909	W.A. Larned
1910	W.A. Larned
1911	W.A. Larned
‡1912	Maurice E. McLoughlin
1913	Maurice E. McLoughlin
1914	R.N. Williams
1915	William M. Johnston
1916	R.N. Williams
§1917	R.L. Murray
1918	R.L. Murray
1919	W.M. Johnston
1920	William T. Tilden
1921	William T. Tilden
1922	William T. Tilden
1923	William T. Tilden
1924	William T. Tilden
1925	William T. Tilden
1926	René Lacoste
1927	René Lacoste
1928	Henri Cochet
1929	William T. Tilden
1930	John H. Doeg
1931	Ellsworth Vines
1932	Ellsworth Vines

1933	Fred J. Perry
1934	Fred J. Perry
1935	Wilmer L. Allison
1936	Fred J. Perry
1937	Don Budge
1938	Don Budge
1939	Bobby Riggs
1940	Donald McNeill
1941	Bobby Riggs
1942	Frederick R. Schroeder, Jr.
1943	Lt. Joseph R. Hunt
1944	Sgt. Frank Parker
1945	Sgt. Frank Parker
1946	Jack Kramer
1947	Jack Kramer
1948	Richard A. Gonzales
1949	Richard A. Gonzales
1950	Arthur Larsen
1951	Frank Sedgman
1952	Frank Sedgman
1953	Tony Trabert
1954	Vic Seixas
1955	Tony Trabert
1956	Ken Rosewall
1957	Malcolm J. Anderson
1958	Ashley Cooper
1959	Neale Fraser
1960	Neale Fraser
1961	Roy Emerson
1962	Rod Laver
1963	Rafael Osuna
1964	Roy Emerson
1965	Manuel Santana
1966	Fred Stolle
1967	John Newcombe
*1968	Arthur Ashe
*1969	Rod Laver
*1970	Ken Rosewall
*1971	Stan Smith
*1972	Ilie Nastase
*1973	John Newcombe
*1974	Jimmy Connors
*1975	Manuel Orantes
*1976	Jimmy Connors
*1977	Guillermo Vilas
*1978	Jimmy Connors
*1979	John McEnroe
*1980	John McEnroe

†No Challenge Round played
§National Patriotic Tournament
‡Challenge Round abolished
*Open Championship

USTA Champions—Men's Doubles

Prior to 1890 the national doubles championship was played in conjunction with the singles tournament. From 1890 to 1906 tournaments were held in the East and West, and the sectional winners at these meets then played off for the privilege of meeting the standing-out champions in the Challenge Round. In 1907 there were three sections competing in preliminary doubles, and this number was increased in subsequent years. In 1917 a play-through Patriotic tournament was held, as no championships were sanctioned that year. The 1918 championship was also a playing-through tournament, the sectional and preliminary doubles and the Challenge Round having been done away with. In 1919 the plan of the qualifying sectional winners was restored, although an exception was made in the case of the Australian teams which were on a visit to the United States at that time, and the last Challenge Round in national doubles was played that year. Since 1920 there have been few changes for the conditions that now prevail. The mixed doubles championship was contested in conjunction with the women's national tournament until 1921, after which it was added to the men's doubles competition. In 1935 the women's doubles championship was added to the doubles championship tournament, and the mixed doubles championship was added to the singles championship tournament.

1881	C.M. Clark—F.W. Taylor
1882	R.D. Sears—J. Dwight
1883	R.D. Sears—J. Dwight
1884	R.D. Sears—J. Dwight
1885	R.D. Sears—J.S. Clark
1886	R.D. Sears—J. Dwight
1887	R.D. Sears—J. Dwight
1888	O.S. Campbell—V.G. Hall
1889	H.W. Slocum, Jr.—H.A. Taylor
1890	V.G. Hall—C. Hobart
1891	O.S. Campbell—Robert Huntington, Jr.
1892	O.S. Campbell—Robert Huntington, Jr.
1893	Clarence Hobart—Fred H. Hovey
1894	Clarence Hobart—Fred H. Hovey
1895	M.G. Chace—R.D. Wrenn
1896	Carr B. Neel—Samuel R. Neel
1897	Leo E. Ware—George P. Sheldon, Jr.
1898	Leo E. Ware—George P. Sheldon, Jr.
1899	Holcombe Ward—Dwight F. Davis
1900	Holcombe Ward—Dwight F. Davis
1901	Holcombe Ward—Dwight F. Davis
1902	Reggie F. Doherty—H. Laurie Doherty
1903	Reggie F. Doherty—H. Laurie Doherty
1904	Holcombe Ward—Beals C. Wright
1905	Holcombe Ward—Beals C. Wright
1906	Holcombe Ward—Beals C. Wright
1907	Fred B. Alexander—Harold H. Hackett
1908	Fred B. Alexander—Harold H. Hackett
1909	Fred B. Alexander—Harold H. Hackett
1910	Fred B. Alexander—Harold H. Hackett
1911	Raymond D. Little—Gustave F. Touchard
1912	Maurice E. McLoughlin—Thomas C. Bundy
1913	Maurice E. McLoughlin—Thomas C. Bundy
1914	Maurice E. McLoughlin—Thomas C. Bundy
1915	William M. Johnston—Clarence J. Griffin
1916	William M. Johnston—Clarence J. Griffin
1917	Fred B. Alexander—Harold A. Throckmorton
1918	William T. Tilden—Vincent Richards
1919	Norman E. Brookes—Gerald Patterson
1920	William M. Johnston—Clarence J. Griffin
1921	William T. Tilden—Vincent Richards

1922	William T. Tilden—Vincent Richards
1923	William T. Tilden—Brian I.C. Norton
1924	Howard Kinsey—Robert Kinsey
1925	R.N. Williams II—Vincent Richards
1926	R.N. Williams II—Vincent Richards
1927	William T. Tilden—Francis T. Hunter
1928	George M. Lott—John Hennessey
1929	George M. Lott—John H. Doeg
1930	George M. Lott—John H. Doeg
1931	Wilmer Allison—John Van Ryn
1932	Ellsworth Vines—Keith Gledhill
1933	George M. Lott—Lester R. Stoefen
1934	George M. Lott—Lester R. Stoefen
1935	Wilmer L. Allison—John Van Ryn
1936	Don Budge—Gene Mako
1937	Gottfried von Cramm—Henner Henkel
1938	Don Budge—Gene Mako
1939	Adrian Quist—John Bromwich
1940	Jack Kramer—Frederick T. Schroeder, Jr.
1941	Jack Kramer—Frederick T. Schroeder, Jr.
1942	Gardnar Mulloy—William Talbert
1943	Jack Kramer—Frank A. Parker
1944	W. Donald McNeill—Robert Falkenburg
1945	Gardnar Mulloy—William Talbert
1946	Gardnar Mulloy—William Talbert
1947	John A. Kramer—Frederick T. Schroeder, Jr.
1948	Gardnar Mulloy—William Talbert
1949	John Bromwich—William Sidwell
1950	John Bromwich—Frank Sedgman
1951	Ken McGregor—Frank Sedgman
1952	Mervyn Rose—Vic Seixas
1953	Rex Hartwig—Mervyn Rose
1954	Vic Seixas—Tony Trabert
1955	Kosei Kamo—Atushi Miyagi
1956	Lew Hoad—Ken Rosewall
1957	Ashley Cooper—Neale Fraser
1958	Alex Olmedo—Hamilton Richardson
1959	Neale Fraser—Roy Emerson
1960	Neale Fraser—Roy Emerson
1961	Charles McKinley—Dennis Ralston
1962	Rafael Osuna—Antonio Palafox
1963	Charles McKinley—Dennis Ralston
1964	Charles McKinley—Dennis Ralston
1965	Roy Emerson—Fred Stolle
1966	Roy Emerson—Fred Stolle
1967	John Newcombe—Tony Roche
*1968	Robert Lutz—Stan Smith
*1969	Ken Rosewall—Fred Stolle
*1970	Pierre Barthes—Niki Pilic
*1971	John Newcombe—Roger Taylor
*1972	Cliff Drysdale—Roger Taylor
*1973	Owen Davidson—John Newcombe
*1974	Robert Lutz—Stan Smith
*1975	Jimmy Connors—Ilie Nastase
*1976	Marty Riessen—Tom Okker
*1977	Bob Hewitt—Frew McMillan
*1978	Robert Lutz—Stan Smith
*1979	John McEnroe—Peter Fleming
*1980	Robert Lutz—Stan Smith

USTA Champions—Women's Singles

The national women's championships were held at the Philadelphia Cricket Club from 1887 to 1920, inclusive. They moved to Forest Hills in 1921, remained there through 1977, and then moved to the USTA's new tennis complex at Flushing Meadow in 1978. Originally the mixed doubles and women's doubles were played in connection with the women's singles championship tournament. In 1921 the mixed doubles, and in 1935 the women's doubles, were transferred and made part of the national doubles championship program. From 1942 to 1945 inclusive the women's doubles, and since 1942 the mixed doubles, were played in connection with the men's championships.

1887	Ellen Hansell
1888	Bertha L. Townsend
1889	Bertha L. Townsend
1890	Ellen C. Roosevelt
1891	Mabel Cahill
1892	Mabel Cahill
1893	Aline Terry
1894	Helen Hellwig
1895	Juliette Atkinson
1896	Bessie Moore
1897	Juliette Atkinson
1898	Juliette Atkinson
1899	Marion Jones
1900	Myrtle McAteer
1901	Bessie Moore
1902	Marion Jones
1903	Bessie Moore
1904	May Sutton
1905	Bessie Moore
1906	Helen Homans
1907	Evelyn Sears
1908	Maud Barger-Wallach
1909	Hazel Hotchkiss
1910	Hazel Hotchkiss
1911	Hazel Hotchkiss
1912	Mary K. Browne
1913	Mary K. Browne
1914	Mary K. Browne
1915	Molla Bjurstedt
1916	Molla Bjurstedt
§1917	Molla Bjurstedt
1918	Molla Bjurstedt
1919	Hazel H. Wightman
1920	Molla B. Mallory
1921	Molla B. Mallory
1922	Molla B. Mallory
1923	Helen Wills
1924	Helen Wills
1925	Helen Wills
1926	Molla B. Mallory
1927	Helen Wills
1928	Helen Wills
1929	Helen Wills
1930	Betty Nuthall
1931	Helen Wills-Moody
1932	Helen H. Jacobs
1933	Helen H. Jacobs
1934	Helen H. Jacobs
1935	Helen H. Jacobs
1936	Alice Marble
1937	Anita Lizana
1938	Alice Marble
1939	Alice Marble
1940	Alice Marble
1941	Sarah Palfrey-Cooke
1942	Pauline Betz
1943	Pauline Betz
1944	Pauline Betz
1945	Sarah P. Cooke
1946	Pauline Betz
1947	Louise Brough
1948	Margaret Osborne DuPont
1949	Margaret Osborne DuPont
1950	Margaret Osborne DuPont
1951	Maureen Connolly
1952	Maureen Connolly
1953	Maureen Connolly
1954	Doris Hart
1955	Doris Hart
1956	Shirley J. Fry
1957	Althea Gibson
1958	Althea Gibson
1959	Maria Bueno
1960	Darlene R. Hard
1961	Darlene R. Hard
1962	Margaret Smith
1963	Maria Bueno
1964	Maria Bueno
1965	Margaret Smith
1966	Maria Bueno
1967	Billie Jean Moffitt-King
*1968	Virginia Wade
*1969	Margaret Smith-Court
*1970	Margaret Smith-Court
*1971	Billie Jean Moffitt-King
*1972	Billie Jean Moffitt-King
*1973	Margaret Smith Court
*1974	Billie Jean Moffitt-King
*1975	Chris Evert
*1976	Chris Evert
*1977	Chris Evert
*1978	Chris Evert
*1979	Tracy Austin
*1980	Chris Evert Lloyd

§National Patriotic Tournament

USTA Champions—Women's Doubles

1890	Ellen C. Roosevelt—Grace W. Roosevelt
1891	Mabel E. Cahill—Mrs. W. Fellowes Morgan
1892	Mabel E. Cahill—A.M. McKinlay
1893	Aline M. Terry—Hattie Butler
1894	Helen R. Helwig—Juliette P. Atkinson
1895	Helen R. Hartwig—Juliette P. Atkinson
1896	Elizabeth H. Moore—Juliette P. Atkinson
1897	Juliette P. Atkinson—Kathleen Atkinson
1898	Juliette P. Atkinson—Kathleen Atkinson
1899	Jane W. Craven—Myrtle McAteer
1900	Edith Parker—Hallie Champlin
1901	Juliette P. Atkinson—Myrtle McAteer
1902	Juliette P. Atkinson—Marion Jones
1903	Elizabeth H. Moore—Carrie B. Neely

1904	May G. Sutton—Miriam Hall
1905	Helen Homans—Carrie B. Neely
1906	Mrs. L.S. Coe—Mrs. D.S. Platt
1907	Marie Weimer—Carrie B. Neely
1908	Evelyn Sears—Margaret Curtis
1909	Hazel V. Hotchkiss—Edith E. Rotch
1910	Hazel V. Hotchkiss—Edith E. Rotch
1911	Hazel V. Hotchkiss—Eleanora Sears
1912	Dorothy Green—Mary K. Browne
1913	Mary K. Browne—Mrs. R.H. Williams
1914	Mary K. Browne—Mrs. R.H. Williams
1915	Hazel Hotchkiss Wightman—Eleonora Sears
1916	Molla Bjurstedt—Eleonora Sears
1917	Molla Bjurstedt—Eleanora Sears
1918	Marion Zinderstein—Eleanor Goss
1919	Marion Zinderstein—Eleanor Goss
1920	Marion Zinderstein—Eleanor Goss
1921	Mary K. Browne—Mrs. R.H. Williams
1922	Marion Zinderstein Jessup—Helen N. Wills
1923	Kathleen McKane—Phyllis H. Covell
1924	Hazel Hotchkiss Wightman—Helen N. Wills
1925	Mary K. Browne—Helen N. Wills
1926	Elizabeth Ryan—Eleanor Goss
1927	Kathleen McKane Godfree—Ermyntrude Harvey
1928	Hazel Hotchkiss Wightman—Helen N. Wills
1929	Phoebe Watson—Peggy Saunders Michell
1930	Betty Nuthall—Sarah Palfrey
1931	Betty Nuthall—Eileen Benentt Whitingstall
1932	Helen Jacobs—Sarah Palfrey
1933	Betty Nuthall—Freda James
1934	Helen Jacobs—Sarah Palfrey
1935	Helen Jacobs—Sarah Palfrey-Fabyan
1936	Marjorie Gladman Van Ryn—Carolin Babcock
1937	Sarah Palfrey-Fabyan—Alice Marble
1938	Sarah Palfrey-Fabyan—Alice Marble
1939	Sarah Palfrey-Fabyan—Alice Marble
1940	Sarah Palfrey-Fabyan—Alice Marble
1941	Sarah Palfrey-Fabyan—Margaret Osborne
1942	Louise Brough—Margaret Osborne
1943	Louise Brough—Margaret Osborne
1944	Louise Brough—Margaret Osborne
1945	Louise Brough—Margaret Osborne
1946	Louise Brough—Margaret Osborne
1947	Louise Brough—Margaret Osborne
1948	Louise Brough—Margaret Osborne-DuPont
1949	Louise Brough—Margaret Osborne-DuPont
1950	Louise Brough—Margaret Osborne-DuPont
1951	Shirley Fry—Doris Hart
1952	Shirley Fry—Doris Hart
1953	Shirley Fry—Doris Hart
1954	Shirley Fry—Doris Hart
1955	Louise Brough—Margaret Osborne-DuPont
1956	Louise Brough—Margaret Osborne-DuPont
1957	Louise Brough—Margaret Osborne-DuPont
1958	Jeanne M. Arth—Darlene Hard
1959	Jeanne M. Arth—Darlene Hard
1960	Maria Bueno—Darlene Hard
1961	Darlene Hard—Lesley Turner
1962	Darlene Hard—Maria Bueno
1963	Robyn Ebbern—Margaret Smith
1964	Billie Jean Moffitt—Karen Hantze Susman
1965	Carole Caldwell-Graebner—Nancy Richey
1966	Maria Bueno—Nancy Richey

1967	Rosemary Casals—Billie Jean Moffitt-King
1968	Maria Bueno—Margaret Smith-Court
*1968	Maria Bueno—Margaret Smith-Court
1969	Margaret Smith-Court—Virginia Wade
*1969	Françoise Durr—Darlene Hard
*1970	Margaret Smith Court—Judy Tegart-Dalton
*1971	Rosemary Casals—Judy Tegart-Dalton
*1972	Françoise Durr—Betty Stove
*1973	Margaret Smith-Court—Virginia Wade
*1974	Rosemary Casals—Billie Jean Moffitt-King
*1975	Margaret Smith Court—Virginia Wade
*1976	Delina Boshoff—Ilana Kloss
*1977	Martina Navratilova—Betty Stove
*1978	Billie Jean Moffitt-King—Martina Navratilova
*1979	Betty Stove—Wendy Turnbull
*1980	Billie Jean Moffitt-King—Martina Navratilova

USTA Champions—Mixed Doubles

1892	Mabel E. Cahill—Clarence Hobart
1893	Ellen C. Roosevelt—Clarence Hobart
1894	Juliette P. Atkinson—Edwin P. Fischer
1895	Juliette P. Atkinson—Edwin P. Fischer
1896	Juliette P. Atkinson—Edwin P. Fischer
1897	Laura Henson—D.L. Magruder
1898	Carrie B. Neely—Edwin P. Fischer
1899	Elizabeth J. Rastall—Albert L. Hoskins
1900	Margaret Hunnewell—Alfred Codman
1901	Marion Jones—Raymond D. Little
1902	Elizabeth H. Moore—Wylie C. Grant
1903	Helen Chapman—Harry F. Allen
1904	Elizabeth H. Moore—Wylie C. Grant
1905	Mr. and Mrs. Clarence Hobart
1906	Sarah Coffin—Edward B. Dewhurst
1907	May Sayres—Wallace F. Johnson
1908	Edith E. Rotch—Nathaniel W. Niles
1909	Hazel V. Hotchkiss—Wallace F. Johnson
1910	Hazel V. Hotchkiss—Joseph R. Carpenter, Jr.
1911	Hazel V. Hotchkiss—Wallace F. Johnson
1912	Mary K. Browne—R.N. Williams II
1913	Mary K. Browne—William T. Tilden
1914	Mary K. Browne—William T. Tilden
1915	Hazel H. Wightman—Harry C. Johnson
1916	Eleonora Sears—Willis F. Davis
1917	Molla Bjurstedt—Irving C. Wright
1918	Hazel Hotchkiss Wightman—Irving C. Wright
1919	Marion Zinderstein—Vincent Richards
1920	Hazel H. Wightman—Wallace F. Johnson
1921	Mary K. Browne—William Johnston
1922	Molla B. Mallory—William T. Tilden
1923	Molla B. Mallory—William T. Tilden
1924	Helen N. Wills—Vincent Richards
1925	Kathleen McKane—John B. Hawkes
1926	Elizabeth Ryan—Jean Borotra
1927	Eileen Bennett—Henri Cochet
1928	Helen N. Wills—John B. Hawkes
1929	Betty Nuthall—George M. Lott, Jr.
1930	Edith Cross—Wilmer L. Allison
1931	Betty Nuthall—George M. Lott, Jr.
1932	Sarah Palfrey—Frederick Perry
1933	Elizabeth Ryan—Ellsworth Vines
1934	Helen H. Jacobs—George M. Lott, Jr.
1935	Sarah Palfrey Fabyan—Enrique Maier
1936	Alice Marble—Gene Mako

1937	Sarah Palfrey Fabyan—Don Budge
1938	Alice Marble—Don Budge
1939	Alice Marble—Harry C. Hopman
1940	Alice Marble—Bobby Riggs
1941	Sarah Palfrey-Cooke—John A. Kramer
1942	Louise Brough—Frederick R. Schroeder, Jr.
1943	Margaret Osborne—William F. Talbert
1944	Margaret Osborne—William F. Talbert
1945	Margaret Osborne—William F. Talbert
1946	Margaret Osborne—William F. Talbert
1947	Louise Brough—John Bromwich
1948	Louise Brough—Thomas P. Brown, Jr.
1949	Louise Brough—Eric Sturgess
1950	Margaret Osborne DuPont—Ken McGregor
1951	Doris Hart—Frank Sedgman
1952	Doris Hart—Frank Sedgman
1953	Doris Hart—Vic Seixas
1954	Doris Hart—Vic Seixas
1955	Doris Hart—Vic Seixas
1956	Margaret Osborne DuPont—Ken Rosewall
1957	Althea Gibson—Kurt Neilsen
1958	Margaret Osborne-DuPont—Neale Fraser
1959	Margaret Osborne-DuPont—Neale Fraser
1960	Margaret Osborne-DuPont—Neale Fraser
1961	Margaret Smith—Robert Mark
1962	Margaret Smith—Fred Stolle
1963	Margaret Smith—Ken Fletcher
1964	Margaret Smith—John Newcombe
1965	Margaret Smith—Fred Stolle
1966	Donna Floyd-Fales—Owen Davidson
1967	Billie Jean Moffitt-King—Owen Davidson
1968	Mary Ann Eisel—Peter Curtis
1969	Patti Hogan—Paul Sullivan
*1969	Margaret Smith-Court—Marty Riessen
*1970	Margaret Smith-Court—Marty Riessen
*1971	Billie Jean Moffitt-King—Owen Davidson
*1972	Margaret Smith-Court—Marty Riessen
*1973	Billie Jean Moffitt-King—Owen Davidson
*1974	Pam Teeguarden—Geoff Masters
*1975	Rosemary Casals—Richard Stockton
*1976	Billie Jean Moffitt-King—Phil Dent
*1977	Betty Stove—Frew McMillan
*1978	Betty Stove—Frew McMillan
*1979	Greer Stevens—Bob Hewitt
*1980	Wendy Turnbull—Marty Riessen

*Open Championship

FRENCH CHAMPIONSHIPS
Paris, France
French Champions—Men's Singles

1891	Briggs
1892	J. Schopfer
1893	L. Riboulet
1894	A. Vacherot
1895	A. Vacherot
1896	A. Vacherot
1897	P. Ayme
1898	P. Ayme
1899	P. Ayme
1900	P. Ayme
1901	A. Vacherot

1902	M. Vacherot
1903	Max Decugis
1904	Max Decugis
1905	Maurice Germot
1906	Maurice Germot
1907	Max Decugis
1908	Max Decugis
1909	Max Decugis
1910	Maurice Germot
1911	Andre Gobert
1912	Max Decugis
1913	Max Decugis
1914	Max Decugis
1915–19	No competition
1920	A.H. Gobert
1921	Jean Samazeuilh
1922	Henri Cochet
1923	Pierre Blanchy
1924	Jean Borotra
1925	René Lacoste
1926	Henri Cochet
1927	René Lacoste
1928	Henri Cochet
1929	René Lacoste
1930	Henri Cochet
1931	Jean Borotra
1932	Henri Cochet
1933	John H. Crawford
1934	Gottfried von Cramm
1935	Fred J. Perry
1936	Gottfried von Cramm
1937	Henner Henkel
1938	Don Budge
1939	W. Donald McNeill
1940–45	No competition
1946	Marcel Bernard
1947	Joseph Asboth
1948	Frank A. Parker
1949	Frank A. Parker
1950	Budge Patty
1951	Jaroslav Drobny
1952	Jaroslav Drobny
1953	Ken Rosewall
1954	Tony Trabert
1955	Tony Trabert
1956	Lew Hoad
1957	Sven Davidson
1958	Mervyn Rose
1959	Nicola Pietrangeli
1960	Nicola Pietrangeli
1961	Manuel Santana
1962	Rod Laver
1963	Roy Emerson
1964	Manuel Santana
1965	Fred Stolle
1966	Tony Roche
1967	Roy Emerson
*1968	Ken Rosewall
*1969	Rod Laver
*1970	Jan Kodes
*1971	Jan Kodes
*1972	Andres Gimeno
*1973	Ilie Nastase

*1974	Bjorn Borg
*1975	Bjorn Borg
*1976	Adriano Panatta
*1977	Guillermo Vilas
*1978	Bjorn Borg
*1979	Bjorn Borg
*1980	Bjorn Borg

French Champions—Men's Doubles

1906	Max Decugis—Maurice Germot
1907	Max Decugis—Maurice Germot
1908	Max Decugis—Maurice Germot
1909	Max Decugis—Maurice Germot
1910	Max Decugis—M. Dupont
1911	Max Decugis—Maurice Germot
1912	Max Decugis—Maurice Germot
1913	Max Decugis—Maurice Germot
1914	Max Decugis—Maurice Germot
1915–19	No competition
1920	Max Decugis—Maurice Germot
1921	Andre Gobert—W.H. Laurentz
1922	Jacques Brugnon—Marcel Dupont
1923	P. Blanchy—Jean Samarzeuilh
1924	Jean Borotra—René Lacoste
1925	Jean Borotra—René Lacoste
1926	Vincent Richards—H. Kinsey
1927	Henri Cochet—Jacques Brugnon
1928	Jean Borotra—Jacques Brugnon
1929	Jean Borotra—René Lacoste
1930	Henri Cochet—Jacques Brugnon
1931	George M. Lott—John Van Ryn
1932	Henri Cochet—Jacques Brugnon
1933	Pat Hughes—Fred J. Perry
1934	Jean Borotra—Jacques Brugnon
1935	Jack Crawford—Adrian Quist
1936	Jean Borotra—Marcel Bernard
1937	Gottfried von Cramm—Henner Henkel
1938	Bernard Destremau—Yvon Petra
1939	Don McNeill—Charles R. Harris
1940–45	No competition
1946	Marcel Bernard—Yvon Petra
1947	Eustace Fannin—Eric Sturgess
1948	Lennart Bergelin—Jaroslav Drobny
1949	Frank Parker—Richard Gonzales
1950	William Talbert—Tony Trabert
1951	Ken McGregor—Frank Sedgman
1952	Ken McGregor—Frank Sedgman
1953	Lew Hoad—Ken Rosewall
1954	Vic Seixas—Tony Trabert
1955	Vic Seixas—Tony Trabert
1956	Don Candy—Robert Perry
1957	Malcolm J. Anderson—Ashley Cooper
1958	Ashley Cooper—Neale Fraser
1959	Nicola Pietrangeli—Orlando Sirola
1960	Neale Fraser—Roy Emerson
1961	Roy Emerson—Rod Laver
1962	Roy Emerson—Neale Fraser
1963	Roy Emerson—Manuel Santana
1964	Roy Emerson—Ken Fletcher
1965	Roy Emerson—Fred Stolle
1966	Clark Graebner—Dennis Ralston
1967	John Newcombe—Tony Roche
*1968	Ken Rosewall—Fred Stolle

*1969	John Newcombe—Tony Roche
*1970	Ilie Nastase—Ion Tiriac
*1971	Arthur Ashe—Marty Riessen
*1972	Bob Hewitt—Frew McMillan
*1973	John Newcombe—Tom Okker
*1974	Dick Crealy—Onny Parun
*1975	Brian Gottfried—Raul Ramirez
*1976	Fred McNair—Sherwood Stewart
*1977	Brian Gottfried—Raul Ramirez
*1978	Gene Mayer—Hank Pfister
*1979	Gene Mayer—Sandy Meyer
*1980	Victor Amaya—Hank Pfister

French Champions—Women's Singles

1897	Cecilia Masson
1898	Cecilia Masson
1899	Cecilia Masson
1900	Cecilia Prevost
1901	Mme. P. Girod
1902	Cecilia Masson
1903	Cecilia Masson
1904	Katie Gillou
1905	Katie Gillou
1906	Katie Fenwick
1907	Mme. de Kermel
1908	Katie Fenwick
1909	Jeanne Mattey
1910	Jeanne Mattey
1911	Jeanne Mattey
1912	Jeanne Mattey
1913	Marguerite Broquedis
1914	Marguerite Broquedis
1915–19	No competition
1920	Suzanne Lenglen
1921	Suzanne Lenglen
1922	Suzanne Lenglen
1923	Suzanne Lenglen
1924	Didi Vlasto
1925	Suzanne Lenglen
1926	Suzanne Lenglen
1927	Ked Bouman
1928	Helen Wills
1929	Helen Wills
1930	Helen Wills-Moody
1931	Cilly Aussem
1932	Helen Wills-Moody
1933	Margaret C. Scriven
1934	Margaret C. Scriven
1935	Hilda Sperling
1936	Hilda Sperling
1937	Hilda Sperling
1938	Simone Mathieu
1939	Simone Mathieu
1940–45	No competition
1946	Margaret Osborne
1947	Patricia C. Todd
1948	Mme. N. Landry
1949	Margaret Osborne DuPont
1950	Doris Hart
1951	Shirley Fry
1952	Doris Hart
1953	Maureen Connolly
1954	Maureen Connolly

1955	Angela Mortimer
1956	Althea Gibson
1957	Shirley Bloomer
1958	S. Koermoczi
1959	Christine Truman
1960	Darlene Hard
1961	Ann Haydon
1962	Margaret Smith
1963	Lesley Turner
1964	Margaret Smith
1965	Lesley Turner
1966	Ann Haydon Jones
1967	Françoise Durr
*1968	Nancy Richey
*1969	Margaret Smith-Court
*1970	Margaret Smith-Court
*1971	Evonne Goolagong
*1972	Billie Jean Moffitt-King
*1973	Margaret Smith-Court
*1974	Chris Evert
*1975	Chris Evert
*1976	Sue Barker
*1977	Mima Jausovec
*1978	Virginia Ruzici
*1979	Chris Evert Lloyd
*1980	Chris Evert Lloyd

French Champions—Women's Doubles

1925	Suzanne Lenglen—Didi Vlasto
1926	Suzanne Lenglen—Didi Vlasto
1927	Mrs. Peacock—E.L. Heine
1928	Mrs. Watson—Eileen Bennett
1929	Lili de Alvarez—Ked Bouman
1930	Helen Wills Moody—Elizabeth Ryan
1931	Eileen B. Whittingstall—Elizabeth Nuthall
1932	Helen Wills Moody—Elizabeth Ryan
1933	Simone P. Mathieu—Elizabeth Ryan
1934	Simone P. Mathieu—Elizabeth Ryan
1935	Margaret Scriven—Kay Stammers
1936	Simone P. Mathieu—Billie Yorke
1937	Simone P. Mathieu—Billie Yorke
1938	Simone P. Mathieu—Billie Yorke
1939	Simone P. Mathieu—Jadwiga Jedrzejowska
1940–45	No competition
1946	Louise Brough—Margaret Osborne
1947	Louise Brough—Margaret Osborne
1948	Doris Hart—Patricia C. Todd
1949	Margaret Osborne DuPont—Louise Brough
1950	Doris Hart—Shirley Fry
1951	Doris Hart—Shirley Fry
1952	Doris Hart—Shirley Fry
1953	Doris Hart—Shirley Fry
1954	Maureen Connolly—Nell Hopman
1955	Beverly B. Fleitz—Darlene Hard
1956	Angela Buxton—Althea Gibson
1957	Shirley Bloomer—Darlene Hard
1958	Rosie Reyes—Yola Ramirez
1959	Sandra Reynolds—Renee Schuurman
1960	Maria Bueno—Darlene Hard
1961	Sandra Reynolds—Renee Schuurman
1962	Sandra Reynolds—Renee Schuurman
1963	Ann H. Jones—Renee Schuurman
1964	Margaret Smith—Lesley Turner

1965	Margaret Smith—Lesley Turner
1966	Judy Tegart—Margaret Smith
1967	Françoise Durr—Gail Sherriff
*1968	Françoise Durr—Ann H. Jones
*1969	Françoise Durr—Ann H. Jones
*1970	Gail S. Chanfreau—Françoise Durr
*1971	Gail S. Chanfreau—Françoise Durr
*1972	Billie Jean Moffitt-King—Betty Stove
*1973	Margaret Smith-Court—Virginia Wade
*1974	Chris Evert—Olga Morozova
*1975	Chris Evert—Martina Navratilova
*1976	Fiorella Bonicelli—Gail S.C. Lovera
*1977	Regina Marsikova—Pam Teeguarden
*1978	Mima Jausovec—Virginia Ruzici
*1979	Betty Stove—Wendy Turnbull
*1980	Kathy Jordan—Anne Smith

French Champions—Mixed Doubles

1925	Suzanne Lenglen—Jacque Brugnon
1926	Suzanne Lenglen—Jacque Brugnon
1927	M. Bordes—Jean Borotra
1928	Eileen Bennett—Henri Cochet
1929	Eileen Bennett—Henri Cochet
1930	Cilly Aussen—William T. Tilden
1931	Betty Nuthall—Patrick D. Spence
1932	Betty Nuthall—Fred J. Perry
1933	Margaret Scriven—Jack H. Crawford
1934	Colette Rosambert—Jean Borotra
1935	Lolette Payot—Marcel Bernard
1936	Billie Yorke—Marcel Bernard
1937	Simone P. Mathieu—Yvon Petra
1938	Simone P. Mathieu—Dragutin Mitic
1939	Sarah Palfrey Fabyan—Elwood T. Cooke
1940–45	No competition
1946	Pauline Betz—Budge Patty
1947	Sheila Summers—Eric Sturgess
1948	Patricia C. Todd—Jaroslav Drobny
1949	Sheila Summers—Eric Sturgess
1950	Barbara Sudfield—Enrique Morea
1951	Doris Hart—Frank Sedgman
1952	Doris Hart—Frank Sedgman
1953	Doris Hart—Vic Seixas
1954	Maureen Connolly—Lew Hoad
1955	Darlene Hard—Gordon Forbes
1956	Thelma Long—Luis Ayala
1957	Vera Puzejova—Jiri Javorsky
1958	Shirley Bloomer—Nicoli Pietrangeli
1959	Yola Ramirez—William Knight
1960	Maria Bueno—Robert Howe
1961	Darlene Hard—Rod Laver
1962	Renee Schuurman—Robert Howe
1963	Margaret Smith—Ken Fletcher
1964	Margaret Smith—Ken Fletcher
1965	Margaret Smith—Ken Fletcher
1966	Annette van Zyl—Frew McMillan
1967	Billie Jean Moffitt-King—Owen Davidson
*1968	Françoise Durr—Jean Claude Barclay
*1969	Margaret Smith-Court—Marty Riessen
*1971	Françoise Durr—Jean Claude Barclay
*1972	Evonne Goolagong—Kim Warwick
*1973	Françoise Durr—Jean Claude Barclay
*1974	Martina Navratilova—Ivan Molina
*1975	Fiorella Bonicelli—Thomas Koch

*1976	Ilana Kloss—Kim Warwick
*1977	Mary Carillo—John McEnroe
*1978	Renata Tomanova—Pavel Slozil
*1979	Wendy Turnbull—Bob Hewitt
*1980	Anne Smith—Billy Martin

Australian Championships
Melbourne, Australia
*Open Championship
#Two championships played. 1977, first January, second December.
Australian Championships—Men's Singles

1905	Rodney W. Heath
1906	Tony Wilding
1907	Horace M. Rice
1908	Fred Alexander
1909	Tony Wilding
1910	Rodney W. Heath
1911	Norman E. Brookes
1912	J. Cecil Parke
1913	E.F. Parker
1914	Arthur O'Hara Wood
1915	Francis G. Lowe
1916–18	No competition
1919	A.R.F. Kingscote
1920	Arthur O'Hara Wood
1921	Rice H. Gemmell
1922	James Anderson
1923	Arthur O'Hara Wood
1924	James Anderson
1925	James Anderson
1926	John Hawkes
1927	Gerald Patterson
1928	Jean Borotra
1929	John C. Gregory
1930	Gar Moon
1931	Jack Crawford
1932	Jack Crawford
1933	Jack Crawford
1934	Fred J. Perry
1935	Jack Crawford
1936	Adrian Quist
1937	Viv McGrath
1938	Don Budge
1939	John Bromwich
1940	Adrian Quist
1941–45	No competition
1946	John Bromwich
1947	Dinny Pails
1948	Adrian Quist
1949	Frank Sedgman
1950	Frank Sedgman
1951	Dick Savitt
1952	Ken McGregor
1953	Ken Rosewall
1954	Mervyn Rose
1955	Ken Rosewall
1956	Lew Hoad
1957	Ashley Cooper
1958	Ashley Cooper
1959	Alex Olmedo
1960	Rod Laver
1961	Roy Emerson

1962	Rod Laver
1963	Roy Emerson
1964	Roy Emerson
1965	Roy Emerson
1966	Roy Emerson
1967	Roy Emerson
1968	Bill Bowrey
*1969	Rod Laver
*1970	Arthur Ashe
*1971	Ken Rosewall
*1972	Ken Rosewall
*1973	John Newcombe
*1974	Jimmy Connors
*1975	John Newcombe
*1976	Mark Edmondson
*1977	Roscoe Tanner#
*1977	Vitas Gerulaitis#
*1978	Guillermo Vilas
*1979	Guillermo Vilas
*1980	Brian Teacher

Australian Champions—Men's Doubles

1905	Tom Tachell—Randolph Lycet
1906	Tony Wilding—Rodney W. Heath
1907	H.A. Parker—Bill A. Gregg
1908	Fred Alexander—Alfred Dunlop
1909	E.F. Parker—J.P. Keane
1910	Horace Rice—Ashley Campbell
1911	Rodney W. Heath—R. Lycett
1912	J.C. Parke—C.P. Dixon
1913	E.F. Parker—A.H. Hedemann
1914	Ashley Campbell—Gerald Patterson
1915	Horace M. Rice—C.V. Todd
1916–18	No competition
1919	Pat O'Hara Wood—R.V. Thomas
1920	Pat O'Hara Wood—R.V. Thomas
1921	R.H. Gennell—R.V. Thomas
1922	Gerald Patterson—John Hawkes
1923	Pat O'Hara Wood—C.B. St. John
1924	Norman E. Brookes—James Anderson
1925	Gerald Patterson—Pat O'Hara Wood
1926	Gerald Patterson—John Hawkes
1927	Gerald Patterson—Jahn Hawkes
1928	Jean Borotra—Jacques Brugnon
1929	Jack Crawford—Harry Hopman
1930	Jack Crawford—Harry Hopman
1931	C. Donahoe—R. Dunlop
1932	Jack Crawford—E.F. Moon
1933	Ellsworth Vines—Keith Gledhill
1934	Fred J. Perry—George Hughes
1935	Jack Crawford—Vic McGrath
1936	Adrian Quist—D.P. Turnbull
1937	Adrian Quist—D.P. Turnbull
1938	Adrian Quist—John Bromwich
1939	Adrian Quist—John Bromwich
1940	Adrian Quist—John Bromwich
1941–45	No competition
1946	Adrian Quist—John Bromwich
1947	Adrian Quist—John Bromwich
1948	Adrian Quist—John Bromwich
1949	Adrian Quist—John Bromwich
1950	Adrian Quist—John Bromwich
1951	Frank Sedgman—Ken McGregor

1952	Frank Sedgman—Ken McGregor
1953	Lew Hoad—Ken Rosewall
1954	Rex Hartwig—Mervyn Rose
1955	Vic Seixas—Tony Trabert
1956	Lew Hoad—Ken Rosewall
1957	Lew Hoad—Neale Fraser
1958	Ashley Cooper—Neale Fraser
1959	Rod Laver—Bob Mark
1960	Rod Laver—Bob Mark
1961	Rod Laver—Bob Mark
1962	Roy Emerson—Neale Fraser
1963	Bob Hewitt—Fred Stolle
1964	Bob Hewitt—Fred Stolle
1965	John Newcombe—Tony Roche
1966	Roy Emerson—Fred Stolle
1967	John Newcombe—Tony Roche
1968	Dick Crealy—Allan Stone
*1969	Roy Emerson—Rod Laver
*1970	Robert Lutz—Stan Smith
*1971	John Newcombe—Tony Roche
*1972	Owen Davidson—Ken Rosewall
*1973	Mal Anderson—John Newcombe
*1974	Ross Case—Geoff Masters
*1975	John Alexander—Phil Dent
*1976	John Newcombe—Tony Roche
*1977	Arthur Ashe—Tony Roche #
*1977	Allan Stone—Ray Ruffels #
*1978	Wojtek Fibak—Kim Warwick
*1979	Peter McNamara—Paul McNamee
*1980	Kim Warwick—Mark Edmondson

Australian Champions—Women's Singles

1922	Mrs. Molesworth
1923	Mrs. Molesworth
1924	Sylvia Lance
1925	Daphne Akhurst
1926	Daphne Akhurst
1927	Esna Boyd
1928	Daphne Akhurst
1929	Daphne Akhurst
1930	Daphne Akhurst
1931	Coral Buttsworth
1932	Coral Buttsworth
1933	Joan Hartigan
1934	Joan Hartigan
1935	Dorothy Round
1936	Joan Hartigan
1937	Nancye Wynne
1938	Dorothy M. Bundy
1939	Emily Westacott
1940	Nancye Wynne
1941–45	No competition
1946	Nancye W. Bolton
1947	Nancye W. Bolton
1948	Nancye W. Bolton
1949	Doris Hart
1950	Louise Brough
1951	Nancye W. Bolton
1952	Thelma C. Long
1953	Maureen Connolly
1954	Thelma C. Long
1955	Beryl Pemrose
1956	Mary Carter
1957	Shirley Fry

1958	Angela Mortimer
1959	Mary Carter-Reitano
1960	Margaret Smith
1961	Margaret Smith
1962	Margaret Smith
1963	Margaret Smith
1964	Margaret Smith
1965	Margaret Smith
1966	Margaret Smith
1967	Nancy Richey
1968	Billie Jean Moffitt-King
*1969	Margaret Smith-Court
*1970	Margaret Smith-Court
*1971	Margaret Smith-Court
*1972	Virginia Wade
*1973	Margaret Smith Court
*1974	Evonne Goolagong
*1975	Evonne Goolagong
*1976	Evonne Goolagong
*1977	Kerry M. Reid #
*1977	Evonne Goolagong #
*1978	Chris O'Neill
*1979	Barbara Jordan
*1980	Hana Mandlikova

Australian Champions—Women's Doubles

1922	Esna F. Boyd—M. Mountain
1923	E. F. Boyd—S. Lance
1924	Daphne Akhurst—Sylvia Lance
1925	Sylvia Lance Harper—Daphne Arkhurst
1926	Mrs. P. O'Hara Wood—E. F. Boyd
1927	Mrs. P O'Hara Wood—Louis Bickerton
1928	Daphne Akhurst—E.F. Boyd
1929	Daphne Akhurst—Louie Bickerton
1930	Mrs. Molesworth—E. Hood
1931	Daphne A. Cozens—Louie Bickerton
1932	Coral Buttsworth—Marjorie Crawford
1933–34	Mrs. Molesworth—Mrs. Westacott
1935	Evelyn Dearman—Nancye W. Lyle
1936–40	Thelma Coyne—Nancye Wynne
1941–45	No competition
1946	Joyce Fitch—Mary Bevis
1947	Thelma Long—Nancye Wynne Bolton
1948	Thelma Long—Nancye Wynne Bolton
1949	Thelma Long—Nancye Wynne Bolton
1950	Louise Brough—Doris Hart
1951	Thelma Long—Nancye Wynne Bolton
1952	Thelma Long—Nancye Wynne Bolton
1953	Maureen Connolly—Julia Sampson
1954	Mary Hawton—Beryl Penrose
1955	Mary Hawton—Beryl Penrose
1956	Mary Hawton—Thelma Long
1957	Althea Gibson—Shirley Fry
1958	Mary Hawton—Thelma Long
1959	Renee Schuurman—Sandra Reynolds
1960	Maria Bueno—Christine Truman
1961	Mary Carter Reitano—Margaret Smith
1962	Margaret Smith—Robyn Ebbern
1963	Margaret Smith—Robyn Ebbern
1964	Judy Tegart—Lesley Turner
1965	Margaret Smith—Lesley Turner
1966	Carol Caldwell-Graebner—Nancy Richey
1967	Lesley Turner—Judy Tegart
1968	Karen Krantzcke—Kerry Melville

*1969 Margaret Smith-Court—Judy Tegart
*1970 Margaret Smith-Court—Judy T. Dalton
*1971 Margaret Smith-Court—Evonne Goolagong
*1972 Kerry Harris—Helen Gourlay
*1973 Margaret Smith-Court—Virginia Wade
*1974 Evonne Goolagong—Peggy Michel
*1975 Evonne Goolagong—Peggy Michel
*1976 Evonne Goolagong—Helen Gourlay
*1977 Dianne Fromholtz—Helen Gourlay #
*1977 Finals rained out #
*1978 Betsy Nagelsen—Renata Tomanova
*1979 Judy Chaloner—Dianne Evers
*1980 Martina Navratilova—Betsy Nagelsen

Australian Champions—Mixed Doubles

1922 Esna F. Boyd—John B. Hawkes
1923 Sylvia Lance—Horace M. Rice
1924–25 Daphne Akhurst—John Willard
1926–27 Esna F. Boyd—John B. Hawkes
1928 Daphne Akhurst—Jean Borotra
1929 Daphne Akhurst—Gar Moon
1930 Nell Hall—Harry C. Hopman
1931–33 Mr. & Mrs. John H. Crawford
1934 Joan Hartigan—Gar Moon
1935 Louie M. Bickerton—Christian Boussus
1936–37 Mr. & Mrs. Harry C. Hopman
1938 M. Wilson—John Bromwich
1939 Mr. & Mrs. Harry C. Hopman
1940 Nancye Wynne—Colin Long
1941–45 No competition
1946 Nancye Wynne Bolton—Colin Long
1947 Nancye Wynne Bolton—Colin Long
1948 Nancye Wynne Bolton—Colin Long
1949 Doris Hart—Frank Sedgman
1950 Doris Hart—Frank Sedgman
1951 Thelma Long—George Worthington
1952 Thelma Long—George Worthington
1953 Julia Sampson—Rex Hartwig
1954 Thelma Long—Rex Hartwig
1955 Thelma Long—George Worthington
1956 Beryl Penrose—Neale Fraser
1957 Fay Muller—Malcombe Anderson
1958 Mary Hawton—Bob Howe
1959 Sandra Reynolds—Bob Mark
1960 Jan Lehane—Trevor Fancutt
1961 Jan Lehane—Bob Hewitt
1962 Lesley Turner—Fred Stolle
1963 Margaret Smith—Ken Fletcher
1964 Margaret Smith—Ken Fletcher
1965 Unfinished
1966 Judy Tegart—Tony Roche
1967 Lesley Turner—Owen Davidson
1968 Billie Jean Moffitt-King—Dick Crealy
1969 Not completed
1970–80 Not held

The All-Time Champions*

The Grand Slam tournaments (France, Britain/Wimbledon, U.S., Australia), known as the Big Four, are the leading major championships. By far the most prolific winner of these events in singles, doubles and mixed doubles is Margaret Smith Court: twenty-six singles, twenty-one doubles, nineteen mixed for a total of sixty-six. First among men is also an Australian, Roy Emerson, with twelve singles and sixteen doubles for twenty-eight. Here are the all-time leaders, noting how many of each category (S-D-M) they have won in each of the Big Four, and the years encompassing their triumphs. A select nine have won all the Big Four singles titles: Court, Emerson, Billie Jean King, Doris Hart, Shirley Fry, Maureen Connolly, Don Budge, Fred Perry, and Rod Laver. Budge (1938), Connolly (1953), Laver (1962 and 1969), Court (1970) won them all in one year, thus achieving Grand Slams.

WOMEN

	Aus.	Fr.	Wim.	U.S.	Overall S-D-M	T
Margaret Smith Court, 1960–75	11-8-2	5-4-4	3-2-5	7-7-8	26-21-19	66
Billie Jean Moffitt King, 1961–80	1-0-1	1-1-2	6-10-4	4-6-3	12-17-10	39
Margaret Osborne DuPont, 1941–60	*	2-3-0	1-5-1	3-13-9	6-21-10	37
Louise Brough, 1942–57	1-1-0	0-3-0	4-5-4	1-12-4	6-21-8	35
Doris Hart, 1948–55	1-1-2	2-5-3	1-4-5	2-4-5	6-14-15	35
Helen Wills-Moody, 1923–38	*	4-2-0	8-3-0	7-4-2	19-9-2	30
Elizabeth Ryan, 1914–34	*	0-4-0	0-12-7	0-1-2	0-17-9	26
Suzanne Lenglen, 1919–26	*	6-2-2	6-6-3	0-0-0	12-8-5	25
Maria Bueno, 1958–68	0-1-0	0-1-1	3-5-0	4-5-0	7-12-1	20
Darlene Hard, 1958–69	*	1-2-2	0-4-2	2-6-0	3-12-4	19
Sarah Palfrey-Cooke, 1930–45	*	0-0-1	0-2-0	2-9-4	2-11-5	18
Alice Marble, 1936–39	*	*	1-2-2	4-4-4	5-6-6	17
Hazel H. Wightman, 1909–28	*	*	0-1-0	4-6-6	4-7-6	17
Shirley Fry, 1950–57	1-1-0	1-4-0	1-3-1	1-4-0	4-12-1	17
Chris Evert Lloyd 1974–80	0-0-0	4-2-0	2-1-0	5-0-0	11-3-0	14
Evonne Goolagong Cawley, 1971–80	4-5-0	1-0-1	2-1-0	0-0-0	7-6-1	14
Simone Mathieu, 1933–39	*	2-6-2	0-3-0	0-0-0	2-9-2	13
Maureen Connolly, 1951–54	1-1-0	2-1-1	3-0-0	3-0-0	9-2-1	12
Françoise Durr, 1967–76	0-0-0	1-5-3	0-0-1	0-2-0	1-7-4	12
Lesley Turner, 1961–67	0-3-2	2-2-0	0-1-1	0-1-0	2-7-3	12
Rosemary Casals, 1967–75	0-0-0	0-0-0	0-5-2	0-3-1	0-8-3	11
Althea Gibson, 1956–58	0-1-0	1-1-0	2-3-0	2-0-1	5-5-1	11

MEN

	Aus.	Fr.	Wim.	U.S.	Overall S-D-M	T
Roy Emerson, 1959–71	6-3-0	2-6-0	2-3-0	2-4-0	12-16-0	28
John Newcombe, 1965–76	2-5-0	0-3-0	3-6-0	2-3-1	7-17-1	25
Frank Sedgman, 1949–52	2-2-2	0-2-2	1-3-2	2-2-2	5-9-8	22
Rod Laver, 1959–71	3-4-0	2-1-1	4-1-2	2-0-0	11-6-3	20
William T. Tilden, 1913–30	*	0-0-1	3-0-0	7-5-4	10-5-5	20
Jean Borotra, 1925–36	1-1-1	1-5-2	2-3-1	0-0-1	4-9-5	18
John Bromwich, 1938–50	2-8-1	0-0-0	0-2-2	0-3-1	2-13-4	19
Fred Stolle, 1962–69	0-3-1	1-2-0	0-2-3	1-3-2	2-10-6	18
Ken Rosewall, 1953–72	4-3-0	2-2-0	0-2-0	2-2-1	8-9-1	18
Neale Fraser, 1957–62	0-3-1	0-3-0	1-2-0	2-3-3	3-11-4	18
Adrian Quist, 1936–50	3-10-0	0-1-0	0-2-0	0-1-1	3-14-1	18
H. Laurie Doherty, 1897–06	*	*	5-8-0	1-2-0	6-10-0	16
Henri Cochet, 1926–32	*	4-3-2	2-2-0	2-0-0	8-5-2	15
Vic Seixas, 1952–56	0-1-0	0-2-1	1-0-4	1-2-3	2-5-8	15
Jack Crawford, 1929–35	4-4-1	1-1-1	1-1-1	0-0-0	6-6-3	15
Bob Hewitt, 1961–79	0-2-1	0-1-2	0-5-2	0-1-1	0-9-5	15
Reggie F. Doherty, 1897–05	*	*	4-8-0	0-2-0	4-10-0	14
Don Budge, 1936–38	1-0-0	1-0-0	2-2-2	2-2-2	6-4-4	14
Tony Roche, 1965–76	0-3-1	1-2-0	0-5-1	0-1-0	1-11-2	14
Lew Hoad, 1953–57	1-3-0	1-1-1	2-3-0	0-1-0	4-8-1	13
Fred J. Perry, 1933–36	1-1-0	1-0-1	3-0-2	3-0-0	8-1-3	12
Jacques Brugnon, 1925–34	0-1-0	0-5-2	0-4-0	0-0-0	0-10-2	12
Tony Wilding, 1906–14	2-1-0	*	4-4-0	*	6-5-0	11
René Lacoste, 1925–29	*	3-2-0	2-1-0	2-0-0	7-3-0	10
Tony Trabert, 1950–55	0-1-0	2-3-0	1-0-0	2-1-0	5-5-0	10
Bjorn Borg, 1974–80	0-0-0	5-0-0	5-0-0	0-0-0	10-0-0	10

*Big Four records through Dec. 31, 1980.

About the Editors

Bob Gillen was the founding editor of *Tennis Trade* and *Tennis Times,* and the former editor of *Tennis USA* magazine (official publication of the United States Tennis Association) and editor of *Winning Tennis: Strokes and Strategies of the World's Top Pros.* He is presently executive editor of *Ski* magazine and an avid tennis player. He lives in Norwalk, Connecticut.

Michael Bartlett is the former editor of *Golf Canada, Golf Journal,* a senior editor at *Golf Magazine,* the managing editor of *Signature* magazine and now works as an editorial consultant to magazines and does freelance editing and writing. He is the editor of *Bartlett's World Golf Encyclopedia* (Bantam) and *The Golf Book* (Arbor House). He makes his home in Mount Vernon, New York.